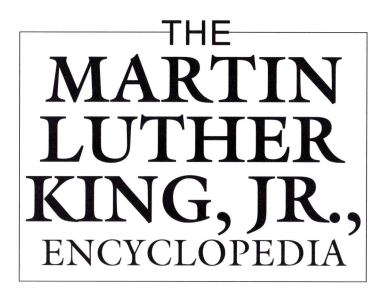

THE
MARTIN LUTHER KING, JR.,
ENCYCLOPEDIA

THE MARTIN LUTHER KING, JR., ENCYCLOPEDIA

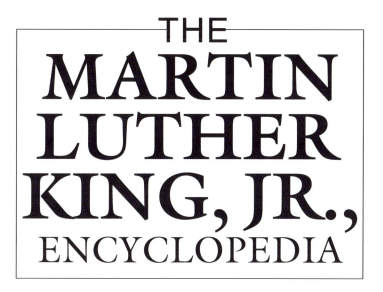

Clayborne Carson

Director and Senior Editor, Martin Luther King, Jr., Papers Project

Tenisha Armstrong

Associate Director, Martin Luther King, Jr., Papers Project

Susan Carson

Contributing Editor

Erin Cook

Contributing Editor

Susan Englander

Associate Director, Martin Luther King, Jr., Papers Project

With the assistance of the King Research and Education Institute

GREENWOOD PRESS

Westport, Connecticut • London

Library of Congress Cataloging-in-Publication Data

The Martin Luther King, Jr., encyclopedia / by Clayborne Carson ... [et al.] ; with the assistance of the King Research and Education Institute.
  p. cm.
  Includes bibliographical references and index.
  ISBN 978–0–313–29440–2 (alk. paper)
  1. King, Martin Luther, Jr., 1929–1968—Encyclopedias. 2. African Americans—Biography—Encyclopedias. 3. African American civil rights workers—Biography—Encyclopedias. 4. Civil rights workers—United States—Biography—Encyclopedias. 5. Baptists—United States—Clergy—Biography—Encyclopedias. 6. African Americans—Civil rights—History—20th century—Encyclopedias. 7. Civil rights movements—United States—History—20th century—Encyclopedias. 8. United States—Race relations—History—20th century—Encyclopedias. I. Carson, Clayborne, 1944–
  E185.97.K5M334 2008
  323.092—dc22   2007035354

British Library Cataloguing in Publication Data is available.

Library of Congress Catalog Card Number: 2007035354
ISBN: 978–0–313–29440–2

First published in 2008

Greenwood Press, 88 Post Road West, Westport, CT 06881
An imprint of Greenwood Publishing Group, Inc.
www.greenwood.com

Printed in the United States of America

∞™

The paper used in this book complies with the Permanent Paper Standard issued by the National Information Standards Organization (Z39.48–1984).

10 9 8 7 6 5 4 3 2 1

Contents

List of Entries

Guide to Related Topics

Parks, Rosa
Popper, Hermine Rich
    Isaacs
Porter, John Thomas
Powell, Mary Louise Stamper
Proctor, Hilda Stewart
Quill, Michael Joseph
Raby, Albert
Ramachandran, G.
Randolph, A. Philip
Ray, Sandy Frederick
Reddick, Lawrence Dunbar
Reeb, James
Reuther, Walter Philip
Robinson, Cleveland
    Lowellyn
Robinson, Jackie
Robinson, Jo Ann Gibson
Rockefeller, Nelson Aldrich
Rodell, Marie Freid
Rogers, Theopholius
    Yelverton, Jr.
Roosevelt, (Anna)
    Eleanor
Rothschild, Jacob
    Mortimer
Rustin, Bayard
Seay, Solomon Snowden, Sr.
Shuttlesworth, Fred Lee
Smiley, Glenn E.
Smith, Kelly Miller
Smith, Lillian Eugenia
Spock, Benjamin
Steele, Charles Kenzie
Taylor, Gardner C.
Thomas, Norman Mattoon
Thurman, Howard
Vivian, Cordy Tindell
Wachtel, Harry H.
Walker, Wyatt Tee
Watson, Melvin Hampton
West, Irene
Wilkins, Roy Ottaway
Williams, Hosea
Wofford, Harris Llewellyn
Wurf, Jerome
Young, Andrew
Young, Whitney Moore

AWARDS
Nobel Peace Prize (1964)
Time Magazine's "Man of the
    Year" (1963)

CELEBRITIES
Angelou, Maya
Baldwin, James Arthur
Belafonte, Harold George, Jr.
Davis, Ossie, and Dee, Ruby
Davis, Sammy, Jr.
Gregory, Dick
Jackson, Mahalia
Robinson, Jackie
Smith, Lillian Eugenia

CHURCHES
Dexter Avenue Baptist
    Church (Montgomery,
    Alabama)
Ebenezer Baptist Church
    (Atlanta, Georgia)
Holt Street Baptist Church
    (Montgomery, Alabama)

CIVIL RIGHTS ACTIVISTS
Abernathy, Ralph David
Anderson, William Gilchrist
Angelou, Maya
Baker, Ella Josephine
Barry, Marion Shepilov, Jr.
Bates, Daisy
Belafonte, Harold George, Jr.
Bevel, James Luther
Blackwell, Randolph T.
Bond, Horace Julian
Borders, William Holmes, Sr.
Boyte, Harry G.
Braden, Anne Gamrell
    McCarty, and Braden,
    Carl James
Brown, Theodore Edward
Bunche, Ralph Johnson
Burroughs, Nannie Helen
Carmichael, Stokely
Carr, Johnnie Rebecca
    Daniels
Challenor, Herschelle
    Sullivan
Chalmers, Allan Knight
Clark, Septima Poinsette
Cotton, Dorothy Foreman
Daniels, Jonathan Myrick
Davis, Ossie, and Dee, Ruby
Durr, Virginia Foster
Evers, Medgar Wiley
Farmer, James

Fauntroy, Walter E.
Forman, James
Gomillion, Charles Goode
Graetz, Robert
Granger, Lester Blackwell
Gray, Fred David, Sr.
Gregory, Dick
Hamer, Fannie Lou
Harding, Vincent Gordon
Hassler, Alfred
Hayling, Robert B.
Heschel, Abraham Joshua
Hollowell, Donald L.
Hooks, Benjamin Lawson
Houser, George Mills
Hughes, Robert E.
Jack, Homer Alexander
Jackson, Jesse Louis
Jackson, Jimmie Lee
Jemison, Theodore Judson
Jones, Clarence Benjamin
King, Alfred Daniel Williams
King, Coretta Scott
King, Martin Luther, Sr.
Lafayette, Bernard
Lawson, James M.
Lee, Bernard Scott
Levison, Stanley David
Lewis, John
Lewis, Rufus
Lowery, Joseph Echols
Malcolm X
Marshall, Thurgood
McKissick, Floyd Bixler
Meredith, James Howard
Moses, Robert Parris
Muste, Abraham Johannes
Nash, Diane Judith
Nixon, Edgar Daniel
O'Dell, Hunter Pitts "Jack"
Parks, Rosa
Peck, James
Porter, John Thomas
Quill, Michael Joseph
Raby, Albert
Randolph, A. Philip
Reddick, Lawrence Dunbar
Reeb, James
Reuther, Walter Philip
Robinson, Cleveland
    Lowellyn
Robinson, Jackie
Robinson, Jo Ann Gibson
Roosevelt, (Anna) Eleanor

Rothschild, Jacob Mortimer
Rustin, Bayard
Seay, Solomon Snowden, Sr.
Shuttlesworth, Fred Lee
Smiley, Glenn E.
Smith, Kelly Miller
Steele, Charles Kenzie
Taylor, Gardner C.
Vivian, Cordy Tindell
Wachtel, Harry H.
Walker, Wyatt Tee
West, Irene
Wilkins, Roy Ottaway
Williams, Adam Daniel
Williams, Hosea
Williams, Robert Franklin
Wofford, Harris Llewellyn
Wurf, Jerome
Young, Andrew
Young, Whitney Moore

CLERGY

Abernathy, Ralph David
Barbour, Josephus Pius
Barth, Karl
Bevel, James Luther
Borders, William Holmes, Sr.
Bristol, James E.
Carey, Archibald J., Jr.
Chalmers, Allan Knight
Davis, George Washington
DeWolf, L. (Lotan) Harold
Dobbs, John Wesley
Fauntroy, Walter E.
Fosdick, Harry Emerson
Graetz, Robert
Graham, William Franklin
Gray, Fred David, Sr.
Gray, William H., Jr.
Heschel, Abraham Joshua
Hooks, Benjamin Lawson
Hughes, Robert E.
Jack, Homer Alexander
Jackson, Jesse Louis
Jackson, Joseph Harrison
Jemison, Theodore Judson
Johns, Vernon
Johnson, Mordecai Wyatt
Kelsey, George Dennis Sale
King, Alfred Daniel
  Williams
King, Martin Luther, Sr.
Lawson, James M.

Lewis, John
Lowery, Joseph Echols
Mays, Benjamin Elijah
McCall, Walter R.
Niebuhr, Reinhold
Porter, John Thomas
Powell, Adam Clayton, Jr.
Ray, Sandy Frederick
Reeb, James
Rogers, Theopholius Yelverton, Jr.
Rothschild, Jacob Mortimer
Seay, Solomon Snowden, Sr.
Shuttlesworth, Fred Lee
Smiley, Glenn E.
Smith, Kelly Miller
Steele, Charles Kenzie
Taylor, Gardner C.
Thurman, Howard
Tilley, John Lee
Tillich, Paul
Vivian, Cordy Tindell
Walker, Wyatt Tee
Watson, Melvin Hampton
Williams, Adam Daniel
Young, Andrew

COURT CASES

Browder v. Gayle, 352 U.S. 903 (1956)
Brown et al. v. Board of Education of Topeka, Kansas, et al., 347 U.S. 483 (1954), 349 U.S. 294 (1955)
New York Times Co. v. Sullivan, 376 U.S. 254 (1964)
State of Alabama v. M. L. King, Jr. (1956 and 1960)

EDUCATIONAL INFLUENCES

Barth, Karl
Boston University
Brightman, Edgar Sheffield
Cook, Samuel DuBois
Crozer Theological Seminary
Davis, George Washington
DeWolf, L. (Lotan) Harold
Dissertation of Martin Luther King, Jr. (1955)
Fosdick, Harry Emerson
Johnson, Mordecai Wyatt
Kelsey, George Dennis Sale

Mays, Benjamin Elijah
Morehouse College
Muste, Abraham Johannes
Niebuhr, Reinhold
Thurman, Howard

EVENTS

Albany Movement
Assassination of Martin Luther King, Jr. (4 April 1968)
Birmingham Campaign (1963)
Chicago Campaign (1966)
Emancipation Proclamation (1863)
Freedom Rides
Freedom Summer (1964)
Institute on Nonviolence and Social Change
Little Rock School Desegregation (1957)
March on Washington for Jobs and Freedom (1963)
Memphis Sanitation Workers' Strike (1968)
Montgomery Bus Boycott (1955–1956)
National Conference on Religion and Race
Operation Breadbasket (1962–1972)
Poor People's Campaign (1967–1968)
Prayer Pilgrimage for Freedom (1957)
Selma to Montgomery March (1965)
Sit-Ins
St. Augustine, Florida (1963–1965)
Summer Community Organization and Political Education (SCOPE) Project
Vietnam War (1961–1975)
Voter Education Project (VEP)
Watts Rebellion (Los Angeles, 1965)
Youth March for Integrated Schools (25 October 1958 and 18 April 1959)

SOUTHERN CHRISTIAN
LEADERSHIP CONFERENCE
(SCLC) COLLEAGUES
Abernathy, Ralph David
Angelou, Maya
Baker, Ella Josephine
Ballou, Maude L. Williams
Bevel, James Luther
Blackwell, Randolph T.
Boyte, Harry G.
Braden, Anne Gamrell
    McCarty, and Braden,
    Carl James
Clark, Septima Poinsette
Cotton, Dorothy Foreman

Evers, Medgar Wiley
Fauntroy, Walter E.
Hooks, Benjamin Lawson
Hunter, Lillie Thomas
    Armstrong
Jackson, Jesse Louis
Jemison, Theodore Judson
Jones, Clarence Benjamin
Lafayette, Bernard
Lawson, James M.
Lee, Bernard Scott
Lowery, Joseph Echols
McDonald, Dora Edith
Moses, Robert Parris
Nash, Diane Judith

O'Dell, Hunter Pitts "Jack"
Ray, Sandy Frederick
Reddick, Lawrence Dunbar
Rustin, Bayard
Seay, Solomon Snowden, Sr.
Shuttlesworth, Fred Lee
Smith, Kelly Miller
Steele, Charles Kenzie
Tilley, John Lee
Vivian, Cordy Tindell
Walker, Wyatt Tee
Williams, Hosea
Young, Andrew

Preface

In 1985, Coretta Scott King asked Stanford University historian Clayborne Carson to edit her late husband's papers. Since accepting her offer, Carson and his staff at the Martin Luther King, Jr., Papers Project at Stanford University have published 6 volumes of a projected 14-volume edition of *The Papers of Martin Luther King, Jr.* As the King Papers Project (now the King Institute) grew, it has built upon the foundation of these scholarly volumes by publishing books and articles intended for various audiences. *The Martin Luther King, Jr., Encyclopedia* is an outgrowth of the King Institute's continuing effort to provide educational resources for students, teachers, researchers, and interested readers of all ages.

The *King Encyclopedia* is based on the extensive historical research originally conducted by the Papers Project staff to produce annotations for the published volumes of King's papers. Unlike other encyclopedias, the *King Encyclopedia* draws heavily upon the Papers Project's vast collection of primary source documents related to King and the movements he inspired. Wherever possible, the authors give preference to the use of contemporaneous documents as sources for the entries. Quotations from these documents are included in many entries to illuminate the relationships among King and the individuals, organizations, events, and other topics included in this encyclopedia.

The encyclopedia begins with a chronology of the most significant events in King's life and civil rights career, followed by a short narrative introduction. This introduction provides a general overview of King's life, beginning with his birth in January 1929 and ending with his untimely death in April 1968. Throughout the introductory essay, and in the entries that follow, the reader will notice that some names, events, organizations, and concepts are presented in bold type to indicate entries that can be found elsewhere in the encyclopedia.

Although King lived only 39 years, his associations during that brief time were vast, making the process of selecting entries for this encyclopedia difficult. The authors devised selection criteria that gave priority to other African American leaders, members of King's family and close relatives, personal and professional associates (including his attorneys, secretaries, and advisors), theological and political sources of influence, religious acquaintances, celebrities who supported his protest campaigns, and political allies and opponents. Major events in King's life, such as his India trip in 1959, and his participation in the Albany Movement in 1961 and 1962, have their own entries. Due to space restrictions, some significant individuals are not given their own entries, but are mentioned in entries concerning their organizational affiliations, or the events or campaigns in which they were prominently involved.

The 285 entries in this encyclopedia are arranged alphabetically. In the interest of providing readers with useful descriptions of each subject, entries begin with a brief explanation of the relationship of the subject to King. The entries are not intended to be a full treatment of any particular topic, but are instead focused on the subject's interactions with King. All entries are followed by a list of sources, which contain secondary literature and primary documents used to produce the entry. The primary document source notes are followed by an archival code, which designates the location of the original or source document using standard abbreviations from the *USMARC Code List for Organizations*. See the list of abbreviations for all codes used. Widely available sources, such as biographical dictionaries and encyclopedias, are not listed. In addition, quotations are cited within the text for the reader's convenience. The encyclopedia concludes with a bibliography containing full citations of the books listed in the source notes of the entries, as well as additional resources pertaining to King's life and work. Many of the entries also are illustrated and information within them can be further accessed through a detailed subject index.

The *King Encyclopedia* was conceived as a reference work that demonstrates the interconnected nature of King's associations, ideas, and activities. The authors hope that this encyclopedia answers many of their questions about Martin Luther King, Jr.'s life and the movements that he inspired.

Acknowledgments

The Martin Luther King, Jr., Encyclopedia has benefited from two decades of research by the King Papers Project, which began as a joint venture of Stanford University and the King Center in Atlanta. Many of the articles in this encyclopedia draw upon the biographical research related to annotations in the published volumes of *The Papers of Martin Luther King, Jr.* Because of the collaborative nature of the project's research effort, this encyclopedia has profited from the efforts of many more individuals than is possible to name here. The following acknowledgments draw attention to those individuals who built on this previous research to produce an encyclopedia intended for general researchers and readers.

Research assistant Madolyn Orr was intensively involved in every stage of the manuscript's production. Her exceptional editing skills and attention to detail greatly improved the quality of the manuscript. Madolyn's enthusiasm and dedication to the difficult task of writing accurate and concise history are very much appreciated.

Special thanks also go to former project editors Adrienne Clay and Kieran Taylor who read early drafts of the articles. Research assistant Louis Jackson checked the manuscript's accuracy and contributed valuable suggestions for revisions. Miranda Worthen, a graduate of Harvard University, also helped with the production of the encyclopedia's manuscript, especially the post-1964 entries. We also appreciate the assistance of Rebecca Hood, Helen Kaufman, and David Leonard.

Although not directly involved in the research or writing of this volume, other staff members provided essential administrative support, especially Project Administrator Jane Abbott and Assistant Administrator Regina Covington.

The King Papers Project has always depended on the skills, dedication, and exceptional talents of Stanford students, working as interns, volunteers, or for academic credit. Undergraduate researchers who worked on the encyclopedia included Alicia Barber, Lisa Brown, Taurean Brown, Lonnie Browne, LaTasha Crow, Adhaar Desai, Robert DeSpain, Kevin Dumolga, Eron Eguavoen, Tim Fleming, Jordan Gilchrist, Adia Gooden, Austin Henderson, Michael Huggins, Kyonne Isaac, Aaron Jackson, Monique King, David Lai, Zoe Levitt, James Locus, Betty Luan, Dagem Mammo, Lauren Mathews, Marina McCoy, Jidenna Mobisson, Jacqueline Palma, Aysha Pamuku, Celia Perry, Ryan Peters, Sam Pressman, Weena Pun, Alison Root, Lisa Ruskin, Anna Sale, Katie Salisbury, Andrew Schneider, Tiana Seymore, Lindsey Smith, Christopher Williams, Katrice Williams, Juliana Yanez, and Reid Yokoyama.

The following students have made significant contributions through the Martin Luther King, Jr., Summer Research Fellowship program: Sarah Allen (Stanford University), Gina Bateson (Stanford University), Vaughn Booker (Dartmouth College), Juliana Boucher (North Carolina State University), Elizabeth Crocker (University of Virginia), Adrienne Denson (Williams College), Joshua Dougherty (Concordia University), Kristin Ferrales (Stanford University), Reygan Harmon (Spelman College), Jessica Harris (Dillard University), Demetrius Hobson (Morehouse College), Kristina Hoeppner (University of California, Davis), Brandon Jackson (Morehouse College), Jeneka Joyce (University of Notre Dame), Monique King (Stanford University), David Lai (Stanford University), Tim Lake (Bowling Green State University), Christopher Lee (Boston College), Treva Lindsey (Oberlin College), James Locus (Stanford University), Katrina Logan (Stanford University), Vernon C. Mitchell, Jr. (University of Missouri, Columbia), Benjamin Peters (University of Washington, Tacoma), Jedediah Peterson (Stanford University), Jennifer Sahrle (CUNY-Geneseo), Anna Sale (Stanford University), Andrew Schneider (Stanford University), Lindsey Smith (Stanford University), Kate Stanley (Stanford University), Eric Stowe (University of Washington, Tacoma), Christopher Williams (Stanford University), and Teresa Yeager (Stanford University). Without the dedicated research of many, this encyclopedia would not be possible.

Introduction

Martin Luther King, Jr., made history, but he was also transformed by his deep family roots in the African American Baptist church, his formative experiences in his hometown of Atlanta, his theological studies, his varied models of religious and political leadership, and his extensive network of contacts in the peace and social justice movements of his time. Although King was only 39 at the time of his death, his life was remarkable for the ways it reflected and inspired so many of the twentieth century's major intellectual, cultural, and political developments.

The son, grandson, and great-grandson of Baptist ministers, Martin Luther King, Jr., named Michael King at birth, was born in Atlanta and spent his first 12 years in the Auburn Avenue home that his parents, the Reverend Michael **King** and Alberta Williams **King**, shared with his maternal grandparents, the Reverend Adam Daniel (A. D.) **Williams** and Jeannie Celeste Williams. After Reverend Williams' death in 1931, his son-in-law became **Ebenezer Baptist Church**'s new pastor and gradually established himself as a major figure in state and national Baptist groups. The elder King began referring to himself (and later to his son) as Martin Luther King.

King's formative experiences not only immersed him in the affairs of Ebenezer but also introduced him to the African-American **social gospel** tradition exemplified by his father and grandfather, both of whom were leaders of the Atlanta branch of the **National Association for the Advancement of Colored People** (NAACP). Depression-era breadlines heightened King's awareness of economic inequities, and his father's leadership of campaigns against racial discrimination in voting and teachers' salaries provided a model for the younger King's own politically engaged ministry. He resisted religious emotionalism and as a teenager questioned some facets of Baptist doctrine, such as the bodily resurrection of Jesus.

During his undergraduate years at Atlanta's **Morehouse College** from 1944 to 1948, King gradually overcame his initial reluctance to accept his inherited calling. Morehouse president Benjamin E. **Mays** influenced King's spiritual development, encouraging him to view Christianity as a potential force for progressive social change. Religion professor George **Kelsey** exposed him to biblical criticism and, according to King's autobiographical sketch, taught him "that behind the legends and myths of the Book were many profound truths which one could not escape" (*Papers* 1:43). King admired both educators as deeply religious yet also learned men and, by the end of his junior year, such academic role models and the example of his father led King to enter the ministry. He described his decision as a response to an "inner urge" calling him to "serve humanity" (*Papers* 1:363). He was ordained during his final semester at Morehouse, and by this time King had also taken his first steps toward political activism. He had responded to the postwar wave of anti-black violence by proclaiming in a letter to the editor of the *Atlanta Constitution* that African Americans were "entitled to the basic rights and opportunities of American citizens" (*Papers* 1:121). During his senior year King joined the Intercollegiate Council, an interracial student discussion group that met monthly at Atlanta's Emory University.

After leaving Morehouse, King increased his understanding of liberal Christian thought while attending **Crozer Theological Seminary** in Pennsylvania from 1948 to 1951. Initially uncritical of liberal theology, he gradually moved toward Reinhold **Niebuhr**'s neo-orthodoxy, which emphasized the intractability of social evil. Mentored by local minister and King family friend J. Pius **Barbour**, he reacted skeptically to a presentation on pacifism by **Fellowship of Reconciliation** leader A. J. **Muste**. Moreover, by the end of his seminary studies King had become increasingly dissatisfied with the abstract conceptions of God held by some modern theologians and identified himself instead with the theologians who affirmed **personalism**, or a belief in the personality of God. Even as he continued to question and modify his own religious beliefs, he compiled an outstanding academic record and graduated at the top of his class.

In 1951, King began doctoral studies in systematic theology at **Boston University**'s School of Theology, which was dominated by personalist theologians such as Edgar **Brightman** and L. Harold **DeWolf**. The papers (including his **dissertation**) that King wrote during his years at Boston University displayed little originality, and some contained extensive plagiarism; but his readings enabled him to formulate an eclectic yet coherent theological perspective. By the time he completed his doctoral studies in 1955, King had refined his exceptional ability to draw upon a wide range of theological and philosophical texts to express his views with force and precision. His capacity to infuse his oratory with borrowed theological insights became evident in his expanding preaching activities in Boston-area churches and at Ebenezer, where he assisted his father during school vacations.

During his stay in Boston, King also met and courted Coretta **Scott**, an Alabama-born Antioch College graduate who was then a student at the New England Conservatory of Music. On 18 June 1953, the two students were married in Marion, Alabama, where Scott's family lived.

Although he considered pursuing an academic career, King decided in 1954 to accept an offer to become the pastor of **Dexter Avenue Baptist Church** in Montgomery, Alabama. In December 1955, when Montgomery black leaders such as Jo Ann **Robinson**, E. D. **Nixon**, and Ralph **Abernathy** formed the **Montgomery Improvement Association** (MIA) to protest the arrest of NAACP official Rosa **Parks** for refusing to give up her bus seat to a white man, they selected King to head the new group. In his role as the primary spokesman of the year-long **Montgomery bus boycott**, King utilized the leadership abilities he had gained from his religious background and academic training to forge a distinctive protest strategy that involved the mobilization of black churches and skillful appeals for white support. With the encouragement of Bayard **Rustin**, Glenn **Smiley**, William Stuart **Nelson**, and other veteran pacifists, King also became a firm advocate of Mohandas **Gandhi's** precepts of **nonviolence,** which he combined with Christian social gospel ideas.

After the U.S. Supreme Court outlawed Alabama bus segregation laws in ***Browder v. Gayle*** in late 1956, King sought to expand the nonviolent civil rights movement throughout the South. In 1957, he joined with C. K. **Steele,** Fred **Shuttlesworth,** and T. J. **Jemison** in founding the **Southern Christian Leadership Conference** (SCLC) with King as president to coordinate civil rights activities throughout the region. Publication of King's memoir of the boycott, ***Stride Toward Freedom: The Montgomery Story*** (1958), further contributed to his rapid emergence as a national civil rights leader. Even as he expanded his influence, however, King acted cautiously. Rather than immediately seeking to stimulate mass desegregation protests in the South, King stressed the goal of achieving black voting rights when he addressed an audience at the 1957 **Prayer Pilgrimage for Freedom.**

King's rise to fame was not without personal consequences. In 1958, King was the victim of his first assassination attempt. Although his house had been bombed several times during the Montgomery bus boycott, it was while signing copies of *Stride Toward Freedom* that Izola Ware **Curry** stabbed him with a letter opener. Surgery to remove it was successful, but King had to recuperate for several months, giving up all protest activity.

One of the key aspects of King's leadership was his ability to establish support from many types of organizations, including labor unions, peace organizations, southern reform organizations, and religious groups. As early as 1956, labor unions, such as the **United Packinghouse Workers of America** and the United Auto Workers, contributed to MIA, and peace activists such as Homer **Jack** alerted their associates to MIA activities. Activists from southern organizations, such as Myles Horton's **Highlander Folk School** and Anne **Braden**'s Southern Conference Education Fund, were in frequent contact with King. In addition, his extensive ties to the **National Baptist Convention** provided support from churches all over the nation; and his advisor, Stanley **Levison**, ensured broad support from Jewish groups.

King's recognition of the link between segregation and colonialism resulted in alliances with groups fighting oppression outside the United States, especially in Africa. In March 1957, King traveled to **Ghana** at the invitation of Kwame **Nkrumah** to attend the nation's independence ceremony. Shortly after returning from Ghana, King joined the **American Committee on Africa**, agreeing to serve as vice chairman of an International Sponsoring Committee for a day of protest against South Africa's **apartheid** government. Later, at an SCLC-sponsored event honoring Kenyan labor leader Tom **Mboya,** King further articulated the connections between the African American freedom struggle and those abroad: "We are all caught in an inescapable network of mutuality" (*Papers* 5:204).

During 1959, he increased his understanding of Gandhian ideas during a month-long visit to **India** sponsored by the **American Friends Service Committee**. With Coretta and MIA historian Lawrence D. Reddick in tow, King met with many Indian leaders, including Prime Minister Jawaharlal **Nehru**. Writing after his return, King stated: "I left India more convinced than ever before that nonviolent resistance is the most potent weapon available to oppressed people in their struggle for freedom" (*Papers* 5:233).

Early the following year, he moved his family, which now included two children—Yolanda and Martin Luther King, III—to Atlanta in order to be nearer to SCLC headquarters in that city and to become co-pastor, with his father, of Ebenezer Baptist Church. (The Kings' third child, Dexter, was born in 1961; their fourth, Bernice, was born in 1963.) Soon after King's arrival in Atlanta, the southern civil rights movement gained new impetus from the student-led lunch counter **sit-in** movement that spread throughout the region during 1960. The sit-ins brought into existence a new protest group, the **Student Nonviolent Coordinating Committee** (SNCC), which would often push King toward greater militancy. King came in contact with students, especially those from Nashville such as John **Lewis**, James **Bevel**, and Diane **Nash**, who had been trained in nonviolent tactics by James **Lawson**. In October 1960, King's arrest during a student-initiated protest in Atlanta became an issue in the national presidential campaign when Democratic candidate John F. **Kennedy** called Coretta King to express his concern. The successful efforts of Kennedy supporters to secure King's release contributed to the Democratic candidate's narrow victory over Republican candidate Richard **Nixon**.

King's decision to move to Atlanta was partly caused by SCLC's lack of success during the late 1950s. Associate director Ella **Baker** had complained that SCLC's Crusade for Citizenship suffered from lack of attention from King. SCLC leaders hoped that with King now in Atlanta, strategy would be improved. The hiring of Wyatt Tee **Walker** as executive director in 1960 was also seen as a step toward bringing efficiency to the organization, while the addition of Dorothy **Cotton** and Andrew **Young** to the staff infused new leadership after SCLC took over the administration of the Citizenship Education Program pioneered by Septima **Clark**. Attorney Clarence **Jones** also began to assist King and SCLC with legal matters and to act as King's advisor.

As the southern protest movement expanded during the early 1960s, King was often torn between the increasingly militant student activists, such as those who participated in the **Freedom Rides**, and more cautious national civil rights leaders. During 1961 and 1962, his tactical differences with SNCC activists surfaced during a sustained protest movement in Albany, Georgia. King was arrested twice during demonstrations organized by the **Albany Movement**, but when he left jail and ultimately left Albany without achieving a victory, some movement activists began to question his militancy and his dominant role within the southern protest movement.

As King encountered increasingly fierce white opposition, he continued his movement away from theological abstractions toward more reassuring conceptions, rooted in African American religious culture, of God as a constant source of support. He later wrote in his book of sermons, *Strength to Love* (1963), that the travails of movement leadership caused him to abandon the notion of God as "theological and philosophically satisfying" and caused him to view God as "a living reality that has been validated in the experiences of everyday life" (141).

During 1963, however, King reasserted his preeminence within the African American freedom struggle through his leadership of the **Birmingham Campaign**. Initiated by SCLC and its affiliate, the **Alabama Christian Movement for Human Rights**, the Birmingham demonstrations were the most massive civil rights protests that had yet occurred. With the assistance of Fred Shuttlesworth and other local black leaders, and with little competition from SNCC and other civil rights groups, SCLC officials were able to orchestrate the Birmingham protests to achieve maximum national impact.

King's decision to intentionally allow himself to be arrested for leading a demonstration on 12 April prodded the Kennedy administration to intervene in the escalating protests. The widely quoted "Letter from Birmingham Jail" displayed his distinctive ability to influence public opinion by appropriating ideas from the Bible, the Constitution, and other canonical texts. During May, televised pictures of police using dogs and fire hoses against young demonstrators generated a national outcry against white segregationist officials in Birmingham. The brutality of Birmingham officials and the refusal of Alabama's governor George C. **Wallace** to allow the admission of black students at the University of Alabama prompted President Kennedy to introduce major civil rights legislation.

King's speech at the 28 August 1963 **March on Washington for Jobs and Freedom**, attended by more than 200,000 people, was the culmination of a wave of civil rights protest activity that extended even to northern cities. In his prepared remarks, King announced that African Americans wished to cash the "promissory note" signified in the egalitarian rhetoric of the Constitution and the Declaration of Independence. Closing his address with extemporaneous remarks, he insisted that he had not lost hope: "I say to you today, my friends, so even though we face the difficulties of today and tomorrow, I still have a dream. It is a dream deeply rooted in the American dream … that one day this nation will rise up and live out the true meaning of its creed: 'we hold these truths to be self-evident, that all men are created equal.'" He appropriated the familiar words of "My Country 'Tis of Thee," before concluding, "when we allow freedom ring, when we let it ring from every village and every hamlet, from every state and every city, we will be able to speed up that day when all of God's children, black men and white men, Jews and Gentiles, Protestants and Catholics, will be able to join hands and sing in the words of the old Negro spiritual, 'Free at last, free at last, thank God Almighty, we are free at last'" (King, *Call*, 82, 85, 87).

Although there was much elation after the March on Washington, less than a month later, the movement was shocked by another act of senseless violence. On 15 September 1963, a dynamite blast at Birmingham's Sixteenth Street Baptist Church killed four young school girls. King delivered the eulogy for three of the four girls, reflecting: "They say to us that we must be concerned not merely about who murdered them, but about the system, the way of life, and the philosophy which produced the murders" (King, *Call*, 96).

St. Augustine, Florida, became the site of the next major confrontation of the civil rights movement. Beginning in 1963, Robert B. **Hayling**, of the local NAACP, had led sit-ins against segregated businesses. SCLC was called in to help in May 1964, suffering the arrest of King and Abernathy. After a few court victories, SCLC left when a biracial committee was formed; however, local residents continued to suffer violence.

King's ability to focus national attention on orchestrated confrontations with racist authorities, combined with his oration at the 1963 March on Washington, made him the most influential African American spokesperson of the first half of the 1960s. He was named *Time* **magazine's "Man of the Year"** at the end of 1963, and was awarded the **Nobel Peace Prize** in December 1964. The acclaim King received strengthened his stature among civil rights leaders but also prompted **Federal Bureau of Investigation** (FBI) director J. Edgar **Hoover** to step up his effort to damage King's reputation.

Hoover, with the approval of President Kennedy and Attorney General Robert **Kennedy**, established phone taps and bugs. Hoover and many other observers of the southern struggle saw King as controlling events, but he was actually a moderating force within an increasingly diverse black militancy of the mid-1960s. Although he was not personally involved in **Freedom Summer** (1964), he was called upon to attempt to persuade the **Mississippi Freedom Democratic Party** delegates to accept a compromise at the Democratic Party National Convention.

As the African American struggle expanded from desegregation protests to mass movements seeking economic and political gains in the North as well as the South, King's active involvement was limited to a few highly publicized civil rights campaigns, such as Birmingham and St. Augustine, which secured popular support for the passage of national civil rights legislation, particularly the **Civil Rights Act of 1964.**

The Alabama protests reached a turning point on 7 March, when state police attacked a group of demonstrators at the start of a march from Selma to the state capitol in Montgomery. Carrying out Governor Wallace's orders, the police used tear gas and clubs to turn back the marchers after they crossed the Edmund Pettus Bridge on the outskirts of Selma. Unprepared for the violent confrontation, King alienated some activists when he decided to postpone the continuation of the **Selma to Montgomery March** until he had received court approval, but the march, which finally secured federal court approval, attracted several thousand civil rights sympathizers, black and white, from all regions of the nation. On 25 March, King addressed the arriving marchers from the steps of the capitol in Montgomery. The march and the subsequent killing of a white participant, Viola Liuzzo, as well as the earlier murder of James **Reeb** dramatized the denial of black voting rights and spurred passage during the following summer of the **Voting Rights Act of 1965**.

After the march in Alabama, King was unable to garner similar support for his effort to confront the problems of northern urban blacks. Early in 1966 he, together with local activist Al **Raby,** launched a major campaign against poverty and other urban problems, and King moved his family into an apartment in Chicago's black ghetto. As King shifted the focus of his activities to the North, however, he discovered that the tactics used in the South were not as effective elsewhere. He encountered formidable opposition from Mayor Richard Daley and was unable to mobilize Chicago's economically and ideologically diverse black community. King was stoned by angry whites in the Chicago suburb of Cicero when he led a march against racial discrimination in housing. Despite numerous mass protests, the **Chicago Campaign** resulted in no significant gains and undermined King's reputation as an effective civil rights leader.

King's influence was damaged further by the increasingly caustic tone of black militancy in the period after 1965. Black radicals increasingly turned away from the Gandhian precepts of King toward the Black Nationalism of **Malcolm X**, whose posthumously published autobiography and speeches reached large audiences after his assassination in February 1965. Unable to influence the black insurgencies that occurred in many urban areas, King refused to abandon his firmly rooted beliefs about racial integration and nonviolence. He was nevertheless unpersuaded by black nationalist calls for racial uplift and institutional development in black communities.

In June 1966, James **Meredith** was shot while attempting a "March against Fear" in Mississippi. King, Floyd **McKissick** of the **Congress of Racial Equality**, and Stokely

Carmichael of SNCC decided to continue his march. During the march, the activists from SNCC decided to test a new slogan that they had been using, **Black Power**. King objected to the use of the term, but the media took the opportunity to expose the disagreements among protestors and publicized the term.

In his last book, ***Where Do We Go from Here: Chaos or Community?*** (1967), King dismissed the claim of Black Power advocates "to be the most revolutionary wing of the social revolution taking place in the United States," but he acknowledged that they responded to a psychological need among African Americans he had not previously addressed (King, *Where Do We Go*, 45–46). "Psychological freedom, a firm sense of self-esteem, is the most powerful weapon against the long night of physical slavery," King wrote. "The Negro will only be free when he reaches down to the inner depths of his own being and signs with the pen and ink of assertive manhood his own emancipation proclamation" (King, *Call*, 184).

Indeed, even as his popularity declined, King spoke out strongly against American involvement in the **Vietnam War**, making his position public in an address, "**Beyond Vietnam**," on 4 April 1967, at New York's Riverside Church. King's involvement in the anti-war movement reduced his ability to influence national racial policies and made him a target of further FBI investigations. Nevertheless, he became ever more insistent that his version of Gandhian nonviolence and social gospel Christianity was the most appropriate response to the problems of black Americans.

In December 1967, King announced the formation of the **Poor People's Campaign**, designed to prod the federal government to strengthen its antipoverty efforts. King and other SCLC workers began to recruit poor people and antipoverty activists to come to Washington, D.C., to lobby on behalf of improved antipoverty programs. This effort was in its early stages when King became involved in the **Memphis sanitation workers' strike** in Tennessee. On 28 March 1968, as King led thousands of sanitation workers and sympathizers on a march through downtown Memphis, black youngsters began throwing rocks and looting stores. This outbreak of violence led to extensive press criticisms of King's entire antipoverty strategy. King returned to Memphis for the last time in early April. Addressing an audience at Bishop Charles J. Mason Temple on 3 April, King affirmed his optimism despite the "difficult days" that lay ahead. "But it really doesn't matter with me now," he declared, "because I've been to the mountaintop [and] I've seen the Promised Land." He continued, "I may not get there with you. But I want you to know tonight, that we, as a people, will get to the Promised Land" (King, *Call*, 222–223). The following evening, the **assassination of Martin Luther King, Jr.,** took place as he stood on a balcony of the Lorraine Motel in Memphis. A white segregationist, James Earl Ray, was later convicted of the crime. The Poor People's Campaign continued for a few months after King's death, under the direction of Ralph Abernathy, the new SCLC president, but it did not achieve its objectives.

Until his death, King remained steadfast in his commitment to the transformation of American society through nonviolent activism. In his posthumously published essay, "A Testament of Hope" (1969), he urged African Americans to refrain from violence but also warned: "White America must recognize that justice for black people cannot be achieved without radical changes in the structure of our society." The "black revolution" was more than a civil rights movement, he insisted. "It is forcing

America to face all its interrelated flaws—racism, poverty, militarism, and materialism" (King, "Testament," 194).

After her husband's death, Coretta Scott King established the Atlanta-based Martin Luther King, Jr., Center for Nonviolent Social Change (also known as the **King Center**) to promote Gandhian–Kingian concepts of nonviolent struggle. She also led the successful effort to honor her husband with a federally mandated **King national holiday**, which was first celebrated in 1986.

SOURCES

Introduction, in *Papers* 1:1–57.

King, "An Autobiography of Religious Development," 12 September–22 November 1950, in *Papers* 1:359–363.

King, "Eulogy for the Young Victims of the Sixteenth Street Baptist Church Bombing," in *Call to Conscience*, Carson and Shepard, eds., 2001, 95–99.

King, "I Have a Dream," in *Call to Conscience,* Carson and Shepard, eds., 2001, 81–87.

King, "I've Been to the Mountaintop," in *A Call to Conscience*, eds. Clayborne Carson and Kris Shepard, New York: Warner Books, 2001, pp. 207–223.

King, "Kick Up Dust," Letter to the Editor, *Atlanta Constitution*, in *Papers* 1:121.

King, "My Trip to the Land of Gandhi," in *Papers* 5:231–238.

King, "Pilgrimage to Nonviolence" in *Papers* 5:419–425.

King, Remarks at Africa Freedom Dinner at Atlanta University, in *Papers* 5:203–204.

King, *Strength to Love*, 1963.

King, "A Testament of Hope," in *Playboy* (16 January 1969): 193–194, 231–236.

King, "Where Do We Go from Here?" in *Call to Conscience*, Carson and Shepard, eds., 2001, 171–199.

King, *Where Do We Go from Here: Chaos or Community?* 1967.

Abbreviations

The primary document source notes are followed by an archival code that designates the location of the original source document using standard abbreviations from *USMARC Code List for Organizations*. Below is the list of abbreviations for all codes used.

ACA-ARC-LNT   American Committee on Africa Papers, Amistad Research Collections, Tulane University, New Orleans, La.

ACCP-DAFL   AFL-CIO Office of the President, George Meany Memorial Archives, Silver Spring, Md.

AFSCR-PPAFS   American Friends Service Committee Records, American Friends Service Committee Archives, Philadelphia, Pa.

AJC-ICHi   Archibald James Carey Collection, Chicago Historical Society, Chicago, Ill.

APRC-DLC   A. Philip Randolph Collection, Library of Congress, Washington, D.C.

ARC-LNT   Amistad Research Collections, Tulane University, New Orleans, La.

BMC-MWalK   Burke Marshall Collection, John F. Kennedy Library, Boston, Mass.

BPD-AB   Birmingham Police Department Surveillance Files, 1947–1980, Birmingham Public and Jefferson County Free Library, Birmingham, Ala.

BRP-DLC   Bayard Rustin Papers, Library of Congress, Washington, D.C.

BSCP-DLC   Brotherhood of Sleeping Car Porters and Maids Records, Library of Congress, Washington, D.C.

CB-CtY   Chester Bowles Collection, Yale University, New Haven, Conn.

CBC   Carl Benkert Collection (In private hands)

CBCR   Cornerstone Baptist Church Records, Brooklyn, N.Y.

CCCSU   Clayborne Carson Collection (In private hands)

CCFA-ICarbs   Christian Century Foundation Archives, Southern Illinois University, Carbondale, Ill.

CKFC	Christine King Farris Collection (In private hands)
CLPAC	Pacifica Radio Archive, Los Angeles, Calif.
CNP	Christopher Niebuhr Papers (In private hands)
CSKC	Coretta Scott Collection (In private hands)
CULC-ICIU	Chicago Urban League Collection, University of Illinois at Chicago Circle, Chicago, Ill.
DABCC	Dexter Avenue King Memorial Baptist Church Collection (In private hands)
DHSTR-WHi	Donald H. Smith Tape Recordings, Wisconsin Historical Society. Madison, Wisc.
DJG-GEU	David J. Garrow Collection, Special Collections, Emory University, Atlanta, Ga.
EBCR	Ebenezer Baptist Church Miscellaneous Records (In private hands)
EMHP-DGU	Eugene McCarthy Historical Project, Georgetown University, Washington, D.C.
ERC-NHyF	Eleanor Roosevelt Collection, General Services Administration, National Archives and Record Service, Franklin D. Roosevelt Library, Hyde Park, N.Y.
FBIDG-NN-Sc	David J. Garrow Federal Bureau of Investigation Collection, Manuscript, Archives and Rare Books Division, Schomburg Center for Research in Black Culture, The New York Public Library, Astor, Lenox and Tilden Foundations, New York, N.Y.
FLSC-GAMK	Fred. L. Shuttlesworth Collection, Martin Luther King, Jr., Center for Nonviolent Social Change, Atlanta, Ga.
FORP-PSC-P	Fellowship of Reconciliation Papers, Swarthmore College Peace Collection, Swarthmore, Pa.
FTaSU	Florida State University, Tallahasee, Fla.
GDL-G-Ar	Georgia Department of Law, Record Group 9, Georgia Department of Archives and History, Atlanta, Ga.
GESP	Glenn E. Smiley Papers (In private hands)
GMF-DAFL	Office of the President, George Meany's Files, George Meany Memorial Archives, Silver Spring, Md.
HAJP-PSC-P	Homer A. Jack Papers, Swarthmore College Peace Collection, Swarthmore, Pa.
HCBP-NcD	Harry C. Boyte Family Papers, Duke University, Durham, N.C.
HG-GAMK	Hazel Gregory Papers, Martin Luther King, Jr., Center for Nonviolent Social Change, Atlanta, Ga.
IElwp	Elmwood Park Public Library, Elmwood Park, Ill.
JBRP-AB	John Bryan Papers, Birmingham Public and Jefferson County Free Library, Birmingham, Ala.

JFKOH-MWalK	John F. Kennedy Oral History Project, John F. Kennedy Library, Boston, Mass.
JFKPP-MWalK	John F. Kennedy Pre-Presidential Papers, John F. Kennedy Library, Boston, Mass.
JMRP-GEU	Jacob M. Rothschild Papers, Special Collections, Emory University, Atlanta, Ga.
JTPP	John T. Porter Papers (In private hands)
JWBP-DMBCH	Jeanetta Welch Brown Papers, Mary McLeod Bethune Council House National Historical Site, Washington, D.C.
JWD-ARC-LNT	John Wesley Dobbs Papers, Amistad Research Collections, Tulane University, New Orleans, La.
LDPF-GAMK	Library Documentation Project Files, Martin Luther King, Jr., Center for Nonviolent Social Change, Atlanta, Ga.
LDRP-NN-Sc	Lawrence Dunbar Reddick Papers, Manuscript, Archives and Rare Books Division, Schomburg Center for Research in Black Culture, The New York Public Library, Astor, Lenox and Tilden Foundations, New York, N.Y.
LEWBP	Lewis Baldwin Papers (In private hands)
LOLP-ICIU	Lloyd O. Lewis Papers, University of Illinois at Chicago Circle, Chicago, Ill.
LSP-GU	Lillian Smith (1897–1966) Papers, University of Georgia Libraries, Athens, Ga.
MCDA-AMC	Montgomery County District Attorney's Files, Montgomery County Courthouse, Montgomery, Ala.
MJGC-MIDW-AL	Martin and Jessie Glaberman Collection, Wayne State University, Walter P. Reuther Library of Labor and Urban Affairs, Archives of Labor History and Urban Affairs, Detroit, Mich.
MLKEC	Martin Luther King Estate Collection (In private hands)
MLKJP-GAMK	Martin Luther King, Jr., Papers, 1950-1968, Martin Luther King, Jr., Center for Nonviolent Social Change, Atlanta, Ga.
MLK/OH-GAMK	Martin Luther King, Jr., Oral History Collection, Martin Luther King, Jr., Center for Nonviolent Social Change, Atlanta, Ga.
MLKP-MBU	Martin Luther King, Jr., Papers, 1954-1968, Howard Gotlieb Archival Research Center, Boston University, Boston, Mass.
MMFR	Montgomery to Memphis Film Research Files (In private hands)
MVC-TMM	Mississippi Valley Collection, Sanitation Workers Strike Collection, Memphis State University, Memphis, Tenn.
NAACPP-DLC	National Association for the Advancement of Colored People Papers, Library of Congress, Washington, D.C.

NCCP-PPPrHi	National Council of the Churches of Christ in the United States of America Papers, Presbyterian Department of History, Philadelphia, Pa.
NF-GEU	Newsweek File, Special Collections, Emory University, Atlanta, Ga.
NHBP-DLC	Nannie H. Burroughs Papers, Library of Congress, Washington, D.C.
NULR-DLC	National Urban League Records, Library of Congress, Washington, D.C.
NYDAR-NNRA	New York District Attorney Records, City of New York, Department of Records and Information Services Archives, New York, N.Y.
ORS	Orsonic Recording Services, Silver Spring, Md.
PGC-GEU	Paul Good Collection, Special Collections, Emory University, Atlanta, Ga.
PV-ARC-LNT	Prestin Valien Collection, Amistad Research Collections, Tulane University, New Orleans, La.
RBOH-DHU	Ralph J. Bunche Oral History Collection, Howard University, Washington, D.C.
RGP	Robert Graetz Papers (In private hands)
RPP-NN-Sc	Richard Parrish Papers (Additions), 1959–1976, Manuscript, Archives and Rare Books Division, Schomburg Center for Research in Black Culture, The New York Public Library, Astor, Lenox and Tilden Foundations, New York, N.Y.
RRML-TxTyU	Robert R. Muntz Library, University of Texas at Tyler, Tyler, Tex.
RWP-DLC	Roy Wilkins Papers, Library of Congress, Washington, D.C.
SCLCR-GAMK	Southern Christian Leadership Conference Records, Martin Luther King, Jr., Center for Nonviolent Social Change, Atlanta, Ga.
SNCCP-GAMK	Student Nonviolent Coordinating Committee Papers, Martin Luther King, Jr., Center for Nonviolent Social Change, Atlanta, Ga.
SOHP-NcU	Southern Oral History Program Collection, University of North Carolina, Chapel Hill, N.C.
SPCC-ScCC	Septima Clark Collection, College of Charleston, Charleston, S.C.
TMAC-GA	T. M. Alexander Collection, Atlanta Public Library, Auburn Avenue Research Center, Atlanta, Ga.
TWUC-NNU-LA	Transport Workers Union Collection, New York University, Robert F. Wagner Labor Archives, New York, N.Y.
UCD-MiDW-AL	UAW Citizenship Department, Roy Reuther Files, Wayne State University, Walter P. Reuther Library of Labor and Urban Affairs, Archives of Labor History and Urban Affairs, Detroit, Mich.

UPWP-WHi	United Packinghouse Workers Papers, Wisconsin Historical Society, Madison, Wisc.
VHC	Vincent Harding Collection (In private hands)
WCFO-KAbE	White House Central Files (Official File), Dwight D. Eisenhower Library, Abilene, Kans.
WHCF-MWalK	White House Central Files, John F. Kennedy Library, Boston, Mass.
WHP-GEU	William B. Hartsfield Papers, Special Collections, Emory University, Atlanta, Ga.
WMYC-NN-Sc	Whitney M. Young Collection, Manuscript, Archives and Rare Books Division, Schomburg Center for Research in Black Culture, The New York Public Library, Astor, Lenox and Tilden Foundations, New York, N.Y.
WONS-KAbE	White House Office, Office of the Special Assistant for National Security Affairs, Dwight D. Eisenhower Library, Abilene, Kans.
WRMP-GAMK	William Robert Miller Papers, 1955–1968, Martin Luther King, Jr., Center for Nonviolent Social Change, Atlanta, Ga.

Chronology

15 January 1929	Michael King (later known as Martin Luther King, Jr.) is born in Atlanta, Georgia.
12 April 1934	King's birth certificate is filed under the name Michael King.
3 May 1936	King is baptized after **Ebenezer Baptist Church**'s two-week annual revival, led by guest evangelist Rev. H. H. Coleman of Macedonia Baptist Church in Detroit.
Summer 1944	King is admitted to **Morehouse College** as an early admissions student.
6 August 1946	The *Atlanta Constitution* publishes King's letter to the editor stating that blacks "are entitled to the basic rights and opportunities of American citizens."
25 February 1948	King is ordained and appointed associate pastor at Ebenezer.
8 June 1948	King receives his bachelor of arts degree in sociology from Morehouse.
14 September 1948	King begins attending **Crozer Theological Seminary** in Chester, Pennsylvania.
May 1950	King is elected student body president at Crozer.
11 January 1951	King is admitted to **Boston University**'s School of Theology.
6 May 1951	King graduates from Crozer with a bachelor of divinity degree.
22 June 1952	King is initiated into Boston's Sigma chapter of the **Alpha Phi Alpha Fraternity**.
18 June 1953	King, Sr., performs the marriage ceremony of King, Jr., and Coretta Scott at the Scott home near Marion, Alabama.
31 October 1954	King is installed as pastor at **Dexter Avenue Baptist Church** in Montgomery, Alabama.
5 June 1955	King is awarded his doctorate from Boston University.
26 August 1955	Rosa **Parks** informs King that he has been elected to the executive committee of the Montgomery branch of the NAACP.

17 November 1955	Yolanda Denise **King**, the Kings' first child, is born.
1 December 1955	Parks is arrested after refusing to give up her bus seat to a white person.
2 December 1955	E. D. **Nixon** calls King to discuss the arrest of Parks and to arrange for a meeting of black leaders at Dexter that evening. King and Ralph **Abernathy** remain at Dexter after the meeting to mimeograph a redrafted leaflet publicizing a one-day bus boycott and the upcoming mass meeting.
3 December 1955	Boycott leaflets are distributed to black residents. Television and radio stations report plans for the Monday boycott and mass meeting at **Holt Street Baptist Church**.
5 December 1955	In the morning, King watches empty buses pass by his home, indicating a successful first day of the boycott. In the afternoon, 18 black leaders meet to plan the evening mass meeting. The group organizes itself as the **Montgomery Improvement Association** (MIA), agrees to an agenda for the mass meeting, and elects its officers, including King as president. Later that evening, several thousand people gather at Holt Street Baptist Church for the first mass meeting of the **Montgomery bus boycott**. King gives the main address.
8 December 1955	King and other members of the MIA executive board meet for four hours with city officials, representatives of the Montgomery City Lines, and members of the Alabama Council on Human Relations. MIA's requests are not approved. At MIA's second mass meeting, held at St. John AME Church, MIA approves the establishment of a carpool system as a temporary alternative to the buses.
17 December 1955	Mayor William A. Gayle appoints a committee composed of eight black leaders, including King, and eight white leaders to resolve the crisis. The committee deadlocks on a resolution offered by the white members to postpone the boycott until 15 January, but agrees to a resolution requesting more courtesy from the bus drivers. The carpool reportedly involves 200 private cars, more than 100 taxis, and 8 gas stations.
26 January 1956	King and five others are stopped for traveling 30 mph in a 25 mph zone. King is arrested, fingerprinted, photographed, and jailed. Abernathy bails him out.
30 January 1956	At 9:15 P.M., while King is speaking before 2,000 congregants at a mass meeting at First Baptist Church, his home is bombed. Coretta Scott **King** and their daughter, Yolanda Denise, are not injured. King addresses a large crowd that gathers outside his house, pleading for **nonviolence**.
21 February 1956	The Montgomery grand jury indicts 115 leaders (later reduced to 89), including King, on misdemeanor charges of violating Alabama's anti-boycott law.

23 February 1956	King surrenders to the sheriff and is immediately released on bond. He agrees to plead guilty to the speeding charge filed against him in January.
24 February 1956	King and other indicted leaders are arraigned in circuit court and plead not guilty to boycott-related charges.
22 March 1956	In his own defense, King testifies on the fourth day of his trial. Judge Eugene Carter finds him guilty of leading an illegal boycott and sentences him to pay a $500 fine plus court costs or serve 386 days in jail. At an evening mass meeting at Holt Street Baptist Church, King announces that the boycott will continue and that his conviction has not lessened his determination.
23 April 1956	Montgomery City Lines informs its drivers that they can no longer enforce segregation on the city buses, but Mayor Gayle announces that Montgomery will continue to enforce state and city segregation laws.
1 May 1956	Montgomery city officials file suit in Montgomery Circuit Court asking for a temporary injunction to restrain the bus company from implementing the desegregation policy.
9 May 1956	Judge Walter B. Jones of the Circuit Court rules that Montgomery and Alabama segregation laws are constitutional and orders Montgomery City Lines to abandon its new policy of not enforcing segregation.
11–12 May 1956	A three-judge U.S. District Court panel hears testimony in *Browder v. Gayle*.
5 June 1956	The U.S. District Court rules two-to-one that segregation on Alabama's intrastate buses is unconstitutional.
26 July 1956	With King presiding, MIA executive board concurs with its legal counsel and agrees to wait until the U.S. Supreme Court reconvenes in the fall to consider its case challenging Alabama segregation laws.
13 November 1956	The Supreme Court confirms the district court's opinion in *Browder* declaring Montgomery and Alabama bus segregation laws unconstitutional.
14 November 1956	King speaks at MIA mass meetings at Hutchinson Street Baptist Church and Holt Street Baptist Church, where 8,000 attendees vote unanimously to end the boycott when the court mandate arrives.
17 December 1956	The Supreme Court rejects Alabama's final appeal.
21 December 1956	Montgomery City Lines resumes full service on all routes. King, Ralph Abernathy, E. D. Nixon, and Glenn **Smiley** are among the first passengers to sit in the section formerly reserved for whites.
23 December 1956	A shotgun blast is fired into the King home.
11 January 1957	While King is still in Montgomery, black leaders in Atlanta name him chairman of the Southern Negro Leaders Conference on

Transportation and Nonviolent Integration (later known as the **Southern Christian Leadership Conference** [SCLC]).

27 January 1957   After a Montgomery police officer finds 12 unexploded sticks of dynamite on the porch of King's home, King calms a gathering crowd by calling for nonviolence.

14 February 1957   The Southern Negro Leaders Conference on Transportation and Nonviolent Integration shorten their name to the Southern Leaders Conference and elect King as president.

18 February 1957   King appears on the cover of *Time* magazine.

2 March 1957   In the afternoon, the Kings leave New York's Idlewild Airport for the Gold Coast with Adam Clayton **Powell**, Ralph **Bunche**, and A. Philip **Randolph**, to participate in the independence celebrations of the new nation of **Ghana**.

6–25 March 1957   King travels to locations around the world including Accra, Kano, Rome, Geneva, Paris, and London.

17 May 1957   At the **Prayer Pilgrimage for Freedom** in Washington, D.C., King delivers "Give Us the Ballot."

13 June 1957   Following a two-hour meeting with Richard **Nixon** in Washington, King tells the press at the Raleigh Hotel that the vice president promised to hold a conference of the President's Committee on Government Contracts in the South.

8 August 1957   The Southern Leaders Conference changes its name to SCLC, and King announces the launching of a "Crusade for Citizenship," a massive voter registration drive in the South.

23 October 1957   The Kings' second child, Martin Luther **King**, III, is born.

19 June 1958   King is elected vice president of the National Sunday School and Baptist Training Union Congress.

23 June 1958   President Dwight D. **Eisenhower** discusses race discrimination with King and other black civil rights leaders at the White House.

September 1958   King's memoir of the Montgomery bus boycott, ***Stride Toward Freedom: The Montgomery Story***, is published.

3 September 1958   While attempting to attend the arraignment of a man accused of assaulting Abernathy, King is arrested outside Montgomery's Recorder's Court and charged with loitering. He is released a short time later on $100 bond.

20 September 1958   During a book signing at Blumstein's department store in Harlem, King is stabbed by Izola Ware **Curry**. He is rushed to Harlem Hospital where a team of doctors successfully removes a seven-inch letter opener from his chest.

3 October 1958   King is released from Harlem Hospital; he begins a three-week convalescence at the Brooklyn parsonage of Sandy **Ray**.

3 February 1959	At New York's Idlewild Airport, the Kings and Lawrence Dunbar **Reddick** depart for a six-week visit to **India** and the Middle East.
6 February 1959	King arrives in Paris; expatriate, African American novelist Richard Wright meets King and his companions at the airport. They dine at Wright's home that evening.
10 February 1959	Indian admirers present garlands to the Kings as they arrive at the Palam Airport in New Delhi. He later meets with India's vice president Sarvepalli Radhakrishnan and has dinner with Indian prime minister Jawaharlal **Nehru** at the Teen Murti Bhavan, Nehru's residence.
11 February 1959	King visits Rajghat and lays a wreath on the Samadhi, the site of **Gandhi**'s cremation.
1 March 1959	King flies to Amadabad where he travels to Sabarmati ashram, the starting point of Gandhi's salt march to the sea.
10–17 March 1959	King departs from New Delhi and travels to Karachi, Beirut, Jerusalem, and Cairo before returning to New York.
13 May 1959	King greets Kenyan leader Tom **Mboya** at Atlanta Municipal Airport. He later delivers remarks at the SCLC-sponsored "Africa Freedom Dinner" in honor of Mboya, held at Atlanta University.
29 November 1959	King announces his resignation from Dexter during Sunday morning services.
31 January 1960	In his final sermon as pastor of Dexter, King delivers "Lessons from History." That evening, the Kings attend a farewell program in their honor at the church.
4 February 1960	King relocates to Atlanta.
17 February 1960	In Atlanta, King is arrested on an Alabama tax violation.
29 February 1960	Facing Alabama perjury charges on his 1956 and 1958 income taxes, King surrenders to state authorities in Montgomery and is released on $4,000 bail.
26 April 1960	A cross is burned on the front lawn of King's home in Atlanta.
28 May 1960	A jury of 12 white men acquits King of falsifying his 1956 tax return.
23 June 1960	In New York, King discusses civil rights with Massachusetts senator John F. **Kennedy** who will become the Democratic presidential candidate in the November election.
18 July 1960	Alabama officials drop charges related to King's 1958 income tax return.
23 September 1960	King pleads guilty to driving with an improper license. He is fined $25 and given a 12-month suspended sentence.
19 October 1960	King and dozens of others are arrested for participating in a **sit-in** demonstration at Rich's department store in Atlanta. King and others are taken to Fulton County Jail after refusing to post bond.

20–24 October 1960	Although charges are dropped against King for his participation in the sit-in demonstration at Rich's, he remains in jail for violating the terms of a suspended sentence he received in September.
25 October 1960	At the DeKalb County courthouse, King is sentenced to four months in a public work camp at Georgia State Prison at Reidsville.
26 October 1960	Before daybreak, Georgia law officials transport King to Georgia State Prison at Reidsville, where he is to begin serving his four-month term. In the evening, presidential candidate John F. Kennedy phones Coretta Scott King to express his concern over King's jailing.
27 October 1960	Following a call to Atlanta Judge J. Oscar Mitchell by Robert F. **Kennedy**, brother and campaign manager of John F. Kennedy, King is freed on $2,000 bond.
30 January 1961	A third child, Dexter Scott **King**, is born to the Kings in Atlanta.
21 May 1961	King addresses freedom riders and black residents at First Baptist Church in Montgomery.
16 October 1961	King meets with President Kennedy and urges him to issue a second Emancipation Proclamation to end racial segregation.
15 December 1961	King responds to an appeal from William G. **Anderson**, president of the **Albany Movement**, to join protests in Albany, Georgia.
16 December 1961	King and Dr. Anderson lead a march through downtown Albany to City Hall but are stopped short of their goal when they are met by Police Chief Laurie **Pritchett**. King, Anderson, and Abernathy, along with the other marchers, are arrested for parading without a permit.
27 February 1962	King and others are tried and convicted for leading the December march in Albany. They are told to return to Albany in July for sentencing.
10 July 1962	With Abernathy, King begins serving a 45-day sentence.
12 July 1962	King leaves jail after his fine is paid by an unidentified person.
27 July 1962	King is arrested at an Albany, Georgia, City Hall prayer vigil and jailed on charges of failure to obey a police officer, obstructing the sidewalk, and disorderly conduct.
10 August 1962	After spending two weeks in jail, King is released.
9 December 1962	King preaches at John Thomas **Porter**'s installation service as pastor of Sixth Avenue Baptist Church in Birmingham, Alabama.
17 January 1963	In Chicago, King delivers "A Challenge to Justice and Love" at the National Conference on Religion and Race to commemorate the 100th anniversary of the **Emancipation Proclamation**.
28 March 1963	The Kings' fourth child, Bernice Albertine **King**, is born.
12 April 1963	After violating a state circuit court injunction against protests, King is arrested in Birmingham.

15 April 1963	President Kennedy calls Coretta Scott King to express concern for her jailed husband.
16 April 1963	Responding to white Birmingham clergymen calling for an end to demonstrations, King writes, "**Letter from Birmingham Jail.**"
3 May 1963	Following an address of encouragement by King at Sixteenth Street Baptist Church, hundreds of children are blasted with fire hoses, which triggers outrage around the world.
June 1963	*Strength to Love* is published.
28 August 1963	King delivers the "**I Have a Dream**" speech at the **March on Washington for Jobs and Freedom.**
22 September 1963	King eulogizes three of the four girls killed in Sixteenth Street Baptist Church bombing in Birmingham, Alabama.
10 October 1963	Robert Kennedy authorizes the **FBI** to wiretap King's telephone in Atlanta, and subsequently approves taps on SCLC's phones.
3 January 1964	King is named "Man of the Year" by *Time* **Magazine.**
9 February 1964	Robert **Hayling**, leader of the movement in **St. Augustine, Florida**, invites King and SCLC to join the struggle.
26 March 1964	King meets **Malcolm X** in the Capitol in Washington, D.C.
June 1964	*Why We Can't Wait* is published.
11 June 1964	King is arrested in St. Augustine.
2 July 1964	King attends the signing of the **Civil Rights Act of 1964**.
20 July 1964	King and SCLC staff launch a People-to-People tour of Mississippi to assist the **Student Nonviolent Coordinating Committee** and the **Congress of Racial Equality** (CORE) in the Mississippi **Freedom Summer** Campaign.
22 August 1964	King testifies before the Credentials Committee prior to the Democratic Convention in Atlantic City, New Jersey.
10 December 1964	King receives the **Nobel Peace Prize** in Oslo, Norway.
2 January 1965	King announces the start of a campaign in Selma, Alabama, aimed at urging the federal government to protect black voting rights through federal legislation.
1 February 1965	King is jailed with more than 200 others after a voting rights march in Selma, Alabama.
21–25 March 1965	King leads **Selma to Montgomery March**.
26 July 1965	King's "People to People" tour of northern cities culminates in a mass march of 30,000 people at Chicago City Hall.
6 August 1965	King is present when President Lyndon B. **Johnson** signs the **Voting Rights Act of 1965**.
17 August 1965	King visits **Watts** after widespread violence erupts in the city the week before.

7 January 1966	King announces the start of the **Chicago Campaign**.
March 1966	King takes over a Chicago slum building and is sued by its owner.
7–26 June 1966	After James Meredith is shot and wounded by a sniper, King; Stokely **Carmichael**, chairman of SNCC; and Floyd **McKissick**, president of CORE, agree to continue the march to encourage black voting in Mississippi.
10 July 1966	At "Freedom Sunday" rally at Soldier's Field, King launches drive to make Chicago an "open city" for housing.
5 August 1966	King is stoned as he leads march through Chicago's southwest side.
1967	***Where Do We Go from Here: Chaos or Community?*** is published.
4 April 1967	King delivers anti-war speech "**Beyond Vietnam**" at the Riverside Church in New York City.
30 October 1967	The Supreme Court upholds the contempt-of-court convictions of King and seven other black leaders who led the 1963 marches in Birmingham, Alabama. King and his aides enter jail to serve five-day sentences.
4 December 1967	King publicly reveals his plans to organize a mass civil disobedience campaign, the **Poor Peoples' Campaign**, in Washington, D.C., to force the government to end poverty.
1968	***The Trumpet of Conscience*** is published. The **King Center** is established by Coretta Scott King.
28 March 1968	King leads a march of approximately 6,000 protestors in support of **Memphis sanitation workers' strike**.
3 April 1968	King delivers his last speech, "**I've Been to the Mountaintop**," at the Mason Temple in Memphis.
4 April 1968	King is **assassinated** in Memphis.
9 April 1968	King is buried in Atlanta.
1985	The Martin Luther King, Jr., Papers Project, later called the **Martin Luther King, Jr., Research and Education Institute**, is initiated by Coretta Scott King with Clayborne Carson, Stanford history professor, as the senior editor.
20 January 1986	The Martin Luther King, Jr., **federal holiday** is celebrated for the first time.

ABERNATHY, RALPH DAVID (1926–1990)

As Martin Luther King's closest friend and advisor, Ralph Abernathy became a central figure in the civil rights struggle during the **Montgomery bus boycott**. "Abernathy infused his audiences with new life and ardor. The people loved and respected him as a symbol of courage and strength," King wrote in *Stride Toward Freedom* (73–74).

Abernathy was born on 11 March 1926 to William L. and Louivery Bell Abernathy of Linden, Alabama. His father, the son of a slave, supported his family of 12 as a farmer while serving as deacon of the local Baptist church.

Abernathy graduated from Linden Academy and then served overseas with the United States Army toward the end of World War II. He was ordained as a Baptist minister in 1948, and two years later he received a BS in mathematics at Alabama State College in Montgomery. He later earned an MA in sociology from Atlanta University (1958).

While a graduate student at Atlanta University, Abernathy heard King preach at **Ebenezer Baptist Church**. In his autobiography, Abernathy recalled "burning with envy" at King's "learning and confidence," and he immediately saw King as a "man with a special gift from God" (Abernathy, 89). Abernathy introduced himself to King that day and their friendship began.

In 1952 Abernathy became pastor of Montgomery's First Baptist Church. He was active in the **National Association for the Advancement of Colored People**, and chaired the State Sunday School and Baptist Training Union Congress' committee on the *Brown v. Board of Education* ruling. He issued a report urging ministers to fight against segregation, writing, "Our business as Christians is to get rid of a system that creates bad men" (*Papers* 2:35).

Shortly after the arrest of Rosa **Parks** on 1 December 1955, E. D. **Nixon** contacted Abernathy to discuss the idea of a bus boycott. Abernathy, King, and other community leaders met to create a new organization to guide the protest movement. At Abernathy's suggestion, the new organization was called the **Montgomery Improvement Association** (MIA).

The different styles of Abernathy and King combined to create an effective and inspiring message at the boycott's weekly mass meetings. While King emphasized the philosophical implications of **nonviolence** and the movement, Abernathy helped

King and Ralph Abernathy greet supporters during a rally marking the end of the Selma to Montgomery March. © 1965 Matt Herron/Take Stock.

energize the people into positive action. "Now," he would tell the audience following King's address, "let me tell you what that means for tomorrow morning" (Raines, 54).

In January 1957, shortly after Abernathy's home and church were bombed, Abernathy joined with King and African American leaders to form the organization that was eventually called the **Southern Christian Leadership Conference** (SCLC). The organization was designed to support the movement to peacefully implement the Supreme Court's decision outlawing bus segregation by coordinating the action of local protest groups throughout the South. King was elected president of SCLC, and Abernathy became financial secretary-treasurer.

In November 1959, King announced to his **Dexter Avenue Baptist Church** congregation that he would be moving to Atlanta to be closer to SCLC headquarters. In January 1960, King officially announced Abernathy as the new president of the MIA: "[Abernathy] has proven his ability as a leader.... and I predict that under his leadership, Montgomery will grow to higher heights and new and creative things will be done" (*Papers* 5:354).

Abernathy struggled with meeting the commitments of the MIA and his ministry in Montgomery and SCLC in Atlanta. King helped remedy the problem by recommending that West Hunter Baptist Church in Atlanta hire Abernathy in late 1960. King informed a member of the church, "Ralph is a dynamic and able preacher, an exceptionally good administrator and organizer, and a great community leader. I am sure that he could give to West Hunter a type of leadership that would both double its membership and its spiritual impact in the community" (*Papers* 5:581). Abernathy accepted the position and moved to Atlanta in 1961.

King and Abernathy provided a great deal of support to one another. The two were jailed together 17 times. Abernathy recalled that their time in jail together allowed them to "make plans and draw strength from one another" (Abernathy, 254). At King's request, Abernathy became vice-president of SCLC, because King knew that should he die, Abernathy would be able to lead the organization.

After King's **assassination** in 1968, Abernathy became SCLC's president. To prepare for the challenges ahead, he fasted for seven days and nights, telling the *New York Post* that he "needed to pray and fast for strength that I might carry on as he requested, and as the board of directors of SCLC unanimously requested, in nonviolence. I want to hold no ill will in my heart toward the assassin or anyone else for taking the life of my dearest friend, closer to me than a blood brother" (Michaelson, "On the Other Side").

Abernathy followed through with the march that King had planned to lead in support of the **Memphis sanitation workers**. He also continued efforts to organize the **Poor People's Campaign** in Washington, D.C., the last major movement of SCLC. Yet, despite Abernathy's commitment to SCLC, the organization never found the same kind of success it had under King's leadership. After resigning his position in SCLC in 1977, Abernathy made an unsuccessful bid for Congress. He remained pastor of West Hunter Baptist Church and formed the Foundation for Economic Enterprises Development, an organization designed to improve black economic opportunities.

SOURCES
Abernathy, *And the Walls Came Tumbling Down*, 1989.
Introduction, in *Papers* 2:35.
King, Address delivered during "A Salute to Dr. and Mrs. Martin Luther King" at Dexter Avenue Baptist Church, 31 January 1960, in *Papers* 5:351–357.
King, *Stride Toward Freedom*, 1958.
King to Samuel L. Spear, 16 December 1960, in *Papers* 5:581–582.
Judy Michaelson, "On the Other Side of the Mountain," *New York Post*, 13 April 1968.
Raines, *My Soul Is Rested*, 1983.

ACMHR. *See* Alabama Christian Movement for Human Rights.

ACOA. *See* American Committee on Africa.

"ADVICE FOR LIVING" (1957–1958)

With the successful conclusion of the **Montgomery bus boycott** in 1956 and the establishment of the **Southern Christian Leadership Conference** the following year, Martin Luther King became a national civil rights spokesman and his opinions, even on personal matters, attracted considerable interest. Thus, in 1957 *Ebony* magazine invited King to write a monthly column entitled "Advice for Living." Responding to readers' questions about marital infidelity, sexuality, birth control, capital punishment, atomic weapons testing, and race relations, King's column reflected his moral and religious convictions and his thoughts on a wide range of issues.

In the summer of 1957 King accepted an invitation to write the column from Lerone Bennett, Jr., a fellow **Morehouse** graduate and associate editor of *Ebony* magazine. In the 5 September 1957 edition of *Ebony*'s sister publication, *Jet*, an advertisement for King's forthcoming "Advice for Living" column recommended that readers "let the man that led the Montgomery boycott lead you into happier living" (*Papers* 4:267n). Letters immediately flooded *Ebony*'s mailbox, and the already busy Baptist minister began drafting responses to a range of queries. King's advice revealed his evolving attitudes on a number of controversial issues. For example, he insisted that God did not approve of the death penalty and affirmed that "individuals marry, not races" (*Papers* 4:305; 357). Reassuring a boy who asked about his sexual feelings toward other boys, King advised seeing "a good psychiatrist" (*Papers* 4:348–349). King continued publishing the column until December 1958, when his doctor advised him to limit his commitments following his September 1958 stabbing.

SOURCE

King, "Advice for Living," in *Papers* 4:267–269; 279–281; 305–307; 326–328; 348–350; 356–357; 374–376; 392–394; 401–402; 417–418; 443–445; 459–460; 471–473; 503–505; 520–522; 540–542.

AFSC. *See* American Friends Service Committee.

AGAPE

For Martin Luther King, the concept of *agape* stood at the center of both his spiritual belief in a knowable God and his assertion that love and **nonviolence** were essential to remedying America's race problems. He defined agape as "purely spontaneous, unmotivated, groundless, and creative. It is the love of God operating in the human heart" (*Papers* 6:325).

In his December 1957 sermon "The Christian Way of Life in Human Relations," delivered before the General Assembly of the **National Council of the Churches of Christ in America** (NCC), King referred to three different types of love: *eros*, romantic love; *philia*, the reciprocal affection between friends; and *agape*, the highest form of love. King explored agape in many of his sermons in order to help illuminate the concept of Christian love.

In papers written during his graduate studies at **Crozer Theological Seminary** and **Boston University**, King credited theologians Anders Nygren and Paul **Tillich** with helping to inform his definition of agape. In his paper "Contemporary Continental Theology," King quoted Nygren's 1932 book *Agape and Eros* in characterizing agape as a "spontaneous and uncaused" kind of love that is "indifferent to human merit" (*Papers* 2:127). He drew on Tillich in his **dissertation**, claiming, "The only basic and adequate symbol for God's love is agape" (*Papers* 2:441). In his dissertation, King argued that only a person can express love and used this rationale as justification for **personalism**, the belief in a personal God, one to whom people could relate. Harry Emerson **Fosdick** also influenced King's thinking on agape. In his discussion on love, King used language very similar to Fosdick's 1946 sermon "On Being Fit to Live With."

In many of his sermons King spoke of agape as a way to explain the use of nonviolence in race relations. "At the center of nonviolence stands the principle of love," said King before the NCC. "When we rise to love on the agape level," he continued, "we love men not because we like them, not because their attitudes and ways appeal to us, but we love them because God loves them. Here we rise to the position of loving the person who does the evil deed while hating the deed that the person does" (*Papers* 6:324; 325).

SOURCES

Fosdick, *On Being Fit to Live With*, 1946.

King, "A Comparison of the Conceptions of God in the Thinking of Paul Tillich and Henry Nelson Wieman," 15 April 1955, in *Papers* 2:339–544.

King, "A View of the Cross Possessing Biblical and Spiritual Justification," 29 November 1949–15 February 1950, in *Papers* 2:263–267.

King, "The Christian Way of Life in Human Relations," Address delivered at the General Assembly of the National Council of Churches, 4 December 1957, in *Papers* 6:322–328.

King, "Contemporary Continental Theology," 13 September 1951–15 January 1952, in *Papers* 2:113–139.

Nygren, *Agape and Eros*, 1932.

AJC. *See* American Jewish Congress.

ALABAMA CHRISTIAN MOVEMENT FOR HUMAN RIGHTS (ACMHR)

At the invitation of ACMHR's president, Fred **Shuttlesworth**, Martin Luther King and the **Southern Christian Leadership Conference** (SCLC) arrived in Birmingham, Alabama, in 1963 to collaborate on the "Project C" campaign. Tensions quickly surfaced between the local organization and the very visible SCLC, as Shuttlesworth came to resent actions taken by SCLC and King without his input.

The ACMHR was founded in Birmingham, Alabama, on 5 June 1956, after Alabama Attorney General John **Patterson** outlawed the **National Association for the Advancement of Colored People** in the state. Immediately afterward Shuttlesworth called a meeting of local ministers and community leaders at Sardis Baptist Church. The *Birmingham News* reported that the ACMHR "was formed here last night amid roars of an estimated 1,000 Negroes approving a 'march to complete freedom'" ("Negroes Roar Approval"). Shuttlesworth was named ACMHR president by acclamation.

In its Declaration of Principles, the ACMHR announced, "we express publicly our determination to press forward persistently for Freedom and Democracy, and the removal from our society any forms of Second Class Citizenship" ("The Original Declaration of Principles," June 2006). Following the example of the **Montgomery Improvement Association**, the ACMHR defied bus segregation in 1956 and 1958, attempted to integrate Birmingham's schools and railroad stations in 1957, and championed the student **sit-ins** in 1960 and the **Freedom Rides** in 1961. The ACMHR became affiliated with SCLC in 1957.

With the backing of SCLC in April and May of 1963, the ACMHR conducted a sustained campaign of marches and nonviolent action to protest segregation in Birmingham. The ACMHR and SCLC sought to desegregate public facilities and attain equal employment opportunities for Birmingham's black citizens by targeting the city's downtown shopping district. Their demonstrations were met with arrests, assault by fire hoses and police dogs, and imprisonment. Although the campaign proved a success, Shuttlesworth expressed frustration that negotiations with white businessowners resulted in an agreement to end the **Birmingham Campaign** without ACMHR participation.

In 1969 Shuttlesworth left his position as ACMHR president, and vice president Edward Gardner took his place. In 2006, 60 black churches received historic plaques to commemorate their role in the Birmingham movement. By that time, 15 of those churches, including Shuttleworth's Bethel Baptist and the Sixteenth Street Baptist Church, were listed on the National Register of Historic Places.

SOURCES

"About 'The Movement' and the Movement Churches," *Birmingham Historical Society Newsletter* (June 2006): 2.

"Documenting and Listing Movement Churches on the National Register of Historic Places," *Birmingham Historical Society Newsletter* (June 2006): 4.

Eskew, *But for Birmingham,* 1997.

Don McKee, "Dogs and Hoses Used to Stall Negro Trek at Birmingham," *Birmingham News,* 4 May 1963.

"Negroes Roar Approval at Rights Meeting," *Birmingham News,* 6 June 1956, reprinted in *Birmingham Historical Society Newsletter* (June 2006): 3.

"The Original Declaration of Principles," *Birmingham Historical Society Newsletter* (June 2006): 2.

ALBANY MOVEMENT

Formed on 17 November 1961 by representatives from the **Student Nonviolent Coordinating Committee** (SNCC), the **National Association for the Advancement of Colored People**, the Ministerial Alliance, the Federation of Women's Clubs, and the Negro Voters League, the Albany Movement conducted a broad campaign in Albany, Georgia, that challenged all forms of segregation and discrimination. King and the **Southern Christian Leadership Conference** (SCLC) temporarily joined the coalition, attracting national publicity to Albany. Although the Albany Movement was successful in mobilizing massive protests during December 1961 and the following summer, it secured few concrete gains.

SNCC members Charles Sherrod and Cordell Reagon traveled to Albany in October 1961 to galvanize the black community into direct action protests against institutionalized segregation. Albany had experienced little protest activity prior to SNCC's arrival; however, black residents were dissatisfied with the city commission's failure to address the community's grievances. Sherrod and Reagon led workshops on nonviolent tactics for Albany residents in anticipation of a showdown with local police. On 1 November, the Interstate Commerce Commission's (ICC) ban of racial segregation in

Police Chief Laurie Pritchett tells King and William G. Anderson that they are under arrest for parading without a permit in Albany, Georgia, 16 December 1961. © Bettmann/Corbis.

interstate bus terminals went into effect. This was an opportune time for Sherrod and Reagon to test segregation policies in the city. They sent nine students from Albany State College to conduct a **sit-in** at the bus terminal. Although none of them was arrested, their actions inspired local black leaders to found the Albany Movement. William G. **Anderson**, a local doctor, and Slater King, a realtor, were elected president and vice president, respectively.

The Albany Movement aimed to end all forms of racial segregation in the city, focusing initially on desegregating travel facilities, forming a permanent biracial committee to discuss further desegregation, and the release of those jailed in segregation protests. Through the course of the campaign, Albany protesters utilized various methods of **nonviolence**, including mass demonstrations, jail-ins, sit-ins, boycotts, and litigation. Notably, in addition to student activists, the campaign involved large numbers of black adults of varied class backgrounds.

Albany police chief Laurie **Pritchett** responded to the demonstrations with mass arrests, but refrained from public brutality and thereby minimized negative publicity. By December 1961 more than 500 protesters were jailed, and negotiations with city officials began. Anderson called on King to help reinvigorate the Movement. Anderson's decision to involve King caused some consternation with SNCC members who worried that King's style of leadership would cause local blacks to "feel that only a particular individual could save them and would not move on their own to fight racism and exploitation" (Forman, 255). Nevertheless, King arrived in Albany on 15 December and spoke at a mass meeting at Shiloh Baptist Church. "It may look dark now, maybe we don't know what tomorrow and the next day will bring," King told the crowd. "But if you will move on out of the taxi lane of your own despair, move out of the taxi lane of your worries and fears, and get out in the take off lane and move out on the wings of faith, we will be able to move up through the clouds of disappointment" (King, 15 December 1961). The following day King, Anderson, and Ralph **Abernathy** joined hundreds of black citizens behind bars on charges of parading without a permit and obstructing the sidewalk. King's involvement attracted national media attention and inspired more members of the black community to join the protests. This did not go unnoticed by city government, and soon after King's arrest city officials and Albany Movement leaders came to an agreement: if King left Albany the city would comply with the ICC ruling, and release jailed protesters on bail. However, after King left Albany the city failed to uphold the agreement, and protests and subsequent arrests continued into 1962. News reports across the country portrayed the failure of early Albany protests as "one of the most stunning defeats" in King's career (Miller, "A Loss for Dr. King").

Behind the scenes, reports of organizational conflict between SCLC and SNCC may have marred the campaign. A *New York Times* article published two days after King's 16 December arrest claimed that the growing break between SCLC and SNCC was due to "competition for financial support and power," and that this would have "important implications for the future of the civil rights movement throughout the South" (Sitton, "Negro Groups Split"). Another article noted that King's organization "took steps that seemed to indicate they were assuming control. But the student group moved immediately to recapture its dominant position on the scene." The article predicted "tragic consequences" if the differences between the organizations were not curbed (Sitton, "Rivalries Beset Integration Campaigns"). Responding to the reports of disunity in the campaign, King said, "If there was an indication of division, it grew out of a breakdown of communications. The unity is far greater than our inevitable points of disagreement" ("Dr. King Is Freed").

Six months later, on 10 July 1962, King and Abernathy were found guilty of having paraded without a permit in December 1961. They were ordered to pay $178 or serve 45 days in jail. They chose to serve the time. As King explained from jail, "We chose to serve our time because we feel so deeply about the plight of more than 700 others who have yet to be tried.... We have experienced the racist tactics of attempting to bankrupt the movement in the South through excessive bail and extended court fights. The time has now come when we must practice civil disobedience in a true sense or delay our freedom thrust for long years" (King, "A Message from Jail"). With King in jail, demonstrations and arrests increased. On 12 July, Chief Pritchett notified King and Abernathy that their bail had been paid by an unidentified black man, and they were released. After his release, Abernathy joked, "I've been thrown out of lots of places in my day, but never before have I been thrown out of jail" (Lewis, 159).

Following his third Albany arrest on 27 July, King agreed on 10 August 1962 to leave Albany and announce a halt to demonstrations, effectively ending his involvement in the Albany Movement. Although local efforts continued in conjunction with SNCC, the ultimate goals of the Movement were not met by the time of King's departure. King blamed much of the failure on the campaign's wide scope, stating in a 1965 interview, "The mistake I made there was to protest against segregation generally rather than against a single and distinct facet of it. Our protest was so vague that we got nothing, and the people were left very depressed and in despair" ("Martin Luther King: A Candid Conversation"). The experiences in Albany, however, helped inform the strategy for the **Birmingham Campaign** that followed less than a year later. King acknowledged that "what we learned from our mistakes in Albany helped our later campaigns in other cities to be more effective" ("Martin Luther King: A Candid Conversation").

Sources
Branch, *Parting the Waters*, 1988.
Carson, *In Struggle*, 1981.
"Dr. King Is Freed," *New York Times*, 19 December 1961.
Forman, *The Making of Black Revolutionaries*, 1972.
King, Address delivered to a Mass Meeting during the Albany Movement, 16 December 1961, IElwp.
King, "A Message from Jail," *New York Amsterdam News*, 14 July 1962.
Lewis, *King*, 1970.
"Martin Luther King: A Candid Conversation with the Nobel Prize-Winning Leader of the Civil Rights Movement," *Playboy* 12 (January 1965): 65–68; 70–74; 76–78.
David Miller, "A Loss for Dr. King—New Negro Roundup: They Yield," *New York Herald Tribune*, 19 December 1961.
Claude Sitton, "Negro Groups Split on Georgia Protest," *New York Times*, 18 December 1961.
Claude Sitton, "Rivalries Beset Integration Campaigns," *New York Times*, 24 December 1961.

ALPHA PHI ALPHA FRATERNITY

In 1956, Martin Luther King was given the Alpha Award of Honor for "Christian leadership in the cause of first class citizenship for all mankind" at the 50th-anniversary convention of Alpha Phi Alpha (*Papers* 3:339). King called the event one of the happiest moments of his life and said that the award gave him "renewed courage to continue in the great and momentous struggle for justice" (King, 21 August 1956).

Founded in 1906 at Cornell University in Ithaca, New York, Alpha Phi Alpha was the first fraternity created by African American students. Operating under the guiding principles of scholarship, fellowship, good character, and the uplifting of humanity, the fraternity counts Thurgood **Marshall**, W.E.B. Du Bois, and King among its notable members. King joined the Boston Sigma chapter of Alpha in June 1952, while a student at **Boston University**. Fraternity brothers supported King during the **Montgomery bus boycott**, sitting behind him at his trial and donating money to the **Montgomery Improvement Association**.

During the civil rights movement King spoke at Alpha chapters throughout the country, and members continued to financially support his campaigns. In 1984 Alpha Phi Alpha initiated a campaign for a Martin Luther King, Jr., Memorial on the National Mall in Washington, D.C. In 1996 President Bill Clinton signed congressional legislation authorizing the memorial, which broke ground in November 2006.

SOURCES

Alpha Phi Alpha Fraternity, Membership Certificate for Martin Luther King, Jr., 22 June 1952, in *Papers* 2:155a.
King, "The Birth of a New Age," Address delivered on 11 August 1956 at the 50th Anniversary of Alpha Phi Alpha in Buffalo, 1956, in *Papers* 3:339–346.
King to Huger, 21 August 1956, MLKP-MBU.
Frank L. Stanley to King, 22 March 1956, in *Papers* 3:201–202.

AMERICAN COMMITTEE ON AFRICA (ACOA)

Founded in 1953, the American Committee on Africa (ACOA) was dedicated to supporting African liberation struggles and informing the American public about African issues. As one of the first national organizations dedicated to anti-colonial struggles in Africa, the organization played host to countless African leaders in the United States. Martin Luther King served on the national committee from 1957 until his death.

ACOA grew out of the ad hoc group Americans for South African Resistance, which was created by civil rights activists George **Houser**, Bayard **Rustin**, and Bill Sutherland of the **Congress of Racial Equality** (CORE) to support the 1952 Campaign to Defy Unjust Laws called by the African National Congress. In 1954 Houser traveled to Africa to meet with leaders of liberation struggles throughout the continent, including Chief Albert **Lutuli** and Walter Sisulu in South Africa, and Kwame **Nkrumah** in Ghana. When he returned he committed himself to ACOA full time, serving as executive director until 1981.

Based in New York, the organization lobbied the United Nations (UN) and the U.S. government to support African independence movements. The organization arranged meetings for African leaders on their trips to the United States and published pamphlets, a magazine, and reports on liberation struggles for both public and policy-making audiences. ACOA raised funds to support African university students, churches, and anti-colonial activists and refugees fleeing colonial regimes through direct appeals and special events. In 1966 Houser created the Africa Fund in an effort to manage tax-exempt donations for African causes.

Founded by pacifists, ACOA emphasized the nonviolent methods available to create social change, such as economic and cultural disengagement from South Africa. However, when confronted with the overwhelming military force of the French colonial regime in Algeria, ACOA supported the main group opposing French rule, the National Liberation Front, despite its use of guerilla warfare. Houser believed ACOA's role should be to influence global and U.S. policy and inform the U.S. public about anti-colonial struggles but not to justify the violence of those struggles. As debate on Algeria began at the UN, King added his signature to a 1959 ACOA petition titled "A Call for Peace in Algeria," which advocated a local African referendum to determine Algeria's future. King balanced his concerns about apartheid and colonialism with his dedication to **nonviolence** when he spoke at the 10 December 1965 Human Rights Day celebration organized by ACOA. King called on all nations to boycott South Africa to "demonstrate the international potential of nonviolence" (King, 10 December 1965).

King participated in many other ACOA campaigns, including acting as vice-chair of the 1957 "Declaration of Conscience" against apartheid. In 1962 he co-sponsored an "Appeal for Action against Apartheid" and was an early participant in the American Negro Leadership Conference on Africa, a group of African American leaders organized by ACOA to make recommendations on U.S. policy in Africa.

In 2001 ACOA merged with its sister organizations, the Africa Fund and the Africa Policy Information Center, to form Africa Action, which continues to work on economic, political, and social justice issues in Africa, and to help shape U.S. policy and the role of multinational institutions toward Africa.

SOURCES
Houser, *No One Can Stop the Rain*, 1989.
King, Address to the South Africa Benefit of the ACOA, 10 December 1965, MLKJP-GAMK.

AMERICAN FEDERATION OF LABOR AND CONGRESS OF INDUSTRIAL ORGANIZATIONS (AFL-CIO)

Following the 1955 merger of the American Federation of Labor (AFL) with the Congress of Industrial Organizations (CIO), the AFL-CIO became an ally of civil rights organizations. Martin Luther King spoke of the shared goals of the civil rights and labor movements, noting in his 1961 address to the fourth AFL-CIO national convention that both African Americans and union members were fighting for "decent wages, fair working conditions, livable housing, old age security, health and welfare measures, conditions in which families can grow, have education for their children, and respect in the community" (King, 11 December 1961).

The AFL was founded in 1886 as an umbrella organization for unions of skilled craft workers. In 1926, under the leadership of A. Philip **Randolph**, the Brotherhood of Sleeping Car Porters became affiliated with the AFL. The AFL gained organizing momentum during the New Deal era after the passage of the National Labor Relations Act in 1935. The CIO, which first emerged as an AFL committee, split from its parent organization in the late 1930s. When the AFL and CIO amalgamated, the 1955 merger agreement included a civil rights clause calling for non-discrimination in union privileges.

During the years that followed, the AFL-CIO and some of its major constituent unions supported the civil rights struggle by providing financial and legal assistance, and moral support. Most prominent among those unions were the **United Packinghouse Workers of America**, led by Ralph **Helstein**; District 65 of the Retail, Wholesale, and Department Store Union; and the United Auto Workers. During the **Montgomery bus boycott** George Meany, the AFL-CIO's newly elected president, sent a telegram to President Dwight D. **Eisenhower** urging him to investigate the violence aimed at Martin Luther King and E. D. **Nixon.** He also communicated his dismay to Georgia's governor Ernest **Vandiver** regarding the "shocking and unusual penalty" imposed on King after he was sentenced to four months in prison for an October 1960 **sit-in** arrest (Meany, 26 October 1960). When King addressed the AFL-CIO's fourth convention in 1961, he dubbed the AFL-CIO and the civil rights movement "the two most dynamic and cohesive liberal forces in the country," and called on the organization to "deal effectively with discrimination and provide financial aid for [the] struggle in the South" (King, 11 December 1961).

The AFL-CIO's support was not unconditional. Its executive council declined to support the 1963 **March on Washington for Jobs and Freedom**, adopting a position of neutrality; however, many international and local unions were present in substantial numbers. Meany and King also disagreed about the **Vietnam War**. After giving his controversial **"Beyond Vietnam"** speech in 1967, King attended a conference of the National Leadership Assembly for Peace, made up of union leaders who disputed the AFL-CIO's official support of U.S. intervention in Vietnam.

In 1968, black **Memphis sanitation workers** in the American Federation of State, County, and Municipal Employees Local 1733, an AFL-CIO affiliate, went on strike for better working conditions. The strike lasted 65 days and involved nearly 1,300 men. Although King was occupied with the **Poor People's Campaign** at the time, he traveled to Memphis repeatedly to support the strike and drew national attention to the workers' cause. King was assassinated during his third trip.

In the decades following King's death, labor groups were instrumental in advocating for the enactment of a **national holiday** to celebrate King's legacy.

SOURCES

Draper, *Conflict of Interests*, 1994.
Honey, *Going Down Jericho Road*, 2007.
William P. Jones, "Working-Class Hero," *The Nation* (30 January 2006).
King, Address at the fourth constitutional convention of the AFL-CIO, 11 December 1961, MLKP-MBU.
Meany to Vandiver, 26 October 1960, ACCP-DAFL.

AMERICAN FRIENDS SERVICE COMMITTEE (AFSC)

Throughout the modern civil rights movement, the similarity of the social ideals of Martin Luther King and the American Friends Service Committee (AFSC) led them to work on the same side of racial issues.

In 1917 a group of Quakers formed the AFSC to give conscientious objectors a non-military public service alternative during World War I. The organization began its anti-racism work in the 1920s and, in 1933, began sponsoring a yearly summer institute on race relations at Swarthmore College that lasted until 1941. In 1944 the

AFSC created a Race Relations Department, which encouraged business leaders to hire minorities and established visiting lectureships at white universities for African American academics. Within months of the start of the **Montgomery bus boycott**, AFSC contacted King to learn more about the campaign.

In 1959 the AFSC arranged for King and Coretta Scott **King** to visit **India**. The AFSC representative in India, James **Bristol**, accompanied the Kings throughout their visit. Later that year, the AFSC southern program began working in Prince Edward County, Virginia, where the local school board had closed public schools rather than give in to court-ordered desegregation. Together with the **National Association for the Advancement of Colored People** and the Southern Regional Council, the AFSC placed dozens of students with host families in school districts throughout the country. In 1963 the AFSC opened the Free School in Prince Edward County, where integrated faculty taught 1,500 African Americans and 6 white children.

In 1963 King's colleague, James **Lawson**, interested the AFSC in a copy of a letter King had written while in jail in Birmingham, Alabama. The AFSC gained permission from King to publish and distribute 50,000 copies of "**Letter from Birmingham City Jail**." That same year, the AFSC nominated King for the **Nobel Peace Prize**, an honor the international Friends organization had received in 1947.

Long-time AFSC staff member Stephen G. Cary noted that working with Martin Luther King and being a part of the civil rights movement "played a big role in the AFSC's evolving understanding of nonviolence" (Sutters, "AFSC in History"). The organization's experience in the South reinforced its decision to expand the AFSC's mission to work not just against war, but against the roots of violence: "injustice, poverty, and oppression" (Sutters, "AFSC in History"). The AFSC continues its social justice work today, operating in 22 countries and 9 regions of the United States.

SOURCES

Introduction, in *Papers* 5:2–12.

King, "Letter from Birmingham City Jail" (Philadelphia: American Friends Service Committee, May 1963).

Jack Sutters, "AFSC in History—MLK for January 2001," American Friends Service Committee, http://www.afsc.org/about/hist/king.htm.

Jack Sutters, "AFSC's Civil Rights Efforts, 1925–1950," American Friends Service Committee, http://www.afsc.org/about/hist/race.htm.

AMERICAN JEWISH CONGRESS (AJC)

The American Jewish Congress (AJC) served as an ecumenical partner to Martin Luther King in the struggle for civil rights. In 1958 King spoke to the AJC convention declaring, "My people were brought to America in chains. Your people were driven here to escape the chains fashioned for them in Europe. Our unity is born of our common struggle for centuries, not only to rid ourselves of bondage, but to make oppression of any people by others an impossibility" (*Papers* 4:407).

The AJC was founded in 1918 by Rabbi Stephen S. Wise, *Hadassah* founder Henrietta Szold, U.S. Supreme Court Justice Louis Brandeis, and other prominent Jews in response to the suffering of Jewish people during World War I. In 1920 a domestic agenda was added to the issues abroad. In 1946 the AJC published a *Jewish Affairs* pamphlet entitled *Action for Unity*, which discussed effective ways to promote "'good will' and better race relations," and analyzed seven strategies—exhortation, education, participation, revelation, negotiation, contention, and prevention—for "improving community inter-relations" (Watson, 3; 4).

King's first official contact with the organization came in January 1957, when AJC president Israel Goldstein responded to a telegraphed request from King and other black leaders for "support and advice for the deliberations" of the Southern Negro Leaders Conference (a precursor of the **Southern Christian Leadership Conference**), held at **Ebenezer Baptist Church** in Atlanta on 10–11 January 1957 (*Papers* 4:98n). Goldstein condemned the bombing of four black Montgomery, Alabama, churches and two parsonages in the early morning of 10 January, stating: "All Americans dedicated to the democratic way of life join us in decrying the violence that has been employed in defiance of the law of the land and the spirit of human brotherhood" (Goldstein, 11 January 1957).

King's advisor Stanley **Levison** served on the organization's Manhattan Division Board and arranged for King to speak at the AJC's 1958 National Biennial Convention in Miami Beach, Florida. Addressing the 1,500 delegates and guests, King called on the AJC to "assist in the development of platforms from which white moderates, liberals, and others may speak and act toward effective ends," asserting: "This is a time for vigorous and positive action" (*Papers* 4:409; 410).

Joachim Prinz, the organization's newly elected president, met King at the 1958 convention. Prinz, who was expelled from Nazi Germany in 1937, became a steadfast supporter of King. Prinz picketed a New York City Woolworth five-and-dime store in 1960 to protest discrimination against African Americans at the store's lunch counters. In 1963, he was one of 10 founding chairmen of the **March on Washington for Jobs and Freedom**, addressing the crowd shortly before King's famous "**I Have a Dream**" speech.

Four days after King's **assassination**, Prinz joined Coretta Scott **King**, Ralph **Abernathy**, and other religious and labor leaders in a silent mass march through the streets of Memphis, Tennessee, to honor King's memory and press for an end to the sanitation strike that had brought King to the city. Prinz's commitment to the civil rights of all Americans and the AJC's long-standing dedication to that cause assured King of a strong ally in the Jewish community.

SOURCES
American Jewish Congress, *All about the American Jewish Congress*, 1993.

Goldstein to Ebenezer Baptist Church, 11 January 1957, RWP-DLC.

King, Address delivered at the National Biennial Convention of the American Jewish Congress, in *Papers* 4:406–410.

Prinz to King, 28 October 1958, in *Papers* 4:517–518.

Maxwell M. Rabb to King, 11 January 1957, in *Papers* 4:98.

Watson, *Action for Unity*, 1946.

ANDERSON, WILLIAM GILCHRIST (1927–)

The civil rights campaign in southwest Georgia gained national attention when Martin Luther King accepted the invitation of **Albany Movement** president W. G. Anderson to assist local leaders in their desegregation efforts in late 1961.

Born in Americus, Georgia, on 12 December 1927, Anderson graduated from Alabama State College (1949) and later received his DO from the University of Osteopathic Medicine and Health Sciences in Des Moines, Iowa. Anderson taught in the Atlanta public school system and at the Atlanta School of Mortuary Science before starting a private osteopathic medical practice in Albany, Georgia.

In November 1961 the **Student Nonviolent Coordinating Committee** (SNCC) arrived in Albany and began testing the Interstate Commerce Commission's ban on racial segregation in interstate bus terminals. No arrests were made initially, but local leaders joined together to form the Albany Movement. Anderson was elected president of the organization, which consisted of members of SNCC, the local ministerial alliances, the Federation of Women's Clubs, the Negro Voters League, and other groups. As the movement in Albany assumed the daunting task of desegregating all public facilities in the city, local leaders sought assistance from a more experienced civil rights group. As a long-time friend and classmate of **Southern Christian Leadership Conference** secretary-treasurer Ralph **Abernathy**, Anderson and his wife were able to persuade King to lend his leadership and support to the Albany Movement.

In July 1962 Anderson attracted national attention with his performance on the television news show *Meet the Press*, where he successfully defended the movement to hostile white newsmen. Anderson was standing in for King, who was imprisoned at the time for his role in the Albany demonstrations. The following year Anderson, with several other Albany leaders, was indicted on charges of conspiring to injure a juror. These charges stemmed from the 1963 picketing of an Albany grocery store owned by Carl Smith, a former juror who helped acquit a sheriff in the murder of a black man. While the Albany leaders maintained that they were picketing the store because of Smith's failure to promote black employees, Smith believed he was picketed in retaliation for his role in the verdict. Living in Detroit, Michigan, and no longer president of the Albany Movement, Anderson was extradited to Albany for a trial in October 1963 that resulted in a mistrial. After moving to Detroit, Anderson completed his training in general surgery at the Art Center Hospital and maintained a successful group medical practice until 1984. After leaving the practice, Anderson served as associate dean of Kirksville College of Osteopathic Medicine.

SOURCES

Carson, *In Struggle*, 1981.

Jenkins, *Open Dem Cells*, 2000.

"Leaders Sentenced on Perjury Charge," *Student Voice*, 30 December 1963.

ANGELOU, MAYA (1928–)

In 1960 Maya Angelou, a single mother and struggling actress, accepted the position of northern coordinator for the New York office of the **Southern Christian Leadership Conference** (SCLC). It was in this capacity that Angelou first met Martin Luther King. Although she worked with SCLC for only six months, King was "grateful" for her contribution, particularly the coordination of several fundraising ventures (Angelou, 107).

Born Marguerite Johnson in St. Louis, Missouri, on 4 April 1928, Angelou was raised by her paternal grandmother after her parents divorced. At age 16 Angelou gave birth to a son, Guy, and took various jobs to help support him. After moving to

New York to pursue a dancing career, she was cast in a production of *Porgy and Bess* that toured Europe and Africa.

After hearing King speak at a church in Harlem in early 1960, Angelou resolved to help SCLC raise funds by staging a revue, "Cabaret for Freedom." The revue was a rousing success, with well-known black celebrities Sidney Poitier, Ossie **Davis**, Ruby **Dee**, and Lorraine Hansberry attending opening night.

Following Bayard **Rustin**'s departure from SCLC in 1960, Angelou succeeded him as director of the New York office. After two months on the job, Angelou met King on one of his visits to New York. In her autobiography, *The Heart of a Woman,* she discussed her first impressions of King: "He was shorter than I expected and so young. He had an easy friendliness, which was unsettling" (Angelou, 107).

In late 1960 Angelou met Vusumzi Make, a South African freedom fighter. The two were married in January 1961. That month Angelou officially resigned from her position and wished King, SCLC, and the cause "a year of unlimited strides." In poetic style typical of Angelou, she closed the letter: "I join with millions of black people the world over in saying 'You are our leader'" (Angelou, 31 January 1961).

In 1962, Angelou moved to Cairo with Guy and her new husband and took a job as editor of the *Arab Observer*, a position she held for over a year. After her marriage ended, Angelou and her son lived in Ghana for several years before moving back to the United States in 1966. Her first novel, *I Know Why the Caged Bird Sings,* was published in 1970 to critical acclaim. Angelou went on to write four other volumes of her autobiography, published several volumes of poetry, and appeared on Broadway and in films. Angelou has served as Reynolds Professor of American Studies at Wake Forest University in Winston-Salem, North Carolina, since 1981.

SOURCES

Angelou, *Heart of a Woman*, 1981.
Angelou to King and Wyatt Tee Walker, 31 January 1961, MLKP-MBU.

APARTHEID (1948–1994)

Martin Luther King believed South Africa was home to "the world's worst racism" and drew parallels between struggles against apartheid in South Africa and struggles against "local and state governments committed to 'white supremacy'" in the southern United States (*Papers* 5:401). In a statement delivered at the 1962 American Negro Leadership Conference King declared: "Colonialism and segregation are nearly synonymous … because their common end is economic exploitation, political domination, and the debasing of human personality" (Press release, 28 November 1962).

Apartheid (meaning "apartness" in Afrikaans) was the legal system for racial separation in South Africa from 1948 until 1994. The Popular Registration Act of 1950 classified all South Africans into three categories: bantu (blacks), coloureds (those of mixed race), and white. Later, a fourth category, "Asians," was added. Throughout the 1950s regulations created separate residency areas, job categories, public facilities, transportation, education, and health systems, with social contact between the races strictly prohibited.

The nonviolent resistance of anti-apartheid demonstrators was often met with government brutality, including the massacre of 72 demonstrators in Sharpeville in 1960.

King called the massacre "a tragic and shameful expression of man's inhumanity to man" and argued that it "should also serve as a warning signal to the United States where peaceful demonstrations are also being conducted by student groups. As long as segregation continues to exist; as long as Gestapo-like tactics are used by officials of southern communities; and as long as there are governors and United States senators [who] arrogantly defy the law of the land, the United States is faced with a potential reign of terror more barbaric than anything we see in South Africa" (*Papers* 5:399–400).

Shortly after the Sharpeville massacre, the African National Congress (ANC) abandoned its adherence to **nonviolence** and created an armed wing, conducting acts of sabotage against the apartheid regime. Despite his commitment to nonviolence, King recognized that "in South Africa even the mildest form of nonviolent resistance [was met] with years of imprisonment" or worse (King, 7 December 1964). He believed that the only nonviolent solution to apartheid was an international economic and political boycott of South Africa, and called on governments to demonstrate the "international potential of nonviolence" through economic sanctions (King, "Let My People Go," December 1965).

Although the struggle against apartheid lasted for more than four decades, the United States and Great Britain did approve economic sanctions against South Africa in 1985. The dismantling of apartheid began in the early 1990s, when South African President F. W. de Klerk legalized formerly banned political parties and released political prisoners. In 1994 a new constitution was written, and ANC leader Nelson Mandela became president in the country's first fair and open elections.

SOURCES

King, "Let My People Go," *Africa Today* (December 1965): 9–11.
King, "On South African Independence," 7 December 1964, ARC-LNT.
King to Claude Barnett, 24 March 1960, in *Papers* 5:399–400.
King to Dwight D. Eisenhower, 26 March 1960, in *Papers* 5:400–402.
Press release, American Negro Leadership Conference, 28 November 1962, SCLCR-GAMK.

ASSASSINATION OF MARTIN LUTHER KING, JR. (4 APRIL 1968)

At 6:05 P.M. on Thursday, 4 April 1968, Martin Luther King was shot dead while standing on a balcony outside his second-floor room at the Lorraine Motel in Memphis, Tennessee. News of King's assassination prompted major outbreaks of racial violence, resulting in more than 40 deaths nationwide and extensive property damage in over 100 American cities. James Earl Ray, a 40-year-old escaped fugitive, later confessed to the crime and was sentenced to a 99-year prison term. During King's funeral a tape recording was played in which King spoke of how he wanted to be remembered after his death: "I'd like somebody to mention that day that Martin Luther King Jr., tried to give his life serving others" (King, "Drum Major Instinct," 85).

King had arrived in Tennessee on Wednesday, 3 April, to prepare for a march the following Monday on behalf of **striking Memphis sanitation workers**. As he prepared to leave the Lorraine Motel for a dinner at the home of Memphis minister Samuel "Billy" Kyles, King stepped out onto the balcony of room 306 to speak with **Southern Christian Leadership Conference** (SCLC) colleagues standing in the parking area below. An assassin fired a single shot that caused severe wounds to the lower right side of his face. SCLC aides rushed to him, and Ralph **Abernathy** cradled King's head.

Others on the balcony pointed across the street toward the rear of a boarding house on South Main Street where the shot seemed to have originated. An ambulance rushed King to St. Joseph's Hospital, where doctors pronounced him dead at 7:05 P.M.

President Lyndon B. **Johnson** called for a national day of mourning to be observed on 7 April. In the following days, public libraries, museums, schools, and businesses were closed, and the Academy Awards ceremony and numerous sporting events were postponed. On 8 April King's widow, Coretta Scott **King**, and other family members joined thousands of participants in a march in Memphis honoring King and supporting the sanitation workers. King's funeral service was held the following day in Atlanta at **Ebenezer Baptist Church**. It was attended by many of the nation's political and civil rights leaders, including Jacqueline Kennedy, Vice President Hubert Humphrey, and Ralph **Bunche**. **Morehouse College** President Benjamin **Mays** delivered the eulogy, predicting that King "would probably say that, if death had to come, I am sure there was no greater cause to die for than fighting to get a just wage for garbage collectors" (Mays, 9 April 1968). Over 100,000 mourners followed two mules pulling King's coffin through the streets of Atlanta. After another ceremony on the Morehouse campus, King's body was initially interred at South-View Cemetery. Eventually, it was moved to a crypt next to the Ebenezer Church at the **King Center**, an institution founded by King's widow.

Shortly after the assassination, a policeman discovered a bundle containing a 30.06 Remington rifle next door to the boarding house. The largest investigation in **Federal Bureau of Investigation** (FBI) history led its agents to an apartment in Atlanta. Fingerprints uncovered in the apartment matched those of James Earl Ray, a fugitive who had escaped from a Missouri prison in April 1967. FBI agents and police in Memphis produced further evidence that Ray had registered on 4 April at the South Main Street roominghouse and that he had taken a second-floor room near a common bathroom with a view of the Lorraine Motel.

The identification of Ray as a suspect led to an international manhunt. On 19 July 1968 Ray was extradited to the United States from Britain to stand trial. In a plea bargain, Tennessee prosecutors agreed in March 1969 to forgo seeking the death penalty when Ray pled guilty to murder charges. The circumstances leading to the plea later became a source of controversy, when Ray recanted his confession soon after being sentenced to a 99-year term in prison.

During the years following King's assassination, doubts about the adequacy of the case against Ray were fueled by revelations of the extensive surveillance of King by the FBI and other government agencies. Beginning in 1976 the House Select Committee on Assassinations, chaired by Representative Louis Stokes, re-examined the evidence concerning King's assassination, as well as that of President John F. **Kennedy**. The committee's final report suggested that Ray may have had co-conspirators. The report nonetheless concluded that there was no convincing evidence of government complicity in King's assassination.

After recanting his guilty plea, Ray continued to maintain his innocence, claiming to have been framed by a gun-smuggler he knew as "Raoul." In 1993 Ray's lawyer, William F. Pepper, sought to build popular support to reopen Ray's case by staging a televised mock trial of Ray in which the "jury" found him not guilty. In 1997 members of King's family publicly supported Ray's appeal for a new trial, and King's son

Dexter Scott **King** supported Ray's claims of innocence during a televised prison encounter. Despite this support Tennessee authorities refused to reopen the case, and Ray died in prison on 23 April 1998.

Even after Ray's death, conspiracy allegations continued to surface. In 1999, on behalf of King's widow and children, Pepper won a token civil verdict of wrongful death against Lloyd Jowers, owner of Jim's Grill, a restaurant across the street from the Lorraine Motel. Although the trial produced considerable testimony that contradicted the original case against Ray, the Justice Department announced in 2000 that its own internal investigation, launched in 1998 at the King family's request, had failed to find sufficient evidence to warrant a further investigation.

SOURCES

Homer Bigarts, "Leaders at Rites," *New York Times*, 10 April 1968.
Honey, *Going Down Jericho Road*, 2007.
King, "Drum Major Instinct," in *Knock at Midnight*, ed. Carson and Holloran, 1998.
Mays, Eulogy, 9 April 1968, MLKJP-GAMK.
Pepper, *Orders to Kill*, 1995.
Posner, *Killing the Dream*, 1998.

AZIKIWE, NNAMDI (1904–1996)

In November 1960 Martin Luther King traveled to Lagos, then Nigeria's capital city, to attend the inauguration of Nnamdi Azikiwe as Nigeria's first governor-general of African descent. Azikiwe, who later became the first president of Nigeria and was a life-long advocate of African independence, personally invited King to take part in the official inauguration festivities in a letter dated 26 October 1960.

Azikiwe was born 16 November 1904 in northern Nigeria and attended mission schools in Lagos. In 1925 he left for the United States, where he studied political science, earning a BA (1930) and MA (1932) from Lincoln University in Pennsylvania. While a graduate student at the University of Pennsylvania, Azikiwe met Marcus Garvey and other leaders of the Back to Africa movement. In 1934 Azikiwe returned to Africa where he joined the Nigerian Youth Movement and founded the *West African Pilot* and several other periodicals that advocated independence from Britain. After more than a decade of working as a writer, Azikiwe was elected to the Nigerian Legislative Council in 1947 and began a career in government.

When King traveled to Nigeria in 1960 the liberation struggles there and in other African nations were having a profound impact on the American civil rights movement. Noting that Azikiwe and other African leaders were "popular heroes on most Negro college campuses," King called the African liberation movement "the greatest single international influence on American Negro students," offering the young people hope and guidance in their own struggle for freedom (King, "The Time for Freedom"). Azikiwe was elected the first president of Nigeria in 1963, but was removed from office by a military coup in 1966.

SOURCE

King, "The Time for Freedom Has Come," *New York Times*, 10 September 1961.

BAKER, ELLA JOSEPHINE (1903–1986)

Rejecting Martin Luther King's charismatic leadership, Ella Baker advised student activists organizing the **Student Nonviolent Coordinating Committee** (SNCC) to promote "group-centered leaders" rather than the "leader-centered" style she associated with King's **Southern Christian Leadership Conference** (SCLC) (Baker, 19 June 1968). It was this grassroots leadership that Baker credited for the success and longevity of the movement: "You see, I think that, to be very honest, the movement made Martin rather than Martin making the movement. This is not a discredit to him. This is, to me, as it should be" (Baker, 19 June 1968).

Born in Norfolk, Virginia, on 13 December 1903, Baker was raised on the same land her grandparents had worked as slaves. Baker's childhood was marked early on by the activist spirit of her mother, a member of the local missionary association, who called on women to act as agents of social change in their communities.

After graduating from Shaw University in 1927, Baker moved to New York, where she served as national director of the Young Negroes Cooperative League. In 1938 Baker joined the staff of the **National Association for the Advancement of Colored People** (NAACP) as an assistant field secretary and later as director of branches. Unable to redirect the organization's focus toward grassroots organizing, Baker resigned from her position in 1946. She joined the NAACP again in 1952 as president of the New York City branch. In 1956 Baker, along with Stanley **Levison** and Bayard **Rustin**, co-founded **In Friendship**, an organization founded to provide aid to local movements in the South.

In January 1958 Baker moved to Atlanta to organize SCLC's Crusade for Citizenship, a campaign to help enforce voting rights for black citizens. She ran SCLC's Atlanta headquarters, and after Executive Director John **Tilley** resigned in April 1959 she filled in until a permanent director was hired the following year.

In addition to her criticism of SCLC's organizing philosophy, Baker also experienced conflicts with her male colleagues. Andrew **Young** described Baker as a "determined woman" and went on to say: "The Baptist church had no tradition of women in independent leadership roles, and the result was dissatisfaction all around" (Young, 137).

Following the February 1960 **sit-ins** in Greensboro, North Carolina, Baker and King called a conference of student activists at Shaw University. The result of this April meeting was a student-led organization known as the **Student Nonviolent Coordinating Committee** (SNCC). Already serving in an advisory capacity to the growing student movement, Baker left SCLC in August 1960.

In addition to continuing her involvement as an advisor to SNCC, Baker served as a consultant to the Southern Conference Education Fund throughout the mid-1960s and helped organize the **Mississippi Freedom Democratic Party**. She returned to New York in the late 1960s and remained active in the civil rights struggle until her death in 1986.

SOURCES

Baker, Interview by John Britton, 19 June 1968, RBOH-DHU.
Grant, *Ella Baker*, 1998.
King to John Lee Tilley, 3 April 1959, in *Papers* 5:179.
Ransby, *Ella Baker and the Black Freedom Movement*, 2003.
Reddick, "Notes on Southern Christian Leadership Conference Administrative Committee Meeting," April 1959, in *Papers* 5:171–179.
Young, *An Easy Burden*, 1996.

BALDWIN, JAMES ARTHUR (1924–1987)

Commissioned by *Harper's Magazine* to write on the civil rights movement, Baldwin first became acquainted with Martin Luther King during a trip through the South in 1957. Baldwin's exposure to King and southern racism had a profound influence on his writing and helped deepen his lifelong commitment to social justice. In a 1960 letter to King Baldwin wrote: "I am one of the millions, to be found all over the world but more especially here, in this sorely troubled country, who thank God for you" (*Papers* 5:461).

The oldest of nine children, James Baldwin was born on 2 August 1924. At a young age, Baldwin showed promise as an exceptional orator and writer, and at age 14 he became a child preacher at Harlem's Fireside Pentecostal Assembly, only to reject the ministry three years later. In 1942 he graduated from the politically progressive De Witt Clinton High School in the Bronx, marking the end of his formal education. After working a series of service jobs to support his family, Baldwin moved to Greenwich Village, where he dedicated himself to writing. In 1946 Baldwin published his first article in *The Nation* magazine, and by 1948 he had become a well-known essayist, winning the Rosenwald Fellowship that enabled him to move to Paris to write. While in Europe, Baldwin completed his first and most acclaimed novel, *Go Tell It on the Mountain* (1953). In 1957 Baldwin returned to the United States, becoming a commentator on the civil rights movement.

After the 1961 publication of Baldwin's *Nobody Knows My Name*, a collection of essays exploring race relations in the United States, King wrote the author, offering the following words of appreciation: "Your analysis of the problem is always creative and penetrating. Your honesty and courage in telling the truth to white Americans, even if it hurts, is most impressive" (King, 26 September 1961).

Although sometimes critical of King's nonviolent methods, Baldwin remained an influential voice for civil rights reform. Baldwin attended the 1963 **March on Washington**, and his most powerful collection of essays, *The Fire Next Time*, which predicted a dangerous race war if relations did not improve in the United States, was published following the march. In December 1987 James Baldwin died of stomach cancer in his home in southern France.

SOURCES

Baldwin, "The Dangerous Road before Martin Luther King," *Harper's Magazine* (February 1961): 33–42.
Baldwin, *The Fire Next Time*, 1963.
Baldwin to King, 26 May 1960, in *Papers* 5:460–461.
King to Baldwin, 26 September 1961, MLKP-MBU.
Weatherby, *James Baldwin*, 1989.

BALLOU, MAUDE L. WILLIAMS (1926–)

After King's election as president of the **Montgomery Improvement Association** (MIA) at the start of the **Montgomery bus boycott**, Maude Ballou became Martin Luther King's personal secretary. Upon leaving Montgomery, Alabama, in January 1960, King praised Ballou as "a real associate and a real encouraging person in this total struggle" (*Papers* 5:355).

Ballou was born in Fairhope, Alabama, and raised in Mobile. She received a BS in business administration in 1947 from Southern University in Baton Rouge, Louisiana. After marrying music instructor Leonard Ballou, she and her husband relocated to Montgomery, Alabama, in 1952. Ballou met Jo Ann **Robinson** before the start of the bus boycott and talked with her about how to obtain better conditions for blacks in Montgomery (Ballou, 23 July 1998).

After becoming King's secretary at the MIA, Ballou helped coordinate carpools during the boycott. She often responded on King's behalf to his correspondence. Ballou accompanied King when he moved to Atlanta in 1960, staying with the King family and assisting him in establishing his office at the **Southern Christian Leadership Conference** headquarters there. Ballou left that summer to rejoin her family in Petersburg, Virginia, where her husband had accepted a position at Virginia State College.

SOURCES

Ballou, Interview by King Papers Project staff, 23 July 1998.
King, Address delivered during "A Salute to Dr. and Mrs. Martin Luther King" at Dexter Avenue Baptist Church, 31 January 1960, in *Papers* 5:351–357.

BARBOUR, JOSEPHUS PIUS (1894–1974)

As a student at **Crozer Theological Seminary**, Martin Luther King, Jr., spent a great deal of time at J. Pius Barbour's home in Chester, Pennsylvania, and often preached at Barbour's church, Calvary Baptist Church. Barbour called King "the greatest orator on the American platform," but also warned King in an article written for the newsletter of the **National Baptist Convention** (NBC), "Why God selected you, I don't know. All I know is that he has, and you are in a dangerous place" (Barbour, "Sermons and Addresses," September 1956).

Born on 8 June 1894 in Galveston, Texas, Barbour attended the same college and seminary as King, earning his BA from **Morehouse College** in 1917 and a masters of theology from Crozer Theological Seminary in 1937. During the 1920s he served as pastor of Day Street Baptist Church in Montgomery, Alabama, and then pastored Calvary Baptist Church in Chester from 1933 until his death in 1974. Barbour was a member of the executive board of the NBC and served as the editor of the *National Baptist Voice*.

King and Barbour corresponded frequently during King's life, and Barbour often offered gratuitous advice in a jocular tone. Soon after King moved to Montgomery in 1954 Barbour cautioned, "Don't get stuck there. Move on to a big metropolitan center in THE NORTH, or some town as ATLANTA. You will dry rot there" (*Papers* 2:565). Writing in the *Voice* during the **Montgomery bus boycott**, Barbour informed his fellow Baptists that he had "heard Mike argue dearly all night about Gandhi" while attending Crozer. Barbour recalled that King argued that "no minority can afford to adopt a policy of violence. Just a matter of arithmetic, Dr., he used to say" (Barbour, "Meditations on Rev. M. L. King, Jr.").

SOURCES

Barbour, "Meditations on Rev. M. L. King, Jr., of Montgomery, Ala.," *National Baptist Voice*, March 1956.
Barbour, "Sermons and Addresses at the Convention," *National Baptist Voice*, September 1956.
Barbour to King, 21 July 1955, in *Papers* 2:564–566.

BARRY, MARION SHEPILOV, JR. (1936–)

As the first chairman of the **Student Nonviolent Coordinating Committee** (SNCC), Marion Barry often looked to Martin Luther King, Jr., and the **Southern Christian Leadership Conference** (SCLC) for guidance and support. Despite the ideological differences that developed between SNCC and SCLC, Barry maintained a strong relationship with King throughout the 1960s.

Born in Itta Bena, Mississippi, on 6 March 1936, Marion Barry was the son of sharecroppers. Despite economic hardships he graduated from LeMoyne College (1958) in Memphis, Tennessee, where he was chapter president of the **National Association for the Advancement of Colored People** and was nearly expelled for denouncing a racist comment made by a trustee. Later, while pursuing a graduate degree in chemistry at Fisk University, Barry attended student workshops on **nonviolence** led by Vanderbilt divinity student James **Lawson**. In 1960 Barry played a key role in the student **sit-ins** at Nashville lunch counters.

In April 1960 Barry and fellow Nashville students Diane **Nash** and John **Lewis** joined other student protest leaders at a meeting in Raleigh, North Carolina, which resulted in the formation of SNCC. Barry was elected chairman of the organization. While SNCC was organized as an autonomous, student-led organization, the students depended upon SCLC for resources and Barry looked to King as a mentor. In a letter written to King shortly after a 1960 arrest in Atlanta, Barry praised the jailed leader's commitment to the struggle: "Thanks to you for your deep commitment to the concept of no violence, and your vision of a free society which makes possible this student movement" (*Papers* 5:531).

Barry resigned as chairman of SNCC in the fall of 1960 but remained involved in the organization throughout the decade, helping to organize the **Mississippi Freedom Democratic Party** challenge, and supporting protest campaigns in McComb, Mississippi; Knoxville, Tennessee; and Washington, D.C.

During his time in Washington, Barry became an advocate for the District's poor, black communities. His career as an elected official began in the 1970s, when he served on the school board and city council. In 1978 he was elected mayor of the city, a position he held until 1990 when he resigned due to a drug conviction. Barry returned to the city council in 1992 and was elected to a fourth term as mayor in 1994.

SOURCES
Carson, *In Struggle*, 1981.
SNCC to King, 26 October 1960, in *Papers* 5:530–531.

BARTH, KARL (1886–1968)

In a 2 January 1952 paper written during his first year of doctoral studies at **Boston University**, Martin Luther King, Jr., criticized Karl Barth's view that "God is the unknowable and indescribable God" (*Papers* 2:98). In his paper "Karl Barth's Conceptions of God," King wrote, "Most of my criticisms stem from the fact that I have been greatly influenced by liberal theology, maintaining a healthy respect for reason and a strong belief in the immanence as well as the transcendence of God" (*Papers* 2:104). King did, however, acknowledge that Barth's view that "man is not sufficient unto himself for life" was "a necessary corrective for a liberalism that at times becomes all [too] shallow" (*Papers* 2:106).

Barth was a Swiss Reformed Church theologian born in Basel, Switzerland. His father, Fritz Barth, was a professor of the New Testament and early church history at the University of Bern. Barth studied at a number of universities between 1904 and 1909, including Bern and the University of Marburg in Germany. After his ordination as a pastor in 1908, and the publication of *Epistle to the Romans* (1933), which established his reputation as a theologian, he became a professor of reformed theology at various German universities despite never receiving a doctorate. In 1935 Barth was fired from his position at the University of Bonn and exiled from Germany for refusing to take an oath of loyalty to Adolf Hitler.

Barth held that theology should be God-centered, based solely on the Bible, faith, and the figure of Jesus Christ—and not focused on individuals. As an adherent of liberal theology King defended **personalism**, the notion that God is knowable through the life of Jesus and through individual religious experience. Barth and King met briefly in 1962 while attending separate events at Princeton University. King was a keynote speaker at an annual civil rights conference and Barth preached at ceremonies marking the 150th anniversary of Princeton Chapel. A photograph records their stroll on campus. Barth died in Basel at the age of 82.

SOURCES
Barth, *Epistle to the Romans*, 1933.
King, "After Christmas, What?" 28 December 1952, in *Papers* 6:128–129.
King, "Christ, the Center of Our Faith," 1953–1955, in *Papers* 6:201–202.
King, "Karl Barth's Conception of God," 2 January 1952, in *Papers* 2:95–107.

BATES, DAISY (1914–1999)

Daisy Lee Gaston Bates, a civil rights advocate, newspaper publisher, and president of the Arkansas chapter of the **National Association for the Advancement of Colored People** (NAACP), advised the nine students who desegregated Central High School in Little Rock, Arkansas, in 1957. Martin Luther King offered encouragement to Bates during this period, telling her in a letter that she was "a woman whom everyone KNOWS has been, and still is in the thick of the battle from the very beginning, never faltering, never tiring" (*Papers* 4:446).

Bates was born in 1914 in the small town of Huttig, Arkansas. Following the murder of her biological mother and the disappearance of her father, family friends Orlee and Susan Smith raised her. At an early age she developed a disdain for discrimination, recalling in her autobiography, *The Long Shadow of Little Rock*, an incident when a local butcher told her, "Niggers have to wait 'til I wait on the white people" (Bates, 8).

At the age of 15 she met L. C. Bates, a journalist and insurance salesman whom she married in 1941. The pair soon founded the *Arkansas State Press*, an avidly pro–civil rights newspaper. Bates became an outspoken critic of segregation, using the paper to call for an improvement in the social and economic conditions of blacks throughout Arkansas. When the Supreme Court issued the **Brown v. Board of Education** decision in 1954 that outlawed segregation in public schools, the *State Press* began clamoring for integration in Little Rock schools. As the state president of the NAACP, a position she had assumed in 1952, Bates worked closely with the black students who volunteered to desegregate Central High School in the fall of 1957. The story of the "Little Rock Nine" quickly became national news when white residents rioted and threatened the physical safety of Bates and the students.

During this time King reached out to the Arkansas civil rights leader. In a 26 September 1957 telegram sent during the **Little Rock school desegregation** crisis, King urged Bates to "adhere rigorously to a way of non-violence," despite being "terrorized, stoned, and threatened by ruthless mobs." He assured her: "World opinion is with you. The moral conscience of millions of white Americans is with you." In May 1958 King stayed with Bates and her husband when he spoke at the Arkansas Agricultural and Mechanical College commencement, and soon afterward invited her to be the Women's Day speaker at **Dexter Avenue Baptist Church** in October of that year. During the same year, Bates was elected to the executive committee of King's **Southern Christian Leadership Conference**.

The only woman to speak at the 1963 **March on Washington for Jobs and Freedom**, Bates later moved to Mitchellville, Arkansas, and became director of the Mitchellville Office of Equal Opportunity Self-Help Project. In 1999, following a series of strokes, she died at the age of 84.

SOURCES

Bates, *Long Shadow of Little Rock*, 1962.

"Dr. King Asks Non-Violence in Little Rock School Crisis," 26 September 1957, in *Papers* 4:279.

King to Bates, 1 July 1958, in *Papers* 4:445–446.

BELAFONTE, HAROLD GEORGE, JR. (1927–)

Harry Belafonte, a supporter of Martin Luther King, Jr., and the civil rights movement, used his celebrity as a beloved entertainer to garner funding for the movement. In her autobiography, Coretta Scott **King** said of Belafonte, "Whenever we got into trouble or when tragedy struck, Harry has always come to our aid, his generous heart wide open" (Scott King, 144–145).

Belafonte was born in Harlem, New York, to West Indian parents. As a child Belafonte suffered from dyslexia and left high school to join the U.S. Navy. Like most African Americans serving during World War II, Belafonte was relegated to manual labor.

Harry Belafonte and King share a laugh at the Washington, D.C., airport in 1963. © 1963 Matt Herron/Take Stock.

After his tour of duty, Belafonte returned to New York City and worked odd jobs before beginning his acting career. He studied acting at Erwin Piscator's Dramatic Workshop at the New School for Social Research. After joining the American Negro Theater in Harlem, Belafonte met Paul Robeson and Sidney Poitier, who became a lifelong friend.

Although best known for his success as a singer and actor, Belafonte continually used his public stature to advance the black freedom struggle. As one of the country's most popular entertainers during the 1950s, Belafonte appeared with Coretta Scott King and Duke Ellington at the "Salute to Montgomery," a December 1956 fundraising event in New York. While participating in the May 1957 **Prayer Pilgrimage for Freedom** in Washington, D.C., Belafonte reportedly remarked to a friend: "We play a hit and run game up here. We come down here like this and say our piece and then it's all over. But the Rev. Martin Luther King has to go back and face it all over again" (*Papers* 4:373n).

During the 1960s Belafonte continued to provide financial assistance to the **Southern Christian Leadership Conference**, most notably during the **Birmingham Campaign**. In late March 1963 Belafonte invited prominent individuals to a meeting at his New York apartment, where King and Fred **Shuttlesworth** discussed plans for the Birmingham Campaign and appealed for financial support to be used primarily for bail money. Without hesitation, Belafonte organized a committee to raise funds for the movement. While King was held in a Birmingham jail, Belafonte raised $50,000, allowing the campaign to proceed.

After King's **assassination** in 1968, Belafonte served as an executor of King's estate and chaired the Martin Luther King, Jr., Memorial Fund. Afterward he continued to support national and international civil rights and humanitarian issues.

SOURCES

Belafonte to King, 26 February 1958, in *Papers* 4:373.

King, *Autobiography of Martin Luther King, Jr.*, ed. Carson, 1998.

(Scott) King, *My Life with Martin Luther King, Jr.*, 1969.

BEVEL, JAMES LUTHER (1936–)

Credited by Martin Luther King with initiating the Children's Crusade during the **Birmingham Campaign** of 1963, James Bevel emerged as a civil rights leader from the ranks of the Nashville, Tennessee, student movement. Bevel was at King's side during many of the major campaigns of the **Southern Christian Leadership Conference** (SCLC) and was at the Lorraine Motel at the time of King's **assassination** in 1968.

Bevel was born in Itta Bena, Mississippi, on 19 October 1936. He served in the U.S. Naval Reserve in 1954 and 1955 before entering the American Baptist Theological Seminary in Nashville, Tennessee. He was ordained as a Baptist minister in 1959 and went on to pastor the Chestnut Grove Baptist Church. During this period Bevel joined with fellow seminarian John **Lewis**, Diane **Nash** from Fisk University, and Vanderbilt's James **Lawson** in the Nashville movement to initiate a local **sit-in** campaign in early February 1960. That same year, Bevel and the other Nashville activists attended the founding meeting of the **Student Nonviolent Coordinating Committee** (SNCC) at Shaw University. Bevel and Nash helped lead the **Freedom Rides** in 1961 and married later that year. In 1962 Bevel left SNCC to become Mississippi field secretary for SCLC.

(L to R) Ralph Abernathy, Andrew Young, King, and Coretta Scott King confer with James Bevel, the Southern Christian Leadership Conference's vanguard organizer in Selma, during the last leg of the Selma to Montgomery March, 25 March 1965. Courtesy of Adele Saunders.

Bevel and Nash moved to Alabama in the spring of 1963 and played leading roles, along with Dorothy **Cotton**, Andrew **Young**, Bernard **Lee**, Fred **Shuttlesworth** and the **Alabama Christian Movement for Human Rights**, in the campaign to desegregate Birmingham. As the number of adult participants willing to go to jail dwindled, Bevel began recruiting black students from Birmingham's high schools, colleges, and churches to participate in the protests. Mass demonstrations by students triggered a violent police response that brought national attention to Birmingham. One week later, city leaders reached an accord with movement leaders.

As he prepared to work on the Alabama voter registration movement that would later culminate in the 1965 **Selma to Montgomery March**, Bevel informed King that more staff was needed to build a nonviolent movement in Alabama.

Bevel feared that activists who were not committed to **nonviolence** were conducting "demonstration[s] for the sake of demonstrating," and that these tactics resulted in "rioting and deaths." He advised, "In order to off-set these trends, the non-violent must project and execute a program that will [allow] more Negroes to become convinced of the effectiveness of non-violence and the principles of it." Bevel further implored King to put "the whole non-violent staff" on the Alabama project (Bevel, 13 April 1964). His pressure paid off, and at the May 1964 executive staff meeting King recommended that SCLC increase its presence in Alabama. Bevel led this effort as the head of SCLC's Direct Action Department.

Bevel moved to **Chicago** in 1965 to begin laying the groundwork for a nonviolent northern civil rights drive. Bevel went on to become national director of the Spring Mobilization Committee to End the War in **Vietnam** in 1967 and, the following year, joined King in the effort to win the **Memphis sanitation workers strike**. Bevel left SCLC after King's death and became involved in the Republican Party and the 1995 Million Man March.

SOURCES

Bevel, Memo to King, 13 April 1964, MLKJP-GAMK.
Honey, *Going Down Jericho Road*, 2007.
Lewis, *Walking with the Wind*, 1998.

"BEYOND VIETNAM" (4 APRIL 1967)

On 4 April 1967 Martin Luther King delivered his seminal speech at Riverside Church condemning the **Vietnam War**. Declaring "my conscience leaves me no other choice," King described the war's deleterious effects on both America's poor and Vietnamese peasants and insisted that it was morally imperative for the United States to take radical steps to halt the war through nonviolent means (King, "Beyond Vietnam," 139).

King's anti-war sentiments emerged publicly for the first time in March 1965, when King declared that "millions of dollars can be spent every day to hold troops in South Viet Nam and our country cannot protect the rights of Negroes in Selma" (King, 9 March 1965). King told reporters on *Face the Nation* that as a minister he had "a prophetic function" and as "one greatly concerned about the need for peace in our world and the survival of mankind, I must continue to take a stand on this issue" (King, 29 August 1965). In a version of the "Transformed Nonconformist" sermon given in January 1966 at **Ebenezer Baptist Church**, King voiced his own opposition to the Vietnam War, describing American aggression as a violation of the 1954 Geneva Accord that promised self-determination.

In early 1967 King stepped up his anti-war proclamations, giving similar speeches in Los Angeles and Chicago. The Los Angeles speech, called "The Casualties of the War in Vietnam," stressed the history of the conflict and argued that American power should be "harnessed to the service of peace and human beings, not an inhumane power [unleashed] against defenseless people" (King, 25 February 1967).

On 4 April, accompanied by Amherst College professor Henry Commager, Union Theological Seminary President John Bennett, and Rabbi Abraham Joshua **Heschel**, at an event sponsored by **Clergy and Laymen Concerned about Vietnam**, King spoke to over 3,000 at New York's Riverside Church. The speech was drafted from a collection of volunteers, including Spelman professor Vincent **Harding** and Wesleyan professor John Maguire. King's address emphasized his responsibility to the American people and explained that conversations with young black men in the ghettos reinforced his own commitment to **nonviolence**.

King followed with an historical sketch outlining Vietnam's devastation at the hands of "deadly Western arrogance," noting, "we are on the side of the wealthy, and the secure, while we create a hell for the poor" (King, "Beyond Vietnam," 146; 153). To change course, King suggested a five point outline for stopping the war, which included a call for a unilateral ceasefire. To King, however, the Vietnam War was only the most pressing symptom of American colonialism worldwide. King claimed that America made "peaceful revolution impossible by refusing to give up the privileges and the pleasures that come from the immense profits of overseas investments" (King, "Beyond Vietnam," 157). King urged instead "a radical revolution of values" emphasizing love and justice rather than economic nationalism (King, "Beyond Vietnam," 157).

The immediate response to King's speech was largely negative. Both the *Washington Post* and *New York Times* published editorials criticizing the speech, with the *Post* noting that King's speech had "diminished his usefulness to his cause, to his country, and to his people" through a simplistic and flawed view of the situation ("A Tragedy," 6 April 1967). Similarly, both the **National Association for the Advancement of Colored People** and Ralph **Bunche** accused King of linking two disparate issues, Vietnam and civil rights. Despite public criticism, King continued to attack the Vietnam War on both moral and economic grounds.

Sources

Branch, *At Canaan's Edge*, 2006.
"Dr. King's Error," *New York Times*, 7 April 1967.
King, "Beyond Vietnam," in *A Call to Conscience*, ed. Carson and Shepard, 2001.
King, "The Casualties of the War in Vietnam," 25 February 1967, CLPAC.
King, Interview on *Face the Nation*, 29 August 1965, RRML-TxTyU.
King, Statement on voter registration in Alabama, 9 March 1965, MLKJP-GAMK.
King, Transformed Nonconformist, 16 January 1966, CSKC.
"A Tragedy," *Washington Post*, 6 April 1967.

BIRMINGHAM CAMPAIGN (1963)

In April 1963 King and the **Southern Christian Leadership Conference** (SCLC) joined with Birmingham, Alabama's existing local movement, the **Alabama Christian Movement for Human Rights** (ACMHR), in a massive direct action campaign to attack the city's segregation system by putting pressure on Birmingham's merchants during the Easter season, the second biggest shopping season of the year. As ACMHR founder Fred **Shuttlesworth** stated in the group's "Birmingham Manifesto," the campaign was "a moral witness to give our community a chance to survive" (ACMHR, 3 April 1963).

The campaign was originally scheduled to begin in early March 1963, but was postponed until 2 April when the relatively moderate Albert **Boutwell** defeated Birmingham's segregationist commissioner of public safety, Eugene "Bull" **Connor**, in a run-off mayoral election. On 3 April the desegregation campaign was launched with a series of mass meetings, direct actions, lunch counter **sit-ins**, marches on City Hall, and a

Sixteenth Street Baptist Church in Birmingham, Alabama, after a bomb exploded on 15 September 1963, killing four girls from the congregation. © 1963 Matt Herron/Take Stock.

boycott of downtown merchants. King spoke to black citizens about the philosophy of **nonviolence** and its methods, and extended appeals for volunteers at the end of the mass meetings. With the number of volunteers increasing daily, actions soon expanded to kneel-ins at churches, sit-ins at the library, and a march on the county building to register voters. Hundreds were arrested.

On 10 April the city government obtained a state circuit court injunction against the protests. After heavy debate, campaign leaders decided to disobey the court order. King declared: "We cannot in all good conscience obey such an injunction which is an unjust, undemocratic and unconstitutional misuse of the legal process" (ACMHR, 11 April 1963). Plans to continue to submit to arrest were threatened, however, because the money available for cash bonds was depleted, so leaders could no longer guarantee that arrested protesters would be released. King contemplated whether he and Ralph **Abernathy** should be arrested. Given the lack of bail funds, King's services as a fundraiser were desperately needed, but King also worried that his failure to submit to arrests might undermine his credibility. King concluded that he must risk going to jail in Birmingham. He told his colleagues: "I don't know what will happen; I don't know where the money will come from. But I have to make a faith act" (King, 73).

On Good Friday, 12 April, King was arrested in Birmingham after violating the anti-protest injunction and was kept in solitary confinement. During this time King penned the "**Letter from Birmingham Jail**" on the margins of the *Birmingham News*, in reaction to a statement published in that newspaper by eight Birmingham clergymen condemning the protests. King's request to call his wife, Coretta Scott **King**, who was at home in Atlanta recovering from the birth of their fourth child, was denied. After she communicated her concern to the Kennedy administration, Birmingham officials permitted King to call home. Bail money was made available, and he was released on 20 April 1963.

In order to sustain the campaign, SCLC organizer James **Bevel** proposed using young children in demonstrations. Bevel's rationale for the Children's Crusade was that young people represented an untapped source of freedom fighters without the prohibitive responsibilities of older activists. On 2 May more than 1,000 African American students attempted to march into downtown Birmingham, and hundreds were arrested. When hundreds more gathered the following day, Commissioner Connor directed local police and fire departments to use force to halt the demonstrations. During the next few days images of children being blasted by high-pressure fire hoses, clubbed by police officers, and attacked by police dogs appeared on television and in newspapers, triggering international outrage. While leading a group of child marchers, Shuttlesworth himself was hit with the full force of a fire hose and had to be hospitalized. King offered encouragement to parents of the young protesters: "Don't worry about your children, they're going to be alright. Don't hold them back if they want to go to jail. For they are doing a job for not only themselves, but for all of America and for all mankind" (King, 6 May 1963).

In the meantime, the white business structure was weakening under adverse publicity and the unexpected decline in business due to the boycott, but many business owners and city officials were reluctant to negotiate with the protesters. With national pressure on the White House also mounting, Attorney General Robert **Kennedy** sent Burke **Marshall**, his chief civil rights assistant, to facilitate negotiations between prominent black citizens and representatives of Birmingham's Senior Citizen's Council, the city's business leadership.

The Senior Citizen's Council sought a moratorium on street protests as an act of good faith before any final settlement was declared, and Marshall encouraged campaign leaders to halt demonstrations, accept an interim compromise that would provide partial success, and negotiate the rest of their demands afterward. Some black negotiators were open to the idea, and although the hospitalized Shuttlesworth was not present at the negotiations, on 8 May King told the negotiators he would accept the compromise and call the demonstrations to a halt.

When Shuttlesworth learned that King intended to announce a moratorium he was furious—about both the decision to ease pressure off white business owners and the fact that he, as the acknowledged leader of the local movement, had not been consulted. Feeling betrayed, Shuttlesworth reminded King that he could not legitimately speak for the black population of Birmingham on his own: "Go ahead and call it off … When I see it on TV, that you have called it off, I will get up out of this, my sickbed, with what little ounce of strength I have, and lead them back into the street. And your name'll be Mud" (Hampton and Fayer, 136). King made the announcement anyway, but indicated that demonstrations might be resumed if negotiations did not resolve the situation shortly.

By 10 May negotiators had reached an agreement, and despite his falling out with King, Shuttlesworth joined him and Abernathy to read the prepared statement that detailed the compromise: the removal of "Whites Only" and "Blacks Only" signs in restrooms and on drinking fountains, a plan to desegregate lunch counters, an ongoing "program of upgrading Negro employment," the formation of a biracial committee to monitor the progress of the agreement, and the release of jailed protesters on bond ("The Birmingham Truce Agreement," 10 May 1963).

Birmingham segregationists responded to the agreement with a series of violent attacks. That night an explosive went off near the **Gaston** Motel room where King and SCLC leaders had previously stayed, and the next day the home of King's brother Alfred Daniel **King** was bombed. President John F. **Kennedy** responded by ordering 3,000 federal troops into position near Birmingham and making preparations to federalize the Alabama National Guard. Four months later, on 15 September, Ku Klux Klan members bombed Birmingham's Sixteenth Street Baptist Church, killing four young girls. King delivered the eulogy at the 18 September joint funeral of three of the victims, preaching that the girls were "the martyred heroines of a holy crusade for freedom and human dignity" (King, 18 September 1963).

SOURCES

ACMHR, "Birmingham Manifesto," 3 April 1963, MLKJP-GAMK.

ACMHR, Press release, Statement by M. L. King et al., 11 April 1963, JBRP-AB.

"The Birmingham Truce Agreement," 10 May 1963, in *Eyes on the Prize,* ed. Carson et al., 1991.

Douglas Brinkley, "The Man Who Kept King's Secrets," *Vanity Fair* (April 2006).

Eskew, *But for Birmingham,* 1997.

Hampton and Fayer, with Flynn, *Voices of Freedom,* 1990.

King, Address delivered at mass meeting, 6 May 1963, MLKJP-GAMK.

King, Eulogy for Carol Denise McNair et al., 18 September 1963, MLKJP-GAMK.

King, *Why We Can't Wait,* 1964.

BLACK NATIONALISM

Achieving major national influence through the Nation of Islam (NOI) and the **Black Power** movement of the 1960s, proponents of black nationalism advocated economic self-sufficiency, race pride for African Americans, and black separatism. Reacting against white racial prejudice and critical of the gap between American democratic ideals and the reality of segregation and discrimination in America, in the 1960s black nationalists criticized the methods of Martin Luther King, Jr., the **Southern Christian Leadership Conference**, and other organizations that sought to reform American society through nonviolent interracial activism. In his 1963 "**Letter from Birmingham Jail**," King described himself as standing between the forces of complacency and the "hatred and despair of the black nationalist" (King, 90).

The historical roots of black nationalism can be traced back to nineteenth-century African American leaders such as abolitionist Martin Delany, who advocated the emigration of northern free blacks to Africa, where they would settle and assist native Africans in nation-building. Delany believed that this development would also uplift the status and condition of African Americans who remained, calling them "a nation within a nation ... really a broken people" (Painter, "Martin R. Delany").

Twentieth-century black nationalism was greatly influenced by Marcus Garvey, a Jamaican immigrant to the United States who founded the United Negro Improvement Association (UNIA) in 1914. In an essay titled "The Future as I See It," Garvey insisted that the UNIA was "organized for the absolute purpose of bettering our condition, industrially, commercially, socially, religiously and politically." Garvey and the UNIA also promoted black emigration to Africa as a program of "national independence, an independence so strong as to enable us to rout others if they attempt to interfere with us" ("Speech by Marcus Garvey"). One of the UNIA's main efforts was to establish black-owned businesses, the best known being the Black Star Line, a firm that planned to transport people and goods to Africa. Although 35,000 investors flocked to buy five-dollar shares of Black Star Line stock, the shipping firm and the UNIA's other commercial ventures failed. Garvey was convicted of mail fraud in 1923 and eventually deported, but he remained a heroic figure to many future black nationalists.

During the economic depression of the 1930s, Farrad Muhammad, a Detroit peddler, founded another significant organization of black nationalists, the NOI. The NOI sought to develop an intentionally separate and economically self-sufficient black community governed by a revised version of the Muslim faith. Muhammad's claim that whites were "blue-eyed devils" seeking to oppress blacks made him a controversial figure. When Farrad Muhammad disappeared in 1934 after various factions in the NOI battled for dominance, his disciple Elijah Muhammad became the sect's leader.

By the late 1950s NOI minister **Malcolm X** had emerged as the group's most dynamic and popular spokesperson. Early on, Malcolm X's oratory combined calls for racial independence with criticisms of mainstream civil rights leaders who cooperated with whites. In his November 1963 speech "Message to the Grass Roots," Malcolm X defined land as "the basis of freedom, justice and equality," and declared: "A revolutionary wants land so he can set up his own nation, an independent nation. These Negroes aren't asking for any nation—they're trying to crawl back on the plantation.... If you're afraid of black nationalism, you're afraid of revolution. And if you love revolution, you love black nationalism" (Malcolm X, "Message to the Grass Roots," 9–10).

Following the defeat of the **Mississippi Freedom Democratic Party** in 1964 and a trend of rising violence against civil rights workers and supporters, many activists became increasingly skeptical of the power of nonviolent resistance to influence the white-dominated power structure in America. Stokely **Carmichael**'s appointment in May 1966 as chair of the **Student Nonviolent Coordinating Committee** (SNCC) signaled an organizational shift toward exclusive black self-determination in SNCC's approach to civil rights. In June 1966 Carmichael began to use the slogan "Black Power" to promote racial self-respect and increased power for blacks in economic and political realms. He asserted that the "concern for black power addresses itself directly to ... the necessity to reclaim our history and our identity from the cultural terrorism and depredation of self-justifying white guilt" (Carmichael, "Toward Black Liberation"). Rather than publicly criticize black nationalists, King preferred to focus on the social forces and conditions that brought black nationalist philosophies such as "Black Power" to the fore. He called their departure from interracial cooperation in civil rights work "a response to the feeling that a real solution is hopelessly distant because of the inconsistencies, resistance and faintheartedness of those in power" (King, *Where*, 33).

King remained fundamentally opposed to black nationalists' rejection of American society as irreparably unjust and to later black nationalists' abandonment of **nonviolence**. Because of their view that "American society is so hopelessly corrupt and enmeshed in evil that there is no possibility of salvation from within," King felt black

nationalist movements rejected "the one thing that keeps the fire of revolutions burning: the ever-present flame of hope" (King, *Where*, 44; 46).

SOURCES

Carmichael, "Toward Black Liberation," *Massachusetts Review* 7 (Autumn 1966): 639–651.

Carson, *In Struggle*, 1981.

Garvey, "The Future as I See It," in *Look for Me All Around You*, ed. Louis J. Parascandola, 2005.

King, "Letter from Birmingham Jail," in *Why We Can't Wait*, 1964.

King, Press conference, 24 February 1965, MLKJP-GAMK.

King, *Where Do We Go from Here*, 1967.

Lomax, *When the Word Is Given*, 1963.

Malcolm X, "Message to the Grass Roots," in *Malcolm X Speaks*, ed. George Breitman, 1965.

Nell Irwin Painter, "Martin R. Delany: Elitism and Black Nationalism," in *Black Leaders of the
Nineteenth Century*, ed. Litwack and Meier, 1991.

"Speech by Marcus Garvey," 7 September 1921, in *The Marcus Garvey and Universal Negro
Improvement Association Papers*, Vol. 4, ed. Hill, Tolbert, and Forczek, 1985.

BLACK POWER

Although African American writers and politicians used the term "Black Power" for years,
the expression first entered the lexicon of the civil rights movement during the Meredith
March Against Fear in the summer of 1966. Martin Luther King, Jr., believed that Black Power
was "essentially an emotional concept" that meant "different things to different people," but
he worried that the slogan carried "connotations of violence and separatism" and opposed its
use (King, 32; King, 14 October 1966). The controversy over Black Power reflected and perpe-
tuated a split in the civil rights movement between organizations that maintained that nonviolent methods were the only way to achieve civil rights goals and those organizations that had
become frustrated and were ready to adopt violence and black separatism.

On 16 June 1966, while completing the march begun by James **Meredith**, Stokely
Carmichael of the **Student Nonviolent Coordinating Committee** (SNCC) rallied a
crowd in Greenwood, Mississippi, with the cry, "We want Black Power!" Although
SNCC members had used the term during informal conversations, this was the first
time *Black Power* was used as a public slogan. Asked later what he meant by the term,
Carmichael said, "When you talk about black power you talk about bringing this
country to its knees any time it messes with the black man ... any white man in this
country knows about power. He knows what white power is and he ought to know
what black power is" ("Negro Leaders on 'Meet the Press'"). In the ensuing weeks,
both SNCC and the **Congress of Racial Equality** (CORE) repudiated **nonviolence**
and embraced militant separatism with Black Power as their objective.

Although King believed that "the slogan was an unwise choice," he attempted to
transform its meaning, writing that although "the Negro is powerless," he should seek
"to amass political and economic power to reach his legitimate goals" (King, October
1966; King, 14 October 1966). King believed that "America must be made a nation in
which its multi-racial people are partners in power" (King, 14 October 1966). Carmichael, on the other hand, believed that black people had to first "close ranks" in solidarity with each other before they could join a multiracial society (Carmichael, 44).

Although King was hesitant to criticize Black Power openly, he told his staff on 14
November 1966 that Black Power "was born from the wombs of despair and disappointment. Black Power is a cry of pain. It is in fact a reaction to the failure of White

Power to deliver the promises and to do it in a hurry … The cry of Black Power is really a cry of hurt" (King, 14 November 1966).

As the **Southern Christian Leadership Conference**, the **National Association for the Advancement of Colored People**, and other civil rights organizations rejected SNCC and CORE's adoption of Black Power, the movement became fractured. In the late 1960s and early 1970s, Black Power became the rallying call of black nationalists and revolutionary armed movements like the Black Panther Party, and King's interpretation of the slogan faded into obscurity.

SOURCES

"Black Power for Whom?" *Christian Century* (20 July 1966): 903–904.

Branch, *At Canaan's Edge*, 2006.

Carmichael and Hamilton, *Black Power*, 1967.

Carson, *In Struggle*, 1981.

King, Address at SCLC staff retreat, 14 November 1966, MLKJP-GAMK.

King, "Is It Not Enough to Condemn Black Power," October 1966, MLKJP-GAMK.

King, Statement on Black Power, 14 October 1966, TMAC-GA.

King, *Where Do We Go from Here*, 1967.

"Negro Leaders on 'Meet the Press,'" 89th Cong., 2d sess., *Congressional Record* 112 (29 August 1966): S 21095–21102.

BLACKWELL, RANDOLPH T. (1927–1981)

Randolph T. Blackwell served as field director of the **Voter Education Project** (VEP) in Atlanta, Georgia, before joining the **Southern Christian Leadership Conference** (SCLC) as program director in 1964. When Blackwell announced his plans to leave SCLC in 1966, Martin Luther King believed his coordinating efforts for SCLC were crucial and pleaded with him to stay.

Blackwell was born on 10 March 1927 in Greensboro, North Carolina. He dated his political awakening to the spring of 1943, when he heard a talk by Ella **Baker**, then field director of the **National Association for the Advancement of Colored People** (NAACP). He joined the NAACP's Youth Council the next day and worked on local campaigns until he was drafted into the Army in 1945. After his discharge two years later, Blackwell resumed his civil rights work and ran for the North Carolina General Assembly while simultaneously earning a BS in sociology from North Carolina A & T University in 1949.

Blackwell worked on a successful desegregation campaign in Washington, D.C., while earning his law degree from Howard University (1953). He continued working with the NAACP after he began his first teaching post at Winston-Salem Teacher's College in 1953. Blackwell became associate professor of government at Alabama A & M College near Huntsville in 1954, and when **sit-ins** began there in 1962 Blackwell emerged as a movement leader.

In 1963 Blackwell left teaching to become field director of VEP, a non-partisan voter registration program administered by the Southern Regional Council with the support of SCLC, the NAACP, the **Congress of Racial Equality**, the **National Urban League**, and the **Student Nonviolent Coordinating Committee**. Blackwell was selected as SCLC's program director in August 1964.

Blackwell and Hosea **Williams** disagreed over supervision of field operations. After King refused to intercede on his behalf in this and other administrative matters,

Blackwell took a leave of absence in 1966. His leave became permanent when he was appointed director of Southern Rural Action, an economic development organization working in the Deep South.

Blackwell's work helping poor communities achieve economic and political self-reliance earned him many awards, including the Martin Luther King, Jr., Nonviolent Peace Prize in 1976 and the National Bar Association's Equal Justice Award in 1978. Southern Rural Action worked in Plains, Georgia, then-governor Jimmy Carter's hometown, and when Carter was elected president Blackwell was appointed director of the Department of Commerce's Office of Minority Business Enterprise. Blackwell held that post from 1977 to 1979 before returning to Atlanta to become the local director of the Office of Minority Business Programs and Development.

SOURCE
Garrow, *Bearing the Cross*, 1986.

BOND, HORACE JULIAN (1940–)

Student activist Julian Bond first met Martin Luther King in 1960 when he was a student at **Morehouse College**. The two became better acquainted when Bond joined the small staff of the **Student Nonviolent Coordinating Committee** (SNCC), which shared an office with the **Southern Christian Leadership Conference** (SCLC). In 1966, when Bond was refused his elected seat in the Georgia House of Representatives, King preached against the legislature's action and organized a march in support of Bond.

Bond was born in Nashville, Tennessee, on 14 January 1940. His father, Horace Mann Bond, became the first African American president of Lincoln University in 1945. After finishing high school, Bond entered Morehouse College in 1957.

Bond's political awakening began in early 1960 when he heard about the student **sit-ins** in Greensboro, North Carolina. Deciding to take similar action in Atlanta, Bond and fellow Morehouse student Lonnie King created the Committee on Appeal for Human Rights. Shortly thereafter, Bond attended a student conference sponsored by SCLC at Shaw University in Raleigh, North Carolina, where young activists decided to form SNCC. Bond was later hired as SNCC's communications director.

In the autumn of 1961 King co-taught a small philosophy seminar at Morehouse with his former professor, Dr. Samuel Williams. Bond wrote that the class "became a class in 'movement,' and laid before us two of the greater minds I will ever know" (Bond, "If Alive Today"). Shortly after taking the class Bond dropped out of Morehouse to work full-time for SNCC.

In 1965 a prior federal court decision forced the creation of new state congressional districts in Georgia. SNCC had been working on voter registration in the rural South and recognized the reapportionment as an opportunity to put forward candidates who would support a civil rights agenda. Bond, like King, lived in the newly created 136th House District in Atlanta, which was 95 percent African American. The 25-year-old ran for his district's seat in the Georgia House of Representatives, and won 82 percent of the vote with an untraditional door-to-door campaign.

A few days before Bond was to take office SNCC put out a press release opposing the **Vietnam War** and proposing civil rights work as an alternative to the draft. Bond publicly supported the press release, and the Georgia legislature, calling his stance treasonous, voted to refuse him his seat. King returned early from a trip to California, issued a press release calling the legislature's act "unconscionable," and led a protest rally to the state house (King, 12 January 1966). In his sermon at **Ebenezer Baptist Church** that Sunday, King praised Bond as "a young man who dared to speak his mind," using the incident as the foundation from which to preach on the biblical injunction to be a non-conformist: "If you're going to be a Christian, take the gospel of Jesus Christ seriously, you must be a dissenter, you must be a non-conformist" (King, 16 January 1966).

With King as a co-plaintiff, Bond appealed the Georgia legislature's decision to the U.S. Supreme Court, which ruled unanimously in his favor on 5 December 1966. He took his seat the following month. At the 1968 Democratic National Convention Bond co-chaired a challenge to the Georgia delegation, seconded the nomination of peace candidate Eugene McCarthy for president, and was nominated for the vice-presidency, but withdrew his name because he did not meet the minimum age required by the U.S. Constitution. In 1971 Bond returned to Morehouse College to earn a BA in English, and also became the first president of the Southern Poverty Law Center. He became a Georgia state senator in 1974 and served until 1986. Since leaving the State Senate Bond has held academic positions at American University and the University of Virginia. In 1998 Bond became chairman of the **National Association for the Advancement of Colored People**.

SOURCES

Bond, "If Alive Today, He'd Tell Movement to 'March On,'" *Atlanta Journal Constitution*, 14 January 1978.
Bond, Interview by Milton Viorst, November 1974, RBOH-DHU.
Branch, *At Canaan's Edge*, 2006.
Carson, *In Struggle*, 1981.
King, Statement on refusal to seat Julian Bond, 12 January 1966, MLKJP-GAMK.
King, Transformed Nonconformist, sermon at Ebenezer, 16 January 1966, MLKJP-GAMK.
Neary, *Julian Bond*, 1971.

BORDERS, WILLIAM HOLMES, SR. (1905–1993)

Shortly before the **Montgomery bus boycott** ended, prominent Atlanta minister William Holmes Borders sent an encouraging letter to Martin Luther King, writing, "May God continue to bless you that you may reach higher heights. Your future is unlimited." He continued, "There is no position in any church, religious body, University … which you could not fill" (*Papers* 3:485).

Born in Macon, Georgia, Borders was a third-generation minister. He earned his BA (1929) from **Morehouse College**, his BD (1932) from Garrett Theological Seminary, and his MA from Northwestern University in 1936. The following year Borders became pastor of Atlanta's Wheat Street Baptist Church, a few blocks away from his rival, Martin Luther **King**, Sr., at **Ebenezer Baptist Church**. Under his leadership, which spanned five decades, the church developed a complex of businesses, housing, and nonprofit organizations. His sermons were broadcast on the radio from the early 1940s until 1972. He published a compilation of his early sermons, *Seven Minutes at the "Mike" in the Deep South*, in 1949.

Borders was a leader in many of Atlanta's civil rights campaigns. He led voter registration efforts in the 1930s and, in 1947, was instrumental in the hiring of Atlanta's first black police officers. In December 1956, at the **Montgomery Improvement Association's** (MIA) first **Institute on Non-Violence and Social Change**, Borders spoke on the "Social Aspects of the Christian Gospel." The following year Borders and five other ministers, leaders of the Triple L Movement (Love, Law, and Liberation), were arrested for occupying bus seats reserved for whites and brought a test case against Georgia's segregation laws. The action resulted in a 1959 court decision striking down the law and integrating Atlanta's public transit system. Borders later chaired the Student-Adult Liaison Committee, which negotiated the desegregation of Atlanta's lunch counters in 1961. Upon Borders' death, congressional representative and civil rights activist John **Lewis** remarked, "We are deeply indebted to this soldier of the cross" (Hardie, "Words, Deeds").

SOURCES

Borders, *Seven Minutes at the "Mike" in the Deep South*, 1943.
Borders to King, 19 December 1956, in *Papers* 3:484–485.
Borders to King, 6 April 1957, in *Papers* 4:153–154.
Ann Hardie, "Words, Deeds of Reverend William Holmes Borders, Sr., Recalled," *Atlanta Journal-Constitution*, 30 November 1993.

BOSTON UNIVERSITY

After graduating from **Crozer Theological Seminary** in 1951, Martin Luther King pursued his doctoral studies in systematic theology at Boston University's School of Theology. King's desire to study at Boston University was influenced by his increasing interest in **personalism**, a philosophy that emphasizes the necessity of personal religious experience in understanding God. Two of the country's leading personalist theologians, Edgar S. **Brightman** and L. Harold **DeWolf**, taught at Boston University and helped to refine King's concept of the theory. King stated in his graduate application that Crozer professor and Boston University graduate Raymond Bean's "great influence over me has turned my eyes toward his former school" (*Papers* 1:390).

At Boston University Brightman and DeWolf became King's primary mentors. King also broadened his studies by taking several classes on the history of philosophy that examined the works of Reinhold **Niebuhr**, Alfred North Whitehead, Plato, and Hegel. King's tenure at Boston University culminated with the completion of his **dissertation**, entitled "A Comparison of the Conceptions of God in the Thinking of Paul Tillich and Henry Nelson Wieman." Although King had not previously studied either **Tillich** or Wieman, he was interested in their denial of both the personality of God and of the possibility of personal knowledge of God, which contrasted greatly with his earlier studies of personalism.

Outside the classroom King helped organize, and participated in, the Dialectical Society, a dozen African American theological students who met monthly to discuss philosophical and theological ideas and their application to the black situation in the United States. A classmate of King's, W. T. Handy, described the group as "solving the problems of the world, politically, socially, and in the theological realm" (*Papers* 2:161). King also delivered sermons at local churches and developed a reputation as a powerful preacher.

Although King received satisfactory grades at Boston University, later analysis would reveal that many of King's essays and his dissertation relied upon appropriated words and ideas for which he failed to provide adequate citations. King's plagiarism escaped detection during his lifetime, and his professors had little reason to suspect him of such, based on his success in the classroom. King completed his dissertation in April 1955 and received his PhD that June. He was not able to attend his graduation ceremony due to financial restraints and his wife Coretta Scott **King**'s pregnancy.

SOURCES

W. T. Handy to King, 18 November 1952, in *Papers* 2:160–164.

Introduction, in *Papers* 2:1–25.

King, "A Comparison of the Conceptions of God in the Thinking of Paul Tillich and Henry Nelson Wieman," 15 April 1955, in *Papers* 2:339–544.

King, Fragment of Application to Boston University, September–December 1950, in *Papers* 1:390.

BOUTWELL, ALBERT (1904–1978)

During the **Birmingham Campaign** of 1963, Martin Luther King addressed Mayor Albert Boutwell in his "**Letter from Birmingham Jail**," writing that he hoped the Birmingham mayor would see the wisdom of not resisting desegregation.

The grandson of two Confederate veterans, Boutwell was born 13 November 1904 in Montgomery, Alabama. After earning an LLB from the University of Alabama in 1928, he began practicing law in Birmingham, Alabama. Boutwell was elected to the State Senate in 1946 and served for three terms until 1958. During this time, he served as Chairman of the Interim Legislative Committee on Segregation in the Public Schools and authored the 1956 Alabama Pupil Placement Act, which successfully maintained segregation in Alabama's public schools after the *Brown v. Board of Education* decision. In 1958 he was elected lieutenant governor of Alabama for the 1959 to 1963 term.

When the city of Birmingham held its first election for mayor in 1963, after changing from a commission form of government, Boutwell ran against Public Safety Commissioner Theophilus Eugene "Bull" **Connor**, a vehement segregationist. Hoping for Connor's defeat, the **Southern Christian Leadership Conference** (SCLC) and the **Alabama Christian Movement for Human Rights**, headed by Fred **Shuttlesworth**, postponed their planned desegregation campaign until after the election. On 2 April 1963 Boutwell defeated Connor by 7,982 votes to become mayor of Birmingham, an outcome that Connor attributed to a 10,000-strong "Negro bloc vote" that favored Boutwell's more moderate stance ("Connor Blames Negro Vote").

Although newspaper coverage after Boutwell's victory projected racial progress in Birmingham under the new mayor, King and his aides were not so optimistic. Dubbed by Shuttlesworth as "just a dignified Bull Connor," Boutwell had declared that he would not tolerate violence and would "arrest, jail, and punish anyone who disturbs the peace or safety of our citizens" (King, 55; Spotswood, "Boutwell, Connor Push Campaigns"). After being elected, he urged Birmingham's citizens, both black and white, to ignore the movement in Birmingham.

King was arrested on Good Friday, 12 April 1963, for violating an injunction against the desegregation protest and was imprisoned. In his "Letter from Birmingham Jail," King declared that while Boutwell was less harsh than Connor he was still, like Connor, a segregationist.

On 10 May 1963 a truce declared between movement leaders and Birmingham's leading businessmen ended the Birmingham Campaign. Later that year, Boutwell told the Birmingham School Board that he felt that the city's integration was "not in the best interest of our school children" (Baker, "Now Wallace Faces"). Boutwell served as mayor of Birmingham until 1967, when he lost a bid for reelection. He died 3 February 1978.

SOURCES

Robert E. Baker, "Now Wallace Faces a Homegrown Challenge," *Washington Post*, 8 September 1963.

"Boutwell Defeats Connor by Margin of 7,982 Votes," *Birmingham World,* 6 April 1963.

"Connor Blames Negro Vote for Birmingham Loss," *Birmingham World*, 16 April 1963.

Eskew, *But for Birmingham*, 1997.

King, "Letter from Birmingham Jail," in *Why We Can't Wait*, 1964.

James Spottswood, "Boutwell, Connor Push Campaigns," *Birmingham News*, 10 March 1963.

BOWLES, CHESTER BLISS (1901–1986)

Chester Bowles greatly influenced Martin Luther King, Jr., early on in his career. As ambassador to **India** and a key member of the Democratic Party, Bowles was a powerful voice of support for King's methods and message of **nonviolence**. Bowles and his wife were early financial supporters of the **Montgomery bus boycott**, and when King wrote to Dorothy Bowles in 1956 to express his appreciation for their support, he described her husband as "one of the greatest statesmen of our nation and of our age" (*Papers* 3:466).

Chester Bliss Bowles was born on 5 April 1901 in Springfield, Massachusetts, to Charles Allen and Nellie Harris Bowles. He received his BS from Yale University in 1924 and started an advertising firm in 1929. He served as governor of Connecticut from 1949 to 1951, and after posts with the United Nations he was appointed ambassador to India in 1951. While in India he became very popular with the Indian government, as well as with the people of India, for his unpretentious and personable style. Bowles' time in India provided him with a deep appreciation for Gandhian principles of nonviolence and the potential of mass movements to affect social change. Upon his return to the United States in 1953, he was elected to the U.S. House of Representatives for Connecticut, serving one term from 1959 to 1961. He worked with the John F. **Kennedy** administration as undersecretary of state and was reappointed as ambassador to India in 1963, a position he held until 1969.

Bowles wrote King in 1957, urging him to go to **India** and offering to put him in contact with people who had worked with **Gandhi**, including Prime Minister Jawaharlal **Nehru**. Bowles compared King's role in the Montgomery bus boycott to the nonviolent campaigns led by Gandhi, stating: "In America you are developing techniques which will not only establish American Negroes as first class citizens, but will do this in a way that earns the respect of all Americans, North and South, white and Negro. The Gandhian method achieves this object not by hurting anyone but by making everyone better" (Bowles, 28 January 1957).

Bowles was the first to telephone Coretta Scott **King** on behalf of the John F. Kennedy campaign during the 1960 presidential race, offering support after King was sentenced to four months in prison following a parole violation. Bowles, with help from King, Harris **Wofford**, and Bayard **Rustin**, used his position as chairman of the 1960 Democratic Platform Committee to draft the strongest civil rights policy ever adopted by the Democratic Party. Following his retirement in 1969, Bowles continued to publish books. His last book, *Mission to India,* was published in 1974.

SOURCES
Bowles to King, 28 January 1957, MLKP-MBU.
King to Bowles, 28 October 1957, in *Papers* 4:303–304.
King to Bowles, 24 June 1960, in *Papers* 5:478–480.
King to Dorothy S. Bowles, 5 December 1956, in *Papers* 3:466.

BOYTE, HARRY G. (1911–1977)

Appointed special assistant to Martin Luther King in 1963, Harry Boyte became the **Southern Christian Leadership Conference**'s (SCLC) first white employee. "I was impressed with Harry's dedication to the basic questions of freedom and human dignity," King explained. "It is wonderful to find a *southern* white person" who has "risen above the paternalism so many southern whites have in their relationship to Negroes" (Boyte, August 1963).

Boyte was born in North Carolina in 1911. After graduating from Elon College in North Carolina, he pursued graduate training in political science at American University. In 1942 Boyte began a 17-year career with the American Red Cross, traveling in Africa and Europe and working in Washington, D.C., before settling in the Atlanta office in 1946.

In 1959 Boyte resigned from the Red Cross to commit himself full time to civil rights. As the chairman of the Greater Atlanta Council on Human Relations, Boyte registered his dismay with Georgia Governor Ernest **Vandiver**'s "inaccurate, unjust" and threatening comments toward King, when he warned that King would be kept under close surveillance after his move to Atlanta. Boyte defended King's work, writing, "Not only his personal character but his public ministry have at all times been in keeping with a strict observance of the laws as well as a humane and Christian concern for the rights of all citizens of the community and state where he has resided" (Boyte and Hocking, 4 December 1959). Boyte also sent King a personal letter of welcome assuring him of his "complete support" in his "efforts to eliminate discrimination in the South" (Boyte, 18 February 1960).

In Atlanta in 1961, Boyte became Southern Director of the Unitarian Service Committee, an organization working to desegregate schools in the South. After approximately six months, Boyte left Atlanta for Charlotte, North Carolina, where he worked with Robert F. **Williams**. The following year he moved to Prince Edward County, Virginia, where he helped the **American Friends Service Committee** run schools for African American students after the local school board closed public schools rather than give in to court mandated desegregation. In 1963 King asked Boyte to join the staff of SCLC in the dual position of special assistant to the president and research and information secretary. He later became director of the Dialogue Department of SCLC, organizing community workshops, interdenominational retreats, and campus discussions to help multiracial groups work against "human misery and alienation" (SCLC, 1965). Boyte continued to run Operation Dialogue until he retired in the summer of 1966.

SOURCES
Boyte, Essay on Harry G. Boyte, August 1963, HCBP-NcD.
Harry Boyte, Jr., Interview by King Papers Project staff, 9–10 April 2007.

Boyte and Richard Hocking to Vandiver, 4 December 1959, LDRP-NN-Sc.
Boyte to King, 18 February 1960, MLKP-MBU.
SCLC, Dialogue: A Search for Reconciliation, 1965, CSKC.

BRADEN, ANNE GAMRELL McCARTY (1924–2006), AND BRADEN, CARL JAMES (1914–1975)

Martin Luther King first met Anne Braden in September 1957 at the 25th anniversary celebration of **Highlander Folk School**. As field organizers for the Southern Conference Educational Fund (SCEF), an organization committed to ending segregation through direct action, advocacy, and education, Anne and Carl Braden epitomized southern white radical thought and practice. In his "**Letter from Birmingham Jail**," King singled out Anne Braden as one of the white southerners who understood and was committed to the civil rights movement.

Born in Louisville, Kentucky, in 1924, Anne McCarty graduated from Randolph-Macon Women's College in 1943. Four years later she went to work at the *Louisville Times*, where she met Carl Braden, a journalist and union organizer. Carl Braden, originally from Portland, a poor white section of Louisville, had grown up imbued with the socialist teachings of Eugene Debs. The couple married in 1948 and became public relations directors for the Congress of Industrial Organizations. In that year they also supported the newly organized Progressive Party.

In 1954 the Bradens purchased a home in a white Louisville neighborhood and, in an effort to promote integration, sold it to a black family. After the home was bombed, Kentucky officials arrested the Bradens for plotting to incite insurrection. Anne Braden described the incident in her 1958 memoir, *The Wall Between*, which became a National Book Award finalist. Unable to secure jobs at southern newspapers, the couple became field organizers for SCEF, an organization accused of having Communist ties.

In 1957 the Bradens became co-editors of the organization's monthly newsletter, the *Southern Patriot*. As the newsletter grew in stature, it increased coverage of national civil rights activities, sometimes including material written by King. Most notably, in 1960 the Bradens published contrasting perspectives on the role of violence as an instrument of social change, written by King and Robert F. **Williams**. King admired Anne Braden's work with the newspaper and praised her for writing "about our struggle in eloquent and prophetic terms" (King, "Letter from Birmingham Jail," 89).

As King's visibility in the movement increased, he was often criticized for his association with the Bradens, due to their alleged Communist ties. In February 1959, when Carl Braden was sentenced to 12 months in prison for refusing to testify before the House Un-American Activities Committee, King's colleagues from the **Southern Christian Leadership Conference** (SCLC) advised him to distance himself from the couple's legal problems. However, in an October 1959 letter to Anne he expressed his hope that the couple would become permanently associated with SCLC.

After the U.S. Supreme Court upheld Carl Braden's conviction in February 1961, Anne Braden mounted a clemency campaign for her husband and asked King to initiate a petition. King initially did not respond to Anne's entreaties but, shortly before Braden entered prison on 1 May 1961, King attended a reception in Atlanta in Braden's honor and consented to sign a petition supporting clemency. "I think Martin did compromise on occasions when he thought it was the best tactic, but I don't think he was ever doing those things for personal aggrandizement," Braden said. "In our case, there was absolutely nothing he was going to get out of signing our petition except a lot of trouble" (Fosl, 274).

After more than two decades in the civil rights struggle, the Bradens became executive directors of SCEF in 1967. They retired in 1972 due to ideological conflicts within the organization. After Carl suffered a fatal heart attack in 1975, Anne, along with other former SCEF members, created the Southern Organizing Committee for Economic and Social Justice. Anne remained a vocal and consistent voice for civil rights reform until her death in 2006.

SOURCES

Braden to King, 14 October 1958, in *Papers* 4:510–511.
Braden v. United States, 365 U.S. 431 (1961).
Fosl, *Subversive Southerner*, 2002.
King, "The Great Debate: Is Violence Necessary to Combat Injustice?" *Southern Patriot*, January 1960, in *Papers* 5:300.
King to Anne Braden, 7 October 1959, in *Papers* 5:306–307.
King, "Letter from Birmingham Jail," in *Why We Can't Wait*, 1964.

BRADEN, CARL JAMES. *See* Braden, Anne Gamrell McCarty and Braden, Carl James.

BRIGHTMAN, EDGAR SHEFFIELD (1884–1953)

Five years after Edgar Brightman's death, Martin Luther King, Jr., wrote that his mentor from **Boston University**'s School of Theology gave him "the metaphysical and philosophical grounding for the idea of a personal God" (*Papers* 4:480). Brightman believed that personal experience was at the center of all faith and that "all religion is of, by, and for persons. Religion ascribes a unique value to persons and has a unique interest in their welfare and their salvation" (Brightman, "Religion as Truth," 73). His scholarship greatly influenced King's personal philosophy of religion from the time of his early graduate studies at **Crozer Theological Seminary**.

Brightman was born in Holbrook, Massachusetts, on 20 September 1884, to George Edgar and Mary Sheffield Brightman. He received his STB in 1910 and his PhD in 1912 from Boston University. Brightman taught at Wesleyan University from 1915 to 1919 and then returned to Boston University, where he was appointed to the chair named for his mentor, Borden Parker Bowne, Professor of Philosophy, in 1925.

King became aware of Brightman's ideas while at Crozer. In a 1949 school paper written for professor George W. **Davis**, King agreed with Brightman's idea that any individual can know God. King read Brightman's A *Philosophy of Religion* (1940), which led him to reflect on his own spiritual life. King commented: "How I long now for that religious experience which Dr. Brightman so cogently speaks of throughout his book. It seems to be an experience, the lack of which life becomes dull and meaningless" (*Papers* 1:415–416).

In his application to Boston University in 1950, King stated, "my thinking in philosophical areas has been greatly influenced by some of the faculty members there, particularly Dr. Brightman" (*Papers* 1:390). After matriculating, King attended Brightman's Philosophy of Religion class and his Seminar on Philosophy. Brightman died just 16 months after King began his graduate studies at Boston University, and

King continued his work in the ideologies of **personalism** with Brightman's colleague and former student, L. Harold **DeWolf**.

SOURCES

Edgar S. Brightman, "Religion as Truth," in *Contemporary American Theology*, ed. Vergilius Ferm, 1932.

Courses at Boston University, 1951–1952, 1952–1953, in *Papers* 2:18.

Introduction, in *Papers* 1:51, 56.

Introduction, in *Papers* 2:5.

King, "A Conception and Impression of Religion Drawn from Dr. Brightman's Book Entitled *A Philosophy of Religion*," 28 March 1951, in *Papers* 1:407–416.

King, Fragment of Application to Boston University, September–December 1950, in *Papers* 1:390.

King, "My Pilgrimage to Nonviolence," 1 September 1958, in *Papers* 4:473–481.

Walter G. Muelder, "Edgar S. Brightman: Person and Moral Philosopher," in *The Boston Personalist Tradition*, ed. Paul Deats and Carol Robb, 1986.

BRISTOL, JAMES E. (1912–1992)

As a peace activist and president of the Quaker Center in New Delhi, **India**, an affiliate of the **American Friends Service Committee** (AFSC), James Ellery Bristol served as host of Martin Luther King, Jr.'s month-long tour of India in 1959.

Born in 1912 in Philadelphia, Bristol began his career as an outspoken pacifist after receiving degrees from Gettysburg College and Lutheran Theological Seminary. In 1935 Bristol became pastor of Grace Lutheran Church in Camden, New Jersey. He spent 18 months in prison for refusing to serve in the military during World War II and, after his release in 1943, left the pulpit to work with peace organizations in Philadelphia. In 1947 he joined the AFSC, an organization founded by Quakers in 1917 to provide conscientious objectors an opportunity to aid civilian war victims. In 1957 Bristol was transferred to New Delhi, where he became director of the Quaker Center, a position that led to his first meeting with King.

In December 1958, after the Gandhi Smarak Nidhi invited the Kings to tour India, Bristol, with the assistance of King's representative Bayard **Rustin** and the AFSC in Philadelphia, arranged an itinerary. When the Kings arrived in Bombay in February 1959, Bristol accompanied them as they toured India, speaking at public gatherings and meeting local dignitaries. Bristol chronicled the trip in a series of letters to his wife, Dorothy, expressing frustration that the focus of the trip was being "thought of in terms of the *return* to U.S.A. and what will make an impact and produces an effect there" (Bristol, 25 February 1959). Nevertheless, he reported to the AFSC that the "net effect of the King trip seems to have been very, very good!" (*Papers* 5:137n). Following the Kings' visit, Bristol continued to work for the AFSC until his retirement in 1977. He remained active in the organization through 1986, and continued his peace advocacy until his death in 1992.

SOURCES

Bristol to Dorothy Bristol, 25 February 1959, AFSCR-PPAFS.

Bristol to Johnson, 10 March 1959, in *Papers* 5:137–142.

Introduction, in *Papers* 5:4–12.

G. Ramachandran to King, 27 December 1958, in *Papers* 4:552–553.

With the Kings in India, A Souvenir of Dr. Martin Luther King's Visit to India, February–March 1959 (New Delhi, India: Gandhi National Memorial Fund, 1959), WRMP-GAMK.

BROWDER V. GAYLE, 352 U.S. 903 (1956)

Aurelia S. Browder v. William A. Gayle challenged the Alabama state statutes and Montgomery, Alabama, city ordinances requiring segregation on Montgomery buses. Filed by Fred **Gray** and Charles D. Langford on behalf of four African American women who had been mistreated on city buses, the case made its way to the U.S. Supreme Court, which upheld a district court ruling that the statute was unconstitutional. Gray and Langford filed the federal district court petition that became *Browder v. Gayle* on 1 February 1956, two days after segregationists bombed King's house. The original plaintiffs in the case were Aurelia S. Browder, Susie McDonald, Claudette Colvin, Mary Louise Smith, and Jeanatta Reese, but outside pressure convinced Reese to withdraw from the case in February. Gray made the decision not to include Rosa **Parks** in the case to avoid the perception that they were seeking to circumvent her prosecution on other charges. Gray "wanted the court to have only one issue to decide—the constitutionality of the laws requiring segregation on the buses" (Gray, 69). The list of defendants included Mayor William A. Gayle, the city's chief of police, representatives from Montgomery's Board of Commissioners, Montgomery City Lines, Inc., two bus drivers, and representatives of the Alabama Public Service Commission. Gray was aided in the case by Thurgood **Marshall** and other **National Association for the Advancement of Colored People** attorneys.

Because *Browder v. Gayle* challenged the constitutionality of a state statute, the case was brought before a three-judge U.S. District Court panel. On 5 June 1956, the panel ruled two-to-one that segregation on Alabama's intrastate buses was unconstitutional, citing **Brown v. Board of Education** as precedent for the verdict. King applauded the victory but called for a continuation of the **Montgomery bus boycott** until the ruling was implemented.

On 13 November 1956, while King was in the courthouse being tried on the legality of the boycott's carpools, a reporter notified him that the U.S. Supreme Court had just affirmed the District Court's decision on *Browder v. Gayle*. King addressed a mass meeting at **Holt Street Baptist Church** the next evening, saying that the decision was "a reaffirmation of the principle that separate facilities are inherently unequal, and that the old *Plessy* Doctrine of separate but equal is no longer valid, either sociologically or legally" (*Papers* 3:425).

On 17 December 1956, the Supreme Court rejected city and state appeals to reconsider their decision, and three days later the order for integrated buses arrived in Montgomery. On 20 December 1956 King and the **Montgomery Improvement Association** voted to end the 381-day Montgomery bus boycott. In a statement that day, King said: "The year-old protest against city buses is officially called off, and the Negro citizens of Montgomery are urged to return to the buses tomorrow morning on a non-segregated basis" (*Papers* 3:486–487). The Montgomery buses were integrated the following day.

SOURCES

Gray, *Bus Ride to Justice*, 1995.

King, Address to MIA mass meeting at Holt Street Baptist Church, 14 November 1956, in *Papers* 3:424–433.

King, Statement on Ending the Bus Boycott, 20 December 1956, in *Papers* 3:485–487.

BROWN, THEODORE EDWARD (1915–1983)

As a champion of the black labor movement, Ted Brown worked closely with Martin Luther King, Jr., throughout the civil rights movement. The two men became particularly close when Brown became president of the American Negro Leadership Conference on Africa in 1962. Throughout the 1960s, Brown and King collaborated on projects supporting African liberation struggles and an end to **apartheid** in South Africa.

Born in New Brunswick, New Jersey, in 1915, Brown worked his way through college as a porter. He studied at Columbia, received his BA from Northwestern, and earned a certificate from Harvard Business School in 1944. In 1946 he joined the Brotherhood of Sleeping Car Porters and was appointed editor of the Brotherhood's magazine, *Black Worker*. Brown quickly became the protégé of A. Philip **Randolph**, and Randolph recommended him for the position of assistant director of the civil rights department at the **American Federation of Labor and Congress of Industrial Organizations** (AFL-CIO) in 1956.

In his position at the AFL-CIO, Brown mobilized African American workers around labor and civil rights issues. He encouraged collaboration between the AFL-CIO and King's **Southern Christian Leadership Conference**, recognizing that the only organizations to boast more African American members than the trade unions were churches.

In 1958 Brown supplied King with a detailed paper on African Americans in the trade union movement for King's book *Stride Toward Freedom*. King incorporated several paragraphs of Brown's paper in the book, acknowledging his contribution in the preface. Brown was the secretary for the **Negro American Labor Council** (NALC), and when he was dismissed from the AFL-CIO in 1961, he believed it was because of his support for the NALC. Several months later King wrote a letter of reference for Brown, praising his "unswerving devotion to the ideals of American democracy ... and his intellectual ability" (King, 12 June 1961). After leaving NALC, Brown became president of the American Negro Leadership Conference on Africa, where King was a committee member. In 1969 Brown was appointed special assistant to the director of the information staff at the United States Agency for International Development. He served as the agency's special assistant on Africa from 1973 until 1977. He died in 1983 at the age of 68.

SOURCES

Introduction, in *Papers* 4:32.
King, *Stride Toward Freedom*, 1958.
King to R. Sargent Shriver, 12 June 1961, MLKP-MBU.

BROWN ET AL., V. BOARD OF EDUCATION OF TOPEKA, KANSAS, ET AL., 347 U.S. 483 (1954), 349 U.S. 294 (1955)

While speaking at an annual luncheon of the National Committee for Rural Schools on 15 December 1956, Martin Luther King, Jr., reflected on the importance of *Brown v. Board of Education*: "To all men of good will, this decision came as a joyous daybreak to end the long night of human captivity. It came as a great beacon light of hope to millions of colored people throughout the world who had had a dim vision of the promised land of freedom and justice ... this decision came as a legal and sociological deathblow to an evil that had occupied the throne of American life for several decades" (*Papers* 3:472).

Brown v. Board of Education (1954) was a consolidation of five school desegregation cases: *Brown v. Board of Education of Topeka, Kansas*; *Briggs v. Elliot*; *Davis v. County School Board of Prince Edward County, Virginia*; *Bolling v. Sharpe*; and *Belton v. Gebhart*. These cases were designed to challenge the "separate but equal" doctrine established in the U.S. Supreme Court's 1896 *Plessy v. Ferguson* decision, and because of their common legal challenge the Supreme Court combined the cases and decided them together. The **National Association for the Advancement of Colored People** (NAACP) Legal Defense and Education Fund's chief counsel, Thurgood **Marshall**, managed the case. He was well aware that the Fund's reputation and national racial progress were reliant on the outcome of *Brown*.

Social psychologist Kenneth Clark testified in the lower courts that segregation causes black children "to reject themselves and their color and accept whites as desirable" (Williams, 202). Clark had traveled to Clarendon County, South Carolina, to administer a test he and his wife, Mamie, had developed. In the test, black children were shown two dolls, a white doll and a black doll, and asked for their opinions of each. The Clarks' findings indicated that feelings of inferiority existed at an early age, as children generally considered the white dolls prettier and smarter than the black dolls.

The Supreme Court's unanimous *Brown* decision, handed down on 17 May 1954, determined that the *Plessy* doctrine of "separate but equal" had no place in education and violated the equal protection clause of the Fourteenth Amendment. Chief Justice Earl Warren wrote: "To separate [blacks] from others of similar age and qualifications solely because of their race generates a feeling of inferiority as to their status in the community that may affect their hearts and minds in a way unlikely ever to be undone" (347 U.S. 483 [1954]). With this decision, racial segregation in schools became unconstitutional.

Initial excitement over the *Brown* victory dwindled, however, when desegregation of schools was not mandated as quickly as had been hoped. Marshall and his staff were disappointed that the Court did not impose a desegregation deadline on southern school districts. The NAACP prepared briefs suggesting that school desegregation transpire before fall 1956 and went to court again to argue for this relief. In *Brown v. Board II*, the Court focused on ways to quickly integrate school districts. The Court recognized that different districts would need to implement different techniques to end segregation, and Warren ruled on 31 May 1955 that school districts were required to desegregate only "with all deliberate speed" (349 U.S. 294 [1955]).

Sources

Brown et al., v. Board of Education of Topeka, Kansas, et al., 347 U.S. 483 (1954), 349 U.S. 294 (1955).

King, "Desegregation and the Future," Address delivered at the Annual Luncheon of the National Committee for Rural Schools, 15 December 1956, in *Papers* 3:471–479.

Kluger, *Simple Justice*, 1975.

Williams, *Thurgood Marshall*, 1998.

BUNCHE, RALPH JOHNSON (1904–1971)

Dr. Ralph Johnson Bunche contributed to the African American freedom struggle and peacekeeping efforts worldwide through his involvement with the United Nations (UN) and several civil rights organizations. Bunche had great admiration for Martin

Luther King, Jr., writing in 1956, "You and our fellow Negro citizens of Montgomery are doing heroic work in the vineyards of democracy. Your patient determination, your wisdom and quiet courage are constituting an inspiring chapter in the history of human dignity" (*Papers* 3:134).

Bunche was born 7 August 1904 in Detroit, Michigan, to Fred Bunch and Olive Agnes Johnson. After being orphaned at the age of 13, Bunche moved to Los Angeles where he added an "e" to his last name and was raised by his maternal grandmother, Lucy Taylor Johnson, who fostered his determination to succeed.

In 1927 Bunche graduated summa cum laude from the University of California at Los Angeles with a BA in international relations. The following year, he received an MA in government from Harvard University and helped establish the Political Science Department at Howard University in Washington, D.C. In 1929 Bunche returned to Harvard and received his PhD in government and international relations in 1934.

In 1936 Bunche helped establish the National Negro Congress, which sought to bring together African American leaders in many fields to push for labor and civil rights. Beginning in 1938, Bunche assisted Swedish sociologist Gunnar Myrdal in writing *An American Dilemma* (1944), a study of black and white race relations in the United States.

Ralph Abernathy, King, and Ralph Bunche help lead the Selma to Montgomery March, 21 March 1965, wearing leis given to them by a group of marchers from Hawaii. © 1965 Matt Herron/Take Stock.

Bunche joined the UN Secretariat in 1947, where he developed the guidelines under which many territories gained nationhood. He was awarded the **Nobel Peace Prize** in 1950 for his work as head of a UN peace-seeking Palestine commission that negotiated armistice between the new state of Israel and Arab nations. Bunche was the first person of color to receive the prize. In 1955 Bunche became UN Undersecretary General for Special Political Affairs. As undersecretary, Bunche was the highest ranking American at the UN at the time. In 1963 President John F. **Kennedy** awarded Bunche the Medal of Freedom, the U.S. government's highest civilian award.

Despite illnesses, Bunche demonstrated with King at the 1963 **March on Washington** and the 1965 **Selma to Montgomery March**. He was an active member on the board of the **National Association for the Advancement of Colored People**, which he served from 1949 until his death.

Although they had similar interests, Bunche did not always agree with King. In 1967 he joined many civil rights supporters in their criticism of King's public statements against the **Vietnam War**. Bunche asserted that King's public position on the war would alienate supporters of the civil rights movement. In an interview, Bunche said: "Right now, I am convinced, he is making a very serious tactical error which will do much harm to the civil rights struggle. I refer to the merging in his recent speeches of the civil rights movement and the crusade against United States involvement in

Vietnam." Responding to his critics, King maintained that "no one can pretend that the existence of the war is not profoundly affecting the destiny of civil rights progress" (Sibley, "Bunche Disputes"). In June 1971 Bunche retired from his United Nations post due to serious illness. He died on 9 December 1971 at the age of 67.

SOURCES

Bunche to King, 22 February 1956, in *Papers* 3:134.

John Sibley, "Bunche Disputes Dr. King on Peace," *New York Times*, 13 April 1967.

Urquhart, *Ralph Bunche*, 1993.

BURROUGHS, NANNIE HELEN (1879–1961)

Nannie Helen Burroughs was an educator, religious leader, and social activist who helped found the Women's Auxiliary of the **National Baptist Convention** (NBC). In August 1954 she invited Martin Luther King, Jr., the young son of her friends, Martin Luther **King**, Sr., and Alberta Williams **King**, to address the Women's Auxiliary on "The Vision of the World Made New." In a letter to King, Jr., thanking him for his speech, she wrote: "What your message did to their thinking and to their faith is 'bread cast upon the water' that will be seen day by day in their good works in their communities" (*Papers* 2:296).

Born in Orange, Virginia, in 1879, Burroughs moved to Washington, D.C., where she attended high school, in 1883. She worked in Louisville, Kentucky, from 1898 to 1909, as a bookkeeper and editorial secretary of the Foreign Mission Board of the NBC. After helping to found the Women's Auxiliary of the NBC, Burroughs convinced the group to establish the National Training School for Women and Girls in 1909. She served as president of that institution until her death in 1961. In 1964 the school was renamed the Nannie Helen Burroughs School.

As part of a network of strong black club women in the first half of the twentieth century, Burroughs was active in the National Association of Colored Women, the National Association of Wage Earners, and the Association for the Study of Negro Life and History. A well-known speaker and writer, she was appointed by President Herbert Hoover to chair a special committee on housing for African Americans. She appeared with Carter G. Woodson and Alain Locke at a meeting of the Association for the Study of Negro Life and History in 1927, and her talk was reported in the *Journal of Negro History*: "By a forceful address Miss Nannie H. Burroughs emphasized the duty the Negro owes to himself to learn his own story" (6).

Burroughs continued to support King until her death. During the **Montgomery bus boycott** in 1956, she wrote King's mother, Alberta, expressing her interest in the "calm, sure way that Junior is standing up for right and righteousness" (Burroughs, 4 February 1956). After King was stabbed in 1958, she telegrammed: "As a friend of yours and of the great cause to which you are giving the last ounce of your devotion I am praying for you" (Burroughs, 25 September 1958).

SOURCES

Burroughs to Alberta Williams King, 4 February 1956, NHBP-DLC.

Burroughs to King, 3 August 1954, in *Papers* 2:282–283.

Burroughs to King, 21 September 1954, in *Papers* 2:295–296.

Burroughs to King, 25 September 1958, CSKC.

"Proceedings of the Annual Meeting of the Association for the Study of Negro Life and History held at Pittsburgh, October 24, 25, and 26, 1927," *Journal of Negro History* 13, no. 1 (January 1928): 1–6.

C

CALCAV. *See* Clergy and Laymen Concerned about Vietnam.

CAREY, ARCHIBALD J., JR. (1908–1981)

An influential Chicago minister and politician, Archibald Carey maintained a close relationship with Martin Luther King, Jr., In 1957 Carey visited the King home while participating in the **Montgomery Improvement Association**'s annual **Institute on Nonviolence and Social Change**.

Carey was born in Chicago in 1908, the son and grandson of ministers. He received degrees from Northwestern University's Garrett Biblical Institute and Chicago-Kent College of Law. During his professional life he wore many hats: lawyer, bank president, politician, judge, and minister. He was pastor of Woodlawn AME Church in Chicago from 1930 to 1949 before moving to Quinn Chapel AME Church, Chicago's second oldest Protestant church, where he served until 1967. Carey also served as Republican alderman of Chicago's Third Ward (1947 to 1955) and was an alternate member of the United States delegation to the Eighth General Assembly of the United Nations in 1953. In 1955 President Dwight **Eisenhower** appointed Carey vice-chair and, later, chairman of the President's Committee on Government Employment Policy. By 1966 Carey had changed his party affiliation to Democrat and was elected as a circuit court judge in Cook County, Illinois, a position he held at the time of his death in April 1981.

During the **Montgomery bus boycott**, King enlisted Carey's aid by appointing him chairman of a Chicago committee that was asked to inform the headquarters of Montgomery's bus company of the concerns of black Montgomery residents. During April 1956, Carey also helped organize an "Hour of Prayer" in Chicago that raised $2,500 for the MIA.

King's "I Have a Dream" address at the 1963 **March on Washington for Jobs and Freedom** parallels themes in Carey's address at the 1952 Republican National Convention in Chicago, which concluded: "from every mountain side, let freedom ring. Not only from the Green Mountains and the White Mountains of Vermont and New Hampshire; not only from the Catskills of New York; but from the Ozarks in Arkansas, from the Stone Mountain in Georgia, from the Great Smokies of Tennessee and from the Blue Ridge Mountains of Virginia" (Carey, 8 July 1952).

SOURCES

Carey, Address to the Republican National Convention, 8 July 1952, AJC-ICHi.

King, "I Have a Dream," 28 August 1963.

King to Carey, 27 December 1955, in *Papers* 3:93–95.

CARMICHAEL, STOKELY (1941–1998)

As chairman of the **Student Nonviolent Coordinating Committee** (SNCC), Stokely Carmichael challenged the philosophy of **nonviolence** and interracial alliances that had come to define the modern civil rights movement, calling instead for "**Black Power**." Although critical of the "Black Power" slogan, King acknowledged that "if Stokely Carmichael now says that nonviolence is irrelevant, it is because he, as a dedicated veteran of many battles, has seen with his own eyes the most brutal white violence against Negroes and white civil rights workers, and he has seen it go unpunished" (King, 33–34).

Carmichael was born on 29 June 1941 in Port-of-Spain, Trinidad. He moved to New York when he was 11, joining his parents, who had settled there 9 years earlier. Carmichael attended the elite Bronx High School of Science, while he met veteran black radicals and Communist activists. In 1960, as a senior in high school, Carmichael learned about the **sit-in** movement for desegregation in the South and joined activists from the **Congress of Racial Equality** (CORE) protesting in New York against Woolworth stores, a chain that maintained segregated lunch counters in the South.

Carmichael enrolled as a philosophy major at Howard University in 1960 and joined the university's Nonviolent Action Group, which was affiliated with SNCC. In addition to working against segregation in Washington, D.C., Carmichael traveled south on the **Freedom Rides**. When the freedom riders traveled to Mississippi, Carmichael was arrested for the first time. King's **Southern Christian Leadership Conference** (SCLC) awarded Carmichael a scholarship designed to support arrested students, and he continued his studies at Howard. Throughout his four years in college, Carmichael participated in civil rights activities ranging from the **Albany Movement** to New York hospital strikes.

After graduating in 1964, Carmichael joined SNCC's staff full time, working on the Mississippi **Freedom Summer** project and the **Mississippi Freedom Democratic Party**. Carmichael found himself frustrated by what he saw as unsuccessful agitation for political rights, and grew skeptical of the prospects for interracial activism within the existing political structure.

After the **Selma to Montgomery March** in March 1965, Carmichael stayed in Alabama to help rural African Americans outside Selma form the Lowndes County Freedom Organization, an all black, independent political group that became known as the Black Panther Party. (Activists Bobby Seale and Huey Newton would later borrow the Black Panther symbol when organizing the Black Panther Party in Oakland, California in October 1966.) He recalled how people in Lowndes County responded to King's leadership: "People loved King ... I've seen people in the South climb over each other just to say, 'I touched him! I touched him!' ... The people didn't know what was SNCC." When asked, "You one of Dr. King's men?" he replied, "Yes, Ma'am, I am" (Carson, 164).

Carmichael had always seen nonviolence as a tactic, rather than a guiding principle. In May 1966 Carmichael replaced John **Lewis** as chairman of SNCC, a move that signaled a shift in the student movement from an emphasis on nonviolence and integration toward black militancy. One month later, Carmichael, King, and CORE's Floyd **McKissick** collectively organized a march supporting James **Meredith**, who had been wounded by a sniper on the second day of his planned 220-mile walk from Memphis, Tennessee, to Jackson, Mississippi. Although Carmichael and King respected one another, the two men engaged in a fierce debate over the future of the civil rights movement, black radicalism, and the potential for integration. When the march reached Greenwood, Mississippi, Carmichael was arrested for the 27th time. At a rally upon his release, he called for "Black Power." King disapproved of the slogan's violent connotations, and Carmichael admitted he had used the term during the march in order to force King to take a stand on the issue. Although King initially resisted publicly opposing Carmichael and Black Power, he admitted a break between those still committed to nonviolence and those willing to use any means necessary to achieve freedom.

King and Carmichael did come to agree on public opposition to the **Vietnam War**. Carmichael encouraged King to speak out against the war while advisors such as Stanley **Levison** cautioned him that such opposition might have an adverse effect on financial contributions to SCLC. Nearly a month after delivering his "**Beyond Vietnam**" address at New York's Riverside Church in April 1967, King preached "Why I Am Opposed to the War in Vietnam" at **Ebenezer Baptist Church**, with Carmichael seated in the front row at his invitation. King declared before the congregation: "There is something strangely inconsistent about a nation and press that will praise you when you say be nonviolent toward Jim Clark, but will curse you and damn you when you say be nonviolent toward little brown Vietnamese children" (King, 30 April 1967). Carmichael joined the congregation in giving King a standing ovation.

Although Carmichael opposed the decision to expel whites from SNCC, in the later 1960s he joined with black nationalists in stressing racial unity over class unity as a basis for future black struggles. After relinquishing the SNCC chairmanship in 1967, Carmichael made a controversial trip to Cuba, China, North Vietnam, and finally to Guinea. Returning to the United States with the intention of forming a black united front throughout the nation, he accepted an invitation to become prime minister of the militant Oakland-based Black Panther Party. In 1969 he left the Black Panthers after disagreeing with the party's willingness to work with radical whites.

Carmichael changed his name to Kwame Ture and moved to Guinea, where he conferred with exiled Ghanaian leader Kwame **Nkrumah.** He helped form the All-African People's Revolutionary Party in 1972 and urged African American radicals to work for African liberation and Pan-Africanism. Carmichael died of cancer in Guinea on 15 November 1998 at the age of 57.

SOURCES

Branch, *At Canaan's Edge*, 2006.
Carmichael with Thelwell, *Ready for Revolution*, 2003.
Carson, *In Struggle*, 1981.
Garrow, *Bearing the Cross*, 1986.
King, *Where Do We Go from Here*, 1967.
King, "Why I Am Opposed to the War in Vietnam," 30 April 1967, MLKEC.

CARR, JOHNNIE REBECCA DANIELS (1911–)

As an Alabama native and civil rights activist, Johnnie Carr was an active participant in the **Montgomery bus boycott**. She recalled hearing Martin Luther King speak for the first time at a meeting of the **National Association for the Advancement of Colored People** (NAACP) in August 1955, and was impressed by the "flow of his words and the way that he expressed them while just talking about ordinary things" (Garrow, 529).

Johnnie Rebecca Daniels, the youngest of six children, was born in 1911. She grew up near Montgomery, Alabama, on a farm owned by her parents, John Daniels and Anna Richmond Daniels. Carr attended the Montgomery Industrial School for African American Girls, where she befriended classmate Rosa Louise McCauley, later known as Rosa **Parks**.

In 1927, when Carr was in the seventh grade, her school closed. Aware of her mother's difficulties supporting the family since her father died, she decided to get married at the age of sixteen to Jack Jordan. After the marriage dissolved, Carr worked and went to school while her mother cared for her two children. After finishing junior high school, she took a course in practical nursing, a career choice that allowed her to make $12 more a week than she did working as a domestic.

Carr became active in numerous clubs and organizations, including the NAACP, where she worked closely with E. D. **Nixon** and childhood friend Rosa Parks. According to Carr, before the boycott people were depressed and bitter because they "didn't have any opportunities to participate in things that we felt that as citizens we should've been given.... we finally realized that it's not whether you have achieved in life, but whether you are a human being, that you should have an opportunity" (Carr, "Interview," 527–528). During the boycott Carr was part of the carpool, served on committees, and spoke at mass meetings. She recalled, "Those of us who had automobiles felt that if other people who did not have cars would sacrifice and walk, we could certainly sacrifice our time and use our automobiles to help transport these people" (Carr, 1970). In 1957 she gave a speech at the Women's Auxiliary of the Baptist State Convention of Illinois describing the bus boycott.

In 1964 Carr's son, Arlam, was a test applicant to white Montgomery schools that led to a successful lawsuit ending segregation in Montgomery schools. Since 1967 Carr has served as president of the **Montgomery Improvement Association**.

SOURCES
Carr, Interview by William Porter, 1970, MLK/OH-GAMK.
Carr, "Interview: Johnnie Carr, 17 July 1977," by Steven M. Millner, in *Walking City*, ed. Garrow, 1989.
Williams, *Johnnie*, 1996.

CHALLENOR, HERSCHELLE SULLIVAN (1938–)

As a student at Spelman College in 1960, Herschelle Sullivan participated in the October 1960 **sit-in** at Rich's, a department store in Atlanta, and was subsequently arrested with Martin Luther King. In a handwritten letter penned while King was in Fulton County Jail, he praised the female protesters, including Sullivan, arrested with him for their "intrepid courage, [their] quiet dignity, and [their] undaunted faith in the power of nonviolence." King continued, "It is inspiring enough to see the fellows willingly accepting jail rather than bail, but when young ladies are willing to accept this type of self suffering for the cause of freedom it is both majestic and sublime" (*Papers* 5:528).

Sullivan was born on 5 October 1938 in Atlanta, Georgia. She received a BA from Spelman College, an MA from Johns Hopkins University, and a PhD from Columbia University. Sullivan came to know King as an active participant in the Atlanta student movement and as student body president of Spelman. As an alumnus of **Boston University**, King wrote a letter of recommendation on Sullivan's behalf for the university's school of international relations. He wrote of Sullivan's "deep commitment to noble principles," and wholeheartedly recommended her admission to the university (King, 15 May 1961). Prior to pursuing graduate studies, Sullivan attended summer school at the University of Kentucky, where she participated in Lexington's **Congress of Racial Equality** chapter. Sullivan, who was passionate about social action, was disheartened by the complacency of African Americans in Kentucky and the overall "lack of unity, organization, and clear reasoned strategy" (Sullivan, 28 July 1961). In a letter to King on 28 July 1961, she wrote: "Many of them don't consider themselves Southerners and have assumed what I like to call a 'cool Northern Negro sense of detachment' from the civil rights struggle."

Instead of attending Boston University, Sullivan accepted admission to the Johns Hopkins School of Advanced International Studies in Baltimore based on the college's location. Sullivan continued to write King, keeping him abreast of her graduate studies. While King was jailed during the **Albany Movement** in December 1961, Sullivan joked that the conditions of the Albany jail "cannot possibly equal the luxury of the 'Fulton Bars'" (Sullivan, 16 December 1961). Although Sullivan was overjoyed with King's work in the movement, she felt increasingly isolated from the struggle that she had been so much a part of in 1960. In a 9 March 1962 letter King consoled Sullivan, maintaining that she would have to "adjust to the experience of not being a participant at a particular moment." Although she was no longer actively involved, he felt her "experience at Johns Hopkins will broaden your insights and extend your intellectual horizon. When this is coupled with the great experience that you had in the struggle for freedom and human dignity, you will have a completeness and a maturity that so many students are missing today" (King, 9 March 1962).

After obtaining her PhD from Columbia, Sullivan (later Challenor) held a number of academic positions, including Assistant Professor in the Political Science Department of Brooklyn College (1969 to 1972), congressional fellow for the American Political Science Association (1972 to 1973), and program officer for the Diversity Education and Research Ford Foundation (1973 to 1975). In 1978 she became the director of the United Nations Educational Science and Cultural Organization Washington Liaison Office, a position she held until 1993. That same year, she became dean of Clark Atlanta University's School of Public and International Affairs.

Challenor has received numerous honors recognizing her work as an educator and activist, including a nomination by President Bill Clinton to the National Security Education Board in August 1994.

SOURCES

King to Female Inmates, 19–23 October 1960, in *Papers* 5:527–528.
King to R. M. Millard, 15 May 1961, MLKP-MBU.

King to Sullivan, 9 March 1962, MLKJP-GAMK.
Sullivan to King, 28 July 1961, MLKP-MBU.
Sullivan to King, 16 December 1961, MLKJP-GAMK.

CHALMERS, ALLAN KNIGHT (1897–1972)

Allan Knight Chalmers served as a mentor to Martin Luther King, Jr., during King's years at **Boston University**, and continued to influence King throughout the civil rights movement. In *Stride Toward Freedom*, King's memoir of the **Montgomery bus boycott**, he wrote of Chalmers' commitment to social justice, which was rooted in his optimism and faith in humanity.

Born in Cleveland, Ohio, in 1897, Chalmers received his BA (1917) from Johns Hopkins University and his BD (1922) from Yale University. He joined the faculty at Boston University in 1948 after serving as minister of New York's Broadway Tabernacle Congregational Church for 18 years. During his career, he was chair of the Scottsboro Defense Committee during the 1930s, president of the **National Association for the Advancement of Colored People** (NAACP) Legal Defense and Education Fund, treasurer of the NAACP, and was active in the **Fellowship of Reconciliation** (FOR), the American Civil Liberties Union, and the Religion and Labor Foundation. Chalmers retired from Boston University's faculty in 1962.

Chalmers was a personal and professional supporter of King and the movement. In early 1956, as treasurer of the NAACP, he wrote to King promising to support the Montgomery bus boycott: "We will back you at the national level without any question" (*Papers* 3:173). In December 1960 he organized a meeting of leaders from various civil rights organizations, such as FOR, the **American Friends Service Committee**, the **National Council of the Churches of Christ in America**, **Congress of Racial Equality**, and **Student Nonviolent Coordinating Committee**, to discuss how they could cooperate to move desegregation forward in the South.

Earlier in 1960 Chalmers had expressed his personal concern for King after meeting with civil rights supporters in New York. In a 6 March letter, he told King: "It is possible that the strenuousness of the job that you are up against plus the pressure even of such friends as we are has filled your program so full that your opportunities for reflection have been taken away." Chalmers warned: "A man gets thin if he does not read, becomes inaccurate if he does not write, but most of all loses a profoundness if he does not think" (*Papers* 5:435n). Chalmers remained active in the NAACP Legal Defense and Education Fund and in other peace, religious, and political groups until his death.

SOURCES
Chalmers to King, 14 March 1956, in *Papers* 3:173–174.
King, *Stride Toward Freedom*, 1958.
King to Chalmers, 18 April 1960, in *Papers* 5:435–437.

CHICAGO CAMPAIGN (1966)

On 7 January 1966, Martin Luther King and the **Southern Christian Leadership Conference** (SCLC) announced plans for the Chicago Freedom Movement, a campaign that marked the expansion of their civil rights activities from the South to northern cities. King believed that "the moral force of SCLC's nonviolent movement

King and his wife, Coretta, clean an apartment shortly after moving into a Chicago ghetto in early 1966. © AP / Wide World Photos.

philosophy was needed to help eradicate a vicious system which seeks to further colonize thousands of Negroes within a slum environment" (King, 18 March 1966). King and his family moved to one such Chicago slum at the end of January so that he could be closer to the movement.

Groundwork for the Chicago Campaign began in the summer of 1965. In July, Chicago civil rights groups invited King to lead a demonstration against de facto segregation in education, housing, and employment. The Coordinating Council of Community Organizations (CCCO), convened by Chicago activist Albert **Raby**, subsequently asked SCLC to join them in a major nonviolent campaign geared specifically at achieving fair housing practices. King believed that turning SCLC's attention to the North made sense: "In the South, we always had segregationists to help make issues clear.... This ghetto Negro has been invisible so long and has become visible through violence" (Cotton, 26–28 August 1965). Indeed, after riots in **Watts**, Los Angeles, in August 1965, it seemed crucial to demonstrate how nonviolent methods could address the complex economic exploitation of African Americans in the North.

CCCO had already organized mass nonviolent protests in the city and was eager to engage in further action. In addition to tapping into this ready-made movement, Chicago politics made the city a good choice for a northern campaign. Mayor Richard Daley had a high degree of personal power and was in a position to directly mandate changes to a variety of racist practices. In addition to targeting racial discrimination in housing, SCLC launched **Operation Breadbasket**, a project under the leadership of Jesse **Jackson**, aimed at abolishing racist hiring practices by companies working in African American neighborhoods.

The campaigns had gained momentum through demonstrations and marches, when race riots erupted on Chicago's West Side in July 1966. During a march through an all-white neighborhood on 5 August, black demonstrators were met with racially fueled hostility. Bottles and bricks were thrown at them, and King was struck by a rock. Afterward he noted: "I have seen many demonstrations in the south but I have never seen anything so hostile and so hateful as I've seen here today" ("Dr. King Is Felled by Rock").

Throughout the summer, King faced the organizational challenges of mobilizing Chicago's diverse African American community, cautioning against further violence and working to counter the mounting resistance of working-class whites who feared the impact of open housing on their neighborhoods. King observed, "Many whites who oppose open housing would deny that they are racists. They turn to sociological arguments … [without realizing] that criminal responses are environmental, not racial" (King, 118–119).

By late August, Mayor Daley was eager to find a way to end the demonstrations. After negotiating with King and various housing boards, a summit agreement was announced in which the Chicago Housing Authority promised to build public housing with limited height requirements, and the Mortgage Bankers Association agreed to make mortgages available regardless of race. Although King called the agreement "the most significant program ever conceived to make open housing a reality," he recognized that it was only "the first step in a 1,000-mile journey" (King, 26 August 1966; Halvorsen, "Cancel Rights Marches").

Following the summit agreement, some SCLC staff stayed behind to assist in housing programs and voter registration. King himself stayed in Chicago until taking time off in January 1967 to write *Where Do We Go from Here: Chaos or Community?* Jackson also continued his Chicago branch of Operation Breadbasket with some success, though city officials failed to take concrete steps to address issues of housing despite the summit agreement. King, in a 24 March 1967 press conference, said, "It appears that for all intents and purposes, the public agencies have [reneged] on the agreement and have, in fact given credence to [those] who proclaim the housing agreement a sham and a batch of false promises" (King, 24 March 1967).

SOURCES

Dorothy Cotton, Minutes from the executive staff meeting, 26–28 August 1965, SCLCR-GAMK.

"Dr. King Is Felled by Rock," *Chicago Tribune*, 6 August 1966.

David Halvorsen, "Cancel Rights Marches," *Chicago Tribune*, 27 August 1966.

Hampton, Fayer, and Flynn, *Voices of Freedom*, 1990.

King, Address at the Palmer House, 26 August 1966, CULC-ICIU.

King, Interview by Mr. Smith, 18 March 1966, MLKJP-GAMK.

King, Press conference at Liberty Baptist Church, 24 March 1967, MLKJP-GAMK.

King, *Where Do We Go from Here*, 1967.

CIVIL RIGHTS ACT OF 1964

In an 11 June 1963 speech broadcast live on national television and radio, President John F. **Kennedy** unveiled plans to pursue a comprehensive civil rights bill in Congress, stating, "This nation, for all its hopes and all its boasts, will not be fully free until all its citizens are free" ("President Kennedy's Radio-TV Address," 970). King congratulated Kennedy on his speech, calling it "one of the most eloquent, profound and unequivocal pleas for justice and the freedom of all men ever made by any president" (King, 12 June 1963).

The earlier Civil Rights Act of 1957, the first law addressing the legal rights of African Americans passed by Congress since Reconstruction, had established the Civil Rights division of the Justice Department and the U.S. Civil Rights Commission to investigate claims of racial discrimination. Before the 1957 bill was passed Congress had, however, removed a provision that would have empowered the Justice Department to enforce the **Brown v. Board of Education** decision. A. Philip **Randolph** and other civil rights leaders continued to press the major political parties and presidents Dwight D. **Eisenhower** and John **F. Kennedy** to enact such legislation and to outlaw segregation. The civil rights legislation that Kennedy introduced to Congress on 19 June 1963 addressed these issues, and King advocated for its passage.

In an article published after the 1963 **March on Washington for Jobs and Freedom** that posed the question, "What next?" King wrote, "The hundreds of thousands who marched in Washington marched to level barriers. They summed up everything in a word—NOW. What is the content of NOW? Everything, not some things, in the President's civil rights bill is part of NOW" (King, "In a Word—Now").

Following Kennedy's assassination in November 1963, King continued to press for the bill as did newly inaugurated President Lyndon B. **Johnson**. In his 4 January 1964 column in the **New York Amsterdam News**, King maintained that the legislation was "the order of the day at the great March on Washington last summer. The Negro and his compatriots for self-respect and human dignity will not be denied" (King, "A Look to 1964").

The bill passed the House of Representatives in mid-February 1964, but became mired in the Senate due to a filibuster by southern senators that lasted 75 days. When the bill finally passed the Senate, King hailed it as one that would "bring practical relief to the Negro in the South, and will give the Negro in the North a psychological boost that he sorely needs" (King, 19 June 1964). On 2 July 1964, Johnson signed the new Civil Rights Act of 1964 into law with King and other civil rights leaders present. The law's provisions created the Equal Employment Opportunity Commission to address race and sex discrimination in employment and a Community Relations Service to help local communities solve racial disputes; authorized federal intervention to ensure the desegregation of schools, parks, swimming pools, and other public facilities; and restricted the use of literacy tests as a requirement for voter registration.

SOURCES

Carson et al., ed., *Eyes on the Prize*, 1991.

Kennedy, "President Kennedy's Radio-TV Address on Civil Rights," *Congressional Quarterly* (14 June 1963): 970–971.

King, "In a Word—Now," *New York Times Magazine*, 29 September 1963.

King, "A Look to 1964," *New York Amsterdam News*, 4 January 1964.

King, Statement on the passage of the Civil Rights Act of 1964, 19 June 1964, MLKJP-GAMK.

King to Kennedy, 12 June 1963, DJG-GEU.

Kotz, *Judgment Days*, 2005.

CLARK, JAMES GARDNER (1922–2007)

A notorious foe of the African American freedom struggle, James Clark served as sheriff of Dallas County, Alabama, from 1955 to 1967. After years of antagonizing local civil rights workers, Clark clashed with Martin Luther King and the **Southern Christian**

Leadership Conference (SCLC) during 1965 voting rights protests in Selma, Alabama. Clark's brutality became a rallying point for King, who said: "Until Sheriff Clark is removed, the evils of Selma will not be removed" (Herbers, "Dr. King Urges").

Clark was born in Alabama in 1922. Prior to serving as sheriff, he worked as an assistant revenue commissioner for the state of Alabama. In February 1963 the **Student Nonviolent Coordinating Committee** began a voter education and registration campaign in Selma, the seat of Dallas County, where a mere 242 of the 15,000 eligible African American voters were registered. By October 1963 Clark had arrested hundreds of civil rights activists. Frustrated by their limited success, in December 1964 local black activists asked King and SCLC to come to Selma. Aware of the violence that Clark and his officers routinely employed, King believed that a confrontation in Selma might attract the national attention necessary to pressure President Lyndon B. **Johnson** to call for voting rights legislation. On 2 January 1965, SCLC sent staff members to begin a protest campaign.

After initially refraining from violent confrontations, on 19 January Clark pulled Amelia Boynton, a local black civil rights activist, out of a voter registration line and pushed her down the street into a waiting patrol car. King denounced Clark: "It is a tragedy when a man becomes so depraved and so sick that he will grab a woman and push and shove and all but kick her in the process as if he were dealing with some wayward dog" (King, 20 January 1965). A week later, Clark's violent behavior landed him on the front page of the *New York Times*, when a cameraman captured him beating a 53-year-old woman over the head with his nightstick as two officers held her down. Clark's brutal tactics prompted a federal court to issue a restraining order prohibiting Clark from employing intimidation and harassment. Clark was fined later that year for violating the order by interfering with registration applicants.

In the weeks following Boynton's arrest, King was also arrested, along with hundreds of black citizens seeking to exercise their constitutional rights. Commenting on how effective Clark's racist aggression was at attracting popular attention, one SCLC staff member reportedly said: "We should put him on the staff" (Garrow, *Bearing*, 381).

The showdown between Clark and civil rights activists climaxed on 7 March 1965, when Clark and his men brutally attacked civil rights demonstrators seeking to march from Selma to Montgomery. National television coverage of Clark's deputies using clubs, whips, and tear gas prompted Johnson to submit legislation that became the **Voting Rights Act of 1965**.

The violent events of 1965 eventually turned Clark's constituency against him, and in 1966 he lost his bid for reelection as county sheriff to Selma's public safety director, Wilson Baker, a moderate who had disapproved of Clark's tactics. After losing the election, Clark became active with the John Birch Society, touring the country to speak about his experience in Selma.

SOURCES

Fager, *Selma, 1965*, 1974.

Garrow, *Bearing the Cross*, 1986.

Garrow, *Protest at Selma*, 1978.

John Herbers, "Dr. King Urges Selma Negroes to Wage a More Militant Drive," *New York Times*, 18 February 1965.

King, Statement against Sheriff Clark, 20 January 1965, MLKJP-GAMK.

CLARK, SEPTIMA POINSETTE (1898–1987)

A pioneer in grassroots citizenship education, Septima Clark was called the "Mother of the Movement" and the epitome of a "community teacher, intuitive fighter for human rights and leader of her unlettered and disillusioned people" (McFadden, "Septima Clark," 85; King, July 1962).

The daughter of a laundrywoman and a former slave, Clark was born 3 May 1898 in Charleston, South Carolina. In 1916 she graduated from secondary school and, after passing her teacher's exam, taught at a black school on Johns Island, just outside of Charleston. For more than 30 years, she taught throughout South Carolina, including 18 years in Columbia and 9 in Charleston.

Clark pursued her education during summer breaks. In 1937 Clark studied under W.E.B. Du Bois at Atlanta University before eventually earning her BA (1942) from Benedict College in Columbia, and her MA (1946) from Virginia's Hampton Institute. Clark also worked with the YWCA and participated in a class action lawsuit filed by the **National Association for the Advancement of Colored People** (NAACP) that led to pay equity for black and white teachers in South Carolina. In 1956 South Carolina passed a statute that prohibited city and state employees from belonging to civil rights organizations. After 40 years of teaching, Clark's employment contract was not renewed when she refused to resign from the NAACP.

By the time of her firing in 1956, Clark had already begun to conduct workshops during her summer vacations at the **Highlander Folk School** in Monteagle, Tennessee, a grassroots education center dedicated to social justice. Rosa **Parks** participated in one of Clark's workshops just months before she helped launch the **Montgomery bus boycott**. After losing her teaching position, Myles Horton hired Clark full time as Highlander's director of workshops. Believing that literacy and political empowerment are inextricably linked, Clark taught people basic literacy skills, their rights and duties as U.S. citizens, and how to fill out voter registration forms.

When the state of Tennessee forced Highlander to close in 1961, the **Southern Christian Leadership Conference** (SCLC) established the Citizenship Education Program (CEP), modeled on Clark's citizenship workshops. Clark became SCLC's director of education and teaching, conducting teacher training and developing curricula. King appreciated Clark's "expert direction" of the CEP, which he called "the bulwark of SCLC's program department" (King, 11 August 1965). Although Clark found that most men at SCLC "didn't respect women too much," she thought that King "really felt that black women had a place in the movement" (Clark, 25 July 1976; McFadden, "Septima Clark," 93).

After retiring from SCLC in 1970, Clark conducted workshops for the American Field Service. In 1975 she was elected to the Charleston, South Carolina, School Board. The following year, the governor of South Carolina reinstated her teacher's pension after declaring that she had been unjustly terminated in 1956. She was given a Living Legacy Award by President Jimmy Carter in 1979 and published her second memoir, *Ready from Within*, in 1986.

SOURCES

Clark, Interview by Jacquelyn Hall, 25 July 1976, SOHP-NcU.

Clark, *Ready from Within*, 1986.

Clark, *Septima Clark and the Civil Rights Movement*, 1986.

Clark to King, 30 July 1956, in *Papers* 3:328–329.

Clark with LeGette Blythe, *Echo in My Soul*, 1962.

King, Annual report delivered at SCLC's Ninth Annual National Convention, 11 August 1965, MLKJP-GAMK.

King, Review and endorsement of Septima Clark's book, July 1962, SPCC-ScCC.

Grace Jordan McFadden, "Septima P. Clark and the Struggle for Human Rights," in *Women in the Civil Rights Movement*, ed. Vickie L. Crawford et al., 1990.

CLERGY AND LAYMEN CONCERNED ABOUT VIETNAM (CALCAV)

In October 1965, 100 clergy members met in New York to discuss what they could do to challenge U.S. policy on **Vietnam**. Believing that a multi-faith organization could lend credible support to an anti-war movement often labeled as Communist, they created the Clergy Concerned about Vietnam. Martin Luther King, Jr., was one of the few black members and the only member from the South. After the group opened its membership to laypeople and changed its name to National Emergency Committee of Clergy and Laymen Concerned about Vietnam (CALCAV), King used the organization's platform in April 1967 for his widely acclaimed "**Beyond Vietnam**" speech that condemned the war in Vietnam.

In February and April 1967 King delivered two speeches devoted entirely to Vietnam. On 25 February 1967, King delivered "The Causalities of the War in Vietnam." He was eager to ensure his message would not be distorted and approached CALCAV to organize a public event where he could situate his position within the broader religious opposition to the war. CALCAV hired a publicist exclusively for the event, which was held at Riverside Church in New York City on 4 April 1967. King's speech, which drew over 3,000 people, provided his most significant endorsement of the anti-war movement to date. CALCAV published and distributed 100,000 copies of the Riverside speeches and King accepted an invitation to be co-chair of the organization.

Later that month, CALCAV endorsed "Vietnam Summer," a campaign promoted by King and the noted pediatrician Benjamin **Spock** to mobilize grassroots anti-war activists in preparation for the 1968 elections. Throughout the summer and fall, CALCAV chapters engaged in civil disobedience by protecting draft resisters, a departure from their more moderate tactics, such as petitions and vigils. The organization's second national mobilization was timed to coincide with the February 1968 release of a study commissioned by CALCAV documenting American war crimes in Vietnam. At the gathering, King led 2,500 CALCAV supporters in silent prayer at Arlington National Cemetery's Tomb of the Unknowns.

Following King's **assassination**, CALCAV increased civil disobedience activities, protesting against Dow Chemical (producer of napalm) and Honeywell (maker of anti-personnel weapons). By 1971 CALCAV had turned its attention to several other social justice issues, dropping "about Vietnam" from its name to become simply Clergy and Laymen Concerned (CALC). During the subsequent decades, CALC supported sanctions against South Africa, a nuclear weapons freeze, and the end of U.S. military involvement in Central America.

SOURCE

Hall, *Because of Their Faith*, 1990.

COFO. *See* Council of Federated Organizations.

COLEMAN, JAMES PLEMON (1914–1991)

As governor of Mississippi, James P. Coleman wrote Martin Luther King in 1956 to dissuade him from making a visit to the state to speak at the fifth annual meeting of the Mississippi Regional Council of Negro Leadership. Regarding King's visit, Coleman announced that "it would be a tragedy to have professional agitators like [Adam Clayton] Powell and King come to the state and fan the fires anew" (*Papers* 4:220).

Coleman was born on 9 January 1914, in Ackerman, Mississippi. He attended the University of Mississippi from 1932 to 1935 but left before completing a degree. In 1939, he received his LLB from George Washington University in Washington, D.C. After returning to Ackerman, Coleman served as district attorney, circuit court judge, and, briefly, as a Mississippi Supreme Court justice before being elected to a full term as Mississippi attorney general in 1951. He was elected governor of the state in 1955.

In 1956 Coleman sent a telegram to King urging him to postpone a scheduled visit to Mississippi, stating: "I feel it my duty as governor of Mississippi to inform you that conditions in our state are now more tranquil than at any time in recent months and in view of your record your appearance here will be a great disservice to our Negro people" (*Papers* 3:220). The next day, King responded that, in fact, he was not scheduled to visit Mississippi, but if he were, he would feel obligated to "come to Mississippi in spite of [Coleman's] most cautious warning. You stated that in view of my record my coming to Mississippi would be a great injustice to the Negro people. I think if you would observe my record very carefully you would discover that it is more the record of a peace maker than a peace breaker" (*Papers* 3:221).

After serving a full term as governor, Coleman joined the state legislature in 1959. Coleman was criticized for his support of President John F. **Kennedy** during the 1960 presidential campaign; Kennedy later used federal troops to integrate the University of Mississippi. Coleman attempted to run for governor again in 1963 but was defeated by Paul B. Johnson, a more extreme segregationist. In 1965 President Lyndon B. **Johnson** nominated Coleman to fill a vacancy on the U.S. Court of Appeals for the Fifth Circuit. As a federal judge, Coleman was responsible for implementing desegregation changes that he had opposed as governor. He retired from the court in 1984.

SOURCES
Coleman to King, 23 April 1956, in *Papers* 3:220–221.
King to Coleman, 24 April 1956, in *Papers* 3:221.

COMMUNISM

In the Cold War climate of the 1950s and 1960s, the threat of communism galvanized public attention. In 1953 Martin Luther King called communism "one of the most important issues of our day" (*Papers* 6:146). As King rose to prominence he frequently had to defend himself against allegations of being a Communist, though his view that "Communism and Christianity are fundamentally incompatible" did not change (King, *Strength*, 93). Although sympathetic to communism's core concern with social justice, King complained that with its "cold atheism wrapped in the garments of materialism, communism provides no place for God or Christ" (*Strength*, 94).

MARTIN LUTHER KING.... AT COMMUNIST TRAINING SCHOOL

PICTURED (Foreground),

(1) Martin Luther King of the Montgomery Boycott and the Birmingham riots, backed up by the Kennedys,

(2) Abner W. Berry of the Central Committee of the Communist Party,

(3) Aubrey Williams, pres. of the Southern Conference Education Fund, Inc., the Transmission Belt in the South for the Communist Party,

(4) Myles Horton, director of Highlander Folk School for Communist Training, Monteagle, Tenn.

These "four horsemen" of racial agitation have brought tension, disturbance, strife and violence in their advancement of the Communist doctrine of "racial nationalism."

This image, showing King (second from right) at Highlander Folk School in 1957, appeared widely throughout the South as part of an effort to discredit King and the civil rights movement because of southern claims that Highlander was a Communist training school. © AP / Wide World Photos.

King first studied communism on his own while a student at **Crozer Theological Seminary** in 1949. In his 1958 memoir, he reported that although he rejected communism's central tenets, he was sympathetic to Marx's critique of capitalism, finding the "gulf between superfluous wealth and abject poverty" that existed in the United States morally wrong (*Stride*, 94). Writing his future wife, Coretta Scott, during the first summer of their relationship, he told her that he was "more socialistic in my economic theory than capitalistic. And yet I am not so opposed to capitalism that I have failed to see its relative merits" (*Papers* 6:123; 125).

King began preaching on "Communism's Challenge to Christianity" in 1952, repeating sermons on the same theme throughout his career and including one as a chapter in his 1963 volume of sermons, **Strength to Love**. Communism's presence demanded "sober discussion," he preached, because "Communism is the only serious rival to Christianity" (*Strength*, 93). King critiqued communism's ethical relativism, which allowed evil and destructive means to justify an idealistic end. Communism, wrote King, "robs man of that quality which makes him man," that is, being a "child of God" (*Strength*, 95).

Despite King's consistent rejection of communism, in 1962 his associations with a few alleged Communists prompted the **Federal Bureau of Investigation** (FBI) to launch an investigation into his alleged links with the Communist Party. In 1976 the U.S. Senate committee reviewing the FBI's investigation of King noted: "We have seen no evidence establishing that either of those Advisers attempted to exploit the civil rights movement to carry out the plans of the Communist Party" (Senate Select Committee, *Book III*, 85). From wiretaps initiated in 1963, the FBI fed controversial information to the White House and offered it to "friendly" reporters in an effort to discredit King. In 1964 King told an audience in Jackson, Mississippi, he was "sick and tired of people saying this movement has been infiltrated by Communists.... There are as many Communists in this freedom movement as there are Eskimos in Florida" (Herbers, "Rights Workers").

In 1963 King bowed to the wishes of the **Kennedy** administration and fired SCLC employee Jack **O'Dell** after the FBI alleged that he was a Communist. King also agreed to cease direct communication with his friend and closest white advisor, Stanley **Levison**, although he eventually resumed contact with him in March 1965. FBI surveillance and bugs tracked King's political associations and produced evidence of King's extramarital sexual activities—information that was later leaked to some reporters.

In 1965 King faced questions from journalists on **Meet the Press** about his association with Tennessee's **Highlander Folk School,** which had been branded a "Communist training school" on billboards that appeared throughout Alabama during the **Selma to Montgomery March** and showed King attending a Highlander workshop. King defended the school, saying that it was not Communist and noted that "great Americans such as Eleanor Roosevelt, Reinhold Niebuhr, Harry Golden, and many others" had supported the school (King, 28 March 1965).

King's position on the war against Communists in northern Vietnam, like his overall position on communism, was rooted in his Christian belief in brotherhood. Indeed, in the summer of 1965 the press reported King's off-the-cuff remarks to a **Southern Christian Leadership Conference** rally in Virginia: "We're not going to defeat Communism with bombs and guns and gases…. We must work this out in the framework of our democracy" ("Dr. King Declares"). In his 1967 book, **Where Do We Go from Here: Chaos or Community?** King decried America's "morbid fear of Communism," arguing that it prevented people from embracing a "revolutionary spirit and … declaring eternal opposition to poverty, racism, and militarism" (King, *Where*, 190).

SOURCES
Branch, *At Canaan's Edge*, 2006.
"Dr. King Declares U.S. Must Negotiate in Asia," *New York Times*, 3 July 1965.
John Herbers, "Rights Workers Report Attacks," *New York Times*, 27 July 1964.
King, "Communism's Challenge to Christianity," 9 August 1953, in *Papers*: 6:146–150.
King, Interview on Meet the Press, 28 March 1965, SCLCR-GAMK.
King, "Let Us Be Dissatisfied," *Gandhi Marg*, 12 (July 1968): 218–229.
King, *Strength to Love*, 1963.
King, *Stride Toward Freedom*, 1958.
King, *Where Do We Go from Here*, 1967.
King to Coretta Scott, 18 July 1952, in *Papers*: 6:123–126.
Senate Select Committee to Study Governmental Operations with Respect to Intelligence Activities, *Book III: Supplementary Detailed Staff Reports on Intelligence Activities and the Rights of Americans*, 94th Cong., 2d sess., 1976, S. Rep. 82–86; 94–755.

CONGRESS OF INDUSTRIAL ORGANIZATIONS. *See* American Federation of Labor and Congress of Industrial Organizations (AFL-CIO).

CONGRESS OF RACIAL EQUALITY (CORE)

Founded in 1942 by an interracial group of students in Chicago, the Congress of Racial Equality (CORE) pioneered the use of nonviolent direct action in America's civil rights struggle. Along with its parent organization, the **Fellowship of Reconciliation** (FOR), CORE members provided advice and support to Martin Luther King during the **Montgomery bus boycott**. King worked with CORE throughout the late 1950s and into the mid-1960s, when CORE abandoned its dedication to nonviolence and adopted black separatist policies.

Early CORE activists James **Farmer**, Bayard **Rustin**, Homer **Jack**, and George **Houser** had all been affiliated with FOR, an international peace and justice organization. Influenced by **Gandhi**, in the 1940s CORE used **sit-ins** and other nonviolent direct actions to integrate Chicago restaurants and businesses. In 1947 CORE organized the Journey of Reconciliation, a multi-state integrated bus ride through the upper South in order to test the previous year's Supreme Court ruling against segregation in interstate travel. This precursor to the 1961 **Freedom Rides** was met with minimal violence, although several of the riders were arrested, and two were sentenced to work on a chain gang in North Carolina.

In the first weeks after the start of the Montgomery bus boycott, CORE-affiliated activists such as James **Peck**, Rustin, and Jack visited King. Jack wrote to his colleagues, "I never expected to see such a disciplined, effective protest in the South in 1956," and suggested CORE send field workers to support the movement (Jack, 9 March 1956). During the Montgomery bus boycott, CORE publicized King's work in its pamphlets. In October 1957 King agreed to serve on CORE's Advisory Committee.

In the following years, King's organization, the **Southern Christian Leadership Conference** (SCLC), worked with CORE on several projects, including the 1959 and 1960 Prayer Pilgrimage for Public Schools in support of integrated education, the **Voter Education Project**, and the **Chicago Campaign**. CORE supported southern blacks during the **sit-in** movement of 1960; CORE field secretaries traveled through the South, advising student activists on nonviolent methods.

CORE organized the Freedom Rides in the spring of 1961. Modeled after the earlier Journey of Reconciliation, the rides took an integrated group through the Deep South. Although King supported the rides, he considered them too dangerous to participate in himself. In Anniston, Alabama, one bus was firebombed, and its fleeing passengers were forced into an angry white mob. As the violence against the Freedom Rides increased, CORE considered halting the project. A Freedom Ride Coordinating Committee was formed by representatives of the **Student Nonviolent Coordinating Committee**, CORE, and SCLC to sustain the rides.

Following the Freedom Rides, CORE concentrated on voter registration. In 1962, along with other civil rights groups, CORE joined the **Council of Federated Organizations** (COFO), which coordinated the activities of local and national civil rights organizations in Mississippi. COFO's efforts culminated in the 1964 **Freedom Summer** and the **Mississippi Freedom Democratic Party** (MFDP), which challenged the state's all-white official delegation at the Democratic National Convention of 1964.

The murder of three CORE workers, Michael Schwerner, Andrew Goodman, and James Chaney, in Mississippi in the summer of 1964, coupled with the limited success of MFDP, led many activists, including some in CORE, to become disenchanted with **nonviolence**. By 1966 a power struggle within CORE forced Farmer to step down as national director, leaving the more militant Floyd **McKissick** in his place. After King worked with McKissick during the summer of 1966 on the Meredith March Against Fear, CORE adopted a platform based on **Black Power** and limited white involvement in the organization.

Following King's **assassination**, McKissick called him "the last prince of nonviolence" and declared that nonviolence was "a dead philosophy" ("McKissick Says Nonviolence"). From this point, CORE focused its efforts on **black nationalism** and political self-determination in the black community.

SOURCES

Arsenault, *Freedom Riders*, 2006.

Jack, Memo to those interested in nonviolent resistance as witnessed in Montgomery Bus Boycott, 9 March 1956, BRP-DLC.

"McKissick Says Nonviolence Has Become Dead Philosophy," *New York Times*, 5 April 1968.

Milton Viorst, "Core and the Pacifist Roots of Civil Rights," in *Civil Rights Since 1787*, ed. Birnbaum and Taylor, 2000.

CONNOR, THEOPHILUS EUGENE "BULL" (1897–1973)

An ardent segregationist who served for 22 years as commissioner of public safety in Birmingham, Alabama, Bull Connor used his administrative authority over the police and fire departments to ensure that Birmingham remained, as Martin Luther King described it, "the most segregated city in America" (King, 50). In 1963 the violent response of Connor and his police force to demonstrations during the **Birmingham Campaign** propelled the civil rights movement into the national spotlight.

Connor was born on 11 July 1897, in Selma, Alabama. After the death of his mother when he was eight, Connor traveled the country with his father, who moved from place to place as a railroad telegrapher. Connor never graduated from high school, but he learned telegraphy from his father and used this skill to gain employment at radio stations, eventually becoming a radio announcer.

Connor's political career began in 1934, when he used his popularity as a Birmingham sportscaster to win a seat in the Alabama House of Representatives. After serving a term in the House, he was elected to the Birmingham City Commission, where he became known for his uncompromising opposition to integration.

When Birmingham voted to convert from a city commission system to a mayor/council system in 1962, Connor ran for mayor. Although he was defeated by Albert **Boutwell** in a run-off election the following spring, Connor refused to vacate his office and still maintained control of the city's police and fire departments when the **Southern Christian Leadership Conference** and **Alabama Christian Movement for Human Rights** launched a massive assault on segregation in the city in April 1963. In King's 1964 account of the campaign, *Why We Can't Wait*, he characterized Connor as "a racist who prided himself on knowing how to handle the Negro and keep him in his 'place'" (King, 49).

During the first days of the campaign, Connor avoided violent confrontations between police and protesters. Adopting a strategy that had successfully thwarted demonstrations in **Albany**, Georgia, Birmingham police jailed wave after wave of protesters without abuse. On 2 May 1963, when campaign leaders called on young students to sustain the protest, police arrested more than 900 "Children's Crusade" participants.

On 3 May, however, Connor ordered firemen to use their hoses on protesters and onlookers, and as the demonstrators fled from the force of the hoses, Connor directed officers to pursue them with dogs. During the following days, television reports and newspapers across the country showed images of police and firemen using hoses, dogs, and batons to force demonstrators from downtown Birmingham.

National outrage forced John F. **Kennedy**'s administration to send a negotiator, Burke **Marshall**, to Birmingham. The Birmingham Campaign ended on 10 May when an agreement was reached between black leaders and representatives of Birmingham's business community that moved the city toward desegregation. On 23 May 1963, the Alabama Supreme Court ordered Connor and the other city commissioners to vacate their offices. Within a year, Connor won election to the Alabama Public Service Commission, where he served as president until 1972.

SOURCES

Eskew, *But for Birmingham*, 1997.
King, *Why We Can't Wait*, 1964.

COOK, SAMUEL DuBOIS (1928–)

Black educator Samuel DuBois Cook entered **Morehouse College** with his friend Martin Luther King, Jr., when both were 15 years of age and took part in the Morehouse early admission program during World War II. At Morehouse, Cook became student body president and founded the campus chapter of the **National Association for the Advancement of Colored People**. Cook supported the **Montgomery bus boycott**, writing to King in March 1956: "You have achieved that rare combination of social action and love" (*Papers* 3:204).

Born 21 November 1928, in Griffin, Georgia, Cook graduated from Morehouse in 1948 and went on to receive his PhD (1955) from Ohio State University. He taught at Southern University and Atlanta University before becoming the first black professor to hold a regular faculty appointment at a white southern university, when he accepted a position at Duke in 1966.

As chair of the Political Science Department at Atlanta University, Cook participated in the civil rights movement, moderating "Town Meeting" forums between activists such as King and students in the early 1960s. Cook was very grateful that King took time from his busy schedule to participate in campus dialogue, writing to him: "Truly, you are as committed to the life of mind and spirit as you are to social reconstruction and redemption." He called King "one of the major prophets and noblest spirits of contemporary culture" (Cook, 13 October 1961).

In 1975 Cook became the president of Dillard University, serving until his retirement in 1997. During his tenure at Dillard he initiated a Japanese language studies program (the first at a historically black college) and founded the Center for Black-Jewish Relations. Cook was the first black president of the Southern Political Science Association. In 1997 the Samuel DuBois Cook Society at Duke University was founded in his honor. Cook has served on the board of trustees of the **King Center** in Atlanta since its founding.

SOURCES

Branch, *Parting the Waters*, 1988.
Cook to King, 23 March 1956, in *Papers* 3:203–204.
Cook to King, 13 October 1961, MLKP-MBU.

CORE. *See* Congress of Racial Equality.

COTTON, DOROTHY FOREMAN (1930–)

Recognized as "the highest ranking woman in SCLC during most of the '60s," Dorothy Foreman Cotton served as director of the **Southern Christian Leadership Conference**'s (SCLC) Citizenship Education Program (CEP) at the peak of the civil rights movement, a position that situated her in Martin Luther King, Jr.'s inner circle of executive staff (Cotton, 3 May 1990).

Born Dorothy Lee Foreman in 1930, Cotton spent her childhood in Goldsboro, North Carolina, where she and her three sisters were raised by their father, a tobacco factory worker, after the death of their mother in 1934. Upon graduating from high school, Cotton left for Shaw University in Raleigh, North Carolina, where she paid for her tuition by working as university president Robert Prentiss Daniel's housekeeper. When he accepted a position as president of Virginia State College in Petersburg, Virginia, Cotton transferred there to complete her undergraduate degree in English and library science. She and George J. Cotton were married shortly after graduation, before she went on to complete her master's degree in speech therapy at **Boston University**.

Cotton's involvement with the civil rights movement began in the late 1950s, when she joined Gillfield Baptist Church in Petersburg and met its pastor, Wyatt Tee **Walker**. Under his leadership she became involved in local protests targeting segregation, and eventually became secretary of the Petersburg Improvement Association. Cotton first met King at a dinner while she was working in Petersburg, and recalls that he had "some intangible magnetic quality.... That something that made people want to be with him ... because he had a way of *really being* with you when he was with you" (Cotton, 3 May 1990).

In 1960, when King invited Walker to come to Atlanta to serve as SCLC's executive director, Cotton joined the organization as Walker's administrative assistant. Her work became more focused the following year, when she became SCLC's educational consultant. She was later promoted to education director of the CEP in 1963. Cotton described her responsibility as helping "people realize that they have within themselves the stuff it takes to bring about a new order" (Cotton, 9). She was active in teaching literacy, citizenship, and nonviolent protest tactics, and motivated others to become registered voters and active political participants. She spent much of her time with the CEP, traveling throughout the South and conducting educational programs with Andrew **Young** and Septima **Clark**.

As one of SCLC's most important leaders, Cotton worked closely with King. In a telegram acknowledging his nomination for the **Nobel Peace Prize**, she expressed her admiration for "the seriousness and devotion with which you hold your noble charge" (Cotton, 31 January 1964). Cotton was a member of the group of close family, friends, and colleagues who accompanied King to Oslo, Norway, when he received the Nobel Prize in 1964. Her relationship with King was not limited to SCLC work, as she pointed out that those working for the organization "were all friends as well as staff." This friendship showed her a side of him that "was fun to be with ... he was the life of the party" (Cotton, 3 May 1990).

Cotton retired from SCLC in 1972. Following her departure, she held jobs relating to public service and social action, including director of the federal Child Development/Head Start program of the Jefferson County Committee for Economic Opportunity in Birmingham, Alabama, and vice president for field operations at the **King**

Center in Atlanta. In 1982 she accepted a position with Cornell University as their director of student activities. In the early 1990s, Cotton returned to her civil rights background and began leading seminars and workshops on leadership development and social change.

SOURCES

Cotton, "CEP: Challenge to the 'New Education,'" *Soul Force* (November 1969): 9.
Cotton, Interview by Clayborne Carson, 3 May 1990, CCCSU.
Cotton to King, 31 January 1964, MLKP-MBU.

COUNCIL OF FEDERATED ORGANIZATIONS (COFO)

The Council of Federated Organizations (COFO) was a coalition of national and regional organizations engaged in civil rights activities in Mississippi. Established in 1962 with the goal of maximizing the efforts of the **Student Nonviolent Coordinating Committee** (SNCC), the **Congress of Racial Equality**, and the **National Association for the Advancement of Colored People** (NAACP), the organization focused on voter registration and education. Under the leadership of SNCC activist Robert **Moses**, and staffed primarily by SNCC activists, COFO launched the Mississippi **Freedom Summer** Project in 1964. In describing the difficulties faced by COFO and Freedom Summer workers, Martin Luther King, Jr., said: "Our nation sent out Peace Corps Volunteers throughout the under-developed nations of the world and none of them experienced the kind of brutality and savagery that these voter registration workers have suffered here in Mississippi" (King, 22 July 1964).

One of COFO's first efforts in Mississippi was the fall 1963 Freedom Vote, a mock election for Mississippi governor and lieutenant governor held to protest the mass disenfranchisement of black citizens in the state. COFO sought to demonstrate that without discriminatory registration procedures and fear of white reprisals, blacks would vote in large numbers. With the help of northern students, more than 80,000 ballots were cast for COFO president and NAACP state president Aaron Henry, and minister Edwin King. This success led to COFO's organization of the Mississippi Freedom Summer project, which brought hundreds of northern white college students to the state to assist COFO. The project opened on a tragic note when three civil rights workers, James Chaney, Michael Schwerner, and Andrew Goodman, disappeared in late June 1964. When they were found murdered in early August, King called the killings "an attack on the very concept of a democratic society" (King, 4 August 1964). Confronting ongoing violence and harassment, Freedom Summer volunteers canvassed neighborhoods, registered voters, developed public health programs, and taught literacy and civics in "Freedom Schools."

Freedom Summer included the formation of the **Mississippi Freedom Democratic Party** (MFDP), an interracial political party that challenged the all-white official state delegation at the 1964 Democratic National Convention in Atlantic City, New Jersey. COFO hoped to generate national party pressure to change state election practices, but garnered little support from national officials of the Democratic Party. President Lyndon B. **Johnson** approved offering the MFDP a compromise of two seats as at-large delegates, which MFDP rejected.

Conflicts over the rejection of Johnson's compromise increased existing tensions among COFO's member organizations. Most of the summer's volunteers returned to college in the fall, and COFO Director Moses resigned at the end of 1964. Weakened by substantial losses in its leadership, workforce, and funding, COFO disbanded in 1965.

SOURCES

Carson, *In Struggle*, 1981.

King, Statement in support of Mississippi Freedom Democratic Party, 22 July 1964, MLKJP-GAMK.

King, Statement on the deaths of Michael Henry Schwerner, Andrew Goodman, and James Earl Chaney, 4 August 1964, MLKJP-GAMK.

McAdam, *Freedom Summer*, 1988.

CROZER THEOLOGICAL SEMINARY

After completing his undergraduate work at **Morehouse College** in 1948, Martin Luther King attended Crozer Theological Seminary near Chester, Pennsylvania. King was drawn to the school's unorthodox reputation and liberal theological leanings. It was at Crozer that King strengthened his commitment to the Christian **social gospel**, developed his initial interest in Gandhian ideas, was first exposed to pacifism, and developed his ideas about **nonviolence** as a method of social reform.

Crozer opened in the fall of 1868 as the new home of the University of Lewisburg Theology Department. Although founded by Baptists, Crozer adopted a nondenominational approach to religious education, gaining a reputation as a theologically liberal institution.

As 1 of only 11 black students at the seminary in 1948, King was initially self-conscious. He said of his early experience at Crozer, "If I were a minute late to class, I was almost morbidly conscious of it and sure that everyone noticed it." He recalled being "grimly serious for a time. I had a tendency to overdress, to keep my room spotless, my shoes perfectly shined and my clothes immaculately pressed" (Peters, 72). Through the years he became more comfortable, developing meaningful relationships with classmates and professors. He was elected class president in his third year.

King studied preaching with Robert Keighton, beginning his first term with Keighton's class Preaching Ministry. King drafted an assignment for that class that revealed many of his early conceptions of the role of preaching, which he called "one of the most vital needs in our society, if it is used correctly" (*Papers* 6:71). King's commitment to addressing societal needs and ills was evident in his closing words: "I must be concerned about unemployment, slums, and economic insecurity. I am a profound advocator of the social gospel" (*Papers* 6:72).

In November 1949 King was introduced to pacifism in a lecture by A. J. **Muste** of the **Fellowship of Reconciliation**. Although not immediately convinced of the practicality of Muste's position, King later attended a sermon by Mordecai **Johnson**, president of Howard University, and learned of the life and teachings of Mohandas K. **Gandhi**. It was through Gandhi's emphasis on love and nonviolence that King discovered the method of social reform that he had been seeking. King was also greatly inspired by George Washington **Davis**, who expanded his knowledge of social gospel philosophies and introduced him to the writings of Reinhold **Niebuhr**.

In 1951, the year of King's graduation from Crozer, Dean Charles Battan praised him as "one of our most outstanding students" and someone who exhibited "fine preparation, an excellent mind, and a thorough grasp of the material" (*Papers* 1:390–391).

King graduated from Crozer with honors as class valedictorian and was also the recipient of the Pearl Plafker award for scholarship. In 1970 the seminary merged with Colgate Rochester Divinity School in Rochester, New York.

SOURCES

Battan, "Martin L. King," 1951, in *Papers* 1:390–392.

Introduction, in *Papers* 1:46, 48, 54–55.

King, "Pilgrimage to Nonviolence," in *Papers* 4:473–481.

King, "Preaching Ministry," in *Papers* 6:69–72.

King, *Stride Toward Freedom*, 1958.

William Peters, "Our Weapon Is Love," *Redbook* (August 1956): 72.

CURRY, IZOLA WARE (1916–)

On 20 September 1958, Izola Ware Curry, a 42-year-old mentally disturbed woman, stabbed Martin Luther King, Jr., while he signed copies of his book, **Stride Toward Freedom**, at Blumstein's Department Store in Harlem, New York. Curry approached King with a seven-inch steel letter opener and drove the blade into the upper left side of his chest. King was rushed to Harlem Hospital, where he underwent more than two hours of surgery to repair the wound. Doctors operating on the 29-year-old civil rights leader said: "Had Dr. King sneezed or coughed, the weapon would have penetrated the aorta.… He was just a sneeze away from death" (*Papers* 4:499n).

Born in Adrian, Georgia, Curry moved to New York at the age of 20 to begin work as a cook and housekeeper. Shortly after her relocation, Curry developed paranoid delusions about the **National Association for the Advancement of Colored People**, Martin Luther King, Jr., and other civil rights leaders. After stabbing King, Curry was arrested at the scene and found carrying a loaded gun. When questioned by police at New York's 28th Precinct, she accused civil rights leaders of "boycotting" and "torturing" her as well as causing her to lose jobs and forcing her to change her religion (Curry, 21 September 1958). Curry also suggested that dangerous connections were being forged between the civil rights movement and the Communist Party. After authorities informed her that she was being charged with felonious assault and possession of firearms, she reportedly replied: "I'm charging him [King] as well as he's charging me … I'm charging him with being mixed up with the Communists" ("Dr. King's Knifer").

King with his mother, Alberta Williams King, and wife, Coretta Scott King, in Harlem Hospital, 30 September 1958, while he was recovering from a stab wound inflicted by Izola Curry. © AP / Wide World Photos.

When King received word of his attacker's mental state, he expressed his sympathy and issued the following statement upon returning home to Montgomery, Alabama:

I am deeply sorry that a deranged woman should have injured herself in seeking to injure me. I can say, in all sincerity, that I bear no bitterness toward her and I have felt no resentment from the sad moment that the experience occurred. I know that we want her to receive the necessary treatment so that she may become a constructive citizen in an integrated society where a disorganized personality need not become a menace to any man. (*Papers* 4:513)

Following the stabbing, Curry was placed in Bellevue Hospital for observation and was found not competent to stand trial. On 20 October 1958, she was diagnosed as a paranoid schizophrenic and committed to Matteawan State Hospital for the Criminally Insane.

SOURCES

Curry, Statement to Howard Jones, 21 September 1958, NYDAR-NNRA.
Dexter Avenue Baptist Church to King, 21 September 1958, in *Papers* 4:498–499.
"Dr. King's Knifer Sent to Bellevue," *New York Times*, 22 September 1958.
King, Statement upon Return to Montgomery, 24 October 1958, in *Papers* 4:513–514.
Pearson, *When Harlem Nearly Killed King*, 2002.

DANIELS, JONATHAN MYRICK (1939–1965)

A seminary student who responded to Martin Luther King's call for participants in the **Selma to Montgomery March**, Daniels was shot and killed by a deputy sheriff in Hayneville, Alabama, who was later acquitted of the crime. King described the acquittal by an all-white jury as a "gross miscarriage of justice," noting that Daniels was one of at least 26 killed in the struggle for civil rights between 1960 and 1965 (King, "The Verdict").

Born 20 March 1939 in Keene, New Hampshire, Daniels graduated as the valedictorian of his class from the Virginia Military Institute in 1961, and was remembered by one of his friends as "a militant Christian" (Dewar, "Slain Civil Rights Aide Gave VMI Valedictory"). After a year at Harvard University, Daniels enrolled at the Episcopal Theological School in Cambridge, Massachusetts. In March 1965 Daniels heard of King's summons for clergy to march from Selma to Montgomery.

After hearing the speech King gave at the end of the march, Daniels wrote to his mother that King was "certainly one of the greatest men of our times" (Eagles, 42). He decided to remain in the South and began to work with the Episcopal Society for Cultural and Racial Unity, embracing **nonviolence** on religious grounds. Daniels initially helped to integrate St. Paul's Episcopal Church in Selma by persistently attending services with an interracial group.

During a demonstration in Fort Deposit on 14 August 1965, Daniels and several other civil rights workers were arrested and driven to the county jail in Hayneville, 20 miles away. Released on 20 August with another white priest and two black women, Daniels was attempting to arrange transportation home when this group of four approached a white-owned store in Hayneville, where they were confronted by Hayneville Special Deputy Sheriff Thomas L. Coleman. Coleman ordered them to leave and abruptly shot Daniels, killing him instantly.

Coleman was acquitted six weeks later by an all-white jury in what the Alabama attorney general dubbed a "callous disregard for the taking of a human life" (Nelson, "Jury Acquits"). In 1994 the Episcopalian Church added Daniels to its list of martyrs to be remembered annually.

Sources

Helen Dewar, "Slain Civil Rights Aide Gave VMI Valedictory," *Washington Post*, 29 August 1965.

Eagles, *Outside Agitator*, 1993.

King, "Address at the Conclusion of the Selma to Montgomery March," in *A Call to Conscience*, ed. Carson and Shepard, 2001.

King, "The Verdict," *New York Amsterdam News*, 20 November 1965.

Jack Nelson, "Jury Acquits Deputy in Rights Death," *Los Angeles Times*, 1 October 1965.

DAVES, JOAN (1919–1997)

Literary agent Joan Daves began working with Martin Luther King, Jr., in October 1957, after he had begun preliminary work on his first book, **Stride Toward Freedom: The Montgomery Story**. In 1964, Daves accompanied King to Europe when he accepted the **Nobel Peace Prize**.

Born Liselotte Davidson in Berlin on 14 November 1919, Daves escaped the Nazi regime in the mid-1930s and fled to Paris and Britain before emigrating to the United States in 1940. Daves worked for Interscience Publishers and, in 1942, she became an editor at Harper & Brothers. Daves co-founded the literary agency of Marie **Rodell** and Joan Daves, Inc., and later established the Joan Daves Agency.

Daves and Rodell managed King's contracts, negotiated motion picture productions, arranged publicity for *Stride*, and worked with editorial assistant Hermine **Popper** to help guide the writing of the manuscript when concerns over King's busy schedule threatened to delay the publication of the book. Daves remained King's literary agent for his next three books, **Strength to Love** (1963), **Why We Can't Wait** (1964), and **Where Do We Go from Here: Chaos or Community?** (1967) and continued to work with King's literary property until her death in 1997.

SOURCES

Daves to King, 18 October 1957, in *Papers* 4:286–287.

Hermine I. Popper to King, 21 March 1958, in *Papers* 4:386, 388.

DAVIS, BENJAMIN JEFFERSON, JR. (1903–1964)

Benjamin J. Davis, Jr., was chairman of the New York State district of the Communist Party and an acquaintance of Martin Luther King, Jr., King and Davis were both from prominent Atlanta families, and despite their ideological differences, their relationship was characterized by a great degree of mutual respect. In a letter to Davis, King once wrote: "Your words are always encouraging, and although we do not share the political views I find a deeper unity of spirit with you that is after all the important thing" (*Papers* 5:442).

Davis was born in Dawson, Georgia, on 8 September 1903, to Benjamin Davis, Sr., and Jimmie W. Porter. In 1909 the family moved to Atlanta, where Benjamin, Sr., became active in Republican Party politics and founded the *Atlanta Independent*, a weekly African American newspaper. A graduate of Amherst College, Davis, Jr., earned a degree from Harvard Law School in 1929 and began practicing law three years later in Atlanta. The young attorney gained international attention when he was hired in 1932 by the International Labor Defense to represent Angelo Herndon, a young African American Communist. Defending Herndon not only brought Davis great renown, but also intensified his own Communist sensibilities. In 1935, he left the legal profession in Atlanta for New York City where he become the editor of the

American Communist Party's periodicals the *Negro Liberator* and, later, the *Daily Worker*. In New York he became active in municipal politics, succeeding Adam Clayton **Powell**, Jr., as Harlem's representative on the New York City Council in 1943. Davis encountered legal problems of his own surrounding his involvement with the Communist Party and, in 1949, lost his bid for a third term on the City Council. He was convicted later that year for violating the Smith Act, a 1940 law that criminalized any act that was seen as advocating an overthrow of the United States government, and spent five years in a federal penitentiary.

Although Davis remained a member of the Communist Party until his death in 1964, throughout the 1950s he developed an increasing admiration for King. Following King's stabbing in 1958 by Izola **Curry**, Davis donated blood at Harlem Hospital to help the injured leader, writing in a letter: "Had the blood been needed it was there. Just as blood knows no race or color—it knows no politics." In that same letter Davis called support for King "a duty" and wished the minister "the best of everything and great success in your work" (Davis, January 1959). King later wrote to Davis that "a friend like yourself … gives me renewed courage and vigor to carry on" (*Papers* 5:443).

In 1962, Davis was again indicted for his association with the Communist Party, this time for violating the McCarran Internal Security Act by failing to register the Communist Party as an agent of the Soviet Union. Davis remained committed to his political ideology and died in 1964 while awaiting trial for these charges.

SOURCES
Davis to King, January 1959, MLKP-MBU.
King to Davis, 23 April 1960, in *Papers* 4:442–443.

DAVIS, GEORGE WASHINGTON (1902–1960)

As Martin Luther King recuperated from surgery after his September 1958 stabbing, he received a warm letter from his mentor at **Crozer Theological Seminary**, George W. Davis, expressing his "moral and spiritual support" (*Papers* 4:512). King replied, "Your words came as a great spiritual lift to me and were of inestimable value in giving me strength and courage to face the ordeal of this trying period" (*Papers* 4:528). Davis' classes exposed King to **social gospel** teachings and greatly influenced his concepts of God and Christian faith.

Born in Pittsburgh, Pennsylvania, to Benjamin Ivor Davis, a steel mill union activist, and his wife Catherine Kaiser Davis, Davis attained his BD (1928) and ThM (1929) at Rochester Theological Seminary, and his PhD (1932) at Yale University. Davis served as pastor of Baptist churches in Maine and Ohio before becoming professor of theology at Crozer in 1938, where he remained for the rest of his career.

King began his studies with Davis during his second term at Crozer in 1949. It was in Davis' classroom that King was introduced to the work of theologians such as Walter Rauschenbusch, a proponent of the social gospel, and Edgar **Brightman**, an advocate of **personalism** and King's advisor at **Boston University**. King took more than one quarter of his courses at Crozer with Davis, who served as his academic advisor there. In a 1950 evaluation of King, Davis commented on his "exceptional intellectual ability" and predicted that King "should make an excellent minister or teacher" (*Papers* 1:334).

After King's graduation in 1951, the two men enjoyed a collegiality that endured until the end of Davis' life. While studying for his doctorate at Boston University, King fondly remembered Davis' classroom as being "saturated with a warm evangelical liberalism" (*Papers* 2:223). In 1953, King wrote to Davis "that theologically speaking, I find myself still holding to the liberal position." He admitted that he had become "more sympathetic towards the neo-orthodox position" because it provided "a necessary corrective for a liberalism that became all too shallow and too easily capitulated to modern culture" (*Papers* 2:223–224). In 1958, Davis sent a copy of his book *Existentialism and Theology* (1957) to King with the inscription: "With my warm compliments and with cherished memories of our days together as professor and student, friend and friend, on Crozer campus, and in my home" (*Papers* 4:528). Although King's theological beliefs continued to evolve after his years at Crozer, he remained committed to certain aspects of the liberal theology first introduced to him by Davis.

SOURCES
Courses at Crozer Theological Seminary, in *Papers* 1:48.
Davis, Crozer Theological Seminary Placement Committee: Confidential Evaluation of Martin Luther King, Jr., in *Papers* 1:334.
Davis to King, 17 October 1958, in *Papers* 4:512.
King, "The Place of Reason and Experience in Finding God," 13 September–23 November 1949, in *Papers* 1:230–236.
King to Davis, 1 December 1953, in *Papers* 2:223–224.
King to Davis, 8 November 1958, in *Papers* 4:528–529.
Smith and Zepp, *Search for the Beloved Community*, 1974.

DAVIS, OSSIE (1916–2005), AND DEE, RUBY (1922–)

Regarded by Martin Luther King as "close personal friends," Ossie Davis and Ruby Dee were among the celebrities involved in efforts to publicize and fund the work of King and the **Southern Christian Leadership Conference** (King, 11 April 1961).

Born 18 December 1917 in Cogdell, Georgia, Davis left the South in 1935 and hitchhiked to Washington, D.C. At Howard University Davis majored in English and studied drama with the intent of becoming a playwright. After he dropped out of college in 1939, he moved to Harlem to begin his career on the stage.

Born Ruby Ann Wallace in Cleveland, Ohio, Dee was raised in Harlem. She joined the American Negro Theater while attending Hunter College (BA, 1945). Dee made her Broadway debut in a 1943 play named "South Pacific" (different from the better-known musical of the same name). In 1946, she met up-and-coming actor Ossie Davis when he starred in the play, "Jeb," a show about a returning World War II veteran who faced down the Ku Klux Klan; Dee was an understudy in the play.

Dee and Davis married in 1948, and as a couple they often staged benefits for civil rights groups and labor unions. In 1957, Davis authored a dramatic rendering of the **Montgomery bus boycott**, called "Montgomery Footprints." His 1961 Broadway hit "Purlie Victorious" in which he starred with Dee dealt with racial issues. Dee starred in the Broadway hit, "A Raisin in the Sun," which won the 1959 Drama Critics Circle Award for best American play.

The couple first encountered King in 1956 at Adam Clayton **Powell**'s Abyssinian Baptist Church in Harlem. Davis noted King's "mellifluous, rolling baritone" and his commanding speaking style, "building one tower of rhetoric after another" (Davis and Dee, 250; 251). Although they did not share King's commitment to **nonviolence**, Davis and Dee enthusiastically embraced King as "a new leader of the black church and community" (Davis and Dee, 251). The following year, Dee, along with fellow entertainer Sammy **Davis**, Jr., attended the **Prayer Pilgrimage for Freedom**, organized by Harry **Belafonte** and others, at the Lincoln Memorial in Washington, D.C. Years later at the same site, she and Davis participated in the 1963 **March on Washington**.

Although Dee and Davis supported King, they questioned his call for nonviolence. In 1964 they privately reprimanded him for meeting with New York's Mayor Robert Wagner in the aftermath of police brutality following riots in Harlem, and for calling for restraint from the African American community. "The mayor needs you, Dr. King. But not nearly so much as we, your own people, do," they chided. "We implore that you will move at once to reassure that people and the leadership of the Harlem Community that their dilemma at this painful hour is much more important to you than the mayor's" (Davis and Dee, 28 July 1964). When King was assassinated in 1968, they traveled to Atlanta to attend his funeral.

SOURCES

Davis and Dee, *With Ossie and Ruby*, 1998.
Davis and Dee to King, 28 July 1964, BRP-DLC.
King, "Give Us the Ballot," Address delivered at the Prayer Pilgrimage for Freedom, 17 May 1957, in *Papers* 4:208–215.
King to Gordon R. Hitchens, 11 April 1961, MLKP-MBU.

DAVIS, SAMMY, JR. (1925–1990)

A popular African American entertainer, Sammy Davis, Jr., lent his fame and talents to several events in support of Martin Luther King and the **Southern Christian Leadership Conference** (SCLC).

Born in New York City to vaudeville performers Elvera Sanchez and Sammy Davis, Sr., Davis, Jr., was performing on stage at the age of three. Early in his career, Davis played the club circuit with the Will Mastin Trio, a vaudeville company. As a solo act, Davis found success in motion pictures, music, and on Broadway in the popular *Mr. Wonderful* (1956) and *Golden Boy* (1960s). Throughout the sixties, he was a prominent member of the acclaimed "Rat Pack."

On 27 January 1961, Davis, along with fellow Rat Packers Frank Sinatra and Dean Martin, joined other notable performers such as Harry **Belafonte**, Mahalia **Jackson**, and Tony Bennett at New York City's Carnegie Hall for a "Tribute to Martin Luther King, Jr." Advertised as a "tribute to the greatest civil rights leader to emerge in the South since the Civil War," the event raised over $50,000, a large portion of which was donated to the SCLC ("Tribute to King," 27 January 1961). Davis also performed at the King-headlined "Freedom Rally" in Los Angeles on 18 June 1961, and at the March on Montgomery in 1965. In a 1961 letter to Davis, King thanked the entertainer for his support and spoke of the changing role of black artists in the civil rights movement: "Not very long ago, it was customary for Negro artists to hold themselves aloof from the struggle for equality.... Today, greats like Harry Belafonte, Sidney

Poitier, Mahalia Jackson, and yourself, of course, are not content to merely identify with the struggle. They actively participate in it, as artists and as citizens, adding the weight of their enormous prestige and thus helping to move the struggle forward" (King, 28 March 1961).

Davis similarly admired King's work, and in an interview with Alex Haley in 1966, Davis proclaimed: "I would give him my good eye. That's what I think of Dr. King. He's one of the great men of our time. They should retire the Nobel Peace Prize with his name on it" (Davis, 487).

In 1968, Davis received the prestigious Spingarn Medal from the **National Association for the Advancement of Colored People** for his best-selling 1965 autobiography, *Yes I Can.* He was widely criticized in 1972 for supporting President Richard **Nixon** before withdrawing his support during the Watergate scandal. Davis continued to perform until his death from throat cancer in 1990.

SOURCES
Davis, *Sammy Davis, Jr., Reader,* ed. Early, 2001.
King to Davis, 28 March 1961, MLKP-MBU.
"Tribute to King," 27 January 1961, JWBP-DMBCH.

DEE, RUBY. *See* Davis, Ossie and Dee, Ruby.

DeWOLF, L. (LOTAN) HAROLD (1905–1986)

In a letter to DeWolf after completing his PhD, Martin Luther King, Jr., wrote to his former **dissertation** advisor: "Both your stimulating lectures and your profound ideas will remain with me so long as the cords of memory shall lengthen. I have discovered that both theologically and philosophically much of my thinking is DeWolfian" (King, 2 June 1955).

DeWolf was born in Columbus, Nebraska, and received his AB (1924) and STB (1926) from Nebraska Wesleyan University, and his PhD (1935) from **Boston University**. DeWolf served as a Methodist pastor in Nebraska and Massachusetts between 1926 and 1936, and taught in the Department of Philosophy at Boston University from 1934 until 1944, when he became professor of systematic theology in the School of Theology.

DeWolf became King's dissertation advisor at Boston University following the death of Edgar S. **Brightman**. In his 1955 reader's report, DeWolf concluded that King's work promised to be "an excellent and useful scholarly achievement" (*Papers* 2:334). By then, King had become minister at **Dexter Avenue Baptist Church** in Montgomery, Alabama. He expressed regrets to DeWolf that he would not be able to attend his own graduation due to financial concerns and his wife Coretta Scott **King**'s first pregnancy: "Without her presence, the whole experience would be somewhat incomplete to me" (King, 2 June 1955).

King remained in contact with DeWolf after graduation. In an August 1956 letter to King during the **Montgomery bus boycott**, DeWolf wrote: "Your letter is a renewing inspiration to me as has been the marvelous leadership which you have given to our people in the south land during these last months." He concluded his letter by writing, "May He bring to you victory for *all* the people, for which you are making such great sacrifices" (*Papers* 3:364).

DeWolf facilitated the 1964 donation of King's personal papers to Boston University, traveling to Atlanta to help pack the boxes for shipment. He left Boston University in 1965 to become dean and professor of systematic theology at Wesley Theological Seminary in Washington, D.C. He retired in 1972.

DeWolf's publications include *A Theology of the Living Church* (1953), *The Case for Theology in Liberal Perspective* (1959), *Responsible Freedom: Guidelines to Christian Action* (1971), and *Crime and Justice in America: A Paradox of Conscience* (1975).

Sources

DeWolf, First Reader's Report, in *Papers* 2:333–334.
Introduction, in *Papers* 2:5–6.
King to DeWolf, 2 June 1955, DABCC.

DEXTER AVENUE BAPTIST CHURCH (MONTGOMERY, ALABAMA)

In 1954, Martin Luther King began his first full-time pastorship at Dexter Avenue Baptist Church in Montgomery, Alabama. While at Dexter, King became president of the **Montgomery Improvement Association** (MIA) and led his congregation and the black community during the **Montgomery bus boycott**.

Founded in 1877, Dexter was originally called the Second Colored Baptist Church. Congregants met in a hall that had been used as a slave trader's pen until 1885, when the first worship service was held in the basement of the current structure. On Thanksgiving Day in 1889, the first service was held in the sanctuary, and the church was renamed Dexter Avenue Baptist Church. The church began its activist tradition under the leadership of King's predecessor, Vernon **Johns**, whose militant words and boldness kindled the spirit of resistance for blacks at Dexter and throughout Montgomery.

King accepted the call to pastor Dexter while completing his doctoral studies at **Boston University**. In his acceptance speech, delivered on 2 May 1954, King admitted to his new congregation: "I have no pretense to being a great preacher or even a profound scholar. I certainly have no pretence to infallibility—that is reserved for the height of the divine rather than the depth of the human." He continued: "I come to you with only the claim of being a servant of Christ, and a feeling of dependence on his grace for my leadership. I come with a feeling that I have been called to preach and to lead God's people" (*Papers* 6:166). Shortly after accepting this position, he proposed a list of recommendations for the revitalization of the church, which were accepted without changes or revisions. King insisted that every church member become a registered voter and a member of the **National Association for the Advancement of Colored People**. He also organized a social and political action committee, "for the purpose of keeping the congregation intelligently informed concerning the social, political, and economic situation" (*Papers* 2:290).

On 2 December 1955, King conducted a meeting in the basement of the Dexter Avenue Church, which resulted in the decision to launch the Montgomery bus boycott, and three days later the MIA was founded. As MIA president, King organized and helped direct the boycott from his office in the lower half of the sanctuary. He continued to serve as president of the MIA after the boycott, a commitment that, at times, compromised his efficacy as Dexter's pastor.

In November 1959, King resigned from Dexter and joined his father the following February as co-pastor at Atlanta's **Ebenezer Baptist Church** in order to more effectively lead the **Southern Christian Leadership Conference**, headquartered in that city. In his resignation to Dexter's congregation, King admitted that "a multiplicity of new responsibilities poured in upon me in almost staggering torrents. So I ended up futilely attempting to be four or five men in one" (*Papers* 5:329). In 1976, the city of Montgomery added the church, which was renamed the Dexter Avenue King Memorial Church in 1973, to a list of designated historic sites.

SOURCES
Evans and Alexander, *Dexter Avenue Baptist Church, 1877–1977*, 1978.
King, Acceptance Speech, 2 May 1954, in *Papers* 6:166–167.
King, Draft, Resignation from Dexter Avenue Baptist Church, 29 November 1959, in *Papers* 5:328–329.
King, "Recommendations to the Dexter Avenue Baptist Church for the Fiscal Year 1954–1955," 5 September 1954, in *Papers* 2:287–294.
SCLC Press Release, "Dr. King Leaves Montgomery for Atlanta," 1 December 1959, in *Papers* 5:330–331.

DIGGS, CHARLES C., JR. (1922–1998)

The first African American to be elected to Congress from Michigan, Charles C. Diggs made significant contributions to the struggle for civil rights through his business and political ties. In an April 1956 telegram to Martin Luther King, Diggs commended the **Montgomery Improvement Association** president for his "cherished leadership in the fight for equality," that he described as an "indestructible monument which will defy the ravages of time" (*Papers* 3:218).

Diggs was born on 2 December 1922, in Detroit. He attended the University of Michigan (1940 to 1942) and Fisk University (1942 to 1943) before joining the Army Air Corps in 1943. After his honorable discharge in 1945, he graduated from Wayne State University School of Mortuary Science (1945 to 1946) and began working with his family's business, the House of Diggs funeral home.

In his first year at the Detroit College of Law (1951 to 1952), Diggs was elected to the Michigan State Senate, where he served until 1954, when he won a seat in Congress with the slogan "Make Democracy Live." Diggs was passionate about civil rights for Africans and African Americans. In 1955, prompted by the murder of Emmett **Till** and the realization that Tallahatchie County in Mississippi did not have any African American registered voters, Diggs advocated slashing Mississippi's representation in Congress in proportion to its disenfranchised African American population. Diggs then made an unsuccessful request to President Dwight **Eisenhower** for a special session of Congress to address civil rights.

In 1956, Diggs raised nearly $4,500 from his radio program, House of Diggs, to aid the **Montgomery bus boycott**. He attended King's boycott violation trial in Montgomery and joined the **Southern Christian Leadership Conference** (SCLC) advisory board in 1957. As an elected official, Diggs was interested in the low rates of African American registered voters in the South, and shared his views on the problem with King. In March 1958, King expressed his deep gratitude to Diggs for his interest and "wise and judicial counsel" on African American voter registration. Three months after that letter, Diggs followed up with King and suggested that SCLC consider South Carolina as a focal point for registration activities (*Papers* 4:389).

As the chairman of the African Affairs Subcommittee of the House of Representative's Committee on Foreign Relations, Diggs strongly advocated ending **apartheid** in South Africa. In 1969, he became a founding member of the Congressional Black Caucus, a group of African American representatives and senators working to promote black interests.

In 1978, Diggs was convicted of illegally diverting office operating funds to pay his own personal expenses. Although his conviction did not prevent him from winning reelection, he resigned from his congressional seat in 1980. After serving seven months in prison, he went back to the family funeral business in Michigan, where he resided until his death in 1998.

SOURCES

Christopher, *America's Black Congressmen*, 1971.
Diggs to King, 20 April 1956, in *Papers* 3:218.
Introduction, in *Papers* 3:15.
King to Diggs, 25 March 1958, in *Papers* 4:389.

DISSERTATION OF MARTIN LUTHER KING, JR. (1955)

During his third year of doctoral work at **Boston University**, Martin Luther King wrote **Crozer Theological Seminary**'s George **Davis**, his former advisor, about his progress in graduate school. He disclosed that he had begun to research his dissertation and that the late Edgar **Brightman**, his first mentor at Boston, and his current dissertation advisor, L. Harold **DeWolf**, were both "quite impressed" with his course work. "So far, my Dissertation title is: 'A comparison of the conception of God in the thinking of Paul Tillich and Henry Nelson Wieman.' I am finding the study quite fascinating. If there are no basic interruptions, I hope to complete it by the end of the coming summer" (*Papers* 2:224). Davis commended King on selecting "an excellent dissertation topic" and expressed his confidence that King would "do a good piece of work with it" (*Papers* 2:225).

King passed his final doctoral examination in February 1954, and his dissertation outline was approved by Boston University's graduate school on 9 April, shortly before he accepted the call to pastor **Dexter Avenue Baptist Church**. King's letter of acceptance to Dexter's congregation specified that he be "granted an allowance of time to complete my work at Boston University," though he would be "able to fill the pulpit at least once or twice per month." He also asked that the church cover his expenses during the completion of his dissertation, "including traveling expenses" (*Papers* 2:260).

King chose to focus his dissertation research on **Tillich** and Wieman due to their status as influential religious thinkers and as representatives of divergent views on the nature of God. King's comparison of Tillich's and Wieman's concepts of God reflected his adherence to **personalism**, which proceeds from the belief that God possesses a personality and can therefore have a relationship with human beings. King's analysis of Tillich's and Wieman's theological concepts as "unsatisfactory" and "inadequate as philosophical and religious world-views" followed from his belief that God was a living force, "responsive to the deepest yearnings of the human heart; this God both evokes and answers prayer" (*Papers* 2:532; 533; 512). He found that both Wieman and Tillich rejected the conception of a personal God, which resulted in "a rejection of the rationality, goodness, and love of God in the full sense of the words. An impersonal 'being-itself' or 'creative event' cannot be rational or good, for these attributes are of personality" (*Papers* 2:506). In the end, King pointed out the two theologians' views of God are not "basically sound" because they "render real religious experience impossible" (*Papers* 2:532).

Recent scholarship by the Martin Luther King, Jr., Papers Project of the **King Institute** has revealed that as a student at Crozer and Boston, King frequently appropriated the words of other writers without proper attribution. Volumes I and II of *The Papers of Martin Luther King, Jr.*, have demonstrated that while his bibliographies contained the authors and books that he drew on in his own compositions, his papers often lacked the footnotes and quotation marks that identified his use of these sources in his text. His habit of plagiarizing others' work, intentionally or not, can be found in the various drafts of his dissertation. King borrowed from several secondary sources without proper citation, including a dissertation written by fellow Crozer student Jack Boozer for DeWolf three years earlier, and a review of Tillich's *Systematic Theology* written by one of King's former professors.

King's professors did not detect this pattern in his scholarship. After King submitted the first draft of his dissertation, DeWolf filed a report observing that he had sent his specific criticisms, "most of them formal or minor," to the candidate. DeWolf reminded King to submit an abstract of the dissertation "early" to allow proper time for revision and to clearly set forth his thesis statement (*Papers* 2:333). That said, DeWolf projected that the finished version would be an "excellent and useful scholarly achievement" (*Papers* 2:334). S. Paul Schilling, the dissertation's second reader, approved the draft as well.

King turned in the final version of his dissertation by the 15 April 1955 deadline, returning to Boston for his oral defense. Graduate faculty at Boston University voted to confer the PhD on King in May 1955; however, due to financial difficulties and Coretta Scott **King**'s pregnancy, he was unable to attend graduation.

SOURCES

Carson et al., "Martin Luther King, Jr., as Scholar: A Reexamination of His Theological Writings," *Journal of American History* 78 (June 1991): 93–105.

Davis to King, 7 December 1953, in *Papers* 2:225–226.

DeWolf, First Reader's Report, 26 February 1955, in *Papers* 2:333–334.

Introduction, in *Papers* 1:49–50.

Introduction, in *Papers* 2:22–26.

King, "A Comparison of the Conceptions of God in the Thinking of Paul Tillich and Henry Nelson Wieman," 15 April 1955, in *Papers* 2:339–544.

King to Davis, 1 December 1953, in *Papers* 2:223–224.

King to Dexter Avenue Baptist Church, 14 April 1954, in *Papers* 2:260.

King Papers Project, "The Student Papers of Martin Luther King, Jr.: A Summary Statement on Research," *Journal of American History* 78 (June 1991): 23–31.

Schilling, Second Reader's Report, 26 February 1955, in *Papers* 2:334–335.

DOBBS, JOHN WESLEY (1882–1961)

John Wesley Dobbs founded a number of civil rights organizations in Atlanta in the 1930s and 1940s. A King family friend, Dobbs heard Martin Luther King, Jr., preach one of his early sermons at **Ebenezer Baptist Church** and said, hugging him: "Young man, you're gonna deliver. You've got the stuff!" (Pomerantz, 161).

Born near Marietta, Georgia, Dobbs spent two years at **Morehouse College** before entering the U.S. Railway Mail Service where he worked for 32 years. Dobbs was elected Grand Master of the Most Worshipful Prince Hall Lodge of the Free and Accepted Masons, Jurisdiction of Georgia, in 1932, and was reelected yearly until his death. During the 1930s and 1940s, he founded the Georgia Voters League and the Atlanta Civic and Political League, and was co-founder of the Atlanta Negro Voters League.

The Martin Luther **King**, Sr., and Dobbs families became well acquainted when the King family moved to Boulevard Street, near the Dobbs' house, in 1941. June Dobbs Butts, one of Dobbs' daughters, recalled, "We kids formed a club comprised of the three King children, the two Burney first cousins, and ourselves—the two youngest of the six Dobbs sisters" (Butts, "Good memories").

In October 1960, when King was arrested for violating his probation by participating in a **sit-in**, Dobbs testified on his behalf at the trial in DeKalb County, prompting a letter of appreciation from King: "While I cannot at all boast of being worthy of the generous and gracious comments that you made concerning my character, I can assure you that such expressions of support and confidence are of inestimable value for the continuance of my humble efforts" (King, 1 December 1960).

Following Dobbs' death in August 1961, King delivered the invocation at his funeral, praising God "for giving to Atlanta, for giving to Georgia, for giving to the nations, for giving to America, such a noble life" (King, 2 September 1961). In 1994, Atlanta renamed Houston Street, where Dobbs had lived for 52 years, John Wesley Dobbs Avenue.

SOURCES

June Dobbs Butts, "Good memories of a great man's childhood," *Tennessean*, 18 January 1993.

King, Invocation delivered at funeral of John Wesley Dobbs at Big Bethel AME Church, 2 September 1961, JWD-ARC-LNT.

King to Dobbs, 1 December 1960, MLKP-MBU.

Pomerantz, *Where Peachtree Meets Sweet Auburn*, 1996.

"DRUM MAJOR INSTINCT" (1968)

On 4 February 1968, Martin Luther King, Jr., preached "The Drum Major Instinct" from the pulpit of **Ebenezer Baptist Church**. Ironically, two months before his **assassination** on 4 April 1968, he told his congregation what he would like said at his funeral: "I'd like for somebody to say that day that Martin Luther King, Jr., tried to love somebody" (King, "The Drum Major," 185). Excerpts were played at King's nationally televised funeral service, held at Ebenezer on 9 April 1968.

King's sermon was an adaptation of the 1952 homily "Drum-Major Instincts" by J. Wallace Hamilton, a well-known, liberal, white Methodist preacher. Both men tell the biblical story of James and John, who ask Jesus for the most prominent seats in heaven. At the core of their desire was a "drum major instinct—a desire to be out front, a desire to lead the parade" (King, "The Drum Major," 170–171). King warns his congregation that this desire for importance can lead to "snobbish exclusivism" and "tragic race prejudice": "Do you know that a lot of the race problem grows out of the drum major instinct? A need that some people have to feel superior ... and to feel that their white skin ordained them to be first" (King, "The Drum Major," 176; 178). Conversely, King preached that when Jesus responded to the request by James and

John, he did not rebuke them for their ambition, but taught that greatness comes from humble servitude. As King put it, Jesus "reordered priorities," and told his disciples to "Keep feeling the need for being first. But I want you to be first in love" (King, "The Drum Major," 181; 182).

King used Jesus' own life as an example of how the priority of love could provide greatness. In his biographical sketch of Jesus, King preached that Jesus owned nothing, and when public opinion turned against him he was called a "rabblerouser" and a "troublemaker" for "[practicing] civil disobedience" (King, "The Drum Major," 183). King notes that, although by worldly standards Jesus was a failure, no one else has "affected the life of man on this earth as much as that one solitary life" (King, "The Drum Major," 184).

King concluded the February 1968 sermon by imagining his own funeral. Urging the congregation not to dwell on his life's achievements, including his receipt of the **Nobel Peace Prize**, King asked to be remembered as one who "tried to give his life serving others" (King, "The Drum Major," 185). He implored his congregation to remember his attempts to feed the hungry, clothe the naked, and comfort prisoners. "Yes, if you want to say that I was a drum major, say that I was a drum major for justice," King intoned. "Say that I was a drum major for peace. I was a drum major for righteousness. And all of the other shallow things will not matter" (King, "The Drum Major," 185–186).

SOURCES

Branch, *At Canaan's Edge*, 2006.
Hamilton, "Drum-Major Instincts," in *Ride the Wild Horses!*, 1952.
King, "The Drum Major Instinct," in *A Knock at Midnight*, ed. Carson and Holloran, 1998.

DURR, VIRGINIA FOSTER (1904–1999)

On 1 December 1955, Virginia Durr and her husband Clifford went with E. D. **Nixon** to bail Rosa **Parks** out of jail for refusing to give up her seat on a Montgomery, Alabama, bus. Durr later wrote, "That was a terrible sight to me to see this gentle, lovely, sweet woman, whom I knew and was so fond of, being brought down by a matron" (Durr, 280). Parks' arrest prompted the **Montgomery bus boycott** and thrust Martin Luther King into a leadership role.

Daughter of Sterling J. and Anne Patterson Foster of Birmingham, Alabama, Durr attended Wellesley College before she married Clifford Durr of Montgomery in 1926. The Durrs moved to Washington, D.C., and Clifford worked with New Deal programs while Virginia worked to abolish the poll tax before returning to Montgomery in the early 1950s. Virginia Durr was a founding member of the Southern Conference on Human Welfare in 1938, and was present at the organization's meeting in Birmingham when Eleanor **Roosevelt** refused to adhere to the segregated seating in the auditorium. In 1954, the Durrs were accused of being Communist sympathizers and were called to testify before James O. Eastland's Senate International Securities Subcommittee.

In July 1955, Durr arranged a scholarship for Rosa Parks to attend an integration workshop at the **Highlander Folk School**, an experience that inspired Parks to challenge the segregated bus system. After Parks' arrest, the Durrs and Nixon urged her to file a test case against Montgomery's segregation policies.

Throughout the bus boycott, Virginia Durr remained an avid supporter, highlighting the importance of white involvement in the protest. She later recalled that during the year-long boycott, white women in Montgomery would offer rides to the black women who worked in their homes, but "a vast deceit went on. Everybody knew everybody else was lying, but to save face, they had to lie. The black women had to say they weren't taking any part in the boycott. The white women had to say that their maids didn't take any part in the boycott" (Durr, 283).

In February 1959, Coretta and Martin Luther King sent a postcard to Clifford and Virginia from **India**. In Durr's autobiography, she recalled that when King called for people from all over the country to come for the **Selma to Montgomery March** in March 1965, her home in Montgomery filled up with people such as C. Vann Woodward, Sterling professor at Yale; Carl **Braden**; and Lou Pollak, dean of the Yale Law School. She remembered, "I spent all my time making coffee and frying bacon and eggs for them" (Durr, 325). Throughout her life Virginia Durr remained involved with numerous civil and human rights organizations, including the Women's International League for Peace and Freedom.

SOURCES

Durr, *Outside the Magic Circle*, 1985.
Gray, *Bus Ride to Justice*, 1995.
Introduction, in *Papers* 3:3.
Rosenberg and Foner, eds., *Divided Lives*, 1992.

EBENEZER BAPTIST CHURCH (ATLANTA, GEORGIA)

In the fall of 1947, Martin Luther King delivered his first sermon at the pulpit of Ebenezer Baptist Church in Atlanta. Ebenezer's congregation voted to license King as a minister soon afterward, and he was ordained in February 1948. King went on to serve as Ebenezer's associate minister during his breaks from **Crozer Theological Seminary** and from his doctoral studies at **Boston University** School of Theology through early 1954. He returned as co-pastor with his father, Martin Luther **King**, Sr., serving from 1960 until his **assassination** in 1968.

The church was founded in 1886 by its first minister, John Andrew Parker. In 1894 Alfred Daniel **Williams**, King, Jr.'s maternal grandfather, became Ebenezer's second pastor. Under Williams the church grew from 13 members to nearly 750 members by 1913. Williams moved the church twice before purchasing a lot on the corner of Auburn Avenue and Jackson Street and announced plans to raise $25,000 for a new building that would include an auditorium and gallery seating for 1,250 people. In March 1914 the Ebenezer congregation celebrated the groundbreaking for its new building. After the death of Williams in 1931, King, Sr., who had married Williams' daughter Alberta in 1926, became pastor.

With King, Sr., as pastor and his wife, Alberta Williams **King**, serving as musical director, the King family spent much of their time at Ebenezer. King, Jr., later described how his earliest relationships were formed at church: "My best friends were in Sunday School, and it was the Sunday School that helped me to build the capacity for getting along with people" (*Papers* 1:359). While in seminary, King often preached at Ebenezer. He delivered some of his most enduring sermons for the first time at Ebenezer, including "The Dimensions of a Complete Life," "What Is Man?" and "Loving Your Enemies."

After King accepted the pastorate at **Dexter Avenue Baptist Church** in Montgomery, members of Ebenezer's congregation attended his October 1954 installation service, prompting King to express his gratitude: "Your prayers and words of encouragement have meant a great deal to me in my ministry; and you can never know what your presence in such large numbers meant to me at the beginning of my pastorate. I want you to know Ebenezer, that I feel greatly indebted to you; and that whatever success I might achieve in my life's work you will have helped to make it possible" (*Papers* 2:314).

In November 1959, King accepted Ebenezer's call to join his father as co-pastor, a move that brought him closer to the headquarters of the **Southern Christian Leadership Conference**. His first sermon as co-pastor at Ebenezer was "The Three Dimensions of a Complete Life." After King's assassination in 1968, his brother, A. D. Williams **King**, was installed as Ebenezer's co-pastor. King, Sr., continued as pastor until 1975, and Coretta Scott **King** continued to attend services at Ebenezer until her death.

SOURCES

Introduction, in *Papers* 1:6–7, 13, 25–26, 28.

King, "An Autobiography of Religious Development," 12 September–22 November 1950, in *Papers* 1:359–363.

King to The Ebenezer Baptist Church Members, 6 November 1954, in *Papers* 2:313–314.

King, Sr., with Riley, *Daddy King*, 1980.

Lillian D. Watkins, "Certification of Minister's License for Martin Luther King, Jr.," 4 February 1958, in *Papers* 1:150.

EISENHOWER, DWIGHT DAVID (1890–1969)

As the 34th president of the United States, Dwight Eisenhower took office one year before the Supreme Court's historic 1954 ruling in **Brown v. Board of Education** and served during the rise of the modern civil rights movement. Unenthusiastic about the Court's decision, Eisenhower nonetheless used military force to counter segregationists during the **Little Rock school desegregation** crisis of 1957. Martin Luther King later corresponded with Eisenhower regarding school desegregation.

Civil rights leaders meet with President Eisenhower on 23 June 1958. Pictured from left to right: Lester Granger, King, E. Frederic Morrow, Dwight D. Eisenhower, A. Philip Randolph, William Rogers, Rocco Siciliano, Roy Wilkins. Courtesy of the National Archives.

Eisenhower was born in Texas and raised in Abilene, Kansas. He was educated at West Point and began his Army career in 1915. Eisenhower held numerous posts in the U.S. Army until his retirement in 1948, including Supreme Commander of Allied Expeditionary Forces in World War II, and Army Chief of Staff. While serving as Supreme Commander of NATO forces in 1950, Eisenhower was persuaded by the Republican Party to run for president and, in 1952, he won the presidency with Richard **Nixon** as his vice presidential running mate.

In 1954, the Supreme Court ruled in *Brown v. Board of Education* that segregation in education was unconstitutional. Civil rights supporters looked to Eisenhower to enforce compliance with the *Brown* decision, but he avoided endorsing the Supreme Court's decision, a silence that encouraged resistance to school desegregation.

In 1957, a showdown between state and federal officials occurred when nine black students tried to integrate Little Rock, Arkansas' Central High School. As a result of violent opposition to the integration of Central, and Orval Faubus, the state governor's unwillingness to enforce the *Brown* decision, Eisenhower federalized the Arkansas National Guard to protect the students. Although Eisenhower did not agree with court mandated integration, he saw that he had a constitutional obligation to uphold the Supreme Court's ruling. King praised the president for restoring "law and order" in Little Rock: "You should know that the overwhelming majority of southerners, Negro and white stand firmly behind your resolute action" (*Papers* 4:278).

King wrote Eisenhower again in 1958, in light of "continued violence in the South and the dreadful prospect that some areas may close schools rather than integrate in September," and asked that Eisenhower "grant an immediate conference to Negro leaders in Washington, D.C." (*Papers* 4:415). Although Eisenhower had refused previous invitations, he agreed to a 23 June meeting at the White House with King, Lester **Granger** of the **National Urban League**, Roy **Wilkins** of the **National Association for the Advancement of Colored People**, and A. Philip **Randolph** of the Brotherhood of Sleeping Car Porters. Although they praised Eisenhower's actions in Little Rock, the leaders also sought "a planned and integral approach" to the problems of resistance to school integration, black disenfranchisement, and a response by the Justice Department to the bombings and "murderous brutality directed at Negro citizens." They also proposed a White House conference on race relations. Following the meeting, Randolph stated that he and the other leaders were "greatly impressed by [Eisenhower's] general attitude of concern"; however, reporter Louis Lautier observed that King and the other leaders demonstrated an "about face attitude" toward the president after criticizing his call for "patience and forbearance" in racial matters (*Papers* 4:426n; 414n). King renewed his request for a White House conference on racial matters in an October 1958 telegram, but such a gathering did not occur.

Despite his personal opposition to legislating racial equality, Eisenhower signed two civil rights bills in 1957 and 1960. King found the 1957 bill weak in some areas, but felt that it was "far better than no bill at all," and urged the President not to veto it (*Papers* 4:263). After serving two terms in office, Eisenhower retired in 1961 to a farm outside Gettysburg, Pennsylvania. He died on 28 March 1969.

SOURCES

Introduction, in *Papers* 4:26–29.

King, Granger, Wilkins, and Randolph, "Statement to the President of the United States," in *Papers* 4:426–429.

King to Eisenhower, 29 May 1958, in *Papers* 4:414–415.
King to Eisenhower, 25 September 1957, in *Papers* 4:278.
King to Eisenhower, 13 October 1958, in *Papers* 4:509.
King to Nixon, 30 August 1957, in *Papers* 4:262–264.
King to Viva O. Sloan, 1 October 1956, in *Papers* 3:383–384.

EMANCIPATION PROCLAMATION (1863)

Decreed by President Abraham Lincoln on 1 January 1863, the Emancipation Proclamation declared slaves in all confederate states then at war with the Union "forever free" and made them eligible for paid military service in the Union Army.

In 1961 and 1962 Martin Luther King made multiple appeals to President John F. **Kennedy** to issue a second Emancipation Proclamation to outlaw segregation in commemoration of the centennial of the original document. A December 1961 telegram to Kennedy called for "a second Emancipation Proclamation to free all Negroes from second class citizenship" in line with the "defense of democratic principles and practices here" in the United States (King, 18 December 1961). On 17 May 1962, the sixth anniversary of *Brown v. Board of Education*, King sent Kennedy a 75-page appeal to request a "national rededication to the principles of the Emancipation Proclamation and for an executive order prohibiting segregation" (King, 17 May 1962). Clarence B. **Jones**, King's legal advisor, recommended that the **Southern Christian Leadership Conference** send out copies of this appeal to all the major national organizations before 22 September 1962, the 100th anniversary of the earlier issuance of the Emancipation Proclamation as a military order.

At the 28 August 1963 **March on Washington for Jobs and Freedom**, as King stood on the steps of the Lincoln Memorial to deliver his **"I Have a Dream"** speech, he noted that the Emancipation Proclamation gave hope to black slaves. The following year Congress passed the **Civil Rights Act of 1964** as a concrete step towards fulfilling the promise of the Emancipation Proclamation.

SOURCES

King, An appeal to the Honorable John F. Kennedy, 17 May 1962, BRP-DLC.
King, "I Have a Dream," in *A Call to Conscience*, ed. Carson and Shepard, 2001.
King, "The Negro and the Constitution," May 1944, in *Papers* 1:108–111.
King to Kennedy, 18 December 1961, WHCF-MWalK.

EVERS, MEDGAR WILEY (1925–1963)

As field secretary for the **National Association for the Advancement of Colored People** (NAACP) in Mississippi from 1954 until his death in 1963, Medgar Evers played a pivotal role in the civil rights organization's expansion in the South. Although the NAACP leadership sought to challenge segregation in the courts, Evers' interest in direct action methods led him to maintain contact with Martin Luther King and to briefly join the **Southern Christian Leadership Conference** (SCLC) in 1957.

The son of a farmer and domestic worker, Evers was born 2 July 1925, in Decatur, Mississippi. As a child, Evers walked three miles to school each day and was an enthusiastic student who loved to read. In high school he began establishing NAACP branches throughout Mississippi. Drafted into the Army in 1943, Evers' military experience with segregation in the service heightened his commitment to the civil rights struggle.

Upon graduating from Alcorn Agricultural & Mechanical College in 1952, Evers and his wife, Myrlie, moved to Mound Bayou in northwest Mississippi, where he worked for an insurance company and organized local NAACP chapters. After the 1954 **Brown v. Board of Education** decision, Evers sought admission to the University of Mississippi Law School. He was unsuccessful but would later help James **Meredith** gain admittance to "Ole Miss" by putting him in contact with NAACP lawyers.

In December 1954, Evers became the NAACP's first field secretary in Mississippi and soon afterward began receiving threatening phone calls and other types of harassment. Following the 1955 lynching of Emmett **Till** in LeFlore County, Mississippi, Evers and other NAACP officials publicized the crime, sought witnesses, and helped witnesses leave Mississippi after testifying against Till's murderers.

Seeking "to bring first-class citizenship to [the South] as hurriedly as possible," Evers attended one of the first meetings of SCLC in February 1957 and was elected assistant secretary of the organization (Evers, 11 March 1957). When Evers notified NAACP director Roy **Wilkins** of his involvement with SCLC, Wilkins advised against participating in another civil rights group. Evers sent King his letter of resignation in August of that year, stating that he was "highly honored to have had the opportunity to serve" SCLC (*Papers* 4:259). King communicated his regret to Evers, writing: "I certainly appreciate your devotion to the cause of justice and if there is anything that I can do to assist you in your great work please feel free to call on me" (King, 28 August 1957).

In 1958, when SCLC sought to establish a base for activity in Jackson, Mississippi, Evers reported to NAACP officials that he "discouraged" this move. "It will be our design through the NAACP and the Progressive Voters League, of which our leaders are in key positions, to control the present state of affairs," he explained (Evers, 24 January 1958).

In the spring of 1963, Evers announced that blacks in Jackson would begin mass demonstrations and rallies to protest Jackson Mayor Alan Thompson's refusal to appoint a biracial committee to examine Jackson's racial problems. "We are prepared to demonstrate until we get our rights!" Evers proclaimed. "Nobody here is afraid anymore" ("NAACP Moves on Jackson").

On 12 June 1963, Evers was assassinated by a rifle shot in the back while walking up his driveway. That day King told the media: "The brutal murder of Medgar Evers came as shocking and tragic news to all people of good will" (King, 12 June 1963). Evers' funeral was held in Jackson, and his burial at Arlington National Cemetery attracted prominent civil rights leaders from around the nation, including King and Wilkins. Evers was posthumously awarded the NAACP's highest honor, the Spingarn Medal, later in the year. In 1994 Byron de la Beckwith was convicted of Evers' murder. Myrlie Evers continued her husband's activism, serving as the NAACP's first female chairperson from 1995 until 1998.

SOURCES

Evers, *The Autobiography of Medgar Evers*, ed. Evers-Williams and Marable, 2006.
Evers and Szanton, *Have No Fear*, 1997.
Evers to King, 20 August 1957, in *Papers* 4:259.

EVERS, MEDGAR WILEY (1925–1963)

Evers to Ruby Hurley, 24 January 1958, NAACPP-DLC.
Evers to Wilkins, 11 March 1957, NAACPP-DLC.
Myrlie Evers, "He Said He Wouldn't Mind Dying If …," *Life* (28 June 1963): 35–36.
Hampton and Fayer, with Flynn, *Voices of Freedom*, 1990.
King, Statement on the murder of Medgar Wiley Evers, 12 June 1963, MLKJP-GAMK.
King to Evers, 28 August 1957, DABCC.
"NAACP Moves on Jackson, Mississippi," *New York Amsterdam News*, 1 June 1963.

FAMILY HISTORY OF MARTIN LUTHER KING, JR.

Even after becoming a civil rights leader and a **Nobel Peace Prize** winner, in the "quiet recesses" of his heart Martin Luther King, Jr., remained a Baptist preacher. "This is my being and my heritage," he once explained, "for I am also the son of a Baptist preacher, the grandson of a Baptist preacher and the great-grandson of a Baptist preacher" (King, "The Un-Christian Christian"). The tightly knit extended family in which King, Jr., was raised had a profound influence on his worldview. "It is quite easy for me to think of a God of love mainly because I grew up in a family where love was central and where lovely relationships were ever present" (*Papers* 1:360).

King, Jr.'s maternal great-grandfather, Willis Williams, who was born in 1810, was described as "an old slavery time preacher" and an "exhorter" (*Papers* 1:1). In 1846, when Willis joined Shiloh Baptist Church in Greene County, Georgia, its congregation numbered 50 white and 28 black members, with African Americans actively participating in church affairs and serving on church committees. In 1855 nearly a hundred blacks joined the congregation, including 15-year-old Lucrecia (or Creecy) Daniel. She and Willis were married in the late 1850s or early 1860s, and she bore him five children, including Adam Daniel (A. D.) **Williams**, King, Jr.'s grandfather. The family left Shiloh Baptist Church when it, like other southern congregations, divided along racial lines at the end of the Civil War.

Born in Atlanta in April 1873, Jennie Celeste Parks, King, Jr.'s maternal grandmother, was one of thirteen children. Her father, William Parks, supported his family through work as a carpenter. At age 15, Jennie Parks began taking classes at Spelman Seminary, but she left in 1892 without graduating. Married to A. D. Williams on 29 October 1899, she was a deeply pious woman who always kept a Bible nearby and was "a model wife for a minister" (*Papers* 1:7). On 13 September 1903, she gave birth at home to their only surviving child, Alberta Christine **Williams**, the mother of King, Jr., During the early years of the century, the family lived in several houses in the Auburn Avenue area, which was then home to both whites and blacks. The Williamses transformed nearby **Ebenezer Baptist Church** from a struggling congregation without a building in the 1890s into one of black Atlanta's most prominent institutions.

As "First Lady" of Ebenezer, Jennie Williams was involved in most aspects of church governance and headed the Missionary Society for many years. She represented the church in local Baptist organizations and the Woman's Convention, an auxiliary to the **National Baptist Convention**. Known as "Mama" to her grandchildren, she was particularly protective of her first grandson and "could never bear to see him cry" (*Papers* 1:29). Referring to her as "saintly," King, Jr., acknowledged her considerable impact on his childhood. "She was very dear to each of us, but especially to me," he later wrote. "I sometimes think that I was [her] favorite grandchild. I can remember very vividly how she spent many evenings telling us interesting stories" (*Papers* 1:359).

King, Jr.'s paternal ancestors can also be traced back to slavery. King, Jr.'s paternal great-grandfather Jim Long (born ca. 1842) had been used by his owner to breed slaves, conceiving children with several women. Census records show that after the Civil War, Long maintained at least two families in Henry County, Georgia, where he also registered to vote during Reconstruction. Long's relationship with Jane Linsey (born 1855) produced a daughter, Delia, in 1875, who married James Albert King (born 1864) in 1895. Like many families, the Kings were poor; the county tax lists record little personal property for James King.

The family of Delia and James King included nine children. Michael King (who later changed his name to Martin Luther King, Sr.), was born on 19 December 1897, the second child and first son. During his childhood, King, Sr., later recalled, "My mother had babies, worked the fields, and often went during the winter to wash and iron in the homes of whites around town" (*Papers* 1:21). His father's life followed the unchanging seasonal labors of a sharecropper; the rewards were paltry, made even more so by the inability of powerless blacks to prevent cheating by white landlords.

For Delia King and her children, the rituals of the black church offered relief from this life of hardship. Although the family occasionally attended a local Methodist church as well as the Baptist church, they established enduring ties with Floyd Chapel Baptist Church in Stockbridge. Its Sunday services, Wednesday prayer meetings, baptisms, weddings, funerals, and special Christmas and Easter services offered welcome diversions. King, Sr., wrote. "Papa was not religious, and although I don't think he was very enthusiastic about my attending so many church affairs, he never interfered with Mama's taking me" (*Papers* 1:21). Unable to find solace in religion, James King became increasingly cynical in the face of the economic and racial hardships of his life. His family became targets of his angry outbursts, fueled by alcoholism.

On Thanksgiving Day 1926, Martin Luther King, Sr., married Alberta Williams, who gave birth to Willie Christine King (**Farris**) in 1927, Martin Luther King, Jr., in 1929, and Alfred Daniel **King** in 1930. The first 12 years of King's childhood were spent in the home at 501 Auburn Avenue that his parents shared with his maternal grandparents, A. D. and Jennie Celeste Williams. Martin Luther King, Sr., succeeded his father-in-law as Ebenezer's pastor, and Alberta Williams King followed her mother as a powerful presence in Ebenezer's affairs.

SOURCES

Introduction, in *Papers* 1:1–57.
King, "An Autobiography of Religious Development," in *Papers* 1:359–363.
King, "The Un-Christian Christian," *Ebony* 20 (August 1965): 77–80.

FARMER, JAMES (1920–1999)

As co-founder of the **Congress of Racial Equality** (CORE), James Farmer was one of the major leaders of the African American freedom struggle. In a 1997 interview, Farmer said: "I don't see any future for the nation without integration. Our lives are intertwined, our work is intertwined, our education is intertwined" (Smith, "Civil Rights Leader"). Farmer credited Martin Luther King and the **Montgomery bus boycott** with educating the public on nonviolent tactics: "No longer did we have to explain nonviolence to people. Thanks to Martin Luther King, it was a household word" (Farmer, 188).

Farmer was born on 12 January 1920, in Marshall, Texas, where his father taught theology at all-black Wiley College. When Farmer was six months old, his family moved to Holly Springs, Mississippi. Throughout his life, Farmer recounted the story of his mother having to explain why she couldn't buy him a soft drink at a drugstore, an experience he said inspired him at an early age to fight injustice. After graduating from Wiley College in 1938, he enrolled in the Howard University School of Divinity, where he first encountered the teachings of the Indian independence leader, Mohandas K. **Gandhi**. Upon earning his BD in 1941, he declined ordination as a Methodist minister because "I did not feel I could preach the gospel in a segregated church" (Shepard, "A Life on the Front Lines"). Farmer was granted conscientious objector status during World War II and became race relations secretary for the **Fellowship of Reconciliation**, a pacifist organization.

A year later, in 1942, Farmer co-founded CORE with an interracial group of University of Chicago students. In the 1940s CORE pioneered the strategies of nonviolent direct action, including the tactics of **sit-ins**, jail-ins, and **Freedom Rides** later used in the civil rights movement during the 1960s. After a brief stint at the **National Association for the Advancement of Colored People** in the late 1950s, Farmer became the first national director of CORE in 1961. That same year, Farmer mobilized CORE to conduct interracial Freedom Rides designed to test the Supreme Court ruling on interstate bus transportation in the South. The group had organized a similar test in 1947, called the "Journey of Reconciliation," which ended in the riders' arrests.

The 1961 freedom riders faced violent resistance along their journey. Upon reaching Montgomery, Alabama, Farmer encountered a rioting mob that threatened to break into Ralph **Abernathy**'s First Baptist Church where freedom riders and other protesters were meeting with King, who was present to offer support. When King tried to mobilize help, U.S. Attorney General Robert **Kennedy** asked Farmer to agree to a cooling-off period and to suspend the integrated rides. Farmer replied: "Please tell the attorney general that we have been cooling for 350 years. If we cool off any more, we will be in a deep freeze. The Freedom Ride will go on" (Farmer, 206). With the protection of U.S. marshals and the Alabama National Guard, the riders continued their journey. Arrested in Jackson, Mississippi, in the act of integrating a restaurant at the bus terminal, Farmer and the riders refused to make bond and spent 40 days at the Parchman State Penitentiary. Two years later, Farmer's imprisonment in Plaquemine, Louisiana, for protesting police brutality prevented him from speaking at the 1963 **March on Washington for Jobs and Freedom**, an event co-sponsored by CORE.

As the influence of **black nationalism** took hold of CORE, Farmer stepped down as National Director in 1966, and cut all ties to the organization 10 years later. After being defeated by Democratic candidate Shirley Chisholm in the 1968 congressional race for New York's 12th district, he served in Richard **Nixon**'s administration in what was then the Department of Health, Education, and Welfare, where he was charged with increasing the role of minorities in the agency.

In 1980 Farmer moved to Fredericksburg, Virginia, where he wrote his autobiography, *Lay Bare the Heart* (1985) and taught at Mary Washington College. President Bill Clinton awarded Farmer the Presidential Medal of Freedom, the nation's highest civilian honor, in 1998. He died the following year at age 79.

SOURCES

Farmer, *Lay Bare the Heart*, 1985.

Scott Shepard, "A Life on the Front Lines: Ending Racism Has Been an Epic Battle for James Farmer," *Atlanta Journal-Constitution*, 6 April 1997.

J. Y. Smith, "Civil Rights Leader James Farmer Dies," *Washington Post*, 10 July 1999.

FARRIS, (WILLIE) CHRISTINE KING (1927–)

In a 1986 article in *Ebony* magazine, Christine King Farris described her brother Martin Luther King as "no saint, ordained as such at birth. Instead, he was an average and ordinary man, called by a God, in whom he had deep and abiding faith, to perform extraordinary deeds." Farris added that "the best way each of us can celebrate Martin's life" is to "join in the struggle for freedom, peace and justice" (Farris, "Young Martin").

King with his sister, Christine, in 1930. Courtesy of Christine King Farris.

Born on 11 September 1927, in Atlanta, Georgia, Christine was the first child of Martin Luther **King**, Sr., and Alberta Williams **King**. Her brother Martin was born in 1929, and her younger brother, Alfred Daniel **King**, in 1930. The three siblings spent their early years in the home of their grandparents, A. D. **Williams**, who died in 1931, and Jennie Celeste Williams, who died a decade later. In her *Ebony* article, Christine recounted that Martin "got into his share of boyhood trouble" and found any excuse imaginable to get out of completing household chores. Christine's decision to step forward during a church revival meeting became the stimulus for a decisive moment in her younger brother's religious life. "My sister was the first one to join the church that morning," Martin King would later write, "and after seeing her join I decided that I would not let her get ahead of me, so I was the next" (*Papers* 1:361).

Farris later traced her love of reading to the hours her aunt, Ida Worthem, spent reading to her and her brothers. This "laid the foundation" for her future as a reading professor (Farris, "Young Martin"). Farris received her BA in economics from Spelman College in 1948 on the same day

King received his BA in sociology from **Morehouse College**. She then attended Columbia University Teacher's College to pursue a master's degree in the social foundations of education (1950) and a master's in special education (1958). Farris planned to teach, but her initial applications with the Atlanta Board of Education were repeatedly denied. Her father recalled that she was qualified, but the board was angry because he had for 11 years struggled to equalize teacher salaries, "forcing white teachers to live on the same rates of pay blacks worked for" (King, Sr., 135). After King, Sr., called the mayor to intervene, Christine was welcomed to her first teaching position at W. H. Crogman Elementary School. She went on to become Associate Professor of Education at Spelman College followed by an appointment as an adjunct professor at Morehouse College and Atlanta University.

Farris married Isaac Newton Farris on 19 August 1960, and they had two children—Isaac Newton Farris, Jr., and Angela Christine Farris. In addition to focusing on her family and career, Farris was, for many years, vice chair and treasurer of the **King Center**. Farris has been active for several years in the International Reading Association and various church and civic organizations, including the **National Association for the Advancement of Colored People** and the **Southern Christian Leadership Conference**.

SOURCES

Farris, Willie Christine King, "The Young Martin: From Childhood Through College," *Ebony*, January 1986.

Farris, *My Brother Martin*, 2003.

Introduction, in *Papers* 1:26.

King, "An Autobiography of Religious Development," 12 September–22 November 1950, in *Papers* 1:359–363.

King, Sr., with Riley, *Daddy King*, 1980.

FAUNTROY, WALTER E. (1933–)

While attending Virginia Union University in 1953, Walter Fauntroy was asked by Wyatt Tee **Walker** to make a room available for Martin Luther King, who was traveling from Atlanta to Boston to attend graduate school. Several years after their meeting, Fauntroy recalled the "lasting effect" of King's visit, particularly the impact of two sermons that King had shared with him. "When first I heard your name mentioned in connection with the Montgomery bus boycott, I thanked God that He had placed in that crisis the man with the message for our time," Fauntroy wrote to King in June 1960 (*Papers* 5:470).

Fauntroy was born on 6 February 1933, in Washington, D.C. He graduated from Virginia Union University in 1955 and received a BD from Yale Divinity School in 1958. The following year, he was called to the pulpit of New Bethel Baptist Church in Washington, D.C.

In 1960, Fauntroy contacted King in hopes of linking his organizing efforts in Washington, D.C., with those of the **Southern Christian Leadership Conference** (SCLC). King welcomed an affiliation with Fauntroy's group and indicated that Fauntroy might serve "a most meaningful role" in SCLC (King, 18 June 1960). The following year, King appointed Fauntroy to the role of regional representative of SCLC. By 1964, Fauntroy was involved in many SCLC-sponsored events, including the **March**

on Washington for Jobs and Freedom, where he helped coordinate medical, health, and sanitation facilities. About three months after the March on Washington, Fauntroy represented SCLC by carrying the torch from the eternal flame at John F. **Kennedy**'s grave to ceremonies presided over by President Lyndon B. **Johnson** at the Lincoln Memorial. Fauntroy's loyalty to SCLC was rewarded in 1964 when King named him director of the new SCLC bureau established in Washington, D.C. Fauntroy's main responsibilities as director included serving as King's spokesman on Capitol Hill, keeping SCLC abreast of matters pertaining to the civil rights movement, and acting as liaison between SCLC and various departments of the federal government. In addition to his work with SCLC, Fauntroy was appointed vice-chairman of D.C.'s first city council by President Johnson in 1967.

After King's **assassination** in April 1968, Fauntroy served as national director of the **Poor People's Campaign**, eventually leaving SCLC in 1971. From 1971 to 1990 he was D.C.'s representative in Congress. During his tenure, he was a founding member of the Congressional Black Caucus and served as the committee's chairman from 1981 to 1983. In 1984, he was arrested after conducting a **sit-in** at the South African embassy in protest of the U.S. policy against **apartheid**. In 1990, after a failed bid for mayor of Washington, D.C., Fauntroy returned to preaching at New Bethel.

SOURCES

"Capital's House Delegate Held in Embassy Sit-In," *New York Times*, 22 November 1984.

Fauntroy, Interview by King Papers Project staff, 6 March 2002.

Fauntroy to King, 10 June 1960, in *Papers* 5:469–470.

King to Fauntroy, 18 June 1960, MLKP-MBU.

SCLC, "SCLC Sets Up New Washington Bureau; Names Walter E. Fauntroy as Director," *Newsletter*, February 1964.

FBI. *See* Federal Bureau of Investigation.

FEDERAL BUREAU OF INVESTIGATION (FBI)

The U.S. Federal Bureau of Investigation (FBI) began monitoring Martin Luther King, Jr., in December 1955, during his involvement with the **Montgomery bus boycott**, and engaged in covert operations against him throughout the 1960s. FBI director J. Edgar Hoover was personally hostile toward King, believing that the civil rights leader was influenced by Communists. This animosity increased after April 1964, when King called the FBI "completely ineffectual in resolving the continued mayhem and brutality inflicted upon the Negro in the deep South" (King, 23 April 1964). Under the FBI's domestic counterintelligence program (COINTELPRO) King was subjected to various kinds of FBI surveillance that produced alleged evidence of extramarital affairs, though no evidence of Communist influence.

The FBI was created in 1909 as the Justice Department's unit to investigate federal crimes. Hoover became FBI director in 1924 and served until his death in 1972. Throughout the 1930s the FBI's role expanded when President Franklin D. Roosevelt asked the FBI to research "subversives" in the United States, and Congress passed a series of laws increasing the types of federal crimes falling under the FBI's jurisdiction. During World War II, the FBI was further authorized to investigate threats to national security. This loosely defined mission formed the heading under which the FBI began to investigate the civil rights movement.

The FBI initially monitored King under its Racial Matters Program, which focused on individuals and organizations involved in racial politics. Although the FBI raised concerns as early as March 1956, that King was associating with card-carrying members of the Communist Party, King's alleged ties with communism did not become the focus of FBI investigations under the existing Communist Infiltration Program (COMINFIL), designed to investigate groups and individuals subject to Communist infiltration, until 1962. In February 1962, Hoover told Attorney General Robert **Kennedy** that Stanley **Levison**, one of King's closest advisors, was "a secret member of the Communist Party" (Hoover, 14 February 1962). In the following months, Hoover deployed agents to find subversive material on King, and Robert Kennedy authorized wiretaps on King's home and **Southern Christian Leadership Conference** (SCLC) offices in October 1963.

Hoover responded to King's criticisms of the Bureau's performance in civil rights cases by announcing at a press conference in November 1964, that King was the "most notorious liar in the country" (Herbers, "Dr. King Rebuts Hoover"). Surprised by the accusation, King replied that he could only have sympathy for Hoover as he must be "under extreme pressure" to make such a statement (Herbers, "Dr. King Rebuts Hoover"). King asked an intermediary to set up a meeting between himself and Hoover to understand what had led to the comment. Andrew **Young**, a King aide who was present at the meeting, recalled that there was "not even an attitude of hostility" between the two, but at about this same time, the FBI anonymously sent King a compromising tape recording of him carousing in a Washington, D.C., hotel room, along with an anonymous letter that SCLC staff interpreted as encouraging King to commit suicide to avoid public embarrassment (Senate Select Committee, 167).

Hoover continued to approve investigations of King and covert operations to discredit King's standing among financial supporters, church leaders, government officials, and the media. When King condemned the **Vietnam War** in a speech at Riverside Church on 4 April 1967, the FBI "interpreted this position as proof he 'has been influenced by Communist advisers'" and stepped up their covert operations against him (Senate Select Committee, 180). The FBI considered initiating another formal COINTELPRO against King and fellow anti-war activist Dr. Benjamin **Spock** in 1967, when the two were rumored to be contemplating a run for the presidency, but ruled it out on the grounds that such a program would be more effective after the pair had officially announced their candidacy.

In August 1967, the FBI created a COINTELPRO against "Black Nationalist–Hate Groups," which targeted SCLC, King, and other civil rights leaders. King was identified as a target because the FBI believed that he could become a "messiah" who could unify black nationalists "should he abandon his supposed 'obedience' to 'white liberal doctrines' (nonviolence) and embrace black nationalism" (Senate Select Committee, 180). In the last few months of King's life, the FBI intensified its efforts to discredit him and to "neutralize" SCLC (Senate Select Committee, 180).

According to a U.S. Senate Committee convened in the 1970s to investigate the FBI's domestic intelligence operations, the impact of the FBI's efforts to discredit SCLC and King on the civil rights movement "is unquestionable" (Senate Select

Committee, 183). The committee determined that: "Rather than trying to discredit the alleged Communists it believed were attempting to influence Dr. King, the Bureau adopted the curious tactic of trying to discredit the supposed target of Communist Party interest—Dr. King himself" (Senate Select Committee, 85).

Though some civil rights activists were aware that they were under surveillance, they still had to rely upon the Bureau to investigate racial discrimination cases. After the passage of the **Civil Rights Act of 1964** the FBI's jurisdiction in segregation and voting rights cases expanded significantly, and the FBI's arrests in the Mississippi triple murder case during Freedom Summer demonstrated some measure of public commitment to civil rights investigations.

After King's **assassination** in 1968, the FBI successfully launched a large scale investigation to find his killer.

SOURCES

FBI Special Agent in Charge, Mobile, memo to Hoover, 4 January 1956, in *Papers* 3:96.

John Herbers, "Dr. King Rebuts Hoover Charges," *New York Times*, 20 November 1964.

Hoover, Memo to Robert F. Kennedy, 14 February 1962, FBIDG-NN-Sc.

King, Statement on J. Edgar Hoover's charge of alleged Communist infiltration of the Civil Rights Movement, 23 April 1964, MLKJP-GAMK.

O'Reilly, *Racial Matters*, 1989.

Senate Select Committee, *Book III: Supplementary Detailed Staff Reports*, 94th Cong., 2d sess., 1976, S. Rep. 94–755.

FELLOWSHIP OF RECONCILIATION (FOR)

Martin Luther King's relationship with the Fellowship of Reconciliation (FOR) began during the **Montgomery bus boycott**, when FOR veteran Bayard **Rustin** and FOR national field secretary Glenn E. **Smiley** came to Montgomery, Alabama, to help support local efforts to challenge racial segregation nonviolently. King also developed a cordial relationship with former FOR chairman A. J. **Muste**, whose absolute pacifism King had questioned while a student at **Crozer Theological Seminary**.

Pacifist Christians in England and Germany founded FOR at the outbreak of World War I as a way of working toward peace while their countries were at war. The U.S. chapter of FOR was established in 1915 and worked to support conscientious objectors. After the war, the organization expanded its mission to work for labor rights and an end to racism. FOR members helped create other organizations dedicated to antiracism and national self-determination work, including the **Congress of Racial Equality** and the **American Committee on Africa**.

Early in his public career, King's understanding of **Gandhi**'s ideas expanded following spring 1956 meetings with Rustin and Smiley, two FOR-affiliated activists who had pioneered the application of Gandhian techniques to American race relations. Rustin, who until 1953 had been a race relations secretary for FOR, spent a week in Montgomery, Alabama, in the early months of the bus boycott and shared his expertise in nonviolent theory and practice during strategy meetings of the **Montgomery Improvement Association**. Smiley arrived in Montgomery shortly after Rustin and was initially unimpressed by King's understanding of Gandhian nonviolence but gave him several books on the subject. After his early contacts with Rustin, Smiley, Homer **Jack**, Muste, and other proponents of Gandhian nonviolence, King became more likely to refer explicitly to Gandhi's teachings. Eager to publicize the Montgomery bus boycott's successful use of nonviolent techniques, FOR produced a documentary film entitled "Walking to Freedom," and a comic book titled "Martin Luther King and the Montgomery Story."

Former FOR staffers continued to offer training on nonviolence throughout the South after the boycott ended. FOR veteran James **Lawson**, based in Nashville, Tennessee, was especially prominent, offering workshops to participants in the **Freedom Rides**, church groups, and college students.

Although FOR members remained active in civil rights issues, in the mid-1960s the organization turned its attention to the **Vietnam War**. Through Muste, FOR encouraged King to speak out against the war and introduced him to anti-war activists such as Thich Nhat Hanh, whom King nominated for the 1967 **Nobel Peace Prize**. FOR raised money for medical aid to victims of the war in **Vietnam** and advocated the release of Vietnamese political prisoners.

SOURCES
Branch, *At Canaan's Edge*, 2006.
Carson, *In Struggle*, 1981.
Fellowship of Reconciliation, "Martin Luther King and the Montgomery Story," November–December 1957, in *Papers* 4:300–301.
Introduction, in *Papers* 3:17–21.
King, "My Pilgrimage to Nonviolence," 1 September 1958, in *Papers* 4:473–481.
Lawson to King, 3 November 1958, in *Papers* 4:522–524.
Rustin to King, 8 March 1956, in *Papers* 3:163–164.

FOR. *See* Fellowship of Reconciliation.

FORMAN, JAMES (1928–2005)

Nearly a decade older than most civil rights activists involved in the **Student Nonviolent Coordinating Committee** (SNCC), James Forman gained the respect of SNCC's staff through his militancy and organizational prowess. At times, his more confrontational, revolutionary style clashed with Martin Luther King, Jr.'s nonviolent, faith-based approach to civil rights activism.

Born 4 October 1928 in Chicago, Forman spent his early childhood living with his grandmother on a farm in Marshall County, Mississippi. At the age of six, he returned to Chicago, where he attended a Roman Catholic grammar school. Forman graduated with honors from Englewood High School in 1947 and went on to serve in the Air Force before enrolling at the University of Southern California in 1952. After suffering a beating and arrest by police during his second semester, Forman transferred to Roosevelt University in Chicago, where he became a leader in student politics and headed the university's delegation to a conference of the National Student Association in 1956. Forman received his BA in 1957 and moved east to attend graduate school at **Boston University**.

During the late 1950s, Forman gradually became involved in the expanding Southern civil rights movement. In 1958 he covered the **Little Rock school desegregation** crisis for the *Chicago Defender*. In late 1960, Forman went to Fayette County, Tennessee, to assist sharecroppers who had been evicted for registering to vote. That summer, he was jailed with other freedom riders protesting segregated facilities in Monroe,

North Carolina. After his sentence was suspended, Forman agreed to become executive secretary of SNCC.

Forman's occasional criticism of King was not simply a rhetorical exercise, but reflected a genuine concern about the direction King was leading the movement. He specifically questioned King's top-down leadership style, which he saw as undermining the development of local grassroots movements. For example, following W. G. **Anderson**'s invitation to King to join the **Albany Movement**, Forman criticized the move because he felt "much harm could be done by interjecting the Messiah complex." He recognized that King's presence "would detract from, rather than intensify" the focus on ordinary people's involvement in the movement (Forman, 255). Forman echoed the concerns of those in SNCC and the broader civil rights movement who saw the potential dangers of relying too heavily upon one dynamic leader.

Following the defeat of the **Mississippi Freedom Democratic Party** in 1964, Forman and other SNCC workers went to Guinea at the invitation of that nation's government. After his return, Forman became increasingly outspoken in his criticisms of the federal government and cautious liberalism. Within SNCC, he encouraged staff to become more aware of Marxism and **Black Nationalism**. He was, however, critical of the black separatist faction within SNCC who expelled whites from the organization. Forman joined with other black militants, including the Black Panther Party (BPP), in calling for greater alliances between black and white radicals. Though still working for SNCC, in early 1968 Forman became the BPP's minister of foreign affairs and sought to build ties between African Americans and revolutionaries in the Third World.

Later in 1968, Forman also joined forces with the League of Revolutionary Black Workers, and in April 1969 he and other League members took control of the National Black Economic Development Conference in Detroit, where Forman was scheduled to speak. He read a "Black Manifesto" that demanded that white churches pay half a billion dollars to blacks as reparations for previous exploitation. A month later he interrupted a service at New York's Riverside Church to read the manifesto again, and later that year he resigned from SNCC.

A prolific writer, Forman authored many books on the civil rights movement and black revolutionary theory, including *Sammy Younge, Jr.: The First Black College Student to Die in the Black Liberation Movement* (1968), and his autobiography, *The Making of Black Revolutionaries* (1972). He received a master's degree in African and Afro-American History from Cornell University (1980) and a PhD from the Union of Experimental Colleges and Universities (1982). In 1981, he published his thesis, "An Examination of the Question of Self-Determination and Its Application for the African American People," in which he advocated an autonomous black nation in the Black Belt region of the United States. Forman died of colon cancer in 2005 at the age of 76.

SOURCE
Carson, *In Struggle*, 1981.

FOSDICK, HARRY EMERSON (1878–1969)

Harry Emerson Fosdick, the founding minister of Riverside Church in New York City, was regarded by Martin Luther King, Jr., as "the greatest preacher of this century" (*Papers* 4:536). One of liberal Protestantism's most influential voices, Fosdick was a proponent of ecumenical Christianity, pacifism, and civil rights, whose radio sermons and writings reached millions. King frequently drew on themes and passages from Fosdick's sermons.

Fosdick was born in Buffalo, New York, and earned his BA at Colgate University (1900), his BD at Union Theological Seminary (1903), and his MA at Columbia University (1908). Fosdick became pastor of New York City's First Presbyterian Church in 1919. He sparked national controversy in the 1920s for challenging Christian fundamentalism's literal reading of the Bible and rejection of historical biblical analysis, and was forced to resign from First Presbyterian in 1925 because of it. After his resignation, millionaire John D. Rockefeller, Jr., asked Fosdick to head Park Avenue Baptist Church. When he declined because he did not "want to be known as the pastor of the richest man in the country," Rockefeller responded: "Do you think that more people will criticize you on account of my wealth than will criticize me on account of your theology?" (Fiske, "Harry Emerson Fosdick Dies"). Fosdick accepted on the condition that the church be nondenominational, and the nonsectarian Riverside Church was born.

As Riverside's pastor until 1946, and a professor of practical theology at Union Theological Seminary, Fosdick was a visible proponent of **social gospel** Christianity. Fosdick greatly influenced King's commitment to the social gospel, and his mark is apparent in King's sermons. King repeatedly echoed Fosdick's call that the Christian church should "be a fountainhead of a better social order" and that "any church that pretends to care for the souls of people but is not interested in the slums that damn them, the city government that corrupts them, and the economic order that cripples them" is, in King's words, "a dry, passive do nothing religion in need of new blood" (*Papers* 6:176).

In a copy of his own 1958 memoir of the boycott, *Stride Toward Freedom*, King inscribed, "If I were called upon to select the foremost prophets of our generation, I would choose you to head the list" (King, November 1958). After receiving the book, Fosdick replied, "We are all unpayably in your debt, not only for what you did but for putting the story down where thousands of people can read it" (*Papers* 4:537).

SOURCES

Edward B. Fiske, "Harry Emerson Fosdick Dies; Liberal Led Riverside Church," *New York Times*, 6 October 1969.
Fosdick, *The Living of These Days*, 1956.
Fosdick to King, 17 November 1958, in *Papers* 4:536–537.
"Fosdick to Quit Riverside Church; Retirement Date Set for May 1946," *New York Times*, 6 June 1945.
King, Inscription to Harry Emerson Fosdick, November 1958, PrRE.
King, *Stride Toward Freedom*, 1958.
King, "What Is Man?" Sermon at Dexter Avenue Baptist Church, 11 July 1954, in *Papers* 6:174–179.

FREEDOM RIDES

During the spring of 1961, student activists from the **Congress of Racial Equality** (CORE) launched the Freedom Rides to challenge segregation on interstate buses and bus terminals. Traveling on buses from Washington, D.C., to Jackson, Mississippi, the riders met violent opposition in the Deep South, garnering extensive media attention and eventually forcing federal intervention from John F. **Kennedy**'s administration. Although the campaign succeeded in securing an Interstate Commerce Commission (ICC) ban on segregation in all facilities under their jurisdiction, the Freedom Rides fueled existing tensions between student activists and Martin Luther King, Jr., who publicly supported the riders, but did not participate in the campaign.

The Freedom Rides were first conceived in 1947 when CORE and the **Fellowship of Reconciliation** organized an interracial bus ride across state lines to test a Supreme Court decision that declared segregation on interstate buses unconstitutional. Called the Journey of Reconciliation, the ride challenged bus segregation in the upper parts of the South, avoiding the more dangerous Deep South. The lack of confrontation, however, resulted in little media attention and failed to realize CORE's goals for the rides. Fourteen years later, in a new national context of **sit-ins**, boycotts, and the emergence of the **Southern Christian Leadership Conference** (SCLC) and the **Student Nonviolent Coordinating Committee** (SNCC), the Freedom Rides were able to harness enough national attention to force federal enforcement and policy changes.

Following an earlier ruling, *Morgan v. Virginia* (1946), that made segregation in interstate transportation illegal, in 1960 the U.S. Supreme Court ruled in *Boynton v. Virginia* that segregation in the facilities provided for interstate travelers, such as bus terminals, restaurants, and restrooms, was also unconstitutional. Prior to the 1960 decision, two students, John **Lewis** and Bernard **Lafayette**, integrated their bus ride home from college in Nashville, Tennessee, by sitting at the front of a bus and refusing to move. After this first ride, they saw CORE's announcement recruiting volunteers to participate in a Freedom Ride, a longer bus trip through the South to test the enforcement of *Boynton*. Lafayette's parents would not permit him to participate, but Lewis joined 12 other activists to form an interracial group that underwent extensive training in nonviolent direct action before launching the ride.

On 4 May 1961, the freedom riders left Washington, D.C., in two buses and headed to New Orleans. Although they faced resistance and arrests in Virginia, it was not until the riders arrived in Rockhill, South Carolina, that they encountered violence. The beating of Lewis and another rider, coupled with the arrest of one participant for using a whites-only restroom, attracted widespread media coverage. In the days following the incident, the riders met King and other civil rights leaders in Atlanta for dinner. During this meeting, King whispered prophetically to *Jet* reporter Simeon Booker, who was covering the story, "You will never make it through Alabama" (Lewis, 140).

The ride continued to Anniston, Alabama, where, on 14 May, riders were met by a violent mob of over 100 people. Before the buses' arrival, Anniston local authorities had given permission to the Ku Klux Klan to strike against the freedom riders without fear of arrest. As the first bus pulled up, the driver yelled outside, "Well, boys, here they are. I brought you some niggers and nigger-lovers" (Arsenault, 143). One of the buses was firebombed, and its fleeing passengers were forced into the angry white mob. The violence continued at the Birmingham terminal where Eugene "Bull" **Connor**'s police force offered no protection. Although the violence garnered national media attention, the series of attacks prompted James **Farmer** of CORE to end the campaign. The riders flew to New Orleans, bringing to an end the first Freedom Ride of the 1960s.

The decision to end the ride frustrated student activists, such as Diane **Nash**, who argued in a phone conversation with Farmer: "We can't let them stop us with violence. If we do, the movement is dead" (Ross, 177). Under the auspices and organizational support of SNCC, the Freedom Rides continued. SNCC mentors were wary of this decision, including King, who had declined to join the rides when asked by Nash and Rodney Powell. Farmer continued to express his reservations, questioning whether continuing the trip was "suicide" (Lewis, 144). With fractured support, the organizers had a difficult time securing financial resources. Nevertheless, on 17 May 1961, seven men and three women rode from Nashville to Birmingham to resume the Freedom Rides. Just before reaching Birmingham, the bus was pulled over and directed to the Birmingham station, where all of the riders were arrested for defying segregation laws. The arrests, coupled with the difficulty of finding a bus driver and other logistical challenges, left the riders stranded in the city for several days.

Federal intervention began to take place behind the scenes as Attorney General Robert **Kennedy** called the Greyhound Company and demanded that it find a driver. Seeking to diffuse the dangerous situation, John Seigenthaler, a Department of Justice representative accompanying the freedom riders, met with a reluctant Alabama Governor John **Patterson**. Seigenthaler's maneuver resulted in the bus's departure for Montgomery with a full police escort the next morning.

At the Montgomery city line, as agreed, the state troopers left the buses, but the local police that had been ordered to meet the freedom riders in Montgomery never appeared. Unprotected when they entered the terminal, riders were beaten so severely by a white mob that some sustained permanent injuries. When the police finally arrived, they served the riders with an injunction barring them from continuing the Freedom Ride in Alabama.

During this time, King was on a speaking tour in Chicago. Upon learning of the violence, he returned to Montgomery, where he staged a rally at Ralph **Abernathy**'s First Baptist Church. In his speech, King blamed Governor Patterson for "aiding and abetting the forces of violence" and called for federal intervention, declaring that "the federal government must not stand idly by while bloodthirsty mobs beat nonviolent students with impunity" (King, 21 May 1961). As King spoke, a threatening white mob gathered outside. From inside the church, King called Attorney General Kennedy, who assured him that the federal government would protect those inside the church. Kennedy swiftly mobilized federal marshals, who used tear gas to keep the mob at bay. Federal marshals were later replaced by the Alabama National Guard, who escorted people out of the church at dawn.

As the violence and federal intervention propelled the freedom riders to national prominence, King became one of the major spokesmen for the rides. Some activists, however, began to criticize King for his willingness to offer only moral and financial support but not his physical presence on the rides. In a telegram to King the president of the Union County **National Association for the Advancement of Colored People** branch in North Carolina, Robert F. **Williams**, urged him to "lead the way by example.... If you lack the courage, remove yourself from the vanguard" (Williams, 31 May 1961). In response to Nash's direct request that King join the rides, King replied that he was on probation and could not afford another arrest, a response many of the students found unacceptable.

On 29 May 1961, the Kennedy administration announced that it had directed the ICC to ban segregation in all facilities under its jurisdiction, but the rides continued.

Students from all over the country purchased bus tickets to the South and crowded into jails in Jackson, Mississippi. With the participation of northern students came even more press coverage. On 1 November 1961, the ICC ruling that segregation on interstate buses and facilities was illegal took effect.

Although King's involvement in the Freedom Rides waned after the federal intervention, the legacy of the rides remained with him. He, and all others involved in the campaign, saw how provoking white southern violence through nonviolent confrontations could attract national attention and force federal action. The Freedom Rides also exposed tactical and leadership rifts between King and more militant student activists, which continued until King's death in 1968.

SOURCES

Arsenault, *Freedom Riders*, 2006.
"Bi-Racial Group Cancels Bus Trip," *New York Times*, 16 May 1961.
Carson, *In Struggle*, 1981.
Garrow, *Bearing the Cross*, 1986.
King, Statement at mass meeting supporting freedom riders, 21 May 1961, MMFR.
Lewis, *Walking with the Wind*, 1998.
Peck, *Freedom Ride*, 1962.
Ross, *Witnessing and Testifying*, 2003.
Williams to King, 31 May 1961, MLKP-MBU.

FREEDOM SUMMER (1964)

Although the **Student Nonviolent Coordinating Committee** (SNCC) had labored for civil rights in rural Mississippi since 1961, the organization found that intense and often violent resistance by segregationists in rural areas of Mississippi would not allow for the kind of direct action campaigns that had been successful in urban areas such as Montgomery and Birmingham. The 1964 Freedom Summer project was designed to draw the nation's attention to the violent oppression experienced by Mississippi blacks who attempted to exercise their constitutional rights, and to develop a grassroots freedom movement that could be sustained after student activists left Mississippi.

When SNCC activist Robert **Moses** launched a voter registration drive in Mississippi in 1961, he confronted a system that regularly used segregation laws and fear tactics to disenfranchise black citizens. In 1962, he became director of the **Council of Federated Organizations**, a coalition of organizations led by SNCC that coordinated the efforts of civil rights groups within the state. Capitalizing on the successful use of white student volunteers in Mississippi during a 1963 mock election called the "Freedom Vote," Moses proposed that northern white student volunteers take part in a large number of simultaneous local campaigns in Mississippi during the summer of 1964.

Letters to prospective volunteers alerted them to conditions in Mississippi, explaining the likelihood of arrest, the need for bond money and subsistence funds, and the requirement that drivers obtain Mississippi licenses for themselves and their cars. Volunteers were also asked to prepare for the experience by reading several books, including King's memoir of the **Montgomery bus boycott**, *Stride Toward Freedom*, and Lillian **Smith**'s novel *Killers of the Dream*.

On 14 June 1964 the first group of summer volunteers began training at Western College for Women in Oxford, Ohio. Of the approximately 1,000 volunteers, the majority were white northern college students from middle and upper class backgrounds.

The training sessions were intended to prepare volunteers to register black voters, teach literacy and civics at Freedom Schools, and promote the **Mississippi Freedom Democratic Party**'s (MFDP) challenge to the all-white Democratic delegation at that summer's Democratic National Convention in Atlantic City, New Jersey.

Just one week after the first group of volunteers arrived in Oxford, three civil rights workers were reported missing in Mississippi. James Chaney, a black Mississippian, and two white northerners, Michael Schwerner and Andrew Goodman, disappeared while visiting Philadelphia, Mississippi, to investigate the burning of a church. The abduction of the three civil rights workers intensified the new activists' fears, but Freedom Summer staff and volunteers moved ahead with the campaign.

Voter registration was the cornerstone of the summer project. Although approximately 17,000 black residents of Mississippi attempted to register to vote in the summer of 1964, only 1,600 of the completed applications were accepted by local registrars. Highlighting the need for federal voting rights legislation, these efforts created political momentum for the **Voting Rights Act of 1965**.

In an effort to address Mississippi's separate and unequal public education system, the summer project established 41 Freedom Schools attended by more than 3,000 young black students throughout the state. In addition to math, reading, and other traditional courses, students were also taught black history, the philosophy of the civil rights movement, and leadership skills that provided them with the intellectual and practical tools to carry on the struggle after the summer volunteers departed.

At Moses' invitation King visited Greenwood, Mississippi, to show the support of the **Southern Christian Leadership Conference** for the summer project and to encourage black Mississippians to vote despite acts of violence and intimidation. Less than three weeks after King's visit, the murdered bodies of Chaney, Goodman, and Schwerner were found. King characterized their brutal deaths as "an attack on the human brotherhood taught by all the great religions of mankind" (King, 4 August 1964).

Freedom Summer activists also worked to make the MFDP a viable alternative to Mississippi's "Jim Crow" Democratic convention delegation. King publicly supported the MFDP, telling the 1964 convention's credentials committee, "If you value your party, if you value your nation, if you value democratic government you have no alternative but to recognize, with full voice and vote, the Mississippi Freedom Democratic Party" (King, 22 August 1964). While the MFDP was initially unsuccessful, some of its members were seated at the 1968 convention.

Freedom Summer marked one of the last major interracial civil rights efforts of the 1960s, as the movement entered a period of divisive conflict that would draw even sharper lines between the goals of King and those of the younger, more militant faction of the black freedom struggle.

SOURCES

Carson, *In Struggle*, 1981.

King, Statement before the Credentials Committee, 22 August 1964, MLKJP-GAMK.

King, Statement on the deaths of Michael Schwerner, Andrew Goodman, and James Chaney, 4 August 1964, MLKJP-GAMK.

Martinez, *Letters from Mississippi*, 1965.

McAdam, *Freedom Summer*, 1988.

G

GANDHI, MOHANDAS K. (1869–1948)

Upon his death, Mohandas K. Gandhi was hailed by the *London Times* as "the most influential figure India has produced for generations" ("Mr. Gandhi"). Gandhi protested against racism in South Africa and colonial rule in India using nonviolent resistance. A testament to the revolutionary power of **nonviolence**, Gandhi's approach directly influenced Martin Luther King, Jr., who argued that the Gandhian philosophy was "the only morally and practically sound method open to oppressed people in their struggle for freedom" (*Papers* 4:478).

King first encountered Gandhian ideas during his studies at **Crozer Theological Seminary**. In a talk prepared for George **Davis**' class, Christian Theology for Today, King included Gandhi among "individuals who greatly reveal the working of the Spirit of God" (*Papers* 1:249). In 1950, King heard Mordecai **Johnson**, president of Howard University, speak of his recent trip to India and Gandhi's nonviolent resistance techniques. King situated Gandhi's ideas of nonviolent direct action in the larger framework of Christianity, declaring that "Christ showed us the way and Gandhi in India showed it could work" (Rowland, "2,500 Here Hail Boycott Leader"). He later remarked that he considered Gandhi to be "the greatest Christian of the modern world" (King, 23 June 1962).

Gandhi was born 2 October 1869, in Porbandar, in the western part of India, to Karamchand Gandhi, chief minister of Porbandar, and his wife Putlibai, a devout Hindu. At the age of 18, Gandhi began training as a lawyer in England. After completing his barrister's degree he returned to India in 1891, but was unable to find well-paid work. In 1893, he accepted a one-year contract to do legal work for an Indian firm in South Africa, but remained for 21 years. It was in South Africa that Gandhi was first exposed to official racial prejudice, and where he developed his philosophy of nonviolent direct action by organizing the Indian community there to oppose race-based laws and socioeconomic repression.

Gandhi returned to India in 1914. In 1919 British authorities issued the Rowlatt Acts, policies that permitted the incarceration without trial of Indians suspected of sedition. In response, Gandhi called for a day of national fasting, meetings, and suspension of work on 6 April 1919, as an act of *satyagraha* (literally, truth-force or love-force), a form of nonviolent resistance. He suspended the campaign of nonviolent resistance a few days later because protesters had responded violently to the police.

Within the next few years, Gandhi reshaped the existing Indian National Congress into a mass movement promoting Indian self-rule through a boycott of British goods and institutions, and leading to the arrests of thousands of satyagrahis. In March 1922, Gandhi was arrested and served two years in prison for sedition.

Gandhi resumed leadership of the Indian National Congress Party in late 1928. In the spring of 1930, Gandhi and 80 volunteers began a 200-mile march to the sea, where they produced salt from seawater to defy the British Salt Laws, which ensured that the British colonial government recovered a tax from the sale of salt. Over 60,000 Indians eventually subjected themselves to imprisonment by making salt. After a year of struggle, Gandhi negotiated a truce with the British government's representative, Lord Irwin, and ended the civil disobedience campaign.

By late 1931, Irwin's successor had resumed political repression. Gandhi revived the satyagraha movement and was soon imprisoned by the British government. While in prison, Gandhi fasted to protest the policy of separate electorates for "untouchables," India's lowest caste, within India's new constitution. The fast elicited public attention and resulted in a historic 1947 resolution making the practice of discrimination against untouchables illegal. In August 1947, Britain transferred governing power to a partitioned India, creating the two independent states of India and Pakistan. Despite Gandhi's urgings, partition was accompanied by violence and rioting. On 30 January 1948, Gandhi was assassinated while entering a prayer meeting in Delhi.

Gandhi and his philosophy were of special interest to the progressive African American community. Referring to the African American freedom struggle, Gandhi had called the practice of segregation "a negation of civilisation" ("Letter from Gandhi"). Howard **Thurman** met with Gandhi in 1935, Benjamin **Mays** in 1936, and William Stuart **Nelson** in 1946. King's colleagues Bayard **Rustin**, James **Lawson,** and Mordecai Johnson had also visited India.

Gandhi's philosophy directly influenced King, who first employed strategies of nonviolent direct action in the 1955 to 1956 **Montgomery bus boycott**. In 1959, King traveled to **India** with his wife, Coretta Scott **King**, and Lawrence D. **Reddick** on a visit co-sponsored by the **American Friends Service Committee** and Gandhi Smarak Nidhi (Gandhi Memorial Fund). King met with the Gandhi family, as well as with Indian activists and officials, including Prime Minister Jawaharlal Nehru, during the five-week trip. In his 1959 Palm Sunday sermon, King preached on the significance of Gandhi's 1928 salt march and his fast to end discrimination against India's untouchables. King ultimately believed that the Gandhian approach of nonviolent resistance would "bring about a solution to the race problem in America" (*Papers* 4:355).

Sources

Introduction, in *Papers* 5:3.

King, "His Influence Speaks to World Conscience," 30 January 1958, in *Papers* 4:354–355.

King, "My Pilgrimage to Nonviolence," 1 September 1958, in *Papers* 4:473–481.

King, Palm Sunday Sermon on Mohandas K. Gandhi, delivered at Dexter Avenue Baptist Church, 22 March 1959, in *Papers* 5:145–157.

King, "Six Talks in Outline," 13 September–23 November 1949, in *Papers* 1:242–251.

King to Harold Edward Fey, 23 June 1962, MLKJP-GAMK.

"Letter from Gandhi," *Baltimore Afro-American*, 7 February 1948.

"Mr. Gandhi," *London Times*, 31 January 1948.

Stanley Rowland, Jr., "2,500 Here Hail Boycott Leader," *New York Times*, 26 March 1956.

GANDHI SOCIETY FOR HUMAN RIGHTS

The Gandhi Society for Human Rights (also known as the Gandhi Society) was the brainchild of Harry **Wachtel**, a prominent New York attorney who was introduced to Martin Luther King, Jr., by Clarence B. **Jones**, King's trusted legal advisor. Upon King's solicitation, Wachtel joined Jones in defending four ministers of the **Southern Christian Leadership Conference** (SCLC) in a libel suit, *New York Times v. Sullivan*, stemming from an advertisement in the *New York Times*. Wachtel met with King in New York in early 1962 and discussed the formation of a tax-exempt fund to cover expenses related to the suit and to channel needed financial support to the nonviolent civil rights movement. With King's endorsement, Wachtel, Jones, and another New York lawyer, Theodore W. Kheel, founded the Gandhi Society for Human Rights. King was made honorary president, and Jones functioned as general counsel and acting executive director.

The founders arranged to launch the Gandhi Society at a luncheon at the Sheraton-Carlton Hotel in Washington, D.C., on 17 May 1962. King invited a number of distinguished individuals to serve on the board of directors and attend the luncheon, based on Jones' insistence that the publicity generated would benefit the society. Senators Jacob Javits (R-NY), Clifford Case (R-NJ), and Hubert Humphrey (D-MN) accepted invitations to serve as honored guests at the luncheon.

King and Kheel, acting president of the Gandhi Society, spoke at the luncheon of about 90 people. King noted that 17 May marked the anniversary of the historic *Brown v. Board of Education* decision that made school segregation unconstitutional; and that 1962 was the 100th anniversary of President Lincoln's **Emancipation Proclamation**, which paved the way for the abolition of slavery; and of Henry David Thoreau's death, whose ideas on civil disobedience inspired Mahatma **Gandhi**. King told the luncheon that "on these overlapping anniversaries of liberal triumphs," it was fitting to "form a new society dedicated to progress through non-violence" which "is [now] woven into the fabric of American life" (King, 17 May 1962). King also revealed that earlier in the day SCLC had sent President John F. **Kennedy** a "landmark" document asking for the issuance of an executive order proclaiming all forms of segregation to be contrary to the U.S. Constitution (King, 17 May 1962).

On 29 June 1962, the first informal meeting of the new organization's board of directors was held in New York. An executive committee elected that day, which included King, went on to write a mission statement defining the activities of the society to include legal defense and aid for civil rights cases, educational materials propagating nonviolent methods and voter registration activities, and financial assistance to other organizations for civil rights projects. Mordecai **Johnson**, president emeritus of Howard University; William **Kunstler**, special counsel to the American Civil Liberties Union; and Benjamin **Mays**, president of **Morehouse College**, were some of the distinguished members of the Gandhi Society's board.

The Gandhi Society was not without its detractors. *Christian Century* published a 13 June 1962 editorial that accused King of channeling reformist energies toward "a new kind of American sectarianism" ("A Gandhi Society?"). King vehemently denied these accusations in a letter to the editor, stating that Gandhi, "a man who never embraced Christianity," was "the greatest Christian of the modern world" (King, 27 June 1962).

By January 1964, the organization's financial situation led Jones to secure a $6,000 loan to cover the organization's overdrawn back account. King later donated $25,000 of his 1964 **Nobel Peace Prize** money to the Gandhi Society. Federal inaction in processing the society's application for tax-exempt status continued to hinder its fundraising activities. Wachtel reported to King on 11 August 1965 that the nonprofit status had been granted by the U.S. Treasury Department, but just a few days later he wrote to King of the many other difficulties facing the organization. In September 1965, Wachtel formally proposed that the Society be renamed the American Foundation on Nonviolence and reconstituted with former board members of the Gandhi Society. The name was changed later that year.

SOURCES

"A Gandhi Society?" *Christian Century* 79 (13 June 1962): 735–736.
"Gandhi Society Explained," *Christian Century* 79 (1 August 1962): 929–930.
Garrow, *Bearing the Cross,* 1986.
King, Address at the formation of the Gandhi Society for Human Rights, 17 May 1962, MLKJP-GAMK.
King to Harold Edward Fey, 27 June 1962, CCFA-ICarbS.

GASTON, ARTHUR GEORGE (1892–1996)

Millionaire entrepreneur A. G. Gaston acted as an intermediary between white moderates and civil rights leaders in Birmingham, Alabama, during the 1960s. Although he favored nonconfrontational methods of civil rights reform, Gaston expressed his support for the "guiding principals and commitment" of Martin Luther King and the **Southern Christian Leadership Conference** (Gaston and Shores, 30 September 1963).

Gaston was born on 4 July 1892, in Demopolis, Alabama. He graduated from the Tuggle Institute in Birmingham and, in 1923, started the Booker T. Washington Insurance Co. with $500. Building on the insurance company, Gaston developed a business empire estimated at more than $30 million, which included the Smith and Gaston Funeral Home, the Gaston Motel, and the Citizens Federal Savings and Loan. While they were in Birmingham Gaston provided Martin Luther King, Jr., and other civil rights leaders with rooms at the Gaston Motel, the city's only first-class accommodation that accepted blacks.

As a successful and prominent businessman, Gaston chose to walk a line of careful moderation in an attempt to balance his loyalty to the black community with his commitment to the business community. He initially opposed King's 1963 push for protest during the **Birmingham Campaign**, preferring to give newly elected Mayor Albert **Boutwell** a chance to follow through with his promised changes. Once the demonstrations were met with violence by segregationists, Gaston gave King his vote of confidence and bailed him out of jail in April 1963. In retaliation for Gaston's support of the campaign, militant segregationists bombed his motel and his home later that year. Following the deaths of four African American girls in the bombing of Sixteenth Street Baptist Church, Gaston joined King in a meeting with President John F. **Kennedy** to urge a federal response to the bombing. The meeting resulted in the appointment of federal mediators who would negotiate between the white and black communities in Birmingham. Gaston continued to be an active member of the

Birmingham business community until his death from stroke complications on 19 January 1996 at the age of 103.

SOURCES

Eskew, *But for Birmingham*, 1997.
Gaston and Arthur D. Shores, 30 September 1963, FLSC-GAMK.

GHANA TRIP (1957)

In March 1957, Martin Luther King, Jr., and his wife Coretta Scott **King** traveled to West Africa to attend Ghana's independence ceremony. King's voyage was symbolic of a growing global alliance of oppressed peoples and was strategically well timed; his attendance represented an attempt to broaden the scope of the civil rights struggle in the United States on the heels of the successful **Montgomery bus boycott**. King identified with Ghana's struggle; furthermore, he recognized a strong parallel between resistance against European colonialism in Africa and the struggle against racism in the United States.

King was invited to the independence ceremony by Ghana's new Prime Minister, Kwame **Nkrumah**. King's friend Bayard **Rustin** coordinated the invitation with the help of Bill Sutherland, a civil rights activist and pacifist who was then working for Nkrumah's finance minister, K. A. Gbedemah. King's trip was funded by the **Montgomery Improvement Association** and the **Dexter Avenue Baptist Church**, his congregation.

King arrived in Accra, the Gold Coast (soon to be Ghana) on 4 March and attended a reception where he met then Vice President Richard **Nixon**. King told Nixon: "I want you to come visit us down in Alabama where we are seeking the same kind of freedom the Gold Coast is celebrating" ("M. L. King Meets"). The next day, King attended the ceremonial closing of the old British Parliament. At the ceremony, the recently incarcerated Nkrumah and his ministers wore their prison caps, symbolizing their struggle to win Ghana's freedom. King wrote: "When I looked out and saw the prime minister there with his prison cap on that night, that reminded me of that fact, that freedom never comes easy. It comes through hard labor and it comes through toil" (*Papers* 4:163).

At midnight on 6 March, King attended the official ceremony in which the British Union Jack was lowered and the new flag of Ghana was raised and the British colony of the Gold Coast became the independent nation of Ghana. King later recalled: "As we walked out, we noticed all over the polo grounds almost a half a million people. They had waited for this hour and this moment for years" (*Papers* 4:159). King's reaction to the Ghanaians' triumph was outwardly emotional. "Before I knew it, I started weeping. I was crying for joy. And I knew about all of the struggles, and all of the pain, and all of the agony that these people had gone through for this moment" (*Papers* 4:160).

Also in attendance at the ceremony were many prominent American activists, politicians, and educators: A. Philip **Randolph**, Ralph **Bunche**, Mordecai **Johnson**, Horace Mann Bond, Senator Charles **Diggs**, Congressman Adam Clayton **Powell**, and Vice President Nixon. The honor of inclusion in this impressive group indicated King's prominence as a civil rights figure both at home and abroad.

Interviewed while in Ghana, King told radio listeners, "This event, the birth of this new nation, will give impetus to oppressed peoples all over the world. I think it will have worldwide implications and repercussions—not only for Asia and Africa, but also for America.… It renews my conviction in the ultimate triumph of justice. And it seems to me that this is fit testimony to the fact that eventually the forces of justice triumph in the universe, and somehow the universe itself is on the side of freedom and justice. So that this gives new hope to me in the struggle for freedom" (*Papers* 4:146).

Despite falling ill for several days, the Kings had a private lunch with Nkrumah and met with anti-**apartheid** activist and Anglican priest Michael Scott and peace activist Homer **Jack**. King departed from Ghana for New York by way of Nigeria, Rome, Geneva, Paris, and London. In London, the Kings had lunch with Trinidadian writer and political activist C. L. R. **James**, who was very impressed by the success of the **Montgomery bus boycott**.

SOURCES

Introduction, in *Papers* 4:7–10.

King, "The Birth of a New Nation," Sermon delivered at Dexter Avenue Baptist Church, 7 April 1957, in *Papers* 4:155–167.

King, Interview by Etta Moten Barnett, 6 March 1957, in *Papers* 4:145–148.

"M. L. King Meets Nixon in Ghana," *Pittsburgh Courier*, 16 March 1957.

GOLDWATER, BARRY M. (1909–1998)

When conservative Arizona Senator Barry M. Goldwater ran for president in 1964, Martin Luther King, Jr., expressed his opposition, explaining: "I feel that the prospect of Senator Goldwater being president of the United States so threatens the health, morality, and survival of our nation that I can not in good conscience fail to take a stand against what he represents" (King, 16 July 1964). Goldwater lost the election to President Lyndon **Johnson** in a landslide, winning majorities only in his native Arizona and five states of the Deep South.

Born in Phoenix in 1909, when Arizona was still a territory, Goldwater's family was part of the city's elite. After completing high school at a military academy in Virginia, he enrolled in the University of Arizona at Tucson in 1928. When his father died the following year, Goldwater dropped out of college to manage his family's department store. He joined the Air Force during World War II, flying missions from India and China. When he returned to Phoenix after the war, he was elected to the city council.

In 1952, Goldwater was elected to the Senate on a pledge to reduce federal spending and fight **communism**. Reelected in 1958, Goldwater opposed social welfare programs and continued to criticize the Supreme Court on its school integration stance. He voted against the **Civil Rights Act of 1964**. King said of Goldwater's voting record, "While not himself a racist, Mr. Goldwater articulates a philosophy which gives aid and comfort to the racists" (King, 16 July 1964). King feared that Goldwater's position that "civil rights must be left, by and large to the states" meant "leaving it to the Wallaces and the Barnetts" (King, "The Republican Presidential Nomination"). Electing Goldwater, King said, would plunge the country into a "dark night of social disruption" (King, 21 September 1964).

In the month before the election, King's **Southern Christian Leadership Conference** launched a nationwide "get out the vote" drive. Although King called the campaign "bipartisan," he wrote: "The principles of states' rights advocated by Mr. Goldwater diminish us and would deny to Negro and white alike, many of the privileges and opportunities of living in American society" (King, 9 October 1964). When Johnson defeated Goldwater, King declared, "The American people made a choice … to build a great society, rather than to wallow in the past" (King, "A Choice and a Promise").

Despite his defeat in the presidential election, Arizona reelected Goldwater to the Senate in 1968, 1974, and 1980. He supported the **Vietnam War** and stood by President Richard **Nixon** during the Watergate controversy until tapes irrefutably demonstrated Nixon's involvement. Despite his conservatism, Goldwater was critical of the religious right, supported gay rights, and defended abortion. After retirement in 1987, he continued to speak publicly on social issues until his death in 1998.

SOURCES
Goldwater with Casserly, *Goldwater*, 1988.
King, "A Choice and a Promise," *New York Amsterdam News*, 5 December 1964.
King, Interview by Ronald Allison, 21 September 1964, MLKJP-GAMK.
King, "The Presidential Nomination," *New York Amsterdam News*, 25 April 1964.
King, Press release, Statement regarding drive to get out the vote, 9 October 1964, MLKJP-GAMK.
King, The Republican presidential nomination, 1 April 1964, MLKJP-GAMK.
King, Statement on Republican nomination of Senator Barry Goldwater, 16 July 1964, MLKJP-GAMK.

GOMILLION, CHARLES GOODE (1900–1995)

Educator and community activist Charles Gomillion worked at the Tuskegee Institute for more than 40 years. As president of the Tuskegee Civic Association, he worked with Martin Luther King, Jr., and the **Southern Christian Leadership Conference** to increase African American voter registration in the South. Gomillion was the lead plaintiff in the landmark 1960 civil rights case *Gomillion v. Lightfoot*, which led the Supreme Court to declare gerrymandering unconstitutional.

Gomillion was born in Johnston, South Carolina, in 1900. Although his parents encouraged his education, Johnston's African American school only ran three months of the year. Gomillion left home at 16 to attend secondary school at Paine College, a Methodist school in Augusta, Georgia, where he completed high school and some college before dropping out to help his aging parents. After working as a junior high school principal, he returned to Paine to finish college and began teaching at Tuskegee Institute in 1928. Gomillion continued his own studies in sociology, eventually earning a PhD from Ohio State University when he was 59 years old.

In the 1930s, Gomillion attempted to register to vote several times, starting in 1934, and was finally successful in 1939. Throughout the 1940s and 1950s, Gomillion, by then the dean of students at Tuskegee, worked to register voters, which prompted the state legislature to redraw the borders of the city in 1957 to maintain white political power. Tuskegee's municipal boundaries were gerrymandered to create a 28-sided shape that retained every white person within the new city boundaries and excluded all but 12 African Americans. Gomillion brought suit to contest the redistricting in *Gomillion v. Lightfoot*.

King sought Gomillion's advice for his book, **Stride Toward Freedom**, and thanked him for his "significant suggestions and real encouragement" in the book's preface

(King, 11). After the Supreme Court ruled in his favor in *Gomillion v. Lightfoot*, Gomillion encouraged the Tuskegee Civic Association to work for collaboration between whites and blacks. However, by the mid-1960s, the prospect of interracial politics was met with firm resistance from local African Americans who had been thoroughly excluded for so long. Gomillion left the Tuskegee Civic Association and, in 1970, retired from Tuskegee Institute.

SOURCES

William A. Elwood, "An Interview with Charles G. Gomillion," *Callaloo*, 40 (Summer 1989): 576–599.

Gomillion v. Lightfoot, 364 U.S. 339 (1960).

King, *Stride Toward Freedom*, 1958.

GRAETZ, ROBERT (1928–)

As the white minister of an African American congregation in Montgomery, Alabama, Graetz's home was bombed several times and he was harassed by white residents for his participation in the **Montgomery bus boycott**. In Martin Luther King, Jr.'s memoir of the boycott, *Stride Toward Freedom*, King recalled that Graetz served to remind those who were boycotting that "many white people as well as Negroes were applying the 'love-thy-neighbor-as-thyself' teachings of Christianity in their daily lives" (King, 74).

Born in Clarksburg, West Virginia, in 1928, Graetz graduated from Capital University in 1950. He received his BD from Evangelical Lutheran Theological Seminary just before arriving in Montgomery in 1955 to become pastor of Trinity Lutheran Church. After the boycott began, Graetz sent a letter to white ministers in Montgomery explaining the protest's objectives and asking them to "consider this matter prayerfully and carefully, with Christian love" (Graetz, 7 December 1955). Graetz, a member of the executive board of the **Montomgery Improvement Association**, participated in the boycott carpool, driving African Americans to work or shopping for several hours each day. After articles about his involvement appeared in local newspapers, sugar was poured in his car's gasoline tank, and he received many threatening phone calls. On 25 August 1956, while he and his family were at **Highlander Folk School** for a workshop with Rosa **Parks**, his house was bombed.

At the 14 November 1956 mass meeting held to celebrate the *Browder v. Gayle* ruling by the Supreme Court outlawing segregation on the city buses, Ralph **Abernathy** asked Graetz to read from scripture. King recalled that more than 8,000 people crowded into two churches that night, and when Graetz read the biblical passage, "'When I was a child, I spoke as a child, I understood as a child, I thought as a child: but when I became a man, I put away childish things,' the congregation burst into applause … they knew they had come of age, had won new dignity" (King, 161).

After Graetz's home was bombed again in January 1957, he left Montgomery to become pastor of St. Philip Lutheran Church in Columbus, Ohio. He remained active in civil rights issues, operating a street ministry in Washington, D.C., in the late 1960s, and then advocating in support of gay rights.

SOURCES

Graetz, *Montgomery*, 1991.

Graetz to Christian Brothers, 7 December 1955, RGP.

King, *Stride Toward Freedom*, 1958.

GRAHAM, BILLY. *See* Graham, William Franklin.

GRAHAM, FRANK PORTER (1886–1972)

A United Nations mediator and former University of North Carolina (UNC) president, Frank Porter Graham was an ardent supporter of Martin Luther King, Jr., Graham told King: "In your stand for nonviolence you [speak] for the immortal teachings of Jesus and the proved techniques of Gandhi, ultimately victorious over bombs, for faith over fear, understanding over prejudice, and love over hate" (Graham, 11 January 1957).

Graham was born in 1886, in Fayetteville, North Carolina, where his father was the superintendent of public schools. He graduated from college and law school at UNC and then received an MA in history from Columbia University. After serving in the Marines during World War I, he returned to North Carolina to teach history at UNC. Graham was outspoken in support of trade unions and public welfare, and authored an "Industrial Bill of Rights" calling for improved working conditions and protection of freedom of speech and assembly ("Seek to Clarify").

In 1930 Graham was elected president of UNC. In 1946 President Harry S. **Truman** appointed Graham to the President's Committee on Civil Rights. Among other recommendations, the Committee's report suggested that Congress enact laws to end segregation, lynching, police discrimination, and voting prerequisites like the poll tax. When North Carolina Senator J. Melville Broughton died in 1949, the governor appointed Graham to fill the vacancy. Graham lost his bid for the Democratic nomination in 1950, saying of his opponents, "First they tried the red issue and failed, then they tried the black issue and won" ("Frank Graham at 80"). Graham then joined the United Nations as a representative to India and Pakistan, where he tried to negotiate peace in Kashmir. He remained at the United Nations for 19 years.

During the summer of 1957, King and Graham spent time together at a **Morehouse College** commencement where they were both honored. In December 1957 King asked Graham to serve on the National Advisory Committee of the Crusade for Citizenship, a program of the **Southern Christian Leadership Conference** (SCLC). Graham accepted.

Graham made regular financial contributions to SCLC and, in 1962, he accepted King's invitation to join the board of directors of the **Gandhi Society for Human Rights**. As a member of the board of trustees of the Southern Regional Council, Graham wrote a resolution supporting King in his efforts in Selma in 1965.

Coming to King's defense against black leaders advocating a turn toward violent self-defense, Graham said, "Those Negro leaders decrying Martin Luther King and Roy Wilkins and looking down on them as out of date should really see they are standing on the shoulders of those they're looking down on" ("Frank Graham at 80"). Graham retired in 1967 and moved back to Chapel Hill, North Carolina. He died in 1972 at the age of 85.

Sources

"Frank Graham at 80: Liberal Still," *New York Times*, 15 October 1966.

Graham, "Students 'Standing Up' for the American Dream," *New South*, 15, nos. 7, 8 (1960): 3–7.

Graham to King, 11 January 1957, MLKJP-GAMK.

GRAHAM, WILLIAM FRANKLIN (1918–)

In a 1957 interview, popular evangelist William "Billy" Graham commended Martin Luther King for providing "an example of Christian love" as a means of confronting America's race problem (Moore, 454). Although both men were evangelical ministers who opposed racism and segregation, their approach to social issues differed. In contrast to King's tactic of nonviolent direct action, Graham believed that conversion was the most effective route to racial harmony and social change.

Graham was born 7 November 1918, on a farm near Charlotte, North Carolina. During his studies at Florida Bible Institute at St. Petersburg, he was ordained as a Southern Baptist minister in 1939. He then received a BA (1943) from Wheaton College in Illinois. From 1943 to 1945, he was pastor of the First Baptist Church in Western Springs, Illinois. In 1947 Graham began his evangelical ministry, and in 1950 he founded the Billy Graham Evangelistic Association in Minneapolis, Minnesota.

Graham and King first met during the **Montgomery bus boycott**. In May 1957, Graham opened his summer-long New York Crusade, whose executive committee included King's clerical compatriots Thomas Kilgore and Gardner **Taylor**. Graham preached from the steps of Sandy **Ray**'s Cornerstone Baptist Church in July as part of his crusade calling for "anti-segregation legislation" ("Graham Says Country"). Graham later invited King to participate in the New York Crusade, and on 18 July 1957, King joined him on the platform at Madison Square Garden. King led the congregation in a prayer, calling "for a warless world and for a brotherhood that transcends race or color" (*Papers* 4:238). Writing Graham after his appearance, King praised his commitment to hold nonsegregated revivals, commenting: "You have courageously brought the Christian gospel to bear on the question of race" (*Papers* 4:265). In the summer of 1960, King and Graham traveled together to the Tenth Baptist World Congress of the Baptist World Alliance. Graham held integrated crusades in Birmingham, Alabama, on Easter 1964 in the aftermath of the bombing of the Sixteenth Street Baptist Church, and toured Alabama again in the wake of the violence that accompanied the **Selma to Montgomery March** in 1965.

Tensions between the two leaders emerged in 1958 when the sponsoring committee of a crusade in San Antonio, Texas, arranged for Graham to be introduced by that state's segregationist governor, Price Daniel. King objected to Daniel's appearance as an "endorsement of racial segregation and discrimination" (*Papers* 4:457). Graham's advisor, Grady Wilson, replied that "even though we do not see eye to eye with him on every issue, we still love him in Christ" (*Papers* 4:458). Graham and King would also come to differ on the **Vietnam War**. After King's "**Beyond Vietnam**" speech denouncing U.S. intervention in Vietnam, Graham castigated him and others for their criticism of American foreign policy. Following King's **assassination** in 1968, Graham mourned that America had lost "a social leader and a prophet" (Graham, 696).

Sources

Graham, *Just as I Am*, 1997.

Graham, "No Color Line in Heaven," *Ebony*, August 1957.

"Graham Says Country Needs 'Anti-segregation Legislation,'" *Baltimore Afro-American*, 27 July, 1957.

King, Invocation at Billy Graham Evangelistic Association Crusade, 18 July 1957, in *Papers* 4:238.

King to Graham, 31 August 1957, in *Papers* 4:264–265.

King to Graham, 23 July 1958, in *Papers* 4:457–458.

Edward L. Moore, "Billy Graham and Martin Luther King, Jr.: An Inquiry into White and Black Revivalistic Traditions," Ph.D. diss., Vanderbilt University, 1979.

Wilson to King, 28 July 1958, in *Papers* 4:458.

GRANGER, LESTER BLACKWELL (1896–1976)

As national executive secretary of the **National Urban League** from 1941 to 1961, Lester Granger was a champion of integration and equal treatment for African Americans. Granger and Martin Luther King became acquainted in 1957, and the following year they and other civil rights leaders met with President Dwight **Eisenhower** to push for civil rights reform. King praised Granger's "dedicated and magnificent leadership" of the Urban League and appreciated his friendship (King, 28 September 1960).

Granger was born in Newport News, Virginia, on 16 September 1896. He graduated from Dartmouth College in 1918, and served in the military during World War I. After the war, Granger became an industrial relations officer for the Newark, New Jersey, chapter of the Urban League. He continued work for the organization while teaching high school and college in North Carolina and as a social worker in New Jersey. In 1934, he became the business manager of the League's magazine, *Opportunity*. In 1940, he became the organization's assistant executive secretary and was appointed national executive secretary the following year. During World War II, he pushed for integration in the military and was awarded the Navy Medal for Distinguished Civilian Service and the President's Medal for Merit in recognition of his efforts.

Shortly after the Southern Negro Leaders Conference (a precursor to the **Southern Christian Leadership Conference**, SCLC) was held in Atlanta in January 1957, Granger sent a telegram to King commending the "conference for the forthright steps you are taking to find practical solutions for the critical problems that Negro citizens are facing today" (Granger, 16 January 1957). Although Granger declined King's later invitation to serve on the advisory board of SCLC's "Crusade for Citizenship," citing a lack of time, he made it clear that he admired the campaign as "a significant step toward full citizenship rights" (Granger, 27 December 1957).

In 1958, when planning a meeting with President Dwight D. **Eisenhower**, King suggested that Granger and Roy **Wilkins**, president of the **National Association for the Advancement of Colored People**, be included despite the White House's preference that the meeting only involve King and A. Philip **Randolph**. The four leaders met with Eisenhower on 23 June 1958, and discussed voting rights, Department of Justice protections against racial violence, and the pace of school integration after the *Brown v. Board of Education* decision.

In 1960, King gave an address at the National Urban League's golden anniversary celebration. "For fifty long years," King told the gathering, "you have worked assiduously to improve the social and economic conditions of Negro citizens through interracial teamwork. Under the dedicated leadership of Lester B. Granger, your purposes have always been noble and your work has always been creatively meaningful" (*Papers* 5:499). King suggested that the Urban League and "more militant civil rights organizations" like SCLC had different, although equally important, roles in the "struggle to free the Negro" (*Papers* 5:506–507). Granger retired from the Urban League in 1961 and moved to New Orleans, Louisiana, where he taught at Dillard University. He died on 9 January 1976.

SOURCES

Granger to King, 16 January 1957, MLKP-MBU.

Granger to King, 27 December 1957, MLKP-MBU.

Introduction, in *Papers* 4:27–28.

King, "The Rising Tide of Racial Consciousness," Address at the Golden Anniversary Conference of the National Urban League, 6 September 1960, in *Papers* 5:499–508.

King to Granger, 28 September 1960, NULR-DLC.

GRAY, FRED DAVID, SR. (1930–)

Martin Luther King once described lawyer and activist Fred Gray as "the brilliant young Negro who later became the chief counsel for the protest movement" (King, 41). Gray provided legal advice to Rosa **Parks**, King's **Montgomery Improvement Association**, the local branch and state conference of the **National Association for the Advancement of Colored People**, and the Montgomery Progressive Democratic Association.

Born on 14 December 1930, in Montgomery, Alabama, Gray was ordained a Christian minister as a teenager and, following high school, he received a BS from Alabama State College for Negroes (1951) and an LLB from Case Western Reserve University in Cleveland, Ohio (1954). Gray then returned to Montgomery to open his private law practice while also serving as minister to the Holt Street Church of Christ. Gray recalled that he was anxious to return to Montgomery to "destroy everything segregated" (Gray, 19).

During the **Montgomery bus boycott**, Gray's leadership and legal counsel played a crucial role in the successful desegregation of Montgomery buses. He defended Claudette Colvin and Rosa Parks against charges of disorderly conduct for refusing to give up their seats to white passengers. Gray also filed the petition that challenged the constitutionality of Alabama state laws mandating segregation on buses (***Browder v. Gayle***). In November 1956, the Supreme Court affirmed the lower court ruling that racial segregation on public transportation was unconstitutional.

Gray recalled that he and King occasionally had differences of opinion on what action should be taken to ensure that rights were protected: "There were times when Dr. King said, 'Fred, I understand what you say the law is, but our conscience says that the law is unjust and we cannot obey it. So, if we are arrested we will be calling on you to defend us'" (Gray, 63).

Gray was involved in many other civil rights cases, including *Gomillion v. Lightfoot*, which challenged the Alabama legislature after it redrew the boundaries of the city of Tuskegee, Alabama, to exclude black neighborhoods, thereby denying African Americans the right to vote in municipal elections. Gray also fought for African American rights to education, the freedom to march peacefully, and the right to participate in juries, and opposed injustices like the infamous Tuskegee syphilis study that purposely left affected black men untreated.

In 1970, Gray was elected to the Alabama State Legislature as a representative from Tuskegee. With this election, he became one of the first two African American officials to serve in the legislature since the Reconstruction era. In 1979, President Jimmy

Carter nominated Gray to the U.S. District Court for the Middle District of Alabama, but Gray withdrew his name in August 1980, after opposition from conservative opponents. Gray received the American Bar Association's Equal Justice Award (1977), the **Southern Christian Leadership Conference**'s Drum Major Award (1980), and the World Conference of Mayors' Legal Award (1985). He was elected president of the Alabama State Bar Association in 2001.

SOURCES
Gray, *Bus Ride to Justice*, 1995.
King, *Stride Toward Freedom*, 1958.

GRAY, WILLIAM H., JR. (1911–1972)

William Gray was part of the network of black ministers throughout the country who supported Martin Luther King, Jr., and the civil rights movement. As pastor of Bright Hope Baptist Church in Philadelphia, Gray raised $1,500 for the **Montgomery Improvement Association** (MIA) in 1956.

Gray was born in Richmond, Virginia, in 1911. He received his BS from Bluefield State College and his MA (1934) and PhD (1942) from the University of Pennsylvania. He served as president of Florida Agricultural and Mechanical University at Tallahassee from 1944 to 1949, before succeeding his father as pastor of Bright Hope Baptist. Gray was active in civic affairs in Philadelphia, serving on the police advisory board, the civil service commission, and the housing authority.

Gray and King met in 1949, when King was a student at nearby **Crozer Theological Seminary**. Gray wrote his friend, Martin Luther **King**, Sr., saying: "He seems to be quite a fine young gentleman, and I am sure that you and Mrs. King must be proud of the record he is making for himself and his family" (*Papers* 1:210). King, Jr., appeared often at Bright Hope to raise money for the MIA, and when Gray's daughter, Marian, was active in the **sit-ins** of 1960, King, Jr., sent Gray a letter congratulating her "courageous activities," adding: "When I read it, my heart was throbbing with joy. You see, my friend, that is that old fighting spirit in you coming out anew" (*Papers* 5:408).

When King, Jr., was arrested in the Atlanta sit-ins of 1960, Gray sent telegrams to Mayor William **Hartsfield**, the *Atlanta Daily World*, and Rich's department store protesting King's treatment. Throughout the 1960s Gray worked to integrate Pennsylvania's state teachers' colleges.

SOURCES
Gray to King, Sr., 8 October 1949, in *Papers* 1:210.
King to Gray, 28 February 1956, in *Papers* 3:145–146.
King to Gray, 6 April 1960, in *Papers* 5:408–409.

GREGG, RICHARD B. (1885–1974)

Pacifist, writer, and activist Richard Gregg was the first American to publish a book on **nonviolence**. Gregg's *The Power of Nonviolence*, published in 1934, explained **Gandhi**'s nonviolent principles and his methodology of social change. In the foreword to the book's second edition (1959), Martin Luther King affirmed that "new ways of solving conflicts, without violence, must be discovered and put into operation" (*Papers* 5:99). In 1957, when King was asked by an official from the **National Association for** the **Advancement of Colored People** to name the books that most influenced him, he included Gregg's book along with those of Gandhi, Henry David Thoreau, and Walter Rauschenbusch.

Gregg was born in Colorado Springs, Colorado, in 1885. He attended Harvard, receiving his BA in 1907 and a law degree in 1911. His work in industrial relations led him to read Gandhi's work and travel to India in 1925 to study with him. Gregg spent four years in India, including seven months at Gandhi's ashram. Upon his return, he wrote *The Power of Nonviolence*. Gregg was involved in the **Fellowship of Reconciliation** (FOR) throughout most of his adult life and influenced many of the founders of the **Congress of Racial Equality**.

When the **Montgomery bus boycott** first began, nonviolence was not mentioned at the mass meetings, and many of the leaders had armed guards protecting them. Former FOR staff member, Bayard **Rustin**, arrived during the boycott's third month and encouraged King to make a philosophical commitment to nonviolence. When FOR's Glenn **Smiley** arrived shortly thereafter, he brought with him *The Power of Nonviolence*. King read it immediately and wrote Gregg, "I don't know when I have read anything that has given the idea of non-violence a more realistic and depthful interpretation. I assure you that it will be a lasting influence in my life" (*Papers* 3:244–245).

King and Gregg corresponded on the application of nonviolence in Montgomery. Gregg cautioned King not to despair if there were failures in discipline during the protest, reminding him that Gandhi also faced this. "You are doing something big enough to call for all your energy and devotion and endurance," he told King. "The whole world will be grateful to you" (*Papers* 3:268). Gregg traveled to India again and reported to King after the boycott that he "heard echoes of [his] struggle in Montgomery" (Gregg, 27 October 1958). Gregg also provided King with the names of people to meet when he traveled to **India** in 1959.

SOURCES

Gregg to King, 20 May 1956, in *Papers* 3:267–269.

Gregg to King, 27 October 1958, MLKP-MBU.

King, Foreword to Richard B. Gregg, *Power of Nonviolence*, 1959, in *Papers* 5:99.

King to Gregg, 1 May 1956, in *Papers* 3:244–245.

King to Gregg, 18 December 1958, in *Papers* 4:547–549.

Joseph Kip Kosek, "Richard Gregg, Mohandas Gandhi, and the Strategy of Nonviolence," *Journal of American History* 91, no. 4 (2005): 1318–1348.

GREGORY, DICK (1932–)

As an active participant in the civil rights movement, comedian Dick Gregory became a close ally of Martin Luther King. In a 14 May 1965 letter to Gregory, King extolled his contributions to the **Southern Christian Leadership Conference** (SCLC) and civil rights, stating that he had been "so dedicated and significant" that the movement would "always remain indebted to [him]."

Born Richard Claxton Gregory on 12 October 1932, in St. Louis, Missouri, Gregory was one of six siblings raised alone by his mother. He attended Southern Illinois University at Carbondale, winning the school's Outstanding Athlete Award in 1953. After serving in the Army, where he performed as a comedian in Special Service Shows, Gregory began a career in standup comedy in the late 1950s.

Gregory used his celebrity to bring attention to civil rights causes, participating in picket lines and voter registration efforts and performing at rallies and fundraisers. On 18 June 1961, he acted as the master of ceremonies at a freedom rally in Los Angeles, where King was the featured speaker. Gregory soon became a valuable resource for the SCLC, joining King in numerous fundraising events. When Wyatt Tee **Walker** sent Gregory an advance copy of King's 1964 book *Why We Can't Wait*, he recognized him as one of "a few people around this nation who have been especially close to the work of the Southern Christian Leadership Conference and for whom Dr. King has an especial affection" (Walker, 4 May 1964). Gregory also toured to raise funds for the **Student Nonviolent Coordinating Committee**'s 1964 **Freedom Summer** and participated in a 1965 freedom rally on the last night of the **Selma to Montgomery March**.

Gregory continued his activism after King's **assassination**, protesting the **Vietnam War** and running for U.S. president on the Peace and Freedom Party ticket in 1968. During the 1970s and 1980s, he turned his attention to issues of nutritional health and spiritual growth. Gregory was in the vanguard of performers who used their talents to promote civil rights and King's methods of **nonviolence**.

SOURCES

Gregory with Lipsyte, *Nigger*, 1964.
King to Gregory, 14 May 1965, MLKJP-GAMK.
Walker to Gregory, 4 May 1964, MLKJP-GAMK.

.

HAMER, FANNIE LOU (1917–1977)

When Fannie Lou Hamer testified before the credentials committee of the 1964 Democratic National Convention, she told the world about the torture and abuse she experienced in her attempt to register to vote. Martin Luther King wrote that her "testimony educated a nation and brought the political powers to their knees in repentance, for the convention voted never again to seat a delegation that was racially segregated" (King, "Something Happening in Mississippi").

Born to sharecroppers in Montgomery County, Mississippi, in 1917, Fannie Lou was the youngest of 20 children. She grew up on a Sunflower County plantation and in the mid-1940s she married Perry Hamer, a tractor driver on a nearby plantation. For the next 18 years, she worked as a sharecropper and a timekeeper for the plantation owner.

In 1962 Robert **Moses** and other members of the **Student Nonviolent Coordinating Committee** (SNCC) came to Sunflower County to register black voters. Inspired by what she learned from SNCC workers, Hamer attempted to register to vote. When her landlord and employer learned of her attempt, he fired Hamer and forced her to leave her home. For her determination to register, Hamer suffered repeated threats. In 1962, on her way to Septima **Clark**'s citizenship school in Charleston, North Carolina, Hamer was so severely beaten in the Winona, Mississippi, jail that she suffered kidney damage and was made partially blind. In 1963, Hamer, then in her forties, became the oldest SNCC employee and worked as a field secretary for the organization. By the time she cast her first vote in 1964, she was already very active in politics. "I cast my first vote for myself, because I was running for Congress," she recalled (Hamer, "An Oral History").

In 1964, Hamer helped organize the **Mississippi Freedom Democratic Party** (MFDP), an alternative to the state's white-controlled Democratic Party. When the MFDP challenged the all-white Mississippi delegation at the 1964 Democratic National Convention in Atlantic City, New Jersey, Hamer gave an impassioned account of the violence she and other civil rights activists had suffered while attempting to register. Although news networks started a live broadcast of her testimony, President Lyndon B. **Johnson** scheduled a live address at the same time, forcing networks to break away from her speech. Hamer closed her testimony, which was later

Fannie Lou Hamer (with microphone), a leader of the Mississippi Freedom Democratic Party, sings with Stokely Carmichael (in hat), Eleanor Holmes, Ella Baker (in sunglasses), and others outside the Democratic National Convention in Atlantic City, New Jersey, August 1964. © 1964 Matt Herron/Take Stock.

broadcast in full on the evening news, by stating: "If the Freedom Democratic Party is not seated now, I question America" (Lee, 89). Speaking after Hamer and the other MFDP delegates, King told the committee, you "cannot imagine the anguish and suffering they have undergone to get to this point," and urged the committee to recognize the MFDP (King, 22 August 1964).

Both King and Hamer participated in negotiations with vice presidential nominee Hubert Humphrey in the days following Hamer's testimony. In a compromise backed by Johnson, the MFDP delegates were offered two at-large seats and a promise that the 1968 conventions would bar any state delegation that discriminated against blacks. While King supported the committee's compromise, Hamer was adamant that her entire delegation should be seated, telling the group: "We didn't come all this way for no two seats!" (Carson, 126). Although MFDP failed to unseat the regular Mississippi delegation and only won two at-large seats, their efforts had a lasting impact on the democratic process.

Hamer, like King, was motivated by faith. Although she was only semi-literate, she had committed countless verses of the bible to memory. Reflecting on the **Nobel Peace Prize** he was awarded a few months after the MFDP challenge, King thanked the "great people," like the "Fannie Lou Hamers" whose "discipline, wise restraint, and majestic courage has led them down a nonviolent course in seeking to establish a reign of justice and a rule of love across this nation of ours" (King, "A Mighty Army of Love").

Hamer continued her career in political organizing and civil rights work as a delegate to the 1968 Democratic National Convention, where she berated authorities for failing to provide justice for King's **assassination**. In 1969, Hamer helped found the Freedom Farms Corporation, a nonprofit farming cooperative organized to alleviate hunger among poor blacks and whites in Mississippi. She remained active in civic affairs in Mississippi throughout her life and continued to speak and give interviews about the civil rights movement until her death in 1977.

Sources

Carson, *In Struggle*, 1981.

Hamer, "An Oral History with Fannie Lou Hamer," University of Southern Mississippi, http://www.lib.usm.edu/~spcol/crda/oh/hamer.htm?hamertrans.htm (accessed January 10, 2007).

King, "A Mighty Army of Love," *SCLC Newsletter* 2 (October–November 1964): 7–8.

King, "Something Happening in Mississippi," 17 October 1964, *New York Amsterdam News*, 17 October 1964.

King, "Statement before Credentials Committee," 22 August 1964, MLKJP-GAMK.

Lee, *For Freedom's Sake*, 1999.

Watters and Cleghorn, *Climbing Jacob's Ladder*, 1967.

HARDING, VINCENT GORDON (1931–)

Vincent Harding, Martin Luther King's colleague and a theologian, historian, and nonviolent activist, reflected upon the last year of King's life, writing, "Martin looked more beleaguered, harassed, and desperate than I had ever seen him before" (Introduction to "Unfulfilled Dreams," 189). Having met King in 1958, Harding had a long sense of perspective.

Born in Harlem on 25 July 1931, Harding was raised by his mother in the city's West Indian community. Harding recalled that his "primary community was a Black church" (Carby and Edwards, "Vincent Harding," 220). The church, according to Harding, "was an offshoot of the Black Seventh-Day Adventist denomination," and represented "a kind of nonconformist Christianity" (Carby and Edwards, "Vincent Harding," 220). Growing up, Harding's mother had difficulty making ends meet and supported the two of them with domestic jobs and government checks. After graduating from City College of New York with a BA in history, he received an MS in journalism from Columbia University.

Harding drove South in the fall of 1958 as part of an interracial pastoral team and met King as he recovered at his Atlanta home from a stab wound inflicted by Izola **Curry**. "He and Coretta were very gracious," Harding recalled, and King told him: "'You ought to come down here and work with us.' So that call reverberated" (Berger, "I've Known Rivers"). From 1961 until 1964 he worked with his wife Rosemarie as a representative of the North American Mennonite Churches in the southern freedom struggle. Their base was in Atlanta at Mennonite House, which they had founded. Harding remarked on their joint decision to go South: "I think the fundamental decision was to give ourselves to the struggle for as long as seemed right" (Carby and Edwards, "Vincent Harding," 225).

Harding engaged in a wide variety of social and political campaigns in the South. In retrospect, Harding remarked that "the fundamental racist nature of the U.S. meant we were of necessity striking at the heart of the situation. When Black people were involved, especially in the South, normal political activities, such as voter registration, became essentially and fundamentally radical" (Carby and Edwards, "Vincent Harding," 226). Harding was involved in the **Albany Movement** and was arrested for leading a demonstration at Albany City Hall in July 1962. He led a workshop on **nonviolence** as an approach to social change at the sixth annual **Southern Christian Leadership Conference** (SCLC) convention in Birmingham, Alabama, in September 1962, and was involved in the Greater Atlanta Peace Fellowship, which protested the proliferation of nuclear arms. In early January 1964, King asked Harding to draft a "critical analysis of the nonviolent movement," with an emphasis on "new directions that the nonviolent movement must take in '64 and in years to come" to catalyze a discussion of these issues for an SCLC retreat attended by Harding later that month (King, 3 January 1964).

Following the 1965 completion of his PhD in history from the University of Chicago, Harding accepted an invitation to become chair of the History and Sociology Department at Atlanta's Spelman College. Harding recalled that as a result of this opportunity and of his growing awareness of the **Vietnam War**: "I became very concerned that I not go to a teaching situation with young people without having some greater clarity about that war" (Berger, "Extended Interview"). To prepare, Harding studied Vietnam's history and, in the process, "decided to write something to the SCLC convention.... And what I wrote was essentially an open letter to Martin and the delegates" (Berger, "Extended Interview"). In this letter, Harding asserts: "It is my personal opinion that our nation is wrong in what it now does in Vietnam, and has been wrong for more than two decades.... I believe, too, that we as a nation are called upon to repent of the arrogance that took us into Vietnam in the first place" (Harding, 8 August 1965).

As American involvement in the Vietnam War escalated, in 1967 King publicly opposed the war. Harding recalled that King joined with **Clergy and Laymen Concerned about Vietnam** "to make a major anti–Vietnam War presentation at Riverside Church and he asked me to prepare a draft of what he might say. Essentially, the speech that he gave on April 4, 1967, was what I drafted.... I feel very strongly that the speech and his unflinching role in expressing and organizing opposition to the war—and to the foreign and domestic policy it represented—as well as his ineluctable movement toward the call for nonviolent revolution in the U.S., were among the major reasons for his **assassination**.... But I know that at his best Martin was his own man, and he would not have made the speech if he had not claimed it fully as his own" (Carby and Edwards, "Vincent Harding," 229). King's speech, "**Beyond Vietnam**," caused a storm of criticism in the press and from supporters of U.S. foreign policy, such as Billy **Graham** and Ralph **Bunche**. However, Harding recalled that, for King, "the most hurtful criticism was in the movement," from civil rights leaders such as Roy **Wilkins** and Whitney **Young** (Harding, 28 June 2007).

After King's **assassination** in 1968, Harding worked with Coretta Scott **King** to establish the **King Center** in Atlanta and was the Center's first director. At that time, he also worked with other scholars to create the Institute of the Black World, based on the idea that "the whole study of the Black experience ... ought to be essentially defined by Black people," and that "our academic work, our intellectual work, be carried on in the service of the continuing struggle" (Carby and Edwards, "Vincent

Harding," 232). Harding was professor of religion and social transformation at Denver's Iliff School of Theology from 1981 until his retirement in 2004. In 1996 he published a collection of essays entitled *Martin Luther King: The Inconvenient Hero*, illuminating the last years of King's life and the necessity of moving beyond King's "**I Have a Dream**" speech. In 1997, Harding and his wife founded Veterans of Hope, an initiative on religion, culture, and participatory democracy that emphasizes nonviolent and grassroots approaches to social change.

SOURCES

Rose Marie Berger, "Extended Interview with Vincent G. Harding," *Sojourners* (April 2007), http://www.sojo.net/index.cfm?action=magazine.article&issue=soj0704&article=070421x.

Rose Marie Berger, "'I've Known Rivers': The Story of Freedom Movement Leaders Rosemarie Freeney Harding and Vincent Harding," *Sojourners: Faith, Politics, Culture*, http://www.sojo.net/index.cfm?action=news.display_archives&mode=current_opinion&article=CO_040311_berger.

Branch, *At Canaan's Edge*, 2006.

Branch, *Parting the Waters*, 1988.

Carby and Edwards, "Vincent Harding," in *Visions of History*, ed. Abelove et al., 1983.

Harding, Interview by King Papers Project staff, 28 June 2007.

Harding, Introduction to "Unfulfilled Dreams," by Martin Luther King, Jr., in *A Knock at Midnight*, ed. Carson and Holloran, 1998.

Harding, *Martin Luther King*, 1996.

Harding, "An Open Letter of Concern to the SCLC Convention," 8 August 1965, VHC.

King to Vincent Harding, 3 January 1964, MLKJP-GAMK.

HARTSFIELD, WILLIAM BERRY (1890–1971)

As mayor of Atlanta, William B. Hartsfield helped negotiate desegregation of the city's businesses. When Martin Luther King and others were arrested during a demonstration in 1960, Hartsfield personally saw that the charges were dropped. King expressed his appreciation for Hartsfield's leadership over the years in a 1965 letter, where he told the former mayor, "I will never forget the great role you played" in the city's civil rights successes (King, 15 March 1965).

Hartsfield was born in Atlanta on 1 March 1890. He studied business and law and was admitted to the Georgia Bar Association in 1917. He joined the Atlanta City Council in 1923, and went on to serve in the State Legislature a decade later. In 1937, he was elected mayor of Atlanta and served until his retirement in 1961. In recognition of his unprecedented 23 terms, he was given the title Mayor Emeritus of Atlanta.

Within the segregationist leadership of the South, Hartsfield was a moderate on civil rights issues. Martin Luther **King**, Sr., even campaigned for Hartsfield in 1953, winning the mayor's appreciation. When 80 students, along with King, Jr., were arrested for participating in **sit-ins** at segregated lunch counters and restaurants on 19 October 1960, Hartsfield intervened. He brokered a truce by calling several dozen black leaders and student representatives to meet at City Hall. Afterward, Hartsfield announced that demonstrations would be halted for 30 days in exchange for the release of jailed students. King stayed in jail to face a hearing on whether his arrest violated his probation for a previous traffic offense. He remained in custody until 27 October, when a phone call from Attorney General Robert F. **Kennedy** to the judge in charge of the case prompted his release on bail. Although Hartsfield's later negotiations among the local parties broke down and the demonstrations were renewed, the Chamber of Commerce and African American leaders eventually signed an agreement in early 1961.

After King was awarded the **Nobel Peace Prize** in 1964, the city of Atlanta struggled with how to welcome him home without causing strife among the still divided population. Mayor Emeritus Hartsfield agreed to sponsor a dinner honoring King. When Hartsfield passed away in 1971, the city of Atlanta renamed the airport in his honor.

SOURCES

"Atlanta Negroes Suspend Sit-ins," *New York Times*, 23 October 1960.
Branch, *Parting the Waters*, 1988.
Introduction, in *Papers* 5:36–40.
King to Hartsfield, 15 March 1965, WHP-GEU.
"Tribute to Dr. King Disrupted in Atlanta," *New York Times*, 29 December 1964.

HASSLER, ALFRED (1910–1991)

As editor of *Fellowship*, the magazine of the **Fellowship of Reconciliation**, Alfred Hassler helped publish a comic book, "Martin Luther King and the Montgomery Story," to publicize the **Montgomery bus boycott**. Martin Luther King thanked Hassler for his support, stating: "You have done a marvelous job of grasping the underlying truth and philosophy of the movement" (*Papers* 4:303).

Born in Allentown, Pennsylvania, Hassler attended the Brooklyn Polytechnic Institute and Columbia University. He was a conscientious objector during World War II and joined the staff of *Fellowship* in 1942. In 1958, he joined Albert Bigelow on his yacht, *Golden Rule*, sailing to Europe and the Soviet Union to protest nuclear testing. From 1960 to 1974 he served as executive secretary of the United States Fellowship of Reconciliation and was also president of the International Confederation for Disarmament and Peace.

In 1965, Hassler was part of a group of clergy who traveled to Vietnam to meet with religious leaders. King sent a cablegram to Hassler, stating: "Please know that you have my prayers and deepest support as you seek to establish the dialogue between conflicting parties" (King, 5 July 1965). As a result of his trips to Vietnam, in 1970 Hassler founded the Dai Dong project, linking environmental problems, war, and poverty issues. He was the author of several books including *Diary of a Self-Made Convict* (1954) and *Saigon, U.S.A.* (1970).

SOURCES

King to Hassler, 28 October 1957, in *Papers* 4:302–303.
King to Hassler, 5 July 1965, FORP-PSC-P.

HAYLING, ROBERT B. (1929–)

As a civil rights leader from **St. Augustine, Florida**, Dr. Robert B. Hayling worked closely with Martin Luther King and the **Southern Christian Leadership Conference** (SCLC) to desegregate the nation's oldest city. King praised Hayling's "driving spirit," and wrote that his "dedication and sacrifice in the civil rights movement [could] never be measured" (King, 1964).

The son of a college professor, Hayling grew up in Tallahassee, Florida. He graduated from Florida A&M University (BS, 1951) and was commissioned a second lieutenant in the Air Force before being trained as a dentist at Meharry Medical School in Nashville, Tennessee. In 1960, Dr. Hayling set up his dental practice in St. Augustine. He was shocked by the extreme racism he witnessed in St. Augustine, although he served both white and black patients.

By 1963, Hayling was advisor to the **National Association for the Advancement of Colored People** (NAACP) Youth Council in St. Augustine. Made up mainly of high school students, the group was more strident in its demands for desegregation than much of the adult population. In early 1963, Hayling threatened public demonstrations against segregated facilities and urged Vice President Lyndon **Johnson** not to attend the city's 400th anniversary celebrations if they were segregated as planned. Although Johnson's insistence led officials to integrate the celebrations, city officials ignored their additional promise to set up a biracial committee to address the concerns of the black population.

Continued protests led by Hayling were uniformly met with resistance by white residents, city officials, and the police. During the summer and fall of 1963, black residents faced violence at the hands of white segregationists. In a controversial move, Hayling stated publicly that he had armed himself and others in the black community, arguing that the police were unable or unwilling to protect them. In September 1963, Hayling and two others were beaten and nearly killed at a Ku Klux Klan rally. The NAACP distanced itself from Hayling's militant statements, and after months of escalation and grand jury findings that blamed racial tensions on Hayling and other activitists, Hayling resigned from the NAACP and turned to SCLC for support in St. Augustine.

SCLC organized a high-profile desegregation campaign for Easter week, 1964. Hayling's approach to dealing with white violence had been very provocative, and SCLC's first step was to train the community in the techniques of nonviolent direct action. SCLC recruited white northern college students to spend their spring vacations in St. Augustine and began a series of night marches, pickets, and **sit-ins**. Hundreds were arrested, including Hayling, King, and Mary Peabody—the elderly mother of the sitting governor of Massachusetts—which brought national media attention to St. Augustine.

Over the next several months, Hayling and SCLC officials led demonstrations and sought redress in the courts. When an 18 June 1964 grand jury suggested that SCLC withdraw for a 30-day cooling-off period, Hayling and King released a joint statement declaring, "There will be neither peace nor tranquility in this community until the righteous demands of the Negro are fully met" (King, 18 June 1964).

After Florida's Governor Farris Bryant declared his intention, on 30 June 1964, to set up a biracial commission to address race relations in St. Augustine, SCLC left the city the next day, anticipating that President Johnson would sign the **Civil Rights Act of 1964** into law on 2 July. City business leaders pledged to follow the new law, but de facto segregation continued as white business owners who integrated suffered intimidation, pickets, and boycotts by segregationists. Hayling and others in the black community felt abandoned by SCLC's abrupt departure and some appealed for King's return to St. Augustine. Although SCLC contributed further financial support to

St. Augustine, the organization never returned to the city, and the St. Augustine group was left to bear the brunt of white backlash on its own.

With his dental practice financially nonviable after the loss of his white patients and the safety of his wife and children uncertain, Hayling decided to move to Ft. Lauderdale, Florida, in 1966. Hayling is the first black dentist in the state to be elected to the local, regional, and state bodies of the American Dental Association. In 2003, nearly four decades after he left St. Augustine, the city's mayor issued a Certificate of Recognition for Hayling's "contributions to the betterment of our society," and a street was named after him.

SOURCES

City of St. Augustine, "Proclamation: Certificate of Recognition," 20 June 2003, http://www.ci. staugustine.fl.us/pressreleases/6_03/proclamations/robhayling.html.

Colburn, *Racial Change and Community Crisis*, 1985.

Hartley, "The St. Augustine Racial Disorders of 1964" in *St. Augustine, Florida, 1963–1964*, ed. David Garrow, 1989.

King and Hayling, "Answer to presentment of Grand Jury," 18 June 1964, PGC-GEU.

King to Hayling, 1964, MLKJP-GAMK.

HELSTEIN, RALPH (1908–1985)

For more than 20 years Ralph Helstein led the United Packinghouse Workers of America (UPWA), a union Martin Luther King called a "pioneer" of the civil rights movement (King, 21 May 1962). In 1964, Helstein became one of King's closest advisers, meeting with him frequently to discuss the direction of the **Southern Christian Leadership Conference** (SCLC) and to help draft his public statements. King had great respect for Helstein's "dedication to the peaceful achievement of human dignity" and described his union's support of SCLC as "a mighty fortress protecting us" (King, 24 April 1962; King, 21 May 1964).

Helstein was born in Duluth, Minnesota, in 1908. He received both his undergraduate and law degrees from the University of Minnesota and took a position as the labor compliance officer of the state's National Recovery Administration in 1934. He began working with the Minnesota affiliate of the Congress of Industrial Organizations (CIO) in 1939, and in 1942 was named general counsel for the Packinghouse Workers Organizing Committee, renamed the UPWA in 1943. Three years later, Helstein was elected international president of UPWA.

Helstein's first move as UPWA president was to lead the union in an 82-day strike against the top U.S. meatpacking companies. Although the strike failed to achieve the pay raise Helstein sought, it consolidated the union's grassroots strength and proved its radicalism in relation to the other major unions at the time. Under Helstein's leadership, the union focused on equal rights for minorities, creating an Anti-Discrimination Department whose leaders worked with King during the **Montgomery bus boycott** and donated money to support the protest.

In October 1957 King was the keynote speaker at the union's Third National Anti-Discrimination Conference. The union had raised $11,000 in workplace collections, which they donated to SCLC. King recalled that the meatpackers' "generous gift was really the means by which our then infant organization was able to begin its work across the south" (King, 17 May 1961). When the UPWA came under attack by the

House Un-American Activities Commission for its alleged Communist sympathies, Helstein asked King to serve on an advisory commission to oversee the implementation of an explicitly anti-Communist ethical code. King returned the compliment in 1962 when he asked Helstein to become a member of the board of directors of the new **Gandhi Society for Human Rights**.

In June 1964 Helstein joined a small group of King's closest advisors known as "the research committee." Harry **Wachtel**, one of King's lawyers and advisors, coordinated the committee, and for the next few years Helstein joined conference calls or traveled to New York to meet with King and the committee in Wachtel's office. When the UPWA merged with the Amalgamated Meat Cutters union in 1968, Helstein became vice president and special counsel. He worked with the union until 1972 and died in Chicago in 1985.

SOURCES

Halpern, *Down on the Killing Floor*, 1997.
Halpern and Horowitz, *Meatpackers*, 1996.
Horowitz, "Negro and White, Unite and Fight!" 1997.
King, Address at the Thirteenth Constitutional Convention of the United Packinghouse, Food and Allied Workers, 21 May 1962, UPWP-WHi.
King to Helstein, 24 April 1962, UPWP-WHi.
King to Members of United Packinghouse Workers of America, 17 May 1961, UPWP-WHi.

HESCHEL, ABRAHAM JOSHUA (1907–1972)

Abraham Joshua Heschel was a Jewish theologian and philosopher with a social consciousness that led him to participate in the civil rights movement. Considered "one of the truly great men" of his day and a "great prophet" by Martin Luther King, Jr., Heschel articulated to many Jewish Americans and African Americans the notion that they had a responsibility for each other's liberation and for the plight of all suffering fellow humans around the world ("Conversation with Martin Luther King," 2).

Heschel was born in 1907 in Warsaw, Poland, to Rabbi Moshe Mordecai and Reizel Perlow Heschel. He received his PhD from the University of Berlin (1933), as well as a liberal rabbinic ordination from the Hochschule für die Wissenschaft des Judentums (1934). Heschel then succeeded Martin Buber as the director of the Central Organization for Jewish Adult Education in Frankfurt, Germany, until his deportation by the Nazis in 1938. Heschel taught in Warsaw and London before emigrating to the United States in 1940. In 1945, he became professor of Jewish ethics and mysticism at New York's Jewish Theological Seminary of America, a post he held for the rest of his life.

As a theologian deeply interested in studying the relationship between God and humankind, Heschel believed that when one understands the spark of the divine that exists within each person, he or she cannot harbor hatred for fellow human beings. A prolific scholar, Heschel also used his writings to express that social concern was an outlet for religious piety in noted works such as *Man Is Not Alone: A Philosophy of Religion* (1951) and *God in Search of Man: A Philosophy of Judaism* (1955).

In his opening address at the National Conference on Religion and Race in Chicago on 14 January 1963, at which King was also a featured speaker, Heschel maintained that Americans had the chance to find redemption through their efforts to combat racism: "Seen in the light of our religious tradition, *the Negro problem is God's gift to America*, the test of our integrity, a magnificent spiritual opportunity" (Fierman, 34). Heschel also viewed ecumenism as the necessary means to attack this social ill.

A social consciousness infused with an ecumenical approach brought Heschel and King together again on 19 November 1963, when both men addressed the United Synagogue of America's Golden Jubilee Convention in New York. King expressed his deep accord with Heschel's cause—which was to stand against the Soviet Union's treatment of its Jewish population—by restating his own view that "injustice anywhere is a threat to justice everywhere." King stated that he could not neglect the plight of his "brothers and sisters who happen to be Jews in Soviet Russia" (King, 15). In March 1965, Heschel responded to King's call for religious leaders to join the **Selma to Montgomery March** for voting rights. The march was spiritually fulfilling for Heschel, and he recalled feeling like his "legs were praying" as he walked next to King (Heschel, "Theological Affinities," 175). When King delivered his famous address against the **Vietnam War** at Riverside Church on 4 April 1967, Heschel followed him as a speaker and ended his own presentation saying, "I conclude with the words of Dr. King: 'The great initiative of this war is ours. The initiative to stop it must be ours'" (Heschel, 4 April 1967).

King later remarked that "Rabbi Heschel is one of the persons who is relevant at all times, always standing with prophetic insights" to guide persons with a social consciousness ("Conversation with Martin Luther King," 2). Both men were driven by the notion of a collective responsibility for the fate of all mankind and believed that the struggle to overcome injustice must be ecumenical.

SOURCES

"Conversation with Martin Luther King," *Conservative Judaism* 22, no. 3 (Spring 1968): 1–19.
Fierman, *Leap of Action*, 1990.
Heschel, Address at Riverside Church, 4 April 1967, CSKC.
Heschel, *God in Search of Man*, 1955.
Heschel, *Man Is Not Alone*, 1951.
Heschel, *No Religion Is an Island*, ed. Harold Kasimow and Byron L. Sherwin, 1991.
Susanna Heschel, "Theological Affiniites in the Writings of Abraham Joshua Heschel and Martin Luther King, Jr.," in *Black Zion*, ed. Chireau and Deutsch, 2000.
Kaplan, *Spiritual Radical*, 2007.
King, "What Happens to Them Happens to Me—and to You," *United Synagogue Review* (Winter 1964): 15.

HIGHLANDER FOLK SCHOOL

On 2 September 1957, Martin Luther King joined with the staff and the participants of a leadership training conference at Highlander Folk School to celebrate its 25th anniversary. In his closing address to the conference, King praised Highlander for its "noble purpose and creative work," and contribution to the South of "some of its most responsible leaders in this great period of transition" (*Papers* 4:270).

In 1932, Myles Horton, a former student of Reinhold **Niebuhr**, established the Highlander Folk School in Monteagle, Tennessee. The school, situated in the Tennessee hills, initially focused on labor and adult education. By the early 1950s, however, it shifted its attention to race relations. Highlander was one of the few places in the

King with folk singer Pete Seeger, Charis Horton (daughter of Myles Horton), Rosa Parks, and Ralph Abernathy at Highlander Folk School's 25th anniversary seminar, September 1957. Courtesy of the Highlander Research and Education Center Archives.

South where integrated meetings could take place, and served as a site of leadership training for southern civil rights activists. Rosa **Parks** attended a 1955 workshop at Highlander four months before refusing to give up her bus seat, an act that ignited the **Montgomery bus boycott**.

Led by Septima **Clark**, Esau Jenkins, and Bernice Robinson, Highlander developed a citizenship program in the mid-1950s that taught African Americans their rights as citizens while promoting basic literacy skills. Reflecting on his experiences with the Citizenship Schools and the emergence of new leaders from "noncharismatic people" who attended the training, Horton concluded that "educational work during social movement periods provides the best opportunity for multiplying democratic leadership" (Horton, *Long Haul*, 127).

Horton, who claimed he had first met King during the civil rights leader's junior year at **Morehouse College**, invited King to participate in Highlander's anniversary celebration in 1957. While attending the celebration, an undercover agent sent by the Georgia Commission on Education took a photograph of King. The photo was sent throughout the South and used as a propaganda tool against King, with claims that it showed him attending a Communist training school.

Highlander continued to be a center for developing future leaders of the movement such as Marion **Barry**, Diane **Nash,** and James **Bevel**. It was closed in 1961 when the

Tennessee government revoked its charter on falsified charges that the school was being run for profit and that it did not fulfill its nonprofit requirements. The **Southern Christian Leadership Conference** (SCLC) took over the citizenship program that year, feeling that it offered, according to King, a plus for SCLC and the movement "in filling the need for developing new leadership as teachers and supervisors and providing the broad educational base for the population at large through the establishment of Citizenship Schools conducted by these new leaders throughout the South" (King, January 1961). Under the leadership of SCLC and the supervision of Clark, Dorothy **Cotton,** and Andrew **Young**, the schools eventually trained approximately 100,000 adults. In August 1961, Horton opened another school in Knoxville, Tennessee, called the Highlander Research and Education Center. He and the Center participated in the 1968 **Poor People's Campaign** and, after King's **assassination**, erected a tent complex at Resurrection City in Washington, D.C., holding workshops until police closed the encampment in June 1968.

SOURCES

Adams with Horton, *Unearthing Seeds of Fire*, 1975.
Anne Braden to King, 23 September 1959, in *Papers* 5:290–293.
Glen, *Highlander*, 1988.
Horton with Judith Kohl and Herbert Kohl, *Long Haul*, 1990.
King, "Leadership Training Program and Citizenship Schools," January 1961, SCLCR-GAMK.
King, "A Look to the Future," Address at Highlander Folk School's 25th Anniversary meeting, 2 September 1957, in *Papers* 4:269–276.
King to Braden, 7 October 1959, in *Papers* 5:306–307.

HOLIDAY. *See* King National Holiday.

HOLLOWELL, DONALD L. (1917–2004)

During Donald Hollowell's career as a prominent civil rights attorney, he represented Martin Luther King several times, beginning in October 1960, when King was arrested for his participation in a **sit-in** at Rich's, a department store in Atlanta.

Hollowell was born in Wichita, Kansas, in 1917. At his father's insistence, Hollowell dropped out of high school at age 18 to help support his family. He immediately enlisted in the Army's all-black 10th Cavalry, and during six years in the service he earned his high school diploma. He later enrolled at Lane College in Jackson, Tennessee. Hollowell re-enlisted during World War II and rose to the rank of captain. After the war, he earned a law degree from Loyola University in Chicago in 1951. In 1961, Hollowell made history as the lead attorney in *Holmes v. Danner*, which desegregated the University of Georgia.

Hollowell defended King in October 1960, after King remained in Fulton County Jail for four days following his participation in an Atlanta sit-in. The sit-in charges were dropped, but he was subsequently charged with violating probation and sentenced to four months hard labor at Reidsville State Prison in Georgia. After one day in prison, King was released due to intervention by the **Kennedy** administration, and Hollowell successfully appealed his sentence to the Georgia Court of Appeals.

In December 1961, King was again in need of Hollowell's services after he and Ralph **Abernathy** were arrested for parading without a permit in Albany, Georgia.

Seven months after his arrest, King and Abernathy were found guilty and sentenced to 45 days in jail or a $178 fine. They chose to serve out the 45-day sentence.

In 1964, when Hollowell ran for Fulton County Superior Court Judge, King provided him with several members of the SCLC staff to aid the campaign. King also urged voters to reward Hollowell "with a vote ... for the long fight he has waged in behalf of justice and freedom" (King, 9 September 1964). Hollowell's bid was unsuccessful.

Under President Lyndon B. **Johnson**'s administration, Hollowell became the first black man to head the southeastern regional office for the Equal Employment Opportunity Commission, which he directed from 1966 to 1976. Hollowell served as president of the **Voter Education Project** from 1971 to 1986 and was the recipient of countless awards, including the **National Association for the Advancement of Colored People** Legal Defense and Education Fund's Lawyer of the Year (1965), and the Civil Liberties Award from the ACLU (1967). In 2002, he received an honorary Doctor of Laws degree from the University of Georgia, the same university he had helped to desegregate 40 years earlier.

SOURCES

Introduction, in *Papers* 5:37–39.
King, "Radio spot announcement by Martin Luther King, Jr.," 9 September 1964, MLKJP-GAMK.

HOLT STREET BAPTIST CHURCH (MONTGOMERY, ALABAMA)

On 5 December 1955, the first day of the **Montgomery bus boycott**, thousands of Montgomery's black citizens gathered at Holt Street Baptist Church for the first mass meeting of the **Montgomery Improvement Association** (MIA). Martin Luther King, Jr., delivered his first address as MIA president, telling the crowd, "There comes a time when people get tired of being trampled over by the iron feet of oppression" (*Papers* 3:72).

First organized in 1909 as part of Bethel Baptist Church, Holt Street Baptist Church was built in 1913 on the corner of South Holt Street and Bullock Street in Montgomery. Under the pastorship of A. W. Wilson for more than 50 years, the church was a frequent site of protest meetings during the boycott.

In his memoir, *Stride Toward Freedom*, King recalled that he had a mere 20 minutes to prepare the 5 December address, one of the most important speeches of his career. He found himself torn between delivering a speech militant enough to keep the boycotters motivated yet "moderate enough to keep this fervor within controllable and Christian bounds" (King, 59). King spoke of the injustices suffered by black bus passengers like Rosa **Parks**, and reminded the crowd of its Christian faith that justified protests grounded in **nonviolence**. He concluded, "When the history books are written in the future, somebody will have to say, 'There lived a race of people, a *black* people, "fleecy locks and black complexion," a people who had the moral courage to stand up for their rights. And thereby they injected a new meaning into the veins of history and civilization'" (*Papers* 3:74). Thundering applause followed King's speech and Ralph **Abernathy** read the resolutions drawn up by Abernathy, King, and others on the resolution committee. The crowd overwhelmingly voted in favor of the resolutions, including not to ride the buses until their demands were met.

Throughout the boycott, Holt Street served as a meeting place for strategic planning sessions as well as other mass meetings. On 25 June 1956, more than 5,000 protesters at Holt Street voted to continue the protest after the federal district court decision in **Browder v. Gayle**. Holt Street was also the site of the MIA's annual **Institute on Nonviolence and Social Change**.

SOURCES

Uriah J. Fields, "Minutes of Montgomery Improvement Association Founding Meeting," 5 December 1955, in *Papers* 3:68–70.

King, MIA Mass Meeting at Holt Street Baptist Church, 5 December 1955, in *Papers* 3:71–79.

King, "The Montgomery Story," Address at the 47th Annual NAACP Convention, 27 June 1956, in *Papers* 3:299–310.

King, *Stride Toward Freedom*, 1958.

Seay, *I Was There by the Grace of God*, 1990.

HOOKS, BENJAMIN LAWSON (1925–)

A Baptist minister serving on the executive board of Martin Luther King's **Southern Christian Leadership Conference** (SCLC), Benjamin Hooks had a long career in law, business, and the judiciary before becoming the executive director of the **National Association for the Advancement of Colored People** (NAACP) in 1977.

Hooks was born in Memphis, Tennessee, on 31 January 1925. After studying pre-law at LeMoyne College in Memphis, he served with the Army in Italy during World War II. Although he had experienced segregation his entire life, he found it particularly humiliating that the Italian prisoners of war he guarded were able to eat in restaurants where he could not. When he returned to the United States, he went back to school, first at Howard University in Washington, D.C., and then at DePaul University in Chicago, where he earned a law degree in 1948.

Hooks practiced law in Memphis from 1949 to 1965. In 1956 he was ordained and became pastor of the Greater Middle Baptist Church. He attended an SCLC conference in 1959, and became a member of the SCLC executive board. In 1962, King wrote Hooks that his sermon at **Ebenezer**'s Youth Day had "made a tremendous impact on our young people and our membership as a whole" (King, 9 April 1962).

Hooks was appointed to a judgeship on the Shelby County Criminal Court in Tennessee in 1965, becoming the first black criminal court judge in the South since Reconstruction. Despite his new role, he maintained his church positions and interest in civil rights activism, becoming a lifetime NAACP member.

During the **Memphis Sanitation Workers' Strike**, Hooks visited King and was in the audience at the Mason Temple on the stormy night of 3 April 1968, when King gave his last public address, **"I've Been to the Mountaintop."** Hooks wrote in his autobiography that he knew at the time that he had "witnessed a unique historical event … we had heard a speech unlike any that we had heard before or would likely hear again" (Hooks, 74).

In 1972, President Richard **Nixon** nominated Hooks to become one of seven commissioners of the Federal Communications Commission (FCC), making him the first black person to serve on the FCC. While on the commission Hooks advocated increasing the number of black-owned television and radio stations. Hooks left the FCC to become executive director of the NAACP in 1977. In his 15-year tenure at the NAACP, Hooks increased membership and lifted the organization out of debt. The NAACP awarded him its Spingarn Medal in 1986.

Hooks retired in 1993, returning to Fisk University, where the Benjamin Hooks Chair on Social Justice is named after him. He also taught at the University of Memphis, which established the Benjamin L. Hooks Institute for Social Change in 1996.

SOURCES
Abernathy, *And the Walls Came Tumbling Down*, 1989.
"Benjamin Hooks Installed as Professor of Social Justice at Fisk Univ.," *Jet*, 15 November 1993.
Garrow, *Bearing the Cross*, 1986.
Hooks with Guess, *March for Civil Rights*, 2003.
King to Hooks, 9 April 1962, MLKJP-GAMK.
Scott Minerbrook, "Being Denied," *U.S. News and World Report*, 22 July 1991.

HOUSER, GEORGE MILLS (1916–)

An original founder of the **Congress of Racial Equality** (CORE), Houser expanded his activism for racial justice internationally in 1953, when he established the **American Committee on Africa** (ACOA). Martin Luther King, Jr., who was a member of ACOA's national committee, regularly corresponded with Houser, writing that he felt an "abiding concern" for Houser and his work opposing colonialism and South African **apartheid** (King, 21 March 1963).

Born to Methodist missionary parents, Houser grew up in the Philippines and various parts of the United States. As a student at the University of Denver and then at New York's Union Theological Seminary, he worked for racial and economic justice. A committed pacifist, Houser, along with seven other seminarians, protested mandatory registration for the newly instituted draft in 1940. The "Union Eight," as they came to be known, were sentenced to a year in federal prison.

When he emerged from prison, Houser completed his studies at Chicago Theological Seminary and joined the **Fellowship of Reconciliation** (FOR) in 1941. In 1942, together with FOR colleagues Bayard **Rustin** and James **Farmer**, Houser founded CORE in order to pursue nonviolent direct action against segregation. Houser led **sit-ins** at segregated restaurants, movie theaters, and roller-skating rinks, and protested racial discrimination in housing. In 1947, Houser and Rustin organized the Journey of Reconciliation, which sent an integrated group of 16 men on a multi-state bus tour of the South to test the Supreme Court's *Morgan v. Virginia* decision, which ruled that interstate travel could not be segregated. The campaign served as a model for the **Freedom Rides** of 1961.

In 1953, Houser created ACOA to support anti-colonial struggles throughout Africa and end apartheid. In December 1962, after preparing with Houser, King and other African American leaders met with President John F. **Kennedy** to discuss U.S. policy in Africa. In a speech at a Human Rights Day rally organized by Houser on 10 December 1965, King called U.S. economic support to South Africa "the shame of our nation" and urged all nations to boycott South Africa in a demonstration of the "international potential of nonviolence" (King, 10 December 1965).

In 1966, Houser founded The Africa Fund, which he directed alongside ACOA until 1981. The following year, he addressed the United Nations' Special Committee against Apartheid on the 30th anniversary of the Campaign of Defiance against Unjust Laws in South Africa. Houser's autobiography, *No One Can Stop the Rain*, was published in 1989, and he continues to speak and write on Africa. ACOA and The Africa Fund merged with the Africa Policy Information Center in 2001 under the name Africa Action.

SOURCES

D'Emilio, *Lost Prophet*, 2003.
Houser, *No One Can Stop the Rain*, 1989.
Houser to Friend, 12 November 1959, in *Papers* 5:320–321.
King, Address to the South Africa benefit of ACOA, 10 December 1965, MLKJP-GAMK.
King to Houser, 21 March 1963, ACA-ARC-LNT.

HUGHES, ROBERT E. (1928–)

As executive director of the **Alabama Council on Human Relations** (ACHR), Robert Hughes helped organize the first negotiating session between the **Montgomery Improvement Association** (MIA) and the Montgomery, Alabama, city commission. A Methodist minister who met with Martin Luther King and other ministers in the MIA on Monday mornings, Hughes saw King as someone not seeking leadership. "It was cast on him," he wrote of King's MIA role. He was "needed for this position" (Hughes, 24 August 1985).

Hughes was born in Gadsden, Alabama, in 1928. He received his BA from the University of Alabama in 1949, a master's in divinity from Emory University (1952), and an MST from **Boston University** (1967). He became pastor of the Methodist Rockford Circuit in Alabama in 1953, but left the following year to serve as the first director of the ACHR. Through their shared interests, Hughes became friends with King, who was the first vice president of the Montgomery chapter of the ACHR. After facilitating the first meeting between the MIA and the city of Montgomery on 8 December 1955, Hughes continued to work behind the scenes to bridge the gap between the races. He occasionally gave guest sermons at **Dexter Avenue Baptist Church** when King was called out of town.

In 1960, as part of *New York Times v. Sullivan*, Hughes was called before a grand jury in Bessemer, Alabama. Refusing to turn over the records of the ACHR and expose its members to possible harassment, he spent Labor Day weekend in jail. Shortly thereafter he was assigned to missionary work in Southern Rhodesia. In 1962, he reported to King that following King's arrest in Albany "a group of ninety Africans in a remote valley far up in the Inyanga Mountains knelt in prayer in your behalf." He went on to ask, "Have you ever considered the power of world-wide prayer—at the same moment praying for the same thing???" (Hughes, December 1962). He remained in Southern Rhodesia until 1964, when the government declared him and his wife "prohibited immigrants" for supporting the liberation movement there, and subsequently they moved to Zambia (Dorothy Hughes, 27 October 1964).

Upon returning from Africa, Hughes became a conciliator and mediator of the U.S. Community Relations Service in 1967. He remained with the federal agency, created by the **Civil Rights Act of 1964**, until he retired in 1994. He later served as the Pacific Northwest coordinator of the Peace with Justice program of the United Methodist Church.

SOURCES

Hughes, Interview by David Garrow, 24 August 1985, DJG-GEU.

"Hughes Punished by Church for Conscience Sake," *Christian Century* (21 September 1960): 1077–1078.

Hughes to King and Coretta Scott King, December 1962, CSKC.

Dorothy Hughes to King, 27 October 1964, CSKC.

King, *Stride Toward Freedom*, 1958.

Morgan, *A Time to Speak*, 1964.

HUNTER, LILLIE THOMAS ARMSTRONG (1929–)

After Martin Luther King, Jr., became pastor at **Dexter Avenue Baptist Church**, he hired Lillie Hunter as church secretary. King cherished Hunter's loyalty to him. "When you have to work with people like me, you have to have a lot of patience," King jokingly said of Hunter at a reception held in his honor upon his relocation to Atlanta, Georgia, in January 1960 (*Papers* 5:355).

While working at Dexter, Hunter was also a student at Alabama State College. Nearly two months into the **Montgomery bus boycott**, Hunter was in a car with King when he was arrested for an alleged traffic violation as part of the "get tough" campaign by city officials. In February 1960, a month after King left Montgomery for Atlanta to be closer to the **Southern Christian Leadership Conference** (SCLC) headquarters, Hunter submitted her letter of resignation to Dexter and moved to Atlanta. She worked as the bookkeeper for SCLC and secretary to Ralph **Abernathy** until she left the organization in 1970. As a loyal employee and cherished friend, Hunter traveled with King's party to Norway when he received the **Nobel Peace Prize** in 1964.

SOURCE

King, Address delivered during "A Salute to Dr. and Mrs. Martin Luther King" at Dexter Avenue Baptist Church, 31 January 1960, in *Papers* 5:351–357.

"I HAVE A DREAM" (28 AUGUST 1963)

Martin Luther King's famous "I Have a Dream" speech, delivered at the 28 August 1963 **March on Washington for Jobs and Freedom**, synthesized portions of his previous sermons and speeches, with selected statements by other prominent public figures.

King had been drawing on material he used in the "I Have a Dream" speech in his other speeches and sermons for many years. The finale of King's April 1957 address, "A Realistic Look at the Question of Progress in the Area of Race Relations," envisioned a "new world," quoted the song "My Country 'Tis of Thee," and proclaimed that he had heard "a powerful orator say not so long ago, that ... Freedom must ring from every mountainside.... Yes, let it ring from the snow-capped Rockies of Colorado.... Let it ring from Stone Mountain of Georgia. Let it ring from Lookout Mountain of Tennessee. Let it ring from every mountain and hill of Alabama. From every mountainside, let freedom ring" (*Papers* 4:178–179).

In King's 1959 sermon "Unfulfilled Hopes," he describes the life of the apostle Paul as one of "unfulfilled hopes and shattered dreams" (*Papers* 6:360). He notes that suffering as intense as Paul's "might make you stronger and bring you closer to the Almighty God," alluding to a concept he later summarized in "I Have a Dream": "unearned suffering is redemptive" (*Papers* 6:366).

In September 1960, King began giving speeches referring directly to the American Dream. In a speech given that month at a conference of the North Carolina branches of the **National Association for the Advancement of Colored People**, King referred to the unexecuted clauses of the preamble to the U.S. Constitution and spoke of America as "a dream yet unfulfilled" (*Papers* 5:508). He advised the crowd that "we must be sure that our struggle is conducted on the highest level of dignity and discipline" and reminded them not to "drink the poisonous wine of hate," but to use the "way of nonviolence" when taking "direct action" against oppression (*Papers* 5:510).

King continued to give versions of this speech throughout 1961 and 1962, then calling it "The American Dream." Two months before the March on Washington, King stood before a throng of 150,000 people at Cobo Hall in Detroit to expound upon making "the American Dream a reality" (King, "I Have a Dream," 70). King repeatedly exclaimed, "I have a dream this afternoon" (King, "I Have a Dream," 71). He articulated the words of the prophets Amos and Isaiah, declaring that "justice will roll down like waters, and righteousness like a mighty stream," for "every valley shall be exalted, and every hill and mountain shall be made low" (King, "I Have a Dream," 72). As he had done numerous times in the previous two years, King concluded his message imagining the day "when all of God's children, black men and white men, Jews and Gentiles, Protestants and Catholics, will be able to join hands and sing with the Negroes in the spiritual of old: Free at last! Free at last! Thank God Almighty, we are free at last!" (King, "I Have a Dream," 73).

As King and his advisors prepared his speech for the conclusion of the 1963 march, he solicited suggestions for the text. Clarence **Jones** offered a metaphor for the unfulfilled promise of constitutional rights for African Americans, which King incorporated into the final text: "America has defaulted on this promissory note insofar as her citizens of color are concerned" (King, "I Have a Dream," 82). Several other drafts and suggestions were posed. References to Abraham Lincoln and the **Emancipation Proclamation** were sustained throughout the countless revisions. King recalled that he did not finish the complete text of the speech until 3:30 A.M. on the morning of 28 August.

Later that day, King stood at the podium overlooking the gathering. Although a typescript version of the speech was made available to the press on the morning of the march, King did not merely read his prepared remarks. He later recalled: "I started out reading the speech, and I read it down to a point ... the audience response was wonderful that day.... And all of a sudden this thing came to me that ... I'd used many times before.... 'I have a dream.' And I just felt that I wanted to use it here.... I used it, and at that point I just turned aside from the manuscript altogether. I didn't come back to it" (King, 29 November 1963).

The following day in the *New York Times*, James Reston wrote: "Dr. King touched all the themes of the day, only better than anybody else. He was full of the symbolism of Lincoln and Gandhi, and the cadences of the Bible. He was both militant and sad, and he sent the crowd away feeling that the long journey had been worthwhile" (Reston, "'I Have a Dream ...'").

SOURCES

Carey to King, 7 June 1955, in *Papers* 2:560–561.

Hansen, *The Dream*, 2003.

King, "Address at Cobo Hall," in *A Call to Conscience*, ed. Carson and Shepard, 2001.

King, "I Have a Dream," in *A Call to Conscience*, ed. Carson and Shepard, 2001.

King, Interview by Donald Smith, 29 November 1963, DHSTR-WHi.

King, "The Negro and the American Dream," Excerpt from Address at the Annual Freedom Mass Meeting of the North Carolina State Conference of Branches of the NAACP, 25 September 1960, in *Papers* 5:508–511.

King, "A Realistic Look at the Question of Progress in the Area of Race Relations," Address at St. Louis Freedom Rally, 10 April 1957, in *Papers* 4:167–179.

King, "Unfulfilled Hopes," Sermon delivered at Dexter Avenue Baptist Church, 5 April 1959, in *Papers* 6:359–367.

James Reston, "'I Have a Dream ...': Peroration by Dr. King Sums Up a Day the Capital Will Remember," *New York Times*, 29 August 1963.

INDIA TRIP (1959)

From the early days of the **Montgomery bus boycott**, Martin Luther King, Jr., referred to India's Mahatma **Gandhi** as "the guiding light of our technique of nonviolent social change" (*Papers* 5:231). Following the success of the boycott in 1956,

King contemplated traveling to India to deepen his understanding of Gandhian principles.

That same year, Jawaharlal **Nehru**, India's prime minister, made a short visit to the United States. Although unable to arrange a meeting with King, Nehru made inquiries through his diplomatic representatives concerning the possibility of King visiting India in the future. King secured funds for his trip to India from the Christopher Reynolds Foundation, the **Montgomery Improvement Association**, the **Southern Christian Leadership Conference**, and **Dexter Avenue Baptist Church**. While King made travel plans from Montgomery, the co-sponsors of King's trip, **American Friends Service Committee** and the Gandhi Smarak Nidhi (Gandhi National Memorial Fund), headed by Secretary G. **Ramachandran**, began arranging for King to meet with Indian officials and Gandhian activists during his stay.

On 3 February 1959, King, his wife, Coretta Scott **King**, and Lawrence **Reddick** began a five-

The Kings, Lawrence Dunbar Reddick, Indian parliamentarian Sucheta Kripalani, G. Ramachandran, and others upon King's arrival in New Delhi, India, on 10 February 1959. © AP / Wide World Photos.

week tour of India. Upon their arrival at New Delhi's Palam Airport on 10 February, King was feted by G. Ramachandran and Sucheta Kripalani of the Gandhi Smarak Nidhi.

King told a group of reporters gathered at the airport, "To other countries I may go as a tourist, but to India I come as a pilgrim" (*Papers* 5:126). Throughout their visit, King, Coretta, and Reddick received invitations to hundreds of engagements. "The people showered upon us the most generous hospitality imaginable…. Virtually every door was open so that our party," King recalled, "was able to see some of India's most important social experiments and talk with leaders in and out of Government, ranging from Prime Minister Nehru to village councilmen and Vinoba Bhave, the sainted leader of the land reform movement" (*Papers* 5:232; 143).

King's popularity in India revealed the extent to which the Montgomery bus boycott had been covered in India and throughout the world. "We were looked upon as brothers with the color of our skins as something of an asset," King recalled. "But the strongest bond of fraternity was the common cause of minority and colonial peoples in America, Africa and Asia struggling to throw off racialism and imperialism" (*Papers* 5:233). The African American and Indian overlapping experiences with racism and common philosophy of liberation sparked numerous conversations, and King shared his views on the race question before university groups and at public meetings. In addition, King discussed his views of **nonviolence** with various heads of state, including Nehru and India's vice president Sarvepalli Radhakrishnan.

Gandhians accepted King openly and praised him for his efforts in Montgomery, which they looked upon as an example of the potential of nonviolence outside of India. King's meetings with satyagrahis and his interactions with the Gandhi family reinforced his belief in the power of nonviolent resistance and its potential usefulness throughout the world—even against totalitarian regimes. In a discussion with African students who were studying in India, King talked about the true nature of nonviolent resistance (*Papers* 5:234).

As he traveled throughout India, King reflected on the similarities and differences between India and the United States. He observed that although India was rife with poverty, overpopulation, and unemployment, the country nonetheless had a low crime rate and strong spiritual quality. Moreover, the bourgeoisie—whether white, black, or brown—had similar opportunities. Upon his return from India, King compared the discrimination of India's untouchables with America's race problems, noting that India's leaders publicly endorsed integration laws. "This has not been done so largely in America," King wrote. He added, "Today no leader in India would dare to make a public endorsement of untouchability. But in America, every day some leader endorses racial segregation" (*Papers* 5:143).

King's trip to India had a profound influence on his understanding of nonviolent resistance and his commitment to America's struggle for civil rights. In a radio address made during his final evening in India, King reflected: "Since being in India, I am more convinced than ever before that the method of nonviolent resistance is the most potent weapon available to oppressed people in their struggle for justice and human dignity. In a real sense, Mahatma Gandhi embodied in his life certain universal principles that are inherent in the moral structure of the universe, and these principles are as inescapable as the law of gravitation" (*Papers* 5:136).

SOURCES

Account by Lawrence Dunbar Reddick of Press Conference in New Delhi on 10 February 1959, in *Papers* 5:125–129.
Introduction, in *Papers* 5:4–7.
King, Farewell Statement for All India Radio, 9 March 1959, in *Papers* 5:135–136.
King, "My Trip to the Land of Gandhi," July 1959, in *Papers* 5:231–238.
King, Statement upon Return from India, 18 March 1959, in *Papers* 5:142–143.

IN FRIENDSHIP

On 5 January 1956, one month after the start of the **Montgomery bus boycott**, New York–based In Friendship was formed to direct economic aid to the South's growing civil rights struggle. Founded by Ella **Baker**, Stanley **Levison**, Bayard **Rustin**, and representatives from more than 25 religious, political, and labor groups, In Friendship sought to assist grassroots activists who were "suffering economic reprisals because of their fight against segregation" (In Friendship, 17 February 1956). During its three years of operation, the organization contributed thousands of dollars to support the work of Martin Luther King and the **Montgomery Improvement Association** (MIA). In a letter to George Lawrence, chairman of In Friendship during the bus boycott, King stated, "We are very grateful to 'In friendship' for the interest that it has taken in our struggle" (*Papers* 3:408).

In May 1956, the organization joined with the Brotherhood of Sleeping Car Porters to hold a civil rights rally in New York City's Madison Square Garden. Proceeds from the event went to the MIA and the **National Association for the Advancement of Colored People**. In addition, $10,000 was deposited into the Victory Savings Bank in Columbia, South Carolina, to enable the bank to issue loans to needy tenant farmers.

On 5 December 1956, In Friendship held its second major fundraiser, a concert at New York's Manhattan Center to commemorate the first anniversary of the start of the bus boycott. In a 23 November letter to concert organizers Ruth Bunche and Aminda Wilkins, King described how boycotters were forced to walk to work because of a recent legal ban on carpools and how drivers were being targeted for economic retaliation. He wrote, "These factors mean that we are unfortunately in grave need of funds for carrying on the most critical phase of our struggle" (*Papers* 3:437). The event, which featured Coretta Scott **King**, Duke Ellington, Harry **Belafonte**, and Tallulah Bankhead, raised nearly $2,000 for the MIA. Coretta King spoke at the event, telling the northern crowd the story of the old woman who said, "It used to be that my soul was tired while my feet rested. Now my feet are tired, but my soul is resting" (King, 5 December 1956).

In Friendship continued to aid the movement after the bus boycott came to an end. Funds were raised to assist in the preparations for the January 1957 Southern Negro Leaders Conference, the founding gathering of the **Southern Christian Leadership Conference** (SCLC). The organization later contributed $500 toward King's 1957 trip to **Ghana** and secured a $4,000 grant for his 1959 **India trip**. During the late 1950s, In Friendship disbanded after funds dwindled as donors began directing their contributions directly to movement groups and Baker, Levison, and Rustin became involved with SCLC.

SOURCES

In Friendship, Memo, 17 February 1956, NAACPP-DLC.
King to George Lawrence, 30 October 1956, in *Papers* 3:407–408.
King to Ruth Bunche and Aminda Wilkins, 23 November 1956, in *Papers* 3:437–438.
(Scott) King, Address at Montgomery anniversary concert, 5 December 1956, CB-CtY.
Ransby, *Ella Baker and the Black Freedom Movement*, 2003.

INSTITUTE ON NONVIOLENCE AND SOCIAL CHANGE

In December 1956, the **Montgomery Improvement Association** (MIA) held the first of its annual conferences on nonviolent direct action, called the Institute on Nonviolence and Social Change. The theme of the 1956 institute was "Freedom and Dignity Through Love," and it included an address by Martin Luther King, Jr.

In addition to King's address at the opening of the mass meeting, the 1956 institute included a forum with T. J. **Jemison** of Baton Rouge, C. K. **Steele** of Tallahassee, Fred **Shuttlesworth** of Birmingham, and B. D. Lambert of Montgomery; a Women's Night with featured addresses by Lillian **Smith** and Nannie H. **Burroughs**; seminars on **nonviolence** presented by Glenn **Smiley**, William Holmes **Borders**, and Gardner **Taylor**; and a closing address by J. H. **Jackson** of the **National Baptist Convention**.

Institutes held in the following years typically included mass meetings, public forums, seminars on nonviolence, women's nights and youth nights, and other public events. To broaden the presentation topics, experts on various aspects of civil rights and nonviolent resistance, such as Harris **Wofford** and James **Lawson**, were brought to Montgomery to join MIA leaders in discussions and addresses on nonviolent tactics, voter registration, and citizen education.

The **Southern Christian Leadership Conference** (SCLC) also held institutes on nonviolence. In 1959, in Atlanta, SCLC, the **Fellowship of Reconciliation**, and the

Congress of Racial Equality conducted the Institute on Nonviolent Resistance to Segregation. William Stuart **Nelson** and Richard **Gregg**, internationally known scholars of nonviolence, gave addresses, and Ella **Baker**, James Lawson, Will Campbell, Ralph **Abernathy**, and King led discussion groups. Institutes subsequently sponsored by SCLC featured activists such as Wyatt Tee **Walker** and Dorothy **Cotton**.

SOURCES
Gregg to King, 2 April 1956, in *Papers* 3:211–212.
Nelson to King, 21 March 1956, in *Papers* 3:182–183.

"I'VE BEEN TO THE MOUNTAINTOP" (3 APRIL 1968)

"We've got some difficult days ahead," Martin Luther King, Jr., told an overflowing crowd in Memphis, Tennessee, on 3 April 1968, where the city's sanitation workers were striking. "But it really doesn't matter with me now, because I've been to the mountaintop … I've seen the Promised Land. I may not get there with you. But I want you to know tonight, that we, as a people, will get to the Promised Land" (King, "I've Been," 222–223). Less than 24 hours after these prophetic words, King was assassinated by James Earl Ray.

King had come to Memphis two times before to give aid to the **Memphis Sanitation Workers' Strike**. On 18 March, he spoke at a rally before 15,000 people and vowed to return the following week to lead a march. James **Lawson** and King led a march on 28 March, which erupted in violence and was immediately called off. Against the advice of his colleagues in the **Southern Christian Leadership Conference**, King returned to Memphis on 3 April 1968, seeking to restore **nonviolence** back to the movement in Memphis.

After arriving in Memphis, King was exhausted and had developed a sore throat and a slight fever. He asked Ralph **Abernathy** to take his place at that night's scheduled mass meeting at Bishop Charles Mason Temple. As Abernathy took the podium he could sense the disappointment of the crowd, which had turned out in the hundreds to hear King speak. Abernathy called King at the hotel and convinced him to brave the bad weather and come down to the temple. When King arrived, the crowd gave him a standing ovation. After Abernathy introduced King, the 39-year-old leader took the podium and began to speak to the audience extemporaneously. "Something is happening in Memphis," King said. "Something is happening in our world" (King, "I've Been," 207). Surveying great times in history, including Egypt, the Roman Empire, the Renaissance, and the Civil War, King said he would "be happy" if God allowed him "to live just a few years in the second half of the twentieth century" (King, "I've Been," 209).

As King recalled the events in **Birmingham** in 1963, he painted a bleak picture of the times, yet said this was the best time in which to live. As King concluded his speech, he began to reminiscence about his near fatal stabbing in September 1958. He exclaimed that he would have missed the emergence of the student **sit-ins** in 1960, the **Freedom Rides** in 1961, the **Albany Movement** in 1962, the **March on Washington for Jobs and Freedom** in 1963, and the **Selma to Montgomery March** in 1965.

In a prophetic finale to his speech, King revealed that he was not afraid to die: "Like anybody, I would like to live a long life—longevity has its place. But I'm not concerned about that now. I just want to do God's will.… And so I'm happy tonight; I'm not worried about anything; I'm not fearing any man. Mine eyes have seen the glory of the coming of the Lord" (King, "I've Been," 222–223). Witnesses, including Abernathy, Andrew **Young**, and James Jordan said King had tears in his eyes as he took his seat. "This time it just seemed like he was just saying, 'Goodbye, I hate to leave,'" Jordan supposed (Honey, 424). On 4 April, while King waited for a limousine to take him to dinner at Reverend Billy Kyles' home, he was fatally shot on the balcony of the Lorraine Motel.

SOURCES

Abernathy, *And the Walls Came Tumbling Down*, 1989.
Honey, *Going Down Jericho Road*, 2007.
King, "I've Been to the Mountaintop," in *A Call to Conscience*, ed. Carson and Shepard, 2001.
Young, *An Easy Burden*, 1996.

JACK, HOMER ALEXANDER (1916–1993)

Social activist Homer Jack was an early supporter of the **Montgomery bus boycott**. He corresponded with Martin Luther King and visited Montgomery during March 1956 to gain first-hand information about the boycott. Afterward he sent a newsletter to his colleagues in the civil rights and peace community describing the movement: "The Gandhian flavor was not apparent at the beginning.... It grew naturally." He concluded, "They have conducted a disciplined campaign which would, in many aspects, have made Mahatma Gandhi very proud" (Jack, 9 March 1956).

Jack was born in Rochester, New York, and attended Cornell University, earning a master's degree and doctorate in science. He went on to earn a BD from Meadville Theological School. He served as executive secretary of the Chicago Council against Racial and Religious Discrimination before assuming the pastorate of the Unitarian Church of Evanston, Illinois, in 1948. A founder of the **Congress of Racial Equality**, Jack was also active in the **Fellowship of Reconciliation** and the **National Association for the Advancement of Colored People**.

In 1957, *Christian Century* published Jack's "Conversation in Ghana," reporting on a meeting between King and anti-**apartheid** Anglican priest Michael Scott that he attended during Ghana's independence celebrations. According to Jack, the two clergymen discussed the "passing of an old age of racism and colonialism," and King told Scott that **nonviolence** in Alabama "did something to the oppressors; so it will even in South Africa." King predicted that the willingness to suffer "will eventually make the oppressor ashamed of his own method" (Jack, "Conversation").

Jack was also concerned with international political developments. When Jack left the pastorate of the Unitarian Church of Evanston to serve as associate executive director of the **American Committee on Africa** (ACOA) in 1959, King wrote in support, "Homer Jack is certainly one of the most dedicated persons that I have ever met. He combines the fact-finding mind of a social scientist with the great insights of a religious prophet" (King, 25 May 1959).

In 1960 Jack left ACOA to become the executive director of the **National Committee for a Sane Nuclear Policy** (SANE) which he had co-founded in 1957. Jack was eager to promote the involvement of international organizations in domestic concerns. In 1963, he wrote King that the national board of SANE had passed a statement "urging that mutual cooperation between the civil rights and peace movements be explored" (Jack, 21 June 1963).

Throughout his life Jack continued to work for world peace, serving the World Conference on Religion and Peace from 1970 to 1983 and founding the United Nations Non-Governmental Committee on Disarmament in the early 1970s. Jack also was the editor of two books on Gandhi, *The Wit and Wisdom of Gandhi* (1951) and *The Gandhi Reader: A Source Book of His Life and Writings* (1956).

SOURCES

Gandhi, *The Gandhi Reader*, ed. Jack, 1956.

Gandhi, *The Wit and Wisdom of Gandhi*, ed. Jack, 1951.

Jack, "Conversation in Ghana," *Christian Century* (10 April 1957): 446–448.

Jack, "To those interested in non-violent resistance aspects of the Montgomery, Alabama, protest against segregation on the city buses," 9 March 1956, BRP-DLC.

Jack to King, 21 June 1963, SCLCR-GAMK.

King to Dale O'Brien, 25 May 1959, MLKP-MBU.

JACKSON, JESSE LOUIS (1941–)

In 1966, Jesse Jackson began to lead **Operation Breadbasket**, a **Southern Christian Leadership Conference** (SCLC) program in Chicago. Often seen as Martin Luther King's protégé, Jackson quickly earned a place among King's inner circle. Although King found Jackson's ambition troubling at times, SCLC executive vice president Andrew **Young** called Jackson "a natural-born leader" (*Frontline*, "Interview with Andrew Young").

Jackson was born in Greenville, South Carolina, on 8 October 1941 to an unmarried, teenage mother. Jackson was both an honor student and class president in high school, and he received an athletic scholarship to the University of Illinois in 1959. He moved back to South Carolina after one year, however, transferring to Greensboro's North Carolina A & T College. In Greensboro, he became active in the civil rights movement, joining the local **Congress of Racial Equality** chapter and participating in **sit-ins** and demonstrations. Aware of SCLC's work at the time, a precocious Jackson wrote King: "Dear Sir, I don't think you'll ever bring God to Albany, Georgia. For He's wise enough to wait till E=MC^2 brings change there. Best of luck, though" (Jackson, 7 August 1962).

In 1964, Jackson graduated from college and moved to Chicago on a Rockefeller grant to study at Chicago Theological Seminary. In March 1965, he organized a group of fellow students to drive down to Selma, Alabama, answering King's call for supporters of the local voting rights campaign. Before returning to Chicago, Jackson asked Ralph **Abernathy** for a staff position with SCLC in order to lay the groundwork for a **Chicago Campaign**. Although King hardly knew Jackson, he took a chance and hired him.

In January 1966, King moved to Chicago to launch SCLC's northern movement. Jackson soon dropped out of seminary to help King full time, becoming the Chicago coordinator of SCLC's economic development and empowerment program, Operation Breadbasket. King was impressed by Jackson's ability to lead Breadbasket, saying, "We knew he was going to do a good job, but he's done better than a good job." Jackson was soon promoted to national leader of Operation Breadbasket. King told a Chicago audience that no one could be "more effective" than Jackson (King, 6 January 1968).

Despite King's praises of Jackson's work, a few days before King's **assassination** he criticized Jackson for following his own agenda rather than supporting the group. Jackson, hurt by his mentor's disapproval, told him, "Everything's going to be all right" (Frady, 225). King angrily replied that everything was not going to be alright and that he needed Jackson and all of the SCLC staff to work toward a common vision for America. King and Jackson reconciled in Memphis, Tennessee, after King called Jackson in Chicago and asked him to join him. Jackson was talking with King from below the balcony of the Lorraine Motel when King was killed.

After King's death in April 1968, Jackson continued to run Operation Breadbasket. Following in King's footsteps, he was ordained a Baptist minister. Newspaper articles after King's death called him "King's successor," and wrote of him as "the most persuasive black leader on the national scene" ("Emerging Rights Leader"). Despite tensions among the SCLC leadership, Jackson stayed with SCLC until 1971, when he formed his own organization, People United to Save Humanity (PUSH). In 1984, Jackson founded the National Rainbow Coalition, a social justice organization, and sought the Democratic Party's presidential nomination, winning 3.5 million votes and helping to register a million new voters. In his second bid for the nomination in 1988, Jackson won several primaries before being defeated by Massachusetts Governor Michael Dukakis. In 1996, the National Rainbow Coalition merged with PUSH to form the Rainbow/PUSH Coalition. Jackson's latest organization, the Wall Street Project, continues Operation Breadbasket's mission to create economic opportunity for minorities.

SOURCES

Branch, *At Canaan's Edge*, 2006.
"Emerging Rights Leader Jesse Louis Jackson," *New York Times*, 24 May 1968.
Frady, *Jesse*, 1996.
Frontline, "Interview with Andrew Young," Public Broadcasting Service (PBS), http://www.pbs. org/wgbh/pages/frontline/jesse/interviews/young.html (accessed 30 November 2006).
Jackson to King, 7 August 1962, CSKC.
King, "Prelude to Tomorrow," 6 January 1968, MLKJP-GAMK.
Landess and Quinn, *Jesse Jackson and the Politics of Race*, 1985.

JACKSON, JIMMIE LEE (1938–1965)

On the night of 18 February 1965, an Alabama state trooper shot Jimmie Lee Jackson in the stomach as he tried to protect his mother from being beaten at Mack's Café. Jackson, along with several other African Americans, had taken refuge there from troopers breaking up a night march protesting the arrest of James Orange, a field secretary for the **Southern Christian Leadership Conference** (SCLC) in Marion, Alabama. Jackson died from his wounds eight days later. Speaking at his funeral, Martin Luther King called Jackson "a martyred hero of a holy crusade for freedom and human dignity" (King, 3 March 1965).

Jimmie Lee Jackson was born in Marion, Alabama, on 16 December 1938. At age 26, the former soldier was the youngest deacon in his church, the father of a young daughter, and worked as a laborer.

Throughout late 1963 and 1964, local black activists in Selma and nearby Marion campaigned for their right to vote. By the time King and the SCLC arrived in Selma on 2 January 1965 to support the campaign, Jackson had already attempted to register to vote several times. King chose to bring SCLC to the region because he was aware of the brutality of local law enforcement officials, led by the sheriff of Dallas County, James G. **Clark**. King thought that unprovoked and overwhelming violence by whites against nonviolent blacks would capture the attention of the nation and pressure Congress and President Lyndon **Johnson** to pass voting rights legislation.

On the night Jackson was shot, he marched with his sister, mother, 82-year-old grandfather, and other protesters from Zion United Methodist Church, where King's colleague C. T. **Vivian** had just spoken, toward the city jail where Orange had been imprisoned earlier that day. When the local police, aided by state troopers, violently broke up the march, demonstrators ran back to the church, nearby houses, and businesses for safety. In the melee, Jackson and his family sought refuge with others in Mack's Café. Troopers followed the protesters inside and began beating people. After Jackson was shot, troopers chased him outside and continued to beat him until he collapsed. In addition to Jackson, at least half a dozen others were hospitalized for the blows they received from troopers.

King visited Jackson at the Good Samaritan Hospital in Selma four days after he was shot. Jackson was conscious, and King recalled his words during the eulogy he delivered to the overflowing Zion Church: "I never will forget as I stood by his bedside a few days ago … how radiantly he still responded, how he mentioned the freedom movement and how he talked about the faith that he still had in his God. Like every self-respecting Negro, Jimmie Jackson wanted to be free … We must be concerned not merely about who murdered him but about the system, the way of life, the philosophy, which produced the murderer" (King, 3 March 1965). Many were enraged that no case was opened against James Bonard Fowler, the Alabama state trooper who shot Jackson. Fowler acknowledged shooting Jackson at close range in an affidavit given the night of the shooting and told his story publicly in 2005 for an article in *Sojourners* magazine. He claimed that Jackson attempted to take his pistol from him, and called the shooting self-defense. Marion police chief T. O. Harris claimed that protesters had attacked law enforcement officers with rocks and bottles, but news reporters on the scene saw troopers beating protesters as they tried to escape, and black witnesses said no bottles were ever thrown. Forty years later, in May 2007, Fowler was indicted for Jackson's murder.

In the weeks following Jackson's death, SCLC organized a march from **Selma to Montgomery**, the state capitol. An SCLC brochure explained that Jackson's death was "the catalyst that produced the march to Montgomery." On 7 March 1965, the day the march first set off from Selma, Sheriff Jim **Clark**'s deputies attacked demonstrators with tear gas, batons, and whips. Images of the attack were nationally televised and at least one network interrupted regular programming to broadcast the violence of "Bloody Sunday." Two white civil rights workers, Viola Liuzzo and Reverend James **Reeb**, were later killed during the campaign. In August, the **Voting Rights Act of 1965** was signed into law.

Sources

Branch, *Pillar of Fire*, 1998.

John Fleming, "Former Trooper Arraigned in 1965 Murder Case," *Anniston Star*, 11 July 2007.

John Fleming, "Who Killed Jimmy Lee Jackson?" *Sojourners Magazine* 34 (April 2005): 20–24.

Garrow, *Protest at Selma*, 1978.

King, Eulogy for Jimmie Lee Jackson, 3 March 1965, MMFR-INP.

SCLC, *Let There Be Understanding … of the Call to Boycott in Alabama* (Atlanta: SCLC, April 1965).

JACKSON, JOSEPH HARRISON (1900–1990)

As a controversial leader of the **National Baptist Convention** (NBC), J. H. Jackson often clashed with other Baptist ministers, including Martin Luther King, Jr., who believed Jackson's opposition to the use of civil disobedience to achieve civil rights was too conservative.

Born on 11 September 1900, near Rudyard, Mississippi, Jackson received a BA from Jackson College (1926), a BD from Colgate Rochester Divinity School (1932), and an MA from Creighton University (1934). He was ordained a Baptist minister at the age of 22 and became pastor of First Baptist Church in Macomb, Mississippi. Jackson ministered in several locations before moving to Chicago in 1941, to serve as pastor of Olivet Baptist Church, a position he held until his death in 1990. In 1953, Jackson was elected president of the NBC, which he headed for the next three decades.

In 1956, some religious leaders urged King to run for NBC president, citing the need for dynamic new leadership. Gil B. Lloyd, pastor of Mount Zion Baptist Church in Seattle, solicited King: "As we stand at the threshold of momentous decision on Christian integration, while taking the long-range view of the future of our Negro Baptist ranks, we *must have a new leadership* which embodies religious zeal with scholarship, group loyalty with clear thinking, and administration with integrity" (*Papers* 3:443–444). Despite Lloyd's pleas and those of another black minister, King did not campaign for the presidency.

The following year, dissatisfaction with Jackson's NBC leadership intensified. The then four-term president was accused by some ministers of flouting NBC's constitutional tenure limit and of being slow to support the burgeoning civil rights movement. In the midst of the rumblings, Jackson became suspicious that King would use his influence to capture the presidency himself, or elect an opposing candidate. In July 1957, Martin Luther **King**, Sr., wrote Jackson attempting to diffuse the situation: "These fellows are lying about M. L., Jr., saying that he is against you and he is going to vote against you. You can take it from me, M. L. is not going to have one thing to do with it one way or another" (King, Sr., 29 July 1957).

Prior to the September 1958 convention, King was elected vice president of the National Sunday School and Baptist Training Union Congress, NBC's educational arm. King sought to place like-minded ministers in NBC hierarchy and requested that Jackson appoint Ralph **Abernathy** chairman of the Social Action Commission. Jackson rejected the recommendation, despite King's efforts to lobby on Abernathy's behalf. Although they were both NBC leaders, King and Jackson disagreed on civil rights tactics. Although Jackson had supported the **Montgomery bus boycott** in 1956 and donated money to the **Montgomery Improvement Association**, he advocated seeking change through the court system, rather than by direct action.

The dynamics of King and Jackson's relationship changed drastically in 1960, at the NBC convention in Philadelphia. King and other ministers were frustrated by Jackson's leadership and eager to unseat him. They organized support for Reverend

Gardner **Taylor**, an opposing candidate for the NBC presidency. Amid convention floor tumult and parliamentary wrangling, each candidate left the convention convinced he was the rightful president.

At the 1961 convention held in Kansas City, Missouri, Jackson and Taylor both claimed the presidency, causing pandemonium. In the midst of intense debate that eventually turned physical, Jackson supporter Reverend Arthur G. Wright toppled off the dais, suffered a head trauma, and later died of his injuries. Jackson was quoted as saying: "The method of campaign for the presidency was due largely to Brother King. His backers marched in boldly and took over the convention.... This disregard for convention officers and the pushing of folks off the platform was the result of an election campaign so vicious it produced violence" ("Calls Dr. King"). In a telegram to Jackson, King admonished the leader for "giving impetus to a conspiracy which had as its goal a homicide. Such an unwarranted, untrue, and unethical statement is libelous to the core and can do irreparable harm to the freedom movement in which I am involved." King clarified that he was not present during the debate and demanded that Jackson "retract [the] statement immediately and urge the press to give as much attention to the retraction as it gave to the original accusation" (King, 10 September 1961). More than 30 religious leaders, including Benjamin **Mays**, Fred **Shuttlesworth**, Kelly Miller **Smith**, and Sandy **Ray** also protested Jackson's remarks, sending the embattled NBC leader a telegram reading: "Whatever may be our differences within the denomination, this uncalled for and provoked attack (credited to you) upon one of the greatest men of our time will only serve the purposes of the segregationist forces in America who are determined to suppress the Negro community all over the nation" (Mays, 12 September 1961). Jackson later claimed his statement had been taken out of context.

As a result of Jackson's controversial remarks, conservative tactics, and tepid support of civil rights efforts, King and other dissenting NBC members left to form a new organization, the **Progressive National Baptist Convention**. Jackson remained NBC president until 1982, when he was replaced by T. J. **Jemison**.

SOURCES

"Calls Dr. King 'Master Mind' of Fatal Riot," *Chicago Tribune*, 10 September 1961.
Introduction, in *Papers* 4:17–18.
King, Sr., to Jackson, 29 July 1957, EBCR.
King to Jackson, 10 September 1961, MLKP-MBU.
Lloyd to King, 28 November 1956, in *Papers* 3:443–444.
Mays, et al., to Jackson, 12 September 1961, MLKP-MBU.
Paris, *Black Religious Leaders*, 1991.

JACKSON, MAHALIA (1911–1972)

As the "Queen of Gospel," Mahalia Jackson sang all over the world, performing with the same passion at the presidential inauguration of John F. **Kennedy** that she exhibited when she sang at fundraising events for the African American freedom struggle. A great champion of the civil rights movement, Martin Luther King called her "a blessing to me … [and] a blessing to Negroes who have learned through [her] not to be ashamed of their heritage" (King, 10 January 1964).

Jackson was born in New Orleans on 26 October 1911. Her father worked three jobs and her mother, a maid, died when Jackson was young. Raised in a devout Baptist family, Jackson grew up singing in choirs. She moved to Chicago at the age of 16 and continued to sing in storefront churches and toured with a gospel quintet. Jackson released her first album in 1934, but it was her 1947 album, "Move on Up a Little Higher," that brought Jackson fame. The album sold eight million copies and Jackson quickly became an international celebrity, performing sold-out shows at Carnegie Hall and later hosting her own radio and television shows in Chicago.

Already an icon, Jackson met Ralph **Abernathy** and King at the 1956 **National Baptist Convention**. King later asked if she could perform in Montgomery for the foot soldiers of the newly successful bus boycott. On 17 May 1957, she joined King on the third anniversary of the **Brown v. Board of Education** decision, singing at the **Prayer Pilgrimage for Freedom** in Washington, D.C. She subsequently appeared often with King, singing before his speeches and for **Southern Christian Leadership Conference** (SCLC) fundraisers. In a 1962 SCLC press release, King wrote that Jackson "has appeared on numerous programs that helped the struggle in the South, but now she has indicated that she wants to be involved on a regular basis" (King, 10 October 1962).

Jackson performed "I Been 'Buked and I Been Scorned" before King took the podium at the 1963 **March on Washington for Jobs and Freedom**. Later expressing his gratitude to Jackson, King wrote: "When I got up to speak, I was already happy. I couldn't help preaching. Millions of people all over this country have said it was my greatest hour. I do not know, but if it was, you, more than any single person helped to make it so" (King, 10 January 1964).

Jackson said she hoped her music could "break down some of the hate and fear that divide the white and black people in this country" (Whitman, "Mahalia Jackson"). In addition to the inspiration that her singing provided the movement, Jackson also contributed financially.

After King's **assassination**, Jackson honored his last request by singing "Precious Lord" at his funeral. When Jackson herself died of heart failure in 1972 at age 60, Coretta Scott **King** commented that "the causes of justice, freedom, and brotherhood have lost a real champion whose dedication and commitment knew no midnight" (Whitman, "Mahalia Jackson").

SOURCES

Introduction, in *Papers* 4:14.
King, Press release, "Mahalia Joins Dr. King in Freedom Crusade," 10 October 1962, HG-GAMK.
King to Jackson, 10 January 1964, MLKJP-GAMK.
Alden Whitman, "Mahalia Jackson, Gospel Singer and a Civil Rights Symbol, Dies," *New York Times*, 28 January 1972.

JAMES, C. L. R. (1901–1989)

As an historian, cultural critic, and intellectual, Cyril Lionel Robert James internationalized Pan-Africanist ideas while making contributions to global Leftist political thought. After speaking to Martin Luther King in 1957, James wrote his colleagues that the **Montgomery bus boycott** was "one of the most astonishing events of endurance by a whole population that I have ever heard of" (James, 25 March 1957).

James was born on 4 January 1901, in Port of Spain, Trinidad, and educated at the Queens Royal College. He worked in the fields of journalism, academia, and politics, but was particularly concerned with black independence movements and the politics of colonialism. In 1938, he published his influential book, *The Black Jacobins: Toussaint L'Ouverture and the San Domingo Revolution*, a study of the slave revolts that led to the independence of Haiti. That same year, James left England for the United States, during which time he met with Leon Trotsky in Mexico. In 1953, he was expelled from the United States for passport violations and returned to London but remained involved in the Johnson-Forest Tendency, a small group of U.S. radicals and Marxist theorists.

On 24 March 1957, during King's return trip from **Ghana**, he spoke with James and other black intellectuals about the freedom struggle in the United States, specifically the Montgomery bus boycott. James saw parallels between King's Gandhian conception of **nonviolence** and Ghanaian leader Kwame **Nkrumah**'s "positive action." James gave King several books to read and promised to send him a copy of *Black Jacobins*. He later wrote that Marxist organizations would be "making a fundamental mistake" by not recognizing that the nonviolent movements in Ghana and Montgomery were "a technique of revolutionary struggle characteristic of our age" (*Papers* 4:150n).

In 1958, James returned to Trinidad and was barred once again from entering the United States until 1970. He was influential to many **Black Power** proponents, and spent the last years of his life teaching and lecturing across the globe. Following his death, the C. L. R. James Society was formed.

SOURCES

Buhle, *C.L.R. James*, 1988.
James to King, 5 April 1957, in *Papers* 4:149–150.
James to Martin and Jessie Glaberman, 25 March 1957, MJGC-MiDW-AL.
King to James, 30 April 1957, in *Papers* 4:194.

JEMISON, THEODORE JUDSON (1919–)

T. J. Jemison led a bus boycott in Baton Rouge, Louisiana, in 1953, which served as a model for the **Montgomery bus boycott**. Martin Luther King called Jemison three days after the Montgomery protest began, and reported in his memoir that "his painstaking description of the Baton Rouge experience was invaluable" (King, 75). Jemison later recalled the importance of his friend, King, to the movement: "The Christian rearing had given him a burning desire that the whites could not understand. It was sort of like a peace that the world can't give and the world can't take away" (Jemison, 12 April 1972).

Jemison was born in Selma, Alabama, the youngest of the six children of Henrietta and David V. Jemison, who served as president of the **National Baptist Convention** (NBC) from 1940 to 1953. Jemison earned a BS from Alabama State College in Montgomery, Alabama, and a Master's of Divinity from Virginia Union University. He became pastor of Mount Zion Baptist Church in Staughton, Virginia, in 1945, and organized the first local **National Association for the Advancement of Colored People** chapter there. He was called to pastor Mount Zion First Baptist Church of Baton Rouge in 1949.

In early 1953, after years of enduring a Jim Crow system that mandated that black passengers stand behind empty seats reserved for whites on busy bus routes, Jemison and other black leaders in Baton Rouge convinced the city council to modify the seating ordinance to a first-come, first-served basis. The bus drivers, however, did not want to enforce the new system. The state attorney general ruled that the new ordinance violated state segregation laws and, in June 1953, black people in Baton Rouge boycotted the buses for eight days. Mass meetings were held every night, and carpools were organized. The boycott ended with a compromise that allowed mostly first-come, first-served seating, with the first two short rows designated for whites, while the rear long rows were for blacks. Dissatisfied with the mild reform, Jemison took the city to court and eventually won full integration of the city's buses. After King spoke to Jemison in December 1955, he took Jemison's suggestion that the **Montgomery Improvement Association** transportation committee help to organize the carpools.

Jemison was one of the founding members of the **Southern Christian Leadership Conference** and served on the organization's executive board until the late 1950s, when his duties as NBC secretary increased. He held the post until 1982, when he ousted J. H. **Jackson** as president. The relationship between King and Jemison became strained in 1961 when Jemison chose to remain loyal to Jackson as King and his allies turned away from the NBC and formed the **Progressive National Baptist Convention**.

Jemison's election in 1982, however, signaled the end of NBC's conservative stance and brought the organization more in line with those, like King, who favored **social gospel** Christianity. On this subject Jemison stated: "I feel that the National Baptist Convention, U.S.A., Inc., and the philosophy of Dr. King can be reunited" (Carter, 22). Jemison served as president until 1994, when term limits prevented his reelection.

Sources

Carter, *Born to Be President*, 1984.
Fairclough, *Race and Democracy*, 1995.
Jemison, Interview by Judy Barton, 12 April 1972, MLK/OH-GAMK.
Jemison to King, 21 October 1956, in *Papers* 3:402.
Jemison v. National Baptist Convention, 720 A.2d 275 (D. C. App. 1998).
King, *Stride Toward Freedom*, 1958.

JOHNS, VERNON (1892–1965)

In 1954, Martin Luther King, Jr., succeeded Vernon Johns as minister of **Dexter Avenue Baptist Church**. Reverend Johns had a lasting affect on King both personally and professionally. In *Stride Toward Freedom,* his memoir of the **Montgomery bus boycott**, King described Johns as "a brilliant preacher with a creative mind" and "a fearless man, [who] never allowed an injustice to come to his attention without speaking out against it" (King, 38). King found an example in Johns, a preacher who was able to use his religious position in the community to challenge his congregation to be less provincial.

Vernon Johns was born in Darlington Heights, Virginia, in 1892. He graduated from Virginia Theological Seminary and College in 1915 (AB), and earned a BD from Oberlin College three years later. Prior to his pastorship at Dexter Avenue Baptist Church, Johns pastored churches in Virginia, Pennsylvania, and West Virginia.

As Dexter's pastor from 1947 to 1952, Johns was an early proponent of civil rights activity in Montgomery, urging his congregation to challenge the traditional status quo. In response to discrimination on city buses, Johns once disembarked in protest and demanded a refund. He was well known for his controversial sermon topics, such as "It Is Safe to Kill Negroes in Montgomery," and he also shocked his middle-class congregation by selling farm produce outside the church. His early activism and challenges to the power structure paved the way for Dexter's congregation to receive King's socially active ministry and enabled King to take a leading role in the Montgomery bus boycott.

King and Johns were both frequent guests at Ralph **Abernathy**'s Montgomery home. Abernathy recalled that on one occasion, the three of them talked "about the situation at Dexter Avenue" and "about the oppression of our people and the growing belief that a sea of changes was taking place" (Abernathy, 125; 126).

Following his departure from Dexter, Johns continued to speak at churches and colleges throughout the United States. At King's request, he returned to Dexter as guest preacher for its 79th anniversary service. In addition to his speaking engagements, Johns also served as the director of the Maryland Baptist Center from 1955 to 1960 and was active in Farm and City Enterprises, Inc., an economic cooperative that enabled farmers to sell their goods directly to the consumer. In 1960, Johns wrote King requesting his assistance with raising capital for the cooperative, noting that he had been successfully speaking to groups that couldn't book King. He teased King: "It takes a mighty big man to enjoy hearing an audience say how glad it is the invited speaker couldn't get there!" (*Papers* 5:455). Johns continued to preach until his death in 1965, which—ironically—was within a week of delivering a sermon entitled "The Romance of Death."

SOURCES

Abernathy, *And the Walls Came Tumbling Down*, 1989.
Branch, *Parting the Waters*, 1988.
Introduction, in *Papers* 2:29–30.
Johns to King, 8 May 1960, in *Papers* 5:455–456.
King, *Stride Toward Freedom*, 1958.
King to Howard Thurman, 31 October 1955, in *Papers* 2:583–584.
King to Johns, 18 September 1956, in *Papers* 3:372.

JOHNSON, LYNDON BAINES (1908–1973)

President Johnson's five years in office brought about critical civil rights legislation and innovative anti-poverty programs through his Great Society initiative, though his presidency was marred by mishandling of the war in Vietnam. Though Martin Luther King, Jr., called Johnson's 1964 election "one of America's finest hours" and believed that Johnson had an "amazing understanding of the depth and dimension of the problem of racial injustice," King's outspoken opposition to the **Vietnam War** damaged his relationship with Johnson and brought an end to an alliance that had enabled major civil rights reforms in America (King, 4 November 1964; King, 16 March 1965).

Johnson was born in rural Texas on 27 August 1908. He graduated from Southwest Texas State Teachers College in 1930 and briefly taught in Texas public schools before becoming secretary to a Texas congressman in Washington, D.C. In 1937, Johnson was elected to serve out the term of a Texas representative who had died in office. In 1948 he was elected a senator, becoming Democratic whip, then minority leader. In 1954, Johnson became the second youngest man ever to be named Senate

King meets with President Lyndon B. Johnson at the White House on 3 December 1963, shortly after the death of President John F. Kennedy. Courtesy of the Chicago History Museum.

majority leader. From this position of power, Johnson used his political leverage to engineer passage of the 1957 and 1960 Civil Rights Acts.

When John F. **Kennedy** secured the Democratic Party's presidential nomination in 1960, he surprisingly chose Johnson as his running mate, hoping the Texas senator would appeal to southern voters. Shortly after winning the election, Kennedy named Johnson chairman of the President's Committee on Equal Employment Opportunity. With Johnson's encouragement, on 11 June 1963, Kennedy framed civil rights in moral terms for the first time during a national address.

Following the assassination of President Kennedy on 22 November 1963, Johnson challenged Congress to pass the civil rights legislation that had been deadlocked at the time of Kennedy's death. King publicly supported Johnson, saying that Johnson had taught him to recognize that there were "new white elements" in the South "whose love of their land was stronger than the grip of old habits and customs" and expressed optimism that Johnson's term would benefit African Americans (King, 1964).

On 2 July 1964 Johnson signed the **Civil Rights Act of 1964**, a far reaching bill he hoped would "eliminate the last vestiges of injustice in America" (Kenworthy, "President Signs Civil Rights Bill"). King stood behind Johnson as he signed the bill into law. A month later they clashed over the recognition of delegates from the integrated **Mississippi Freedom Democratic Party** (MFDP) at the Democratic National Convention of 1964. MFDP sought recognition as the legitimate Democratic Party delegation from Mississippi instead of the all-white "regular" delegation. However, Johnson feared this change would cost him southern Democratic votes in the upcoming election against Republican Barry **Goldwater** and recommended a compromise that King eventually supported.

Later that year Johnson won a decisive victory in the 1964 election, garnering the widest popular margin in presidential history. King had campaigned actively for Johnson and welcomed the victory saying, "The forces of good will and progress have triumphed" (King, 4 November 1964). In the first months of Johnson's elected term, King joined a voting rights campaign in Selma, Alabama, where less than two percent of eligible black voters had been able to register to vote. The brutality of white law enforcement during the **Selma to Montgomery March** stirred Johnson to send a voting rights bill to Congress. When introducing the bill, Johnson reflected publicly on the poverty and racism he had encountered teaching high school to Mexican immigrant children in Texas. King called Johnson's speech "one of the most eloquent, unequivocal, and passionate pleas for human rights ever made by the President of the United States" (King, 16 March 1965). Johnson signed the **Voting Rights Act of 1965** into law on 6 August.

During the first four years of Johnson's tenure as president, he deflected the criticisms of King that were fed to him almost daily by **Federal Bureau of Investigation** (FBI) Director J. Edgar Hoover, who nursed personal animosity toward King. Johnson saw King as a natural ally for his civil rights agenda, soliciting King's advice on civil rights matters and collaborating on tactics for pushing legislation through Congress. This relationship, coupled with Johnson's civil rights record, made King initially hesitant to speak out against his administration's policies in Vietnam. When asked his opinion by journalists in March 1965, King cautiously stated that he was "sympathetic" to Johnson's predicament but did not believe that "violence can solve the problem" (King, 6 March 1965). In late 1966 King's last phone call to Johnson was made to discuss Vietnam.

In the months that followed, Johnson attempted to meet with King on two occasions, but King canceled both engagements. Johnson was bewildered and asked his aides to find out why King was avoiding him. On 4 April 1967, the answer was revealed to Johnson in a speech, "**Beyond Vietnam**," that King delivered at New York's Riverside Church in conjunction with **Clergy and Laymen Concerned about Vietnam**. In his speech, King said that he was moved to "break the betrayal of my own silences and to speak from the burnings of my own heart" against the war in Vietnam, and in a devastating indictment of Johnson's policies, King called the United States government "the greatest purveyor of violence in the world today" (King, "Beyond Vietnam," 141; 143). Shocked by King's address and feeling personally betrayed, Johnson caved in to Hoover's pressure and asked his press secretary to distribute the FBI's information about King's ties with alleged Communist Stanley **Levison** to reliable reporters.

A year later, at a press conference for the **Poor People's Campaign**, King announced that he would not support Johnson in the 1968 presidential election. "I was a strong supporter," King recalled. "I voted for President Johnson and saw great hope there, and I'm very sorry and very sad about the course of action that has followed" (King, 26 March 1968). On 31 March 1968, Johnson shocked the nation by declaring that he would not seek reelection, and pledged that he would spend the remainder of his term seeking "an honorable peace" in Vietnam ("Transcript").

Four days later, on 4 April 1968, King was **assassinated**. Johnson wrote in his memoir that he had rarely felt a "sense of powerlessness more acutely than the day Martin Luther King, Jr., was killed" (Johnson, 173). Less than a week later, Johnson invoked King's memory when he signed into law the Civil Rights Act of 1968. Among other provisions, the bill barred discrimination in federally funded housing and created new penalties for threatening or injuring persons exercising their civil rights. In his final year as president, Johnson halted bombing in North Vietnam and pressed for peace talks. He would not, however, live to see peace in Vietnam; he died of a heart attack at his Texas ranch on 22 January 1973.

SOURCES

Branch, *At Canaan's Edge*, 2006.

Henry with Curry, *Aaron Henry*, 2000.

Johnson, *Vantage Point*, 1971.

E. W. Kenworthy, "President Signs Civil Rights Bill; Bids All Back It," *New York Times*, 3 July 1964.

King, "Beyond Vietnam," in *A Call to Conscience*, ed. Carson and Shepard, 2001.

King, Press conference on the Poor People's Campaign and the 1968 presidential elections, 26 March 1968, MMFR.

King, Press statement on Johnson, 16 March 1965, MLKJP-GAMK.

King, Statement on election of Johnson, 4 November 1964, MLKJP-GAMK.

King, Statement on President Johnson, 1964, MLKJP-GAMK.

King, Statement on Vietnam, 2 March 1964, MLKJP-GAMK.

King, Statement on Vietnam, 6 March 1965, MLKJP-GAMK.

Kotz, *Judgment Days*, 2005.

"Transcript of the President's Address on the Vietnam War and His Political Plans," *New York Times*, 1 April 1968.

JOHNSON, MORDECAI WYATT (1890–1976)

When Martin Luther King, Jr., went to the Fellowship House of Philadelphia one Sunday afternoon in 1950 to hear Mordecai Wyatt Johnson preach, he was treated to a message on **Gandhi** "so profound and electrifying" that he was propelled to buy "a half-dozen books" on the nonviolent revolutionary (King, 96).

Johnson was born in Paris, Tennessee, on 12 January 1890, to the Reverend Wyatt and Carolyn Freeman Johnson. He earned his BA from Atlanta Baptist College—now **Morehouse College**—in 1911 and was a professor of English, History, and Economics at Morehouse from 1911 to 1913. He went on to obtain a second BA from the University of Chicago (1913), a BD from Rochester Theological Seminary (1921), an STM from Harvard University the following year, a DD from Howard University (1923) and a second DD from the Gammon Theological Seminary (1928). Ordained as a Baptist minister in 1916, he served as pastor of the First Baptist Church in Charleston, West Virginia, from 1917 to 1926. In 1926, Johnson became the first African American president of Howard University, a post he held for 34 years.

Viewed as a somewhat polarizing figure during his presidency at Howard, Johnson had what most close associates and relatives considered a "Messianic Complex." One phrase he offered frequently on public occasions was, "The Lord told me to speak, but He did not tell me when to stop" (Logan, 249). Such command and conviction captivated King when he heard Johnson speak, in 1950, of his journey to India and of Gandhi's nonviolent resistance.

Following the **Montgomery bus boycott**, Johnson awarded King an honorary Doctor of Laws degree from Howard University. Expressing his admiration for King's spiritual, moral, and political leadership, Johnson described King as a man who had "revitalized religion in America" so that a "weak and conforming Christian church" could become "an instrument of redemptive social power" (Johnson, 15 July 1957). When Johnson offered King the deanship of Howard's School of Religion in 1957, King declined due to his commitment to nonviolent action in the South. Johnson understood and lauded King as "intellectually and spiritually" fit for the work (Johnson, 3 August 1957).

Johnson retired from Howard University in 1960, but continued to speak out on issues relating to the Cold War and the plight of Third World nations. Like King, Johnson believed that the United States could combat Communist influences through generosity as opposed to militarism, insisting that a policy of economic aid and political involvement would be far greater for these nations than armed conflict.

SOURCES

Johnson, "President Johnson's Citations: Martin Luther King," 15 July 1957, MLKP-MBU.
Johnson to King, 3 August 1957, MLKP-MBU.
Kapur, *Raising Up a Prophet*, 1992.
King, *Stride Toward Freedom*, 1958.
Logan, *Howard University*, 1969.

JONES, CLARENCE BENJAMIN (1931–)

In 1962, Martin Luther King wrote a letter recommending his lawyer and advisor, Clarence B. Jones, to the New York State Bar, stating: "Ever since I have known Mr. Jones, I have always seen him as a man of sound judgment, deep insights, and great dedication. I am also convinced that he is a man of great integrity" (King, 29 May 1962).

Jones was born on 8 January 1931 to parents who were domestic workers in Philadelphia, Pennsylvania, and was raised in a foster home and a boarding school in New England. He attended Columbia University beginning in 1949, but his college education was interrupted by military service. Jones was drafted into the Army in August 1953, but was given an "undesirable" discharge as a security risk in April 1955 for refusing to sign the Armed Forces Loyalty Certificate stating that he was not a member of the Communist Party. **Federal Bureau of Investigation** reports compiled in 1957 identified Jones as a member and leader of the Labor Youth League, described as a Communist Party front organization, during his years at Columbia. His discharge status was later changed to "honorable" on appeal.

Following his discharge, Jones returned to Columbia to complete his BA in 1956. That year he began attending **Boston University** School of Law, obtaining his LLB in 1959. He and his wife Anne moved to Altadena, California, where Jones established a practice in entertainment law.

Jones joined the team of lawyers defending King in the midst of King's 1960 tax fraud trial; the case was resolved in King's favor in May 1960. Jones and his family relocated to New York to be close to the Harlem office of the **Southern Christian Leadership Conference** (SCLC), and he joined the firm of Lubell, Lubell, and Jones as a partner. In 1962, Jones became general counsel for the **Gandhi Society for Human Rights**, SCLC's fundraising arm. Later that year, Jones would advise King to write president John F. **Kennedy** on the Cuban missile crisis. He urged King to make a statement because "your status as a leader requires that you not be silent about an event and issues so decisive to the world" (Jones, 1 November 1962).

Jones accompanied King, Wyatt Tee **Walker**, Stanley **Levison**, Jack **O'Dell**, and others to the SCLC training facility in Dorchester, Georgia, for an early January 1963 strategy meeting to plan the **Birmingham Campaign**. Following King's 12 April arrest in Birmingham for violating a related injunction against demonstrations, Jones secretly took King's handwritten response from jail to eight Birmingham clergymen who had denounced the protests in the newspaper. It was typed and circulated among the Birmingham clergy and later printed and distributed nationally as "**Letter from Birmingham Jail**." Jones helped secure bail money for King and the other jailed protesters by flying to New York to meet with New York Governor Nelson **Rockefeller**, who gave Jones the bail funds directly from his family's vault at Chase Manhattan Bank.

Jones continued to function as King's lawyer and advisor through the remainder of his life, assisting him in drafting the "**I Have a Dream**" speech and preserving King's copyright of the momentous address; acting as part of the successful defense team for the SCLC in *New York Times v. Sullivan*; serving as part of King's inner circle of advisers, called the "research committee"; and contributing with Vincent **Harding** and Andrew **Young** to King's "**Beyond Vietnam**" address at New York's Riverside Church on 4 April 1967.

After King's death, Jones served as one of the negotiators during the 1971 prison riot at Attica, and was editor and part owner of the *New York Amsterdam News* from 1971 to 1974. In summing up his sentiments on King's life, Jones remarked in a 2007 interview: "Except for Abraham Lincoln and the Emancipation Proclamation of 1963, Martin Luther King, Jr., in 12 years and 4 months from 1956 to 1968, did more to achieve political, economic, and social justice in America than any other event or person in the previous 400 years" (Jones, 18 May 2007).

SOURCES

Douglas Brinkley, "The Man Who Kept King's Secrets," *Vanity Fair*, No. 548 (April 2006).

Jones, Interview by King Papers Project staff, 18 May 2007.

Jones to King, 1 November 1962, MLKP-MBU.

King, *A Call to Conscience*, ed. Carson and Shepard, 2001.

King to Committee on Character and Fitness of the Appellate Division of the Supreme Court of the State of New York, 29 May 1962, MLKJP-GAMK.

K

KATZENBACH, NICHOLAS DeBELLEVILLE (1922–)

As Deputy and U.S. Attorney General during the **Kennedy** and **Johnson** administrations, Nicholas Katzenbach was a key governmental figure during the civil rights struggles of the 1960s. Although sometimes critical of Katzenbach's positions, Martin Luther King praised him as someone who "made significant contributions to the parade of progress in human relations" (King, "My Dream").

Katzenbach was born in Philadelphia, Pennsylvania, in 1922, the son of Edward L. Katzenbach, Attorney General of New Jersey, and Marie Hilson Katzenbach, a New Jersey state education official. His studies at Princeton were interrupted by World War II, during which he was a prisoner of war in both Italy and Germany. Following his release, he received his BA from Princeton (1945), his LLB from Yale (1947), and was a Rhodes Scholar at Oxford University in 1949. Katzenbach taught law at Yale and the University of Chicago during the 1950s. In 1961, Katzenbach was appointed Assistant Attorney General in charge of the Justice Department's Office of Legal Counsel by President John F. Kennedy and was promoted to Deputy Attorney General the following year. In 1964, after Robert F. **Kennedy**'s resignation, Katzenbach was appointed Attorney General. During the final years of Lyndon B. Johnson's presidential administration, Katzenbach served as the Under Secretary of State.

While at the Department of Justice, in 1961 Katzenbach urged Alabama officials to protect the freedom riders, and later intervened to enforce court orders to desegregate the University of Alabama and the University of Mississippi.

King met with Katzenbach on several occasions. Their correspondence primarily centered on Katzenbach's efforts to draft and secure passage of the **Civil Rights Act of 1964** and the **Voting Rights Act of 1965**. Katzenbach also intervened in the **Selma to Montgomery March** (1965), asking that King not lead marchers across the Edmund Pettus Bridge in defiance of Governor George **Wallace** and the local police force. King rejected the advice, replying: "Mr. Attorney General, you have not been a black man in America" (Greenberg, "Martin Luther King, Jr., and the Law," 17109). Following King's **assassination** and the conclusion of the Johnson administration, Katzenbach went on to work as general counsel for IBM.

SOURCES

Garrow, *Bearing the Cross*, 1986.

Jack Greenberg, "Martin Luther King, Jr., and the Law," *Congressional Record* 114 (17 May 1968): 17109.

Katzenbach, Interview by King Papers Project staff, 2 March 2007.

King, "My Dream: Great Expectations," *Chicago Defender*, 11–17 December 1965.

KELSEY, GEORGE DENNIS SALE (1910–1996)

The only instructor to award Martin Luther King, Jr., an A as an undergraduate at **Morehouse College**, George D. Kelsey was a theologian and educator who helped to convince King that a career in ministry would enable him to address issues of social justice and racial reform.

Kelsey was born in 1910 in Columbus, Georgia. He received his AB from Morehouse College (1934), his BD from Andover Newton Theological School (1937), and his PhD from Yale University (1946). Kelsey joined the Morehouse faculty in 1938 as professor of Religion and Philosophy and served as director of the School of Religion from 1945 to 1948. An ordained minister in the American Baptist Convention, he became associate director in the field department of the Federal Council of Churches in 1948 and retained the position until 1952, after the organization became the **National Council of Churches of Christ** in 1950. Kelsey joined the faculty of Drew University in 1951, a post he held until his retirement in 1976.

During King's junior year at Morehouse, his burgeoning sociopolitical views intersected with Kelsey's **social gospel** approach when King enrolled in his Bible course. To King's father, Kelsey was a teacher who "saw the pulpit as a place both for drama, in the old-fashioned, country Baptist sense, and for the articulation of philosophies that address the problems of society" (*Papers* 1:42). The younger King, uncertain about pursuing ministry as a vocation, was greatly impressed by Kelsey's use of higher biblical criticism in addressing theological issues.

King enjoyed his undergraduate studies in the social sciences and had been leaning toward a career in law or medicine; however, the ministry became a more tangible choice when he learned from Kelsey "that behind the legends and myths of the Book were many profound truths which one could not escape" (*Papers* 1:362). King had questioned "whether religion, with its emotionalism in Negro churches, could be intellectually respectable as well as emotionally satisfying," but Kelsey encouraged King to synthesize the religious notions of his upbringing with the secular education he received (*Papers* 1:44). He saw that King "stood out in class not simply academically, but in the sense that he absorbed the teachings of Jesus with his whole being" (*Papers* 1:155). In his letter recommending King for admission to **Crozer Theological Seminary**, Kelsey noted this shift in King's academic performance and described him as "being quite serious about the ministry and as having a call rather than a professional urge" (*Papers* 1:155).

King continued his close relationship with Kelsey beyond his college years, and Kelsey continued to provide King with financial and moral support during the **Montgomery bus boycott**. Kelsey believed King was "conducting activities in the finest Mosaic and prophetic tradition" (*Papers* 3:146). King sent Kelsey an early draft of a chapter of *Stride Toward Freedom*, trusting Kelsey's scholarship and asserting he would not like to have any of it published without Kelsey's "critical suggestions" (*Papers* 4:391).

Upon announcement of King's 1964 **Nobel Peace Prize**, Kelsey sent King a heartfelt congratulation. The Kelseys and the Kings remained family friends, with Kelsey inviting Martin and Coretta to stay with him and his wife whenever King traveled north.

SOURCES

Introduction, in *Papers* 1:42–44.

Kelsey to Charles E. Batten, 12 March 1948, in *Papers* 1:155.

Kelsey to King, 28 February 1956, in *Papers* 3:146.

King, "An Autobiography of Religious Development," *Papers* 1:359–363.

King to Kelsey, 31 March 1958, in *Papers* 4:391–392.

William Peters, "Our Weapon Is Love," *Redbook*, August 1956, 42–43, 71–73.

KENNEDY, JOHN FITZGERALD (1917–1963)

The 1960 presidential campaign between Democrat John F. Kennedy and Republican candidate Richard **Nixon** proved to be one of the closest elections in U.S. history, and one in which Martin Luther King, Jr., and the civil rights movement played a pivotal role.

Born 29 May 1917 to a wealthy and politically prominent Boston family, Kennedy graduated from Harvard University in 1940. After serving in the Navy during World War II, he followed his father into politics and served three terms in the U.S. House of Representatives and eight years in the Senate before securing the Democratic Party's nomination for president in 1960.

During the 1960 presidential campaign, Kennedy interceded when King was convicted for a probation violation after participating in a **sit-in** in Atlanta. Following the recommendations of campaign advisors, Kennedy called Coretta Scott **King** to offer his sympathy and his brother, Robert F. **Kennedy**, made phone calls that helped hasten King's release on bail from Georgia State Prison at Reidsville. In a statement following his release, King told reporters he owed "a great debt of gratitude to Senator Kennedy and his family," and downplayed the candidate's political motivations: "I'm sure that the senator did it because of his real concern and his humanitarian bent" (*Papers* 5:39). Though pressed by reporters, King declined to endorse Kennedy, explaining that it would be inappropriate for him to do so as the leader of the nonpartisan **Southern Christian Leadership Conference**. On election day, Kennedy defeated Nixon by less than one percent of the popular vote, a margin of victory that highlighted the importance of African American support.

Initially Kennedy proceeded cautiously with respect to civil rights. Despite pleas from King and other civil rights leaders for federal intervention during the violence surrounding the **Freedom Rides** and the **Albany Movement**, the Kennedy administration produced little policy progress on civil rights for racial minorities. In 1962, Kennedy slowly began to move forward a civil rights agenda with his administration's participation in the creation of the **Voter Education Project**. Later that year, he sent federal troops to Oxford, Mississippi, to quell riots at the University of Mississippi following its integration by James **Meredith**.

The 1963 **Birmingham Campaign**, headed by SCLC and local leaders, proved to be a catalyst for increased federal involvement in the struggle. The national media showed images of peaceful demonstrators being attacked by police dogs and high-powered water hoses sweeping people down the street, and Kennedy had little choice but to increase efforts to restore peace. On 11 June 1963, he directly addressed national concerns over civil rights: "We are confronted primarily with a moral issue. It is as old as the scriptures and as clear as the American Constitution. The heart of the question is whether all Americans are to be afforded equal rights and equal opportunities, whether we are going to treat our fellow Americans as we want to be treated" (Kennedy, "President Kennedy's Radio," 970). Kennedy followed his speech by introducing to Congress a comprehensive civil rights bill that primarily focused on the desegregation of schools, restaurants, hotels, and similar public facilities.

As Kennedy's proposed legislation was filibustered in Congress, King and other civil rights leaders pressured the president for action and proceeded with plans for the **March on Washington for Jobs and Freedom**, scheduled for late August. In a meeting with King, Kennedy initially expressed concern about the march and its effect on the pending civil rights bill. King assured Kennedy of the event's peaceful intentions and the president did not request the demonstration's cancellation.

Two weeks after the March on Washington, a dynamite blast at the Sixteenth Street Baptist Church in Birmingham, Alabama, killed four girls. King was devastated by the killings, writing to Kennedy: "In a few hours I will be going to Birmingham. I will sincerely plead with my people to remain non violent.… I am convinced that unless some steps are taken by the federal government to restore a sense of confidence in the protection of life, limb and property my pleas shall fall on deaf ears and we shall see the worst racial holocaust this nation has ever seen" (King, 15 September 1963). A few days later Kennedy met with King and other leaders regarding federal intervention in the civil rights struggle.

Kennedy's civil rights legislation remained stalled in Congress when he was assassinated on 22 November 1963. King wrote an epitaph to the slain president in a column appearing in the **New York Amsterdam News**, a month after Kennedy's death. Proclaiming that we can all learn something from Kennedy in death, King wrote that the former president's death "says to all of us that this virus of hate that has seeped into the [veins] of our nation, if unchecked, will lead inevitably to our moral and spiritual doom." Concluding his eulogy, King described Kennedy's life as a challenge to "move forward with more determination to rid our nation of the vestiges of racial segregation and discrimination" ("What Killed JFK?"). It would take another eight months of battles with southern politicians before the **Civil Rights Act** was signed on 2 July 1964.

SOURCES

Introduction, in *Papers* 5:38–40.
Kennedy, "President Kennedy's Radio-TV Address on Civil Rights," *Congressional Quarterly* (14 June 1963): 970–971.
King, Interview after Release from Georgia State Prison at Reidsville, 27 October 1960, in *Papers* 5:535–536.
King, Statement on Presidential Endorsement, 1 November 1960, in *Papers* 5:537, 540.
King, "What Killed JFK?" *New York Amsterdam News*, 21 December 1963.
King to Kennedy, 15 September 1963, WHCF-MWalK.

KENNEDY, ROBERT FRANCIS (1925–1968)

As U.S. Attorney General from 1961 to 1964, Robert F. Kennedy served as one of the most trusted advisors to his brother, President John F. **Kennedy**, on matters of civil rights. Although Martin Luther King boldly criticized the attorney general and the Department of Justice for its failure to investigate civil rights violations, he wrote Kennedy in 1964 praising him for his efforts to pass the **Civil Rights Act of 1964**: "Your able, courageous and effective work in guiding the Civil Rights Act of 1964 through both Houses of Congress has earned for you an even warmer spot in the hearts of freedom loving people the world over. I add to theirs my sincere and heartfelt thanks" (King, 24 June 1964).

Born on 20 November 1925, Robert Kennedy was the seventh of nine children of Joseph Patrick and Rose Kennedy. Despite a mediocre academic performance in high school, Kennedy was admitted to Harvard University in 1944. He joined the Navy during World War II, but was discharged following an injury. Kennedy resumed his studies at Harvard, graduating in 1948. He went on to attend University of Virginia Law School and earned his LLB in 1951.

Kennedy's political career began in 1946, when he helped manage the Massachusetts congressional campaign of his brother, John F. Kennedy. For the next several years, Kennedy assisted with his brother's campaigns for the U.S. Senate in 1952 and his presidential campaign in 1960. Between campaigns, Kennedy served as legal assistant to Senator Joseph R. McCarthy during the infamous House Un-American Activities Commission hearings. He also served on the John McClellan Committee of the U.S. Senate, which was charged with investigating organized crime.

During the 1960 presidential campaign, King participated in a **sit-in**, a direct violation of his probation stemming from driving with an invalid license in 1960. John F. Kennedy phoned Coretta Scott **King** to offer his support and Robert Kennedy then initiated a series of contacts with Ernest **Vandiver**, governor of Georgia, which eventually led to King's release. Robert Kennedy downplayed the significance of the phone call to the press, explaining that he had been pressed to act because of the numerous calls to Kennedy headquarters. After his brother was elected president by a narrow margin over Richard **Nixon**, Kennedy was appointed Attorney General of the United States.

The relationship between Attorney General Kennedy and the civil rights movement was tested when King and several hundred protesters were threatened by an angry mob outside of a Montgomery church, where King was holding a mass meeting in support of the **Freedom Rides**. As the mob grew more hostile, King feared for the people inside and phoned Kennedy, asking him to intervene. Kennedy assured King that federal marshals were on the way to Montgomery and proposed a cooling-off period for the Freedom Rides. James **Farmer** and Diane **Nash** rejected the idea of a halt to the demonstrations. Federal marshals arrived to protect the protesters, but as the siege continued the marshals were eventually replaced by the Alabama State National Guard under Governor John **Patterson**'s control—a decision that greatly disappointed King.

Although the Kennedy administration was the first to give substantial attention to the southern freedom struggle, King continuously challenged Robert Kennedy and the Department of Justice to make a greater commitment to civil rights. A week after the melee in Montgomery, King sent Kennedy a formal complaint accusing the Justice Department of not enforcing the Interstate Commerce Commission ruling after four students in Atlanta were arrested for seeking to use bus terminals on an integrated basis. "It appears," King wrote, "that only swift and decisive action by your department will make it clear to every citizen the right of unencumbered travel regardless of race, creed or color" (King, 29 May 1961).

Between 1961 and 1963, King registered a number of complaints with Kennedy and the Department of Justice regarding the violence faced by civil rights workers in

Albany, Georgia; **Birmingham**, Alabama; and Jackson, Mississippi. In one of Kennedy's standard responses to King, he expressed that the president's "strong conviction that these matters should be satisfactorily settled through negotiation between the city commission and Negro citizens" (Kennedy, 2 September 1962).

As King's stature as a national leader heightened, he was closely scrutinized by J. Edgar Hoover and the **Federal Bureau of Investigation** (FBI). In early 1962, King's relationship with two suspected Communists, Jack **O'Dell** and Stanley **Levison**, caused alarm within the FBI. Harris **Wofford** warned King against associating with O'Dell and Levison, a warning President Kennedy repeated to King. King asked O'Dell to resign, but found it difficult to sever relations with Levison, who was a trusted advisor. In October 1963, Robert Kennedy authorized the wiretapping of King's home and office in response to his ongoing relationship with Levison.

After the assassination of President Kennedy in 1963, Robert Kennedy continued to serve as Attorney General under President Lyndon **Johnson** until September 1964. That November, he was elected to the U.S. Senate to represent New York. As a senator, Kennedy spoke out against America's involvement in the **Vietnam War**. In March 1966, King applauded Kennedy's statement against the war, invoking the legacy of his brother, the former president: "Your great brother carried us far in new directions with his concept of a world of diversity; your position advances us to the next step which requires us to reach the political maturity to recognize and relate to all elements produced by the contemporary colonial revolutions" (King, 2 March 1966). The following year, King delivered his most comprehensive speech on the war, "**Beyond Vietnam**," to a crowd of over 3,000 people at Riverside Church in New York.

While campaigning for the presidency on 4 April 1968, Kennedy learned of King's **assassination** during a speech at a rally in Indianapolis, Indiana. Kennedy informed the largely black audience of King's death, cautioning them not to be "filled with hatred and distrust at the injustice of such an act, against all white people," for "Martin Luther King dedicated his life to love and to justice for his fellow human beings, and he died because of that effort" (Kennedy, 4 April 1968). Just two months later, Kennedy was assassinated in California while campaigning for the presidency.

SOURCES

Arsenault, *Freedom Riders*, 2006.
Introduction, in *Papers* 5:38–39.
Kennedy, Statement on death of King, 4 April 1968, EMHP-DGU.
Kennedy to King, 2 September 1962, MLKJP-GAMK.
King, *A Call to Conscience*, ed. Carson and Shepard, 2001.
King to Kennedy, 29 May 1961, MLKP-MBU.
King to Kennedy, 24 June 1964, BMC-MWalK.
King to Kennedy, 2 March 1966, MLKJP-GAMK.
Wofford, *Of Kennedys and Kings*, 1980.

KING, ALBERTA WILLIAMS (1903–1974)

Alberta Williams King, mother of Martin Luther King, Jr., was born in Atlanta in 1903, the only surviving child of Jennie Celeste Williams and Adam Daniel **Williams**, pastor of Atlanta's **Ebenezer Baptist Church**. King often spoke of the positive influence his mother had on his moral development, deeming her "the best mother in the world" (*Papers* 1:161). In a piece he wrote as a student at **Crozer Theological Seminary**, he described his mother as being "behind the scene setting forth those motherly cares, the lack of which leaves a missing link in life" (*Papers* 1:360).

Williams attended high school at Spelman Seminary and went on to enroll in Hampton Normal and Industrial Institute, where she obtained her teaching certificate. Before attending Hampton, Williams met a young minister named Michael **King**. Shortly after completing school, Williams and King announced their engagement during Sunday services at Ebenezer Baptist Church. Because the local school board did not allow married women in the classroom, Williams taught only briefly before her marriage on Thanksgiving Day 1926. After their wedding, the newlyweds moved into an upstairs bedroom in the Williams' home on Auburn Avenue, where King, Jr., and his two siblings, Willie Christine and Alfred Daniel, were born.

After the death of A. D. Williams in 1931, Michael King succeeded his father-in-law as Ebenezer's pastor and began using the name Martin Luther King. Alberta Williams King followed in her mother's footsteps as a powerful presence in Ebenezer's affairs. She founded the Ebenezer choir and was an organist there from 1932 to 1972. She

King family portrait, January 1939. Clockwise from upper left: Alberta Williams King, Martin Luther King, Sr., Jennie Celeste Parks Williams (Alberta's mother), A. D. King, Christine King, and Martin Luther King, Jr., Courtesy of Christine King Farris.

was also organist for the Women's Auxiliary of the **National Baptist Convention** from 1950 to 1962, and was active in the YWCA, the **National Association for the Advancement of Colored People**, and the Women's International League for Peace and Freedom.

As a mother, Alberta worked diligently to instill a sense of self-respect within her three children. King remembered his childhood as one of harmony spent "in a very congenial home situation," with parents who "always lived together very intimately" (*Papers* 1:360). King, Jr., maintained a close relationship with his mother throughout his life. Writing to her from the Connecticut tobacco farm where he worked during the summer while a high school student, he requested, "Mother dear, I want you to send me some fried chickens and rolls" (*Papers* 1:116). Four years later, as a first-year student at Crozer, he wrote his mother, "I met a fine chick in Phila who has gone wild over the old boy" (*Papers* 1:161). Although her soft-spoken nature compelled her to avoid the publicity that accompanied her son's international renown, she remained a constant source of strength to the King family, especially after King, Jr.'s **assassination**.

In 1974, as she played the organ during Sunday services at Ebenezer, Alberta Williams King was shot by Marcus Chenault, a 21-year-old man from Ohio who claimed, "All Christians are my enemies" ("Atlanta: Another King Killed"). Alberta Williams King died later that day at the age of 70.

SOURCES

"Atlanta: Another King Killed," *Newsweek* (8 July 1974): 33–34.

Introduction, in *Papers* 1:1, 7, 13, 18–19, 24–30.

King, "An Autobiography of Religious Development," 12 September–22 November 1950, in *Papers* 1:359–363.

King to Alberta Williams King, 18 June 1944, in *Papers* 1:115–116.

King to Alberta Williams King, October 1948, in *Papers* 1:161–162.

KING, ALFRED DANIEL WILLIAMS (1930–1969)

Although Alfred Daniel King, called A. D. by family and friends, lived in the shadows of his famous brother, Martin Luther King, Jr., he was a participant in the African American freedom struggle, often appearing at his brother's side in movements in Atlanta and Birmingham.

Alfred Daniel Williams King was born on 30 July 1930, in Atlanta, Georgia. A. D. was the third child of Alberta Williams **King** and Martin Luther **King**, Sr. In contrast to his peacemaking brother, Martin, A. D. was, according to his father, "a little rough at times" and "let his toughness build a reputation throughout our neighborhood" (King, Sr., 126). Less interested in academics than his siblings, A. D. started a family of his own while still a teenager. He was married on 17 June 1950, to Naomi Barber, with whom he had five children. Although as a youth he strongly resisted his father's ministerial urgings, King eventually began assisting his father at **Ebenezer Baptist Church**. In 1959, King graduated from **Morehouse College**, and that same year he left Ebenezer to become pastor of Mount Vernon First Baptist Church in Newnan, Georgia.

A. D. King was arrested with King, Jr., and 70 others while participating in an October 1960 lunch counter sit-in in Atlanta. In 1963, A. D. King became a leader of the **Birmingham Campaign** while pastoring at First Street Baptist Church in nearby Ensley, Alabama. On 11 May 1963 King's house was bombed. In August, after a bomb exploded at the home of a prominent black lawyer in downtown Birmingham, thousands of outraged citizens poured into the city streets intent on revenge. As rocks were thrown at gathering policemen and the situation escalated, A. D. King climbed on top of a parked car and shouted to the rioters in an attempt to quell their fury: "My friends, we have had enough problems tonight. If you're going to kill someone, then kill me.... Stand up for your rights, but with nonviolence" ("Bomb Hits Home in Birmingham").

Like his brother, A. D. was a staunch believer in the importance of maintaining **nonviolence** in direct action campaigns. However, unlike his brother, A. D. was able to remain mostly outside of the media spotlight. As one of his associates said, "Not being in the limelight never seemed to affect him but because he stayed in the background, many people never knew that he was deeply involved, too" (Johnson, "A Rights Activist").

In 1965, King moved to Louisville, Kentucky, where he became pastor at Zion Baptist Church. While there, King continued to fight for civil rights and was successful in a 1968 campaign for an open-housing ordinance. After the **assassination** of King, Jr., in April 1968, there was speculation that A. D. might become president of the **Southern Christian Leadership Conference**. A. D., however, made no effort to assume his brother's role, although he did continue to be active in the **Poor People's Campaign** and in other work on behalf of SCLC. Following the death of King, Jr., A. D. King returned to Ebenezer Baptist Church and, in September 1968, was installed as co-pastor. Praised by his father as "an able preacher, a concerned, loving pastor," A. D. King's life was tragically cut short when he drowned on 21 July 1969, at the age of 38 (King, Sr., 191).

SOURCES

"Bomb Hits Home in Birmingham," *New York Times*, 21 August 1963.
Introduction, in *Papers* 1:26; 43.
Thomas A. Johnson, "A Rights Activist," *New York Times*, 22 July 1969.
King, Sr., with Riley, *Daddy King*, 1980.

KING, BERNICE ALBERTINE (1963–)

The youngest child of Martin Luther King, Jr., and Coretta Scott **King**, Bernice was born 28 March 1963. Mirroring her father's induction to the church at an early age, Bernice was called to the ministry when she was seventeen: "I think that in a sense my calling to the ministry will be the perpetuation of the flame, the spirit of my father living on" (Norment, "The King Family"). She graduated from Spelman College with a BA in psychology in 1985, and went on to earn a JD and Master of Divinity from Emory University in 1990. On 27 March 1988 she delivered her first sermon at **Ebenezer Baptist Church**, the church of her father and grandfather. She was ordained as a minister in 1990, and after serving as assistant minister at Ebenezer from 1990 to 1993, she began serving as a minister at Greater Rising Star Baptist Church in Atlanta. She was impressed by the community programs of the church, and in 1995 became senior pastor in charge of the youth and women's ministries. In 1996 she published a collection of her addresses, *Hard Questions, Heart Answers: Sermons and Speeches*.

The only child of Martin Luther King, Jr., to take up the ministry as a profession, Bernice has often been compared to her father. Andrew **Young** alleged that watching Bernice "makes you believe preaching is hereditary" (Cleage, "Bernice King Carries It On"). Bernice, however, has her own goals. Employing her legal background, she has consulted with youth, especially those in trouble. Although she has spoken out against war in the Persian Gulf and addressed sexism in churches, her approach leans toward a more personal, intimate ministry than a social, political gospel.

SOURCES

Pearl Cleage, "Bernice King Carries It On," *Essence*, January 1989.
Lynn Norment, "The King Family: Keepers of the Dream," *Ebony*, January 1987.

KING, CORETTA SCOTT (1927–2006)

The widow of one of the most influential leaders in the world, Coretta Scott King provided Martin Luther King, Jr., with what he called the "love, sacrifices, and loyalty [without which] neither life nor work would bring fulfillment" (King, *Stride*, 11). An activist in her own right, Coretta King made numerous contributions to the struggle for social justice and human rights throughout her life.

Coretta Scott was born on 27 April 1927, near Marion, Alabama. Her parents, Obadiah "Obie" Scott and Bernice McMurray Scott, were farm owners committed to

Wedding party of Martin Luther King, Jr., and Coretta Scott King, 18 June 1953. (right to left) Christine King, A. D. King, Betty Ann Hill, Martin Luther King, Jr., Naomi Barber King, Coretta Scott King, Martin Luther King, Sr., Edythe Scott, Bernice Scott, Alberta Williams King, Obadiah Scott, and Alveda King (front). Courtesy of Christine King Farris.

ensuring that their children received the best education possible. Scott attended the private Lincoln High School in Marion, where she developed her interest in music. There she took formal vocal lessons, learned to read music, and played several instruments. By the age of 15, she had become the choir director and pianist of her church's junior choir.

After graduating from Lincoln, Scott won a partial scholarship to Antioch College, in Yellow Springs, Ohio, the same university her sister Edythe had attended as the first African American student. While at Antioch, Scott studied voice and music education. She also became a member of the local chapter of the **National Association for the Advancement of Colored People**, as well as the Race Relations and Civil Liberties Committees. In an article, "Why I Came to College," published in *Opportunity* in 1948, Scott wrote that college graduates "had greater freedom of movement: they went on trips; they visited cities; they knew more about the world" (Scott, 42). She later credited Antioch with preparing her for her role in the civil rights movement, stating that "the college's emphasis on service to mankind reinforced the Christian spirit of giving and sharing" and provided "a new self-assurance that encouraged me in competition with all people" (Scott King, 43).

In 1951 Scott enrolled in Boston's New England Conservatory of Music with a grant from the Jessie Smith Noyes Foundation. In early 1952, her friend Mary **Powell** introduced her to King, then a doctoral candidate at **Boston University**'s School of Theology. While initially wary of dating a Baptist minister, she was impressed by his sophistication and intellect and recalled King telling her: "You have everything I have ever wanted in a wife" (Scott King, 53). The two were married at the Scott family home near Marion on 18 June 1953. After the wedding, they returned to Boston to complete their degrees. Coretta Scott King earned her bachelor of music degree in June 1954.

Although Scott King was focused on raising the couple's four children: Yolanda Denise **King** (1955), Martin Luther **King**, III (1957), Dexter Scott **King** (1961), and Bernice Albertine **King** (1963), she continued to play a critical role in many of the civil rights campaigns of the 1950s and 1960s, performing in freedom concerts that included poetry recitation, singing, and lectures related to the history of the civil rights movement. The proceeds from these concerts were donated to the **Southern Christian Leadership Conference**.

Scott King also accompanied her husband around the world, traveling to **Ghana** in 1957 and **India** in 1959. She was particularly affected by the women she met in India. "As we traveled through the land, we were greatly impressed by the part women played in the political life of India, far more than in our own country" (Scott King, 162). In 1962, Coretta Scott King's interest in disarmament efforts took her to Geneva, Switzerland, where she served as a Women's Strike for Peace delegate to the 17-nation Disarmament Conference. Two years later, she accompanied her husband to Oslo for the awarding of the **Nobel Peace Prize**. She later recalled thinking: "What a blessing, to be a co-worker with a man whose life would have so profound an impact on the world" (Scott King, 12).

After King's **assassination** on 4 April 1968, Coretta Scott King devoted much of her life to spreading her husband's philosophy of **nonviolence**. Just days after his death, she led a march on behalf of sanitation workers in Memphis, Tennessee. Later that month, she stood in for her husband at an anti–**Vietnam War** rally in New York. In May 1968, she helped to launch the **Poor People's Campaign**, and thereafter participated in numerous anti-poverty efforts.

With a deep commitment to preserving King's legacy, almost immediately Coretta Scott King began mobilizing support for the Martin Luther King, Jr., Center for Nonviolent Social Change. As founding president of the **King Center**, she guided its construction next to **Ebenezer Baptist Church**, where King had served as co-pastor with his father, Martin Luther **King**, Sr.

Throughout the 1970s and 1980s, Scott King continued to speak publicly and write nationally syndicated columns, and began efforts to establish a **national holiday** in honor of her husband. In 1983, she led an effort that brought more than a half-million demonstrators to Washington, D.C., to commemorate the 20th anniversary of the 1963 **March on Washington for Jobs and Freedom**, where King had delivered his famous "**I Have a Dream**" speech. As chairperson of the Martin Luther King, Jr., Federal Holiday Commission, she successfully formalized plans for the annual celebration of Martin Luther King, Jr., Day, which began in January 1986.

During the 1980s, Coretta Scott King reaffirmed her long-standing opposition to South African **apartheid**, participating in a series of **sit-in** protests in Washington that prompted nationwide demonstrations against South African racial policies. In 1986 she traveled to South Africa and met with Winnie Mandela. She also remained active in various women's organizations, including the National Organization for Women, the Women's International League for Peace and Freedom, and United Church Women.

Throughout her life, Coretta Scott King carried the message of nonviolence and social justice to almost every corner of the globe. On 30 January 2006, Coretta Scott King died in her sleep at a holistic health center in Rosarito Beach, Mexico. She was 78 years old.

SOURCES
Introduction, in *Papers* 2:12–14, 19.
King, *Stride Toward Freedom*, 1958.
(Scott) King, *My Life with Martin Luther King, Jr.*, 1969.
Scott, "Why I Came to College," *Opportunity* 26 (1948): 42, 70.

KING, DEXTER SCOTT (1961–)

On 30 January 1961, Dexter Scott King, the third child of Martin and Coretta Scott **King**, was born. He was named after the church where his father held his first pastorate. In her autobiography, Coretta Scott King wrote how glad she was that both Dexter and young Martin Luther **King**, III had a chance to go with their father on one of his speaking tours in early 1968. She recalled that upon returning from the trip Dexter told her, "You know Mommy, I don't see how my daddy can do so much, and talk to so many people and not even get tired at all" (King, *My Life*, 307).

Dexter attended **Morehouse College** and majored in business administration. Upon becoming chairman, president, and chief executive officer of the **King Center** in 2005, Dexter articulated his vision for his father's legacy: "Our main goal is to educate the public about, and to perpetuate and promote, my father's message of **nonviolence** to people around the world" (King, *Growing*, 200). Dexter also pursued a career in media and entertainment and has starred in and produced films, records, and television specials concerning the civil rights movement. His animated movie, "Our Friend Martin," was nominated for an Emmy award. He is also the author of *Growing Up King: An Intimate Memoir* (2003). *Ebony* magazine has featured Dexter in its "100 Most Influential Black Americans" lists, and he has appeared on numerous talk shows. In 1997, Dexter met with James Earl Ray and stated publicly that he did not believe that Ray was his father's killer.

SOURCES
King, *Growing Up King*, 2003.
(Scott) King, *My Life with Martin Luther King, Jr.*, 1969.

KING, MARTIN LUTHER, SR. (1897–1984)

In a speech expressing his views on "the true mission of the Church," Martin Luther King, Sr., told his fellow clergymen that they must not forget the words of God: "The spirit of the Lord is upon me, because he hath anointed me to preach the Gospel to the poor.… In this we find we are to do something about the brokenhearted, poor, unemployed, the captive, the blind, and the bruised" (King, Sr., 17 October 1940). Martin Luther King, Jr., credited his father with influencing his decision to join the

Martin Luther King, Sr., Alberta Williams King, Martin Luther King, Jr., A. D. King, Christine King, and Joel King (uncle) on the Morehouse College campus, 1948. Courtesy of Christine King Farris.

ministry, saying: "He set forth a noble example that I didn't [mind] following" (*Papers* 1:363).

King, Sr., was born Michael King on 19 December 1897, in Stockbridge, Georgia. The eldest son of James and Delia King, King, Sr., attended school from three to five months a year at the Stockbridge Colored School. "We had no books, no materials to write with, and no blackboard," he wrote, "But I loved going" (King, Sr., 37).

King experienced a number of brutal incidents while growing up in the rural South, including witnessing the lynching of a black man. On another occasion he had to subdue his drunken father who was assaulting his mother. His mother took the children to Floyd Chapel Baptist Church to "ease the harsh tone of farm life" according to King (King, Sr., 26). Michael grew to respect the few black preachers who were willing to speak out against racial injustices, despite the risk of violent white retaliation. He gradually developed an interest in preaching, initially practicing eulogies on the family's chickens. By the end of 1917, he had decided to become a minister.

In the spring of 1918, King left Stockbridge to join his sister, Woodie, in Atlanta. The following year, Woodie King boarded at the home of A. D. **Williams**, minister of **Ebenezer Baptist Church**. King seized the opportunity to introduce himself to the minister's daughter, Alberta **Williams**. Her parents welcomed King into the family circle, eventually treating him as a son and encouraging the young minister to overcome his educational limitations.

179

In March 1924, the engagement of Alberta to Michael King was announced at Ebenezer's Sunday services. Meanwhile, King served as pastor of several churches in nearby College Park, while studying at Bryant Preparatory School. He followed the urging of Alberta Williams and her father to seek admission to **Morehouse College** and was admitted in 1926. King found the work difficult; however, he relied on the help of classmate Melvin H. **Watson**, the son of a longtime clerk at Ebenezer Baptist Church, and Sandy **Ray** of Texas, a fellow seminarian. "We shared an awe of city life, of cars, of the mysteries of college scholarship, and, most of all, of our callings to the ministry," King recalled (King, Sr., 77).

On Thanksgiving Day 1926, Michael Luther King and Alberta Christine Williams were married at Ebenezer. The newlyweds moved into an upstairs bedroom of the Williams' house on Auburn Avenue. The King family quickly expanded, with the birth of Willie Christine in 1927, Michael Luther, Jr., in 1929, and Alfred Daniel Williams in 1930, a month after King, Sr., received his bachelor's degree in theology.

After the death of A. D. Williams in 1931, King, Sr., succeeded his father-in-law as pastor of Ebenezer. According to King's recollections, A. D. Williams inspired him in many ways. Both men preached a **social gospel** Christianity that combined a belief in personal salvation with the need to apply the teachings of Jesus to the daily problems of their black congregations.

The Kings raised their children in what King, Jr., described as "a very congenial home situation," with parents who "always lived together very intimately" (*Papers* 1:360). Hidden from view were his parents' negotiations regarding their conflicting views on discipline. Although King, Sr., believed that the "switch was usually quicker and more persuasive" in disciplining his boys, he increasingly deferred to his wife's less stern but effective approach to childrearing (King, Sr., 130).

In 1934, King, Sr., attended the World Baptist Alliance in Berlin. Traveling by ocean liner to France, he and 10 other ministers also toured historic sites in Palestine and the Holy Land. "In Jerusalem, when I saw with my own eyes the places where Jesus had lived and taught, a life spent in the ministry seemed to me even more compelling," King recalled (King, Sr., 97). A story appearing in the *Atlanta Daily World* upon King's return to Atlanta in August 1934 increased his prominence and relative affluence among Atlanta's elite. This was also reflected in the final transformation of his name from Michael King to Michael Luther King and finally Martin Luther King (although close friends and relatives continued to refer to him and his son as Mike or M. L.).

In Atlanta, King, Sr., not only engaged in personal acts of political dissent, such as riding the "whites only" City Hall elevator to reach the voter registrar's office, but was also a local leader of organizations such as the Atlanta Civic and Political League and the **National Association for the Advancement of Colored People** (NAACP). In 1939, he proposed, to the lack of opposition to more cautious clergy and lay leaders, a massive voter registration drive to be initiated by a march to City Hall. At a rally at Ebenezer of more than 1,000 activists, King referred to his own past and urged black people toward greater militancy. "I ain't gonna plow no more mules," he shouted. "I'll never step off the road again to let white folks pass" (King, Sr., 100). A year later, King, Sr., braved racist threats when he became chairman of the Committee on the Equalization of Teachers' Salaries, which was organized to protest discriminatory policies in teachers' pay. With the legal assistance of the NAACP, the movement resulted in significant gains for black teachers.

Although too young to fully understand his father's activism, King, Jr., later wrote that dinner discussions in the King household often touched on political matters, as King, Sr., expressed his views about "the ridiculous nature of segregation in the South" (*Papers* 1:33). King, Jr., remembered witnessing his father standing up to a policeman who stopped the elder King for a traffic violation and referred to him as a "boy." According to King, Jr., his indignant father responded by pointing to his son and asserting: "This is a boy. I'm a man, and until you call me one, I will not listen to you." The shocked policeman "wrote the ticket up nervously, and left the scene as quickly as possible" (King, *Stride*, 20).

King, Sr., was generally supportive of his son's participation in the civil rights movement; however, during the **Montgomery bus boycott**, he and his wife were very concerned about the safety of King, Jr., and his family. King, Sr., asked a number of prominent Atlantans, such as Benjamin **Mays**, to try to convince King, Jr., not to return to Montgomery; but they were unsuccessful. King, Sr., later wrote, "I could only be deeply impressed with his determination. There was no hesitancy for him in this journey" (King, Sr., 172). King, Sr., traveled with the delegation to Oslo in 1964 to see his son accept the **Nobel Peace Prize**. In his autobiography, King, Sr., recalled, "As M. L. stood receiving the Nobel Prize, and the tears just streamed down my face, I gave thanks that out of that tiny Georgia town I'd been spared to see this and so much else" (King, Sr., 183).

Throughout his life, King, Sr., was a prominent civic leader in Atlanta, serving on the boards of Atlanta University, Morehouse College, and the **National Baptist Convention**. After the **assassination** of King, Jr., he spoke at numerous events honoring his son. A strong supporter of Jimmy Carter, he delivered invocations to the Democratic National Convention in 1976 and 1980. After serving Ebenezer for 44 years, he died in Atlanta in 1984.

SOURCES

Introduction, in *Papers* 3:14.
King, "An Autobiography of Religious Development," 12 September–22 November 1950, in *Papers* 1:359–363.
King, *Stride Toward Freedom*, 1958.
King, Sr., "Moderator's Annual Address," 17 October 1940, CSKC.
King, Sr., with Riley, *Daddy King*, 1980.
"Rev. King Is Royally Welcomed on Return from Europe," *Atlanta Daily World*, 28 August 1934.

KING, MARTIN LUTHER, III (1957–)

The first son of Martin Luther King, Jr., and Coretta Scott **King**, Martin Luther King, III, was born 23 October 1957. He graduated from **Morehouse College** with a BA in political science. He is a popular speaker and a community activist with a special interest in programs that support young people. In 1986 he was elected to the Fulton County Board of Commissioners to represent more than 700,000 Georgia residents, but was defeated in his bid for the chairmanship of the Board in 1993. Dedicated to expanding his father's ideals, Martin was elected the fourth president of the

Southern Christian Leadership Conference in 1997. He served until the end of 2003, leading marches, convening police brutality hearings, and organizing gun buy-back programs. In 2005, he told in *Ebony* magazine, "My father's views were unequivocal, and I have found them to be invaluable to me as guidelines for prayerful consideration of current events and issues" ("What Would King Do Now?").

SOURCE
King, III, "What Would King Do Now?" *Ebony*, January 2005.

KING, YOLANDA DENISE (1955–2007)

The eldest child of Martin Luther King, Jr., and Coretta Scott **King**, Yolanda was born 17 November 1955, less than a month before the launch of the **Montgomery bus boycott**. She and her mother were in the family home when it was bombed on 30 January 1956. The family moved to Atlanta in 1960 and Yolanda became immersed in the activities of her grandparents, aunts, and cousins. According to her father, by the age of six she was aware of the racism that surrounded her. In his "**Letter from Birmingham Jail**," King recalled that he had to explain to Yolanda why she could not go to a new amusement park known as Funtown. He recounted the difficulty of seeing tears in Yolanda's eyes when he told her that black children were not permitted in the park. Coretta Scott King described an incident in her autobiography that occurred when Yolanda was seven. Yolanda reportedly told her friends, "Look, all I want is just to be treated like a normal child" (Scott King, *My Life*, 211). Scott King wrote: "She had articulated, in her childish wisdom, exactly what Martin and I had in mind for our children" (*My Life*, 211).

Yolanda attended drama school and was active in sports and student council. She graduated from Smith College with a BA in theater and African-American studies in 1976, and received an MFA from New York University in 1979. For several years afterward, she collaborated with Attallah Shabazz, daughter of **Malcolm X**, to produce and perform plays as the Nucleus Theatre Group. Yolanda then returned to Atlanta to direct cultural affairs for the **King Center** for Nonviolent Social Change. She served three years as Professor in Residence at Fordham University before moving to Los Angeles in 1990 to found Higher Ground Productions. With Higher Ground, she produced and starred in numerous productions, including "Tracts: A Celebration of the Triumph and Spirit of Martin Luther King, Jr." Yolanda published several books, including *Open My Eyes, Open My Soul* (2003). She died on 15 May 2007.

SOURCES
King, "Letter from Birmingham Jail," in *Why We Can't Wait*, 1964.
(Scott) King, *My Life with Martin Luther King, Jr.*, 1969.

KING CENTER (ATLANTA, GEORGIA)

Established in 1968 by Coretta Scott **King** as "the official, living memorial dedicated to the advancement of the legacy" of Martin Luther King, Jr., the King Center is located in Atlanta's historic Auburn district next to **Ebenezer Baptist Church**. Originally called the Martin Luther King, Jr., Center for Nonviolent Social Change, Inc., the King Center houses the final resting place of Martin and Coretta Scott King.

Its programming focuses on disseminating King's philosophies of **nonviolence** and service to mankind, building international partners to further the "Beloved Community," and overseeing various programs that use King's name.

The King Center established several means to preserve King's legacy for both historical and educational purposes. In 1968, the Library Documentation Project began collecting the records and recollections of activists during the civil rights movement under the guidance of Vincent **Harding**. The King Library and Archives at the King Center stores the result of this project, with over 14,000 pieces of King's correspondence, extensive audiovisual documentation, oral histories, and records of many of the most involved organizations. Collections housed at the Library include the records of the **Southern Christian Leadership Conference**, the **Student Nonviolent Coordinating Committee,** the **Congress of Racial Equality**, and the **Mississippi Freedom Democratic Party**.

The King Center spearheaded the campaign to petition Congress to pass legislation establishing the **King National Holiday**. Following a 1983 demonstration at the Lincoln Memorial commemorating the 20th anniversary of the 1963 **March on Washington for Jobs and Freedom**, Congress passed legislation establishing the third Monday in January as a federal holiday to honor King. The King Center currently sponsors educational programs and encourages people to remember the holiday through service as "a day on, not a day off."

In 1985, the King Center initiated the King Papers Project to further study and disseminate King's philosophies and beliefs and to create educational materials regarding his life and the movements that he inspired.

By the early 1990s, the King Center had become one of Atlanta's top tourist attractions, with more than 650,000 people visiting the physical site annually. Upon founding president Coretta Scott King's retirement in 1995, Dexter **King** became the King Center's president and CEO.

SOURCE

The King Center, http://www.thekingcenter.org (accessed 12 July 2007).

KING NATIONAL HOLIDAY

The establishment of a national holiday honoring Martin Luther King, Jr., marked the culmination of a long campaign that began soon after King's **assassination** and ended on 2 November 1983, with the signing of legislation by President Ronald Reagan. Public Law 98-144 designated the third Monday in January as an annual federal holiday in King's honor, and the first official celebration took place on 20 January 1986.

King's 1968 assassination prompted various efforts to pay homage to the slain civil rights leader. Many communities throughout the nation reacted by naming streets, schools, and other public landmarks after King. Congressman John Conyers (D–MI) initially introduced a bill calling for a national holiday only four days after King's assassination, but this proposal garnered little support until the numbers of African Americans elected to Congress increased and King holiday campaigns at the local and state levels gained momentum. The Congressional Black Caucus' persistent attempts to pass King holiday legislation gained support from the **Southern Christian**

Leadership Conference (SCLC), which King had led since its founding in 1957. In the early 1970s the SCLC gathered petitions bearing 3 million signatures in support of the King holiday. In 1973, the first state King holiday bill (sponsored by Assemblyman Harold Washington) was signed into law in Illinois, and in 1974, similar legislation was passed in Massachusetts and Connecticut. Most other states followed suit during the following decade.

During the late 1970s, King's widow, Coretta Scott **King**, and the Atlanta-based **King Center** that she founded played an increasingly important role in mobilizing popular support for a holiday. In 1979, Coretta Scott King urged passage of a national King holiday bill when she testified before the Senate Judiciary Committee and joint hearings of Congress. In addition, Coretta Scott King directed King Center staff to begin intensive organizing of a nationwide citizens lobby for the holiday and garnered more than 300,000 signatures on a petition before the end of the year. With support from the Jimmy Carter administration, the King holiday bill emerged for the first time from congressional committees, but in November 1979 the bill was defeated by five votes in a floor vote in the House of Representatives.

The setback did not end the national campaign. Singer Stevie Wonder composed a song celebrating King's birth, and his hit recording of the birthday song further increased the holiday's popular support. On 15 January 1983, more than 100,000 people rallied at the Washington Monument to express support for the King holiday movement. With financial support from Wonder, a lobbying office was opened in Washington, D.C., and eventually this effort secured more than 6 million signatures on petitions to Congress in support of a King national holiday. The King Center began working with Wonder to organize an observance of the 20th anniversary of the 1963 **March on Washington for Jobs and Freedom**. More than half a million people attended this commemoration march and the rally at the Lincoln Memorial, where they heard speakers call upon the Senate and President Reagan to enact King holiday legislation.

A few weeks before the march took place, the House passed a bill creating the King holiday by an overwhelming vote of 338–90. But the subsequent Senate debate concerning the bill was nonetheless contentious, continuing into the fall of 1983. North Carolina Senator Jesse Helms sought to diminish King's reputation by calling for the release of **Federal Bureau of Investigation** surveillance tapes on King that had been sealed by court order until the year 2027, while other senators complained that another paid holiday would be too costly. Senator Edward M. Kennedy (D–MA) vigorously defended King against the allegations of Helms, noting that no evidence of ties between King and the Communist Party had been uncovered. When the Senate finally voted on the bill on 19 October, the packed galleries included numerous prominent proponents of the holiday, including Coretta Scott King, SCLC President Joseph E. **Lowery**, and **National Association for the Advancement of Colored People** Executive Director Benjamin **Hooks**. The holiday bill was finally approved by a vote of 78–22 (37 Republicans and 41 Democrats voted in favor; 18 Republicans and 4 Democrats voted against).

After the holiday bill became law, the King Center gained congressional support to establish a King Federal Holiday Commission, which introduced a variety of commemorative activities, including tree planting ceremonies and the distribution of posters, newsletters, and guides citing the principles of King's **nonviolence** teachings. In the 1990s the King holiday theme became "Remember—Celebrate—Act. A Day On, Not a Day Off." As with other federal holidays, the observance of the King holiday applied only to federal workers rather than employees of state and local governments or of private institutions, but by January 1989 the number of states celebrating a King holiday had grown to 44 and, in June 1999, New Hampshire became the final state to pass some form of King holiday legislation.

SOURCE

Encyclopedia of American Holidays and National Days, ed. Travers, 2006.

KING INSTITUTE. *See* Martin Luther King, Jr., Research and Education Institute at Stanford University.

KUNSTLER, WILLIAM MOSES (1919–1995)

From the freedom riders to the "Chicago Seven," William Kunstler defended political and social activists for four decades. Martin Luther King and Kunstler first met during the 1961 **Freedom Rides**. King asked Kunstler to take on several cases throughout the 1960s and praised him for the "magnificent job" he had done as a civil rights attorney (King, 30 December 1963).

Kunstler was born in New York City on 7 July 1919. After graduating from Yale in 1941, he served in the Philippines in World War II. When he returned to the United States, he attended Columbia Law School, graduating in 1948, and opened a law practice with his brother. He taught at Pace College's Business School from 1951 to 1960, and at New York Law School from 1949 to 1961. In 1961, while working with the American Civil Liberties Union (ACLU), Kunstler defended freedom riders challenging segregation on interstate bus travel.

In 1961, King asked Kunstler to speak at the **Southern Christian Leadership Conference** (SCLC) annual convention on the legal implications of the Freedom Rides. Kunstler subsequently took on several cases referred to him by King or SCLC, ranging from defending Fred **Shuttlesworth** in an appeal stemming from a 1958 Birmingham bus protest to representing the **Mississippi Freedom Democratic Party** in their struggle to unseat the Mississippi convention delegation. Kunstler's wife, Lotte, participated as a demonstrator in the **Albany Movement**, and the couple arranged a fundraiser for King near their home in Westchester, New York.

Kunstler also served on the board of directors of the **Gandhi Society for Human Rights**, a charitable nonprofit group committed to providing "front line emergency legal assistance in lower courts, particularly where nonviolent demonstrations involve mass arrests and imprisonment" (Kunstler, *Deep*, 93). Kunstler chronicled some of his civil rights work in his book, *Deep in My Heart*, for which King and James **Forman**, executive secretary of the **Student Nonviolent Coordinating Committee**, each wrote a foreword.

From 1964 to 1972, Kunstler served as director of the ACLU. In 1966, he also co-founded the Center for Constitutional Rights. By the late 1960s, Kunstler was representing black militants H. Rap Brown and Stokely **Carmichael**, as well as white anti-war radicals such as Abbie Hoffman and Tom Hayden. During his successful defense of the "Chicago Seven," protesters arrested during the 1968 Democratic National Convention, Kunstler's quick wit and sharp retorts initially earned him a sentence of more than four years in prison for contempt, but the sentence was later overturned.

Throughout his career, Kunstler remained staunchly committed to defending people and movements who were widely unpopular. In the fall of 1992, Kunstler returned to New York Law School to teach a seminar on constitutional law. Three years later, he died of a heart attack.

Sources

King to Kunstler, 30 December 1963, MLKJP-GAMK.
Kunstler, *Deep in My Heart*, 1966.
Kunstler, *My Life as a Radical Lawyer*, 1994.
Langum, *William M. Kunstler*, 1999.

LAFAYETTE, BERNARD (1940–)

A student activist in the Nashville, Tennessee, **sit-in** campaign of 1960, and a long-time staff member of the **Student Nonviolent Coordinating Committee** (SNCC), Bernard Lafayette gained a reputation as a steadfast proponent of **nonviolence** before Martin Luther King offered him the position of program director of the **Southern Christian Leadership Conference** (SCLC) in 1967.

Lafayette was born in Tampa, Florida, on 19 July 1940. In 1958 he moved to Nashville to attend American Baptist Theological Seminary. As a freshman, Lafayette began attending weekly meetings arranged by James **Lawson**, a representative of the **Fellowship of Reconciliation** who had contacted King during the **Montgomery bus boycott**. Throughout 1958 and 1959, in partnership with Nashville's SCLC affiliate, Lawson taught **nonviolence** techniques to Lafayette and his fellow Nashville students, including John **Lewis**, James **Bevel**, and Diane **Nash**. Energized by Lawson's classes and a weekend retreat at the **Highlander Folk School**, Lafayette and his friends began conducting **sit-ins** at segregated restaurants and businesses in 1959. When Ella **Baker**, under the auspices of SCLC, organized a conference of students on Easter weekend in 1960, Lafayette attended this conference that gave birth to SNCC.

Prior to the Supreme Court's 1960 ruling in *Boynton v. Virginia* declaring segregation in interstate travel facilities unconstitutional, Lafayette and Lewis integrated an interstate bus on their way home from seminary by sitting at the front and refusing to move. Months later, in 1961, he answered a **Congress of Racial Equality** announcement recruiting students to participate in the **Freedom Rides**. Although unable to join the first ride because his parents refused to permit him to participate, Lafayette and other Nashville students volunteered to continue the rides after the first group of freedom riders was attacked in Alabama. In Montgomery, Lafayette's group was attacked by members of the Ku Klux Klan. King met with Lafayette, Nash, and Lewis and then negotiated on their behalf with the White House and the Department of Justice to ensure their protection in Montgomery and a military escort on their continued journey to Mississippi. In Mississippi, Lafayette was arrested and served 40 days in Parchman Penitentiary, only to be rearrested upon his release for contributing to the delinquency of minors because the students he recruited to ride the buses were all under 18 years of age.

In 1962 Lafayette became the director of SNCC's Alabama Voter Registration Project. The following February, he and his wife, Colia, began running voter registration clinics in Selma, Alabama. In the summer of 1963, the pair was hired by the **American Friends Service Committee** to begin testing nonviolent methods in Chicago. When King launched SCLC's **Chicago Campaign** he appointed Lafayette, still there in 1966, to help plan and execute the campaign's direct action program.

After King hired him as SCLC's program coordinator in 1967, Lafayette took on responsibility for the 1968 **Poor People's Campaign**. Following King's **assassination**, Lafayette continued to work on the campaign with Ralph **Abernathy**. Lafayette received his MEd from Harvard University in 1972 and a doctorate in 1974. He served as a scholar in residence at the **King Center**. After teaching at several universities, he was named president of his alma mater, American Baptist Theological Seminary, in 1993. He later became the director of the Center for Nonviolence and Peace Studies at the University of Rhode Island.

SOURCES

Arsenault, *Freedom Riders*, 2006.
Lewis, *Walking with the Wind*, 1998.

LAWSON, JAMES M. (1928–)

As a minister who trained many activists in nonviolent resistance, James Lawson made a critical contribution to the civil rights movement. In his 1968 speech, "**I've Been to the Mountaintop**," Martin Luther King spoke of Lawson as one of the "noble men" who had influenced the black freedom struggle: "He's been going to jail for struggling; he's been kicked out of Vanderbilt University for this struggling; but he's still going on, fighting for the rights of his people" (King, "I've Been," 214).

The son of Philane May Cover and James Morris Lawson, Sr., Lawson was born in Uniontown, Pennsylvania, in 1928. He earned his AB from Baldwin-Wallace College in 1951 and his STB from **Boston University** in 1960. A draft resister, Lawson was imprisoned in 1951 for refusing to register with the armed forces. Following his parole from prison in 1952, he traveled to India and performed missionary work with the Methodist Church. While in India, he deepened his study of **Gandhi**'s use of **nonviolence** to achieve social and political change. In 1956, Lawson returned to the United States and resumed his studies at Oberlin College's School of Theology from 1956 to 1957, and Vanderbilt University from 1958 to 1960.

When Lawson and King met in 1957, King urged Lawson to move to the South and begin teaching nonviolence on a large scale. Later that year, Lawson transferred to Vanderbilt University in Nashville, Tennessee, and organized workshops on nonviolence for community members and students at Vanderbilt and the city's four black colleges. These activists, who included Diane **Nash**, Marion **Barry**, John **Lewis**, Bernard **Lafayette**, and James **Bevel**, planned nonviolent demonstrations in Nashville, conducting test **sit-ins** in late 1959. In February 1960, following lunch counter sit-ins initiated by students at a Woolworth's store in Greensboro, North Carolina, Lawson and several local activists launched a similar protest in Nashville's downtown stores. More than 150 students were arrested before city leaders agreed to desegregate some lunch counters. The discipline of the Nashville students became a model for sit-ins in other southern cities. In March 1960 Lawson was expelled from Vanderbilt because of his involvement with Nashville's desegregation movement.

Lawson and the Nashville student leaders were influential in the founding conference of the **Student Nonviolent Coordinating Committee** (SNCC), held April 1960. Their commitment to nonviolence and the Christian ideal of what Lawson called "the redemptive community" helped to shape SNCC's early direction (Lawson, 17 April 1960). Lawson co-authored the statement of purpose adopted by the conference, which emphasized the religious and philosophical foundations of nonviolent direct action.

Lawson was involved with the **Fellowship of Reconciliation** from 1957 to 1969, SNCC from 1960 to 1964, and the **Southern Christian Leadership Conference** (SCLC) from 1960 to 1967. For each organization, he led workshops on nonviolent methods of protest, often in preparation for major campaigns. He also participated in the third wave of the 1961 **Freedom Rides**. In 1968, at Lawson's request, King traveled to Memphis, Tennessee, to draw attention to the plight of striking sanitation workers in the city. It was during this campaign that King was assassinated on 4 April 1968.

Lawson continued to work with various civil rights groups following King's **assassination**. In 1973, he became a board member of SCLC and served as president of the Los Angeles chapter from 1979 to 1993. He was also the pastor of Holman United Methodist Church in Los Angeles from 1974 to 1999.

SOURCES

Arsenault, *Freedom Riders*, 2006.

Carson, *In Struggle*, 1981.

Richard Deats, "Fighting Prejudice Through Creative Nonviolence: An Interview with Jim Lawson," *Fellowship*, November/December 1999.

Introduction, in *Papers* 5:23, 28.

King, "I've Been to the Mountaintop," 3 April 1968, in *A Call to Conscience*, ed. Carson and Shepard, 2001.

Lawson, Interview by King Papers Project staff, 23 November 1998.

Lawson, "Statement of Purpose," 17 April 1960, SNCCP-GAMK.

Lawson to King, 3 November 1958, in *Papers* 4:522–524.

LEE, BERNARD SCOTT (1935–1991)

Bernard Lee, student leader of the Alabama **sit-in** movement, was Martin Luther King's personal assistant and traveling companion throughout the 1960s. A member of King's inner circle, Lee defended King from pushy reporters, shepherded him to engagements, provided a sounding board for new ideas, and readily joined in during spare moments of levity. King publicly commended Lee's "devotion to civil rights" and made funding Lee's travel expenses a prerequisite for accepting invitations (King, 63).

Born in Norfolk, Virginia, on 2 October 1935, Lee attended the local public schools. He served in the Air Force during the Korean War and then enrolled in Montgomery's Alabama State College in 1958. On 25 February 1960, Lee led a group of 35 students to the state capitol, where they attempted to order food at the segregated cafeteria. Alabama's Governor John **Patterson** responded by threatening to withhold funding from Alabama State unless the school president, H. Councill **Trenholm**, expelled Lee and his fellow protesters. The president complied.

King spoke with Lee at a rally the evening after the protest and invited Lee to have dinner with him and his fellow preachers Ralph **Abernathy** and Fred **Shuttlesworth**. By April, Lee was touring New York with King and had become the chairman of the student division of the Committee to Defend Martin Luther King and the Struggle for Freedom in the South, a group committed to fundraising for King's legal expenses. Lee moved to Atlanta, where the **Southern Christian Leadership Conference** (SCLC) was based, continuing his coursework at Morris Brown College, where he was promptly elected class president.

In October 1960, King and Lee were arrested together while sitting-in at Rich's, an Atlanta department store. Throughout 1960 and 1961, Lee toured schools and churches throughout the South, speaking on SCLC's behalf. Although he was a founding member of the **Student Nonviolent Coordinating Committee** (SNCC), Lee left SNCC to work exclusively with SCLC in 1961, becoming the organization's official student liaison and, later, field secretary. In the summer of 1961, Lee was arrested along with several other SCLC members participating in the **Freedom Rides** initiated by the **Congress of Racial Equality**. Later that year, Lee became the first SCLC representative arrested in support of the **Albany Movement** in Albany, Georgia. King was arrested there soon after.

As King's chief travel companion, Lee accompanied him on "people-to-people" tours, took part in the 1963 **Birmingham Campaign**, and served as King's representative raising money and recruiting volunteers throughout the nation.

Lee shared high moments—such as when King found out he had been awarded the **Nobel Peace Prize**—as well as low ones, when he listened to a tape made by the **Federal Bureau of Investigation** with an accompanying anonymous letter that urged King to commit suicide or face public humiliation. They marched together from **Selma to Montgomery** in 1965 and in the Meredith March against Fear in 1966. When King moved to Chicago in 1966, Lee's name appeared on the lease to his apartment after several landlords refused to rent to King.

In the months before King was assassinated, Lee worked with him on the **Poor People's Campaign** and in support of the **Memphis Sanitation Workers' Strike**. Lee was one of the first to rush to King's side when he was shot on 4 April 1968, and joined Abernathy at the hospital where King was pronounced dead.

After King's death, Lee continued to work on the Poor People's Campaign and later served as vice president of SCLC. Lee joined the Community Services Administration under President Jimmy Carter and was special assistant for religious affairs to Washington, D.C.'s Mayor Marion **Barry**. In 1985, Lee received his Master's in Divinity from Howard University, where he had also earned his Bachelor's degree. Throughout the 1980s, Lee served as chaplain at the Lorton Correctional Complex in Virginia. Lee died of heart failure in 1991, at the age of 55.

SOURCES
Abernathy, *And the Walls Came Tumbling Down*, 1989.
Branch, *At Canaan's Edge*, 2006.
Branch, *Pillar of Fire*, 1998.
King, *Why We Can't Wait*, 1964.

"LETTER FROM BIRMINGHAM JAIL" (1963)

As the events of the **Birmingham Campaign** intensified on the city's streets, Martin Luther King, Jr., composed a letter from his prison cell in Birmingham in response to local religious leaders' criticisms of the campaign: "Never before have I written so long a letter. I'm afraid it is much too long to take your precious time. I can assure you that it would have been much shorter if I had been writing from a comfortable desk, but what else can one do when he is alone in a narrow jail cell, other than write long letters, think long thoughts and pray long prayers?" (King, *Why*, 94–95).

King's 12 April 1963 arrest for violating Alabama's law against mass public demonstrations took place just over a week after the campaign's commencement. In an effort to revive the campaign, King and Ralph **Abernathy** had donned work clothes and marched from Sixth Avenue Baptist Church into a waiting police wagon. The day of his arrest, eight Birmingham clergy members wrote a criticism of the campaign that was published in the *Birmingham News*, calling its direct action strategy "unwise and untimely" and appealing "to both our white and Negro citizenry to observe the principles of law and order and common sense" ("White Clergy Urge").

Following the initial circulation of King's letter in Birmingham as a mimeographed copy, it was published in a variety of formats: as a pamphlet distributed by the **American Friends Service Committee** and as an article in periodicals such as *Christian Century*, *Christianity and Crisis*, the *New York Post*, and *Ebony* magazine. The first half of the letter was introduced into testimony before Congress by Representative William Fitts Ryan (D–NY) and published in the *Congressional Record*. One year later, King revised the letter and presented it as a chapter in his 1964 memoir of the Birmingham Campaign, **Why We Can't Wait**, a book modeled after the basic themes set out in "Letter from Birmingham Jail."

In *Why We Can't Wait*, King recalled in an author's note accompanying the letter's republication how the letter was written. It was begun on pieces of newspaper, continued on bits of paper supplied by a black trustee, and finished on paper pads left by King's attorneys. After countering the charge that he was an "outside agitator" in the body of the letter, King sought to explain the value of a "nonviolent campaign" and its "four basic steps: collection of the facts to determine whether injustices exist; negotiation; self-purification; and direct action" (King, *Why*, 79). He went on to explain that the purpose of direct action was to create a crisis situation out of which negotiation could emerge.

The body of King's letter called into question the clergy's charge of "impatience" on the part of the African American community and of the "extreme" level of the campaign's actions ("White Clergymen Urge"). "For years now, I have heard the word 'Wait!'" King wrote. "This 'Wait' has almost always meant 'Never'" (King, *Why*, 83). He articulated the resentment felt "when you are forever fighting a degenerating sense of 'nobodiness'—then you will understand why we find it difficult to wait" (King, *Why*, 84). King justified the tactic of civil disobedience by stating that, just as the Bible's Shadrach, Meshach, and Abednego refused to obey Nebuchadnezzar's unjust laws and colonists staged the Boston Tea Party, he refused to submit to laws and injunctions that were employed to uphold segregation and deny citizens their rights to peacefully assemble and protest.

King also decried the inaction of white moderates such as the clergymen, charging that human progress "comes through the tireless efforts of men willing to be co-workers with God, and without this hard work, time itself becomes an ally of the forces of social stagnation" (King, *Why*, 89). He prided himself as being among "extremists" such as Jesus, the prophet Amos, the apostle Paul, Martin Luther, and Abraham Lincoln, and observed that the country as a whole and the South in particular stood in need of creative men of extreme action. In closing, he hoped to meet the eight fellow clergymen who authored the first letter.

SOURCES

Garrow, *Bearing the Cross*, 1986.

King, "A Letter from Birmingham Jail," *Ebony* (August 1963): 23–32.

King, "From the Birmingham Jail," *Christianity and Crisis* 23 (27 May 1963): 89–91.

King, "From the Birmingham Jail," *Christian Century* 80 (12 June 1963): 767–773.

King, "Letter from Birmingham City Jail" (Philadelphia: American Friends Service Committee, May 1963).

King, "Letter from Birmingham Jail," in *Why We Can't Wait*, 1964.

Reverend Martin Luther King Writes from Birmingham City Jail—Part I, 88th Cong., 1st sess., *Congressional Record* (11 July 1963): A 4366–4368.

"White Clergymen Urge Local Negroes to Withdraw from Demonstrations," *Birmingham News*, 13 April 1963.

LEVISON, STANLEY DAVID (1912–1979)

In 1956 Stanley Levison, a Jewish attorney from New York, began raising funds to support the **Montgomery bus boycott** and became acquainted with Martin Luther King, Jr., The two men developed a close relationship in which Levison not only advised King, but also aided him with the day-to-day administrative demands of the movement. In 1963, the **Federal Bureau of Investigation** (FBI) used King's relationship with Levison, who they believed to be a Communist functionary, to justify surveillance of King.

Born in New York City on 2 May 1912, Levison studied at the University of Michigan, Columbia University, and the New School for Social Research before earning two law degrees from St. John's University. As treasurer of the Manhattan branch of the **American Jewish Congress**, Levison became a champion of left-wing causes and supported the defense of Julius and Ethel Rosenberg and the campaign against the McCarran Internal Security Act. In the early 1950s the FBI considered Levison to be a major financial coordinator for the Communist Party in the United States and began to monitor his activities.

In the mid-1950s Levison turned his attention to the civil rights struggle. In 1956 Levison, Bayard **Rustin**, and Ella **Baker** created **In Friendship**, an organization that raised money for southern civil rights activists and organizations, including the **Montgomery Improvement Association** (MIA). Together they formulated the concept of a regional "congress of organizations" dedicated to mass action grounded in **nonviolence**, an idea that would later develop into the **Southern Christian Leadership Conference** (SCLC) (*Papers* 4:491).

Throughout King's career, Levison drafted articles and speeches for him, prepared King's tax returns, and raised funds for SCLC. In 1958 Levison helped King edit **Stride Toward Freedom** and secured a book contract with Harper & Brothers. In almost all instances, he performed these services without compensation. When King offered payment, Levison refused. "My skills," he wrote King, "were acquired not only in a cloistered academic environment, but also in the commercial jungle.... I looked forward to the time when I could use these skills not for myself but for socially constructive ends. The liberation struggle is the most positive and rewarding area of work anyone could experience" (*Papers* 5:103).

The FBI's interest in Levison was suddenly rekindled in 1959, when the bureau learned of Levison's connection with King and the movement. FBI chief J. Edgar Hoover believed that Levison was a Communist agent, and that through Levison international **communism** influenced King's actions. He brought this concern to the attention of Attorney General Robert **Kennedy**, and Harris **Wofford** was enlisted by the Kennedy administration to warn King to end his relationship with Levison. Unwilling to lose a trusted advisor because of vague allegations, King refused to act on the administration's request for over a year. In March 1962 Robert Kennedy authorized the FBI to begin electronic surveillance of Levison, including his contact with King.

Just before a 22 June 1963 White House meeting with civil rights leaders, Burke **Marshall** and Robert Kennedy separately repeated the warning to King, and this time included a recommendation to also fire Jack **O'Dell**. King demurred and requested proof of Levison's threat to national security. After the meeting President John F. **Kennedy** took King aside and repeated the request that he ban Levison and O'Dell directly.

Over the next months King debated how to handle the requests to cease contact with Levison. Levison, however, valued the administration's support for the movement and took the initiative to cut off all visible ties with King. He continued to advise King on important matters indirectly, often using Clarence **Jones** as an intermediary. In October 1963, evidence of the ongoing relationship helped convince Robert Kennedy to approve wiretaps in King's home and office.

Throughout the 1960s, Levison continued to lend King practical and moral support. Following the **Selma to Montgomery March** in 1965, Levison wrote King: "For the first time, whites and Negroes from all over the nation physically joined the struggle in a pilgrimage to the deep south." For Levison, Selma was a turning point in King's status as a leader: "It made you one of the most powerful figures in the country—a leader now not merely of Negroes, but of millions of whites" (Levison, 7 April 1965).

In early 1967, when King became determined to participate in a public denunciation of the **Vietnam War** organized by **Clergy and Laymen Concerned about Vietnam**, Levison counseled him to refrain. Levison felt that King's planned speech, "**Beyond Vietnam**," was unbalanced and would have disastrous consequences to SCLC's fundraising campaign and King's personal prestige.

A year after publicly speaking out against the Vietnam War, King was assassinated in Memphis, Tennessee. Andrew **Young**, another of King's trusted advisors, called Levison a few hours afterward to tell him the news. Young wrote in his autobiography that "Martin had confided in Stan his worries and doubts and hopes ever since Montgomery and had defied the FBI and the president of the United States for their friendship. I knew he ... would want to hear from one of us personally" (Young, 467).

After a long battle with diabetes and cancer, Levison died at his home in New York City in 1979. Upon hearing of his death, Coretta Scott **King** called him "one of my husband's loyal and supportive friends" whose "contributions to the labor, civil rights, and peace movements" are relatively unknown ("Civil Rights Strategist").

SOURCES

Branch, *Parting the Waters*, 1989.

"Civil Rights Strategist S. D. Levison Dies," *Los Angeles Times*, 17 September 1979.

Friedman, *What Went Wrong?*, 1995.

Garrow, *The FBI and Martin Luther King, Jr.*, 1981.

Levine, *Bayard Rustin*, 2000.

Levison to King, 8 January 1959, in *Papers* 5:103–104.

Levison to King, 7 April 1965, MLKJP-GAMK.

Rustin to King, 23 December 1956, in *Papers* 3:491–494.

Senate Select Committee, *Book III: Supplementary Detailed Staff Reports on Intelligence Activities and the Rights of Americans*, 94th Cong., 2d sess., 1976, S. Rep. 94-755.

Theoharis, ed., *From the Secret Files of J. Edgar Hoover*, 1991.

Young, *An Easy Burden*, 1996.

LEWIS, JOHN (1940–)

Celebrated as one of the civil rights movement's most courageous young leaders, John Lewis, a founding member and chairman of the **Student Nonviolent Coordinating Committee** (SNCC), greatly contributed to student movements of the 1960s. He described Martin Luther King as "the person who, more than any other, continued to influence my life, who made me who I was" (Lewis, 412).

Born on 21 February 1940, Lewis was raised on a farm near Troy, Alabama, where his parents were sharecroppers. Lewis was first exposed to King and his ideas when he heard one of the young minister's sermons on the radio. This was a revolutionary moment for Lewis who thought of King as a "Moses" of his people; one who used "organized religion and the emotionalism within the Negro church as an instrument, as a vehicle, toward freedom" (Allen, "John Lewis"). Inspired by this idea of the **social gospel**, Lewis began preaching in local churches when he was 15 years old. Upon graduating from high school, Lewis enrolled in the American Baptist Theological Seminary in Nashville.

Lewis' first direct encounter with King occurred in the summer of 1958, when he traveled to Montgomery to seek King's help in suing to transfer to Troy State University, an all-white institution closer to his home. Lewis met with King, Ralph **Abernathy**, and Fred **Gray** at Abernathy's First Baptist Church, and they decided they would contribute their financial and legal assistance to "the boy from Troy," as King called him (Lewis, 68). Lewis' parents, however, feared the potential repercussions of the lawsuit. Lewis acknowledged these sentiments and returned to American Baptist that fall.

While in Nashville, Lewis attended direct action workshops led by James **Lawson** and came to embrace the Gandhian philosophy of **nonviolence**. Lewis became heavily involved in the Nashville movement and participated in a series of student **sit-ins** in early 1960 that aimed to integrate movie theaters, restaurants, and other businesses. In April 1960, he helped form SNCC and later participated in the **Freedom Rides** of 1961. During this campaign, Lewis realized the potential implications of his involvement in the movement after being severely beaten by white youth. Faced with jeopardizing his ability to graduate from American Baptist by being incarcerated for participation in a demonstration, he stated: "This is [the] most important decision in my life, to decide to give up all if necessary for the Freedom Ride, that Justice and Freedom might come to the Deep South" (Branch, 395).

Lewis received his BA from the American Baptist Theological Seminary in 1961. Acknowledging him as "one of the most dedicated young men in our movement," the **Southern Christian Leadership Conference** (SCLC) elected him to their board the following year in an attempt to bring more young people into the organization (SCLC, 16 May 1962). In 1963 he was chosen by acclamation as the chairman of SNCC. As leader of the organization, Lewis often found himself torn between his allegiance to SNCC and his relationship with King. Lewis told King that "it has always been a deep concern of mine that there has not been enough communication between S.C.L.C. and SNCC," however, this was not a sentiment shared by other members of either group (Lewis, 11 April 1964). Lewis' decision to "maintain a liaison with Dr. King and the SCLC" earned him much criticism within SNCC (Lewis, 379). Lewis, however, valued King as the man who had ultimately set him on his life's path, and chose to uphold strong ties with both him and SNCC.

As chairman of SNCC, Lewis participated in many of the civil rights movement's most momentous events. On 28 August 1963, he delivered one of the keynote speeches at the **March on Washington for Jobs and Freedom**. Fellow civil rights leaders had advised Lewis to revise his speech because of its blunt criticisms of the federal government's inaction, but the final version was still regarded as "the most controversial and militant speech at the March," proclaiming that "we march today for jobs and freedom, but we have nothing to be proud of" and asking in an accusatory manner, "Which side is the federal government on?" (Lewis, 28 August 1963). Lewis went on to play a crucial role in the 1964 **Freedom Summer** by coordinating voter registration drives and community action programs in Mississippi.

On 7 March 1965, Lewis and Hosea Williams led several hundred protest marchers across the Edmund Pettus Bridge in Selma, Alabama in a demonstration aimed at drawing attention to increased voting rights in the South. The march came to be known as "Bloody Sunday," because of the brutal beatings that many of the marchers received from state troopers; Lewis himself was severely attacked and suffered a fractured skull. Lewis' involvement with SNCC ended the following year when Stokely **Carmichael** won a bid for the chairmanship, and Lewis perceived that the organization was heading in a militant direction that conflicted with his "personal commitment to nonviolence" (Carson, 231).

Lewis continued his civil rights involvement in later years as the head of voter registration initiatives run by the Southern Regional Council and the **Voter Education Project**. In 1977 President Jimmy Carter chose him to head ACTION, a federal volunteer agency. He attempted to enter government that same year with a House congressional campaign but was unsuccessful. He served on Atlanta's city council from 1982 to 1986, when he defeated Julian **Bond** in the Democratic congressional primary and was elected to the House of Representatives, where he has served 11 terms.

Sources

Archie Allen, "John Lewis: Keeper of the Dream," *New South* 26 (Spring 1971):15–25.

Branch, *Parting the Waters*, 1988.

Carson, *In Struggle*, 1981.

Lewis, Speech delivered at the March on Washington for Jobs and Freedom, 28 August 1963, SNCCP-GAMK.

Lewis, *Walking with the Wind*, 1998.

Lewis to King, 11 April 1964, MLKJP-GAMK.

SCLC, Minutes from board meeting, 16 May 1962, MLKJP-GAMK.

LEWIS, RUFUS (1906–1999)

Long-time voter registration activist Rufus Lewis nominated his pastor, Martin Luther King, Jr., as president of the **Montgomery Improvement Association** (MIA) at the founding meeting on 5 December 1955. Lewis organized the Citizen Coordinating Committee in 1954 with Jo Ann **Robinson** and E. D. **Nixon** "to develop united efforts in voting, to get more people registered and to create civic consciousness." Lewis attributed the success of the boycott to the unity of the black community: "The mass meetings help to keep the spirit up in the minds of the common man. Negroes know what they want, although it's expressed by someone else" (Lewis, 20 January 1956).

Lewis was born in Montgomery on 30 November 1906, and graduated from Fisk University in 1931. A librarian and athletic coach at Alabama State College from the mid-1930s to 1941, he later taught night school for World War II veterans. In 1958, after his wife's death, he began operating her family's funeral business. A member of **Alpha Phi Alpha** fraternity and the **National Association for the Advancement of Colored People**, Lewis organized the Citizens Club, a social club that provided voter registration assistance in 1952. Lewis also traveled throughout the South training voter registration workers.

Once described by King as having "an inextinguishable passion for social justice," Lewis headed the MIA's transportation committee and co-chaired its committee on registration and voting (King, May 1958). He offered his Citizens Club as the MIA headquarters when they had trouble securing space, only to rescind his offer when he was warned that his license could be suspended. Lewis continued chairing the registration and voting committee after the end of the boycott and sent King a letter asking him to support a get-out-the-vote drive in 1958.

Lewis was active in the Democratic Party in Alabama, serving as the first president of the Montgomery County Democratic Conference. In 1976, he was elected to the Alabama House of Representatives, resigning in 1977 when President Jimmy Carter appointed him a U.S. Marshall and he became the first African American from the Middle District of Alabama to hold the position.

Sources

Uriah J. Fields, "Minutes of Montgomery Improvement Association Founding Meeting," 5 December 1955, in *Papers* 3:68–70.

King, Draft, Chapter IV of *Stride Toward Freedom*, May 1958.

King, *Stride Toward Freedom*, 1958.

Lewis, Interview by Donald Ferron, 20 January 1956, PV-ARC-LNT.

LITTLE ROCK SCHOOL DESEGREGATION (1957)

Three years after the U.S. Supreme Court ruled unanimously in ***Brown v. Board of Education*** that separate educational facilities are inherently unequal, nine African American students—Minnijean Brown, Terrance Roberts, Elizabeth Eckford, Ernest Green, Thelma Mothershed, Melba Patillo, Gloria Ray, Jefferson Thomas, and Carlotta Walls—attempted to integrate Central High School in Little Rock, Arkansas. The students, known as the Little Rock Nine, were recruited by Daisy **Bates**, president of the Arkansas branch of the **National Association for the Advancement of Colored People** (NAACP). As president of the **Montgomery Improvement Association,**

Martin Luther King wrote President Dwight D. **Eisenhower** requesting a swift resolution allowing the students to attend school.

On 4 September 1957, the first day of school at Central High, a white mob gathered in front of the school, and Governor Orval Faubus deployed the Arkansas National Guard to prevent the black students from entering. In response to Faubus' action, a team of NAACP lawyers, including Thurgood **Marshall**, won a federal district court injunction to prevent the governor from blocking the students' entry. With the help of police escorts, the students successfully entered the school through a side entrance on 23 September 1957. Fearing escalating mob violence, however, the students were rushed home soon afterward.

Observing the standoff between Faubus and the federal judiciary, King sent a telegram to President Eisenhower urging him to "take a strong forthright stand in the Little Rock situation." King told the president that if the federal government did not take a stand against the injustice it would "set the process of integration back fifty years. This is a great opportunity for you and the federal government to back up the longings and aspirations of millions of peoples of good will and make law and order a reality" (King, 9 September 1957). Aware that the Little Rock incident was becoming an international embarrassment, Eisenhower reluctantly ordered troops from the Army's 101st Airborne Division to protect the students, who were shielded by federal troops and the Arkansas National Guard for the remainder of the school year. In a 25 September telegram, King praised the president's actions: "I wish to express my sincere support for the stand you have taken to restore law and order in Little Rock, Arkansas.... You should know that the overwhelming majority of southerners, Negro and white, stand firmly behind your resolute action" (*Papers* 4:278).

At the end of the school year, Ernest Green became the first African American to graduate from Central High School. King attended his graduation ceremony. In honor of their momentous contributions to history and the integration of the Arkansas public school system, in 1958 the Little Rock Nine were honored with the NAACP's highest honor, the Spingarn Medal.

Before schools opened in the fall of 1958, Faubus closed all four of Little Rock's public high schools rather than proceed with desegregation, but his efforts were short lived. In December 1959, the Supreme Court ruled that the school board must reopen the schools and resume the process of desegregating the city's schools.

SOURCES

Bates, *Long Shadow of Little Rock*, 1962.
Hampton, Fayer, and Flynn, *Voices of Freedom*, 1990.
King to Eisenhower, 9 September 1957, MLKJP-GAMK.
King to Eisenhower, 25 September 1957, in *Papers* 4:278.
"National Affairs," *Time*, 7 October 1957.
Williams, *Thurgood Marshall*, 1998.

LOWERY, JOSEPH ECHOLS (1921–)

Minister and civil rights activist Joseph E. Lowery was a member of Martin Luther King's inner circle of confidantes and colleagues. Lowery was a founding executive committee member of the **Southern Christian Leadership Conference** (SCLC), and was made a vice president in the late 1950s. Lowery continued to work for SCLC after King's death, serving as president from 1977 through 1997.

Lowery was born in Huntsville, Alabama, in 1921. After graduating from high school, he studied at Knoxville College and Alabama Agricultural and Mechanical College before earning a BA (1943) from Paine College, a Methodist institution in Augusta, Georgia. The following year, he enrolled in Paine Theological Seminary to become a Methodist minister. After graduation, Lowery became pastor of the Warren Street United Methodist Church in Mobile, Alabama, where he also became president of the local Alabama Civic Affairs Association.

Lowery and King worked closely throughout the 1950s and 1960s, as both men were committed to using **nonviolence** to achieve social justice. In the aftermath of the **Montgomery bus boycott**, Lowery, King, Fred **Shuttlesworth** and Ralph **Abernathy** formed SCLC to strengthen their work throughout the South.

In 1960, Lowery, Shuttlesworth, Abernathy, and Solomon **Seay** were sued for libel by the Montgomery police commissioner over an advertisement in the *New York Times* that sought to raise funds for King's defense against felony charges related to alleged false statements in his 1956 and 1958 Alabama tax returns. Although an all-white jury initially ordered the defendants to pay $500,000 and Lowery had his car seized and sold at public auction, the U.S. Supreme Court overturned the libel verdict in 1964, in **New York Times v. Sullivan**. In 1961 Lowery moved to Nashville, Tennessee, where he led marches and **sit-ins** against segregation in public facilities and continued to serve SCLC. Three years later, Lowery returned to Alabama, where he served as pastor at St. Paul United Methodist Church in Birmingham until 1968.

Lowery supported King in times of personal crisis, such as when the **Federal Bureau of Investigation** (FBI) sent King an anonymous letter in 1964 urging him to commit suicide. He also aided King practically, tying up loose ends while King was jailed in Selma, Alabama, in February 1965. Following King's **assassination**, Lowery spoke in tribute at his memorial service in Atlanta.

In 1968, Lowery moved to Atlanta to pastor Central United Methodist Church and work with Abernathy, the new president of SCLC. In 1977, after Abernathy resigned, Lowery became president. He led SCLC for 20 years, focusing not only on civil rights in the South, but on human rights issues in the Middle East and South Africa as well. In 1982, Lowery and Jesse **Jackson** led a march from Tuskegee, Alabama, to Washington, D.C., to promote the extension of the **Voting Rights Act of 1965**.

Lowery retired from the church in 1992, and left SCLC in 1997, the year he received the Lifetime Achievement Award **from the National Association for the Advancement of Colored People**. In 2001 Clark Atlanta University established the Joseph E. Lowery Institute for Justice and Human Rights. In February 2006, at Coretta Scott **King**'s funeral, Lowery criticized the current war in Iraq and accused the government of not doing enough to fight poverty.

SOURCES

Abernathy, *And the Walls Came Tumbling Down*, 1989.

Branch, *Parting the Waters*, 1988.

Branch, *Pillar of Fire*, 1998.

Committee to Defend Martin Luther King and the Struggle for Freedom in the South, "Heed Their Rising Voices," 29 March 1960, in *Papers* 5:382.

Introduction, in *Papers* 5:24–26.
King to Fred D. Gray, 14 December 1960, in *Papers* 5:580.
John Malcolm Patterson to King, 9 May 1960, in *Papers* 5:456.

LUTULI, ALBERT J. (c. 1898–1967)

Albert Lutuli, an African nationalist and Zulu chief, was recognized nationally and internationally for his involvement in the fight against **apartheid** in South Africa.

Although Lutuli and Martin Luther King, Jr., rarely worked closely together, they were mutual admirers. In 1959, after reading **Stride Toward Freedom**, King's account of the **Montgomery bus boycott**, Lutuli told a friend that it was the "greatest inspiration" (*Papers* 5:307). As a Christian and president of the African National Congress (ANC), Lutuli shared with King the religiously inspired dream of a peacefully integrated society achieved through nonviolent means. In December 1959 King wrote Lutuli of his admiration: "I admire your great witness and your dedication to the cause of freedom and human dignity. You have stood amid persecution, abuse and oppression with a dignity and calmness of spirit.... One day all of Africa will be proud of your achievements" (*Papers*, 5:344).

Lutuli was born around 1898 in southern Rhodesia. Upon completing a teaching program in 1917, Lutuli took his first job as an elementary school teacher. Two years later he attended Adams College in South Africa where, after earning a higher degree, he remained on faculty for 15 years. During his time at Adams, the devoutly religious Lutuli became a lay preacher. An active member of the Christian community, he served as chairman of the South African Board of the Congregationalist Church of America and as president of the Natal Mission Conference. In 1936 Lutuli accepted the call to serve as chief of the Groutville Reserve Tribe, an area populated by about 5,000 Zulus. For the next 17 years, Lutuli remained chief until he was deposed by the government in 1952.

In 1945, Lutuli was elected provincial executive secretary for the Natal branch of the ANC, an organization formed in 1912 to unite tribes and promote voting rights for blacks. By 1952 Lutuli was president, a position he held until his death. Lutuli's leadership within his tribe and in the ANC coincided with the escalation of discriminatory legislation in South Africa, and a series of new laws systematically disenfranchised all black, Indian, and colored South Africans, pushing them literally and figuratively to the margins of South African society. Due to his vocal dissent against **apartheid**, Lutuli was banned several times from South African public life and confined within a 15-mile radius of his home.

Lutuli's unrelenting dedication to the anti-apartheid movement was acknowledged when he became the first black African to be awarded the **Nobel Peace Prize** in 1960. Almost immediately after receiving the award, Lutuli joined King to issue an Appeal for Action against Apartheid, under the sponsorship of the **American Committee on Africa**, which urged people to protest apartheid through nonviolent actions such as boycotts, demonstrations, and public education.

After returning from Africa in March 1964, James W. King, an Ohio minister, relayed a message from Lutuli to King: "I asked Chief Lutuli what he would want Americans to know. He said: 'Give my highest regards to Martin Luther. It is not often that we see clergymen taking a stand on social issues. It means a lot to us here....

Martin Luther King is my hero'" (King, 25 March 1964). King's respect for Lutuli was such that, in his acceptance of the Nobel Peace Prize in 1964, he honored Lutuli's work in South Africa and forged a link between the civil rights movement and the African Liberation Movement, saying, "You honor, once again, Chief Lutuli of South Africa, whose struggles with and for his people are still met with the most brutal expressions of man's inhumanity to man" (King, 108). Lutuli died in 1967 at age 69.

SOURCES

Bryan to King, 10 October 1959, in *Papers* 5:307–308.
James W. King to King, 25 March 1964, LewBP-INP.
King, *A Call to Conscience*, ed. Carson and Shepard, 2001.
King to Lutuli, 8 December 1959, in *Papers* 5:344–345.

MALCOLM X (1925–1965)

As the nation's most visible proponent of **Black Nationalism**, Malcolm X's challenge to the multiracial, nonviolent approach of Martin Luther King, Jr., helped set the tone for the ideological and tactical conflicts that took place within the black freedom struggle of the 1960s. Given Malcolm X's abrasive criticism of King and his advocacy of racial separatism, it is not surprising that King rejected the occasional overtures from one of his fiercest critics. However, after Malcolm's assassination in 1965, King wrote to his widow, Betty Shabazz: "While we did not always see eye to eye on methods to solve the race problem, I always had a deep affection for Malcolm and felt that he had the great ability to put his finger on the existence and root of the problem" (King, 26 February 1965).

Malcolm Little was born to Louise and Earl Little in Omaha, Nebraska, on 19 May 1925. His father died when he was six years old—the victim, he believed, of a white racist group. Following his father's death, Malcolm recalled, "Some kind of psychological deterioration hit our family circle and began to eat away our pride" (Malcolm X, *Autobiography*, 14). By the end of the 1930s Malcolm's mother had been institutionalized, and he became a ward of the court to be raised by white guardians in various reform schools and foster homes.

Malcolm joined the Nation of Islam (NOI) while serving a prison term in Massachusetts on burglary charges. Shortly after his release in 1952, he moved to Chicago and became a minister under Elijah Muhammad, abandoning his "slave name," and becoming Malcolm X (Malcolm X, "We Are Rising"). By the late 1950s, Malcolm had become the NOI's leading spokesman.

Although Malcolm rejected King's message of **nonviolence**, he respected King as a "fellow-leader of our people," sending King NOI articles as early as 1957 and inviting him to participate in mass meetings throughout the early 1960s (*Papers* 5:491). Although Malcolm was particularly interested that King hear Elijah Muhammad's message, he also sought to create an open forum for black leaders to explore solutions to the "race problem" (Malcolm X, 31 July 1963). King never accepted Malcolm's invitations, however, leaving communication with him to his secretary, Maude **Ballou**.

Despite his repeated overtures to King, Malcolm did not refrain from criticizing him publicly. "The only revolution in which the goal is loving your enemy," Malcolm told

King and Malcolm X meet at the Capitol in Washington, D.C., on 26 March 1964, during the filibuster of the 1964 Civil Rights Act. © AP / Wide World Photos.

an audience in 1963, "is the Negro revolution.... That's no revolution" (Malcolm X, "Message to the Grassroots," 9).

In the spring of 1964, Malcolm broke away from the NOI and made a pilgrimage to Mecca. When he returned he began following a course that paralleled King's—combining religious leadership and political action. Although King told reporters that Malcolm's separation from Elijah Muhammad "holds no particular significance to the present civil rights efforts," he argued that if "tangible gains are not made soon all across the country, we must honestly face the prospect that some Negroes might be tempted to accept some oblique path [such] as that Malcolm X proposes" (King, 16 March 1964).

Ten days later, during the Senate debate on the **Civil Rights Act of 1964**, King and Malcolm met for the first and only time. After holding a press conference in the Capitol on the proceedings, King encountered Malcolm in the hallway. As King recalled in a 3 April letter, "At the end of the conference, he came and spoke to me, and I readily shook his hand." King defended shaking the hand of an adversary by saying that "my position is that of kindness and reconciliation" (King, 3 April 1965).

Malcolm's primary concern during the remainder of 1964 was to establish ties with the black activists he saw as more militant than King. He met with a number of workers from the **Student Nonviolent Coordinating Committee** (SNCC), including SNCC chairman John **Lewis** and Mississippi organizer Fannie Lou **Hamer**. Malcolm saw his newly created Organization of African American Unity (OAAU) as a potential source of ideological guidance for the more militant veterans of the southern civil rights movement. At the same time, he looked to the southern struggle for inspiration in his effort to revitalize the Black Nationalist movement.

In January 1965, he revealed in an interview that the OAAU would "support fully and without compromise any action by any group that is designed to get meaningful immediate results" (Malcolm X, *Two Speeches*, 31). Malcolm urged civil rights groups to unite, telling a gathering at a symposium sponsored by the **Congress of Racial Equality**: "We want freedom now, but we're not going to get it saying 'We Shall Overcome.' We've got to fight to overcome" (Malcolm X, *Malcolm X Speaks*, 38).

In early 1965, while King was jailed in Selma, Alabama, Malcolm traveled to Selma, where he had a private meeting with Coretta Scott **King**. "I didn't come to Selma to make his job difficult," he assured Coretta. "I really did come thinking that I could make it easier. If the white people realize what the alternative is, perhaps they will be more willing to hear Dr. King" (Scott King, 256).

On 21 February 1965, just a few weeks after his visit to Selma, Malcolm X was assassinated. King called his murder a "great tragedy" and expressed his regret that it "occurred at a time when Malcolm X was … moving toward a greater understanding of the nonviolent movement" (King, 24 February 1965). He asserted that Malcolm's murder deprived "the world of a potentially great leader" (King, "The Nightmare of Violence"). Malcolm's death signaled the beginning of bitter battles involving proponents of the ideological alternatives the two men represented.

SOURCES

Maude L. Ballou to Malcolm X, 1 February 1957, in *Papers* 4:117.

Goldman, *Death and Life of Malcolm X*, 1973.

King, "The Nightmare of Violence," *New York Amsterdam News*, 13 March 1965.

King, Press conference on Malcolm X's assassination, 24 February 1965, MLKJP-GAMK.

King, Statement on Malcolm X's break with the Nation of Islam, 16 March 1964, MLKJP-GAMK.

King to Abram Eisenman, 3 April 1964, MLKJP-GAMK.

King to Shabazz, 26 February 1965, MLKJP-GAMK.

(Scott) King, *My Life with Martin Luther King, Jr.*, 1969.

Malcolm X, Interview by Harry Ring over Station WBAI-FM in New York, in *Two Speeches by Malcolm X*, 1965.

Malcolm X, "Message to the Grassroots," in *Malcolm X Speaks*, ed. George Breitman, 1965.

Malcolm X, "We Are Rising from the Dead Since We Heard Messenger Muhammad Speak," *Pittsburgh Courier*, 15 December 1956.

Malcolm X to King, 21 July 1960, in *Papers* 5:491–492.

Malcolm X to King, 31 July 1963, MLKJP-GAMK.

Malcolm X with Haley, *Autobiography of Malcolm X*, 1965.

MARCH ON WASHINGTON FOR JOBS AND FREEDOM (1963)

On 28 August 1963, more than 200,000 demonstrators took part in the March on Washington for Jobs and Freedom in the nation's capital. The march was successful in pressuring the administration of John F. **Kennedy** to initiate a strong federal civil rights bill in Congress. During this event, Martin Luther King delivered his memorable "**I Have a Dream**" speech.

The 1963 March on Washington had several precedents. In the summer of 1941 A. Philip **Randolph**, founder of the Brotherhood of Sleeping Car Porters, called for a march on Washington, D.C., to draw attention to the exclusion of African Americans from positions in the national defense industry. This job market had proven to be closed to blacks, despite the fact that it was growing to supply materials to the Allies in World War II. The threat of 100,000 marchers in Washington, D.C., pushed President Franklin D. Roosevelt to issue Executive Order 8802, which mandated the formation of the Fair Employment Practices Commission to investigate racial discrimination charges against defense firms. In response, Randolph cancelled plans for the march.

Civil rights demonstrators did assemble at the Lincoln Memorial in May 1957 for a **Prayer Pilgrimage for Freedom** on the third anniversary of **Brown v. Board of Education**, and in October 1958, for a **Youth March for Integrated Schools** to protest the lack of progress since that ruling. King addressed the 1957 demonstration, but due to ill health after being stabbed by Izola **Curry**, Coretta Scott **King** delivered his scheduled remarks at the 1958 event.

By 1963, the centennial of the **Emancipation Proclamation**, most of the goals of these earlier protests still had not been realized. High levels of black unemployment, work that offered most African Americans only minimal wages and poor job mobility,

View of the March on Washington for Jobs and Freedom, 28 August 1963. Courtesy of the Library of Congress.

systematic disenfranchisement of many African Americans, and the persistence of racial segregation in the South prompted discussions about a large scale march for political and economic justice as early as 1962. On behalf of the **Negro American Labor Council** (NALC), the **Southern Christian Leadership Conference**, the **Congress of Racial Equality** (CORE), and the **Student Nonviolent Coordinating Committee** (SNCC), Randolph wrote a letter on 24 May 1962 to Secretary Stewart Udall of the Department of the Interior regarding permits for a march culminating at the Lincoln Memorial that fall. Plans for the march were stalled when Udall encouraged the groups to consider the Sylvan Theater at the Washington Monument due to the complications of rerouting traffic and the volume of tourists at the Lincoln Memorial.

In March 1963 Randolph telegraphed King that the NALC had begun planning a June march "for Negro job rights," and asked for King's immediate response (Randolph, 26 March 1963). In May, at the height of the **Birmingham Campaign**, King joined Randolph, James **Farmer** of CORE, and Charles McDew of SNCC in calling for such an action later that year, declaring, "Let the black laboring masses speak!" (King et al., 7 May 1963) After notifying President Kennedy of their intent, the leaders of the major civil rights organizations set the march date for 28 August. The stated goals of the protest included "a comprehensive civil rights bill" that would do away with segregated public accommodations; "protection of the right to vote"; mechanisms for seeking redress of violations of constitutional rights; "desegregation of all public schools in 1963"; a massive federal works program "to train and place unemployed workers"; and "a Federal Fair Employment Practices Act barring discrimination in all employment" ("Goals of Rights March").

As the summer passed, the list of organizations participating in and sponsoring the event expanded to include the **National Association for the Advancement of Colored People** (NAACP), the **National Urban League**, the National Catholic Conference for Interracial Justice, the **National Council of the Churches of Christ in America**, the United Auto Workers (UAW), and many others.

The March on Washington was not universally embraced. It was condemned by the Nation of Islam and Malcolm X who referred to it as "the Farce on Washington," although he attended nonetheless (Malcolm X, 278). The executive board of the **American Federation of Labor-Congress of Industrial Organizations** declined to support the march, adopting a position of neutrality. Nevertheless, many constituent unions attended in substantial numbers.

The diversity of those in attendance was reflected in the event's speakers and performers. They included singers Marian Anderson, Odetta, Joan Baez, and Bob Dylan; Little Rock civil rights veteran Daisy Lee **Bates**; actors Ossie **Davis** and Ruby **Dee**; **American Jewish Congress** president Rabbi Joachim Prinz; Randolph; UAW president Walter **Reuther**; march organizer Bayard **Rustin**; NAACP president Roy **Wilkins**; National Urban League president Whitney **Young** and SNCC leader John **Lewis**.

A draft of John Lewis' prepared speech, circulated before the march, was denounced by Reuther, Burke **Marshall**, and Patrick O'Boyle, the Catholic Archbishop of Washington, D.C., for its militant tone. In the speech's original version Lewis charged that the Kennedy administration's proposed **Civil Rights Act** was "too little and too late," and threatened not only to march in Washington but to "march through the South, through the heart of Dixie, the way Sherman did. We will pursue our own 'scorched earth' policy" (Lewis, 221; 224). In a caucus that included King, Randolph, and SNCC's James **Forman**, Lewis agreed to eliminate those and other phrases, but believed that in its final form his address "was still a strong speech, very strong" (Lewis, 227).

The day's high point came when King took the podium toward the end of the event and moved the Lincoln Memorial audience and live television viewers with what has come to be known as his "I Have a Dream" speech. King commented that "as television beamed the image of this extraordinary gathering across the border oceans, everyone who believed in man's capacity to better himself had a moment of inspiration and confidence in the future of the human race," and characterized the march as an "appropriate climax" to the summer's events (King, "I Have a Dream," 125; 122).

After the march, King and other civil rights leaders met with President Kennedy and Vice President Lyndon B. **Johnson** at the White House, where they discussed the need for bipartisan support of civil rights legislation. Though they were passed after Kennedy's death, the provisions of the **Civil Rights Act of 1964** and **Voting Rights Act of 1965** reflect the demands of the march.

SOURCES

Branch, *Parting the Waters*, 1988.

Carson, *In Struggle*, 1981.

"Goals of Rights March," *New York Times*, 29 August 1963.

King, Address at youth march for integrated schools in Washington, D.C., delivered by Coretta Scott King, 25 October 1958, in *Papers* 4:514–515.

King, "Give Us the Ballot," Address at the Prayer Pilgrimage for Freedom, 17 May 1957, in *Papers* 4:208–215.

King, "I Have a Dream," in *A Call to Conscience*, ed. Carson and Shepard, 2001.

King, *Why We Can't Wait*, 1964.

King, Randolph, Farmer, and McDew, Call for an Emancipation March on Washington for Jobs, 7 May 1963, BRP-DLC.

Lewis, *Walking with the Wind*, 1998.

Malcolm X with Haley, *Autobiography of Malcolm X*, 1965.

Randolph to King, 26 March 1963, MLKJP-GAMK.

MARSHALL, BURKE (1922–2003)

Burke Marshall was head of the Justice Department's Civil Rights Division under Presidents John F. **Kennedy** and Lyndon B. **Johnson**, serving from January 1961 through December 1964. Martin Luther King regularly called and wired Marshall for assistance. John **Lewis**, head of the **Student Nonviolent Coordinating Committee**, and other civil rights leaders were on a first name basis with Marshall. Wyatt Tee **Walker**, executive director of the **Southern Christian Leadership Conference** (SCLC), woke Marshall at 1:00 A.M. to inform him of King's arrest during the 1963 **Birmingham Campaign**.

Marshall was born in Plainfield, New Jersey, on 1 October 1922. He graduated from Yale University in 1943 and served in the army intelligence corps during World War II before returning to Yale for law school. After graduation he worked with Harris **Wofford** at the Washington, D.C., law firm of Covington & Burling, representing prominent clients in antitrust suits. Although he seemed an unqualified choice for the top civil rights position in the Department of Justice, Attorney General Robert **Kennedy** surmised that the job would be best handled by a competent professional with no past political statements on civil rights.

Once in office, Marshall carried the task of litigating voting rights cases and school desegregation in New Orleans. That summer Marshall was faced with the **Freedom Rides**, the major federal racial crisis of Kennedy's term. Although the federal government didn't act until the violence in Alabama was national news, Marshall advised Kennedy to authorize federal protection for the young riders. After the ordeal, Marshall concluded that they had given the Kennedy administration a much-needed impetus to enforce constitutional freedoms.

Voting rights were on the agenda at an amicable April 1962 meeting between Marshall, Attorney General Kennedy, King, and other movement leaders. Afterward Walker thanked Marshall for his "invaluable assistance in removing and confronting many of the problems we face in our work in voter registration" (Walker, 11 April 1962).

Soon thereafter, King was jailed in Albany, Georgia, as part of SCLC's participation in the **Albany Movement**. Marshall telephoned King's wife, Coretta Scott **King**, telling her that he would do whatever he could to obtain King's release. King, however, did not want to be released, as he wished to remain in solidarity with jailed local activists. Eleven days later, after being released, King debated for two hours on the phone with Marshall about whether to obey a federal court injunction against civil rights protests in Albany. In the end, he agreed not to march; however, an impromptu march went ahead without him.

Although King's efforts were sometimes frustrated by Marshall's noncommittal responses to his wires urging investigations into potential civil rights violations that did not clearly fall under federal jurisdiction, nearly every decision the federal government made to become involved in a civil rights claim during his tenure went through Marshall. Occasionally, where there was no immediate legal remedy for an unresolved racial dispute, Marshall personally negotiated between King and the white community. In his book **Why We Can't Wait**, King wrote that Marshall "did an invaluable job of opening channels of communication between our leadership and the top people in the economic power structure" during the Birmingham negotiations (King, 103).

Marshall also had the dubious task of conveying to King the allegations by **Federal Bureau of Investigation** Director J. Edgar Hoover that King was being influenced by two alleged Communists, Jack **O'Dell** and Stanley **Levison**. Although King was slow to act, after further urgings by Attorney General Kennedy and President Kennedy, he cut all contact with O'Dell and agreed to only communicate with Levison through intermediaries.

Marshall was critical to the passage of the **Civil Rights Act of 1964**. After the Act was signed King wrote to Marshall, thanking him for his "able leadership" in securing its passage through Congress (24 June 1964). In his December 1964 letter of resignation, Marshall wrote that he believed the passage of the Civil Rights Act meant that the task of his division was "now a straightforward matter of litigation" to ensure compliance with the law (White House, 18 December 1964). Accepting his resignation, Johnson told Marshall, "During the past four years, the Nation has at long last come to grips with the domestic problem that has been the most difficult and complicated during our entire existence. You have played an extraordinary role in this significant area of human progress.... In 33 years service with the Federal government I have never known any person who rendered a better quality of public service" (White House, 18 December 1964).

After resigning, Marshall continued to assist Johnson with civil rights issues. He served as Johnson's personal envoy during the **Selma to Montgomery March**, walking with Wofford as the march set out from Selma. Marshall returned to the firm of Covington & Burling and then became general counsel at IBM. In 1970 he was named deputy dean at Yale Law School. From 1966 to 1986, Marshall served as chairman of the board of the Vera Institute of Justice, a nonprofit organization committed to making the justice system fair and humane. Marshall died in 2003 at the age of 80.

SOURCES

Arsenault, *Freedom Riders*, 2006.

Branch, *At Canaan's Edge*, 2006.

Branch, *Parting the Waters*, 1988.

Garrow, *Protest at Selma*, 1978.

King, *Why We Can't Wait*, 1964.

King to Marshall, 24 June 1964, MLKJP-GAMK.

Cabell Phillips, "Kennedy Requests Report on Dr. King," *New York Times*, 12 July 1962.

Jack Raymond, "President Phones Justice Aide on Negroes' Jailing in Alabama," *New York Times*, 14 April 1963.

Claude Sitton, "Birmingham Pact Sets Timetable for Integration," *New York Times*, 11 May 1963.

Walker to Marshall, 11 April 1962, SCLCR-GAMK.

White House, Press release, Exchange of Letters Between Lyndon B. (Baines) Johnson and Burke Marshall, Assistant Attorney General, 18 December 1964, MLKJP-GAMK.

Wofford, *Of Kennedys and Kings*, 1980.

MARSHALL, THURGOOD (1908–1993)

As an attorney fighting to secure equality and justice through the courts, Thurgood Marshall helped build the legal foundation for Martin Luther King's challenges to segregation. On 6 February 1958, King wrote Marshall to express his gratitude for Marshall's efforts in the **Montgomery bus boycott**: "We will remain eternally grateful to you and your staff for the great work you have done for not only the Negro in particular but American Democracy in general" (*Papers* 4:360).

Born in Baltimore, Maryland, Marshall grew up in a middle class, politically active black family, and was taught early on to challenge injustice. Marshall earned his BA from Lincoln University in 1930. Unable to enroll at University of Maryland because of its Jim Crow admission policy, Marshall attended Howard University Law School (JD, 1933). After working in the **National Association for the Advancement of Colored People** (NAACP) national office as an assistant to chief counsel Charles Houston, his former law school professor, Marshall succeeded him as NAACP chief counsel in 1938. In 1940 he began directing the newly created NAACP Legal Defense and Educational Fund. Marshall argued several landmark court cases that banned segregation practices, most notably *Smith v. Allwright* (1944), which won blacks the right to vote in Texas primaries; *Morgan v. Virginia* (1946), which banned segregation on interstate passenger carriers; and *Sweatt v. Painter* (1950), which required the admittance of a qualified black student to the University of Texas Law School.

Marshall's most historic victory came in 1954 with ***Brown v. Board of Education***, in which Marshall argued successfully against the doctrine of "separate but equal," convincing the court that segregated schools were inherently unequal, and beginning the process of school desegregation.

Despite common beliefs in American democracy and integrationist goals, King and Marshall disagreed over tactics. Rather than civil disobedience and demonstrations, Marshall favored legal remedies as more efficient and effective. "I used to have a lot of fights with Martin about his theory about disobeying the law. I didn't believe in that." Marshall recalled. "I thought you did have a right to disobey a law, and you also had a right to go to jail for it. He kept talking about Thoreau, and I told him … 'If I understand it, Thoreau wrote his book in jail. If you want to write a book, you go to jail and write it'" (Marshall, 471). Marshall did acknowledge King as "a great speaker," and conceded that the protests "achieved much. If you put them in the scale, they would weigh very heavy, because it reached people's consciousness" (Marshall, 479).

In 1961 President John F. **Kennedy** appointed Marshall to the Second Circuit Court of Appeals, making him the second African American to serve as a federal appellate judge. From 1965 to 1967, Marshall served under President Lyndon B. **Johnson** as solicitor general, the government's chief appellant lawyer before the Supreme Court, another first for an African American. In 1967 Marshall was confirmed to the Supreme Court, where he remained the first and only African American justice until he retired in 1991.

SOURCES

King to Marshall, 6 February 1958, in *Papers* 4:360.
Marshall, *Thurgood Marshall*, ed. Tushnet, 2001.
Williams, *Thurgood Marshall*, 1998.

MARTIN LUTHER KING, JR., RESEARCH AND EDUCATION INSTITUTE AT STANFORD UNIVERSITY

Established in 2005, the King Institute at Stanford University became the institutional home for the Martin Luther King, Jr., Papers Project as well as a broad range of activities related to King's life, the African American freedom struggle, and other nonviolent struggles for social justice around the world.

The King Institute's principal mission is to publish *The Papers of Martin Luther King, Jr.*, a 14-volume edition of King's most significant correspondence, sermons, published writings, and unpublished manuscripts. In 1985, the **King Center**'s founder and president, Coretta Scott **King,** invited Stanford University historian Clayborne Carson to become the director and senior editor for the King Papers Project. To document King's life and times, the Project's staff assembled copies of thousands of documents from hundreds of archives and private collections.

Building upon the research required for the *Papers*, the King Project, and later the King Institute, also initiated other related research and educational activities. These include a website, www.kinginstitute.info, that provides an online archive of King-related documents and audiovisual materials; the King Research Fellows Program, which provides research opportunities for students from Stanford and other universities; the Liberation Curriculum, offering online lesson plans for teachers and students; and various public programs, including King holiday commemorations.

The King Institute's publications include the initial volumes of *The Papers of Martin Luther King, Jr.*, published through the University of California Press: Volume I: *Called to Serve: January 1929–June 1951* (1992); Volume II: *Rediscovering Precious Values: July 1951–November 1955* (1994); Volume III: *Birth of a New Age: December 1955–December 1956* (1997); Volume IV: *Symbol of the Movement: January 1957–December 1958* (2000); Volume V: *Threshold of a New Decade: January 1959–December 1960* (2005); and Volume VI: *Advocate of the Social Gospel, September 1948–March 1963* (2007).

SOURCE

http://www.kingpapers.org.

MAYNARD, AUBRÉ DE LAMBERT (1901–1999)

Director of Surgery at Harlem Hospital, Aubré Maynard successfully operated on Martin Luther King, Jr., following the civil rights leader's 1958 stabbing at a Harlem department store.

Born in Georgetown, Guyana, Maynard and his family immigrated to New York City in 1906. He received his BA from the City College of New York in 1922, and enrolled in New York University Medical School after being told that the teaching hospitals associated with his first choice, Columbia University's College of Physicians and Surgeons, had objections to black doctors having patient contact. Maynard earned his MD in 1926, and became one of the first black interns at Harlem Hospital that year. In 1951 he was president of the Harlem Surgical Society, and in 1952 he was promoted to director of surgery at Harlem Hospital.

On the afternoon of 20 September 1958, King was rushed to Harlem Hospital after being stabbed with a letter opener by Izola **Curry.** With the blade positioned perilously close to King's aorta, the hospital staff determined that, "had Dr. King sneezed or coughed the weapon would have penetrated the aorta.... He was just a sneeze away from death" (*Papers* 4:499n). While New York's Governor W. Averell Harriman waited outside and notable city surgeons looked on from an elevated platform, Maynard successfully removed the blade from King's chest. Ten days after the surgery, King released a statement in which he expressed his gratitude to Maynard and his staff. In the months following the operation, Maynard continued to monitor King's recovery, and declared the civil rights leader fully recovered after an examination on 16 January 1959.

When King won the **Nobel Peace Prize** in 1964, Maynard sent him a congratulatory telegram extolling the leader's achievements: "You fully merit the distinguished honor of the Nobel Prize for Peace" (Maynard, 15 October 1964).

Maynard retired from Harlem Hospital in 1967, and the hospital's cardiac operating suite was named in his honor in 1972. His book, *Surgeons to the Poor: The Harlem Hospital Story*, includes an account of the events surrounding King's stabbing.

SOURCES

Dexter Avenue Baptist Church to King, 21 September 1958, in *Papers* 4:498–499.

King, Statement Issued from Harlem Hospital, 30 September 1958, in *Papers* 4:502.

King to Maynard, 6 January 1959, in *Papers* 5:101–102.

Maynard, *Surgeons to the Poor*, 1978.

Maynard to King, 15 October 1964, MLKJP-GAMK.

Pearson, *When Harlem Nearly Killed King*, 2002.

MAYS, BENJAMIN ELIJAH (1894–1984)

Described by Martin Luther King, Jr., as his "spiritual mentor," Benjamin Mays was a distinguished Atlanta educator who served as president of **Morehouse College** from 1940 to 1967 (Scott King, 249). While King was a student at Morehouse, the two men developed a relationship that continued until King's death in 1968.

Mays was born in Epworth, South Carolina, on 1 August 1894 to former slaves Hezekiah and Louvenia Carter. After briefly attending Virginia Union University, Mays transferred to Bates College in Maine, where he earned his BA in 1920. The following year he was ordained as a Baptist minister. After earning his MA and PhD from the University of Chicago, Mays served as dean of the School of Religion at Howard University from 1934 to 1940.

After becoming president of Morehouse College, Mays delivered weekly addresses at the college's chapel services. King often followed Mays to his office after these sessions to discuss theology and current events. Mays visited King and his parents at their home and became a regular guest at the family's Sunday night dinners. According to King, his ministerial aspirations were deeply influenced by Mays and Morehouse professor George **Kelsey**. "I could see in their lives the ideal of what I wanted a minister to be," King commented in a 1956 interview (Peters, "Our Weapon Is Love"). Mays remarked that the King he met at Morehouse was "mature beyond his years" (Bennett, 27). Mays also had a lasting influence on King's intellectual life. In "Mastering Our Fears," a sermon written nine years after King graduated from Morehouse, he drew on a 1946 newspaper column Mays wrote for the *Pittsburgh Courier*, which argued that black and white people must overcome their mutual fears to improve race relations.

When the Montgomery, Alabama, police indicted over 80 boycott leaders to stop the **Montgomery bus boycott** in 1956, King decided that he should remain involved in the protest, even against the wishes of his father. While the senior King assembled acquaintances to dissuade the younger from continuing to lead the Montgomery bus boycott, it was Mays who heard King's "unspoken plea" and strongly defended his position (King, 145). Morehouse College awarded King an honorary Doctorate of Letters in July 1957, and Mays, reflecting upon King's role in the bus boycott, glowingly referred to him as a man "more courageous in a righteous struggle than most men can ever be, living a faith that most men preach about and never experience" (Mays, July 1957). Mays continued to support King throughout his life, delivering the benediction at the 1963 **March on Washington for Jobs and Freedom** and endorsing King's decision to speak out against the **Vietnam War** in 1967.

After King's **assassination** Mays eulogized him on the Morehouse campus by detailing King's consistent faith in **nonviolence**: "Here was a man who believed with all his might that the pursuit of violence at any time is ethically and morally wrong; that God and the moral weight of the universe are against it; that violence is self-defeating; and that only love and forgiveness can break the vicious circle of revenge" (Mays, *Dr. Benjamin E. Mays*, 247).

Mays remained active throughout the 1970s, becoming the first black president of the Atlanta Board of Education as well as serving on the Advisory Council of the Peace Corps, the board of directors of the United Negro College Fund, and the board of the National Commission for UNESCO. By the time of his death in 1984, Mays had received 28 honorary degrees and the Spingarn Medal, the highest honor awarded by the **National Association for the Advancement of Colored People**.

SOURCES

Bennett, *What Manner of Man*, 1964.
Branch, *Parting the Waters*, 1988.
Garrow, *Bearing the Cross*, 1986.
King, "Mastering Our Fears," 21 July 1957, in *Papers* 6:319–321.
King, *Stride Toward Freedom*, 1958.
(Scott) King, *My Life with Martin Luther King, Jr.*, 1969.
Mays, *Born to Rebel*, 1971.
Mays, *Dr. Benjamin E. Mays Speaks*, ed. Colston, 2002.
Mays, Honorary Degree Citation to Martin Luther King, Jr., *Morehouse College Bulletin* (July 1957): 6–7, LOLP-ICIU.
William Peters, "Our Weapon Is Love," *Redbook* (August 1956), 42–43; 71–73.

MBOYA, THOMAS JOSEPH (1930–1969)

In May 1959, African trade unionist and nationalist Thomas Mboya was honored by Martin Luther King and the **Southern Christian Leadership Conference** (SCLC) at an "Africa Freedom Dinner." Prior to Mboya's keynote address, King delivered introductory remarks noting the link between the American civil rights movement and the African Liberation Movement. "Our struggle is not an isolated struggle," King insisted. "We are all caught in an inescapable network of mutuality" (*Papers* 5:203–204).

Mboya was born 15 August 1930 in Kilima Mbogo, Kenya. He founded the Kenya Local Government Workers' Union, and after many of its leaders were jailed Mboya assumed the leadership of the Kenya Federation of Labour in 1953, distinguishing himself by mediating the Mombasa dockworkers' strike in 1955. Mboya returned to Kenya after studying at Ruskin College in Oxford, England, and was elected to Kenya's Legislative Council in 1957. The same year, he formed the People's Convention Party, over which he presided.

Mboya coordinated an "airlift" of 81 Kenyan students to the United States to attend college, and shortly after attending the "Africa Freedom Dinner," Mboya wrote King requesting financial assistance for a Kenyan student who was to enter Tuskegee

Institute in the fall. In an 8 November 1959 letter to the *New York Times*, Mboya explained: "Nothing constitutes a greater contribution to the struggle against poverty, disease and political subjection in Africa more than the contribution made toward our peoples' educational advancement." With the help of the African-American Students Foundation and its sponsors, Harry **Belafonte**, Jackie **Robinson**, and Sidney Poitier, Mboya raised sufficient funds to cover the students' travel expenses.

King believed that Africans and African Americans shared "a common struggle" against colonialism and segregation and took an active interest in the education of African students (Yette, "M. L. King Supports African Students"). As colonial and post-colonial African governments lacked the will or the capacity to educate their population, King encouraged college presidents in the United States to expand financial aid options available to Africans. He arranged for the **Montgomery Improvement Association** and other Montgomery organizations to fund five Kenyan students to study at American universities and pledged the SCLC and **Dexter Avenue Baptist Church** to fund the living expenses for Kenyan student Nicholas Raballa, who was admitted to Tuskegee Institute.

For the next several years, Mboya worked to lay the foundation for an active Kenya African National Union, Kenya's first black-majority political party, and was instrumental in achieving independence for Kenya in 1963. He was an outspoken critic of government corruption, led by Kenyan President Jomo Kenyatta, and in July 1969, Mboya was assassinated at the age of 39.

SOURCES

King, Remarks at Africa Freedom Dinner at Atlanta University, 13 May 1959, in *Papers* 5:203–204.

King to Tom Mboya, 8 July 1959, in *Papers* 5:242–243.

Mboya to the *New York Times*, 8 November 1959, MLKP-MBU.

S. F. Yette, "M. L. King Supports African Student," *News of Tuskegee Institute*, December 1959.

McCALL, WALTER R. (1923–1978)

A Baptist minister and close friend of Martin Luther King's at both **Morehouse College** and **Crozer Theological Seminary**, Walter McCall described his relationship with King as the type of "friends who share in the totality of your life's experiences." McCall remembered King as "an ordinary student" who "loved the lighter side of life as any normal boy would do" (McCall, 31 March 1970).

McCall was born in Conway, South Carolina, on 23 August 1923, and served in the Army during World War II. Although six years older than King, the two formed a close friendship while at Morehouse. McCall shared King's passion for justice: they were part of a group that considered suing a New Jersey tavern owner who had refused to serve them on the basis of race in 1950. McCall observed a change in King when he entered the seminary. "He began to take his studies more seriously; he began to take preaching more seriously," he recalled. "He would sometimes, if necessary, stay up all night to make certain that he got an idea" (McCall, 31 March 1970).

After completing his studies at Crozer in 1951, McCall attended Temple University and was dean and chaplain at Georgia's Fort Valley State College from 1951 to 1957. McCall and King competed directly for the open **Dexter Avenue Baptist Church** pastorate in early 1954. Following King's trial sermon at Dexter, entitled "The Three

Dimensions of a Complete Life," McCall gave a sermon there entitled "The Four Dimensions of a Complete Life." Dexter awarded its pastorate to King, and McCall wrote to congratulate him.

Earlier in their careers, McCall and King exchanged speaking engagements, with McCall speaking at a Youth Day at Dexter and King speaking at Religious Emphasis Week at Fort Valley State College. McCall offered his support to King in the early stages of the **Montgomery bus boycott**, writing, "*Do not despair. This is your task! Face it with courage. The storm will break!*" (*Papers* 3:118).

In 1957 McCall took over the pastorate at Providence Baptist Church in Atlanta. He went on to serve as director of Morehouse's School of Religion from 1965 to 1969. McCall's last memory of King was three weeks before King's **assassination**, when the two joked about the risks King faced and promised to meet again soon. McCall died on 12 November 1978.

SOURCES

Introduction, in *Papers* 2:29.
McCall, Interview by Herbert Holmes, 31 March 1970, MLK/OH-GAMK.
McCall to King, 5 August 1954, in *Papers* 2:283–284.
McCall to King, 21 October 1954, in *Papers* 2:303–304.
McCall to King, 1 February 1956, in *Papers* 3:117–118.
W. Thomas McGann, Statement on Behalf of Ernest Nichols, *State of New Jersey v. Ernest Nichols*, 20 July 1950, in *Papers* 1:327–328.

McDONALD, DORA EDITH (1925–2007)

Dora McDonald was Martin Luther King's primary personal secretary, trusted confidante, and close family friend from 1960 until his death in 1968. In the preface to King's 1963 book, **Strength to Love**, King thanked McDonald for her "encouraging words" and her efficiency in transferring his handwritten drafts to a typed manuscript. Within King's inner circle, McDonald was an unsung hero of the African American freedom struggle who kept King's life organized and was "his alter ego" (Percy, "King's Secretary Recalls").

McDonald was born on 16 July 1925, in Greeleyville, South Carolina, on her family's farm. The Great Depression forced her father to sell the farm but, despite economic hardships, McDonald was able to attend South Carolina State College (SCSC) in Orangeburg. It was in her junior year at SCSC that McDonald met Benjamin **Mays**, president of **Morehouse College**, who spoke on Easter Sunday at the campus. Mays asked McDonald to work as his secretary after graduation, a position she assumed in June 1947. It was as Mays' secretary that she first met both Martin Luther King, Jr., and Martin Luther **King**, Sr. After leaving Morehouse, she worked at Mutual Federal Savings and Loan Association in Atlanta from 1956 to 1960.

After King moved from Montgomery, Alabama, to Atlanta, Georgia, in February 1960, the civil rights leader was in need of a good secretary. McDonald came highly recommended by Mays. McDonald recalled that initially she did not have strong personal views about the movement but her opinion soon changed. "After I got into my job, and what I was doing, what we were doing, and what the movement meant, I never wanted to be doing something else. I was a part of something momentous" (Percy). She worked with King at the **Southern Christian Leadership Conference**

213

(SCLC) from 1960 to 1968, answering his correspondence, fielding his telephone calls, typing his speeches and manuscripts, and keeping his calendar in order. Having come to rely on McDonald, King often asked her to travel with him.

Over the years, McDonald and King developed a lasting friendship. "He would call me late at night, and I knew he would call me because he couldn't sleep. He could talk to me about anything, possibly things he wouldn't even burden Coretta with.... When he was hurting, I was hurting" (Percy). As the friendship developed, King entrusted McDonald to care for his wife and children in the event of an emergency.

McDonald's life was forever changed by King's **assassination** on 4 April 1968. She left SCLC in 1969, because she "didn't want to be anyone else's secretary at SCLC" (Percy). From 1972 to 1977 she worked in Andrew **Young**'s congressional office, then at IBM until her retirement in 1992. McDonald died of complications from cancer in Atlanta on 13 January 2007, but not before she wrote her memoir, *Secretary to a King* (forthcoming).

SOURCES

King, *Strength to Love*, 1963.
McDonald, *Secretary to a King*, forthcoming.
Dudley Percy, "King's Secretary Recalls Her 'Very Caring' Boss," *Atlanta Constitution*, 28 February 1989.

McKISSICK, FLOYD BIXLER (1922–1991)

As national director of the **Congress of Racial Equality** (CORE) from 1966 to 1968, Floyd McKissick's tenure with the organization was dominated by controversy over **Black Power**. Although the media was quick to focus on areas of disagreement between McKissick and Martin Luther King, the two leaders sought to downplay their differences, stressing their "brotherhood" and areas of mutual respect and agreement (Wehrwein, "Dr. King and CORE Chief").

Born 9 March 1922 in Asheville, North Carolina, McKissick attended **Morehouse College** in Atlanta for a year before leaving to serve in World War II. After the war, McKissick joined CORE and served as the youth chairman for the North Carolina branch of the **National Association for the Advancement of Colored People** (NAACP). He studied at Morehouse again for the 1947–1948 school year, King's last at the college. When he was denied admission to the all-white University of North Carolina (UNC), Chapel Hill, Law School, he enrolled at the law school of North Carolina Central College (NCCC). McKissick brought suit, and with the support of NAACP lawyer Thurgood **Marshall**, a judge ruled in favor of McKissick in 1951 and granted him admission to UNC. Although he had already earned his degree from NCCC, McKissick and three other black students enrolled in UNC law courses that summer.

As an attorney, McKissick defended civil rights activists who were arrested for participating in sit-ins at segregated lunch counters and represented his own children in a public school desegregation lawsuit. In another well-publicized legal challenge against the Tobacco Workers International Union (AFL-CIO), he successfully won the right of black workers admitted to the skilled scale to maintain their seniority. McKissick, who also handled cases for CORE, was elected chairman of CORE's national board in 1963 and became national director three years later.

When James **Meredith** was shot in 1966 while marching from Memphis, Tennessee, to Jackson, Mississippi, McKissick and King decided to resume his march. Stokely **Carmichael**, chairman of the **Student Nonviolent Coordinating Committee** (SNCC), soon joined them, and the three organizations co-led the Meredith March Against Fear. Carmichael's proclamation of "Black Power" quickly exposed growing differences among CORE, SNCC, and the **Southern Christian Leadership Conference** and within the civil rights movement. McKissick embraced Black Power, but defined the term to mean building political and economic power in African American communities.

In the late 1960s, King's and McKissick's philosophies also diverged with respect to **nonviolence**. After the Meredith March, McKissick continued to advocate nonviolence as a tactic in demonstrations, but maintained that black activists had a right to strike back when hit, arguing that "self-defense and nonviolence are not incompatible" (**Meet the Press**, 21 August 1966). King consistently condemned strategies of reprisal and refused to take "programmatic action around defensive violence" (*Meet the Press*, 21 August 1966).

Despite these areas of difference, King and McKissick agreed when opposing the **Vietnam War**, and appeared together in support of black athletes boycotting the 1968 Olympics. When King was assassinated in 1968, McKissick called it "a horror for us, for all Americans that the apostle of nonviolence should be gunned down on an American street" and advocated a national holiday in King's honor ("McKissick Says Nonviolence"; Millones, "Thousands Take Time to Express Grief"). McKissick resigned from CORE later that year.

In July 1972, McKissick received federal funding from the Department of Housing and Urban Development to create Soul City, an integrated community under black and white leadership in North Carolina. A few months later, McKissick caused a stir in the African American community when he switched to the Republican Party and later became a minority campaign chairman for President Richard **Nixon**'s reelection. In 1975 McKissick admitted that the development of Soul City had political implications, but denied any impropriety in government funding for the project. Soul City was declared economically unviable in 1979, and the land was later taken over by the federal government. After returning to the law, McKissick was appointed to a judgeship in the Ninth Judicial District in 1990. He died of lung cancer in 1991, and is buried in Soul City.

SOURCES
Introduction, in *Papers* 1:45n.
King, *Meet the Press*, 21 August 1966, CCCSU.
Wayne King, "McKissick Is Succeeding Although Not 'Supposed To,'" *New York Times*, 22 December 1974.
"McKissick Says Nonviolence Has Become Dead Philosophy," *New York Times*, 5 April 1968.
Meier and Rudwick, *CORE*, 1973.
Peter Millones, "Thousands Take Time to Express Grief and Respect for Dr. King at 2 Rallies Here," *New York Times*, 9 April 1968.
Austin C. Wehrwein, "Dr. King and CORE Chief Act to Heal Rights Breach," *New York Times*, 11 July 1966.

MEASURE OF A MAN, THE (1959)

In August 1958 Martin Luther King, Jr., preached two sermons, "What Is Man?" and "The Dimensions of a Complete Life," at the first National Conference on

Christian Education of the United Church of Christ at Purdue University. Franklin I. Sheeder, executive secretary of the Board of Christian Education and Publication, found the speeches to be "among the finest of our entire program" (Sheeder, 11 September 1958). In response to demands made by conference attendees, Sheeder requested that King allow publication of the addresses. With King's consent, the sermons were published by the Christian Education Press in a short book entitled *The Measure of a Man*. The press and King arranged for proceeds to be shared evenly, after the former had recovered its costs of publication.

King first developed the theme of "What Is Man?" during his seminary days. The earliest available manuscript version of this sermon dates back to July 1954, although records indicate that he may have delivered earlier versions. King believed the sermon's title to be "one of the most important questions confronting any generation," proposing that man is many things: "a biological being," "a being of spirit" who is "made in the image of God" and "sinner in need of God's divine grace" (King, *Measure*, 1; 3; 8; 10). King preached the **social gospel** by issuing a challenge to America's moral conscience and encouraging the nation to act in the interest of all of its citizens. Influenced by Reinhold **Niebuhr**'s philosophy in his book *Moral Man and Immoral Society*, King declared that "our sin is even greater" in "our collective lives" (King, *Measure*, 13). Drawing examples from the socio-political arena, he lamented that Western civilization had "trampled over one billion six hundred million of your colored brothers in Africa and Asia," while America had deviated from its promises of equality in the Declaration of Independence by straying into the "far country of segregation and discrimination" (King, *Measure*, 16). Yet, he asserted, a loving Christian God would forgive Western civilization and America if they would renounce these practices.

King continued to emphasize man's need for God in his second sermon, "The Dimensions of a Complete Life." He begins with the story of John the Baptist, who glimpses the new Jerusalem descending from the heavens. In *Revelation 21:16*, John refers to the completeness of this city of God: "The length and the breadth and the height of it are equal." King interprets the length of life as an individual's personal push to realize ambition, the breadth of life as concern for others and realization of our interdependence, and the height of life as a love for God. King finally asks God: "Help us to discover ourselves, to discover our neighbors, and to discover thee and to make all part of our life" (King, *Measure*, 34). King delivered a version of this sermon in January 1954 when applying to pastor **Dexter Avenue Baptist Church**, where he served until 1959.

The Measure of a Man is the earliest attempt to publish King's sermons in book form. A few years later, Harper & Row published the definitive collection of King's signature sermons, **Strength to Love** (1963), which included the two sermons in *The Measure of a Man*. King continued to preach both of these sermons after their publication.

SOURCES

King, "The Dimensions of a Complete Life," Sermon at Dexter Avenue Baptist Church, 24 January 1954, in *Papers* 6:150–156.
King, *Measure of a Man*, 1959.
King, *Strength to Love*, 1963.

King, "What Is Man?" Sermon at Dexter Avenue Baptist Church, 11 July 1954, in *Papers*
6:174–179.
Niebuhr, *Moral Man and Immoral Society*, 1932.
Sheeder to King, 11 September 1958, MLKP-MBU.

MEET THE PRESS

Created for radio in 1945 by Martha Rountree and Lawrence Spivak, *Meet the Press*
first aired on television in November 1947. Martin Luther King appeared on *Meet the
Press* five times. Though the tone of the program was often antagonistic, King appreciated the chance to reach a national audience and had a cordial relationship with Spivak,
who was the show's producer and a permanent panelist until his retirement in 1975.

Spivak first approached King about appearing on the show in March 1957.
Although King agreed at the time, telling Spivak he was "more than happy to accept
the invitation for such a significant interview," scheduling conflicts delayed his
appearance (King, 29 March 1957). King first addressed the Sunday program on 17
April 1960, during the height of the **sit-in** movement. King discussed the sit-ins and
nonviolence, criticized the federal government's lack of moral leadership, and
defended himself against accusations of being sympathetic to **communism**. After the
program, he received numerous telegrams congratulating him on his performance.

King was next scheduled to appear on the program 29 July 1962, but he was
arrested in Albany, Georgia, on 27 July. Spivak telephoned King in jail and, according
to King's jail diary, begged him to post bail so he could appear on the program. King
refused, suggesting Spivak instead interview his colleague, William G. **Anderson**, a
founder and the president of the **Albany Movement**. The following summer, in the
days leading up to the **March on Washington for Jobs and Freedom**, King appeared
on the program again, this time with Roy **Wilkins** of the **National Association for
the Advancement of Colored People**. The pair explained the purpose of the march
and countered fears that large-scale violence would break out.

King next appeared on *Meet the Press* on 28 March 1965. Special arrangements were
made so that King could record the program from San Francisco, while the panel of
interviewers remained in Washington, D.C. In a heated interview, King defended the
Selma to Montgomery March from the allegation that it was "silly," arguing that the
demonstration had not only been about voting rights, but was also meant to draw
attention to the problems of police brutality and impunity for crimes perpetrated
against civil rights activists.

In 1966, soon after the term "**Black Power**" began to be used among some civil
rights activists, *Meet the Press* broadcasted a special 90-minute show with a panel of
civil rights leaders including King; Wilkins; Whitney **Young**, director of the **National
Urban League**; Floyd **McKissick**, director of the **Congress of Racial Equality**; Stokely
Carmichael, chairman of **Student Nonviolent Coordinating Committee**; and James
Meredith, who had recently been shot while marching to promote voter registration.
The discussion addressed perceived tensions within the civil rights movement and was
later entered in full into the *Congressional Record*.

King's final appearance on *Meet the Press* occurred 13 August 1967, the day before
the annual convention of the **Southern Christian Leadership Conference**, and shortly

after the publication of King's book, **Where Do We Go from Here: Chaos or Community?** Although the discussion focused largely on King's anti–**Vietnam War** views, King also answered questions about recent riots and the 1968 presidential elections.

SOURCES
Garrow, *Bearing the Cross*, 1986.
King, Diary from Albany Jail, 27 July 1962, MLKP-MBU.
King, "Interview on *Meet the Press*," 17 April 1960, in *Papers* 5:428–435.
King to Spivak, 29 March 1957, MLKP-MBU.
"Negro Leaders on 'Meet the Press,'" *Congressional Record* 112 (29 August 1966): 21095–21102.

MEMPHIS SANITATION WORKERS' STRIKE (1968)

The night before his **assassination** in April 1968, Martin Luther King told a group of striking sanitation workers in Memphis, Tennessee: "We've got to give ourselves to this struggle until the end. Nothing would be more tragic than to stop at this point in Memphis. We've got to see it through" (King, "I've Been to the Mountaintop," 217). King believed the struggle in Memphis exposed the need for economic equality and social justice that he hoped his **Poor People's Campaign** would highlight nationally.

On 1 February 1968, two Memphis garbage collectors, Echol Cole and Robert Walker, were crushed to death by a malfunctioning truck. Twelve days later, frustrated by the city's response to the latest event in a long pattern of neglect and abuse of its black employees, 1,300 black men from the Memphis Department of Public Works went on strike. Sanitation workers, led by garbage-collector-turned-union-organizer T. O. Jones and supported by the president of the American Federation of State, County, and Municipal Employees (AFSCME), Jerry **Wurf**, demanded recognition of their union, better safety standards, and a decent wage.

The union, which had been granted a charter by AFSCME in 1964, had attempted a strike in 1966, but failed in large part because workers were unable to arouse the support of Memphis' religious community or middle class. Conditions for black sanitation workers worsened when Henry Loeb became mayor in January 1968. Loeb refused to take dilapidated trucks out of service or pay overtime when men were forced to work late-night shifts. Sanitation workers earned wages so low that many were on welfare and hundreds relied on food stamps to feed their families.

On 11 February, more than 700 men attended a union meeting and unanimously decided to strike. Within a week, the local branch of the **National Association for the Advancement of Colored People** passed a resolution supporting the strike. The strike might have ended on 22 February, when the City Council, pressured by a **sit-in** of sanitation workers and their supporters, voted to recognize the union and recommended a wage increase. Mayor Loeb rejected the City Council vote, however, insisting that only he had the authority to recognize the union and refused to do so.

The following day, after police used mace and tear gas against nonviolent demonstrators marching to City Hall, Memphis' black community was galvanized. Meeting in a church basement on 24 February, 150 local ministers formed Community on the Move for Equality (COME), under the leadership of King's longtime ally, local minister James **Lawson**. COME committed to the use of nonviolent civil disobedience to fill Memphis' jails and bring attention to the plight of the sanitation workers. By the beginning of March, local high school and college students, nearly a quarter of them white, were participating alongside garbage workers in daily marches; and over 100 people, including several ministers, had been arrested.

While Lawson kept King updated by phone, other national civil rights leaders, including Roy **Wilkins** and Bayard **Rustin**, came to rally the sanitation workers. King himself arrived on 18 March to address a crowd of about 25,000—the largest indoor gathering the civil rights movement had ever seen. Speaking to a group of labor and civil rights activists and members of the powerful black church, King praised the group's unity, saying: "You are demonstrating that we can stick together. You are demonstrating that we are all tied in a single garment of destiny, and that if one black person suffers, if one black person is down, we are all down" (King, 18 March 1968). King encouraged the group to support the sanitation strike by going on a citywide work stoppage, and he pledged to return that Friday, 22 March, to lead a protest through the city.

King left Memphis the following day, but the **Southern Christian Leadership Conference**'s (SCLC) James **Bevel** and Ralph **Abernathy** remained to help organize the protest and work stoppage. When the day arrived, however, a massive snowstorm blanketed the region, preventing King from reaching Memphis and causing the organizers to reschedule the march for 28 March. Memphis city officials estimated that 22,000 students skipped school that day to participate in the demonstration. King arrived late and found a massive crowd on the brink of chaos. Lawson and King led the march together but quickly called off the demonstration as violence began to erupt. King was whisked away to a nearby hotel, and Lawson told the mass of people to turn around and go back to the church. In the chaos that followed, downtown shops were looted, and a 16-year-old was shot and killed by a police officer. Police followed demonstrators back to the Clayborn Temple, entered the church, released tear gas inside the sanctuary, and clubbed people as they lay on the floor to get fresh air.

Loeb called for martial law and brought in 4,000 National Guard troops. The following day, over 200 striking workers continued their daily march, carrying signs that read, "I <u>Am</u> a Man" (Honey, 389). At a news conference held before he returned to Atlanta, King said that he had been unaware of the divisions within the community, particularly of the presence of a black youth group committed to "**Black Power**" called the Invaders, who were accused of starting the violence.

King considered not returning to Memphis, but decided that if the nonviolent struggle for economic justice was going to succeed it would be necessary to follow through with the movement there. After a divisive meeting on 30 March, SCLC staff agreed to support King's return to Memphis. He arrived on 3 April and was persuaded to speak by a crowd of dedicated sanitation workers who had braved another storm to hear him. A weary King preached about his own mortality, telling the group, "Like anybody, I would like to live a long life—longevity has its place. But I'm not concerned about that now … I've seen the Promised Land. I may not get there with you. But I want you to know tonight that we, as a people, will get to the Promised Land" (King, "I've Been to the Mountaintop," 222–223).

The following evening, as King was getting ready for dinner, he was shot and killed on the balcony of the Lorraine Motel. While Lawson recorded a radio announcement urging calm in Memphis, Loeb called in the state police and the National Guard and ordered a 7 P.M. curfew. Black and white ministers pleaded with Loeb to concede to the union's demands, but the mayor held firm. President Lyndon B. **Johnson** charged Undersecretary of Labor James Reynolds with negotiating a solution and ending the strike.

On 8 April, an estimated 42,000 people led by Coretta Scott **King**, SCLC, and union leaders silently marched through Memphis in honor of King, demanding that Loeb give in to the union's requests. In front of City Hall, AFSCME pledged to support the workers until "we have justice" (Honey, 480). Negotiators finally reached a deal on 16 April, allowing the City Council to recognize the union and guaranteeing a better wage. Although the deal brought the strike to an end, several months later the union had to threaten another strike to press the city to follow through with its commitment.

SOURCES

Honey, *Going Down Jericho Road*, 2007.

King, "Address at Mass Meeting at the Bishop Charles Mason Temple," 18 March 1968, MVC-TMM.

King, "I've Been to the Mountaintop," *A Call to Conscience*, ed. Carson and Shepard, 2001.

MEREDITH, JAMES HOWARD (1933–)

In Martin Luther King's famous "**Letter from Birmingham Jail**," he called James Meredith, the first African American to integrate the University of Mississippi in 1962, a hero of the civil rights movement. He honored Meredith and others for their strong sense of purpose that allowed them to stand up to the hostility directed at them by opponents of civil rights. In 1966, King praised Meredith once again, after he was

Coretta Scott King, King, Christine King Farris (second row, in sunglasses), and others lead the James Meredith March against Fear into Jackson, Mississippi, 26 June 1966. © 1966 Matt Herron/Take Stock.

wounded on a 220-mile personal journey to encourage African American voter registration.

In June 1933, Meredith was born the 7th of 13 children in rural Kosciusko, Mississippi. Growing up in rural Mississippi was difficult for Meredith, who moved to St. Petersburg, Florida, to live with his aunt and attend public schools superior to those available in Kosciusko. After graduating from high school in 1951, Meredith joined the Air Force, serving nine years before returning to Mississippi and enrolling in Jackson State University.

In January 1961, the night following John F. **Kennedy**'s presidential inauguration, Meredith decided to submit his first application to the University of Mississippi (also known as Ole Miss), which was closed to African American students. His application was rejected twice, but with the help of the **National Association for the Advancement of Colored People**, Meredith legally challenged the university's segregation policy. After enduring extended court battles, the defiance of Mississippi's Governor Ross Barnett, and violent campus riots, Meredith was finally admitted on 1 October 1962.

In a March 1963 letter published in the *New York Amsterdam News*, King asked for the public's support of Meredith, describing him as "a symbol of self-respect and dignity." King asked the public to pray for Meredith and to express to him "how much you appreciate his heroism" (King, "A Letter to Meredith"). Meredith graduated from Ole Miss in August 1963 with a bachelor's degree in political science.

In 1966 Meredith began a "March Against Fear," a solitary march from Memphis, Tennessee, to Jackson, Mississippi, to encourage African American voter registration. When a sniper wounded him on the second day of the march, the **Southern Christian Leadership Conference**, the **Congress of Racial Equality**, and the **Student Nonviolent Coordinating Committee** rallied behind his cause. King, Stokely **Carmichael**, and Floyd **McKissick** were joined by hundreds of others as they completed the march.

By the late 1960s, Meredith had moved to New York and received a law degree from Columbia University. Over the next several years Meredith became more politically involved, making several unsuccessful bids for public office, including a run for the Republican nomination for senator from Mississippi. A local community leader in Mississippi, Meredith organized the Black Man's March to the Library in Memphis to promote reading and writing of standard English, and the Black Man's March for Education to the University of Mississippi.

SOURCES
King, "Letter from Birmingham Jail," in *Why We Can't Wait*, 1963.
King, "A Letter to Meredith," *New York Amsterdam News*, 30 March 1964.

MFDP. *See* Mississippi Freedom Democratic Party.

MIA. *See* Montgomery Improvement Association.

MISSISSIPPI FREEDOM DEMOCRATIC PARTY (MFDP)

In early 1964, as part of **Freedom Summer**, Mississippi civil rights activists affiliated with the **Council of Federated Organizations** in Mississippi launched the Mississippi

King speaks to a crowd holding posters of slain Freedom Summer workers Michael Schwerner, James Chaney, and Andrew Goodman, outside the Democratic National Convention, 25 August 1964. © Bettmann/Corbis.

Freedom Democratic Party (MFDP). Claiming status as "the only democratically constituted body of Mississippi citizens," they appealed to the credentials committee of the Democratic National Convention (DNC) of 1964 to recognize their party's delegation in place of the all-white Democratic Party delegation from Mississippi (Victoria Gray, July 1964). In his statement before the credentials committee, Martin Luther King, Jr., expressed support for the MFDP delegates, calling them "the true heirs of the tradition of Jefferson and Hamilton" (King, 22 August 1964).

Because Mississippi blacks were barred from participating in the meetings of the state's Democratic Party, they decided to form their own party. Mirroring the Democratic Party's official procedure, MFDP held parallel precinct and district caucuses open to all races. With the support of Freedom Summer students and volunteers from the **Student Nonviolent Coordinating Committee** (SNCC), activists gathered signatures of potential black voters for a "freedom registration." Delegates to the DNC in Atlantic City, New Jersey, were elected at MFDP's state convention in Jackson on 6 August 1964.

At the DNC later that month, the **National Association for the Advancement of Colored People, Congress of Racial Equality, Southern Christian Leadership Conference,** and SNCC conducted public and private diplomacy on the MFDP's behalf. In a nationally televised speech before the DNC credentials committee, MFDP delegate Fannie Lou **Hamer** spoke passionately about the violence and intimidation suffered by Mississippi blacks seeking to register to vote, concluding, "If the Freedom Democratic Party is not seated now, I question America" (Carson, 125). King echoed Hamer's sentiment, telling the committee, "Any party in the world should be proud to have a delegation such as this seated in their midst. For it is in these saints in ordinary walks of life that the true spirit of democracy finds its most profound and abiding expression" (King, 22 August 1964).

President Lyndon **Johnson**, however, was fearful of losing white southern votes if the MFDP delegates were seated and advocated a compromise. The credentials committee of the DNC offered to award the MFDP two at-large seats, to seat members of the all-white delegation who would formally promise to support the DNC's candidates in the upcoming elections (rather than campaign for Republican Barry **Goldwater**), and to bar segregated delegations from the 1968 convention.

Although King had told Johnson that he would "do everything in my power to urge [the MFDP] being seated as the only democratically constituted delegation from Mississippi," he supported the compromise (King, 19 August 1964). MFDP delegates and many civil rights activists, however, were disheartened by the Credentials Committee's refusal to seat MFDP delegates. Hamer's response was, "We didn't come all this way for no two seats" (Carson, 126).

When all but three of the regular Mississippi delegation withdrew rather than promise to support the full slate of Democratic candidates, MFDP delegates borrowed passes from sympathetic delegates from other states, symbolically occupied the vacated seats and, when the chairs were removed, stood and sang freedom songs.

Although the MFDP did not gain the recognition it sought at the 1964 convention, it continued to pressure the Democratic Party to create a policy that would prevent the seating of a segregationist delegation and later campaigned for Johnson, recognizing that a Goldwater victory would have devastating implications for the civil rights movement.

For the next three years, MFDP continued to agitate on behalf of disenfranchised black Mississippians. In 1965, the MFDP led a challenge to unseat Mississippi's congressmen on the grounds that they had been elected unconstitutionally. In remarks that were later read in the House, King declared, "I pledge myself and the Southern Christian Leadership Conference to the fullest support of the challenges of the Mississippi Freedom Democratic Party and call upon all Americans to join with me in this commitment" ("Mississippi Challenge," *Congressional Record*, H10941).

In 1968, a group of former MFDP delegates, calling themselves the Loyal Democrats of Mississippi, succeeded in being seated as the sole Mississippi delegation to the DNC.

SOURCES

Carson, *In Struggle*, 1981.
Victoria Gray, Press release, July 1964, MLKJP-GAMK.
Henry with Curry, *Aaron Henry*, 2000.
King, Address to the Credentials Committee, 22 August 1964, MLKJP-GAMK.
King to Johnson, 19 August 1964, MLKJP-GAMK.
"Mississippi Challenge," 89th Cong., 1st sess., *Congressional Record* (19 May 1965): H10941.
Payne, *I've Got the Light of Freedom*, 1995.

MONTGOMERY BUS BOYCOTT (1955–1956)

Sparked by the arrest of Rosa **Parks** on 1 December 1955, the Montgomery bus boycott was a 13-month mass protest that ended with the U.S. Supreme Court ruling that segregation on public buses is unconstitutional. The **Montgomery Improvement Association** (MIA) coordinated the boycott, and its president, Martin Luther King,

On 21 December 1956, the day after the Supreme Court's integration order arrived in Montgomery, Ralph Abernathy, King, Glenn E. Smiley, and others ride a city bus and end the Montgomery bus boycott. © AP / Wide World Photos.

Jr., became a prominent civil rights leader as international attention focused on Montgomery. The bus boycott demonstrated the potential for nonviolent mass protest to successfully challenge racial segregation and served as an example for other southern campaigns that followed. In *Stride Toward Freedom*, King's 1958 memoir of the boycott, he declared the real meaning of the Montgomery bus boycott to be the power of a growing self-respect to animate the struggle for civil rights.

The roots of the bus boycott began years before the arrest of Rosa Parks. The **Womens' Political Council** (WPC), a group of black professionals founded in 1946, had already turned their attention to Jim Crow practices on the Montgomery city buses. In a meeting with Mayor W. A. Gayle in March 1954, the council's members outlined the changes they sought for Montgomery's bus system: no one standing over empty seats; a decree that black individuals not be made to pay at the front of the bus and enter from the rear; and a policy that would require buses to stop at every corner in black residential areas, as they did in white communities. When the meeting failed to produce any meaningful change, WPC president Jo Ann **Robinson** reiterated the council's requests in a 21 May letter to Mayor Gayle, telling him, "There has been talk from twenty-five or more local organizations of planning a city-wide boycott of buses" ("A Letter from the Women's Political Council").

A year after the WPC's meeting with Mayor Gayle, a 15-year-old named Claudette Colvin was arrested for challenging segregation on a Montgomery bus. Seven months later, 18-year-old Mary Louise Smith was arrested for refusing to yield her seat to a white passenger. Neither arrest, however, mobilized Montgomery's black community like that of Rosa Parks later that year.

King recalled in his memoir that "Mrs. Parks was ideal for the role assigned to her by history," and because "her character was impeccable and her dedication deep-rooted" she was "one of the most respected people in the Negro community" (King, 44). Robinson and the WPC responded to Parks' arrest by calling for a one-day protest of the city's buses on 5 December 1955. Robinson prepared a series of leaflets at Alabama State College and organized groups to distribute them throughout the black community. Meanwhile, after securing bail for Parks with Clifford and Virginia **Durr**, E. D. **Nixon**, past leader of the Montgomery chapter of the **National Association for the Advancement of Colored People** (NAACP), began to call local black leaders, including Ralph **Abernathy** and King, to organize a planning meeting. On 2 December, black ministers and leaders met at **Dexter Avenue Baptist Church** and agreed to publicize the 5 December boycott. The planned protest received unexpected publicity in the weekend newspapers and in radio and television reports.

On 5 December, 90 percent of Montgomery's black citizens stayed off the buses. That afternoon, the city's ministers and leaders met to discuss the possibility of extending the boycott into a long-term campaign. During this meeting the MIA was formed, and King was elected president. Parks recalled: "The advantage of having Dr. King as president was that he was so new to Montgomery and to civil rights work that he hadn't been there long enough to make any strong friends or enemies" (Parks, 136).

That evening, at a mass meeting at **Holt Street Baptist Church**, the MIA voted to continue the boycott. King spoke to several thousand people at the meeting: "I want it to be known that we're going to work with grim and bold determination to gain justice on the buses in this city. And we are not wrong.… If we are wrong, the Supreme Court of this nation is wrong. If we are wrong, the Constitution of the United States is wrong. If we are wrong, God Almighty is wrong" (*Papers* 3:73). After unsuccessful talks with city commissioners and bus company officials, on 8 December the MIA issued a formal list of demands: courteous treatment by bus operators; first-come, first-served seating for all, with blacks seating from the rear and whites from the front; and black bus operators on predominately black routes.

The demands were not met, and Montgomery's black residents stayed off the buses through 1956, despite efforts by city officials and white citizens to defeat the boycott. After the city began to penalize black taxi drivers for aiding the boycotters, the MIA organized a carpool. Following the advice of T. J. **Jemison**, who had organized a carpool during a 1953 bus boycott in Baton Rouge, the MIA developed an intricate carpool system of about 300 cars. Robert **Hughes** and others from the Alabama Council for Human Relations organized meetings between the MIA and city officials, but no agreements were reached.

In early 1956, the homes of King and E. D. Nixon were bombed. King was able to calm the crowd that gathered at his home by declaring: "Be calm as I and my family are. We are not hurt and remember that if anything happens to me, there will be others to take my place" (*Papers* 3:115). City officials obtained injunctions against the boycott in February 1956, and indicted over 80 boycott leaders under a 1921 law prohibiting conspiracies that interfered with lawful business. King was tried and convicted on the charge and ordered to pay $500 or serve 386 days in jail in the case *State of Alabama v. Martin Luther King, Jr*. Despite this resistance, the boycott continued.

Although most of the publicity about the protest was centered on the actions of black ministers, women played crucial roles in the success of the boycott. Women such as Robinson, Johnnie **Carr**, and Irene **West** sustained the MIA committees and volunteer networks. Mary Fair Burks of the WPC also attributed the success of the boycott to "the nameless cooks and maids who walked endless miles for a year to bring about the breach in the walls of segregation" (Burks, "Trailblazers," 82). In his memoir, King quotes an elderly woman who proclaimed that she had joined the boycott not for her own benefit but for the good of her children and grandchildren (King, 78).

National coverage of the boycott and King's trial resulted in support from people outside Montgomery. In early 1956 veteran pacifists Bayard **Rustin** and Glenn E. **Smiley** visited Montgomery and offered King advice on the application of Gandhian techniques and **nonviolence** to American race relations. Rustin, Ella **Baker**, and Stanley **Levison** founded **In Friendship** to raise funds in the North for southern civil rights efforts, including the bus boycott. King absorbed ideas from these proponents of nonviolent direct action and crafted his own syntheses of Gandhian principles of nonviolence. He said: "Christ showed us the way, and Gandhi in India showed it could work" (Rowland, "2,500 Here Hail"). Other followers of Gandhian ideas such as Richard **Gregg**, William Stuart **Nelson**, and Homer **Jack** wrote the MIA offering support.

On 5 June 1956, the federal district court ruled in *Browder v. Gayle* that bus segregation was unconstitutional, and in November 1956 the U.S. Supreme Court affirmed *Browder v. Gayle* and struck down laws requiring segregated seating on public buses. The court's decision came the same day that King and the MIA were in circuit court challenging an injunction against the MIA carpools. Resolved not to end the boycott until the order to desegregate the buses actually arrived in Montgomery, the MIA operated without the carpool system for a month. The Supreme Court upheld the lower court's ruling, and on 20 December 1956 King called for the end of the boycott; the community agreed. The next morning, he boarded an integrated bus with Ralph Abernathy, E. D. Nixon, and Glenn Smiley. King said of the bus boycott: "We came to see that, in the long run, it is more honorable to walk in dignity than ride in humiliation. So … we decided to substitute tired feet for tired souls, and walk the streets of Montgomery" (*Papers* 3:486). King's role in the bus boycott garnered international attention, and the MIA's tactics of combining mass nonviolent protest with Christian ethics became the model for challenging segregation in the South.

Sources

Joe Azbell, "Blast Rocks Residence of Bus Boycott Leader," 31 January 1956, in *Papers* 3:114–115.

Baker to King, 24 February 1956, in *Papers* 3:139.

Burks, "Trailblazers: Women in the Montgomery Bus Boycott," in *Women in the Civil Rights Movement*, ed. Crawford et al., 1990.

"Don't Ride the Bus," 2 December 1955, in *Papers* 3:67.

U. J. Fields, Minutes of the MIA Founding Meeting, 5 December 1955, in *Papers* 3:68–70.

Gregg to King, 2 April 1956, in *Papers* 3:211–212.

Indictment, *State of Alabama v. M. L. King, Jr., et al.*, 21 February 1956, in *Papers* 3:132–133.

Introduction, in *Papers* 3:3–7; 17–21; 29.

Jack to King, 16 March 1956, in *Papers* 3:178–179.

Judgment and Sentence of the Court, *State of Alabama v. M. L. King, Jr.*, 22 March 1956, in *Papers* 3:197.

King, Statement on Ending the Bus Boycott, 20 December 1956, in *Papers* 3:485–487.

King, *Stride Toward Freedom*, 1958.

King, Testimony in *State of Alabama v. M. L. King, Jr.*, 22 March 1956, in *Papers* 3:183–196.

King, To the National City Lines, Inc., 8 December 1955, in *Papers* 3:80–81.

"A Letter from the Women's Political Council to the Mayor of Montgomery, Alabama," in *Eyes on the Prize*, ed. Carson et al., 1991.

MIA Mass Meeting at Holt Street Baptist Church, 5 December 1955, in *Papers* 3:71–79.

Nelson to King, 21 March 1956, in *Papers* 3:182–183.

Parks and Haskins, *Rosa Parks*, 1992.

Robinson, *Montgomery Bus Boycott*, 1987.

Stanley Rowland, Jr., "2,500 Here Hail Boycott Leader," *New York Times*, 26 March 1956.

Rustin to King, 23 December 1956, in *Papers* 3:491–494.

MONTGOMERY IMPROVEMENT ASSOCIATION (MIA)

The Montgomery Improvement Association (MIA) was formed on 5 December 1955 by black ministers and community leaders in Montgomery, Alabama. Under the leadership of Martin Luther King, Jr., the MIA was instrumental in guiding the **Montgomery bus boycott**, a successful campaign that focused national attention on racial segregation in the South and catapulted King into the national spotlight. In his memoir, King concluded that as a result of the protest "the Negro citizen in Montgomery is respected in a way that he never was before" (King, 184).

Following the arrest of Rosa **Parks** on 1 December 1955 for failing to vacate her seat for a white passenger on a Montgomery city bus, Jo Ann **Robinson** of the **Women's Political Council** and E. D. **Nixon** launched plans for a one-day boycott of Montgomery buses on 5 December. A planning meeting was held in King's **Dexter Avenue Baptist Church** on 2 December. Ninety percent of the black community stayed off the buses on 5 December, prompting calls for boycott leaders to harness the momentum into a larger protest campaign. At a meeting held at Mt. Zion AME Church on the afternoon of 5 December, Montgomery's black leaders established the MIA to oversee the continuation and maintenance of the boycott and elected King, a young minister new to Montgomery, as its chairman. The organization's overall mission, however, extended beyond the boycott campaign to advance "the general status of Montgomery, to improve race relations, and to uplift the general tenor of the community" (*Papers* 3:185).

The MIA's earliest officers were: Martin Luther King, Jr., president; L. Roy Bennett, first vice president (later replaced by Ralph D. **Abernathy**); Moses W. Jones, second vice president; Erna Dungee, financial secretary; U. J. Fields, recording secretary (later replaced by W. J. Powell); E. N. French, corresponding secretary; E. D. Nixon, treasurer; C. W. Lee, assistant treasurer; and A. W. Wilson, parliamentarian.

Following the MIA's initial meeting, the executive committee drafted the demands of the boycott and agreed that the campaign would continue until these demands were met: courteous treatment by bus operators; first-come, first-served seating; and employment of Negro bus drivers. During the next year the association organized carpools and held weekly mass meetings with sermons and music to keep the African American community mobilized. When fundraising allowed for a paid staff position,

Reverend R. J. Glasco was appointed King's executive secretary. MIA officers negotiated with Montgomery city leaders, coordinated legal challenges to the city's bus segregation ordinance with the **National Association for the Advancement of Colored People**, and supported the boycott financially by raising money through passing the plate at meetings and soliciting support from northern and southern civil rights organizations.

The MIA suffered a setback in the spring of 1956. In February 1956 Montgomery officials indicted 89 boycott leaders, including King, for violating Alabama's 1921 anti-boycott law. King's trial, *State of Alabama v. M. L. King, Jr.*, held 19–22 March, ended with his conviction, but no one else was brought to trial.

In November 1956 the U.S. Supreme Court upheld a federal district court's ruling in *Browder v. Gayle*, putting an end to segregated seating on public buses. The order to desegregate the buses arrived the following month, and on 20 December 1956 King officially called for the end of the boycott.

King emerged as a national figure during the boycott, and the MIA's tactics became a model for the many civil rights protests to follow. Reflecting on his experience with MIA, King said: "I will never forget Montgomery, for how can one forget a group of people who took their passionate yearnings and deep aspirations and filtered them into their own souls and fashioned them into a creative protest, which gave meaning to people and gave inspiration to individuals all over the nation and all over the world" (*Papers* 5:359).

Following its success in Montgomery, the MIA became one of the founding organizations of the **Southern Christian Leadership Conference** in January 1957. Although the MIA lost some momentum after King returned to Atlanta in 1960, the organization, under Abernathy, Solomon **Seay**, and Johnnie **Carr**, continued campaigns throughout the 1960s, focusing on voter registration, local school integration, and the integration of public facilities. Carr was president for over four decades.

SOURCES

Uriah J. Fields, Minutes of Montgomery Improvement Association Founding Meeting, 5 December 1955, in *Papers* 3:68–70.

Introduction, in *Papers* 3:1–33.

King, Address delivered at the MIA's "Testimony of Love and Loyalty," 1 February 1960, in *Papers* 5:358–363.

King, *Stride Toward Freedom*, 1958.

King, Testimony in *State of Alabama v. M. L. King, Jr.*, 22 March 1956, in *Papers* 3:183–196.

MIA, Press release, Bus Protesters Call Southern Negro Leaders Conference on Transportation and Nonviolent Integration, 7 January 1957, in *Papers* 4:94–96.

Robinson, *Montgomery Bus Boycott*, 1987.

MOREHOUSE COLLEGE

In September 1944, Martin Luther King began his studies at Morehouse College in Atlanta, following in the footsteps of his father, Martin Luther **King**, Sr., and his maternal grandfather, A. D. **Williams**. Although King's years at Morehouse were characterized by middling academic performance, his experiences outside the classroom set him on a path toward the ministry and the struggle for civil rights.

Founded in 1867 by William Jefferson White as Augusta Baptist Institute, the school's purpose was to educate newly freed male slaves to teach and become ministers. The school relocated from Augusta to Atlanta in 1879, and was renamed the

Atlanta Baptist Seminary. Later named Atlanta Baptist College at the turn of the twentieth century, it was eventually renamed after American Baptist Home Missionary Society official Henry L. Morehouse.

King, Jr., was admitted to the college in 1944 following his junior year in high school, as the school's enrollment fell with the wartime draft. A friend of King's, Walter R. **McCall**, recalled that King was an "ordinary student" during his time at Morehouse: "I don't think he took his studies very seriously, but seriously enough to get by" (*Papers* 1:38). King did, however, flourish in other areas, winning second prize in the John L. Webb oratorical competition in 1946 and 1948. King was president of the sociology club, as well as a member of the debate team, student council, glee club, and minister's union. King also joined the Morehouse chapter of the **National Association for the Advancement of Colored People** and played on the Butler Street YMCA basketball team.

King's growing awareness of social and political issues while at Morehouse is evident in the surviving writings from his undergraduate years. The summer before his junior year King wrote a letter to the editor of the *Atlanta Constitution*, responding to a series of racially motivated murders in Georgia. In the letter, King summarized the goals of black citizens: "We want and are entitled to the basic rights and opportunities of American citizens: The right to earn a living at work for which we are fitted by training and ability; equal opportunities in education, health, recreation, and similar public services; the right to vote; equality before the law; some of the same courtesy and good manners that we ourselves bring to all human relations" (*Papers* 1:121).

That same year the school paper, the *Maroon Tiger*, published King's article "The Purpose of Education," in which he argued that education had both a utilitarian and a moral function. King asserted that the function of education was "to teach one to think intensively and to think critically" (*Papers* 1:124). The following year, his commitment to social change was strengthened through his involvement with the Intercollegiate Council, an interracial Atlanta student group that met monthly to discuss various social issues. King's participation with white students from Emory University in these meetings helped him to overcome his own anti-white feelings. He later recalled: "As I got to see more of white people, my resentment was softened, and a spirit of cooperation took its place" (*Papers* 1:45n).

Benjamin E. **Mays**, who served as president of Morehouse from 1940 to 1967, played a critical role in King's college experience and was described by King as "one of the great influences in my life" (*Papers* 1:38). Mays believed that black colleges should be "experiment stations in democratic living" and challenged Morehouse students to struggle against segregation rather than accommodate themselves to it (*Papers* 1:37). Mays preached every Tuesday morning in the college's chapel and introduced many students to **Gandhi**'s philosophy of **nonviolence**, which Mays had gained an appreciation for during his travels to **India**.

SOURCES

Introduction, in *Papers* 1:7; 25–26; 36–46.
King, "An Autobiography of Religious Development," in *Papers* 1:359–363.
King, "Kick Up Dust," *Atlanta Constitution*, 6 August 1946, in *Papers* 1:121.
King, "The Purpose of Education," in *Papers* 1:122–124.
William Peters, "Our Weapon Is Love," *Redbook*, August 1956, 41–42; 72–73.

MOSES, ROBERT PARRIS (1935–)

Although he avoided publicity and was reluctant to assert himself as a leader, Robert Parris Moses became one of the most influential black leaders of the southern civil rights struggle. His vision of grassroots, community-based leadership differed from Martin Luther King's charismatic leadership style. Nonetheless, King appreciated Moses' fresh ideas, calling his "contribution to the freedom struggle in America" an "inspiration" (King, 21 December 1963).

Born on 23 January 1935 in New York City, Moses grew up in a housing project in Harlem. He attended Stuyvesant High School, an elite public school, and won a scholarship to Hamilton College in Clinton, New York. He earned a master's degree in philosophy in 1957 from Harvard University and was working toward his doctorate when he was forced to leave because of the death of his mother and the hospitalization of his father. Moses returned to New York and became a mathematics teacher at Horace Mann School.

During the late 1950s Moses became increasingly interested in the civil rights struggle. In 1959 he helped Bayard **Rustin** with the second **Youth March for Integrated Schools** in Washington, D.C. Although he was willing to stuff envelopes along with other office volunteers, Rustin encouraged him to do more, suggesting in 1960 that he use his summer teaching break to go to Atlanta and work with King and the **Southern Christian Leadership Conference** (SCLC). In Atlanta, Moses volunteered to travel on behalf of the **Student Nonviolent Coordinating Council** (SNCC)—then a nascent student organization sharing offices with SCLC—on a recruiting tour of Louisiana, Alabama, and Mississippi, where he met local **National Association for the Advancement of Colored People** activist Amzie Moore. At Moore's request, Moses returned to Mississippi in 1961 to work on voter registration. Initially just a volunteer, Moses quickly joined SNCC's staff of three as the special field secretary for voter registration based in McComb, Mississippi. The following year he was named the co-director of the **Council of Federated Organizations** (COFO), a cooperative of civil rights groups in the state.

As an organizer, Moses nurtured local leaders who could continue the struggle after organizers had departed. He recognized the untapped potential of grassroots activists such as Fannie Lou **Hamer** who, despite only a sixth grade education, became one of SNCC's most effective organizers. "Leadership is there in the people," he later said. "You don't have to worry about where your leaders are, how are we going to get some leaders. The leadership is there. If you go out and work with your people, then the leadership will emerge" (Carson, 303).

Moses developed the idea for the 1964 Mississippi **Freedom Summer** Project, which recruited northern college students to join Mississippi blacks conducting a grassroots voter registration drive. When local blacks were excluded from participating in the all-white "regular" Democratic Party, Moses suggested creating the **Mississippi Freedom Democratic Party** (MFDP), which sought recognition as the representative delegation from Mississippi at the Democratic National Convention of 1964. Moses, King, and MFDP delegates participated in negotiations with vice presidential hopeful Hubert Humphrey. Although King favored a compromise whereby MFDP would be given two at-large seats, Moses and most MFDP delegates held out for full recognition.

Moses resigned from COFO in late 1964. He later commented that his role had become "too strong, too central, so that people who did not need to, began to lean on me, to use me as a crutch" (Carson, 156). He temporarily dropped his surname, going by his middle name, Parris, and began participating in the campaign against the **Vietnam War**. Speaking at the first massive anti-war demonstration on 17 April 1965 at the Washington Monument, Moses linked his opposition to the war to the civil rights struggle. As his involvement in the anti-war movement increased, he took a leave of absence from SNCC to avoid criticisms from fellow members who did not support his stance. Following his trip to Africa in 1965 Moses came to believe that blacks must work independently of whites, and by 1966 Moses had cut off all relationships with whites, even former SNCC activists.

Then separated from his first wife, SNCC worker Dona Richards, Moses moved to Canada to avoid the military draft in 1967. He later remarried and settled in Tanzania, where he and his wife Janet lived for several years before returning to the United States. While Moses was completing his PhD at Harvard, he was awarded a MacArthur Foundation "Genius" award, which he used to promote the Algebra Project, a national program to improve the math literacy skills of children in poor communities.

SOURCES
Burner, *And Gently He Shall Lead Them*, 1994.
Carson, *In Struggle*, 1981.
King to Moses, 10 March 1964, MLKJP-GAMK.
King to Robert and Donna Moses, 21 December 1963, MLKJP-GAMK.
Moses and Cobb, *Radical Equations*, 2001.

MUSTE, ABRAHAM JOHANNES (1885–1967)

A renowned Christian pacifist and a leading member of the **Fellowship of Reconciliation** (FOR), Abraham Johannes Muste was one of the foremost proponents of **nonviolence** in the United States. Muste was a strong supporter of the civil rights movement, as well as a leader in the anti-**Vietnam War** movement. At the end of Muste's life, Martin Luther King said that without Muste, "the American Negro might never have caught the meaning of true love for humanity" (Robinson, 137).

Muste was born in Zierikzee, the Netherlands. In 1891 his family emigrated to Grand Rapids, Michigan, and they became naturalized citizens in 1896. Muste graduated from Hope College and Union Theological Seminary. During the first decades of the twentieth century Muste was heavily involved with Communist and labor movements, and met with Leon Trotsky. He returned to his religious roots and during his years as national chairman (1926 to 1929) and executive secretary (1940 to 1953) of FOR he helped found the **Congress of Racial Equality** and served as a mentor to younger FOR staff members, including Bayard **Rustin**, James **Farmer**, and Jim **Lawson**.

During World War II Muste wrote a tract addressed to black churches called "What the Bible Teaches about Freedom." The pamphlet advocated nonviolent resistance as a biblically sanctioned method of fighting injustice. In it Muste notes that unless "Negroes and whites concerned about abolishing the denial of brotherhood represented by Jim Crow take up the Cross of suffering for its removal, it cannot be done away."

As a student at **Crozer Theological Seminary**, King attended a lecture by Muste and was initially skeptical of his absolute pacifism, believing at the time that war "could serve as a negative good in the sense of preventing the spread and growth of an evil force" (King, 95). After the **Montgomery bus boycott** brought King to national prominence as a proponent of **nonviolence**, he asked Muste to speak at conferences on nonviolence, and Muste invited King to attend meetings advocating worldwide Christian pacifism. After King was stabbed in 1958, Muste wrote to him: "Above any other man, Negro or white, you are now inevitably the instrument both to break down the color bar in this country and to reconcile and heal the people involved" (*Papers* 4:500).

A long-time opponent of the Vietnam War, Muste sought to link King to the antiwar movement, arranging a meeting for him with Thich Nhat Hanh, a prominent Vietnamese monk. He continued to organize events against U.S. involvement in Vietnam until his death in 1967.

SOURCES

King, *Stride Toward Freedom*, 1958.
Muste, *Essays of A. J. Muste*, ed. Nat Hentoff, 1967.
Muste, *What the Bible Teaches about Freedom*, circa 1943.
Muste to King, 23 September 1958, in *Papers* 4:500–501.
Robinson, *Abraham Went Out*, 1981.

NAACP. *See* National Association for the Advancement of Colored People.

NALC. *See* Negro American Labor Council.

NASH, DIANE JUDITH (1938–)

Through her involvement with the **Student Nonviolent Coordinating Committee** (SNCC) and the **Southern Christian Leadership Conference** (SCLC), Diane Nash worked closely with Martin Luther King. In 1962 King nominated Nash for a civil rights award sponsored by the New York branch of the **National Association for the Advancement of Colored People** to acknowledge her exemplary role in the student **sit-ins**. King described Nash as the "driving spirit in the nonviolent assault on segregation at lunch counters" (King, 9 April 1962).

Born in 1938, in Chicago, Illinois, Nash left Chicago to attend Howard University in Washington, D.C., but transferred a year later to Fisk University in Nashville, Tennessee, where she majored in English.

In Nashville, Nash experienced the full effect of the Jim Crow system for the first time. In 1959 she began attending **nonviolence** workshops given by James **Lawson**. Initially a skeptic of nonviolent tactics, Nash began to understand their effectiveness and marveled at the willingness of people to risk their lives for the sake of others. She had the opportunity to practice nonviolent direct action after the Student Central Committee in Nashville organized sit-ins in local department stores. Their sit-ins occurred in conjunction with the wave of sit-ins across the South initiated in Greensboro, North Carolina, on 1 February 1960.

In 1960 Nash attended the founding meeting of SNCC in Raleigh, North Carolina. In 1961 SNCC began supporting 10 students in Rock Hill, South Carolina, who were involved in protest activities and refused to post bail after being arrested. Shortly after arriving in Rock Hill, Nash and three other activists were also jailed for requesting service at a segregated lunch counter. For Nash, "jail without bail" gave protesters the "opportunity to reach the community and society with a great moral appeal and thus bring about basic changes in people and in society" (Garrow, 202). On 17 February

1961 King wrote to Nash, Charles Sherrod, and the other protesters, "You have inspired all of us by such demonstrative courage and faith. It is good to know that there still remains a creative minority who would rather lose in a cause that will ultimately win than to win in a cause that will ultimately lose."

During the spring of 1961 Nash played a crucial role in sustaining **Freedom Rides** initiated by the **Congress of Racial Equality**. From her base in Nashville, she coordinated student efforts to continue the rides into Mississippi and served as a liaison between the press and the United States Department of Justice. Tensions developed between King and SNCC members, including Nash, when King refused to participate in the Freedom Rides himself.

After her leadership role in the Freedom Rides, Nash became head of SNCC's direct action campaigns during the summer of 1961. That same year she married James **Bevel**, a fellow civil rights activist. The two moved to Jackson, Mississippi, where Nash was later convicted of contributing to the delinquency of minors for teaching them nonviolent tactics. Given a choice between paying a fine and jail time, Nash opted to serve her sentence despite being pregnant. The judge suspended her sentence rather than face the possibility of negative publicity for sending a pregnant woman to jail. In 1962 she joined Bevel at SCLC as a field staff organizer. She and Bevel made important contributions to the **Birmingham Campaign**, **March on Washington for Jobs and Freedom**, and the Selma Campaign. Both received the Rosa **Parks** Award from SCLC in 1965.

From the late 1960s onward, Nash taught in Chicago public schools and continued her activism organizing tenants, welfare support, and housing advocates.

Sources

Carson, *In Struggle*, 1981.
Garrow, *Bearing the Cross*, 1986.
Halberstam, *The Children*, 1998.
King to Diane Nash and Charles Sherrod, 17 February 1961, MLKP-MBU.
King to Basil Patterson, 9 April 1962, MLKJP-GAMK.

NATIONAL ASSOCIATION FOR THE ADVANCEMENT OF COLORED PEOPLE (NAACP)

At the time of Martin Luther King, Jr.'s birth in 1929, the National Association for the Advancement of Colored People (NAACP) was already the largest and most influential civil rights organization in the United States. King's father, Martin Luther **King**, Sr., headed Atlanta's NAACP branch; and in 1944, King, Jr., chaired the youth membership committee of the Atlanta NAACP Youth Council. Although King believed in the power of nonviolent direct action, he understood that it worked best when paired with the litigation and lobbying efforts of the NAACP.

The NAACP was formed in 1909 when progressive whites joined forces with W.E.B. Du Bois and other young blacks from the Niagara Movement, a group dedicated to full political and civil rights for African Americans. The NAACP initially focused on ending the practice of lynching, and although lobbying efforts did not persuade Congress to pass anti-lynching laws, the 1919 publication of the NAACP report entitled *Thirty Years of Lynching in the United States* convinced President Woodrow Wilson and other politicians to condemn mob violence.

In 1940 the NAACP established its nonprofit legal arm, the Legal Defense and Educational Fund (LDF). Under the direction of Thurgood **Marshall**, the LDF went on to win the landmark 1954 case ***Brown v. Board of Education***, which ruled that segregated education was unconstitutional. NAACP activists worked at the local level as well. In 1955 NAACP member Rosa **Parks** refused to give up her seat on a Montgomery bus, helping launch the **Montgomery bus boycott** that brought King into the national spotlight.

The NAACP supported the boycott throughout 1956, providing NAACP lawyers and paying legal costs. NAACP Executive Secretary Roy **Wilkins** personally encouraged branches to fundraise for the **Montgomery Improvement Association**. In a 1 May 1956 letter, King thanked Wilkins, saying, "This deep spirit of cooperation from the NAACP will give us renewed courage and vigor to carry on" (*Papers* 3:244). King recognized the benefits of this partnership and encouraged Montgomery churches to become lifetime members of the NAACP. In the summer of 1956, King gave the first of many featured addresses at an NAACP national convention. The following year the NAACP gave King its highest award, the Spingarn Medal. In his appreciation letter, King wrote Wilkins, "I am wholeheartedly with the program of the NAACP. You will have my moral and financial support at all times" (King, 10 July 1957).

In 1957 the NAACP and King's new organization, the **Southern Christian Leadership Conference** (SCLC), began collaborating on civil rights campaigns, beginning with the **Prayer Pilgrimage for Freedom** in Washington, D.C. The next year King and Wilkins met with President Dwight **Eisenhower** to advocate for civil rights legislation. Although tensions surfaced between SCLC and NAACP, both King and Wilkins were quick to publicly deny any discord between the two organizations.

In 1962 NAACP partnered with SCLC, the **Student Nonviolent Coordinating Committee** (SNCC), the **National Urban League**, and the **Congress of Racial Equality** (CORE) to launch the **Voter Education Project**, a grassroots voter registration and mobilization campaign. The organizations joined with the Brotherhood of Sleeping Car Porters the following year to organize the **March on Washington for Jobs and Freedom**. Throughout the mid-1960s, while King continued to partner with the youthful activists of SNCC and CORE, the NAACP sought to distance itself from the more radical, action-oriented organizations. However, by 1966, the NAACP and SCLC were both at odds with CORE and SNCC because these groups began advocating "**Black Power**" and excluding white members.

Despite the NAACP's opposition to King's 1967 public statement against the **Vietnam War**, Wilkins and King continued to work closely on civil rights issues. Both pressed for immediate action to address the needs of urban blacks and blamed the summer race riots of 1967 on a lack of jobs. SCLC and the NAACP were both accused of being too moderate during the late 1960s and early 1970s. The NAACP steadily lost membership during this more radical period, and the political climate under Presidents Richard **Nixon** and Gerald Ford continued to hurt the organization. In 1986 the NAACP moved its headquarters from New York to Baltimore, where it began a slow recovery. Nearly a century old, the NAACP continues to be the strongest national multiracial voice for political, educational, social, and economic equality.

SOURCES

Greenberg, *Crusaders in the Courts*, 1994.

King, "Call to a Prayer Pilgrimage for Freedom," in *Papers* 4:151–153.

King, "The Montgomery Story," Address delivered at the Forty-seventh Annual NAACP Convention, in *Papers* 3:299–310.

King to Wilkins, 1 May 1956, in *Papers* 3:243–244.

King to Wilkins, 10 July 1957, NAACPP-DLC.

NATIONAL BAPTIST CONVENTION (NBC)

Founded in 1895, the National Baptist Convention (NBC) is the major organization of African American Baptists and the nation's largest black religious organization in the United States. Martin Luther King's family was active in the NBC from its founding.

A. D. **Williams**, King's grandfather and an early minister of **Ebenezer Baptist Church**, was present at the NBC's founding meeting at Atlanta's Friendship Baptist Church. Jennie Celeste Williams (see **Family History**), King's grandmother, represented Ebenezer at the Woman's Convention, an NBC auxiliary. After **King**, Sr., became Ebenezer's pastor in 1931, he attended most NBC meetings through the 1930s and 1940s. King, Jr., accompanied his father to the September 1945 NBC meeting in Detroit, Michigan, just before his sophomore year at **Morehouse College**. In 1953 King family friend Sandy **Ray** was one of six ministers who ran for the NBC presidency, losing to Chicago's J. H. **Jackson**.

In 1954, shortly after King, Jr., became pastor of **Dexter Avenue Baptist Church** in Montgomery, Alabama, Nannie H. **Burroughs**, president of the Woman's Convention Auxiliary, invited him to address the group's annual meeting. King delivered a sermon on the convention's theme, "The Vision of a World Made New," condemning colonialism, imperialism, and segregation as well as the church's role in buttressing them. King said that the days of such abominations were limited: "So, like John, we can say we see a new heaven and a new earth. The old order of ungodly exploitation and crushing domination is passing away" (*Papers* 6:183). The following year, King attended the NBC's annual meeting with his mother and his father, who was serving on the convention's board of directors.

Following the **Prayer Pilgrimage for Freedom**, in 1957, King's relative fame and popularity threatened NBC president Jackson, who feared King might oppose him for president. King, Sr., reassured Jackson: "You can take it from me. M. L. is not going to have one thing to do with it one way or another" (*Papers* 4:18). However, in an August 1958 letter to O. Clay Maxwell, president of NBC's National Sunday School and Baptist Training Union (NSSBTU) Congress, King, Sr., revealed his lack of faith in Jackson's leadership and his intent to "avert a split in our Brotherhood" due to Jackson's plans to unseat Maxwell and Nannie Burroughs from their NBC positions. "We are gaining friends, new friends, every day," he advised Maxwell (King, Sr., 30 August 1958). King himself wrote Thomas Kilgore in July 1958, predicting, "I believe in the next few years, we will see a new day and even a new administration in the NBC" (*Papers* 4:447). Before the annual NBC meeting that year, King, Jr., was elected vice president of the NSSBTU.

Tensions in the NBC continued to rise and came to a head during the 1960 annual meeting, when Gardner **Taylor**, a King family friend, ran against Jackson for the presidency. Although Taylor and Jackson both claimed victory, the situation was not resolved until the next convention. In the meantime, Jackson spoke out against the tactics used by the freedom riders to protest interstate bus segregation. His counter to King's position on the importance of direct action protest to the civil rights movement led to his reelection as president at the annual meeting in Kansas City, Kansas, in 1961. During the contentious 1961 convention a Jackson supporter sustained injuries on the convention floor, which caused his death days later. Taylor and L. V. Booth led an NBC walkout that resulted in the formation of the **Progressive National Baptist Convention** in which King, Jr., participated. Jackson, who continued to serve as NBC president until 1982, accused King of "[masterminding] the invasion of the convention floor Wednesday which resulted in the death of a delegate" ("Dr. King Is Accused"). King telegraphed Jackson demanding a retraction. Jackson dismissed the allegation in a 12 September 1961 letter, and later removed King, Jr., from his office as vice president of the NSSBTU. Jackson was succeeded by T. J. **Jemison** in 1982.

SOURCES

"Dr. King Is Accused in Baptist Dispute," *New York Times*, 10 September 1961.
Introduction, in *Papers* 4:17–18.
Jackson to King, 12 September 1961, MLKP-MBU.
King to Martin Luther King, Sr., 24 January 1940, in *Papers* 1:103–104.
King, "The Vision of a World Made New," 9 September 1954, in *Papers* 6:181–183.
King, Sr., to Maxwell, 30 August 1958, EBCR.
King to Jackson, 10 September 1961, MLKP-MBU.
King to Kilgore, 7 July 1958, in *Papers* 4:447.
King to Kilgore, 6 October 1959, in *Papers* 5:305.

NATIONAL COMMITTEE FOR A SANE NUCLEAR POLICY (SANE)

In line with his belief in **nonviolence**, Martin Luther King worked closely with the National Committee for a Sane Nuclear Policy (SANE), often sponsoring the organization's statements. He told a journalist in 1961, "I am a strong believer in disarmament and suspension of nuclear tests" (King, 29 October 1961).

SANE grew out of a meeting of pacifists and anti-nuclear activists in April 1957. Initially conceived as a liberal ad hoc committee to stimulate debate on the hazards of nuclear testing, SANE soon became a leader in the struggle for disarmament. On 15 November 1957, SANE ran a full-page advertisement in the *New York Times* warning Americans: "We are facing a danger unlike any danger that has ever existed." Inspired by the enthusiastic response to its *Times* advertisement, SANE redefined itself as a mass membership organization, gaining 130 chapters and 25,000 members by the following summer.

King became involved with SANE in March 1958, when he joined several other notables in sponsoring the organization's second public advertisement. Over the following years, he sponsored and signed dozens of letters, petitions, brochures, and advertisements for the organization. In 1961 King said, "I don't think the choice is any longer between violence and nonviolence in a day when guided ballistic missiles are carving highways of death through the stratosphere. I think now it is a choice between nonviolence and nonexistence" (King, 29 October 1961).

As the war in **Vietnam** escalated, SANE became more active in the anti-war movement. In 1965, before King's first major speech on Vietnam, Coretta Scott **King** joined with SANE spokesman Benjamin **Spock** to rally against the war in New York and Washington, D.C. Two years later, King, Jr., and Spock co-chaired the spring Mobilization to End the War in Vietnam. Many in SANE's liberal leadership were hesitant to align with the more radical anti-war organizations, however; others like Spock thought it was essential to collaborate effectively with other peace organizations. Although the organization faltered in late 1967, it reinvented itself while campaigning for Senator Eugene McCarthy's presidential race.

After King's death, Coretta Scott King continued to work on behalf of SANE. SANE membership peaked during Ronald Reagan's presidency, and Coretta Scott King was invited to sit on the organization's advisory council. In 1983, commemorating the organization's historic link with the civil rights movement, SANE held a reception for Mrs. King on the 20th anniversary of the **March on Washington for Jobs and Freedom**.

In 1987 SANE merged with the grassroots-based Nuclear Weapons Freeze Campaign, and SANE/FREEZE changed its name to Peace Action in 1993. As the largest grassroots peace network in the United States, Peace Action remains engaged in activism and policy advocacy today.

SOURCES

Katz, *Ban the Bomb*, 1986.
King, Interview by John Freedom on "Face to Face," 29 October 1961, MLKJP-GAMK.
SANE, "We Are Facing a Danger Unlike Any Danger That Has Ever Existed," *New York Times*, 15 November 1957.

NATIONAL CONFERENCE ON RELIGION AND RACE

The National Conference on Religion and Race, held at Chicago's Edgewater Beach Hotel, 14–17 January 1963, brought together representatives of U.S. Catholic, Jewish, and Protestant organizations to discuss America's racial problems, and was hailed by Martin Luther King as "the most significant and historic [convention] ever held for attacking racial injustice" (Pieza, "Rev. King Urges Boycott"). King gave one of the major speeches at the four-day event, convened to commemorate the 100th anniversary of the **Emancipation Proclamation** and subtitled "A Challenge to Justice and Love."

Initiated by a coalition of the **National Council of Churches**, the Synagogue Council of America, and the National Catholic Welfare Conference in April 1962, the conveners invited King to join the steering committee early in the planning process. King accepted the offer and designated Wyatt Tee **Walker** as the **Southern Christian Leadership Conference** representative. In an announcement sent to the press in June 1962, organizers described the purpose of the conference as bringing "the joint moral force of the churches and synagogues to bear on the problem of racial segregation" (National Conference, 21 June 1962). The statement further explained that the meeting would "deal with the distinctive role that religion and religious institutions have to play in removing racial segregation and securing acceptance for all Americans" (National Conference, 21 June 1962).

The conference began on Monday, 14 January 1963, with a statement from President John F. **Kennedy** pledging to do "what is possible to protect and preserve our cherished democratic traditions," which accord full rights to every American regardless of his race, religion, color, or country of national origin (Schwartz, "Meyer Urges All-Faith Bias Action"). Theologian Abraham J. **Heschel** then spoke on "The Religious Basis of Equality of Opportunity," categorizing racism as "universal and evil," and as "man's gravest threat to man, the maximum of hatred for a minimum of reason, the maximum of cruelty for a minimum of thinking" (McCahill, "Historic Parley on Bias Opens Here"). It was at this convention that Heschel and King first met.

King arrived in Chicago on 16 January, and at a press conference that evening he said that the purpose of the conference was to "rectify past moments of apathy" (Hoffman, "Rev. King").

At the close of the conference, attendees adopted "An Appeal to the Conscience of the American People," which concluded: "We call upon all the American people to work, to pray and to act courageously in the cause of human equality and dignity while there is still time, to eliminate racism permanently and decisively, to seize the historic opportunity the Lord has given us for healing an ancient rupture in the human family, to do this for the glory of God" ("Church Parley Issues Appeal to U.S. Conscience").

SOURCES

"Church Parley Issues Appeal to U.S. Conscience," *Chicago Defender*, 19 January 1963.

Dick Hoffmann, "Rev. King: Take Stand against Prejudice," *Daily Herald*, 17 January 1963.

Dolores McCahill, "Historic Parley on Bias Opens Here," *Chicago Sun-Times*, 15 January 1963.

National Conference on Religion and Race, Press release, 21 June 1962, MLKJP-GAMK.

Stanley Pieza, "Rev. King Urges Boycott by Churches to Fight Bias," *Chicago's American*, 16 January 1963.

Donald M. Schwartz, "Meyer Urges All-Faith Bias Action," *Chicago Sun-Times*, 15 January 1963.

NATIONAL COUNCIL OF NEGRO WOMEN (NCNW)

Founded in 1935 by Mary McLeod Bethune, the National Council of Negro Women (NCNW) was the first national coalition of African American women's organizations. The most influential national women's organization during the civil rights movement at the time, the NCNW represented 850,000 members, including Martin Luther King's wife, Coretta Scott **King**. In 1957 King addressed the NCNW at their annual convention, telling the women, "I have long admired this organization, its great work, and its noble purposes" (King, 9 November 1957).

NCNW presidents Vivian C. Mason (1953–1957) and Dorothy I. Height (1957–1998) both worked with King, collaborating on movement strategies and speaking at events together. In the early months of the **Montgomery bus boycott**, Mason raised funds for the boycott and featured Rosa **Parks** as a guest speaker at a May 1956 NCNW conference of women leaders in Washington, D.C. In May 1957 King and Mason shared a podium at the **Prayer Pilgrimage for Freedom**. Later that year, King gave a featured address at the NCNW annual convention, predicting a future of desegregation and urging the audience to "be maladjusted" to segregation and discrimination (King, 9 November 1957). Mason wrote King soon afterward, thanking him for addressing her members: "Your philosophy to treat the sickness of race culture in American life found an echo in their hearts. They want to be counted among the brave and the daring, those who dare to be followers of Christ when all the world seeks mammon" (Mason, 19 November 1957). Mason also proposed turning King's speech into a commercial recording to raise funds for both organizations. Mason and King shared an interest in voter registration and the NCNW collaborated with the **Southern Christian Leadership Conference** (SCLC) on the organization's registration campaign, the Crusade for Citizenship.

Height continued Mason's collaboration with King. Height and King were both sponsors of the 1962 American Negro Leadership Conference on Africa and met with President John F. **Kennedy**, James **Farmer**, A. Philip **Randolph**, Roy **Wilkins**, and Whitney **Young** to share the conference's resolutions. In 1963 the NCNW and SCLC joined with five other national civil rights organizations to form the Council for United Civil Rights Leadership (CUCRL). This organization became the beneficiary of the profits from the sales of recordings of King's "**I Have a Dream**" speech at the **March on Washington for Jobs and Freedom**.

Height visited Birmingham, Alabama, on Mother's Day 1963, at the conclusion of the **Birmingham Campaign**. Height thanked King and the others engaged in the campaign, saying, "Know that the National Council of Negro Women and all of us are hand in hand with you, all of us with our hand in God's hand" (Height, 12 May 1963). Speaking after her, King called Height one of "the great women of our day and age" and praised the women in the Birmingham movement, saying, "We wouldn't have a Birmingham movement if the women were not present in this movement" (King, 12 May 1963). The next month, Height joined the dais guests at a **Gandhi Society for Human Rights** luncheon in King's honor in Washington, D.C.

After King's **assassination**, Height recalled: "Each of us had a feeling that, particularly in the United Civil Rights Leadership group, we had a feeling that we had to re-double our efforts. We saw him cut down right in the middle of what he was doing. And we felt that we wanted to make sure that it was clear that the dream was not killed, but it was the dreamer. That's the way we felt about it" (Height, 14 January 2005). Height remained the president of the NCNW until 1998, when she became chair and president emerita of the organization.

SOURCES

Farmer, *Lay Bare the Heart*, 1985.

Garrow, *Bearing the Cross*, 1986.

Height, Address delivered at New Pilgrim Baptist Church, 12 May 1963, MLKEC.

Height, *Open Wide the Freedom Gates*, 2003.

Height, "We Wanted the Voice of a Woman to Be Heard," in *Sisters in the Struggle*, ed. Thomas and Franklin, 2001.

King, Address delivered at New Pilgrim Baptist Church, 12 May 1963, MLKEC.

King, "A Look to the Future," 9 November 1957, ORS.

Mason to King, 30 April 1956, in *Papers* 3:235–236.

Mason to King, 19 November 1957, MLKP-MBU.

"Transcript: Civil Rights Activist Dorothy Height Remembers Martin Luther King," 14 January 2005, Voice of America. http://www.voanews.com/mediaassets/english/2005_01/Audio/mp3/Rupli-Height%2014Jan05.mp3.

NATIONAL COUNCIL OF THE CHURCHES OF CHRIST IN AMERICA (NCC)

An ecumenical organization comprised of most of the mainline Protestant denominations, the National Council of the Churches of Christ in America (NCC) represented a moderate view toward race relations in America since its inception in 1950, and supported many of Martin Luther King's major campaigns.

The NCC's formation resulted from a merger of several Protestant umbrella organizations. One of them, the Federal Council of Churches, was founded in 1908, and initiated Race Relations Sunday in 1922, an effort by churches to focus the second Sunday of February every year on race issues. The NCC continued this tradition and, during the 1950s, the pamphlets produced by the NCC for Race Relations Sunday contained a "Call to Action" that promoted individual and political approaches toward addressing race in America.

During the **Montgomery bus boycott**, the NCC sent a telegram reassuring Montgomery ministers of its support, calling segregation "a violation of the Gospel of love and human brotherhood" (Blake, 25 February 1956). In early 1957 the NCC also criticized President Dwight D. **Eisenhower**'s refusal to condemn the rise of violence against Southern blacks and circulated the call for the May 1957 **Prayer Pilgrimage for Freedom** held by the **Southern Christian Leadership Conference** (SCLC) at the Lincoln Memorial in Washington, D.C.

Following his rise to prominence in Montgomery, King became closely aligned with the NCC. He contributed to the NCC's 1957 Race Relations Sunday message, "For All … A Non-Segregated Society," writing: "Racial segregation is a blatant denial of the unity which we all have in Christ. Segregation is a tragic evil that is utterly un-Christian" (*Papers* 4:124). He also delivered two addresses during the 1957 NCC annual meeting. King charged: "All too many ministers are still silent while evil rages," but praised the NCC's stand against segregation and noted that such instances "are still far too few" (*Papers* 6:326).

In 1961 Andrew **Young** left a position with the NCC's youth education office to help run the SCLC's Citizenship Education Program, and later he became SCLC's executive director. The next year King agreed to serve on the steering committee of the NCC-sponsored **National Conference on Religion and Race**. King spoke on the last day of the conference, stating: "Honesty impels us to admit that religious bodies in America have not been faithful to their prophetic mission on the question of racial justice. In the midst of a nation rife with racial animosity, the Church too often has been content to mouth pious irrelevancies and sanctimonious trivialities" (King, 17 January 1963). NCC put pressure on legislators to support the **Civil Rights Act of 1964** and was an early critic of the **Vietnam War**. The organization also supported the **Poor People's Campaign**, one of King's last major initiatives.

SOURCES

Eugene Carson Blake to Solomon Seay, 25 February 1956, NCCP-PPPrHi.

George Dugan, "Church Council Asks U.S. to Halt Vietnam Bombing," *New York Times*, 4 December 1965.

Introduction, in *Papers* 4:14–15.

King, "A Challenge to the Churches and Synagogues," 17 January 1963, CSKC.

King, The Christian Way of Life in Human Relations, Address at the General Assembly of the National Council of Churches, 4 December 1957, in *Papers* 6:322–328.

King, "Crisis in America's Cities: An Analysis of Social Disorder and a Plan of Action Against Poverty, Discrimination and Racism in Urban America" (Washington, D.C., National Council of Churches Office of Liaison for the Poor Peoples Campaign, 15 August 1967), FORP-PSC-P.

King, "For All … A Non-Segregated Society," Message for Race Relations Sunday, 10 February 1957, in *Papers* 4:123–125.

National Council of Churches, *That All May Be One: A Message from Race Relations Sunday* (New York: National Council of Churches of Christ, 8 February 1953), CSKC.

NATIONALISM

Martin Luther King often criticized nationalism, whether in the guise of Adolf Hitler's tyranny or Senator Joseph McCarthy's attacks against un-American activities. In 1953, when King was still in graduate school, he preached a sermon against nationalism, saying, "One cannot worship this false god of nationalism and the God of christianity at the same time" (*Papers* 6:133).

Throughout his life, King wrestled with the religious and moral meaning of nationalism. King believed that Christianity championed internationalism, describing a truth for all men: "Not some white and not some black, not some yellow and not some brown, but all flesh shall see it together" (*Papers* 4:166). Notes from his readings of Isaiah, Jeremiah, Ezra, and other biblical verses show that he interpreted passages to refute "nationalistic teachings" and to demonstrate that "God's house is to be a house of prayer for all people" (King, 22 September 1952–28 January 1953). King's internationalism did not preclude loving one's own country, however, and he felt that "no other nation can mean to us what our nation means," but King thought loving one's nation need not turn into "chauvinism and isolationism" (*Papers* 6:133).

When King spoke out against the **Vietnam War**, he urged Americans to move beyond narrow nationalism. On 4 April 1967 at an event organized by **Clergy and Laymen Concerned About Vietnam** he told an audience at Riverside Church in New York City: "I come to this platform tonight to make a passionate plea to my beloved nation" (King, "Beyond Vietnam," 141). He claimed that the soul of America was being poisoned by the war in Vietnam. King stated that he felt compelled to speak for the suffering and helpless in Vietnam as well as the poor in the United States: "Beyond the calling of race or nation or creed is this vocation of sonship and brotherhood.… This I believe to be the privilege and the burden of all of us who deem ourselves bound by allegiances and loyalties … broader and deeper than nationalism" (King, "Beyond Vietnam," 145–146).

Sources

King, "Beyond Vietnam," in *A Call to Conscience*, ed. Carson and Shepard, 2001.
King, "The Birth of a New Nation," Sermon delivered at Dexter Avenue Baptist Church, 7 April 1957, in *Papers* 4:155–167.
King, "The False God of Nationalism," 12 July 1953, in *Papers* 6:132–133.
King, Notecards on Topics from Isaiah, 22 September 1952–28 January 1953, CSKC.
King, *Where Do We Go from Here*, 1967.
King, *Why We Can't Wait*, 1964.

NATIONAL URBAN LEAGUE

Martin Luther King and the **Southern Christian Leadership Conference** (SCLC) joined with the National Urban League in the struggle for African American economic rights. In a 31 July telegram to the organization's officers and delegates on the occasion of its 1963 national convention, King praised the Urban League, writing: "Your tenacious instance in seeking for the Negro community economic justice has paid large dividends." He pledged SCLC's "full support to your ultimate goals of complete economic[,] social[,] and spiritual freedom for all mankind."

Founded in 1910, the National Urban League counseled recent black migrants to urban areas in the North and South, assisted in the training of social workers for this population, and provided educational and increased employment opportunities in industry. The Urban League's board was interracial from its earliest days.

Under the leadership of Lester **Granger**, executive director from 1941 to 1961, the League supported A. Philip **Randolph**'s 1941 March on Washington Movement to combat discrimination against blacks during World War II, and advocated the integration of labor unions. In a 16 January 1957 telegram, Granger sent King greetings during the founding meeting of the SCLC and commended "your conference for the forthright steps you are taking to find practical solutions for the critical problems that Negro citizens are facing today." On 23 June 1958 Granger joined King, Randolph, and Roy **Wilkins** in a meeting with President Dwight D. **Eisenhower** to urge that the 1957 Civil Rights Act be enforced, and that the Department of Justice "act now to protect the right of citizens to register and vote," and promote "non-discrimination in government employment" (*Papers* 4:428–429). League officials also participated in the Leadership Conference on Civil Rights with King, Wilkins, and other civil rights organizations and labor unions to meet with congressional leaders in January 1960 on the progress of a new civil rights bill.

In September 1960 King addressed the Urban League during its Golden Anniversary Conference and characterized the relationship between it and other "more militant civil rights organizations," saying that both types of groups "must accept the other as a necessary partner in the complex yet exciting struggle to free the Negro, and thereby save the soul of America" (*Papers* 5:506; 507).

Leaders such as Whitney M. **Young**, who headed the organization from 1961 until his death in 1971, brought the organization closer to full involvement in the civil rights movement. Although it could not fully join in protests because of its tax-exempt status, the League contributed through different actions, such as hosting meetings—like those held by King, Randolph, and other planners of the **1963 March on Washington for Jobs and Freedom**—at its New York headquarters. Although Young disagreed with King in 1967 regarding his opposition to the **Vietnam War**, the League endorsed SCLC's **Operation Breadbasket** in Chicago that year.

SOURCES

Granger to King, 16 January 1957, MLKP-MBU.

King, "The Rising Tide of Racial Consciousness," Address at the Golden Anniversary Conference of the National Urban League, 6 September 1960, in *Papers* 5:499–508.

King to Officers and Delegates of the Annual Convention of the National Urban League, 31 July 1963, MLKJP-GAMK.

Randolph, Granger, King, and Wilkins, "A Statement to the President of the United States," 23 June 1958, in *Papers* 4:426–429.

Weiss, *Whitney M. Young, Jr.*, 1989.

Wilkins to King, 8 February 1960, in *Papers* 5:366–367.

NBC. *See* National Baptist Convention.

NCC. *See* National Council of the Churches of Christ in America.

NCNW. *See* National Council of Negro Women.

NEGRO AMERICAN LABOR COUNCIL (NALC)

In the wake of the vicious reaction to the 1961 **Freedom Rides**, Negro American Labor Council (NALC) President A. Philip **Randolph** telegraphed Martin Luther King, pledging: "The Negro American Labor Council speaking for thousands of Negro workers is fully behind you—strong in our material and spiritual condemnation of the violence visited upon you[,] we pledge our unstinting aid" (Randolph, 23 May 1961). Founded in 1960, the NALC sought to address the failure of the **American Federation of Labor and Congress of Industrial Organizations** (AFL-CIO) to end racial discrimination in some of its unions.

Dissatisfied with AFL-CIO President George Meany's lack of support for the civil rights movement, Randolph introduced a resolution at the 1959 **National Association for the Advancement of Colored People** convention calling for a black labor organization that would carry out the civil rights program of the AFL-CIO. In July 1959 Randolph called a meeting of African American labor leaders who agreed to form the NALC. Randolph invited King to speak at the NALC's founding convention in May 1960, but King was defending himself against an indictment of tax fraud at the time. In addition to electing Randolph as president, the delegates at the founding convention chose Cleveland **Robinson**, secretary-treasurer of the District 65 Retail, Wholesale, and Department Store Workers Union, as their vice president. The same month, Randolph called once again for the elimination of segregated locals in the AFL-CIO, prompting his censure by the AFL-CIO executive board. King and other African American leaders reproached the AFL-CIO.

By 1962 membership numbers in the NALC began to decline, falling from more than 10,000 members to 4,000 members. The following year, the organization engaged in its best-known action, initiating the **March on Washington for Jobs and Freedom**. Randolph asked for King's support in a 26 March 1963 telegram, beseeching him: "We need the great moral weight of your name on the call" (Randolph, 26 March 1963). Despite the fact that the march was not endorsed by the AFL-CIO, a number of unions sanctioned the event and labor participation was strong.

In 1966 Robinson succeeded Randolph as NALC president. The organization joined with the **Southern Christian Leadership Conference** to help organize workers in Baltimore and Memphis in the late 1960s. During this time, more radical organizations competed with NALC for members, and membership continued to decline. In 1972, recognizing NALC's ineffectiveness, Robinson switched his involvement to the Coalition of Black Trade Unionists, founded that year.

SOURCES
Pfeffer, A. *Philip Randolph*, 1990.
Randolph to King, 23 May 1961, RPP-NN-Sc.
Randolph to King, 26 March 1963, MLKJP-GAMK.

NEHRU, JAWAHARLAL (1889–1964)

The first prime minister of independent India, Jawaharlal Nehru was a follower of Mahatma **Gandhi** and had advocated for India's release from British rule. Nehru's political and social work helped create an independent India in 1947, and inspired Martin Luther King in his own struggle for the freedom of African Americans in the

United States. During King's 1959 **India trip**, which he called "one of the most concentrated and eye-opening experiences" of his life, he met with Nehru (*Papers* 5:232).

Nehru, the son of a wealthy barrister and politician, was born on 14 November 1889, in Allahabad, India. The eldest of three children, Nehru was home schooled until the age of 15, when he continued his education in England. He received a BA (1910) from Trinity College, Cambridge, and, after studying law at Inner Temple in London, Nehru was called to the bar in 1912, and returned to India to practice law. Following his return to India, Nehru joined Gandhi's civil disobedience movement and, in 1923, became general secretary of the All-India Congress Committee.

Nehru served as a source of inspiration for King during the **Montgomery bus boycott**. A year before the two men met, King inscribed a copy of his newly published book, ***Stride Toward Freedom***, to Nehru with the words: "In appreciation for your genuine good-will, your broad humanitarian concern, and the inspiration that your great struggle for India gave to me and the 50,000 Negroes of Montgomery" (November 1958). King and Nehru met on 10 February 1959, at the prime minister's home. During that visit Nehru and King discussed the possibility of Indian universities providing assistance for African American students. Although Nehru supported the proposal, he acknowledged that "nobody in *poor* India had thought about offering scholarships for students from *rich* America" (Reddick, 1968). The two men also discussed methods that relied on **nonviolence**, and the vitality of Gandhianism throughout India.

Nehru and King maintained a casual correspondence until Nehru's death in May 1964. In a telegram to Nehru's daughter, Indira Gandhi, King said that the prime minister's death was a "great loss to the whole world" and that "generations yet unborn will be inspired by his noble life" (King, 27 May 1964). Writing in *The Legacy of Nehru: A Memorial Tribute*, published the year after Nehru's death, King said: "In all of these struggles of mankind to rise to a true state of civilization, the towering figure of Nehru sits unseen but felt at all council tables. He is missed by the world, and because he is so wanted, he is a living force in the tremulous world of today" (King, 67).

Nehru's legacy was carried on by his only child, Indira Gandhi, who served as the third prime minister of independent India until her assassination in 1984. Today Nehru's powerful influence in India is still widely acknowledged.

SOURCES

King, Inscription to Nehru, November 1958, LDPF-GAMK.
King, "My Trip to the Land of Gandhi," July 1959, in *Papers* 5:231–238.
King to Gandhi, 27 May 1964, SCLCR-GAMK.
Nehru, "Martin Luther King, Jr.," in *Legacy of Nehru*, ed. Natwar-Singh, 1965.
Nehru, *Toward Freedom*, 1941.
Nehru to King, 14 January 1959, in *Papers* 5:107–108.
"Notes for Conversation between King and Nehru," 10 February 1959, in *Papers* 5:130.
Reddick, "With King through India: A Personal Memoir," 1968, LDRP-NN-Sc.

NELSON, WILLIAM STUART (1895–1977)

An internationally known expert on **nonviolence**, William Stuart Nelson corresponded regularly with Martin Luther King. When Nelson sent him his 1958 article "Satyagraha: Gandhian Principles of Non-Violent Non-Cooperation," King wrote that it was "one of the best and most balanced analyses of the Gandhian principles of non-violent, noncooperation that I have read" (King, 18 August 1958).

Nelson was born in Paris, Kentucky, in 1895. He served in World War I and went on to receive his BA from Howard University in 1920. After attending schools in France and Germany, he received a BD from Yale (1924) and returned to Howard to teach. In 1931 he became the first black president of Shaw University and, later, the first president of Dillard University. He finished his career at Howard, serving as dean of the School of Religion from 1940 to 1948, dean of the university from 1948 to 1961, and vice president of special projects from 1961 to 1967.

Nelson made several trips to India. In 1946, while visiting as a representative of the **American Friends Service Committee**, he marched with **Gandhi** through Bengal in an effort to help reconcile the Hindu and Muslim communities. He returned to India in 1958 as a Fulbright scholar, but could not stay long enough to accompany King on his trip there in 1959. After King returned home, Nelson wrote that what he had "done in America is proving a source of great encouragement to and re-awakening of people in India, and is thereby serving the cause of non-violence in the very country which has witnessed its most significant demonstration" (Nelson, 10 April 1959).

Nelson was active throughout the civil rights movement, speaking at the 1959 **Institute on Nonviolence and Social Change** and the 1962 convention of the **Southern Christian Leadership Conference**, and joining the **Selma to Montgomery March** in 1965. He remained a member of various peace, religious, and educational groups until his death in 1977.

SOURCES

King to Nelson, 18 August 1958, MLKP-MBU.

Blanche Wright Nelson, "A Tribute to My Husband," *Journal of Religious Thought* (Fall 1978/ Winter 1979): 54–56.

Nelson, "Satyagraha: Gandhian Principles of Non-Violent Non-Cooperation," *Journal of Religious Thought* (Fall 1957/Winter 1958): 15–24.

Nelson to King, 10 April 1959, MLKP-MBU.

NESBITT, ROBERT D. (1908–2002)

In 1954 R. D. Nesbitt recruited Martin Luther King, Jr., to become the pastor at **Dexter Avenue Baptist Church** in Montgomery, Alabama. Nesbitt admired King, observing, "His major strength—in my way of thinking—was his ability to get along with people and his ability to sell himself to individuals. And he did this beautifully" (Nesbitt, 24 January 1972).

Nesbitt was born in Montgomery, Alabama, on 22 November 1908. He was the 12th of 14 children. He received a degree from Virginia Union University in 1928, and went on to work for the Pilgrim Health and Life Insurance Company of Augusta, Georgia, where he was employed for 35 years. Nesbitt was a member of the **National Association for the Advancement of Colored People** and was active in many other civic organizations.

Nesbitt was Dexter's clerk for 35 years, and served terms as chairman of the deacon board, as well as treasurer. Nesbitt was also chairman of Dexter's pulpit selection committee. It was Nesbitt who found Dexter's two previous pastors, Alfred Charles Livingston Arbouin and Vernon **Johns**, neither of whom had satisfied Dexter's officials.

In his search for a pastor to replace Johns, Nesbitt heard about King while traveling in Atlanta. Meeting King at the house of **King, Sr.**, Nesbitt convinced him to preach a trial sermon at Dexter on 17 January 1954. Recalling his first impression of King, Nesbitt said, "He was a very unassuming young man, very humble, and he had a very easy flow of expression" (Jarrett, "A Quiet Deacon"). Dexter's congregation immediately liked the young reverend, but several weeks later King told Nesbitt he was still considering other job options. After further negotiations, Nesbitt persuaded King to accept the call.

Nesbitt served on the executive board of the **Montgomery Improvement Association**, for which he also served as treasurer. He attributed the success of the **Montgomery bus boycott** to the ministers: "The results of the active participation and leadership exemplified by our ministers—whom blacks love more than they do any other personalities—provided the turning point in the movement," he recalled (Jarrett, "A Quiet Deacon").

In 1959 King informed Nesbitt of his plans to resign from Dexter and return to Atlanta. The following year, King was tried for perjury on his 1956 Alabama state tax return (see *State of Alabama v. M. L. King, Jr.*). King's defense team put Nesbitt on the stand, who informed the jury that King had fiercely resisted salary increases offered by the Dexter trustees. King was acquitted.

Nesbitt continued his work with the MIA, writing to supporters in June 1961, seeking money to support the freedom riders as they journeyed through Montgomery. He received a number of honors, such as the Young Men's Christian Association Man of the Year Award in 1987, and the Montgomery Bar Association Liberty Bell Award in 1988.

SOURCES

Branch, *Parting the Waters*, 1988.
Vernon Jarrett, "A Quiet Deacon Unites Black Struggle," *Chicago Tribune*, 2 December 1975.
King to Dexter Avenue Baptist Church, 14 April 1954, in *Papers* 2:260.
King to Pulpit Committee, Dexter Avenue Baptist Church, 10 March 1954, in *Papers* 2:258–259.
Nesbitt, Interview by Judy Barton, 24 January 1972, MLK/OH-GAMK.
Nesbitt to King, 7 March 1954, in *Papers* 2:225.

NEW YORK AMSTERDAM NEWS

In 1962 Martin Luther King began writing a biweekly column for the *New York Amsterdam News*. The column was intended to highlight King's views on contemporary issues, including the efficacy of nonviolence, the state of the civil rights movement, and the role of the church in the freedom struggle.

Founded in 1909 by James Henry Anderson, the *New York Amsterdam News* was a weekly newspaper that reported on issues relevant to the African American community. At its height in the 1940s, the newspaper had a circulation of 100,000 and was one of the four largest African American newspapers in the United States. It published columns by such black notables as W.E.B. Du Bois, Roy **Wilkins**, Adam Clayton **Powell**, Jr., and **Malcolm X**.

In his column King commented on a myriad of issues, including his evolving attitudes on the progress of civil rights reform. In a February 1962 column, King addressed the question, "Are you satisfied with President Kennedy's stand on Civil Rights?" King admitted that the question was complicated given that the Kennedy administration had appointed blacks to key government positions and issued an executive order eliminating employment discrimination. However, King called **Kennedy** "cautious and defensive" when it came to providing the "strong leadership in Civil Rights that is necessary to grapple with the enormity of the problem." King was further dismayed when the president backed "completely away from the most challenging order, namely, an order to end discrimination in Federally assisted housing" (King, "The President's Record").

King used the column to speak out on the issues of the day. He told the Christian church that "moral coercion" and "action in the area of job discrimination" were necessary for social change, writing: "We cannot be a sheltered group of detached spectators chanting and singing on sequestered corners in a world that is being threatened by the forces of evil" (King, "The Church Must Be Firm!"). In December 1963 he charged that John F. Kennedy's death was caused "by a morally inclement climate" that arose from "our constant attempt to cure the cancer of racial injustice with the vasoline of graduation; our readiness to allow arms to be purchased at will and fired at whim" (King, "What Killed JFK?").

The consequence of violence in America was a frequent topic of King's columns. He mourned the death of Malcolm X in a March 1965 column: "Like the murder of Lumumba, the murder of Malcolm X deprives the world of a potentially great leader. I could not agree with either of these men, but I could see in them a capacity for leadership which I could respect" (King, "The Nightmare of Violence"). Following the **Watts rebellion** in Los Angeles later that year, King maintained that the cause of the violence was primarily economic and was "the beginning of a stirring of a deprived people in a society who have been by-passed by the progress of the past decade" (King, "Feeling Alone in the Struggle").

King gave attention to the civil rights movement in his column and paid tribute to unsung heroes of the movement, including Esau Jenkins, Fred **Shuttlesworth**, and James **Meredith**. He continued to write the column through 1966. In 1971 the *New York Amsterdam News* was purchased by Percy E. Sutton, H. Carl McCall, and Clarence B. **Jones**.

SOURCES
King, "The Church Must Be Firm!" *New York Amsterdam News*, 23 November 1963.
King, "Feeling Alone in the Struggle," *New York Amsterdam News*, 28 August 1965.
King, "The Nightmare of Violence," *New York Amsterdam News*, 13 March 1965.
King, "The President's Record," *New York Amsterdam News*, 17 February 1962.
King, "What Killed JFK?" *New York Amsterdam News*, 21 December 1963.

NEW YORK TIMES CO. V. SULLIVAN, 376 U.S. 254 (1964)

The events that led to the 1964 landmark U.S. Supreme Court decision confirming freedom of the press under the First Amendment in *New York Times Co. v. Sullivan* began in March 1960, after Martin Luther King's supporters published a fundraising appeal on the civil rights leader's behalf. The appeal was in response to King's arrest on perjury charges, and so incensed Alabama officials that they brought suit against several black ministers whose names appeared on the advertisement.

On 17 February 1960 two Fulton County sheriff's deputies arrested King at his **Ebenezer Baptist Church** office and took him into custody. A grand jury in Alabama had issued a warrant for King's arrest on two counts of felony perjury for signing fraudulent tax returns for 1956 and 1958. In response to King's indictment, a group of King supporters met in Harry **Belafonte**'s New York apartment to form the Committee to Defend Martin Luther King and the Struggle for Freedom in the South, to raise money for King's defense and for other civil rights initiatives. Under the chairmanship of A. Philip **Randolph**, the committee immediately launched a fundraising campaign aimed at raising $200,000.

In a 3 March press release, the committee denounced the charges against King as a "gross misrepresentation of fact" because King's income had never "even approached" the $45,000 that Alabama officials claimed he earned in 1958 (*Papers* 5:25–26). In response to the perjury charges against King, a felony that could have resulted in a five-year sentence, the committee placed a full-page advertisement in the *New York Times* entitled "Heed Their Rising Voices." The ad sought to demonstrate that King's arrest was politically motivated and part of an effort "to destroy the one man who, more than any other, symbolizes the new spirit now sweeping the South" (*Papers* 5:382). The appeal requested donations that would be divided between King's defense, support for student protesters, and the voting rights struggle, and was signed by 84 King supporters, including Jackie **Robinson** and Eleanor **Roosevelt**.

Alabama officials, particularly governor John **Patterson**, were upset by statements in the ad, which accused Alabama state and local officials of retaliating against students for protesting, and harassing King with repeated arrests. L. B. Sullivan, a Montgomery city commissioner, sued the *New York Times* for libel, and Patterson demanded an immediate retraction. Four Alabama ministers whose names appeared in the advertisement, Ralph **Abernathy**, Solomon S. **Seay**, Fred L. **Shuttlesworth**, and Joseph **Lowery**, were also sued, despite testimony that their names were used without their knowledge or consent. In addition to Sullivan and Patterson, three other Alabama officials each sued the *Times* and the four ministers for $500,000. The Patterson suit also included King as a defendant.

During the trial in Alabama, Sullivan and his lawyers attempted to persuade the jury that the statements made in the ad were libelous, false, and injurious to his reputation. The jury ruled in his favor and the defendants were required to pay $500,000. On appeal the defendants argued that Sullivan's suit violated the First Amendment, but the Alabama Court responded: "The First Amendment of the U.S. Constitution does not protect libelous publications" (*Times v. Sullivan*). The Supreme Court of Alabama affirmed the lower court's decision on 30 August 1962.

In a final attempt to reverse the previous decisions, Herbert Wechsler, a professor at Columbia Law School and specialist on the Constitution and the Supreme Court, was asked to handle the case, in conjunction with Clarence **Jones**, Harry **Wachtel**, and others. Wechsler's arguments persuaded the U.S. Supreme Court to reverse the Alabama decisions based on the suppositions that Sullivan's case lacked proof of "actual malice," lacked evidence that the statements were "of and concerning" Sullivan, and did not produce with convincing clarity evidence that the statements were published with "reckless disregard of whether it was true or false" (*Times v. Sullivan*). Following the U.S. Supreme Court ruling on 9 March 1964, all charges were dropped against the defendants.

SOURCES

Committee to Defend Martin Luther King, Jr. and the Struggle for Freedom in the South, Press release, "Statement on the Indictment of Martin Luther King, Jr.," 3 March 1960, APRC-DLC.

"Committee to Defend Martin Luther King and the Struggle for Freedom in the South," *New York Times*, 29 March 1960, in *Papers* 5:382.

Introduction, in *Papers* 5:24–26.

King, Interview on Arrest following Indictment by Grand Jury of Montgomery County, 17 February 1960, in *Papers* 5:370–372.

Lewis, *Make No Law*, 1991.

New York Times Co. v. Sullivan, 376 U.S. 254 (1964).

Patterson to King, 9 May 1960, in *Papers* 5:456–458.

Tedford, *Freedom of Speech in the United States*, 1985.

NIEBUHR, REINHOLD (1892–1971)

Raised in the **social gospel** tradition of his father's church, Martin Luther King encountered Reinhold Niebuhr's less hopeful philosophy, Christian realism, as a student at **Crozer Theological Seminary** in 1949. King later evaluated Niebuhr's contribution to theology as a rebuttal of "the false optimism characteristic of a great segment of Protestant liberalism" (King, 99).

Niebuhr was born in Wright City, Missouri, the son of a Lutheran minister, Gustave Niebuhr, and his wife Lydia. He attended Yale Divinity School (BD, 1914; MA, 1915) before assuming the pastorate of Bethel Evangelical Church of Detroit in 1915. In 1928 Niebuhr accepted a position at Union Theological Seminary in New York City, where he taught philosophy of religion and applied Christianity for the remainder of his life. As a founder of the journal *Christianity and Crisis*, and the political group Americans for Democratic Action, he exercised considerable influence in American religious and political thought.

Once an advocate of pacifism, Niebuhr served as chairman of the **Fellowship of Reconciliation** from 1931 until 1932. He broke from the movement in 1933 with the publication of his book *Moral Man and Immoral Society* (1932). Niebuhr embraced a new approach to theology and ethics called Christian realism. He argued that a chief reliance on the power of reason through education and moral suasion was naive and misplaced. Citing U.S. racial problems as an example, he declared, "However large the number of individual white men who do and who will identify themselves completely with the Negro cause, the white race in America will not admit the Negro to equal rights if he is not forced to do so" (Niebuhr, 253).

Prior to his initial introduction to the ideas of Niebuhr, King "was absolutely convinced of the natural goodness of man and the natural power of human reason" (*Papers* 5:419). Niebuhr, however, challenged the usefulness of moral idealism in struggles for social justice. In line with this thinking, King also appreciated Niebuhr's interpretation of original sin, writing: "His theology is a persistent reminder of the reality of sin on every level of man's existence" (King, 99). King wrote several papers on Niebuhr in the course of his doctoral studies at **Boston University** and determined that Niebuhr's thought was "the necessary corrective of a kind of liberalism that too easily capitulated to modern culture" (*Papers* 2:278).

King wrote to Niebuhr in preparation for his doctoral **dissertation** comparing Paul **Tillich**'s and Henry Nelson Wieman's concepts of God, asking for assistance with his topic. As he rose to national prominence, King continued to draw on Niebuhr's philosophy as a theological basis for nonviolent civil rights protest. He linked Niebuhr's Christian realism to his own ideas of Gandhian **nonviolence**, calling it "a Niebuhrian stratagem of power" (Branch, 87). King inscribed a copy of his 1958 account of the **Montgomery bus boycott**, *Stride Toward Freedom*, to Niebuhr, praising him as a theologian of "great prophetic vision," with "unswerving devotion to the ideals of freedom and justice" (King, November 1958).

King invited Niebuhr to participate in the **Selma to Montgomery March** in 1965, and Niebuhr responded by telegram: "Only a severe stroke prevents me from accepting … I hope there will be a massive demonstration of all the citizens with conscience in favor of the elemental human rights of voting and freedom of assembly" (Niebuhr, 19 March 1965). Two years later, Niebuhr defended King's decision to speak out against the **Vietnam War**, calling him "one of the greatest religious leaders of our time." Niebuhr asserted: "Dr. King has the right and a duty, as both a religious and a civil rights leader, to express his concern in these days about such a major human problem as the Vietnam War" (Ansbro, 261). Of his country's intervention in Vietnam, Niebuhr admitted: "For the first time I fear I am ashamed of our beloved nation" (Fox, 285).

SOURCES

Ansbro, *Martin Luther King, Jr.*, 2000.
Branch, *Parting the Waters*, 1988.
Fox, *Reinhold Niebuhr*, 1985.
King, Inscription to Reinhold Niebuhr, November 1958, CNP.
King, "Pilgrimage to Nonviolence," 13 April 1960, in *Papers* 5:419–425.
King, *Stride Toward Freedom*, 1958.
King, "The Theology of Reinhold Niebuhr," April 1953–June 1954, in *Papers* 2:269–279.
King to Niebuhr, 1 December 1953, in *Papers* 2:222–223.
Niebuhr, *Moral Man and Immoral Society*, 1932.
Niebuhr to King, 19 March 1965, MLKJP-GAMK.

NIXON, EDGAR DANIEL (1899–1987)

Union leader and civil rights advocate E. D. Nixon helped launch the **Montgomery bus boycott**, the event that propelled Martin Luther King, Jr., into the national spotlight. Described by King as "one of the chief voices of the Negro community in the area of civil rights," and "a symbol of the hopes and aspirations of the long oppressed people of the State of Alabama," Nixon worked behind the scenes to launch the **Montgomery Improvement Association** (MIA) and to then organize and sustain the boycott (King, 39).

The son of a Baptist minister and a maid-cook, Nixon was born on 12 July 1899, in Lowndes County, Alabama. Nixon received only 16 months of formal education, but after working his way up from a job in the train station baggage room, he became a Pullman car porter, a job he held until 1964. In 1928 he joined A. Philip **Randolph**'s Brotherhood of Sleeping Car Porters Union, and later helped form its Montgomery branch, acting as its president for many years. Nixon later said of Randolph's impact on him: "Nobody in all my years influenced me or made me feel like A. Philip Randolph did" (Viorst, 22).

On 1 December 1955 Rosa **Parks** was arrested for refusing to give up her bus seat to a white man. Nixon, former head of the Montgomery **National Association for the Advancement of Colored People** (NAACP), felt her arrest was the perfect case to challenge Montgomery's segregated bus system. Nixon recalled: "When Rosa Parks was arrested, I thought 'this is it!' 'Cause she's morally clean, she's reliable, nobody had nothing on her, she had the courage of her convictions" (Millner, "Interview; E. D. Nixon," 546). Nixon then worked with the **Women's Political Council** to convince black residents to support the boycott.

Together with Clifford Durr, a white attorney, Nixon bailed Parks out of jail and quickly began to mobilize Montgomery's black community. Impressed by King's address to the local NAACP chapter several months earlier, Nixon asked him to host a bus-boycott planning meeting at his church on 2 December. After the successful one-day boycott on 5 December, Montgomery's black leaders met again. King was elected to lead the boycott as president of the newly created MIA, and Nixon was elected treasurer. When some participants suggested forming a secret organization, Nixon chastised them, "Am I to tell our people that you are cowards?" (*Papers* 3:4n).

Nixon supplied the MIA with contacts for various labor and civil rights organizations, which provided both financial and political support for the boycott. In 1957 tensions between King and Nixon developed over leadership and decision making in the MIA. Nixon resigned his post as MIA treasurer in 1957, citing resentment at "being treated as a newcomer" (*Papers* 4:217). However, Nixon maintained respect for King. Referring to King's handling of his arrest in Montgomery on 3 September 1958, Nixon applauded King, "Because of your courage in face of known danger I want to commend you for your stand for the people of color all over the world, and [especially] the people in Montgomery. Your action took the fear out of the Negroes and made the white man see himself as he is" (*Papers* 4:492).

Until his death at the age of 87, Nixon continued to work for civil rights, focusing his later years on improving conditions at housing projects and organizing programs for African American children. Nixon received the Walter White Award from the NAACP in 1985, and in 1986, a year before his death, Nixon's home in Montgomery was placed on the Alabama Register of Landmarks and Heritage.

SOURCES

Introduction, in *Papers* 3:4.
King, *Stride Toward Freedom*, 1958.
Steven M. Millner, "Interview; E. D. Nixon," in *The Walking City*, ed. Garrow, 1989.
Nixon to King, 3 June 1957, in *Papers* 4:217–218.
Nixon to King, 9 September 1958, in *Papers* 4:492.
Raines, *My Soul Is Rested*, 1983.
Viorst, *Fire in the Streets*, 1979.

NIXON, RICHARD MILHOUS (1913–1994)

Richard M. Nixon had a complicated relationship with Martin Luther King, Jr., and the African American freedom struggle. Although King later questioned Nixon's sincerity, while Nixon served as vice president in the 1950s, King commented that with "persons like you occupying such important positions in our nation I am sure that we will soon emerge from the bleak and desolate midnight of man's inhumanity to man" (*Papers* 4:264).

Born 9 January 1913 in Yorba Linda, California, Nixon was the second son of Frank and Hannah Nixon. He was raised in the small town of Whittier, California, where his father owned a gas station and general store. Nixon graduated second in his class from Whittier College in 1934 and received a scholarship to attend Duke University's law school, graduating third in his class in 1937. Nixon returned to Whittier to practice law for several years before moving to Washington, D.C., to work for the tire rationing section of the Office of Price Administration during World War II. In August of 1942 Nixon was commissioned to the Navy and rose to the rank of lieutenant commander while serving in the South Pacific.

Nixon's political career began in 1946, when he was elected to the U.S. House of Representatives for California's 12th congressional district. He gained national attention as a member of the House Un-American Activities Committee and for his role in the prosecution of Alger Hiss, a former employee of the Department of State and an alleged Communist agent. In 1950 Nixon was elected to the U.S. Senate and was later selected as the Republican vice-presidential running mate for Dwight D. **Eisenhower**.

The tone of the relationship between King and Nixon varied over the years. Early on, King had developed an "initial bias" against Nixon because of his tendency to vote with the more conservative right wing of the Republican Party (*Papers* 4:482). This shifted, however, when the two met in March 1957 at ceremonies in **Ghana** celebrating that nation's independence. Nixon later invited King to Washington, D.C., for a meeting on 13 June 1957. This meeting, described by Bayard **Rustin** as a "summit conference," marked national recognition of King's role in the civil rights movement (Rustin, 13 June 1957). Seeking support for a voter registration initiative in the South, King appealed to Nixon to urge Republicans in Congress to pass a pending civil rights bill and to visit the South to express support for civil rights. Optimistic about Nixon's commitment to improving race relations in the United States, King told Nixon, "How deeply grateful all people of goodwill are to you for your assiduous labor and dauntless courage in seeking to make the civil rights bill a reality" (*Papers* 4:264). King was also skeptical, telling a Nixon biographer, "If Richard Nixon is not sincere, he is the most dangerous man in America" (*Papers* 4:483).

Many black leaders, including Martin Luther **King**, Sr., and Jackie **Robinson**, initially supported Nixon's 1960 bid for the presidency. Blacks believed Nixon to be more committed to civil rights reform than President Eisenhower had been, but the attitudes of black voters shifted during the final days of the 1960 presidential campaign. In October 1960 King was sentenced to four months in jail for violating his probation after participating in an Atlanta **sit-in**. After encouragement from Harris Wofford and other advisors, Nixon's opponent, John F. **Kennedy**, phoned Coretta Scott **King** to convey his sympathy. King expressed disappointment that, despite his previously warm relationship with Nixon, "When this moment came, it was like he had never heard of me." King believed Nixon's inaction made him appear as "a moral coward and one who was really unwilling to take a courageous step and take a risk" (King, 9 March 1964). Kennedy's phone call and his campaign's discreet publicity promoting his role in releasing King from jail gained him the support of many black voters, and he defeated Nixon by less than one percent of the popular vote.

Nixon ran an unsuccessful campaign for California governor in 1962, and later narrowly won the 1968 presidential election against Democrat Hubert Humphrey and third-party candidate George **Wallace**. He was reelected in a landslide victory over Democratic opponent Senator George McGovern in 1972. During his terms in office Nixon reversed some of the social and economic welfare policies of predecessor Lyndon B. **Johnson**, vetoing new health, education, and welfare legislation. Seeking southern support for the Republican Party, Nixon supported anti-busing legislation and favored "law and order" policies that were widely seen as directed against black militancy.

In 1974, after his involvement in the Watergate scandal, Nixon became the only U.S. president to ever resign. He continued to comment on foreign affairs and wrote several books before his death in New York City on 22 April 1994.

SOURCES

Ambrose, *Nixon*, 1987.
Introduction, in *Papers* 4:8; 15–17.
Introduction, in *Papers* 5:36–40.
King, Interview by Berl Bernhard, 9 March 1964, JFKOH-MWalK.
King, Statement on Meeting with Richard M. Nixon, 13 June 1957, in *Papers* 4:222–223.
King to Mazo, 2 September 1958, in *Papers* 4:481–483.
King to Nixon, 30 August 1957, in *Papers* 4:262–264.
Rustin to King, 13 June 1957, MLKP-MBU.

NKRUMAH, KWAME (1909–1972)

The first African-born Prime Minister of Ghana, Kwame Nkrumah was a prominent Pan-African organizer whose radical vision and bold leadership helped lead Ghana to independence in 1957. Nkrumah served as an inspiration to Martin Luther King, who often looked to Nkrumah's leadership as an example of nonviolent activism. The evolution of Nkrumah's power in Ghana, however, complicated relations between the two men. Just days after King's **assassination**, Nkrumah expressed disagreement with King's views on **nonviolence**.

Nkrumah was born on 21 September 1909, in the British colony of Nkroful, on the Gold Coast. Although raised in a small fishing village, Nkrumah was educated in the United States. He received both his Bachelor of Arts (1939) and Bachelor of Theology (1942) from Lincoln University and continued his education at the University of Pennsylvania, where he received a Masters of Philosophy and a Masters of Education (1942, 1943). While in college, Nkrumah became increasingly active in the Pan-African movement, the African Students Association of America, and the West African Students' Union. In 1945 Nkrumah played a central role in organizing the Fifth Pan-Africanist Congress.

In 1947 Nkrumah's activism attracted the attention of Ghanaian politician J. B. Danquah, who hired Nkrumah to serve as general secretary of the United Gold Coast Convention, an organization pursuing independence for the British colony. However, ideological differences between the two men led Nkrumah to found his own party, the Convention People's Party (CPP), in 1949. Nkrumah and the CPP sought self-government through the nonviolent strategy of "positive action." Much like King's nonviolent strategies, positive action employed the tactics of protest and strike against colonial administration. In 1951 Nkrumah and the CPP received a decisive majority of votes in Ghana's first general elections, and on 22 March 1952, Nkrumah became the first prime minister of the Gold Coast. It would be five more years before full independence was realized, and the Gold Coast became the self-governed nation of Ghana.

Martin and Coretta **King** attended Ghana's independence ceremony on 6 March 1957, at the invitation of Nkrumah. King was impressed by Nkrumah's leadership and keenly aware of the parallels between Ghanaian independence and the American civil rights movement. While in Ghana, the Kings shared a private meal with Nkrumah, discussing nonviolence and Nkrumah's impressions of the United States. After returning to the United States, King explained the lessons of Nkrumah and the Ghanaian struggle in a series of speeches and sermons. In a 24 April speech, King related a message from Nkrumah and his finance minister: "'Our sympathies are with America and its allies. But we will make it clear thru the United Nations and other diplomatic channels that beautiful words and extensive hand outs cannot be substitutes for the simple responsibility of treating our colored brothers in America as first-class human beings.' So if we are to be a first-class nation, we cannot have second-class citizens" (King, 24 April 1957).

King lauded Nkrumah's leadership through nonviolent positive action. Both men were inspired by the life and teachings of **Gandhi**. In a sermon entitled "The Birth of a New Nation," King said of Ghana's newfound independence, "It reminds us of the fact that a nation or a people can break loose from oppression without violence" (*Papers* 4:162).

As early as 1962 Prime Minister Nkrumah faced the challenges of nation building in the legacy of colonialism. Mounting economic troubles led to increased discontentment with Nkrumah, and Ashanti nationalism further threatened his presidency. King struggled to understand the growing criticism of Nkrumah's leadership, stating: "I'm sure President Nkrumah has made some mistakes. On the other hand I think we would have to see the problems that he has confronted. It is not an easy thing to lift a nation from a tribal tradition into a [democracy] first without having problems" (King, 19 July 1962). In 1966 Nkrumah was removed from power in a coup led by the Ghanaian military and police forces.

In response to King's assassination in 1968, Nkrumah wrote: "Even though I don't agree with [King] on some of his non-violence views, I mourn for him. The final solution of all this will come when Africa is politically united. Yesterday it was Malcolm X. Today Luther King. Tomorrow, fire all over the United States" (Nkrumah, 231). Nkrumah died of cancer in April 1972 while in exile in Conakry, Guinea.

SOURCES
King, Address at the National Press Club, 19 July 1962, MLKJP-GAMK.
King, "The Birth of a New Nation," 7 April 1957, in *Papers* 4:155–167.
King, This Is a Great Time to Be Alive, 24 April 1957, MLKJP-GAMK.
Nkrumah, *Kwame Nkrumah*, 1990.

NOBEL PEACE PRIZE (1964)

On the morning of 14 October 1964, Martin Luther King, sleeping in an Atlanta hospital room after checking in for a rest, was awakened by a phone call from his wife, Coretta Scott **King**, telling him that he had been awarded the Nobel Prize for Peace. Although many in the United States and abroad praised the selection, segregationist

King displays his Nobel Peace Prize medal in Oslo, Norway, 10 December 1964. © AP / Wide World Photos.

Eugene "Bull" **Connor** called it "scraping the bottom of the barrel" ("Cheers and Scorn"). Presenting the award to King in Oslo, Norway, that December, the chairman of the Nobel Committee praised him for being "the first person in the Western world to have shown us that a struggle can be waged without violence. He is the first to make the message of brotherly love a reality in the course of his struggle, and he has brought this message to all men, to all nations and races" (Jahn, "Presentation," 332).

The Nobel Prize was endowed in 1895 by Alfred Nobel, a Swedish industrialist and the inventor of dynamite. Annual awards in physics, chemistry, medicine, literature, and peace began in 1901. The winner of the Peace Prize is selected by a committee appointed by the Norwegian Parliament from nominations submitted by past winners and other select persons. King was nominated by the **American Friends Service Committee**, which had received the prize in 1947.

King departed for Oslo on 4 December 1964, stopping in London for three days to preach at St. Paul's Cathedral and meet with leaders of the peace community. He was accompanied on his trip by a group of **Southern Christian Leadership Conference** (SCLC) staff and members of his family. King accepted the prize on 10 December, in the name of the thousands of people in the civil rights movement who constituted what he termed a "mighty army of love" (King, "Mighty Army of Love"). He called the award, "a profound recognition that nonviolence is the answer to the crucial political and moral questions of our time: the need for man to overcome oppression and violence without resorting to violence and oppression," and discussed ways to overcome the evils of racial injustice, poverty, and war (King, "Address," 106).

Recognizing that SCLC played only one part in the movement, King shared the $54,000 monetary prize with leading civil rights groups, giving $25,000 to the **Gandhi Society for Human Rights**, $12,000 to SCLC, and splitting the remainder among the **Congress of Racial Equality**, the **National Association for the Advancement of Colored People** (NAACP), the NAACP Legal Defense Fund, the **National Council of Negro Women**, the **National Urban League**, and the **Student Nonviolent Coordinating Committee**.

King was feted at events in Europe and at home, where he praised the volunteers in the movement who would never be publicly recognized but who were critical to the success of the nonviolent struggle. King described the award as a reminder to civil rights workers that "the tide of world opinion is in our favor," and pledged to "work even harder to make peace and brotherhood a reality" (King, "Mighty Army of Love"; King, 27 January 1965). When King decided to speak out against the **Vietnam War** in April 1967, he reflected on this promise, calling the prize a "commission," that required him to go "beyond national allegiances" to speak out for peace (King, "Beyond Vietnam," 145).

SOURCES

"Cheers and Scorn for Nobel Award," *New York Times*, 15 October 1964.

Gunnar Jahn, "Presentation," in *Nobel Lectures*, ed. Haberman, vol. 3, 1972.

King, "Acceptance Address for the Nobel Peace Prize," in *A Call to Conscience*, ed. Carson and Shepard, 2001.

King, "Beyond Vietnam," in *A Call to Conscience*, ed. Carson and Shepard, 2001.

King, "Mighty Army of Love," *New York Amsterdam News*, 7 November 1964.

King, "The Struggle for Racial Justice," 27 January 1965, NF-GEU.

NONVIOLENCE

As a theologian, Martin Luther King reflected often on his understanding of nonviolence. He described his own "pilgrimage to nonviolence" in his first book, **Stride Toward Freedom**, and in subsequent books and articles. "True pacifism," or "nonviolent resistance," King wrote, is "a courageous confrontation of evil by the power of love" (King, *Stride*, 80). Both "morally and practically" committed to nonviolence, King believed that "the Christian doctrine of love operating through the Gandhian method of nonviolence was one of the most potent weapons available to oppressed people in their struggle for freedom" (King, *Stride*, 79; *Papers* 5:422).

King was first introduced to the concept of nonviolence when he read Henry David Thoreau's *Essay on Civil Disobedience* as a freshman at **Morehouse College**. Having grown up in Atlanta and witnessed segregation and racism every day, King was "fascinated by the idea of refusing to cooperate with an evil system" (King, *Stride*, 73).

In 1950, as a student at **Crozer Theological Seminary**, King heard a talk by Dr. Mordecai **Johnson**, president of Howard University. Dr. Johnson, who had recently traveled to India, spoke about the life and teachings of Mohandas K. **Gandhi**. Gandhi, King later wrote, was the first person to transform Christian love into a powerful force for social change. Gandhi's stress on love and nonviolence gave King "the method for social reform that I had been seeking" (King, *Stride*, 79).

While intellectually committed to nonviolence, King did not experience the power of nonviolent direct action first-hand until the start of the **Montgomery bus boycott** in 1955. During the boycott, King personally enacted Gandhian principles. With guidance from black pacifist Bayard **Rustin** and Glenn **Smiley** of the **Fellowship of Reconciliation**, King eventually decided not to use armed bodyguards despite threats on his life, and reacted to violent experiences, such as the bombing of his home, with compassion. Through the practical experience of leading nonviolent protest, King came to understand how nonviolence could become a way of life, applicable to all situations. King called the principle of nonviolent resistance the "guiding light of our movement. Christ furnished the spirit and motivation while Gandhi furnished the method" (*Papers* 5:423).

King's notion of nonviolence had six key principles. First, one can resist evil without resorting to violence. Second, nonviolence seeks to win the "friendship and understanding" of the opponent, not to humiliate him (King, *Stride*, 84). Third, evil itself, not the people committing evil acts, should be opposed. Fourth, those committed to nonviolence must be willing to suffer without retaliation as suffering itself can be redemptive. Fifth, nonviolent resistance avoids "external physical violence" and "internal violence of spirit" as well: "The nonviolent resister not only refuses to shoot his opponent but he also refuses to hate him" (King, *Stride*, 85). The resister should be motivated by love in the sense of the Greek word *agape*, which means "understanding," or "redeeming good will for all men" (King, *Stride*, 86). The sixth principle is that the nonviolent resister must have a "deep faith in the future," stemming from the conviction that "The universe is on the side of justice" (King, *Stride*, 88).

During the years after the bus boycott, King grew increasingly committed to nonviolence. An **India trip** in 1959 helped him connect more intimately with Gandhi's legacy. King began to advocate nonviolence not just in a national sphere, but internationally as well: "the potential destructiveness of modern weapons" convinced King that "the choice today is no longer between violence and nonviolence. It is either nonviolence or nonexistence" (*Papers* 5:424).

After **Black Power** advocates such as Stokely **Carmichael** began to reject nonviolence, King lamented that some African Americans had lost hope, and reaffirmed his own commitment to nonviolence: "Occasionally in life one develops a conviction so precious and meaningful that he will stand on it till the end. This is what I have found in nonviolence" (King, *Where*, 63–64). He wrote in his 1967 book, **Where Do We Go from Here: Chaos or Community?**: "We maintained the hope while transforming the hate of traditional revolutions into positive nonviolent power. As long as the hope was fulfilled there was little questioning of nonviolence. But when the hopes were blasted, when people came to see that in spite of progress their conditions were still insufferable … despair began to set in" (King, *Where*, 45). Arguing that violent revolution was impractical in the context of a multiracial society, he concluded: "Darkness cannot drive out darkness: only light can do that. Hate cannot drive out hate: only love can do that. The beauty of nonviolence is that in its own way and in its own time it seeks to break the chain reaction of evil" (King, *Where*, 62–63).

SOURCES
King, "Pilgrimage to Nonviolence," in *Papers* 5:419–425.
King, *Stride Toward Freedom*, 1958.
King, *Where Do We Go from Here*, 1967.

O'DELL, HUNTER PITTS "JACK" (1923–)

A valued organizer and fundraiser who was unapologetic about his early Communist associations, Hunter Pitts "Jack" O'Dell ranks among the most controversial figures of the civil rights movement. His role in the **Southern Christian Leadership Conference** (SCLC) was used by detractors as ammunition against both Martin Luther King, Jr., and the civil rights movement at large. As O'Dell wrote to King upon his departure from SCLC: "Not the least formidable of the obstacles blocking the path to Freedom is the anti-Communist hysteria in our country which is deliberately kept alive by the defenders of the status-quo as a barrier to rational thinking on important social questions" (O'Dell, 12 July 1963).

Born in Detroit, Michigan, on 11 August 1923, O'Dell was raised there by his grandfather, a janitor at a public library, and his grandmother. After graduating from public school, he attended Xavier University in New Orleans from 1941 until 1943. During World War II, he served in the Merchant Marines, and worked as a merchant seaman after the war's end. He was active in the National Maritime Union and during the 1948 presidential election was a leader of "Seamen for Wallace," a group campaigning for Progressive Party presidential candidate Henry Wallace. In 1950 he was forced out of the union and maritime work during an anti-Communist purge. In the late 1950s O'Dell began working for a black insurance company, first in Birmingham and then in Montgomery, where he heard King preach at **Dexter Avenue Baptist Church**. He resigned from the firm after being called to testify before the House Un-American Activities Committee (HUAC) and moved to New York for graduate studies at the New York University School of Management, earning a certificate in 1960. While there, he assisted Bayard **Rustin** and A. Philip **Randolph** in organizing the April 1959 **Youth March for Integrated Schools**, which King addressed.

O'Dell first began work with SCLC as a volunteer in March 1960, and was hired by King in 1961 to manage a mass-mail funding office for SCLC in New York, where he worked closely with King advisor Stanley **Levison**. By January 1962, O'Dell was asked to serve as SCLC's director of voter registration in seven southern states. He worked in this capacity, along with the Citizenship Education Program, until 1963.

In March 1962 Attorney General Robert F. **Kennedy** authorized the **Federal Bureau of Investigation** to begin surveillance of Levison and King, on the assumption that Levison was influenced by the Communist Party. Ten months later, on 26 October 1962, the *New Orleans Times-Picayune* published a story denouncing O'Dell as a Communist who had "infiltrated to the top administrative post" in SCLC and had been carrying out "Communist Party assignments" (Branch, 675). In the wake of this attack, King drafted a letter stating that SCLC was "on guard against any such infiltration," but acknowledging that such accusations and investigations by HUAC were "a means of [harassing] Negroes and whites merely because of their belief in integration" (King, November 1962). Pending an SCLC investigation into the charges, O'Dell submitted a temporary letter of resignation. However, he continued to work with SCLC, attending a key planning session for the upcoming **Birmingham Campaign** at the CEP's training center in Dorchester, Georgia, in early 1963.

On 22 June 1963, King and other civil rights leaders met with President John F. **Kennedy** at the White House. Prior to the meeting King was taken aside by Burke **Marshall**, Robert Kennedy, and President Kennedy, in turn. All three told him that keeping Levison and O'Dell on staff meant opening SCLC to the influence of **communism**, and told King to cut ties with the two men. Though he was not willing to part company with Levison, his closest advisor, two weeks later King wrote to O'Dell asking him to resign from SCLC permanently. King explained that "any allusion to the left brings forth an emotional response which would seem to indicate that SCLC and the Southern Freedom Movement are Communist inspired" (King, 3 July 1963). King described O'Dell's departure as "a significant sacrifice commensurate with the sufferings in jail and through loss of jobs under racist intimidation" (King, 3 July 1963).

O'Dell responded to King's request on 12 July 1963, submitting his final resignation and sharing that his work with SCLC had been "a rewarding experience which I shall always cherish." He expressed hope that "everything that is decent and civilized in our country will inevitably be swept into the orbit of the ever-mounting Negro Freedom Movement as it emerges from the economic and political darkness of segregation" (O'Dell, 12 July 1963). O'Dell went on to work as an associate editor of the journal *Freedomways* magazine for 23 years and served on the National Coordinating Committee to End the War in Vietnam from 1965 until 1972.

SOURCES

Branch, *Parting the Waters*, 1988.

King, Address at the Youth March for Integrated Schools on 18 April 1959, in *Papers* 5:186–188.

King, "Letter to Answer Questions of Communist Infiltration," November 1962, SCLCR-GAMK.

King to O'Dell, 18 January 1963, MLKJP-GAMK.

King to O'Dell, 3 July 1963, MLKJP-GAMK.

O'Dell, Interview by King Papers Project staff, 10 May 2007.

O'Dell to King, 12 July 1963, MLKJP-GAMK.

OPERATION BREADBASKET (1962–1972)

In 1962 the **Southern Christian Leadership Conference** (SCLC) launched Operation Breadbasket in Atlanta. According to King, "The fundamental premise of Breadbasket is a simple one. Negroes need not patronize a business which denies them jobs, or advancement [or] plain courtesy" (King, 11 July 1967). "Many retail businesses and consumer-goods industries," King explained, "deplete the ghetto by selling to Negroes without returning to the community any of the profits through fair hiring practices" (King, January 1967).

Operation Breadbasket was modeled after a selective patronage program developed by Leon Sullivan in Philadelphia, Pennsylvania. King brought Sullivan to Atlanta in October 1962 to meet with local ministers about replicating the program. Breadbasket used the persuasive power of black ministers and the organizing strength of the churches to create economic opportunities in black communities. The group obtained employment statistics for industries selling their products in black communities and, if these statistics demonstrated that blacks were underemployed or restricted to menial positions, ministers from Operation Breadbasket asked the company to "negotiate a more equitable employment practice" (King, January 1967). If the company refused, clergy encouraged their parishioners to boycott selected products and picket businesses selling those products. By 1967 Atlanta's Breadbasket had negotiated jobs bringing a total of $25 million a year in new income to the black community.

Operation Breadbasket expanded to Chicago in 1966 as part of SCLC's **Chicago Campaign**. King called it SCLC's "most spectacularly successful program" in Chicago (King, January 1967). Under the leadership of Chicago Theological Seminary student Jesse **Jackson**, Breadbasket targeted five businesses in the dairy industry. While three companies negotiated to add black jobs immediately, two complied only after boycotts. Chicago Breadbasket went on to target Pepsi and Coca-Cola bottlers, and then supermarket chains, winning 2,000 new jobs worth $15 million a year in new income to the black community in the first 15 months of its operation. Going beyond jobs and patronage for black-owned businesses, Chicago-based Operation Breadbasket became a cultural event, focused around weekly Saturday workshops, which drew thousands to hear Jackson preach in person and on the radio.

Jackson became the national director of Operation Breadbasket's programs in 1967. After King's **assassination** in 1968, Jackson continued to lead the program; however, tensions emerged between Jackson and SCLC's new leader, Ralph **Abernathy**, over fundraising and the location of Breadbasket's national headquarters. Abernathy wanted Jackson to move Breadbasket from Chicago to Atlanta in early 1971, but Jackson refused and resigned from SCLC in December. A week later he launched his own economic empowerment organization called Operation PUSH (People United to Save Humanity). Breadbasket continued through the next year, experiencing several leadership changes before its eventual demise.

SOURCES

Garrow, *Chicago 1966*, 1989.
King, "One Year Later in Chicago," January 1967, SCLCR-GAMK.
King, Press conference, 11 July 1967, MLKJP-GAMK.

PARKS, ROSA (1913–2005)

On 1 December 1955 local **National Association for the Advancement of Colored People** (NAACP) leader Rosa Parks was arrested for refusing to give up her seat to a white passenger on a city bus in Montgomery, Alabama. This single act of nonviolent resistance helped spark the **Montgomery bus boycott**, a 13-month struggle to desegregate the city's buses. Under the leadership of Martin Luther King, Jr., the boycott resulted in the enforcement of a U.S. Supreme Court ruling that public bus segregation is unconstitutional, and catapulted both King and Parks into the national spotlight.

Born in Tuskegee, Alabama, on 4 February 1913, Rosa Louise McCauley Parks grew up in Montgomery and was educated at the laboratory school of Alabama State College. In 1932 she married Raymond Parks, a barber and member of the NAACP. At that time, Raymond Parks was active in the Scottsboro case. In 1943 Rosa Parks joined the local chapter of the NAACP and was elected secretary. Two years later, she registered to vote, after twice being denied.

By 1949 Parks was advisor to the local NAACP Youth Council. Under her guidance, youth members challenged the Jim Crow system by checking books out of whites-only libraries. The summer before Parks' arrest, Virginia **Durr** arranged for Parks to travel to Tennessee's **Highlander Folk School** to attend a workshop entitled "Racial Desegregation: Implementing the Supreme Court Decision." It was there that Parks received encouragement from fellow participant Septima **Clark**, who later joined Highlander's staff in mid-1956.

When Parks was arrested on 1 December 1955, she was not the first African American to defy Montgomery's bus segregation law. Nine months earlier, 15-year-old Claudette Colvin had been arrested for refusing to give up her seat to a white passenger. In October 1955, 18-year-old Mary Louise Smith had been arrested under similar circumstances, but both cases failed to stir Montgomery's black leadership to help launch a mass protest. King wrote of Parks' unique local stature in his memoir, ***Stride Toward Freedom***, where he talked of how her character and dedication made her widely respected in the African American community.

Although many news accounts depicted Parks as a tired seamstress, Parks explained the deep roots of her act of resistance in her autobiography: "I was not tired

On 19 March 1956, Rosa Parks and E. D. Nixon climb the Montgomery County Courthouse steps to attend the beginning of King's trial during the Montgomery bus boycott. © AP / Wide World Photos.

physically, or no more tired than I usually was at the end of a working day. I was not old, although some people have an image of me as being old then. I was forty-two. No, the only tired I was, was tired of giving in" (Parks, 116).

Parks inspired tens of thousands of black citizens to boycott the Montgomery city buses for over a year. During that period she served as a dispatcher to coordinate rides for protesters and was indicted, along with King and over 80 others, for participation in the boycott. Parks also made appearances in churches and other organizations, including some in the North, to raise funds and publicize the **Montgomery Improvement Association** (MIA).

Parks continued to face harassment following the boycott's successful conclusion and decided to move to Detroit to seek better employment opportunities. Shortly before her departure, the MIA declared 5 August 1957 "Rosa Parks Day." A celebration was held at Mt. Zion AME Zion Church, and $800 was presented to Parks. Despite the fanfare, Parks found it hard to believe that her actions launched an entire movement: "I had no idea when I refused to give up my seat on that Montgomery bus that my small action would help put an end to the segregation laws in the South" (Parks, 2).

In 1964 John Conyers, an African American lawyer, received Parks' endorsement of his campaign to represent Detroit in the U.S. House of Representatives. After he won, he hired Parks as an office assistant. She remained with him until her retirement in 1988.

In 1987 she founded the Rosa and Raymond Parks Institute for Self-Development, which provides learning and leadership opportunities for youth and seniors. She was an active supporter of civil rights causes in her elder years. She died in October 2005, at the age of 92.

SOURCES

Introduction, in *Papers* 3:3; 5.
King, *Stride Toward Freedom*, 1958.
Parks, *Rosa Parks*, 1992.
Robinson, *Montgomery Bus Boycott*, 1987.

PATTERSON, JOHN MALCOLM (1921–)

Patterson's gubernatorial term in Alabama was a turbulent one due to his enforcement of state-sponsored segregation and the increase of civil rights activity in Alabama. During his tenure as governor the student **sit-in** movement was taking hold, and Martin Luther King was indicted for perjury for his 1956 and 1958 Alabama income tax returns (see *State of Alabama v. M. L. King, Jr.*). King felt that the charges against him were an "attempt on the part of the state of Alabama to harass me for the role that I have played in the civil rights struggle" (*Papers* 5:371).

Patterson, born in Goldville, Alabama, received his law degree from the University of Alabama in 1949. In 1954 he was elected attorney general of Alabama, and, in reaction to the **Montgomery bus boycott**, in 1956 he successfully barred the **National Association for the Advancement of Colored People** (NAACP) from participating in activities in the state. In conjunction with the case, Patterson served King with a subpoena requiring him to testify regarding the NAACP's policies toward fundraising, collecting dues, and soliciting new members.

After his indictment for perjury in 1960, King's supporters took out a full-page advertisement in the *New York Times* entitled "Heed Their Rising Voices," requesting funds to support King's defense, support student protesters, and the voting rights struggle. The fundraising appeal, however, led to unexpected problems when Patterson and other Alabama officials filed libel suits against the *Times*, King, and four Alabama ministers whose names were used in the advertisement, charging that it contained defamatory statements regarding the student protests. Patterson wrote King in May 1960, demanding that King publish a retraction to the fundraising appeal. The four Alabama ministers became part of the landmark free speech case *New York Times Co. v. Sullivan*, and Patterson dropped his case against King after the U.S. Supreme Court ruled in their favor.

In addition to the lawsuits, the student sit-ins in Montgomery attracted additional publicity in 1960, when Patterson ordered the president of Alabama State College, H. Councill **Trenholm**, to expel students and faculty participating in movement activities. King wrote Patterson expressing his disappointment at the anticipated "purge" of faculty, and affirming the teachers' "academic freedom and the right of citizenship" (*Papers* 5:425; 426). After Patterson threatened to fire Trenholm, the beleaguered college president fired history professor L. D. **Reddick**; Jo Ann **Robinson** and Mary Fair Burks resigned at the close of the spring semester.

Violent attacks against freedom riders in Anniston and Birmingham, Alabama, in 1961 drew media attention again, and the John F. **Kennedy** administration was forced to react. After several attempts to reach Patterson by phone to discuss the attacks on the freedom riders, U.S. Attorney General Robert **Kennedy** sent Assistant Attorney General John Seigenthaler to speak with Patterson. At the conclusion of the meeting, Patterson reluctantly agreed to use state resources to protect the safety of the protesters. Within days of this incident, King hosted a mass meeting at Ralph **Abernathy**'s First Baptist Church in Montgomery to support the freedom riders. As the mass meeting progressed, a mob of whites throwing rocks, bricks, and Molotov cocktails surrounded the church, making it impossible for those in the mass meeting to leave. During the meeting, King took the podium and he placed much of the blame on Patterson, whose "consistent preaching of defiance of the law, his vitriolic public pronouncements, and his irresponsible actions created the atmosphere in which violence could thrive" (King, 21 May 1961). The Kennedy administration used federal marshals to protect the church until they were eventually replaced by Alabama National Guard troops under the governor's control. King and the other protesters remained in the church until the mob was dispersed the following morning.

After Patterson's term as governor ended in 1963 he practiced law in Montgomery. He was defeated in a 1966 bid for governor by Lurleen Wallace, wife of George **Wallace**, Patterson's 1963 successor as Alabama governor and a staunch segregationist. In 1972 he ran unsuccessfully for Chief Justice of the State Supreme Court but was appointed to the State Court of Criminal Appeals in 1984, where he remained until his retirement in 1997.

SOURCES

Arsenault, *Freedom Riders*, 2006.

Committee to Defend Martin Luther King and the Struggle for Freedom in the South, "Heed Their Rising Voices," in *Papers* 5:382.

Introduction, in *Papers* 5:25; 26.

King, Interview on Arrest following Indictment by Grand Jury of Montgomery County, 17 February 1960, in *Papers* 5:370–372.

King, Statement at Mass Meeting Supporting Freedom Rider, 21 May 1961, MLKJP-GAMK.

King to Fred D. Gray, 14 December 1960, in *Papers* 5:580.

King to Patrick Murphy Malin, Roy Wilkins, and Carl J. Megel, 16 June 1960, in *Papers* 5:471–472.

King to Patterson, 14 April 1960, in *Papers* 5:425–426.

King to Patterson, 9 August 1960, in *Papers* 5:495–496.

Patterson, Interview by King Papers Project staff, 18 July 2001.

Patterson to King, 12 July 1956, in *Papers* 3:319–320.

Patterson to King, 9 May 1960, in *Papers* 5:456–458.

PECK, JAMES (1914–1993)

A radical pacifist, trade union proponent, and civil rights activist, James Peck wrote the introduction to a **Congress of Racial Equality** (CORE) reprint of Martin Luther King's article, "Our Struggle: The Story of Montgomery," which originally appeared in *Liberation*. "By encouraging and supporting actions such as that in Montgomery," Peck informed readers, "we who adhere to the principles of nonviolence hope to hasten complete abolition of segregation within our social system" (King, "Our Struggle," 1957).

The son of a wealthy clothier, Peck was born in New York City and briefly attended Harvard University before becoming a full-time activist. Peck was interned for 28 months during World War II as a conscientious objector, and in 1947 he participated in CORE's Journey of Reconciliation. Thereafter, he worked with the War Resisters League and CORE, editing the newsletter *CORElator* for 17 years.

During the **Montgomery bus boycott**, Peck helped the **Montgomery Improvement Association** raise funds by sending the group matchbooks bearing slogans. In 1960 King wrote the introduction to Peck's pamphlet, "Cracking the Color Line: Non-Violent Direct Action Methods of Eliminating Racial Discrimination." In the introduction King praised CORE for using "brains and imagination as well as good-will, self-discipline, and persistence" (*Papers* 5:349).

Peck was the only participant in the original Journey of Reconciliation to join the **Freedom Rides** in 1961. When the bus he was riding arrived in Birmingham, Alabama, he was knocked unconscious and suffered a gash that required 53 stitches to close. In February 1962 Peck sent King a copy of his memoir *Freedom Ride*, informing King that the book's chapter on Montgomery quoted "at length" from King's *Liberation* article (Peck, 19 February 1962).

Although he was ousted from CORE in 1966 when that group adopted **Black Power** policies and abandoned its previous interracialism, Peck continued to be active in the movement to end the **Vietnam War**. He expressed his continuing admiration for King in a June 1966 letter to the **Southern Christian Leadership Conference** leader: "Despite the increasing clamor for 'black power' and 'self-defense,' you adhere to the principles of equality and nonviolence" (Peck, 27 June 1966).

Sources

King, Introduction to *Cracking the Color Line: Non-Violent Direct Action Methods of Eliminating Racial Discrimination*, 1960, in *Papers* 5:349.
King, "Our Struggle," *Liberation* 1 (April 1956): 3–6.
King, "Our Struggle: The Story of Montgomery" (New York: CORE, 1957).
Peck, *Freedom Ride*, 1962.
Peck to King, 19 February 1962, MLKJP-GAMK.
Peck to King, 27 June 1966, MLKJP-GAMK.

PERSONALISM

Central to King's approach to preaching and religion was the concept of a personal and knowable God. King described God in his sermon, "Living Under the Tensions of Modern Life," as "a personal God, who's concerned about us, who is our Father, who is our Redeemer. And this sense of religion and of this divine companionship says to us ... that we are not lost in a universe fighting for goodness and for justice and love all by ourselves" (*Papers* 6:268). King's belief in God as a higher being invested with a personality had its foundation in the theological school of personalism, which, according to King, represented the "theory that the clue to the meaning of ultimate reality is found in personality" (King, 100).

King's personalism developed and matured during his doctoral work at **Boston University** with Edgar **Brightman** and L. Harold **DeWolf**, two proponents of personalist theory. In his **dissertation** King firmly rejected the notion of an abstract God, writing, "The religious man has always recognized two fundamental religious values. One is fellowship with God, the other is trust in his goodness. Both of these imply the personality of God" (*Papers* 2:512). King retreated from any notion that God was, as theologian Karl **Barth** described, "'wholly other.' God is not a process projected somewhere [in] the lofty blue. God is not a divine hermit hiding himself in a cosmic cave.... God is forever present with us" (*Papers* 6:97). To King, God was a personality who could be encountered, comprehensible to any individual and present throughout the universe. King scorned Barth's "disdain for the very use of the word *experience* in a religious context," and contended that "the very idea of God is an outgrowth of experience" (*Papers* 1:231; 233; 234).

King preached that the knowable God maintained a personal interest in each human soul and was most discernable through personal experience and biblical stories of Jesus' life. In an April 1960 *Christian Century* article on his "personal trials," King referred to his stabbing by Izola **Curry** and persistent death threats, writing: "The suffering and agonizing moments through which I have passed over the last few years have also drawn me closer to God. More than ever before I am convinced of the reality of a personal God" (King, "Suffering and Faith").

According to King, Jesus' example in the Bible provided Christians with a personal life path: "God has set us a plan for the building of the soul: the life of Christ as it is revealed in the New Testament" (*Papers* 6:85). In a 1952 Christmas sermon King addressed "the Christlikeness of God," and asserted that Jesus "brought God nearer to earth" (*Papers* 6:129).

Reflecting on the impact that personalism had on his ministry and life, King maintained that his acceptance of personalist theology gave him "metaphysical and philosophical grounding for the idea of a personal God, and it gave me a metaphysical basis for the dignity and worth of all human personality" (King, 100).

Sources

Introduction, in *Papers* 2:1–37.
Introduction, in *Papers* 6:8–9.
King, "After Christmas, What?" 28 December 1952, in *Papers* 6:128–129.
King, "A Comparison of the Conceptions of God in the Thinking of Paul Tillich and Henry Nelson Wieman," 15 April 1955, in *Papers* 2:339–544.
King, "Living Under the Tensions of Modern Life," Sermon delivered at Dexter Avenue Baptist Church, September 1956, in *Papers* 6:262–270.
King, "Mastering Our Evil Selves" / "Mastering Ourselves," 5 June 1949, in *Papers* 6:94–97.
King, "The Place of Reason and Experience in Finding God," in *Papers* 1:230–236.
King, Sermon Conclusions, 30 November 1948–16 February 1949, in *Papers* 6:85.
King, *Stride Toward Freedom*, 1958.
King, "Suffering and Faith," *Christian Century* 77 (27 April 1960): 510.

PNBC. *See* Progressive National Baptist Convention.

POOR PEOPLE'S CAMPAIGN (1967–1968)

Martin Luther King announced the Poor People's Campaign at a staff retreat for the **Southern Christian Leadership Conference** (SCLC) in November 1967. Seeking a "middle ground between riots on the one hand and timid supplications for justice on the other," King planned for an initial group of 2,000 poor people to descend on Washington, D.C., southern states and northern cities to meet with government officials to demand jobs, unemployment insurance, a fair minimum wage, and education for poor adults and children designed to improve their self-image and self-esteem (King, 29 November 1967).

On 4 March 1968, King displays the poster to be used during the upcoming Poor People's Campaign. © AP / Wide World Photos.

Suggested to King by Marion Wright, director of the **National Association for the Advancement of Colored People**'s Legal Defense and Education Fund in Jackson, Mississippi, the Poor People's Campaign was seen by King as the next chapter in the struggle for genuine equality. Desegregation and the right to vote were essential, but King believed that African Americans and other minorities would never enter full citizenship until they had economic security. Through nonviolent direct action, King and SCLC hoped to focus the nation's attention on economic inequality and poverty. "This is a highly significant event," King told delegates at an early planning meeting, describing the campaign as "the beginning of a new co-operation, understanding, and a determination by poor people of all colors and backgrounds to assert and win their right to a decent life and respect for their culture and dignity" (SCLC, 15 March 1968). Many leaders of American Indian, Puerto Rican, Mexican American, and poor white communities pledged themselves to the Poor People's Campaign.

Some in SCLC thought King's campaign too ambitious, and the demands too amorphous. Although King praised the simplicity of the campaign's goals, saying, "it's as pure as a man needing an income to support his family," he knew that the campaign was inherently different from others SCLC had attempted (King, 29 November 1967). "We have an ultimate goal of freedom, independence, self-determination, whatever we want to call it, but we aren't going to get all of that now, and we aren't going to get all of that next year," he commented at a staff meeting on 17 January 1968. "Let's find something that is so possible, so achievable, so pure, so simple that even the backlash can't do much to deny it. And yet something so non-token and so basic to life that even the black nationalists can't disagree with it that much" (King, 17 January 1968).

After King's **assassination** in April 1968, SCLC decided to go on with the campaign under the leadership of Ralph **Abernathy**, SCLC's new president. On Mother's Day, 12 May 1968, thousands of women, led by Coretta Scott **King**, formed the first wave of demonstrators. The following day, Resurrection City, a temporary settlement of tents and shacks, was built on the Mall in Washington, D.C. Braving rain, mud, and summer heat, protesters stayed for over a month. Demonstrators made daily pilgrimages to various federal agencies to protest and demand economic justice. Midway through the campaign, Robert **Kennedy**, whose wife had attended the Mother's Day opening of Resurrection City, was assassinated. Out of respect for the campaign, his funeral procession passed through Resurrection City. The Department of the Interior forced Resurrection City to close on 24 June 1968, after the permit to use park land expired.

Although the campaign succeeded in small ways, such as qualifying 200 counties for free surplus food distribution and securing promises from several federal agencies to hire poor people to help run programs for the poor, Abernathy felt these concessions were insufficient.

SOURCES

Ben A. Franklin, "5,000 Open Poor People's Campaign in Washington," *New York Times*, 13 May 1968.

Ben A. Franklin, "Poor People's Drive Makes Gains, but Fails to Reach Goals," *New York Times*, 30 June 1968.

King, Address at workshop on civil disobedience at SCLC staff retreat, 29 November 1967, MLKJP-GAMK.

King, Address delivered at SCLC staff meeting, 17 January 1968, MLKEC.

Joseph A. Loftus, "City of the Poor Shuts Peacefully," *New York Times*, 25 June 1968.

McKnight, *Last Crusade*, 1998.

SCLC, Press release, "Black and White Together," 15 March 1968, BPD-AB.

POPPER, HERMINE RICH ISAACS (1915–1968)

Hermine Popper, a critic, short story writer, and freelance editor, was hired in early 1958 by publishing house Harper & Brothers to edit Martin Luther King's account of the **Montgomery bus boycott, Stride Toward Freedom** (1958).

Popper was born in New York City and received her BA (1936) from Radcliffe College. Two years later, she became managing editor and film critic of *Theater Arts Magazine*, where she worked until 1947. From 1953 to 1956, Popper served as an editor for Harper & Brothers, before leaving the publishing house to become a freelance book editor.

In Popper's initial review of chapter one of *Stride*, she wrote in a 21 March 1958 letter that it was a "pleasure" to work on the Montgomery project and reassured King that her job was "to convert, as it were, an expert orator's style into a writer's style" (*Papers* 4:386). Although the two primarily exchanged ideas by mail, Popper did visit Montgomery to help expedite the volume's production. In *Stride*, King thanked Popper for her "invaluable editorial assistance," which ultimately led to her involvement in the editing of two of King's later books, **Why We Can't Wait** (1964) and **Where Do We Go from Here: Chaos or Community?** (1967) (King, 11).

Aside from editing, Popper worked for the Urban League of Westchester County for more than 15 years, and wrote short stories appearing in *Harper's* and other prominent magazines. She died of cancer at the age of 53.

SOURCES

King, *Stride Toward Freedom*, 1958.
Popper to King, 21 March 1958, in *Papers* 4:386; 388.

PORTER, JOHN THOMAS (1931–2006)

As someone who was greatly influenced by Martin Luther King in his early days at **Dexter Avenue Baptist Church**, John T. Porter served as one of several key pastoral contacts for the **Birmingham Campaign**.

Porter was born on 4 April 1931, in Birmingham, Alabama. He earned a BS from Alabama State College in 1955 and his BD from **Morehouse College** in 1958. While a student, he served as King's pulpit assistant at Dexter from 1954 to 1955. Porter remembered King's mentorship fondly, remarking: "He was a tremendous inspiration to me during his first year in the pastorate" (Porter, 10 August 1990). After Porter's departure from Dexter King wrote, "We miss you a great deal here at Dexter," and recalled "the devoted service that you rendered to our church while you were here" (King, 15 July 1955).

After receiving his divinity degree from Morehouse College in 1958, Porter served as a pastor at Detroit's First Baptist Institutional Church before being called to Sixth Avenue Baptist Church in Birmingham in December 1962. King preached at Porter's installation service at Sixth Avenue, calling Porter an "eloquent prophet," suited to "this great and challenging city" (King, 9 December 1962).

In addition to opening his church for SCLC in April 1963, he also played an active role in the nonviolent campaign to desegregate Birmingham. Porter disobeyed the Alabama injunction against mass demonstrations, and was jailed two days after King for marching on 14 April, Easter Sunday. A statue now standing in Birmingham's Kelly Ingram Park, the site of many of the demonstrations, commemorates his Easter arrest with ministers Nelson H. Smith and A. D. **King**. Although Porter was an avid supporter and participant in the Birmingham Campaign, he opposed James **Bevel**'s plan to have children march in demonstrations.

Porter served as pastor of Sixth Avenue Baptist Church until 2000, helping the church grow into one of the state's largest, while also serving in the Alabama legislature from 1974 to 1989. He died on 15 February 2006.

SOURCES

King, "A Knock at Midnight," 9 December 1962, JTPP.
King to Porter, 15 July 1955, DABCC.
Porter, Interview by King Papers Project staff, 10 August 1990.

POWELL, ADAM CLAYTON, JR. (1908–1972)

As a minister and congressman, Adam Clayton Powell, Jr., was a prominent and controversial figure in the struggle for civil rights. Although Powell and Martin Luther King were initially supportive of one another's work, King lost trust in Powell in 1960, after the congressman threatened to lie to the press about King's friendship with his advisor Bayard **Rustin**. Despite their differences the two continued to publicly cooperate for several years; however, their relationship further eroded when Powell publicly renounced **nonviolence** in 1968.

Born 29 November 1908, in New Haven, Connecticut, Powell grew up in New York City, where his father was the pastor of Harlem's Abyssinian Baptist Church. After graduating from Colgate University in 1930, Powell returned to Harlem, where he became an assistant pastor at Abyssinian while earning a master's degree in religious education from Columbia University (1932). When his father retired in 1937, Powell became the new pastor of Abyssinian, ministering to a congregation of over 10,000 members. Powell used the pulpit to work for social change, organizing his community around issues related to discrimination in employment and government services. Powell headed the "Don't Buy Where You Can't Work" campaign, which succeeded in opening up jobs to African Americans at New York stores, utility companies, and city buses.

In 1941 Powell became the first African American elected to the New York City Council. He was elected to the U.S. House of Representatives three years later, representing a newly formed congressional district in Harlem. In 1950, in collaboration with the **National Association for the Advancement of Colored People** (NAACP), he put forward a legislative rider barring federal funds from segregated institutions. Although the rider did not pass, Powell reintroduced the legislation so many times that it became known as the Powell Amendment. The amendment's content was eventually incorporated into the **Civil Rights Act of 1964**.

In February 1956 Powell appealed to President Dwight D. **Eisenhower** to support the **Montgomery bus boycott** and take responsibility for "safeguarding the lives, physical security and civil liberties of the 115 Negroes arrested for peaceably and nonviolently trying to obtain what the Constitution promises" (Powell, 22 February 1956). Powell personally contributed to the **Montgomery Improvement Association** and called King a "brilliant young prophet" (Powell, 17 May 1957). At King's invitation, Powell later joined the advisory committee of the **Southern Christian Leadership Conference** (SCLC).

Powell and King traveled together to **Ghana** to celebrate that country's independence in 1957. When Powell was facing a difficult reelection the following year, King pledged his "wholehearted support," writing: "As I see it, the attacks upon you are in reality an effort to destroy the Negroes' political independence, and remove from the legislature an uncompromising voice" (*Papers* 4:421).

In the summer of 1960, Powell threatened to tell the press that King was involved in a homosexual affair with Rustin unless King called off plans to demonstrate at the upcoming Democratic National Convention. "I have always vigorously defended you against your most severe critics," King wrote Powell in response. "In spite of all," King told him, "I will hold nothing in my heart against you and I will not go to the press to answer or condemn you" (*Papers* 5:481). The incident blew over without much public scandal, and relations between King and Powell appeared to normalize. When Powell was named chairman of the House Education and Labor Committee the following year, King wrote him praising his "unswerving dedication and loyalty without compromise to the civil rights struggle of the Negro people" (King, 28 January 1961). As chairman, Powell played a crucial role in moving Lyndon **Johnson**'s progressive War on Poverty legislation through Congress.

Although they continued to encounter patches of disagreement, King spoke occasionally at Abyssinian Baptist Church in the early 1960s, raising funds for SCLC. Powell's influential career was undermined by scandal, including allegations of tax evasion and misuse of government funds. Following an investigation of Powell's conduct, in 1967 the House voted not to seat him. He challenged the decision, winning a special election to fill his own seat, but was barred from Congress. In March 1968 Powell rejected nonviolence and told an assembled crowd of thousands, "The day of Martin Luther King has come to an end" (Johnson, "Cheering Harlem Throngs"). King was **assassinated** less than two weeks later. Powell won reelection, and in 1969 the Supreme Court ruled that his expulsion from Congress was unconstitutional. Powell was reinstated, but without seniority. In 1970 he lost a close reelection bid to Charles Rangel. Powell died two years later on 4 April 1972.

SOURCES

Branch, *At Canaan's Edge*, 2006.

Branch, *Parting the Waters*, 1988.

Introduction, in *Papers* 5:31–32.

Thomas A. Johnson, "Cheering Harlem Throngs Walk with Powell in Rain," *New York Times*, 24 March 1968.

King to Powell, 10 June 1958, in *Papers* 4:420–421.

King to Powell, 24 June 1960, in *Papers* 5:480–481.

King to Powell, 28 January 1961, MLKJP-GAMK.

Powell, "Address at the Prayer Pilgrimage for Freedom," 17 May 1957, MLKP-MBU.

Powell to Eisenhower, 22 February 1956, WCFO-KAbE.

POWELL, MARY LOUISE STAMPER (1918–)

As a friend of Martin Luther King, Jr., Mary Powell helped initiate the courtship between King and Coretta Scott. After his first date with Scott, King told Powell, "I owe you a thousand dollars for introducing me to this girl" (Scott King, 56).

Mary Louise Stamper was born in Atlanta on 7 September 1918. She attended Lincoln Academy in Kings Mountain, North Carolina, and graduated from Spelman College in 1941. She went on to receive her MA from Atlanta University in 1950. She met King while he was studying for his doctorate at **Boston University** and Powell was attending the New England Conservatory of Music. In early 1952, after King asked Powell if she knew of any "nice, attractive young ladies" for him to date, she described Coretta Scott, her schoolmate at the Conservatory, and gave Scott's telephone number to King (Scott King, 53). Scott and King were married the following year.

Powell later exchanged letters with King, encouraging him to use the Christian principle, "Love Thy Enemy" in Montgomery, Alabama. Although Powell was supportive of King's aims, she was sometimes critical of his methods, expressing disapproval of King's encouragement of mass civil disobedience: "If you and others have earned the right to go to jail, it is your [privilege] if you deem it so. But going to jail on a group basis will accomplish little but confusion" (Powell, 29 February 1960).

SOURCES

(Scott) King, *My Life with Martin Luther King, Jr.*, 1969.

Powell to King, 29 February 1960, MLKP-MBU.

PRAYER PILGRIMAGE FOR FREEDOM (1957)

On 17 May 1957, nearly 25,000 demonstrators gathered at the Lincoln Memorial in Washington, D.C., for a Prayer Pilgrimage for Freedom, featuring three hours of spirituals, songs, and speeches that urged the federal government to fulfill the three-year-old *Brown v. Board of Education* decision. The last speech of the day was reserved for Martin Luther King's "Give Us the Ballot" oration, which captured public attention and placed him in the national spotlight as a major leader of the civil rights movement.

On 14 February 1957, King and members of the newly organized Southern Leaders Conference (later known as the **Southern Christian Leadership Conference** [SCLC]) urged Dwight D. **Eisenhower**'s administration to publicly condemn segregationists' unwillingness to comply with the *Brown* decision. In a telegram sent to President Eisenhower, the organizers of the demonstration stated that if Eisenhower would not maintain law and order in the South, "we shall have to lead our people to you in the capitol in order to call the nation's attention to the violence and organized terror directed toward [men], women, and children who merely seek freedom" (*Papers* 4:134). When the Eisenhower administration failed to make a public stand in favor of desegregation, King and Thomas Kilgore, Jr., National Director of the Pilgrimage, solicited financial contributions from leaders throughout the country, and asked them to attend the Prayer Pilgrimage which was being organized by Bayard **Rustin** and others. "We're moving up the highway of freedom toward the city of equality … our nation has a date with destiny and we can't be late," King told an audience in New York, imploring whites and African Americans to join the pilgrimage (Booker, "Date with Destiny").

The pilgrimage was not without internal controversy and civil rights leaders differed on its intent. A. Philip **Randolph** intended the event to relate to his 1941 effort to use the threat of mass protests to secure civil rights reform. When 77 church, labor, and civil rights supporters met on 5 April in Washington to finalize plans for the pilgrimage, moderates Adam Clayton **Powell** and Clarence Mitchell sought to ensure that the pilgrimage would not embarrass the Eisenhower administration, and would instead be used to commemorate the *Brown* decision through prayer.

Although the event attracted less than one half of its intended participants, the pilgrimage featured singing by Mahalia **Jackson**, and speeches from such prominent leaders as Randolph, Powell, Mordecai **Johnson**, Fred **Shuttlesworth**, Roy **Wilkins**, and Charles **Diggs**. But it was King's "Give Us the Ballot" that became the legacy of the pilgrimage. After the event James Hicks of the *New York Amsterdam News* wrote that King was now the "top Negro leader" and that the "Prayer Pilgrimage was the idea of Martin Luther King alone and no other Negro leader in America was enthusiastic about it" (Hicks, "King Emerges"). Hicks' article struck a nerve with Wilkins, head of the **National Association for the Advancement of Colored People** (NAACP), who promptly wrote to the paper to rebuke his claims. Wilkins also sent a letter to King, reminding him that the NAACP had covered many of the expenses of the pilgrimage.

Nonetheless, King had gained national prominence. When King preached at Philadelphia's Zion Baptist Church just two days after the pilgrimage "a crowd estimated at more than 1,800 persons crammed into the church, and hundreds of others who failed to gain admittance stood outside to get a glimpse of the nation's most talked-about leader" (*Papers* 4:15).

SOURCES

James Booker, "'Date with Destiny in DC'—Rev. King," *New York Amsterdam News*, 11 May 1957.

James Hicks, "King Emerges as Top Negro Leader," *New York Amsterdam News*, 1 June 1957.

Introduction, in *Papers* 4:13–17.

King, "Give Us the Ballot," Address delivered at the Prayer Pilgrimage for Freedom, 17 May 1957, in *Papers* 4:208–215.

King to Eisenhower, 14 February 1957, in *Papers* 4:132–134.

PRITCHETT, LAURIE (1926–2000)

As police chief of Albany, Georgia, Laurie Pritchett gained national attention when he effectively thwarted the efforts of the **Albany Movement** in 1961–1962. Pritchett's nonviolent response to demonstrations, including the mass arrests of protesters and the jailing of Martin Luther King, Jr., was seen as an effective strategy in bringing the campaign to an end before the movement could secure any concrete gains.

Pritchett was born on 9 December 1926, in Griffin, Georgia. Pritchett attended Auburn University and South Georgia College before graduating from the National Academy of the **Federal Bureau of Investigation** and the Southern Police Institute at the University of Louisville. An Army veteran, he was also a decorated and distinguished member of numerous law enforcement organizations. By 1961 Pritchett had risen to become Albany's Chief of Police.

In 1961 Charles Sherrod and Cordell Reagon of the **Student Nonviolent Coordinating Committee** (SNCC) began to organize a grassroots movement in Albany, Georgia. Gaining the support of Albany State College students, local ministers, and others in the community, SNCC contested racial segregation in bus and train stations, libraries, parks, and hospitals; and discrimination in jury representation, voting, and employment. Pritchett ordered his officers to enforce the law without using violence in public and to make arrests under laws protecting the public order, rather than under the more legally unstable segregation laws. Pritchett, who had anticipated mass arrests, arranged to have access to jails in nearby cities available for the hundreds of arrested demonstrators. According to King, "Chief Pritchett felt that by directing his police to be nonviolent, he had discovered a new way to defeat the demonstrations" (King, 69).

At the invitation of W. G. **Anderson**, president of the Albany Movement, King and the **Southern Christian Leadership Conference** (SCLC) arrived in Albany in December 1961. King's presence in Albany drew national attention to the protests. When King and Ralph **Abernathy** were found guilty of parading without a permit in July 1962, an anonymous man paid their bail. King wanted to remain in jail to pressure city officials to negotiate in good faith with the Albany Movement, and in a statement following his release, King said: "This is one time that I'm out of jail and I'm not happy to be out" (King, Statement, 12 July 1962). King and Abernathy were arrested again in late July, but were given suspended sentences and released. The judgment brought much relief to Pritchett, who was well aware throughout the campaign that demonstrations increased when King was jailed.

Throughout the movement, white Albany city officials never followed through on any of the compromises reached with protesters. In December 1961 demonstrations were temporarily halted by the promise that bus and train stations would be desegregated, protesters would be released from jail, and a biracial committee would be formed to discuss segregation issues in Albany. Albany city officials stalled on implementing these changes, and did not uphold all parts of the agreement. Despite the dishonesty of some Albany officials, however, King believed Pritchett was inherently a good person. "I sincerely believe that Chief Pritchett is a nice man, a basically decent man, but he's so caught up in a system that he ends up saying one thing to us behind closed doors and then we open the newspaper and he's said something else to the press" (King, Address, 12 July 1962).

In August 1962, King left Albany with no tangible civil rights gains achieved. While many in the press called the movement "one of the most stunning defeats" in King's career, Pritchett was lauded for his use of **nonviolence** ("King Suffered"). Pritchett's nonviolent approach left an indelible imprint on King, who later wrote of his indignation at Pritchett's use of "the moral means of nonviolence to maintain the immoral ends of racial injustice" (King, 99).

After leaving Albany, Pritchett served as chief of police in High Point, North Carolina, until his retirement in 1975. Although King and Pritchett were adversaries in the 1960s, Pritchett later considered King a "close personal friend" (Pritchett, 23 April 1976). He died in 2000, at the age of 73.

SOURCES

Carson, In Struggle, 1981.
King, Address at Shiloh Baptist Church, 12 July 1962, GDL-G-Ar.
King, Statement on release from jail in Albany, Ga., 12 July 1962, MLKJP-GAMK.
King, Why We Can't Wait, 1964.
"King Suffered 'Stunning Defeat Here,' Papers State," Albany Herald, 21 December 1961.
Pritchett, Interview by James Reston, 23 April 1976, SOHP-NcU.

PROCTOR, HILDA STEWART (1905–1984)

In 1958, in addition to her other civil rights activities, Hilda Proctor worked as Martin Luther King's personal secretary for seven months while Maude **Ballou**, his regular assistant, was on maternity leave.

Hilda Stewart Proctor was the great-niece of Harriet Tubman and was born on 5 April 1905, in Boston, Massachusetts, to British parents. During her teenage years, she was a member of the Fellowship of Youths for Peace, a precursor to her involvement with the **Fellowship of Reconciliation** (FOR). Proctor studied religion and social studies at **Boston University** while she continued her education as a violin student at the New England Conservatory of Music. Before working for King, she was employed by several black newspapers, including the **New York Amsterdam News** and the Pittsburgh Courier, where she worked for associate editor George Schuyler. Following her work with these publications, Proctor served as private secretary for the president of Fisk University, Charles S. Johnson.

In March 1958 Proctor moved to Alabama to work as King's secretary in Ballou's absence. King appreciated Proctor's "helpfulness and genuine concern," particularly in the extra assistance she provided while King was in New York recovering from his stabbing in late 1958 (*Papers* 4:550). Although Proctor only worked for King in Alabama until August of that year, the two remained friends through correspondence and occasional visits. Prior to King's 1959 **India trip**, Proctor volunteered to help him with any extra office work he might have: "As any friend would do who is interested in getting you off to India" (*Papers* 4:554). The respect that Proctor had for King's work was evident in a letter she wrote after leaving Montgomery. She complained that in her new community, she "[did] not find the people on fire with the problem that you are giving your life for … I have to watch myself that I do not fall into this complacency" (Proctor, 15 April 1964).

After working for King, Proctor spent time in New York, Hawaii, and Florida. She continued to be active in the civil rights movement, working with such organizations as FOR, the **National Association for the Advancement of Colored People**, and the **National Urban League**. Proctor died on 21 June 1984.

SOURCES
King to Proctor, 22 December 1958, in *Papers* 4:549–550.
Proctor to King, 27 May 1958, in *Papers* 4:412–413.
Proctor to King, 31 December 1958, in *Papers* 4:554.
Proctor to King, 22 May 1959, in *Papers* 5:212–214.
Proctor to King, 15 April 1964, MLKJP-GAMK.
Schuyler, *Black and Conservative*, 1966.

PROGRESSIVE NATIONAL BAPTIST CONVENTION (PNBC)

The Progressive National Baptist Convention (PNBC) grew out of the September 1961 convention of the **National Baptist Convention** (NBC), which was held in Kansas City, Missouri. This event demonstrated the hostility of the NBC's leadership to the use of nonviolent direct action tactics such as those used by the **Southern Christian Leadership Conference** (SCLC), the **Student Nonviolent Coordinating Committee** (SNCC), and the **Congress of Racial Equality** (CORE). NBC president J. H. **Jackson** had previously denounced the tactics of SNCC's lunch counter **sit-ins** and CORE's 1961 **Freedom Rides**, which Martin Luther King endorsed.

A group of younger ministers led by Gardner **Taylor** sought to overthrow Jackson and assume the leadership of the NBC. The convention ended with Jackson's decisive victory over Taylor for president and King's removal as vice president of the NBC's National Sunday School and Baptist Training Union.

After Taylor's defeat, he and other ministers left the NBC to form a splinter organization, PNBC, founded November 1961, in Cincinnati, Ohio. The new Baptist alliance championed the more militant direct action campaigns of SCLC, CORE, and SNCC. After the PNBC's first president, T. M. Chambers, left in 1966, Taylor was elected PNBC president in 1967.

After King's **assassination** in 1968, Taylor remarked in that year's annual address to the PNBC: "As we remember Dr. Martin King's trials and triumphs, we remember our part in them. Progressive Baptists may take justifiable pride in the unassailable fact which must now forever be true, that when he had no spiritual (denominational) home among Black Baptists, cast out from the house of his Fathers, Progressive Baptists gave him a Black Baptist (denominational) residence" (Progressive National Baptist Convention, Inc., "Civil Rights Advocacy and Activism").

SOURCES

Garrow, *Bearing the Cross*, 1986.

Introduction, in *Papers* 5:34.

Progressive National Baptist Convention, Inc., "Civil Rights Advocacy and Activism," http://pnbc.org/index.php?option=com_content&task=view&id=26&Itemid=44.

QUILL, MICHAEL JOSEPH (1905–1966)

Near the end of the **Montgomery bus boycott**, Martin Luther King received a letter of support from the leaders of the Transport Workers Union (TWU) of America. International President Mike Quill and Secretary-Treasurer Matthew Guinan congratulated King "for the mature and courageous leadership you have given not only to the people of Alabama but all Americans in the fight to wipe out the scourge of segregation from our national life" (*Papers* 3:440).

Quill was born in Kilgarvan, County Kerry, Ireland, on 18 September 1905. His family supported the Irish Republican Army (IRA) during Ireland's struggle for independence from Britain, and Quill served in the IRA between 1919 and 1923. He emigrated to the United States in 1926, and remained involved in IRA-supported activities through its U.S. affiliate, Clan na Gael. In New York Quill secured work with the Interborough Rapid Transit subway line. In 1934 he and other members of Clan na Gael helped organize subway workers into the new TWU. In 1935 he was elected president and remained in that office until his death.

The TWU joined the Congress of Industrial Organizations (CIO) in 1937, and the union quickly organized workers for most of New York's subway lines. By the end of World War II, the TWU had expanded to Philadelphia, Chicago, and Miami. Quill was elected head of the New York CIO in 1949, and became a national vice president in 1950. He later opposed the CIO's merger with the American Federation of Labor (AFL) to form the **American Federation of Labor and Congress of Industrial Organizations** (AFL-CIO), in part due to his opposition to racial discrimination in the AFL.

Quill was a consistent advocate for the civil rights movement and for the activities of King and the **Southern Christian Leadership Conference**. He served as a vice chairman of the April 1959 **Youth March for Integrated Schools**. In 1961 Quill invited King to speak at TWU's 11th convention. King accepted, and he called on his audience to be "maladjusted" to "economic conditions that will take necessities from the many to give luxury to the few" and to "the madness of militarism" (King, 5 October 1961). After the speech Quill noted, "If you are looking for maladjusted people, you came to the right place" (King, 5 October 1961). Quill served on the board of directors of the **Gandhi Society for Human Rights** and, in 1963, presented King with a check for $10,000 at a Gandhi Society luncheon. King thanked him in a

14 June letter, writing: "You and the members of your Union have proved to be real and abiding friends of those of us who are struggling for freedom and dignity in the Southland."

In January 1966 Quill collapsed after being jailed in the course of a massive New York transit strike. The strike was settled in favor of the union, but Quill died a few weeks later, on 28 January 1966.

Sources
King, America's Greatest Crisis, 5 October 1961, TWUC-NNU-LA.
King to Quill, 14 June 1963, TWUC-NNU-LA.
Quill to King, 27 November 1956, in *Papers* 3:440.
Quill, *Mike Quill*, 1985.

RABY, ALBERT (1933–1988)

Albert Raby, convener of the coalition of Chicago civil rights groups known as the Coordinating Council of Community Organizations (CCCO), worked closely with Martin Luther King from 1965 to 1967. After King brought the **Southern Christian Leadership Conference** (SCLC) north to launch its **Chicago Campaign** in January 1966, he told an *Ebony* reporter that he had chosen to come to that city "mainly because of Al Raby. I had been watching Al for some time and I must say that I became enormously impressed with his work and with the sincerity of his commitment" ("Dr. King Carries Fight," 102).

Raby was born in Chicago in 1933. After his father died when he was still a baby, his mother struggled to raise four children on her own. Before and after school Raby delivered groceries and sold newspapers, before dropping out entirely without finishing the eighth grade. When he was 20, Raby was drafted into the Army. After his discharge he enrolled in night school, earning his elementary and high school diplomas in two years. He then obtained a certificate in teaching at Chicago Teachers College.

In 1960 Raby began teaching seventh grade at an all-black school. In 1962 he became actively involved in Teachers for Integrated Education, a local movement demanding that the city address inequality in the schools. As the teachers' delegate to the emerging CCCO, Raby was outspoken and soon was selected as the CCCO's convener, making him the group's chief organizer and spokesman. Raby successfully organized a school boycott on 22 October 1963, prompting 300,000 students to stay home from school to demand integrated and improved public education. Demonstrations escalated in June 1965, when Raby and hundreds of others were arrested while blocking a major downtown intersection.

In early July 1965, responding to Raby's appeal for assistance, King agreed to go to Chicago later that month for a three-day mobilization during which he and Raby spoke at over a dozen neighborhood rallies. Seeking to focus attention on the plight of urban African Americans in the North, King and his associates at SCLC decided they should go to Chicago, moving there in January 1966.

Shortly thereafter, Raby and King became co-chairs of a new organization called the Chicago Freedom Movement, a coalition of CCCO, SCLC, and other Chicago civil rights organizations. Throughout the year, the pair collaborated on countless demonstrations, community gatherings, and meetings with city officials while attempting to end racist education, housing, and employment practices. Raby was with King when segregationists in Chicago's Lawn and Gage Park district pelted marchers, who were advocating for open housing, with rocks.

In August 1966 the campaign's efforts culminated in a summit agreement on open housing among real estate businessmen, civic and religious groups, Mayor Richard Daley, and the Chicago Freedom Movement. While the city's business and government leaders agreed to several concessions on housing, the agreement fell short of achieving city-wide desegregation. Although King and Raby continued to work together into 1967, SCLC largely shifted its priorities away from Chicago, leaving behind its **Operation Breadbasket** program under the leadership of Jesse **Jackson**.

Raby resigned from CCCO in 1967 to study history at the University of Chicago. In 1970 he entered politics as a delegate to the Illinois Constitutional Convention, and in 1973 he began working in the administration of Illinois Governor Dan Walker as a liaison to the state's housing authority. After losing a close election for Chicago alderman in 1975, he joined President Jimmy Carter's administration in Washington, D.C. Two years later Raby was in Ghana working as the director of Peace Corps volunteers. He returned to Chicago in 1982 to run the successful election campaign of Chicago's first black mayor, Harold Washington. Raby later served on the city's Human Relations Commission. Raby died of a heart attack in 1988 at the age of 55.

SOURCES

Branch, At Canaan's Edge, 2006.
Coordinating Council of Community Organizations, 90th Cong., 1st sess., Congressional Record 113 (12 July 1967): 18513.
"Dr. King Carries Fight to Northern Slums," Ebony, April 1966, 94–102.
Robert McClory, "The Activist," Chicago Tribune, 17 April 1983.

RAMACHANDRAN, G. (1904–1995)

G. Ramachandran, a disciple of Mahatma **Gandhi**, served as the secretary of the Gandhi Smarak Nidhi (Gandhi National Memorial Fund), which co-sponsored Martin Luther King's 1959 **India trip**. King thanked Ramachandran for his hospitality during his trip to India, writing that Ramachandran's interpretations of Gandhi "left an indelible imprint on my thinking" (*Papers* 5:212).

Born in 1904, in Perumthanni, Kerala, India, Ramachandran graduated from the Visva-Bharati at Santiniketan in 1925. As a disciple of Gandhi, Ramachandran helped lead the salt march in Tamil Nadu and the movement against the treatment of untouchables. In 1947 Ramachandran founded the Gandhigram at Madurai, a rural college based on Gandhian principles.

On 27 December 1958 Ramachandran wrote King, inviting him and Coretta Scott **King** to spend a month in India. "We in India have watched with sympathy and admiration the nonviolent movements of the Negroes in America to achieve their full equality, in law and in spirit," Ramachandran wrote. "It would be good if you could share with the Indian people your own experiences and thoughts," and "study how Mahatma Gandhi evolved the techniques of peaceful action to solve innumerable social and national problems in India" (*Papers* 4:553). King accepted the invitation, visiting India in February and March 1959. King and his party dined with Ramachandran in New Delhi on 6 March.

King remained in contact with Ramachandran for several years after his trip to India. In 1961 Ramachandran asked King to write a statement on the application of Gandhian principles to nuclear disarmament for publication in *Gandhi Marg*, a quarterly journal of Gandhian thought. King complied and composed a bold statement, arguing that the "civilized world stands on the brink of nuclear annihilation. No longer can any sensible person talk glibly about preparation for war. The present crisis calls for sober thinking, reasonable negotiation and moral commitment." Without this kind of nonviolent direct action, King wrote: "The choice is no longer between violence and nonviolence, it is either nonviolence or nonexistence" (King, 23; 24).

Ramachandran remained committed to Gandhian ideals throughout his life, founding the Madhavi Mandiram Loka Seva Trust in 1980, by donating his property to support a self-sustaining village for women and children. He died on 17 January 1995 at the age of 91.

SOURCES

Introduction, in *Papers* 5:2–12.
King, "Gandhi and the World Crisis: A Symposium," *Gandhi Marg* 6, no. 1 (January 1962): 23–24.
King to Ramachandran, 19 May 1959, in *Papers* 5:211–212.
Ramachandran to King, 27 December 1958, in *Papers* 4:552–553.
Ramachandran to King, 6 December 1961, MLKJP-GAMK.
Ramachandran, *Gandhi*, 1967.

RANDOLPH, A. PHILIP (1889–1979)

A. Philip Randolph, whom Martin Luther King, Jr., called "truly the Dean of Negro leaders," played a crucial role in gaining recognition of African Americans in labor organizations (*Papers* 4:527). A socialist and a pacifist, Randolph founded the Brotherhood of Sleeping Car Porters, the first successful black trade union, and the **Negro American Labor Council** (NALC).

The youngest son of a poor preacher deeply committed to racial politics, Randolph was born in Crescent City, Florida, on 15 April 1889. He graduated from Jacksonville's Cookman Institute in 1911, relocating to New York City soon afterward. In 1917 Randolph and Chandler Owen founded the *Messenger*, an African American socialist journal critical of American involvement in World War I.

After the 1925 founding of the Brotherhood of Sleeping Car Porters, Randolph succeeded in gaining recognition of the union from the Pullman Palace Car Company in 1937. When the union signed its first contract with the company, membership rose to nearly 15,000. In 1941 Randolph threatened a march on Washington, D.C., if the federal government did not address racial discrimination in the defense industry. In response, President Franklin D. Roosevelt issued Executive Order 8802, which banned discrimination in the defense industry and established the Fair Employment Practices Commission. Randolph also helped to form the League for Non-Violent Civil Disobedience against Military Segregation, which influenced President Harry S. **Truman**'s decision to desegregate the armed services in 1948.

After the **American Federation of Labor** merged with the **Congress of Industrial Organizations** to form the AFL-CIO in 1955, Randolph was appointed to the new

Bayard Rustin (left) confers with A. Philip Randolph during the Selma to Montgomery March. © 1965 Matt Herron/Take Stock.

organization's executive council, when he became one of its first two black vice presidents. As a labor official, Randolph won significant union support for the civil rights movement and allied with King and other organizations on initiatives like the 1957 **Prayer Pilgrimage for Freedom**.

In 1959 Randolph founded NALC in an effort to effectively present the demands of black workers to the labor movement. Randolph and NALC helped initiate the 1963 **March on Washington for Jobs and Freedom**, during which King delivered his famous "**I Have a Dream**" speech.

Randolph devoted his life to the achievement of both racial and economic equality. On the occasion of Randolph's 70th birthday, King participated in an evening honoring him at New York's Carnegie Hall. King praised Randolph's refusal "to sell his race for a mess of pottage," and credited him with never being "afraid to challenge an unjust state power" or to "speak out against the power structure" (*Papers* 5:350). Randolph died on 16 May 1979 at age 90.

SOURCES

King, Outline of Remarks for "A Salute to A. Philip Randolph," 24 January 1960, in *Papers* 5:350.

King to Randolph, 8 November 1958, in *Papers* 4:527–528.

Pfeffer, *A. Philip Randolph*, 1990.

RAY, SANDY FREDERICK (1898–1979)

Named by Martin Luther King, Jr., as one of the strongest orators in the African American church, Sandy Ray was one of many talented ministers who, through his association with Martin Luther **King**, Sr., served as a role model for King, Jr.

Born in Texas, Ray was King, Sr.'s, closest friend while they attended **Morehouse College**'s three-year minister's degree program. After graduating in 1930, Ray served Baptist churches in LaGrange, Georgia; Chicago, Illinois; Columbus, Ohio; and Macon, Georgia, before being called to Brooklyn, New York's Cornerstone Baptist Church in 1944, where he served as pastor until his death. Ray was one of six candidates nominated for president of the **National Baptist Convention** in 1953. Beginning in 1954, he presided over New York's Empire Missionary Baptist Convention for many years.

Throughout his life, Ray remained close to the Kings. King, Jr., remarked during a March 1956 speech in New York, "I'm glad to see Rev. Sandy Ray out there…. You know, for years he was 'Uncle Sandy' to me. In fact, I did not know he was not related to me by blood until I was 12 years old" (Herndon, "Sidelights of a 'Kingly' Meeting"). Earlier in the month Ray had attended a **Montgomery Improvement Association** mass meeting in support of the **Montgomery bus boycott**. It was at Ray's parsonage at Cornerstone Baptist that King recuperated after being stabbed in September 1958 by Izola Ware **Curry**.

Ray supported the efforts of the **Southern Christian Leadership Conference** by serving as a member of the steering committee for a June 1961 fundraising effort in New York City. He was also a founding member of the board of directors of the **Gandhi Society for Human Rights**. On the afternoon that Ray dedicated Cornerstone Baptist's community center in 1966, King delivered the sermon "Guidelines for a Constructive Church" there. Ray delivered the eulogy at the funeral of King's mother, Alberta Williams **King**, in 1974.

SOURCES

Donald T. Ferron, Notes on MIA mass meeting at Hutchinson Street Baptist Church, in *Papers* 3:150–151.

Cholly Herndon, "Sidelights of a 'Kingly' Meeting in Brooklyn," *New York Amsterdam News*, 31 March 1956.

King, "Guidelines for a Constructive Church," Sermon delivered at Cornerstone Baptist Church, 29 May 1966, CBCR.

King, Sr., with Riley, *Daddy King*, 1980.

REDDICK, LAWRENCE DUNBAR (1910–1995)

On 5 December 1955, Lawrence Reddick attended the first mass meeting of the **Montgomery bus boycott**. Although he recalled feeling "baffled" by what was taking place, he did "realize that something socially significant was happening" and began to take copious notes (Reddick, 235). Throughout 1956 and 1957, as his notes materialized into a manuscript for a book, Reddick became friends with Martin Luther King, Jr., while conducting interviews with the bus boycott leader. In his biography of King, *Crusader without Violence* (1959), Reddick called King a "national asset," claiming that King "symbolizes an idea that meets a fundamental need of our times. His way is needed in the painful transition through which the South is presently passing, and his way is needed by the American nation in a divided world" (Reddick, 233–234). For more than a decade, Reddick chronicled the events of the civil rights movement and assisted King in writing many of his public statements and speeches.

Born in Jacksonville, Florida, Reddick received his BA (1932) and MA (1933) from Fisk University, and his PhD (1939) in history from the University of Chicago. Upon earning his PhD, Reddick was named curator of the Schomburg Collection of Negro Literature at the New York Public Library. Before joining the faculty at Alabama State College in 1956, Reddick taught at a number of colleges, including Atlanta University and the New School for Social Research.

In 1956 King appointed Reddick chairman of the **Montgomery Improvement Association** (MIA) History Committee, to record the events of the bus protest. Having completed his own account of the bus boycott for the spring 1956 issue of *Dissent*, Reddick later agreed to help King recount the events for *Stride Toward Freedom* (1958).

Reddick accompanied King and his wife Coretta Scott **King** on their month-long **India trip** in 1959. On the way the group stopped briefly in Paris, where Reddick introduced the Kings to Richard Wright. Of that meeting, Reddick wrote: "Coretta and I threw in a point now and then but we were content to observe the giants in intellectual action. Both were short and brown-skinned but Dick was intense, always reaching for a thought or phrase while Martin was relaxed and un-spirited" (*Papers* 5:4). Once they arrived in India Reddick meticulously recorded the events of the trip. The publication of *Crusader without Violence* followed the trip.

In January 1960 King praised Reddick for being a "friend, not only to me and to Coretta, but to our total movement" (*Papers* 5:356). Reddick, however, paid a high price for supporting the movement, when he was fired from his post as chair of the Alabama State College History Department by President Councill **Trenholm** at the request of Governor John **Patterson**. In Reddick's defense, King released a statement extolling the historian's "unswerving devotion to the ideals of American democracy, and his basic commitment to the ethical principles of the Christian faith." He further admonished Governor Patterson and the State of Alabama for sinking to "a new low" by "seeking to bring a halt to the creative movement for human rights by making an example of a man who has committed no crime" (King, 16 June 1960). Reddick was fired in June 1960. His colleagues, English teachers and MIA stalwarts Mary Fair Burks and Jo Ann **Robinson**, resigned at the close of the spring semester.

The following fall Reddick began teaching at Coppin State Teachers College in Baltimore, Maryland. Although no longer in Alabama, Reddick continued to work with the **Southern Christian Leadership Conference**, providing content for the organization's newsletter. In addition, Reddick continued to offer King suggestions on his public statements. After it was announced that King would receive the **Nobel Peace Prize** in 1964, Reddick wrote King, offering ideas for his acceptance speech. "I believe that you would want to say that you accept the award for the thousands of Negro Americans and their white friends who have struggled for equality and democracy in America but have resolutely done so nonviolently" (Reddick, 25 November 1964). Reddick further suggested that King connect the civil rights struggle with the international liberation struggle by referring to the peace work in South Africa done by Nobel laureate Albert **Lutuli**. In the handwritten draft of his acceptance speech, King wrote: "You honor the dedicated pilots of our struggle, who have sat at the controls as the freedom movement soared into orbit. You honor, once again, Chief Lutuli of South Africa, whose struggles with and for his people, are still met with the most brutal expression of man's inhumanity to man" (King, "Acceptance Address for the Nobel Peace Prize," 108).

In 1978 Reddick accepted a position teaching African American history at Dillard University in New Orleans. He retired in 1987, after 40 years of teaching. Following his death in 1995 the Association of Third World Studies honored Reddick's academic contributions by establishing the Lawrence Dunbar Reddick Memorial Scholarship Award.

SOURCES

Introduction, in *Papers* 4:31; 5:3, 4, 25.

King, "Acceptance Address for the Nobel Peace Prize," in *A Call to Conscience*, ed. Carson and Shepard, 2001.

King, Address delivered during "A Salute to Dr. and Mrs. Martin Luther King" at Dexter Avenue Baptist Church, 31 January 1960, in *Papers* 5:351–357.

King, Statement on the firing of Reddick, 16 June 1960, MLKP-MBU.

King to Mary Fair Burks, 5 April 1960, in *Papers* 5:406–408.

Reddick, "The Bus Boycott in Montgomery," *Dissent* 3 (Spring 1956): 1–11.

Reddick, *Crusader without Violence*, 1959.

Reddick to King, 25 November 1964, MLKJP-GAMK.

REEB, JAMES (1927–1965)

James Reeb, a white Unitarian minister, became nationally known as a martyr to the civil rights cause when he died on 11 March 1965, in Selma, Alabama, after being attacked by a group of white supremacists. Reeb had traveled to Selma to answer Martin Luther King's call for clergy to support the nonviolent protest movement for voting rights there. Delivering Reeb's eulogy, King called him "a shining example of manhood at its best" (King, 15 March 1965).

Reeb was born on New Year's Day 1927, in Wichita, Kansas. He was raised in Kansas and Casper, Wyoming. After a tour of duty in the Army at the end of World War II, Reeb became a minister, graduating first from a Lutheran college in Minnesota, and then from Princeton Theological Seminary in June 1953. Although ordained a Presbyterian minister, Reeb transferred to the Unitarian Church and became assistant minister at All Souls Church in Washington, D.C., in the summer of 1959. In September 1963 Reeb moved to Boston to work for the **American Friends Service Committee**. He bought a home in a slum neighborhood and enrolled his children in the local public schools, where many of the children were black.

On 7 March 1965, Reeb and his wife watched television news coverage of police attacking demonstrators in Selma as they attempted to march across the Edmund Pettus Bridge on what became known as "Bloody Sunday." The following day, King sent out a call to clergy around the country to join him in Selma in a second attempt at a **Selma to Montgomery March** that Tuesday, 9 March. Reeb heard about King's request from the regional office of the Unitarian Universalist Association on the morning of 8 March, and was on a plane heading south that evening.

As Reeb was flying toward Selma, King was considering whether to disobey a pending court order against the Tuesday march to Montgomery. In the end he decided to march, telling the hundreds of clergy who had gathered at Brown's Chapel, "I would rather die on the highways of Alabama, than make a butchery of my conscience" (King, 9 March 1965). King led the group of marchers to the far side of the bridge, then stopped and asked them to kneel and pray. After prayers, they rose and retreated back across the bridge to Brown's Chapel, avoiding a violent confrontation with state troopers and skirting the issue of whether or not to obey the court order.

Several clergy decided to return home after this symbolic demonstration. Reeb, however, decided to stay in Selma until court permission could be obtained for a full scale march, planned for the coming Thursday. That evening, Reeb and two other white Unitarians dined at an integrated restaurant. Afterward they were attacked by several white men and Reeb was clubbed on the head. Several hours elapsed before Reeb was admitted to a Birmingham hospital where doctors performed brain surgery. While Reeb was on his way to the hospital in Birmingham, King addressed a press conference lamenting the "cowardly" attack and asking all to pray for his protection (King, 10 March 1965). Reeb died two days later.

Reeb's death provoked mourning throughout the country, and tens of thousands held vigils in his honor. President Lyndon B. **Johnson** called Reeb's widow and father to express his condolences, and on 15 March he invoked Reeb's memory when he delivered a draft of the **Voting Rights Act** to Congress. That same day King eulogized Reeb at a ceremony at Brown's Chapel in Selma. "James Reeb," King told the audience, "symbolizes the forces of good will in our nation. He demonstrated the conscience of the nation. He was an attorney for the defense of the innocent in the court of world opinion. He was a witness to the truth that men of different races and classes might live, eat, and work together as brothers" (King, 15 March 1965).

In April 1965 three white men were indicted for Reeb's murder; they were acquitted that December. The Voting Rights Act was passed on 6 August 1965.

SOURCES

Garrow, *Protest at Selma*, 1978.

Howlett, *No Greater Love*, 1966.

Johnson, "Special Message to Congress: The American Promise," 15 March 1965, in *Public Papers of the Presidents: Lyndon B. Johnson, 1965*, bk. 1, 1966.

King, Address to Selma marchers, 9 March 1965, MLJKP-GAMK.

King, Eulogy for James Reeb, 15 March 1965, CBC.

King, Statement on the beating of Orloff Miller, James Reeb, and Clark Olsen, 10 March 1965, MLKJP-GAMK.

King to Elder G. Hawkins, 8 March 1965, NCCP-PPPrHi.

REUTHER, WALTER PHILIP (1907–1970)

On the occasion of the 25th anniversary of the United Auto Workers (UAW), Martin Luther King wrote a letter to union president Walter Reuther, congratulating him and observing: "More than anyone else in America, you stand out as the shining symbol of democratic trade unionism" (King, 17 May 1961). King had a stalwart ally in Reuther, who gave critical backing to the 1963 **March on Washington for Jobs and Freedom** and was a supporter of King's civil rights tactics.

Reuther was born on 1 September 1907, in Wheeling, West Virginia, one of four sons of labor official Valentine Reuther and his wife, Anna. At age 15 Reuther went to work at the Wheeling Steel Corporation, serving as an apprentice tool and die maker. In 1927 he went to Detroit, and by 1931 he was a foreman supervising 40 other tool and die workers at the Ford Motor Company. During these years he completed his high school education and attended Wayne State University for three years.

Reuther left Ford in 1932, and in 1933 he and his brother Victor embarked on a three-year, around-the-world trip, traveling through England, Russia, Central Asia, China, and Japan and observing auto work and the labor movement in these countries. Reuther organized, and became the first president of, West Side Local 174 of the newly formed UAW, increasing membership from 78 to 30,000 members between 1936 and 1937, which was a precursor to the civil rights **sit-ins** of the 1960s.

Reuther was elected national UAW president in 1946, a position he held until his death. That year, he also became vice president of the Congress of Industrial Organizations (CIO), ascended to that body's presidency in 1952, and was at the forefront of the effort to merge the CIO with the American Federation of Labor, forming the **American Federation of Labor and Congress of Industrial Organizations** (AFL-CIO) in 1955. With the amalgamation of the two bodies, Reuther became an AFL-CIO vice president and also served as president of its Industrial Union Department. His tenure in these positions ended when the UAW withdrew from the AFL-CIO in 1968.

During his years as a top labor leader, Reuther took forceful positions inside and outside the labor movement with regard to civil rights. He sat on the national advisory boards of the **National Association for the Advancement of Colored People** and the **Congress of Racial Equality**, urged union locals to participate in the May 1957 **Prayer Pilgrimage for Freedom**, joined the call for protests later that year against South Africa's **apartheid** regime, and was a scheduled speaker at the May 1960 founding convention of the **Negro American Labor Council**. Reuther invited King to be a speaker at the 25th anniversary celebration of the UAW the following year, and in 1965 marched with King in the **Selma to Montgomery March**.

Reuther mobilized the UAW and other unions on behalf of the August 1963 March on Washington. He attempted to obtain the AFL-CIO's endorsement for the march, but president George Meany's tepid support caused Reuther to remark: "The statement is so anemic that you'd have to give it a blood transfusion to keep it alive on its way to the mimeograph machine" (Pomfret, "AFL-CIO Aloof"). Reuther spoke at the event, and later that day said the event "proves beyond doubt … that free men, despite their different points of view, despite their racial and religious differences, can unite on a great moral question like civil rights and the quest for equal opportunity and full citizenship rights" (King et al., 28 August 1963). In March 1965 Reuther marched with King in Selma, Alabama.

After King's **assassination**, Reuther marched with Coretta Scott **King** in Memphis on 8 April, in support of the peaceful resolution of that city's sanitation strike, and donated the largest check from any outside source, $50,000, to the striking sanitation workers. When he and his wife were killed in a 1970 plane crash, Coretta Scott King eulogized Reuther, saying, "He was there in person when the storm clouds were thick" (Flint, "Reuther Praised").

SOURCES

Jerry Flint, "Reuther Praised in Funeral Rites," *New York Times*, 16 May 1970.

King, Reuther, et al., "Transcript of 'March on Washington … Report by the Leaders,'" 28 August 1963, WHCF-MWalK.

King to Reuther, 17 May 1961, MLKP-MBU.

Lichtenstein, *Walter Reuther*, 1995.

John D. Pomfret, "AFL-CIO Aloof on Capital March," *New York Times*, 14 August 1963.

ROBINSON, CLEVELAND LOWELLYN (1914–1995)

In late 1958 Martin Luther King declined an invitation by union official Cleveland Robinson to speak in New York during Negro History Week. In his written response, he noted, "I want you to know that I have been deeply moved by your dedication and your humanitarian concern. You are doing a grand job for all of us" (King, 15 November 1958). Robinson served as one of King's advisors on the labor movement and as a force against racism in labor unions.

Robinson was born on 12 December 1914, in Swabys Hope, a rural parish of Manchester, Jamaica. He immigrated to the United States in 1944 and began working in a Manhattan dry goods store. He soon became active in District 65, Distributive

Workers Union of the Congress of Industrial Organizations, and in 1947, after organizing the store where he worked, he became a full-time organizer with the union. He rose swiftly in the union, becoming vice president in 1950 and secretary-treasurer in 1952. He remained in that position until his retirement from the union in 1992.

In 1960, Robinson joined with A. Philip **Randolph** to form the **Negro American Labor Council** (NALC), an organization that aimed to end discrimination in organized labor. He was elected vice president at the NALC's founding convention that year and, after Randolph's tenure, served as president from 1966 to 1972, when the NALC became the Council of Black Trade Unionists (CBTU).

Robinson participated in the **Prayer Pilgrimage for Freedom** in May 1957, joining King on the event's platform with other labor, civil rights, and religious leaders. The following year, while King convalesced from a stabbing, Robinson and District 65's President David Livingston wrote King, declaring that: "Your suffering will inspire us to renewed determination and greater efforts to fight segregation and discrimination" (Livingston and Robinson, 29 September 1958). Robinson worked as a member of the Board of Directors of the **Gandhi Society for Human Rights**, the fundraising arm of the **Southern Christian Leadership Conference**, and often solicited donations for King from the unions. He was involved in the earliest NALC meetings to plan the 1963 **March on Washington** and acted as the administrative chairman for the march. When King was awarded the **Nobel Peace Prize** in December 1964, Robinson was the event coordinator for the gala honoring King's return to the United States. The event was attended by such notables as Nelson A. **Rockefeller**, Whitney **Young**, James **Farmer**, Dorothy **Height**, and Jackie **Robinson**.

After membership in the NALC declined in the early 1970s, Robinson began working with the CBTU, the successor to the NALC. In addition to union organizing, Robinson was appointed to the New York City Commission of Human Rights. At the time of his death, Robinson was the chairman of the New York State Martin Luther King, Jr., Commission.

SOURCES

King to Robinson, 15 November 1958, MLKP-MBU.

Livingston and Robinson to King, 29 September 1958, BSCP-DLC.

Pfeffer, A. *Philip Randolph*, 1990.

ROBINSON, JACKIE (1919–1972)

Jackie Robinson, the first African American to play major league baseball, used his prestige as a star athlete to garner support for the civil rights movement. Following his retirement from baseball in 1957, Robinson often appeared with Martin Luther King at rallies, fundraising events, and demonstrations. King told Robinson, "You have made every Negro in America proud through your baseball prowess and your inflexible demand for equal opportunity for all" (King, 14 May 1962).

Born 31 January 1919, in Cairo, Georgia, Robinson grew up in Pasadena, California. After graduating from high school he attended Pasadena Junior College and the University of California in Los Angeles (UCLA), where he excelled in baseball, football, basketball, and track. In 1942 Robinson was drafted into the Army. Initially informally barred from Officer Candidate School because of his race, he eventually graduated as a second lieutenant. In July 1944 Robinson was court martialed for resisting a demand to move to the back of an Army bus. Eventually acquitted of the charges, he later received an honorable discharge from the Army.

Robinson was signed by the Brooklyn Dodgers in 1946, and on 15 April 1947 Robinson broke the color line in major league baseball when he took the field as first baseman for the Dodgers. Despite enduring insults, threats, isolation, and aggression on the playing field, Robinson eventually won over teammates and fans with his skill and competitive drive. He was named Rookie of the Year after his first season, and two years later he won the National League batting title and was named Most Valuable Player.

After leaving baseball in 1957, Robinson became an executive at Chock Full O'Nuts Corporation. Robinson also served as chairman of the **National Association for the Advancement of Colored People** (NAACP) Freedom Fund Drive, and later joined its Board of Directors.

In October 1958 Robinson and King served as honorary chairmen of the **Youth March for Integrated Schools** in Washington, D.C. Two years later Robinson raised concerns with King that some people affiliated with the **Southern Christian Leadership Conference** (SCLC) were claiming that the NAACP had outlived its usefulness, but King reassured Robinson that he had "always stressed the need for great cooperation between SCLC and the NAACP" (*Papers* 5:477).

Robinson continued to work with King, and when he became the first African American to be inducted into the Baseball Hall of Fame in 1962, Robinson donated the proceeds of a dinner in his honor to SCLC's voter registration project. In an article King wrote for the **New York Amsterdam News** upon this occasion, King applauded Robinson for choosing "truth" rather than "repose," because "back in the days when integration wasn't fashionable, he underwent the trauma and the humiliation and the loneliness which comes with being a pilgrim walking the lonesome byways toward the high road of Freedom. He was a sit-inner before the sit-ins, a freedom rider before the Freedom Rides" (King, "Hall of Famer").

The following year, Robinson joined the platform guests at the **March on Washington for Jobs and Freedom**. In 1964 he co-founded the interracial Freedom National Bank in Harlem and served as chairman until his death in 1972. In 1966 New York Governor Nelson **Rockefeller** hired him as a Special Assistant for Community Affairs.

Robinson disagreed with King's opposition to the **Vietnam War** and his calls for the United States to stop its bombing campaigns. In an open letter published in his regular *Chicago Defender* newspaper column in May 1967, Robinson questioned King's stance: "I am confused Martin, because I respect you deeply. But I also love this imperfect country" (Robinson, "An Open Letter"). After King called Robinson to elaborate on his beliefs, Robinson replied that despite disagreeing with King, he still saw King as "the finest leader the Negro people have and one of the most magnificent leaders the world has today" (Robinson, "What I Think"). Robinson died of a heart attack in 1972 at the age of 53.

SOURCES

King, "Hall of Famer," *New York Amsterdam News*, 4 August 1962.

King, "The Measure of a Man," *New York Amsterdam News*, 29 September 1962.

King to Robinson, 19 June 1960, in *Papers* 5:475–478.

King to Robinson, 14 May 1962, MLKJP-GAMK.

Rachel Robinson, *Jackie Robinson*, 1996.

Robinson to King, 5 May 1960, in *Papers* 5:454–455.

Robinson, *I Never Had It Made*, 1972.

Robinson, "An Open Letter to Dr. Martin L. King," *Chicago Defender*, 13 May 1967.

Robinson, "What I Think of Dr. Martin L. King," *Chicago Defender*, 1 July 1967.

ROBINSON, JO ANN GIBSON (1912–1992)

An instrumental figure in initiating and sustaining the **Montgomery bus boycott**, Jo Ann Robinson was an outspoken critic of the treatment of African Americans on public transportation. In his memoir, ***Stride Toward Freedom***, Martin Luther King said of Robinson: "Apparently indefatigable, she, perhaps more than any other person, was active on every level of the protest" (King, 78).

Born on 17 April 1912, in Culloden, Georgia, Robinson was the youngest of 12 children. After her father's death, her family sold their farm and moved to Macon, Georgia. Robinson graduated as valedictorian of her high school class and went on to earn her BS from Fort Valley State College, becoming the first person in her family to graduate from college. Robinson taught for five years in Macon's public school system before moving to Atlanta, Georgia, to earn her MA in English from Atlanta University. Following a year of study at Columbia University, she taught briefly at Mary Allen College in Crockett, Texas, before moving to Montgomery in 1949 to teach English at Alabama State College.

In Montgomery Robinson was active in the **Dexter Avenue Baptist Church** and the **Women's Political Council** (WPC). In 1949 Robinson suffered a humiliating experience on a nearly empty public bus when the driver ordered her off for having sat in the fifth row. When she became WPC president in 1950, Robinson made the city's segregated bus seating one of the top priorities of the organization. The WPC made repeated complaints about seating practices and driver conduct to the Montgomery City Commission. After the Supreme Court decision in ***Brown v. Board of Education***, Robinson informed the city's mayor that a bus boycott might ensue if bus service did not improve, but negotiations had yielded little success by late 1955. After Rosa **Parks'** arrest in December 1955, Robinson seized the opportunity to put the long-considered protest into motion. Late that night, she, two students, and John Cannon, chairman of the Business Department at Alabama State, mimeographed and distributed approximately 52,500 leaflets calling for a boycott of the buses.

As King and other civic and religious leaders established the **Montgomery Improvement Association** (MIA) to oversee organization of the boycott, Robinson chose not to accept an official MIA position for fear of jeopardizing her job at Alabama State College. She was, however, named to the executive board because of her WPC position, and King personally asked her to write and edit the weekly *MIA Newsletter*.

Despite Robinson's efforts to work behind the scenes, she was the target of several acts of intimidation. In February 1956 a local police officer threw a stone through her window. Two weeks later, a police officer poured acid on her car. Eventually, the governor ordered state police to guard the homes of boycott leaders.

Robinson took great pride in the eventual success of the boycott. In her memoir, Robinson wrote: "An oppressed but brave people, whose pride and dignity rose to the occasion, conquered fear, and faced whatever perils had to be confronted. The boycott was the most beautiful memory that all of us who participated will carry to our final resting place" (Robinson, 11).

Following the student **sit-ins** at Alabama State in early 1960, Robinson and other supporters of the students resigned their faculty positions rather than endure the tensions that Robinson called "a constant threat to our peace of mind" (Robinson, 169). After teaching for a year at Grambling College in Louisiana, Robinson moved to Los Angeles, where she taught until her retirement in 1976. Her memoir, *The Montgomery Bus Boycott and the Women Who Started It*, was published in 1987.

SOURCES

King, *Stride Toward Freedom*, 1958.
Robinson, *Montgomery Bus Boycott*, 1987.

ROCKEFELLER, NELSON ALDRICH (1908–1979)

Politician and philanthropist Nelson A. Rockefeller was an outspoken supporter of the civil rights movement. Martin Luther King once said of the four-term governor of New York: "If we had one or two governors in the Deep South like Nelson Rockefeller, many of our problems could be readily solved" (Walker, 19 October 1962).

Rockefeller was born 8 July 1908, in Bar Harbor, Maine, into one of the wealthiest families in the country. Concern for the lives of African Americans went back at least three generations to his grandfather, Standard Oil founder John D. Rockefeller, who, with his wife, Laura Spelman Rockefeller, had endowed Spelman College and King's alma mater, **Morehouse College**. Rockefeller graduated from Dartmouth in 1930, and joined the State Department the following year to oversee relations with Latin America. He left five years later to found his own nonprofit organization promoting development in the region. Rockefeller moved in and out of government for the next decade, taking roles in both the Harry S. **Truman** and the Dwight D. **Eisenhower** administrations, and then ran for governor of the state of New York in 1958.

Rockefeller's support for King began during that election year when the two appeared together, along with baseball star Jackie **Robinson** and president of the Brotherhood of Sleeping Car Porters, A. Philip **Randolph**, at a rally sponsored by the **Youth March for Integrated Schools**. After Rockefeller was elected, he used his position to advocate civil rights in the South. When King was arrested at a **sit-in** demonstration in Atlanta in October 1960, Rockefeller used the pulpit of a Brooklyn, New York, church to applaud King's ideals: "We've got to make love a reality in our own country. When the great spiritual leader, the Rev. Dr. Martin Luther King, finds himself in jail today because he had the courage to love, we have a long way to go in America" (Dales, "Governor Turns to Lay Preaching").

In early 1962, Rockefeller offered to help King set up a New York office of the **Southern Christian Leadership Conference** (SCLC), and after King was arrested while supporting the **Albany Movement**, he expressed appreciation for Rockefeller's supportive response at a dinner he co-chaired honoring Robinson's Hall of Fame induction. "Governor Rockefeller probed clearly to the point of our crusade and asked the Federal Government … whether or not the city of Albany, Georgia infringes upon the constitutional rights of Negro citizens with impunity" (King, 20 July 1962).

Rockefeller's financial largesse helped rebuild several bombed churches in the South, and he matched the $25,000 donation King made of his **Nobel Peace Prize** award to the **Gandhi Society for Human Rights**. During the **Birmingham Campaign**, Rockefeller secretly gave Clarence **Jones** money from his family's Chase Manhattan bank to bail local protesters out of jail. King wrote in his *New York Amsterdam News* column that Rockefeller had "a real grasp and understanding of what the Negro revolution is all about, and a commitment to its goals" (King, "The Presidential Nomination").

Although Rockefeller could not join King during his 1965 **Selma to Montgomery March**, Rockefeller wrote that he had "the most profound sympathy and respect for the purpose of this historic mission" (Rockefeller, 18 March 1965). That fall, the governor traveled to Atlanta to join King as the featured speaker at **Ebenezer Baptist Church**'s annual Men's Day celebration.

The following year Rockefeller won his third term as governor of New York. He later appointed Wyatt Tee **Walker**, SCLC's executive director from 1960 to 1964, as his special assistant for urban affairs.

After King's **assassination**, Rockefeller asked the New York legislature to pass "a series of measures vitally affecting the lives of all our Negro citizens: jobs and health, housing, education, and training" (Witkin, "Rockefeller Asks 'Memorial' Laws"). He flew to Atlanta in a chartered jet to attend King's funeral.

Rockefeller announced his third and final bid for the Republican presidential nomination on 30 April 1968, later losing to Richard **Nixon**. Although he was reelected governor of New York in 1970, he resigned in 1973 to devote himself to his charitable work. After Nixon resigned in the wake of the Watergate scandal, President Gerald Ford asked Rockefeller to serve as Vice President of the United States. Rockefeller served the two-year term and then retired from public life. He died of a heart attack on 26 January 1979.

SOURCES

Douglas Dales, "Governor Turns to Lay Preaching," *New York Times*, 24 October 1960.
King, Address at Jackie Robinson Hall of Fame Dinner, 20 July 1962, MLKJP-GAMK.
King, "The Presidential Nomination," *New York Amsterdam News*, 25 April 1964.
Rockefeller to King, 18 March 1965, MLKJP-GAMK.
Wyatt Tee Walker to Hugh Morrow, 19 October 1962, MLKJP-GAMK.
Richard Witkin, "Rockefeller Asks 'Memorial' Laws," *New York Times*, 6 April 1968.

RODELL, MARIE FREID (1912–1975)

Marie F. Rodell served as Martin Luther King, Jr.'s literary agent for the publication of his first book, *Stride Toward Freedom*. Inundated with offers to produce books and films about the **Montgomery bus boycott**, King hired Rodell and Joan **Daves**, Inc., in October 1957. Rodell corresponded with King regarding contract negotiations, editorial decisions, and publicity for *Stride Toward Freedom*.

Born in New York City on 31 January 1912, to Isadore and Elizabeth Freid, Rodell received her BA in 1932 from Vassar College. Following a nine-year career as associate editor in the Mystery Department at Duell, Sloan, and Pearce, Rodell launched her own literary agency with Joan Daves in 1948.

Extensive demands on King's time made it difficult for him to make significant progress on his first book; however, Rodell was adamant that the book be published by the fall of 1958. In a letter to King she conveyed her dissatisfaction with his lack of progress: "The fact that the first draft is still not completed is most disquieting to all of us" (Rodell, 13 March 1958). Despite much difficulty, *Stride* was publicly available by September 1958.

Rodell later became director of the Rachel Carson Trust for Living Environment. The author of three mystery novels, she was the founding secretary of the Mystery Writers of America. Rodell died in New York City in November 1975.

SOURCES

Advertisement for *Stride Toward Freedom*, August 1958, in *Papers* 4:466.
Daves to King, 18 October 1957, in *Papers* 4:286–287.
Rodell to King, 13 March 1958, MLKP-MBU.

ROGERS, THEOPHOLIUS YELVERTON, JR. (1935–1971)

In 1956 T. Y. Rogers became Martin Luther King, Jr.'s assistant at **Dexter Avenue Baptist Church**. King described Rogers as "one of the most promising young men in the Christian Ministry," possessing "a keen and analytical mind" (King, 29 September 1960; King, 25 April 1959).

Rogers was born in Sumter County, Alabama, on 8 October 1935. He graduated from Sumter County Training School in May 1952 before completing a BS at Alabama State College in 1955. In November 1956 Rogers became King's assistant at Dexter. In 1957 Rogers was ordained into the Baptist ministry in a special ceremony at Dexter. He later enrolled at **Crozer Theological Seminary**, where he earned his BD in 1960. During his summer and winter breaks from Crozer, Rogers returned to Dexter to preach.

In 1960 King resigned from Dexter and returned to Atlanta to be closer to the **Southern Christian Leadership Conference** (SCLC) headquarters. Upon his departure, Rogers expressed interest in the vacant pulpit at Dexter. King cautioned Rogers on the difficulty of gaining respect from the congregation: "It is one of the most difficult things in the world for a group of people who once taught you to accept you as their spiritual shepherd" (*Papers* 5:474). Dexter hired a different preacher in late 1960, and Rogers answered the call to Galilee Baptist Church in Philadelphia. He stayed there until 1964, when he returned to the South as pastor of First African Baptist Church in Tuscaloosa, Alabama. King spoke at his installation service in March 1964.

For the next several years, Rogers continued to work closely with SCLC. At the time of his death in 1971, he was serving as SCLC's director of affiliates.

SOURCES

King to Registrar at Boston University School of Theology, 25 April 1959, MLKP-MBU.
King to Rogers, 31 August 1957, in *Papers* 4:266–267.
King to Rogers, 18 June 1960, in *Papers* 5:474–475.
King to Phinehas Smith, 19 September 1960, MLKP-MBU.
"T. Y. Rogers, Member of SCLC Board," *Washington Post*, 27 March 1971.

ROOSEVELT, (ANNA) ELEANOR (1884–1962)

First Lady Eleanor Roosevelt, wife of President Franklin D. Roosevelt, was an advocate for civil rights and an ardent supporter of Martin Luther King from his **Montgomery bus boycott** days until her death six years later. King called Mrs. Roosevelt "perhaps the greatest woman [of] our time," praising "the courage she displayed in taking sides on matters considered controversial" and her "unswerving dedication to high principle and purpose" (King, "Epitaph for Mrs. FDR").

Eleanor Roosevelt was born in New York City on 11 October 1884. Although born into a privileged family, she was orphaned when she was 10 years old and was raised by her maternal grandmother. Sent to school in England at age 15, she learned a sense of public service that compelled her to work in New York City settlements when she returned in 1902. She married her distant cousin, Franklin D. Roosevelt, in 1905 and initially devoted her time to childrearing and supporting her husband's work. In 1920 Roosevelt began working on efforts to expand women's political and economic opportunities. After her husband became president of the United States in 1933, Roosevelt began to hold weekly women-only press conferences and started a syndicated newspaper column, "My Day," which was published for nearly three decades.

As first lady, Roosevelt championed many social justice causes. In the 1930s she joined the **National Association for the Advancement of Colored People** (NAACP), pressuring her husband to pass anti-lynching laws, and gave up her membership in the Daughters of the American Revolution after that organization denied black singer Marion Anderson the right to use their segregated concert hall. She was present at the founding meeting of the Southern Conference on Human Welfare in 1938, and defied Bull **Connor**'s orders when she sat in the aisle rather than submit to segregated seating in the Birmingham, Alabama, auditorium. She advocated against the poll tax and, as World War II began, campaigned to end racial discrimination in the armed forces. Following her husband's death in 1945, Roosevelt joined the board of directors of both the NAACP and the **Congress of Racial Equality**. That same year, President Harry S. **Truman** appointed her one of five delegates to the first United Nations (UN) General Assembly. Roosevelt became the chair of the UN Human Rights Commission and was critical to the drafting of the Universal Declaration of Human Rights.

Roosevelt met Montgomery NAACP activists Rosa **Parks** and E. D. **Nixon** during the **Montgomery bus boycott** and also sent King a telegram inviting him to meet with her. She wrote about the bus boycott in her column, saying, "There must be great pride, not only among the Negroes but among white people all over the country, in the remarkable restraint and courage shown by the Negroes in their struggle for their rights in Montgomery, Ala., and other places in the South." King's "insistence that there be no hatred in this struggle," in Roosevelt's view, was "almost more than human beings can achieve" (Roosevelt, 22 March 1957).

For the next several years, Roosevelt and King enjoyed frequent correspondence. When King was arrested for perjury on his income taxes in February 1960, Roosevelt joined the Committee to Defend Martin Luther King and the Struggle for Freedom in the South. Several months later, in October 1960, King was again arrested for his participation in a sit-in in downtown Atlanta. Of King's arrest Roosevelt wrote: "The people of the world will condemn—not Georgia, unfortunately—the United States for treating as a criminal a man who is looked upon with respect" (Roosevelt, 28 October 1960). In her column she continued to write in support of the **sit-ins**, commending the students' "determination to do away with inequality between races and to have real democracy in the United States" (Roosevelt, 6 February 1961). King expressed his appreciation, writing: "Once again, for all you have done, and I'm sure will continue to do to help extend the fruits of Democracy to our southern brothers, please accept my deep and lasting gratitude" (*Papers* 5:517).

Roosevelt's health began to decline in the fall of 1962. In September, she invited King to be a guest on the first episode of her new television series, "The American Experience," which would focus on civil rights. However, she entered the hospital just before it was scheduled to be taped. Roosevelt died on 7 November 1962. King wrote her family a condolence telegram, reflecting: "Her life was one of the bright interludes in the troubled history of mankind" (King, 8 November 1962).

SOURCES

Committee to Defend Martin Luther King and the Struggle for Freedom in the South, "Heed Their Rising Voices," in *Papers* 5:382.

King, "Epitaph for Mrs. FDR," *New York Amsterdam News*, 24 November 1962.

King to Roosevelt, 6 October 1960, in *Papers* 5:516–517.

King to Roosevelt Family, 8 November 1962, MLKJP-GAMK.

Roosevelt, "My Day," 22 March 1957, ERC-NHyF.

Roosevelt, "My Day," 28 October 1960, ERC-NHyF.

Roosevelt, "My Day," 6 February 1961, ERC-NHyF.

Roosevelt to King, 17 October 1956, in *Papers* 3:400.

ROTHSCHILD, JACOB MORTIMER (1911–1973)

Jacob Mortimer Rothschild was a steadfast supporter of the civil rights movement and racial equality. As a rabbi, he spread ideals of peace and unity to his Atlanta congregation, despite hostile public responses. Rothschild described Martin Luther King as a "spokesman who—like a prophet of ancient Israel—had fearlessly confronted the society of his day with its failures; had sought to rouse men to a vision of their own nobility," and who "has earned his place as the moral leader of our social revolution" (Rothschild, 20 November 1963).

Born in Pittsburgh, Pennsylvania, on 4 August 1911, Rothschild received his AB from the University of Cincinnati and completed his rabbinical studies at Hebrew Union College. He was ordained in 1936, and became the first Jewish chaplain to go into combat during World War II. In 1946 he was offered the pulpit at Atlanta's Hebrew Benevolent Congregation, where he remained until his death in 1973. As early as 1948 Rothschild unsettled congregants and aggravated Atlanta's white community with sermons calling for racial tolerance. Due to his outspokenness, his synagogue was bombed in October 1958. Responding to the bombing, King urged President Dwight D. **Eisenhower** to "convene a White House conference" that "could help recommit our nation to the peaceful settling of differences" (*Papers* 4:509).

King and Rothschild first met through membership in an interracial dinner group in Atlanta, and over the next several years they developed a close relationship. When King wrote "**Letter from Birmingham Jail**" after his April 1963 arrest, Rothschild praised the civil rights leader for his eloquence: "To my mind, it is without question the most moving and significant document I have yet read. May I congratulate you not only on the cogency of its position but on the power of its language and the beauty of its imagery as well" (Rothschild, 10 June 1963).

In 1964, King was awarded the **Nobel Peace Prize**, and Rothschild organized a dinner honoring King. Over 1,400 people, both white and black, gathered at Atlanta's

Dinkler Hotel to congratulate the city's native son in the largest biracial gathering in the history of Atlanta at the time. Many of Atlanta's elite attended, including Mayor Ivan Allen, Jr., Georgia Senator Leroy Johnson, and Archbishop Paul J. Hallinan.

In September 1967 King's friendship with Rothschild was tested, after Rothschild confronted him about "scurrilous" and "untrue" anti-Semitic and anti-Israeli comments reportedly made by staff members of the **Southern Christian Leadership Conference** (SCLC). "Do they really represent the position of the organization which you head and they serve?" Rothschild asked King. "I cannot believe so, particularly in the light of your many speeches in which you have publicly made clear not only the complete absence of any prejudice in your own heart but an empathy and a sympathy for Jews whether in the United States, in the Soviet Union, or in Israel" (Rothschild, 7 September 1967). In a five-page response to Rothschild, King confirmed that SCLC denounced anti-Semitism. He acknowledged that Hosea **Williams** had made the comment attributed to him out of anger, and assured Rothschild that, although he was unaware of any past negative comments made about Jews by James **Bevel** or Andrew **Young**, "I am sure that they were misquoted if any anti-Semitic impressions were given" (King, 28 September 1967).

After King's death, Rothschild delivered the eulogy at a memorial service held for him at the Episcopal Cathedral of St. Philip in Atlanta. Rothschild died on 31 December 1973, after suffering a heart attack. Following his death Coretta Scott **King** called Rothschild a "true neighbor," who would "risk his position, his prestige, and even his life for the welfare of others" (Greene, 435).

Sources

Blumberg, *One Voice*, 1985.
Greene, *Temple Bombing*, 1996.
King to Eisenhower, 13 October 1958, in *Papers* 4:509.
King to Rothschild, 28 September 1967, JMRP-GEU.
Rothschild, *As but a Day*, 1967.
Rothschild, "Introduction of Martin Luther King, Jr.," 20 November 1963, JMRP-GEU.
Rothschild to King, 10 June 1963, MLKJP-GAMK.
Rothschild to King, 7 September 1967, JMRP-GEU.

RUSTIN, BAYARD (1912–1987)

A close advisor to Martin Luther King and one of the most influential and effective organizers of the civil rights movement, Bayard Rustin was affectionately referred to as "Mr. March-on-Washington" by A. Philip **Randolph** (D'Emilio, 347). Rustin organized and led a number of protests in the 1940s, 1950s, and 1960s, including the 1963 **March on Washington for Jobs and Freedom**. While Rustin's homosexuality and former affiliation with the Communist Party led some to question King's relationship with him, King recognized the importance of Rustin's skills and dedication to the movement. In a 1960 letter, King told a colleague: "We are thoroughly committed to the method of nonviolence in our struggle and we are convinced that Bayard's expertness and commitment in this area will be of inestimable value" (*Papers* 5:390).

Born on 17 March 1912, Rustin was one of 12 children raised by his grandparents, Janifer and Julia Rustin, in West Chester, Pennsylvania. Rustin's life-long commitment to **nonviolence** began with his Quaker upbringing and the influence of his grandmother, whose participation in the **National Association for the Advancement of Colored People** (NAACP) resulted in leaders of the black community, such as W.E.B. Du Bois and Mary McLeod Bethune, visiting the Rustin home during Rustin's childhood. After graduating from West Chester High School, Rustin studied intermittently at Wilberforce University, Cheyney State Teachers College, and City College of New York.

While a student at City College of New York in the 1930s, Rustin joined the Young Communist League (YCL). Drawn to what he believed was the Communists' commitment to racial justice, Rustin left the organization when the Communist Party shifted their emphasis away from civil rights activity in 1941. Shortly after his YCL departure, Rustin was appointed youth organizer of the proposed 1941 March on Washington, by trade union leader A. Philip Randolph. During this period he joined the **Fellowship of Reconciliation** (FOR) and co-founded the **Congress of Racial Equality** (CORE). Rustin organized campaigns and led workshops on nonviolent direct action for both organizations, serving as field secretary and then race relations director for FOR. During

Ralph Abernathy, King, and Bayard Rustin leaving the Montgomery County Courthouse following Abernathy and King's indictment for boycotting city buses during the Montgomery bus boycott, 24 February 1956. © AP / Wide World Photos.

World War II he spent more than two years in prison as a conscientious objector. In 1947 Rustin was arrested with other participants of CORE's Journey of Reconciliation, a test of the Supreme Court rulings barring segregation in interstate travel that provided a model for the **Freedom Rides** of 1961. After spending 22 brutal days on a North Carolina chain gang, Rustin published a report in several newspapers that led to reform of the practice of prison chain gangs.

In 1948 Rustin went to India for seven weeks to study the Gandhian philosophy of nonviolence. Several years later, he traveled to Africa on a trip sponsored by FOR and the **American Friends Service Committee**, where he worked with West African independence movements. Despite his successful tenure with FOR, Rustin was asked to resign from the organization in 1953, after his arrest and conviction on charges related to homosexual activity. The following year he was appointed executive secretary of the War Resisters League, a position he held until January 1965.

Rustin became a key advisor to King during the **Montgomery bus boycott**. He first visited Montgomery in February 1956, and published a "Montgomery Diary," in which, upon observing a meeting of the **Montgomery Improvement Association**, he wrote: "As I watched the people walk away, I had a feeling that no force on earth can stop this movement. It has all the elements to touch the hearts of men" (Rustin, "Montgomery Diary," 10).

Rustin provided King with a deep understanding of nonviolent ideas and tactics at a time when King had only an academic familiarity with **Gandhi**. Rustin later recalled: "The glorious thing is that he came to a profoundly deep understanding of nonviolence through the struggle itself, and through reading and discussions which he had in the process of carrying on the protest" (D'Emilio, 230–231). King recognized the advantages of Rustin's knowledge, contacts, and organizational abilities, and invited him to serve as his advisor, well aware that Rustin's background would be controversial to other civil rights leaders. As King's special assistant, Rustin assumed a variety of roles, including proofreader, ghostwriter, philosophy teacher, and nonviolence strategist.

Rustin was also instrumental in the formation of the **Southern Christian Leadership Conference** (SCLC), proposing to King in December 1956 that he create a group that would unite black leaders in the South who possess "ties to masses of people so that their action projects are backed by broad participation of people" (*Papers* 3:493). Rustin developed the agenda and guidelines for discussion for the founding meeting of SCLC in January 1957. Although Rustin helped draft much of King's memoir, *Stride Toward Freedom*, Rustin would not allow his name to be credited in the book, telling an associate: "I did not feel that he should bear this kind of burden" (*Papers* 4:380n).

Rustin was instrumental in organizing the 1957 **Prayer Pilgrimage for Freedom**. He authored several memos to King outlining the goals of the march and advised King on what topics he should cover in his address. With Randolph, he also coordinated the 25 October 1958 and 18 April 1959 **Youth Marches for Integrated Schools**.

In 1963 Randolph began organizing the **March on Washington for Jobs and Freedom**. Despite the concerns of many civil rights leaders, Rustin was appointed deputy director of the march. In less than two months Rustin guided the organization of an event that would bring over 200,000 participants to the nation's capital.

From 1965 until 1979, Rustin served as president, and later as co-chair, of the A. Philip Randolph Institute, an organization of black trade unionists dedicated to racial equality and economic justice. From this position, Rustin promoted his view that future progress for African Americans rested on alliances between blacks, liberals, labor, and religious groups.

Sources

Anderson, *Bayard Rustin*, 1998.
D'Emilio, *Lost Prophet*, 2003.
King to Edward Gotlieb, 18 March 1960, in *Papers* 5:390–391.
Rustin, "Montgomery Diary," *Liberation* (April 1956): 7–10.
Rustin to King, 23 December 1956, in *Papers* 3:491–494.

SANE. *See* National Committee for a Sane Nuclear Policy.

SCLC. *See* Southern Christian Leadership Conference.

SCOPE. *See* Summer Community Organization and Political Education (SCOPE) Project.

SEAY, SOLOMON SNOWDEN, SR. (1899–1988)

In his memoir, ***Stride Toward Freedom,*** Martin Luther King described Solomon Seay as one of the few African American clergymen who, in the years before the **Montgomery bus boycott,** denounced injustice and encouraged blacks to have greater confidence in themselves. Seay observed King's unique contribution to the movement, stating: "He's a Ph.D. with common sense and humility, and not many people have both" (Ferron, 1 March 1956).

Seay was born 25 January 1899, in Macon County, Alabama, to Hagger Warren Seay and Isaac Seay, a railroad tie cutter. He studied at Alabama State College and Talladega College, and began his ministry in 1916. Seay preached at several AME Zion churches in the South before becoming pastor at Mount Zion AME Zion Church in Montgomery, Alabama, in 1947.

As one of the central pastors working to sustain the Montgomery bus boycott, Seay served on the executive board and the negotiating committee of the **Montgomery Improvement Association** (MIA). He believed in social change through **nonviolence** grounded in Christian principles, proclaiming at one mass meeting that "with love in our hearts and God on our side, there are no forces in hell or on earth that can mow us down" (Ferron, 1 March 1956). He called the MIA his "dream organization—one that would really champion the cause of the forgotten masses of our group," and wrote in a letter to MIA board members, "We have, voluntarily or involuntarily, been cata-pulted into a position of responsibility in the world's struggle for human rights and jus-tice" (Seay, 2 April 1958; Seay, 1957).

Seay continued his involvement in civil rights issues after the boycott came to an end. In 1961 Seay's house served as a safe haven for freedom riders beaten by violent mobs in Montgomery. Seay was also one of four pastors sued for libel in the **New York Times Co. v. Sullivan** case. The subsequent trial continued for years before the U.S. Supreme Court finally ruled in the pastors' favor in 1964.

In 1962 Seay was elected MIA president, after King and Ralph **Abernathy** left Montgomery for Atlanta to be closer to the **Southern Christian Leadership Conference** (SCLC). In a statement at the time of his election, Seay declared: "'I have come this far by faith.' Faith in God; faith in the hidden goodness of mankind, and faith in my own outlook on life" (Seay, 25 January 1962). During King's imprisonment in Albany, Georgia, Seay wrote to him that he was "as ever *with Martin with all that I have*" (Seay, 1 August 1962).

In 1972 Seay moved to southern Alabama, where he served as presiding Elder of the Greenville District of the AME Zion church. He retired from the ministry in 1982. His autobiography, *I Was There by the Grace of God*, was published posthumously in 1990.

SOURCES

Donald T. Ferron, Notes on MIA Executive Board meeting, 30 January 1956, in *Papers* 3:109–112.

Donald T. Ferron, Notes on MIA mass meeting, 1 March 1956, PV-ARC-LNT.

King, *Stride Toward Freedom*, 1958.

Manis, *A Fire You Can't Put Out*, 1999.

Seay, *I Was There by the Grace of God*, 1990.

Seay, "My Faith in the Possibility," 25 January 1962, HG-GAMK.

Seay to King, 1 August 1962, MLKJP-GAMK.

Seay to Members of the MIA board, 2 April 1958, RGP.

Seay to Members of the MIA Executive Board, 1957, MLKP-MBU.

SELMA TO MONTGOMERY MARCH (1965)

On 25 March 1965, Martin Luther King led thousands of nonviolent demonstrators to the steps of the capitol in Montgomery, Alabama, after a 5-day, 54-mile march from Selma, Alabama, where local African Americans, the **Student Nonviolent Coordinating Committee** (SNCC), and the **Southern Christian Leadership Conference** (SCLC) had been campaigning for voting rights. King told the assembled crowd: "There never was a moment in American history more honorable and more inspiring than the pilgrimage of clergymen and laymen of every race and faith pouring into Selma to face danger at the side of its embattled Negroes" (King, "Address at the Conclusion of the Selma to Montgomery March," 121).

On 2 January 1965 King and SCLC joined the SNCC, the Dallas County Voters League, and other local African American activists in a voting rights campaign in Selma where, in spite of repeated registration attempts by local blacks, only two percent were on the voting rolls. SCLC had chosen to focus its efforts in Selma because they anticipated that the notorious brutality of local law enforcement under Sheriff Jim **Clark** would attract national attention and pressure President Lyndon B. **Johnson** and Congress to enact new national voting rights legislation.

The campaign in Selma and nearby Marion, Alabama, progressed with mass arrests but little violence for the first month. That changed in February, however, when police attacks against nonviolent demonstrators increased. On the night of 18

King and others march from Selma to Montgomery during the Selma Campaign, 17 March 1965. (L to R): Ralph Abernathy, James Forman, King, S. L. Douglas, John Lewis. © AP / Wide World Photos.

February, Alabama state troopers joined local police breaking up an evening march in Marion. In the ensuing melee, a state trooper shot Jimmie Lee **Jackson**, a 26-year-old church deacon from Marion, as he attempted to protect his mother from the trooper's nightstick. Jackson died eight days later in a Selma hospital.

In response to Jackson's death, activists in Selma and Marion set out on 7 March to march from Selma to the state capitol in Montgomery. While King was in Atlanta, his SCLC colleague Hosea **Williams** and SNCC leader John **Lewis** led the march. The marchers made their way through Selma across the Edmund Pettus Bridge, where they faced a blockade of state troopers and local lawmen commanded by Clark and Major John Cloud, who ordered the marchers to disperse. When they did not, Cloud ordered his men to advance. Cheered on by white onlookers, the troopers attacked the crowd with clubs and tear gas. Mounted police chased retreating marchers and continued to beat them.

Television coverage of "Bloody Sunday," as the event became known, triggered national outrage. Lewis, who was severely beaten on the head, said: "I don't see how President Johnson can send troops to Vietnam—I don't see how he can send troops to the Congo—I don't see how he can send troops to Africa and can't send troops to Selma" (Reed, "Alabama Police Use Gas").

That evening King began a blitz of telegrams and public statements "calling on religious leaders from all over the nation to join us on Tuesday in our peaceful, non-violent march for freedom" (King, 7 March 1965). While King and Selma activists made plans to retry the march again two days later, Federal District Court Judge Frank M. Johnson notified movement attorney Fred Gray that he intended to issue a restraining order prohibiting the march until at least 11 March, and President Johnson pressured King to call off the march until a federal court order could provide protection to the marchers.

Forced to consider whether to disobey the pending court order, after consulting late into the night and early morning with other civil rights leaders and John Doar, the deputy chief of the Justice Department's Civil Rights Division, King proceeded to the Edmund Pettus Bridge on the afternoon of 9 March. He led more than 2,000 marchers, including hundreds of clergy who had answered King's call on short notice, to the site of Sunday's attack, then stopped and asked them to kneel and pray. After prayers they rose and turned the march back to Selma, avoiding another confrontation with state troopers and skirting the issue of whether to obey Judge Johnson's court order. Many marchers were critical of King's unexpected decision not to push on to Montgomery, but the restraint gained support from President Johnson, who issued a public statement: "Americans everywhere join in deploring the brutality with which a number of Negro citizens of Alabama were treated when they sought to dramatize their deep and sincere interest in attaining the precious right to vote" (Johnson, "Statement by the President"). Johnson promised to introduce a voting rights bill to Congress within a few days.

That evening, several local whites attacked James **Reeb**, a white Unitarian minister who had come from Massachusetts to join the protest. His death two days later contributed to the rising national concern over the situation in Alabama. Johnson personally telephoned his condolences to Reeb's widow and met with Alabama Governor George **Wallace**, pressuring him to protect marchers and support universal suffrage.

On 15 March Johnson addressed the Congress, identifying himself with the demonstrators in Selma in a televised address: "Their cause must be our cause too. Because it is not just Negroes, but really it is all of us, who must overcome the crippling legacy of bigotry and injustice. And we shall overcome" (Johnson, "Special Message"). The following day Selma demonstrators submitted a detailed march plan to federal Judge Frank Johnson, Jr., who approved the demonstration and enjoined Governor Wallace and local law enforcement from harassing or threatening marchers. On 17 March Johnson submitted voting rights legislation to Congress.

The federally sanctioned march left Selma on 21 March. Protected by hundreds of federalized Alabama National Guardsmen and **Federal Bureau of Investigation** agents, the demonstrators covered between 7 to 17 miles per day. Camping at night in supporters' yards, they were entertained by celebrities such as Harry **Belafonte** and Lena Horne. Limited by Judge Johnson's order to 300 marchers over a stretch of two-lane highway, the number of demonstrators swelled on the last day to 25,000, accompanied by Assistant Attorneys General John Doar and Ramsey Clark, and former Assistant Attorney General Burke **Marshall**, among others.

During the final rally, held on the steps of the capitol in Montgomery, King proclaimed: "The end we seek is a society at peace with itself, a society that can live with its conscience. And that will be a day not of the white man, not of the black man. That will be the day of man as man" (King, "Address," 130). Afterward a delegation of march leaders attempted to deliver a petition to Governor Wallace, but were rebuffed. That night, while ferrying Selma demonstrators back home from Montgomery, Viola Liuzzo, a housewife from Michigan who had come to Alabama to volunteer, was shot and killed by four members of the Ku Klux Klan. Doar later prosecuted three Klansmen for conspiring to violate her civil rights.

On 6 August, in the presence of King and other civil rights leaders, President John-son signed the **Voting Rights Act of 1965**. Recalling "the outrage of Selma," Johnson called the right to vote "the most powerful instrument ever devised by man for break-ing down injustice and destroying the terrible walls which imprison men because they are different from other men" (Johnson, "Remarks"). In his annual address to SCLC a few days later, King noted that "Montgomery led to the Civil Rights Act of 1957 and 1960; Birmingham inspired the Civil Rights Act of 1964; and Selma produced the voting rights legislation of 1965" (King, 11 August 1965).

SOURCES

Garrow, *Protest at Selma*, 1978.

Johnson, "Remarks in the Capitol Rotunda at the Signing of the Voting Rights Act," 6 August 1966, in *Public Papers of the Presidents: Lyndon B. Johnson, 1965*, bk. 2, 1966.

Johnson, "Special Remarks to the Congress: The American Promise," 15 March 1965, in *Public Papers of the Presidents: Lyndon B. Johnson, 1965*, bk. 1, 1966.

Johnson, "Statement by the President on the Situation in Selma, Alabama," 9 March 1965, in *Public Papers of the Presidents: Lyndon B. Johnson, 1965*, bk. 1, 1966.

King, "Address at Conclusion of the Selma to Montgomery March," in *A Call to Conscience*, ed. Carson and Shepard, 2001.

King, Annual report at SCLC convention, 11 August 1965, MLKJP-GAMK.

King, Statement on violence committed by state troopers in Selma, Alabama, 7 March 1965, MLKJP-GAMK.

King to Elder G. Hawkins, 8 March 1965, NCCP-PPPrHi.

Lewis, *Walking with the Wind*, 1998.

Roy Reed, "Alabama Police Use Gas and Clubs to Rout Negroes," *New York Times*, 8 March 1965.

SHUTTLESWORTH, FRED LEE (1922–)

One of the founding members of the **Alabama Christian Movement for Human Rights** (ACMHR) and the **Southern Christian Leadership Conference** (SCLC), Fred Shuttlesworth brought a militant voice to the struggle for black equality. In 1963 he drew Martin Luther King and the SCLC to Birmingham for a historic confrontation with the forces of segregation. The scale of protest and police brutality of the **Bir-mingham Campaign** created a new level of visibility for the civil rights movement and contributed to the passage of the **Civil Rights Act of 1964**.

Born in Mount Meigs, Alabama, Shuttlesworth was licensed and ordained as a preacher in 1948. He earned an AB (1951) from Selma University and a BS (1953) from Alabama State College. Shuttlesworth served as minister at First Baptist Church in Selma until 1952, and the following year he was called to Bethel Baptist Church in Birmingham.

Shuttlesworth became involved in the local chapter of the **National Association for the Advancement of Colored People** (NAACP) in 1955. When Circuit Judge Walter B. Jones banned the NAACP from activity in the state in 1956, at the urging of Alabama Attorney General John **Patterson**, Shuttlesworth presided over a 4 June planning meeting for a new organization that became the ACMHR. Shuttlesworth led a mass meeting at Sardis Church the next evening, and was declared president by ac-clamation, a post he held until 1969.

In November 1956, after the U.S. Supreme Court ruled that bus segregation in Montgomery was unconstitutional, Shuttlesworth and the ACMHR made plans to challenge segregation on Birmingham's buses. The night before their campaign was to begin, a bomb exploded under Shuttlesworth's parsonage at Bethel Baptist. The house was destroyed, but Shuttlesworth escaped unharmed. The following day, several hundred protesters sat in the sections reserved for whites on Birmingham buses. Twenty-one of the participants were arrested and convicted, and the ACMHR filed suit in federal court to strike down the local law mandating segregation.

Shuttlesworth joined King and C. K. **Steele** in issuing a call for a conference of southern black leaders in January 1957, "in an effort to coordinate and spur the campaign for integrated transportation in the South" (*Papers* 4:94). Held at **Ebenezer Baptist Church** in Atlanta, the meeting laid the foundation for the group that would become SCLC. At a later meeting in August of that year, Shuttlesworth became SCLC's first secretary.

As SCLC struggled through its early years, Shuttlesworth urged the organization to aggressively confront segregation. "I feel that the leadership in Alabama among Negroes is, at this time, much less dynamic and imaginative than it ought to be," he wrote to King in April 1959. "Even in our Southern Christian Leadership Conference, I believe we must move now, or else [be] hard put in the not too distant future, to [justify] our existence" (*Papers* 5:189–190).

In 1963 SCLC joined forces with the ACMHR to protest segregation in Birmingham. SCLC leaders met secretly in January of that year to draw up initial plans for the **Birmingham Campaign**, known as "Project C"—C for confrontation. Shuttlesworth issued the "Birmingham Manifesto," which explained the black community's decision to act. "We act today in full concert with our Hebraic-Christian tradition, the laws of morality and the Constitution of our nation," Shuttlesworth proclaimed. "We appeal to the citizenry of Birmingham, Negro and white, to join us in this witness for decency, morality, self-respect, and human dignity" (Shuttlesworth, 3 April 1963). On 6 April Shuttlesworth led the campaign's first march on city hall.

As the campaign continued, tensions between King and Shuttlesworth increased. As a result of injuries from a march, Shuttlesworth was in the hospital during negotiations that produced a one-day halt to demonstrations. In addition to his opposition to the halt, Shuttlesworth resented being left out of the decision. King, however, was able to convince him to publicly support the decision. The Birmingham Campaign ended two days later, with an agreement between the city's business community and local black leaders that included a commitment to the desegregation of public accommodations, a committee to ensure nondiscriminatory hiring practices in Birmingham, and cooperation in releasing jailed protesters.

Shuttleworth's confrontational style provided a counterbalance to King's more measured approach and served to inspire people to action. In his memoir of the Birmingham Campaign, King praised "the fiery words and determined zeal of Fred Shuttlesworth, who had proved to his people that he would not ask anyone to go where he was not willing to lead" (King, 61).

SOURCES
Eskew, *But for Birmingham*, 1997.
King, *Why We Can't Wait*, 1964.
Manis, *A Fire You Can't Put Out*, 1999.

MIA, Montgomery Improvement Association Press Release, Bus Protesters Call Southern Negro Leaders Conference on Transportation and Nonviolent Integration, 7 January 1957, in *Papers* 4:94.

Shuttlesworth, "Birmingham Manifesto," 3 April 1963, MLKJP-GAMK.

Shuttlesworth to King, 24 April 1959, in *Papers* 5:189–190.

SIT-INS

The sit-in campaigns of 1960 and the ensuing creation of the **Student Nonviolent Coordinating Committee** (SNCC) demonstrated the potential strength of grassroots militancy and enabled a new generation of young people to gain confidence in their own leadership. Martin Luther King, Jr., described the student sit-ins as an "electrifying movement of Negro students [that] shattered the placid surface of campuses and communities across the South," and he expressed pride in the new activism for being "initiated, fed and sustained by students" (*Papers* 5:368).

The sit-ins started on 1 February 1960, when four black students from North Carolina A&T College sat down at a Woolworth lunch counter in downtown Greensboro, North Carolina. The students—Joseph McNeil, Izell Blair, Franklin McCain, and David Richmond—purchased several items in the store before sitting at the counter reserved for white customers. When a waitress asked them to leave, they politely refused; to their surprise, they were not arrested. The four students remained seated for almost an hour until the store closed.

The following morning about two dozen students arrived at Woolworth's and sat at the lunch counter. Although no confrontations occurred, the second sit-in attracted the local media. By day three of the campaign, the students formed the Student Executive Committee for Justice to coordinate protests. The Greensboro protesters eventually agreed to the mayor's request to halt protest activities while city officials sought "a just and honorable resolution," but black students in other communities launched lunch counter protests of their own (Carson, 10). By the end of the month, sit-ins had taken place at more than 30 locations in 7 states, and by the end of April over 50,000 students had participated.

The sustained student protests in Nashville, Tennessee, were particularly well organized. Vanderbilt University student James **Lawson** led workshops on Gandhian **nonviolence** that attracted a number of students from Nashville's black colleges. Many of them, including John **Lewis**, Diane **Nash**, and Marion **Barry**, would later become leaders of the southern civil rights struggle. The Nashville movement proved successful, and the students grew ever more confident in their ability to direct campaigns without adult leadership.

Nonviolence was a central component of the student-led demonstrations; however, many protesters were not met with peaceful responses from the public. Although protesters were routinely heckled and beaten by segregationists and arrested by police, their determination was unyielding. King wrote: "The key significance of the student movement lies in the fact that from its inception, everywhere, it has combined direct action with non-violence. This quality has given it the extraordinary power and discipline which every thinking person observes" (*Papers* 5:450).

Although many of the student sit-in protesters were affiliated with **National Association for the Advancement of Colored People** (NAACP) youth groups, the new student movement offered an implicit challenge to the litigation strategy of the nation's oldest civil rights group. NAACP leaders, for their part, gave public support to the sit-ins, although some privately questioned the usefulness of student-led civil disobedience.

On 16 April, the leaders of the various sit-in campaigns gathered at a conference called by **Southern Christian Leadership Conference** (SCLC) executive director Ella **Baker**. This meeting became the founding conference of SNCC. In a statement prior to the opening of the conference, King emphasized the "need for some type of continuing organization" and expressed his belief that "the youth must take the freedom struggle into every community in the South" (*Papers* 5:427). The 120 students representing 12 southern states voted to establish a youth-centered organization without formal affiliation with any other civil rights group.

In October 1960 Atlanta student leaders convinced King to participate in a sit-in at Rich's, a local department store. King and about 300 students were arrested. The students were later released, but King remained in jail while Georgia officials determined whether his sit-in arrest violated parole conditions King had received a month earlier after driving with a suspended license. After being sentenced to six months of hard labor at Georgia State Prison at Reidsville, presidential hopeful John F. **Kennedy** and his campaign manager and brother, Robert **Kennedy**, helped secure King's release. Their intervention in the case helped contribute to Kennedy's narrow victory over Richard **Nixon** in the presidential election.

By fall 1960, there were signs that the southern civil rights movement had been profoundly transformed by the fiercely independent student protest movement. Those who had participated in the sit-in campaign were determined to continue the direct action tactics that were seizing the initiative from more cautious organizations made up of older people, such as King's SCLC.

SOURCES

Carson, *In Struggle*, 1981.
Introduction, in *Papers* 5:23–40.
King, "The Burning Truth in the South," in *Papers* 5:447–451.
King, "A Creative Protest," 16 February 1960, in *Papers* 5:367–370.
King, "Statement to the Press at the Beginning of the Youth Leadership Conference," 15 April 1960, in *Papers* 5:426–427.

SMILEY, GLENN E. (1910–1993)

Smiley, who rode alongside Martin Luther King on Montgomery's first desegregated bus, served as an advisor to King and the **Montgomery Improvement Association** (MIA) during the **Montgomery bus boycott**. A southern white minister and national field secretary of the **Fellowship of Reconciliation** (FOR), Smiley helped solidify King's understanding of Gandhian **nonviolence**. After interviewing King during the first few months of the boycott, Smiley wrote a colleague: "I believe that God has called Martin Luther King to lead a great movement here, and in the South. But why does God lay such a burden on one so young, so inexperienced, so good? King can be a Negro Gandhi, or he can be made into an unfortunate demagogue destined to swing from a lynch mob's tree" (Smiley, 28 February 1956).

Smiley was born in Loraine, Texas, on 19 April 1910. He studied at McMurry College, Southwestern University, University of Arizona, and University of Redlands.

Smiley worked for 14 years as a Methodist preacher in Arizona and California before joining the **Congress of Racial Equality** (CORE) and FOR in 1942. In 1945 he served time in prison as a conscientious objector.

As national field secretary for FOR, Smiley arrived in Montgomery on 27 February 1956, and was introduced to King by Bayard **Rustin**. He was impressed with King's leadership, but criticized King's willingness to accept a bodyguard. He gave King some books on nonviolence, including *The Power of Nonviolence*, by Richard **Gregg**. In a letter to friends, Smiley wrote, "If [King] can *really* be won to a faith in non-violence there is no end to what he can do. Soon he will be able to direct the movement by the sheer force of being the symbol of resistance" (Smiley, 29 February 1956).

Smiley emphasized to King the need to create dialogue between white and black ministers in the South. In an April 1956 letter to King, Smiley described a prayer meeting of Alabama white ministers who supported a liberal approach to racial issues as something that could "very easily be the most significant thing [he had] done, in that it stands a good chance of being the beginning of a rebuilt 'middle ground' in Alabama" (*Papers* 3:214). Smiley also hoped to establish joint prayer meetings with Montgomery's white and black ministers.

After the court found segregation on buses unconstitutional in **Browder v. Gayle** on 17 December 1956, the MIA released a set of guidelines for riding on newly integrated buses. Smiley helped develop these guidelines with King and other MIA leaders. In a 1986 draft of his autobiography, Smiley recalled that he approached King the night before they rode an integrated Montgomery bus for the first time and asked "to collect [his] salary" by being "the first white man to ride by you tomorrow when we ride the bus for the first time" (Smiley, 1986). Smiley rode alongside King, Ralph **Abernathy**, E. D. **Nixon**, and Fred **Gray** on the first integrated bus in Montgomery on 21 December 1956.

From 1956 to the early 1960s, Smiley organized a number of nonviolence training workshops and conferences with others, including King, Rustin, James **Lawson**, Abernathy, and A. J. **Muste**. Smiley believed nonviolent direct action was essential in the South, calling it "the most promising and adequate tool available" to the movement (Smiley, 11 July 1958). Smiley was also a strong supporter of the student **sit-in** movement in 1960, urging students to attend the Shaw University conference in April that became the birthplace of the **Student Nonviolent Coordinating Committee**.

The extent to which FOR and Smiley claimed credit for the adoption of nonviolence in the Montgomery bus boycott became an issue of contention in the late 1950s. According to Smiley, Abernathy reportedly felt that: "We could never have achieved the success we did in Montgomery had it not been for the Fellowship of Reconciliation and Glenn Smiley" (Smiley, 1986). Smiley stated his own position in a 1957 letter: "It seems clear to me that the F.O.R. has developed in the south a self-conscious, nonviolent movement with King at the head" (*Papers* 5:218n). King acknowledged Smiley's role, noting "his contribution in our overall struggle has been of inestimable value" (*Papers* 4:111). However, he challenged the notion that FOR was responsible for the nonviolent campaign. He wrote to a colleague: "I fear that this impression has gotten out in many quarters because members of the staff of the FOR have spread the idea" (*Papers* 5:218).

In the 1960s, Smiley founded Justice-Action-Peace Latin America, a Methodist-inspired group that organized seminars on nonviolence in Latin American countries from 1967 through the early 1970s. Smiley continued to work with FOR in the 1980s, receiving FOR's Martin Luther King, Jr., Award in 1991.

SOURCES

King to Alfred Hassler, 18 January 1957, in *Papers* 4:111.
King to Hilda Proctor, 1 June 1959, in *Papers* 5:218.
Smiley, Autobiography draft, 1986, GESP.
Smiley to King, 13 April 1956, in *Papers* 3:214.
Smiley to Muriel Lester, 28 February 1956, FORP-PSC-P.
Smiley to William Stuart Nelson, 11 July 1958, GESP.
Smiley to John Swomley, 29 February 1956, FORP-PSC-P.

SMITH, KELLY MILLER (1920–1984)

As a **social gospel** minister, Kelly Miller Smith believed in using his pastorate to promote activism. Smith participated in the founding meeting of the **Southern Christian Leadership Conference** (SCLC) in 1957, and co-founded the Nashville Christian Leadership Council (NCLC) a year later. In a 1961 telegram Smith described Martin Luther King as the "embodiment of the message you bear" (Smith, 19 December 1961).

Smith and his six siblings were raised in a Christian household in Mound Bayou, Mississippi. In 1938 Smith entered Tennessee State University as a music major. Two years later he decided to focus on religious studies and received his BA in religion and music from **Morehouse College** (1942) and his Master of Divinity from Howard University Divinity School (1945).

Smith first served as pastor of Mount Heroden Baptist Church in Vicksburg, Mississippi, before being called to First Baptist Church in Nashville, Tennessee, in 1951. Upon his arrival in Nashville Smith became extremely active in the civil rights struggle. In 1955 he and 12 other parents filed a lawsuit against the Nashville Board of Education for failing to implement the Supreme Court's ***Brown v. Board of Education*** ruling. With this case, his eldest daughter Joy, then six years old, became one of the first African American children to integrate Nashville's public schools in December 1957.

As president of the Nashville chapter of the **National Association for the Advancement of Colored People** from 1956 to 1959, Smith coordinated a voter registration drive that resulted in the addition of hundreds of new African American voters to the rolls. Smith also served on SCLC's executive board from 1957 to 1969. His affiliate organization, NCLC, held workshops directed by James **Lawson** to train students in the use of nonviolent protest techniques. In a June 1960 letter congratulating the students for their nonviolent protest of lunch counter segregation, King wrote that "Nashville provided the best organized and best disciplined group in the whole southern student movement," and acknowledged Smith's "magnificent leadership" (*Papers* 5:466).

Smith was assistant dean of Vanderbilt University Divinity School from 1968 to 1984, and a member of the Morehouse School of Religion's board of directors from 1975 until his death. In 1983 Smith was selected to give the Lyman Beecher Lectures at Yale Divinity School, one of the highest honors in theological education.

Smith remained pastor of First Baptist Church until his death in 1984. Four years before his death, the congregation honored his activism with the establishment of Kelly Miller Smith Towers, Nashville's first minority-owned housing project for the elderly and disabled.

SOURCES

King to Smith, 9 June 1960, in *Papers* 5:466.

Leila A. Meier, "'A Different Kind of Prophet': The Role of Kelly Miller Smith in the Nashville Civil Rights Movement, 1955–1960" (Master's thesis, Vanderbilt University, 1991).

Smith to King, 19 December 1961, MLKJP-GAMK.

SMITH, LILLIAN EUGENIA (1897–1966)

Renowned for her controversial books exploring segregation, white supremacy, and other social mores, author Lillian Smith was an advocate of racial reform in the South. In a 1956 letter to Martin Luther King, Smith expressed a "profound sense of fellowship and admiration" for King's efforts and his commitment to **nonviolence** and asked him to pass along a message to the **Montgomery Improvement Association** (MIA): "Tell them, please, that I am deeply humbled by the goodwill, the self discipline, the courage, the wisdom of this group of Montgomery Negroes" (*Papers* 3:170).

One of nine children in an affluent family, Smith was born on 12 December 1897, in Jasper, Florida. She attended Piedmont College, studied music at the Peabody Conservatory, and took classes at Columbia University. In 1922 she became head of the Music Department at an American Methodist school for Chinese girls in Huchow, China, where she developed an aversion to the arrogance of white colonialism and drew parallels to similar behavior in the segregated South. From 1925 to 1948, Smith managed the Laurel Falls Camp for Girls, founded by her parents in Clayton, Georgia. In 1936 she launched a literary magazine with Paula Snelling. Eventually titled *The South Today*, the magazine was devoted to Southern politics and culture and included works written by African Americans and women.

Smith's first novel, *Strange Fruit* (1944), dealt with the taboo subject of an interracial love affair and was banned in Boston, Massachusetts, as obscene. The controversial bestseller was the first of her several books addressing issues of social change, including *Killers of the Dream* (1949), *The Journey* (1954), and *Now Is the Time* (1955).

Smith's outspoken advocacy in support of the civil rights struggle made her a target for segregationists. In the winter of 1955, two young white boys burned down her house, destroying her correspondence, manuscripts, and works in progress. In a letter to King, Smith wrote, "It is hard to believe they did it because of race. But this lawlessness of the young is a direct result of the lawlessness of their elders, many of whom do not hesitate to say they will not obey the highest law of our land when that law does not suit them" (Smith, 3 April 1956).

Smith wrote a positive review of King's **Montgomery bus boycott** memoir, **Stride Toward Freedom** (1958), predicting that it would become "a classic story—as has Gandhi's salt march—of man demanding justice and discovering that justice first begins in his own heart" (Smith, "And Suddenly Something Happened"). In January 1959 King wrote to Smith: "Of all the reviews that I have read on *Stride Toward Freedom*, I still consider yours the best" (King, 23 January 1959).

Sources

King to Smith, 23 January 1959, LSP-GU.

Loveland, *Lillian Smith*, 1986.

Smith, "And Suddenly Something Happened," *Saturday Review* (20 September 1958): 21.

Smith to King, 10 March 1956, in *Papers* 3:168–170.

Smith to King, 3 April 1956, MLKP-MBU.

SNCC. *See* Student Nonviolent Coordinating Committee.

SOCIAL GOSPEL

In an 18 July 1952 letter, Martin Luther King wrote to his future wife, Coretta Scott, about his beliefs as a minister and proclaimed: "Let us continue to hope, work, and pray that in the future we will live to see a warless world, a better distribution of wealth, and a brotherhood that transcends race or color. This is the gospel that I will preach to the world" (*Papers* 6:126). As a self-described "advocator of the social gospel," King's theology was concerned "with the whole man, not only his soul but his body, not only his spiritual well-being, but his material well-being" (*Papers* 6:72; *Papers* 5:422). His ministry built upon the social gospel of the Protestant church at the turn of the twentieth century and his own family's practice of preaching on the social conditions of parishioners.

The early social gospel movement emerged during the rapidly industrializing American society following the Civil War. Recognizing the injustices of "triumphant capitalism," some progressive ministers prescribed a large dose of "practical Christianity" to right these wrongs and directly address the social needs of the era (Hopkins, 121). One of the most prominent was Walter Rauschenbusch, a German-American who pastored a church in the Hell's Kitchen district of New York in the late nineteenth century. In *Christianity and the Social Crisis*, Rauschenbusch traced the social gospel back to the lives of the Hebrew prophets. He stated that rather than ritualistic ceremonies, the prophets "insisted on a right life as the true worship of God" (Rauschenbusch, 5). This "right life" included the belief that "social problems are moral problems on a large scale" (Rauschenbusch, 6). King read *Christianity and the Social Crisis* at **Crozer Theological Seminary** and wrote that its message "left an indelible imprint on my thinking by giving me a theological basis for the social concern which had already grown up in me" (*Papers* 4:474).

Social gospel proponent Henry Emerson **Fosdick**, popular pastor of New York's Riverside Church during the 1930s and 1940s, was an early influence on King's preaching. Fosdick felt that a church "that pretends to care for the souls of people but is not interested in the slums that damn them, the city government that corrupts them, the economic order that cripples them, and international relationships that, leading to peace or war, determine the spiritual destiny of innumerable souls" would receive divine condemnation (Fosdick, 25). He also emphasized that "the saving of society does depend on things which only high, personal religion can supply" (Fosdick, 38).

King's family put him on a social gospel path, one that had already been cleared by his grandfather, A. D. **Williams**, and father, **King**, Sr. Williams, who was minister of **Ebenezer Baptist Church** at the turn of the twentieth century, helped form the Georgia Equal Rights League in February 1906, and was a founding member of Atlanta's branch of the **National Association for the Advancement of Colored People**. King, Sr., succeeded Williams at Ebenezer and, in a 1940 address to the Atlanta Missionary Baptist Association, he envisioned a "time when every minister will become a registered voter and a part of every movement for the betterment of our people" (*Papers* 1:34). In his unpublished 1973 autobiography, King, Sr., asserted that his ministry was never "solely oriented toward life and death. It has been equally concerned with the here and now, with improving man's lot in *this* life. I have therefore stressed the social gospel" ("A Black Rebel"). Other influences on King's social gospel included **Morehouse College** president and minister Benjamin **Mays**, who regularly spoke against segregation in Tuesday morning chapel at the college during King's years there. He chastised both African Americans who favored a gradualist approach to civil rights and whites who did not "want democracy to function in certain areas: especially in areas that involve Negroes" (Mays, "Three Great Fears").

King's studies of Reinhold **Niebuhr**'s writings at Crozer and **Boston University** tempered his belief in the social gospel's typical confidence in liberal theology and its reliance on human agency as a primary force for change. "While I still believed in man's potential for good, Niebuhr made me realize his potential for evil as well," King later recalled (King, *Stride*, 99). He also appreciated Niebuhr's assertion that "the glaring reality of collective evil" was one explanation for racial hatred (King, *Stride*, 99).

King arrived as pastor at **Dexter Avenue Baptist Church** still "a firm believer in what is called the 'social gospel'" (*Papers* 6:141). King tied this faith to the nonviolent protest that characterized the **Montgomery bus boycott**, noting that "Christ furnished the spirit and motivation" for the boycott (*Papers* 5:423).

King took to task those churches that separated the secular realities of daily life from spiritual needs. His vision of the church's role in social concerns was based on the early church's identity, in his mind, as an institution that shaped social mores and conditions. King believed that God would harshly judge the church's apathy on these matters and, conversely, praise those clergy who would take public stands on issues confronting their parishioners' everyday lives.

King remained a proponent of the social gospel despite the many setbacks the civil rights movement suffered in the later 1960s. In a speech delivered the day before his death, King asserted that "somehow the preacher must have a kind of fire shut up in his bones, and whenever injustice is around he must tell it" (King, "I've Been," 213).

SOURCES

Fosdick, *Hope of the World*, 1933.

Hopkins, *Rise of the Social Gospel*, 1940.

Introduction, in *Papers* 1:1, 10, 14, 34, 38.

Introduction, in *Papers* 6:2.

King, "Accepting Responsibility for Your Actions," 26 July 1953, in *Papers* 6:139–142.

King, "I've Been to the Mountaintop," in *A Call to Conscience*, ed. Carson and Shepard, 2001.

King, "Letter from Birmingham Jail," in *Why We Can't Wait*, 1964.

King, "My Pilgrimage to Nonviolence," 1 September 1958, in *Papers* 4:473–481.

King, "Pilgrimage to Nonviolence," 13 April 1960, in *Papers* 5:419–425.

King, "Preaching Ministry," in *Papers* 6:69–72.

King, *Stride Toward Freedom*, 1958.

King to Coretta Scott, 18 July 1952, in *Papers* 6:123–126.

King. Sr., "A Black Rebel: The Autobiography of M. L. King, Sr.," 1973, MLKJP-GAMK.

Mays, "Three Great Fears," *Pittsburgh Courier*, 17 April 1948.

Rauschenbusch, *Christianity and the Social Crisis*, 1907.

SONGS AND THE CIVIL RIGHTS MOVEMENT

Music and singing played a critical role in inspiring, mobilizing, and giving voice to the civil rights movement. "The freedom songs are playing a strong and vital role in our struggle," said Martin Luther King, Jr., during the **Albany Movement**. "They give the people new courage and a sense of unity. I think they keep alive a faith, a radiant hope, in the future, particularly in our most trying hours" (Shelton, "Songs a Weapon").

The evolution of music in the black freedom struggle reflects the evolution of the movement itself. Calling songs "the soul of the movement," King explained in his 1964 book **Why We Can't Wait** that civil rights activists "sing the freedom songs today for the same reason the slaves sang them, because we too are in bondage and the songs add hope to our determination that 'We shall overcome, Black and white together, We shall overcome someday'" (King, *Why*, 86).

"We Shall Overcome," a song with roots in the **Highlander Folk School** during the labor struggles of the 1940s, became the unofficial anthem of the movement. Wyatt T. **Walker**, executive director of King's **Southern Christian Leadership Conference**, said, "One cannot describe the vitality and emotion this one song evokes across the Southland. I have heard it sung in great mass meetings with a thousand voices singing as one; I've heard a half-dozen sing it softly behind the bars of the Hinds County prison in Mississippi; I've heard old women singing it on the way to work in Albany, Georgia; I've heard the students singing it as they were being dragged away to jail. It generates power that is indescribable" (Carawan, 11).

Professional singers such as Mahalia **Jackson** and Harry **Belafonte** were early and consistent supporters of civil rights reform efforts, but group singing was the most prominent music in the movement. As a community-based campaign led by church leaders, the music of the **Montgomery bus boycott** in 1955–1956 consisted of Baptist and Methodist hymns and traditional Negro spirituals. As King recalled in his memoir of the boycott, **Stride Toward Freedom**, "One could not help but be moved by these traditional songs, which brought to mind the long history of the Negro's suffering" (King, *Stride*, 86). In contrast, beginning with the **sit-in** movements of 1960, black students throughout the South began to take leadership roles in the broader movement. The songs of campaigns led by student activists moved beyond traditional church music. Younger activists made up new lyrics, giving new life to many traditional songs.

In the 1961 **Freedom Rides** songs played a critical role in sustaining morale for those serving time in Mississippi's Hinds County Jail. James **Farmer**, national director of the **Congress of Racial Equality** and a Freedom Ride participant, recalled one night when a voice called from the cell block below to the freedom riders: "Sing your freedom song.… We sang old folk songs and gospel songs to which new words had been written, telling of the Freedom Ride and its purpose" (Wexler, 134). The female freedom riders in another wing of the jail joined in, "and for the first time in history, the Hinds County jail rocked with unrestrained singing of songs about Freedom and Brotherhood" (Wexler, 134).

For many on the staff of the **Student Nonviolent Coordinating Committee** (SNCC), the protests in Albany, Georgia, proved an important training ground in which to learn the techniques for mobilizing the dormant black populace of the Deep South. Perhaps of greatest importance, they became more aware of the cultural dimensions of the black struggle, quickly recognizing the value of freedom songs to convey the ideas of the southern movement and to sustain morale. Bernice Reagon, an Albany student leader who joined SNCC's staff, described the Albany Movement as "a singing movement." Singing had special importance at mass meetings, Reagon observed: "After the song, the differences among us would not be as great" (Reagon, "In Our Hands").

SOURCES

Carawan and Carawan, *We Shall Overcome*, 1963.
Carson, *In Struggle*, 1981.
King, *Stride Toward Freedom*, 1958.
King, *Why We Can't Wait*, 1964.
Reagon, "In Our Hands: Thoughts on Black Music," *Sing Out!* 24 (January/February 1976): 1–2, 5.
Reagon, "Songs of the Civil Rights Movement 1955–1965: A Study in Culture History." PhD diss., Howard University, 1975.
Robert Shelton, "Songs a Weapon in Rights Battle," *New York Times*, 20 August 1962.
Werner, *Change Is Gonna Come*, 1998.
Wexler, *Civil Rights Movement*, 1993.

SOUTHERN CHRISTIAN LEADERSHIP CONFERENCE (SCLC)

With the goal of redeeming "the soul of America" through nonviolent resistance, the Southern Christian Leadership Conference (SCLC) was established in 1957 to coordinate the action of local protest groups throughout the South (King, "Beyond Vietnam," 144). Under the leadership of Martin Luther King, Jr., the organization drew on the power and independence of black churches to support its activities. "This conference is called," King wrote, with fellow ministers C. K. **Steele** and Fred **Shuttlesworth** in January 1957, "because we have no moral choice, before God, but to delve deeper into the struggle—and to do so with greater reliance on non-violence and with greater unity, coordination, sharing, and Christian understanding" (*Papers* 4:95).

The catalyst for the formation of SCLC was the **Montgomery bus boycott**. Following the success of the boycott in 1956, Bayard **Rustin** wrote a series of working papers to address the possibility of expanding the efforts in Montgomery to other cities throughout the South. In these papers, he asked whether an organization was needed to coordinate these activities. After much discussion with his advisors, King invited southern black ministers to the Southern Negro Leaders Conference on Transportation and Nonviolent Integration (later renamed the Southern Christian Leadership Conference) at **Ebenezer Baptist Church** in Atlanta. The ministers who attended released a manifesto in which they called upon white southerners to "realize that the treatment of Negroes is a basic spiritual problem.... Far too many have silently stood by" (*Papers* 4:105). In addition, they encouraged black Americans "to seek justice and reject all injustice" and to dedicate themselves to the principle of **nonviolence** "no matter how great the provocation" (*Papers* 4:104; 105).

SCLC differed from organizations such as the **Student Nonviolent Coordinating Committee** (SNCC) and the **National Association for the Advancement of Colored People**, in that it operated as an umbrella organization of affiliates. Rather than seek individual members, it coordinated with the activities of local organizations like the **Montgomery Improvement Association** and the Nashville Christian Leadership Council. "The life-blood of SCLC movements," as described in one of its pamphlets, "is in the masses of people who are involved—members of SCLC and its local affiliates and chapters" ("This Is SCLC," 1971). To that end, SCLC staff such as Andrew **Young** and Dorothy **Cotton** trained local communities in the philosophy of Christian

(L to R) T. J. Jemison, C. K. Steele, Fred Shuttlesworth, and King concluding the Southern Negro Leaders Conference on Transportation and Nonviolent Integration in Atlanta, 10 January 1957. This meeting laid the foundation for the Southern Christian Leadership Conference. © AP / Wide World Photos.

nonviolence by conducting leadership training programs and opening citizenship schools. Through its affiliation with churches and its advocacy of nonviolence, SCLC sought to frame the struggle for civil rights in moral terms.

SCLC's first major campaign, the Crusade for Citizenship, began in late 1957, sparked by the civil rights bill then pending in Congress. The idea for the crusade was developed at SCLC's August 1957 conference, where 115 African American leaders laid the groundwork for the crusade. The campaign's objective was to register thousands of disenfranchised voters in time for the 1958 and 1960 elections, with an emphasis on educating prospective voters. The crusade sought to establish voter education clinics throughout the south, raise awareness among African Americans that "their chances for improvement rest on their ability to vote," and stir the nation's conscience to change the current conditions (SCLC, 9 August 1957). Funded by small donations from churches and large sums from private donors, the crusade continued through the early 1960s.

SCLC also joined local movements to coordinate mass protest campaigns and voter registration drives all over the South, most notably in Albany, Georgia, Birmingham and Selma, Alabama, and **St. Augustine, Florida**. The organization also played a major role in the **March on Washington for Jobs and Freedom**, where King delivered his "**I Have a Dream**" speech on the steps of the Lincoln Memorial. The visibility that SCLC brought to the civil rights struggle laid the groundwork for passage of the **Civil Rights Act of 1964** and the **Voting Rights Act of 1965**. By the latter half of the decade, tensions were growing between SCLC and more militant protest groups such as SNCC and the **Congress of Racial Equality**. Amid calls for "**Black Power**,"

King and SCLC were often criticized for being too moderate and overly dependent on the support of white liberals.

As early as 1962 SCLC began to broaden its focus to include issues of economic inequality. Seeing poverty as the root of social inequality, in 1962 SCLC began **Operation Breadbasket** in Atlanta to create new jobs in the black community. In 1966 the program spread to Chicago as part of the **Chicago Campaign**. A year later planning began for a **Poor People's Campaign** to bring thousands of poor people to Washington, D.C., to push for federal legislation that would guarantee employment, income, and housing for economically marginalized people of all ethnicities. The **assassination** of King on 4 April 1968 crippled SCLC's momentum and undermined the success of the Poor People's Campaign. The organization, which had often been overshadowed by its leader's prominence, resumed plans for the Washington demonstration as a tribute to King. Under the leadership of SCLC's new president, Ralph **Abernathy**, 3,000 people camped in Washington from 13 May to 24 June 1968.

Headquartered in Atlanta, SCLC is now a nationwide organization with chapters and affiliates located throughout the United States. It continues its commitment to nonviolent action to achieve social, economic, and political justice and is focused on issues such as racial profiling, police brutality, hate crimes, and discrimination.

SOURCES

Fairclough, *To Redeem the Soul of America*, 1987.

King, "Beyond Vietnam," in *A Call to Conscience*, ed. Carson and Shepard, 2001.

King et al., MIA press release, 7 January 1957, in *Papers* 4:94–95.

King, "A Statement to the South and the Nation," Issued by the Southern Negro Leaders Conference on Transportation and Nonviolent Integration, 10 January–11 January 1957, in *Papers* 4:103–106.

SCLC, Press release, 9 August 1957, MLKP-MBU.

"This Is SCLC," 1971, MLKJP-GAMK.

SPOCK, BENJAMIN (1903–1998)

Pediatrician and author Benjamin Spock used his fame to bring attention to the **Vietnam War** and nuclear proliferation. In 1965 he encouraged Martin Luther King to join him in criticizing United States policy in Vietnam. King participated in his first anti-war demonstration in March 1967, alongside Spock.

Born in 1903, Spock trained as a pediatrician and psychoanalyst. His influential book, *Dr. Spock's Baby and Child Care*, sold over 50 million copies and helped revolutionize parenting. Throughout the 1950s and 1960s, Spock taught child development, wrote extensively, lectured around the world, and had his own television program. In 1963 he became the co-chair of the **National Committee for a SANE Nuclear Policy**.

Coretta Scott **King** joined Spock as a featured speaker at a major demonstration against the war in Vietnam in Washington, D.C., in November 1965. There, Spock urged her to pressure her husband to join the peace movement, arguing that "he could become the most important symbol for peace in this country, as well as for world peace" (Scott King, 293). King, Jr., admired Spock's dedication to the peace movement, even suggesting to the World Council of Peace that Spock be awarded the organization's Frederic Joliet-Curie Award.

In January 1967 *Ramparts* magazine published a photo essay on the impact of the war on Vietnamese children, with an introduction written by Spock. The essay deeply affected King; just three months later, he made his most public and comprehensive address against the war, "**Beyond Vietnam**," at Riverside Church. Three weeks later, both men led a march to United Nations Plaza in New York. King and Spock collaborated on "Vietnam Summer," a project to mobilize grassroots peace activists in preparation for the 1968 elections.

Members of the peace movement encouraged Spock and King to compete in the 1968 presidential race on a third-party ticket. Although they declined, Spock did run for president in 1972. In January 1968, Spock, William Sloane Coffin, and three others were indicted for conspiring to counsel young men to violate the draft laws. Spock asked, "What is the use of physicians like myself trying to help parents bring up children, healthy and happy, to have them killed in such numbers for a cause that is ignoble?" ("Baby Doctor for the Millions Dies"). King submitted a statement of complicity supporting those who had been indicted. Spock was tried and found guilty, but the verdict was overturned on appeal. Spock continued his writing and political activity throughout his life. In 1985 he and his second wife wrote a memoir, *Spock on Spock*. He died at the age of 94.

SOURCES
"Baby Doctor for the Millions Dies," *Los Angeles Times*, 17 March 1998.
King, "Beyond Vietnam," in *A Call to Conscience*, ed. Carson and Shepard, 2001.
(Scott) King, *My Life with Martin Luther King, Jr.*, 1969.
William F. Pepper, "The Children of Vietnam," *Ramparts* (January 1967): 44–67.
"What Are You Doing during Vietnam Summer 1967?" *New York Times*, 30 April 1967.

STATE OF ALABAMA V. M. L. KING, JR. (1956 AND 1960)

White officials in Alabama conducted two concerted efforts to defeat Martin Luther King, Jr., and the civil rights movement legally, by indicting King for violating an anti-boycotting law during the **Montgomery bus boycott** and for income tax fraud, in 1956 and 1960, respectively.

On 21 February 1956 King was indicted by the Montgomery County Grand Jury for his boycott of the Montgomery City Lines, Inc. According to the State of Alabama, King and 89 others violated a 1921 statute that outlawed boycotts against businesses. During the four-day trial, which began on 19 March 1956, eight lawyers, led by local attorney Fred **Gray**, defended King by presenting the evils of bus segregation and the abuse that Montgomery blacks had suffered for years from Montgomery bus drivers. Thirty-one witnesses testified to the harassment they had suffered while riding the city buses. Stella Brooks revealed that she stopped riding the buses in 1950, after her husband was killed by Montgomery police. According to Brooks, her husband was shot after demanding a fare refund following a confrontation with the bus driver.

On the final day of the trial, Judge Eugene W. Carter found King guilty and fined him $500 plus an additional $500 for court costs. Rather than pay the fine, King chose to appeal the verdict, and the sentence was converted to 386 days of jail time. Responding to the verdict, King said: "I was optimistic enough to hope for the best but realistic enough to prepare for the worst. This will not mar or diminish in any way my interest in the protest. We will continue to protest in the same spirit of nonviolence and passive resistance, using the weapon of love" (Phillips, "Negro Minister Convicted"). Outside the courthouse, King was greeted by a crowd of 300 cheering supporters. The Court of Appeals rejected King's appeal on 30 April 1957, maintaining that his lawyers missed the 60-day deadline. King paid the fine in December 1957.

King's second indictment came in February 1960, after an Alabama grand jury issued a warrant for his arrest on two counts of felony perjury. The state charged that King had signed fraudulent tax returns for 1956 and 1958. A state audit of King's returns the previous month claimed that he had not reported funds he received on behalf of the **Montgomery Improvement Association** (MIA) and the **Southern Christian Leadership Conference** (SCLC), and still owed the state more than $1,700. In late February a group of King's supporters met in the New York home of Harry **Belafonte** and formed the Committee to Defend Martin Luther King and the Struggle for Freedom in the South. The committee issued press releases denouncing the charges against King as a "gross misrepresentation of fact" because King's income had never "even approached" the $45,000 that Alabama officials claimed King received in 1958 (*Papers* 5:25–26).

King's trial began in Montgomery, Alabama, on 25 May 1960. His lawyers effectively poked holes in the prosecution's case, calling attention to the vagueness of the indictment and arguing that any expense reimbursements King may have received from SCLC were nontaxable income. Testifying in his own defense, King asserted that the tax examiner had revealed that he was "under pressure by his supervisors" to find fault with his returns (*Papers* 5:30). The all-white jury deliberated nearly four hours before returning a "not guilty" verdict. In a statement following the verdict King said: "This represents to my mind great hope, and it reveals that said on so many occasions, that there are hundreds and thousands of people, white people of goodwill in the South" (*Papers* 5:462). Although neither case posed a serious threat to King or the movement, these cases show the extent to which white officials in Alabama went to thwart civil rights gains in the state.

SOURCES

Burns, *Daybreak of Freedom*, 1997.
Indictment, *State of Alabama v. M. L. King, Jr., et al.*, in *Papers* 3:132–133.
Introduction, in *Papers* 3:14–16; 24–26; 30.
"Judgment and Sentence of the Court," *State of Alabama v. M. L. King, Jr., et al.*, in *Papers* 3:197.
King, Statement on Perjury Acquittal, 28 May 1960, in *Papers* 5:462.
King, *Stride Toward Freedom*, 1958.
Wayne Phillips, "Negro Minister Convicted of Directing Bus Boycott," *New York Times*, 23 March 1956.
"Rev. King Tells Why He Paid Fine," *Afro-American*, 7 December 1957.
Testimony in *State of Alabama v. M. L. King, Jr., et al.*, 22 March 1956, in *Papers* 3:183–196.

ST. AUGUSTINE, FLORIDA (1963–1965)

In the spring of 1964, as St. Augustine, Florida, prepared to celebrate its 400th anniversary, Martin Luther King, Jr., and the **Southern Christian Leadership Conference** (SCLC) launched a massive campaign supporting the small local movement to end racial discrimination in the nation's oldest city. King hoped that demonstrations there would lead to local desegregation and that media attention would garner national support for the **Civil Rights Act of 1964**, which was then stalled in a congressional filibuster.

Organized demonstrations reached St. Augustine in the summer of 1963, when Robert B. **Hayling**, a local dentist and advisor to the Youth Council of the city's branch of the **National Association for the Advancement of Colored People** (NAACP), led pickets and **sit-ins** against segregated businesses. The Ku Klux Klan and other whites responded with violence against demonstrators, which escalated through the fall of 1963, when Hayling and three other NAACP members were severely beaten at a Klan rally, then arrested and convicted of assaulting their attackers. In December 1963, after a grand jury blamed the racial crisis on Hayling and other activists, the NAACP asked for Hayling's resignation. St. Augustine activists then turned to SCLC for support.

SCLC had been aware of events in St. Augustine as early as July 1963, when King wrote to the White House questioning federal funding for the city's segregated 400th anniversary celebration. The following spring, after witnessing the activity of white supremacists and the absence of ministerial leadership in the city, SCLC board member C. T. **Vivian** recommended SCLC's support. SCLC recruited white northern college students to participate in demonstrations and sit-ins during Easter week of 1964, and hundreds were jailed. Some were made to stand in a cramped outdoor overflow pen in the late spring heat, while others were put into a concrete "sweatbox" overnight. Bail rose from $100 per person up to $1,000.

King and Ralph Abernathy share a jail cell in St. Augustine, Florida, following their arrest for participating in a sit-in at a segregated restaurant on 11 June 1964. © Bettmann/Corbis.

King visited St. Augustine for the first time on 18 May 1964. Speaking at a Baptist church on 27 May, he told the congregation that segregation would soon be over in St. Augustine "because trouble don't last always" (King, 27 May 1964). In the early morning of 29 May, the house SCLC rented for King in St. Augustine was sprayed by gunfire. On June 11, the day after the Senate voted to end the filibuster of the Civil Rights Act, King, Ralph **Abernathy**, and several others were arrested when they requested service at a segregated restaurant. Throughout June, SCLC led evening marches to the Old Slave Market, often facing counter demonstrations by the Klan, and provoking violence that garnered national media attention.

As the violence continued, King appealed to the federal government for assistance, asking the White House to pressure prominent white citizens to negotiate in good faith. Although by late June 1964 King was eager to leave St. Augustine and focus SCLC efforts on Alabama, he did not want to negatively affect the passage of the **Civil Rights Act**. When, on 18 June 1964, a Grand Jury called on King and SCLC to leave St. Augustine for one month to diffuse the situation, claiming that they had disrupted "racial harmony" in the city, King replied that the Grand Jury's request was "an immoral one," as it asked "the Negro community to give all, and the white community to give nothing." "St. Augustine," he insisted, had "never had peaceful race relations" (King, 19 June 1964).

As the Senate debated the Civil Rights Act, SCLC lawyers began to win court victories in St. Augustine. Judge Bryan Simpson continually ruled in favor of civil rights activists and encouraged SCLC to bring cases against the Ku Klux Klan and other white supremacist organizations. On 30 June 1964 Florida Governor C. Farris Bryant announced the formation of a biracial committee to restore interracial communication in St. Augustine. Although matters were far from resolved, national SCLC leaders left St. Augustine on 1 July, the day before President Lyndon **Johnson** signed the Civil Rights Act into law.

Despite this national success, black residents in St. Augustine continued to face violence and intimidation. Consistent threats and picketing by the Klan led many of the town's businesses to remain segregated. Although SCLC continued to provide some financial support to activists in St. Augustine beyond July 1964, the organization never returned to the city. King observed that St. Augustine had been made to "bear the cross," suffering violence and brutality that helped prompt Congress to pass the Civil Rights Act of 1964 (Colburn, 113).

SOURCES

Colburn, *Racial Change and Community Crisis*, 1985.
King, Address to Baptist Church rally, 27 May 1964, MLKJP-GAMK.
King, "Answer to the Presentment of Grand Jury," 19 June 1964, PGC-GEU.

STEELE, CHARLES KENZIE (1914–1980)

The first vice president of the **Southern Christian Leadership Conference** (SCLC), Reverend C. K. Steele shared Martin Luther King, Jr.'s vision of social equality through nonviolent means. As president of the Inter-Civic Council, Steele led a successful bus boycott in Tallahassee, Florida, in 1956, based on the example set by the **Montgomery Improvement Association** (MIA). Although not widely noted, the efforts of the Inter-Civic Council offered hope to those engaged in what Steele described as "the pain and the promise" of the civil rights movement (Steele, 27 September 1978). He later stated: "Where there is any power … as strong [and] as eternal as love using nonviolence, the promise will be fulfilled" (Steele, 27 September 1978).

Born on 7 February 1914, Steele was raised in the predominantly African American town of Gary, West Virginia, by his parents Lyde Bailor and Henry L. Steele, a miner with the United States Steel and Coal Corporation. Steele began preaching at the young age of 15. He was ordained as a Baptist minister in 1935, and three years later earned his BA degree from **Morehouse College**. After nearly a year of service at Friendship Baptist Church in northeast Georgia, Steele was called to Hall Street Baptist Church in Montgomery, Alabama, during the spring of 1939. In 1941 he married Lois Brock. Steele spent nine years in Montgomery and four at Springfield Baptist Church in Augusta, Georgia, before accepting the pastorate at Bethel Baptist Church in Tallahassee in 1952.

While serving as head of the local **National Association for the Advancement of Colored People** chapter, Steele was also elected president of the Inter-Civic Council

(ICC), an organization formed in May 1956, to direct a bus boycott initiated by black students at Florida A&M University. The ICC absorbed members from all walks of life within the black community, involving laborers, domestic workers, ministers, professionals, businessmen, and teachers. As in Montgomery, the ICC held mass meetings and organized a carpool. Unlike the MIA, which sought to modify existing seating rules, the ICC demanded the full integration of passengers on city buses.

After months of police harassment of the ICC carpool, city officials charged 22 organizers and drivers with operating a transportation system without a franchise, and a municipal judge levied an $11,000 fine against the ICC. In response boycott participants began walking, and the ICC welcomed the Supreme Court's November 1956 decision in **Browder v. Gayle**, which declared bus segregation unconstitutional. Following the decision the ICC called an end to the seven-month boycott. As blacks attempted to ride the buses, violence and intimidation of boycott leaders heightened. Eventually, Tallahassee's bus company did not enforce desegregated seating rules, and the ICC shifted its attention to voter registration and to the desegregation of local stores.

In 1956 Steele joined King as a speaker at **nonviolence** workshops held at the Tuskegee Institute, the annual meeting of the **National Baptist Convention**, and MIA's **Institute on Nonviolence and Social Change**. At SCLC's founding meeting in 1957, Steele was elected the organization's vice president. In March 1960 Steele's son, Henry, was among eight students who chose to go to jail after a demonstration at a Tallahassee chain store. King, evidently pleased by Henry's actions, sent the elder Steele a telegram that read: "Going to jail for a righteous cause is a badge of honor and a symbol of dignity" (*Papers* 5:391).

Although SCLC never launched a major campaign in Tallahassee, Steele supported its efforts in other cities. In Albany, Georgia (see **Albany Movement**), in 1962, Steele led demonstrations while King was incarcerated. Steele also contributed to the **Poor People's Campaign**. After King's **assassination**, Steele and other ICC members organized a "Vigil for Poverty" in Tallahassee to recognize individuals who lacked the basic needs of food, shelter, clothing, education, and employment. C. K. Steele continued his civil rights activism and his ministry at Bethel Baptist Church until he lost his battle with cancer on 19 August 1980.

SOURCES

Branch, *Parting the Waters*, 1988.
Fendrich, *Ideal Citizens*, 1993.
Introduction, in *Papers* 3:27, 30–31.
King to Steele, 19 March 1960, in *Papers* 5:391–392.
Gregory B. Padgett, "C. K. Steele, A Biography." Ph.D. diss., Florida State University, 1994.
Rabby, *Pain and the Promise*, 1999.
Steele, "Non-Violent Resistance: The Pain and the Promise," 27 September 1978, FTaSU.

STRENGTH TO LOVE (1963)

As Martin Luther King prepared for the **Birmingham Campaign** in early 1963, he drafted the final sermons for *Strength to Love*, a volume of his most well known homilies that would be published later that year. He originally proposed the book in early 1957 to Melvin Arnold, head of Harper & Brothers' Religious Books Department. Arnold welcomed King's "proposed collection of sermons; we hope that they will have a heavy emphasis on permanent religious values, rather than on topical events" (Arnold, 5 February 1957). Despite King's best intentions and Arnold's repeated urging for a manuscript, however, King had not produced the promised sermon book by mid-1962.

Although circumstances were far from ideal, King was finally able to start working on the sermons during a fortnight in jail in July 1962, during the **Albany Movement**. Having been arrested for holding a prayer vigil outside Albany City Hall, King and Ralph **Abernathy** shared a jail cell for 15 days that was, according to King, "dirty, filthy, and ill-equipped" and "the worse I have ever seen" (King, "Reverend M. L. King's Diary"). While behind bars, he was able to spend a fair amount of uninterrupted time preparing the drafts for the sermons "Loving Your Enemies," "Love in Action," and "Shattered Dreams," and continued to work on the volume after his release. King sent the first part of the manuscript to his publisher in the early fall, including several sermons that had become King standards, such as "Paul's Letter to American Christians" and "What Is Man?"

His editors praised the first results, seeing *Strength to Love* as the words of a minister who addressed his congregation with messages of "warmth, immediate application, and poetic verve" (Wallis, 3 October 1962). In the process of editing the book, however, many familiar King phrases were removed by Arnold and Charles Wallis. King's assessment of segregation as one of "the ugly practices of our nation," his call that capitalism must be transformed by "a deep-seated change," and his depiction of colonialism as "evil because it is based on a contempt for life" were stricken from the text (*Papers* 6:480; 471; 530). In particular, many of King's vivid anti-military and anti-war statements were deleted. In his draft sermon of "Transformed Nonconformist," for example, he characterized the early Christian church as anti-war: "Its views on war were clearly known because of the refusal of every Christian to take up arms" (*Papers* 6:473). These statements were absent in the sermons' published versions.

King worried that the force of his spoken words would not make the transition to the printed page and wrote in the book's preface that his reservations had "grown out of the fact that a sermon is not an essay to be read but a discourse to be heard. It should be a convincing appeal to a listening congregation." Even as the book went to press, he conceded: "I have not altogether overcome my misgivings" (King, x).

As the first volume of sermons by an African American preacher widely available to a white audience, *Strength to Love* was a landmark work. Despite omissions and changes to the original manuscript, *Strength to Love* remains a concrete testament to King's lifelong commitment to preach the **social gospel**. His fusion of Christian teachings and social consciousness remains in print and continues to promote King's vision of love as a potent social and political force for change, the efficacy of religious faith in surmounting evil, and the vital need for true human integration, or, as he defined it, "genuine intergroup and interpersonal living" (King, 23). This volume brought to the forefront King's identity as a compelling, well-educated, and compassionate preacher at a time when many whites knew him only as a civil rights leader.

SOURCES

Arnold to King, 5 February 1957, MLKP-MBU.

King, Draft of Chapter II, "Transformed Nonconformist," July 1962–March 1963, in *Papers* 6:466–477.

King, Draft of Chapter III, "On Being a Good Neighbor," July 1962–March 1963, in *Papers* 6:478–486.

King, Draft of Chapter XIII, "Our God Is Able," July 1962–March 1963, in *Papers* 6:527–534.

King, "Reverend M. L. King's Diary in Jail," *Jet* (23 August 1962).

King, *Strength to Love*, 1963.

Charles L. Wallis, Editorial notes, 3 October 1962, CSKC.

STRIDE TOWARD FREEDOM: THE MONTGOMERY STORY (1958)

According to Martin Luther King, *Stride Toward Freedom*, his memoir of the **Montgomery bus boycott**, is "the chronicle of 50,000 Negroes who took to heart the principles of nonviolence, who learned to fight for their rights with the weapon of love, and who in the process, acquired a new estimate of their own human worth" (King, 9).

In early 1957 numerous publishers began encouraging King to write a book about the boycott. By October of that year, he signed a contract with Harper & Brothers that was negotiated by his new literary agents, Joan **Daves** and Marie **Rodell**, and began work on the manuscript.

In *Stride Toward Freedom*, King delineates racial conditions in Montgomery before, during, and after the bus boycott. He discusses the origin and significance of the boycott, the roles that residents, civic leaders, and community organizations played in organizing and sustaining the movement, and the reactions of white Montgomery officials and residents. According to King, before the boycott African Americans in Montgomery were victims of segregation and poverty, but after the boycott, when bus desegregation was achieved, they evidenced a new level of self-respect (King, 28; 187). King points out that most African Americans in Montgomery accepted a nonviolent approach because they trusted their leaders when they told them that nonviolence was the essence of active Christianity.

In the chapter "Pilgrimage to Nonviolence," King delves into the intellectual influences that led him to nonviolent philosophy. He discusses the impact made upon his thinking by the works of Thoreau, Marx, Aristotle, Rauschenbusch, and **Gandhi**. King also outlines his understanding of **nonviolence**, which seeks to win an opponent to friendship, rather than to humiliate or defeat him (King, 102).

Throughout the writing process, King was dependent on friends and colleagues who supplied text to aid him in meeting publishing deadlines. Stanley **Levison**, Bayard **Rustin**, and Harris **Wofford** provided significant guidance. In fact, King's discussion of nonviolence is drawn from an address by Wofford. King also received editorial help from Lawrence D. **Reddick**, a professor at Alabama State College, Hermine I. **Popper**, a freelance editor, and Melvin Arnold, of Harper & Brothers.

In revisions of King's manuscript, the meticulous editors from the press made "every effort to see that not even a single sentence can be lifted out of context and quoted against the book and the author" (*Papers* 4:404). For instance, they were extremely cautious about King's discourse on **communism**, and they suggested changes, such as using the phrase "social cooperation" instead of "collectivism," and calling Marxism "a partial truth" instead of "a half truth" (*Papers* 4:405).

Stride Toward Freedom was officially released on 17 September 1958. It was lauded by both the general public and literary critics, who repeatedly labeled it "'must' reading" (Mays, "My View"). In describing the book in 1958, Benjamin **Mays** wrote, "Americans who believe in justice and equality for all cannot afford to miss the book. Negroes can not afford to miss it because it tells us again how we can work against evil with dignity, pride and self-respect" ("My View").

SOURCES

Arnold to King, 5 May 1958, in *Papers* 4:404–405.
Introduction, in *Papers* 4:29–33.
King, *Stride Toward Freedom*, 1958.
Mays, "My View," *Pittsburgh Courier*, 25 October 1958.

STUDENT NONVIOLENT COORDINATING COMMITTEE (SNCC)

The Student Nonviolent Coordinating Committee (SNCC) was founded in April 1960 by young people dedicated to nonviolent, direct action tactics. Although Martin Luther King, Jr., and others had hoped that SNCC would serve as the youth wing of the **Southern Christian Leadership Conference** (SCLC), the students remained fiercely independent of King and SCLC, generating their own projects and strategies. Although ideological differences eventually caused SNCC and SCLC to be at odds, the two organizations worked side by side throughout the early years of the civil rights movement.

The idea for a locally based, student-run organization was conceived when Ella **Baker**, a veteran civil rights organizer and an SCLC official, invited black college students who had participated in the early 1960 **sit-ins** to an April 1960 gathering at Shaw University in Raleigh, North Carolina. Baker encouraged the more than 200 student attendees to remain autonomous, rather than affiliate with SCLC or any of the other existing civil rights groups. King issued a press statement on the first day of the conference, characterizing the time as "an era of offensive on the part of oppressed people" (*Papers* 5:426). He called on the students to form "some type of continuing organization" and "to delve deeper into the philosophy of nonviolence," advising: "Our ultimate end must be the creation of the beloved community" (*Papers* 5:427).

At the Raleigh Conference the students were generally reluctant to compromise the independence of their local protest groups, and voted to establish only a temporary coordinating body. Vanderbilt University theology student James **Lawson**, whose workshops on nonviolent direct action served as a training ground for many of the Nashville student protesters, drafted an organizational statement of purpose that reflected the strong commitment to Gandhian **nonviolence** that characterized SNCC's early years: "We affirm the philosophical or religious ideal of nonviolence as the foundation of our purpose, the presupposition of our faith, and the manner of our action. Nonviolence as it grows from Judaic-Christian traditions seeks a social order of justice permeated by love" (Lawson, 17 April 1960). In May 1960 the group constituted itself as a permanent organization and Fisk University student Marion **Barry** was elected SNCC's first chairman.

SNCC's emergence as a force in the southern civil rights movement came largely through the involvement of students in the 1961 **Freedom Rides**, designed to test a 1960 Supreme Court ruling that declared segregation in interstate travel facilities unconstitutional. The **Congress of Racial Equality** initially sponsored the Freedom Rides that began in May 1961, but segregationists viciously attacked riders traveling through Alabama. Students from Nashville, under the leadership of Diane **Nash**, resolved to finish the rides. Once the new group of freedom riders demonstrated their determination to continue the rides into Mississippi, other students joined the movement.

By the time the Interstate Commerce Commission began enforcing the ruling mandating equal treatment in interstate travel in November 1961, SNCC was immersed in voter registration efforts in McComb, Mississippi, and a desegregation campaign in Albany, Georgia, known as the **Albany Movement**. King and SCLC later joined with SNCC in Albany, but tensions arose between the two civil rights groups. The Albany effort, although yielding few tangible gains, was an important site of development for SNCC.

At the August 1963 **March on Washington for Jobs and Freedom**, SNCC chairman John **Lewis** was one of those scheduled to speak. He intended to criticize John F. **Kennedy**'s proposed civil rights bill as "too little, and too late," and to refer to the movement as "a serious revolution" (Lewis, 28 August 1963). Lewis softened the tone of the delivered speech to appease A. Philip **Randolph** and other march organizers, but remained adamant that SNCC had "great reservations" regarding Kennedy's proposed civil rights legislation (Carson, 94). He warned his audience: "We want our freedom and we want it now" (Carson, 95).

In 1961 organizer Bob **Moses** moved to Jackson, Mississippi, and began organizing young Mississippi residents. Moses, who was firmly committed to non-hierarchical grassroots organizing, joined the SNCC staff and became voter registration director of Mississippi's **Council of Federated Organizations** the following year. He encountered considerable resistance to civil rights reform efforts, but the Mississippi voter registration effort created conditions for racial reform by bringing together three crucial groups: dynamic and determined SNCC field secretaries, influential regional and local civil rights leaders from Mississippi, and white student volunteers who participated in the "Freedom Vote" mock election of October 1963 and **Freedom Summer** (1964). Early in 1964, SNCC supported the formation of the **Mississippi Freedom Democratic Party** in an effort to challenge the legitimacy of the state's all-white Democratic Party.

The voting rights demonstrations that began in 1965 in Selma, Alabama, sparked increasingly bitter ideological debates within SNCC, as some workers openly challenged the group's previous commitment to nonviolent tactics and its willingness to allow the participation of white activists. Distracted by such divisive issues, the day-to-day needs of the group's ongoing projects suffered. In many Deep South communities, where SNCC had once attracted considerable black support, the group's influence waned. Nevertheless, after the **Selma to Montgomery March**, Stokely **Carmichael** and other SNCC organizers entered the rural area between Selma and Montgomery and helped black residents launch the all-black Lowndes County Freedom Organization, later known as the Black Panther Party. Meanwhile, several SNCC workers established incipient organizing efforts in volatile urban black ghettos.

In May 1966 a new stage in SNCC's history began with Carmichael's election as chairman. Because Carmichael identified himself with the trend away from nonviolence and interracial cooperation, his election compromised SNCC's relationships with more moderate civil rights groups and many of its white supporters. During the month following his election, Carmichael publicly expressed SNCC's new political orientation when he began calling for "**Black Power**" during a voting rights march through Mississippi. The national exposure of Carmichael's Black Power speeches brought increased notoriety to SNCC, but the group remained internally divided over its future direction. King responded directly to Carmichael's and SNCC's appeal for Black Power in his 1967 book, *Where Do We Go from Here: Chaos or Community?* King argued, "effective political power for Negroes cannot come through separatism" (King, 48). Opposing exclusive support of black electoral candidates, King continued: "SNCC staff members are eminently correct when they point out that in Lowndes County, Alabama, there are no white liberals or moderates and no possibility for cooperation between the races at the present time. But the Lowndes County experience cannot be made a measuring rod for the whole of America" (King, 49).

Even after the dismissal of a group of SNCC's Atlanta field workers who called for the exclusion of whites, the organization was weakened by continued internal conflicts and external attacks, along with a loss of northern financial backing. The election in June 1967 of H. "Rap" Brown as SNCC's new chair was meant to reduce the controversy surrounding the group. Brown, however, encouraged militancy among urban blacks, and soon a federal campaign against black militancy severely damaged SNCC's ability to sustain its organizing efforts. SNCC became a target of the Counterintelligence Program (COINTELPRO) of the **Federal Bureau of Investigation** (FBI) in a concerted effort at all levels of government to crush black militancy through both overt and covert means.

The spontaneous urban uprisings that followed the **assassination** of King in April 1968 indicated a high level of black discontent. However, by then, SNCC had little ability to mobilize an effective political force. Its most dedicated community organizers had left the organization, which changed its name to the Student National Coordinating Committee. Although individual SNCC activists played significant roles in politics during the period after 1968, and many of the controversial ideas that once had defined SNCC's radicalism had become widely accepted among African Americans, the organization disintegrated. By the end of the decade, FBI surveillance of SNCC's remaining offices was discontinued due to lack of activity.

SOURCES

Carson, *In Struggle*, 1981.
James E. Clayton, "Some in South Defy ICC Order on Depot Signs," *Washington Post*, 2 November 1961.
Introduction, in *Papers* 5:26–28.
King, "Statement to the Press at the Beginning of the Youth Leadership Conference," 15 April 1960, in *Papers* 5:426–427.
King, *Where Do We Go from Here*, 1967.
Lawson, "Statement of Purpose," 17 April 1960, SNCCP-GAMK.
Lewis, Press release, "Text of speech to be delivered at Lincoln Memorial," 28 August 1963, NAACPP-DLC.

SUMMER COMMUNITY ORGANIZATION AND POLITICAL EDUCATION (SCOPE) PROJECT

On 15 June 1965 Martin Luther King addressed the opening orientation session for student volunteers in Atlanta's Summer Community Organization and Political

Education (SCOPE) Project of the **Southern Christian Leadership Conference** (SCLC). He told the assembled volunteers: "This generation of students is found where history is being made" (King, 15 June 1965).

SCOPE took place during the summer of 1965, growing out of SCLC's participation in the **Voter Education Project**, the momentum following the **Selma to Montgomery March**, and SCLC's desire to highlight the voter registration process for blacks while the **Voting Rights Act** was pending before Congress. SCOPE was also inspired by the 1964 **Freedom Summer**, a **Council of Federated Organizations** iniative that mobilized hundreds of white college students to work in the South against segregation and black disenfranchisement. SCLC's Voter Registration and Political Education Director Hosea **Williams** was selected to manage the effort. On 30 April King and SNCC's John **Lewis** announced that the two organizations would work cooperatively to implement programs designed to carry out a program of voter education and political organization across the South (King and Lewis, 30 April 1965).

Despite promises that the Voting Rights Act would be enacted by June 1965, SCOPE began that summer as the bill wended its way through Congress. Its three objectives were local recruitment and community grass-roots organization, voter registration, and political education. Over 1,200 SCOPE workers, including 650 college students from across the nation, 150 SCLC staff members, and 400 local volunteers, served in 6 southern states to register African Americans to vote.

President Lyndon B. **Johnson** signed the Voting Rights Act on 6 August 1965, three days after its enactment in Congress. SCOPE ended only three weeks later, depriving the SCLC workers, students, and local volunteers of federal support during most of the program. King reported that the project's goals had been achieved and projected success in SCLC's future registration efforts.

SOURCES

King, "Let My People Vote," 19 June 1965, *New York Amsterdam News*.
King, "Meaning of Georgia Elections," 3 July 1965, *New York Amsterdam News*.
King, Why Are You Here?, Address delivered at the Summer Community Organization and Political Education (SCOPE) orientation, 15 June 1965, MLKEC.
King and Lewis, Statement on cooperation between Southern Christian Leadership Conference and Student Nonviolent Coordinating Committee, 30 April 1965, SCLCR-GAMK.

TAYLOR, GARDNER C. (1918–)

An eloquent Baptist minister and civil rights proponent, Gardner Taylor was a close friend and political ally of Martin Luther King, Jr., as well as his father, Martin Luther **King**, Sr. In a 1958 telegram to King, Jr., Taylor wrote: "No public position [is] as important to me as our struggle" (Taylor, 6 September 1958).

The son of Reverend Washington and Selina Taylor, Gardner was born in Baton Rouge, Louisiana, and received his AB from Louisiana's Leland College in 1937. Although Taylor was accepted to the University of Michigan Law School, a serious car accident served as "the defining moment" of his life, and instead of attending law school he answered the call to the ministry, becoming the pastor at Concord Baptist Church in the Bedford–Stuyvesant section of Brooklyn (Gilbreath, "The Pulpit King").

Taylor and King became better acquainted when King preached at Concord Baptist shortly before he began his postgraduate work at **Boston University** in 1951. King named Taylor as one of the African American Baptist church's great preachers during a student discussion in those years. Taylor was often at King's side during and after the **Montgomery bus boycott**, hosting King's 1956 New York rally during the boycott, and making that evening's fundraising speech. He visited King at the home of Sandy **Ray** during King's recovery from his stabbing in 1958. He also participated in the 1958 **Youth March for Integrated Schools** at King's behest.

At the 1961 annual convening of the **National Baptist Convention** (NBC), Taylor challenged the legitimacy of conservative incumbent J. H. **Jackson**'s presidency and noted his lackluster support of the civil rights movement. A shoving match over the convention's speaking platform resulted in the injury of one of Jackson's supporters, Reverend Arthur G. Wright, who later died. Jackson charged King with masterminding the turmoil and removed him from the vice-presidency of NBC's National Sunday School and Baptist Training Union. Taylor conceded defeat. The confrontation led to a split by Taylor, King, and others who left the NBC and formed the **Progressive National Baptist Convention**.

Dubbed "the dean of the nation's black preachers," Taylor remained at Concord Baptist Church, one of the largest black churches in New York, until his retirement in 1990 ("American Preaching"). One of the first African Americans elected to the New York City Board of Education in 1958, he was also the first black and first

Baptist president of the New York City Council of Churches. Taylor delivered the benediction at President Bill Clinton's 1997 inauguration and was awarded the Presidential Medal of Freedom in 2000. He authored *How Shall They Preach?* (1977), *The Scarlet Thread* (1981), and *Chariots Aflame* (1988).

SOURCES

"American Preaching: A Dying Art?" *Time*, 31 December 1979, 67.
Michael Eric Dyson, "Gardner Taylor: Poet Laureate of the Pulpit," *Christian Century* 112, no. 1 (1995): 12–16.
Edward Gilbreath, "The Pulpit King," *Christianity Today* 39, no. 14 (11 December 1995): 25–28.
Taylor, *Black Churches of Brooklyn*, 1994.
Taylor to King, 6 September 1958, MLKP-MBU.

THOMAS, NORMAN MATTOON (1884–1968)

When Norman Thomas died in 1968, the *New York Times* called him "the nation's conscience for social justice and social reform" (Whitman, "Norman Thomas"). On the occasion of Thomas' 80th birthday, Martin Luther King wrote: "I can think of no man who has done more than you to inspire the vision of a society free of injustice and exploitation" (King, "The Bravest"). King praised Thomas for speaking out on behalf of oppressed peoples of all kinds, including black sharecroppers, interned Japanese Americans during World War II, and imprisoned conscientious objectors.

Thomas was born in Marion, Ohio, in 1884, into a family of Presbyterian ministers and abolitionists. After graduating from Princeton in 1905, Thomas became a settlement worker in New York City. Ordained in 1910, he became pastor to an East Harlem church serving poor immigrants. At the outbreak of World War I, Thomas joined the nascent **Fellowship of Reconciliation** (FOR) and the American Union Against Militarism. By 1918, he was secretary of FOR, editor of FOR's journal *The World Tomorrow*, and served on the executive board of the American Union. During his tenure with the American Union he co-founded its civil liberties bureau, which later became the American Civil Liberties Union.

Thomas' anti-war activism led to his involvement with the Socialist Party of America. Thomas resigned from his church and FOR positions and became associate editor of *The Nation* magazine. In 1922 he co-directed the League for Industrial Democracy, the education wing of the Socialist Party. Four years later he was spokesman for the party and campaigned for office 15 times between 1924 and 1948, including 6 bids for the presidency.

In the 1950s Thomas denounced with equal vehemence **communism** and the methods of Senator Joseph McCarthy, whose investigations of alleged Communist influence in the American Left threatened activist groups throughout the country. In the first weeks of the **Montgomery bus boycott**, Thomas met with civil rights and union leaders to explore the possibility of organizing northern support for King's movement. Thomas wrote King in March 1956: "I am of the opinion that the intrusion of Northerners in Montgomery will do more harm than good but if there is any help that I can give in the country, I should like to know it" (*Papers* 3:206).

In the following years King and Thomas collaborated on many projects. After King was arrested on a minor tax charge in 1960, Thomas cosigned a fundraising advertisement that eventually led to the landmark **New York Times v. Sullivan** case. Thomas testified before the Senate in support of the 1963 civil rights bill, which became the **Civil Rights Act of 1964**. King and Thomas worked together on the board of the **National Committee for a Sane Nuclear Policy**.

In 1965 King chronicled Thomas' career in an article titled "The Bravest Man I Ever Met." In the article, King recounted an anecdote from the **March on Washington**: "A little Negro boy listened at the Washington Monument to an eloquent orator. Turning to his father, he asked, 'Who is that man?' Came the inevitable answer; 'That's Norman Thomas. He was for us before any other white folks were'" (King, "The Bravest").

King considered it his "good fortune" to work with Thomas both in the cause of racial equality and in the attainment of social justice for all minorities everywhere (King, "The Bravest"). Throughout his many years of activism, Thomas published more than 20 books and authored hundreds of articles. His 70th, 75th, and 80th birthday gatherings were gala events for the American Left.

SOURCES

Committee to Defend Martin Luther King and the Struggle for Freedom in the South, "Heed Their Rising Voices," 29 March 1960, in *Papers* 5:381.

King, "The Bravest Man I Ever Met," *Pageant* (June 1965): 23–29.

Thomas to King, 23 March 1956, in *Papers* 3:206.

Alden Whitman, "Norman Thomas: The Great Reformer, Unsatisfied to the End," *New York Times*, 22 December 1968.

THURMAN, HOWARD (1899–1981)

During his tenure as dean of Marsh Chapel at **Boston University**, theologian and minister Howard Thurman sent Martin Luther King, Jr., and Coretta Scott **King** his 1955 volume on spirituals, *Deep River*. He inscribed the book: "To the Kings—The test of life is often found in the amount of pain we can absorb without spoiling our joy" (*Papers* 6:299). Thurman's commitment to a spiritually and physically integrated society, and to the methods of Gandhian **nonviolence**, served as major influences in King's life.

Born in Daytona, Florida, Thurman attended **Morehouse College**, earning a BA in 1923. After receiving his BD from Rochester Theological Seminary (1926), he did further graduate work at the Oberlin School of Theology and at Haverford College, where he studied under Quaker philosopher Rufus Jones. He returned to Morehouse in 1929, as a philosophy and religion professor. In 1932 he married Sue Bailey, a contemporary of King's mother, Alberta Williams **King**, when both women attended Spelman College. The couple relocated to Washington, D.C., when Thurman joined Howard University's faculty. Three years later, he became dean of Howard's Rankin Memorial Chapel, a position he held until 1943.

In 1935 the Thurmans traveled with Reverend Edward and Phenola Carroll on a "Pilgrimage of Friendship" to Burma, Ceylon, and India at the invitation of the Student Christian Movements of the United States of America and India. The delegation met with Mohandas K. **Gandhi** in February 1936, and discussed the status and history of African Americans and questions of **nonviolence**. Upon their return to the United States, the Thurmans toured and spoke of their experiences with Gandhi.

In 1943 Thurman resigned his position at Howard to help found an integrated church in San Francisco. The doors of the Church for the Fellowship of All Peoples opened for the first time in October 1944, for an inaugural multi-faith service with Thurman and white clergyman Alfred G. Fisk as co-pastors. Thurman remained there as minister until 1953, when he accepted the post of dean of Marsh Chapel and professor of Spiritual Disciplines and Resources at Boston University. According to Thurman, he and King met "informally" during King's last years as a doctoral student: "We watched the World Series on television at our house. Sue and Martin discussed very seriously the possibility of his coming to Fellowship Church; it was then she discovered his commitment to Montgomery" (Thurman, 254). In a 1955 letter written less than a month before the **Montgomery bus boycott**, Thurman communicated his regret that he would not be able to preach at **Dexter Avenue Baptist Church**'s Men's Day Service and passed on "special greetings" from his wife (*Papers* 2:588). During the bus boycott, King's friend and biographer, Lerone Bennett, reported that King "read or reread" Thurman's 1949 work, *Jesus and the Disinherited*, which interprets Jesus' teachings through the experience of the oppressed and the need for a nonviolent response to such oppression (Bennett, 74).

According to Thurman's autobiography, the only time that he and King were able to arrange a "serious talk" came in the fall of 1958, when King was recovering in New York after being stabbed by Izola **Curry** at a book signing (Thurman, 254). The day before their meeting, Thurman recalled having a "vibrant sensation" in which "Martin emerged in my awareness and would not leave" (Thurman, 255). When he met alone with King the following day, he asked how long King's doctor had given him for his convalescence.

> When he told me, I urged him to ask them to extend the period by an additional two weeks. This would give him time away from the immediate pressure of the movement to reassess himself in relation to the cause, to rest his body and mind with healing detachment, and to take a long look that only solitary brooding can provide. The movement had become more than an organization; it had become an organism with a life of its own to which he must relate in fresh and extraordinary ways or be swallowed up by it. (Thurman, 255)

Thurman retired from Boston University in 1965. He directed the Howard Thurman Educational Trust until his death in 1981.

SOURCES

Bennett, Jr., *What Manner of Man*, 1968.
Kapur, *Raising Up a Prophet*, 1992.
King to Thurman, 31 October 1955, in *Papers* 2:583–584.
Thurman, Inscription to King, 1955, in *Papers* 6:229.
Thurman, *Jesus and the Disinherited*, 1949.
Thurman, *With Head and Heart*, 1979.
Thurman to King, 14 November 1955, in *Papers* 2:588.

TILL, EMMETT LOUIS (1941–1955)

The 1955 abduction and murder of 14-year-old Emmett Till helped ignite the civil rights movement. A month after the Till lynching, Martin Luther King stated that it "might be considered one of the most brutal and inhuman crimes of the twentieth century" (*Papers* 6:232). Just three months after Till's body was pulled from the Talla-hatchie River, the **Montgomery bus boycott** began. For most of his life, King would use the Till murder as an example of "the evil of racial injustice," preaching about "the crying voice of a little Emmett Till, screaming from the rushing waters in [Missis-sippi]" (King, 12 May 1963).

Emmett Till was born in Chicago on 25 July 1941. At the age of 14, he was sent by his parents to visit relatives in LeFlore County, Mississippi. Till was reportedly dared by some local boys to enter Bryant's Grocery and talk to the white woman behind the counter, who owned the store. According to William Bradford Huie, a journalist who later interviewed the accused, Till entered and touched Carol Bryant and whistled at her as his friends rushed him away. Four days later, on 28 August, he was abducted from his uncle's home by Bryant's husband, Roy, and Roy's half brother, J. W. Milam. Till's mangled body was found three days later in the Tallahatchie River, with a large cotton-gin fan tied around his neck. He had been brutally beaten and shot through the head.

Till's body was returned to Chicago, where his mother insisted on an open-casket funeral so everyone could see the brutality of her son's death. The **National Associa-tion for the Advancement of Colored People** and other organizations planned demon-strations following the publication of photos of Till's corpse in *Jet* magazine. On 19 September the kidnapping and murder trial of Bryant and Milam began. Till's uncle, Moses Wright, identified the two men as the assailants; but the all-white jury acquit-ted Bryant and Milam of Till's murder.

On 24 January 1956, *Look* magazine published "The Shocking Story of Approved Killing in Mississippi," in which the killers gave details of their crime. The U.S. Department of Justice reopened the case in 2004.

SOURCES

Huie, "The Shocking Story of Approved Killing in Mississippi," *Look* 2, no. 2 (24 January 1956): 46–48, 50.

King, "Pride Versus Humility: The Parable of the Pharisee and the Publican," Sermon at Dexter Avenue Baptist Church, 25 September 1955, in *Papers* 6:230–234.

King, "What a Mother Should Tell Her Child," 12 May 1963, MLKJP-GAMK.

TILLEY, JOHN LEE (1898–1971)

In April 1958 the **Southern Christian Leadership Conference** (SCLC) asked John Lee Tilley, pastor of New Metropolitan Baptist Church in Baltimore, to become the organization's first executive director. Responding to Tilley's appointment, Martin Luther King described him as a "very able man with a great deal of experience and know-how in the area of Human Relations" (King, 9 July 1958). Within one year of Tilley's selection, however, King asked the minister to submit his resignation.

Born in Stem, North Carolina, Tilley received his AB (1925) from Shaw University and his PhB (1927) from the University of Chicago. He later received his MA (1933) at the University of Chicago and his DD (1933) from Shaw, before being named the first dean of Shaw's School of Religion. He left Shaw in 1944, when he became presi-dent of Florida Normal and Industrial College in St. Augustine, a position he held until 1951, when he became pastor of New Metropolitan Baptist Church. Before his appointment to serve as SCLC executive director, Tilley chaired both the **National**

Association for the Advancement of Colored People (NAACP) Register and Vote Campaign and the Baltimore NAACP's Labor Committee. Because of his many commitments, Tilley initially accepted the SCLC position on a part-time basis.

In Tilley's first year as executive director, tensions rose when an SCLC supporter complained of Tilley's inability to devote sufficient time to Atlanta's voter registration drive. Knowing of Tilley's part-time status with SCLC, King defended his executive director. "Dr. Tilley is a man of wide experience," King boasted, "having [led] the city of Baltimore in one of the most successful voting drives to date" (*Papers* 5:115). Three months later, on 3 April 1959, King asked for Tilley's resignation because SCLC's Crusade for Citizenship program was stalled and its treasury overextended. Writing on behalf of SCLC's administrative committee, King noted: "We had hoped that our program would be well developed by now, and that the aims and purposes of the Southern Christian Leadership Conference would have been well established in the minds and hearts of the people all over the nation by this time" (*Papers* 5:180). In closing, King thanked Tilley and hoped that the "present crisis, will not in any way cause you to sever your interest and affection from our conference" (*Papers* 5:180).

On 13 April 1959 Tilley complied with King's request, reminding the SCLC president of his initial agreement to serve as executive director on a temporary and part-time basis. Calling his work with SCLC a "privilege and pleasure," Tilley suggested that "fear and apathy … in regard to voting, jealousies, and the attitude of competition on the part of many individuals and organizations," as well as a lack of sufficient funds and staffing, posed barriers to SCLC's success. In closing, Tilley offered his services to SCLC at a later date if the organization so desired.

In 1961 Tilley returned to Shaw University as the director of public relations and alumni affairs. From 1964 to 1970 he was a visiting lecturer at Howard University's School of Religion. He died on 28 April 1971 in Baltimore.

SOURCES

King to Jesse Hill, Jr., 28 January 1959, in *Papers* 5:114–115.
King to Myles Horton, 9 July 1958, MLKP-MBU.
King to Tilley, 3 April 1959, in *Papers* 5:179–181.
Tilley to King, 26 June 1958, in *Papers* 5:441–443.
Tilley to King, 13 April 1959, in *Papers* 5:182–184.

TILLICH, PAUL (1886–1965)

A theologian who had a major influence on Martin Luther King's religious ideas, Paul Tillich is considered one of the foremost thinkers of Protestantism. In response to Tillich's death in October 1965, King commented: "He helped us to speak of God's action in history in terms which adequately expressed both the faith and the intellect of modern man" (King, October 1965).

Paul Tillich was born on 20 August 1886, in the province of Brandenburg, Germany, to Johannes Tillich, a Lutheran pastor, and his wife, Wilhelmina Mathilde. He studied at a number of German universities before obtaining his PhD at Breslau in 1911. In 1912 he was ordained as a pastor of the Evangelical Lutheran Church in Brandenburg. After serving as a chaplain in the German Army during World War I, he taught theology at the Universities of Berlin, Marburg, Dresden, Leipzig, and Frankfort. Removed from his Frankfort post due to his public support of leftist intellectuals and Jews during the early Nazi regime, Tillich accepted Reinhold **Niebuhr**'s invitation to teach at Union Theological Seminary in New York. Tillich served on the faculty as a professor of philosophical theology from 1933 until his retirement in 1955, and went on to join the faculty at Harvard University. In 1962 he accepted a post as the Nuveen Professor of Theology at the University of Chicago, where he remained until his death.

King first encountered Tillich's writings as a student at **Crozer Theological Seminary** and **Boston University**, but he did not substantively study Tillich's work until choosing his **dissertation** topic, "A Comparison of the Conceptions of God in the Thinking of Paul Tillich and Henry Nelson Wieman," in early 1953. In his dissertation, King expressed disagreement with both men's disavowal of **personalism** and criticized Tillich's abstract notion of God as "little more than a sub-personal reservoir of power" and "a pure absolute devoid of consciousness and life" (*Papers* 2:534). King did, however, praise both men's "cry against the humanism of our generation … that has had all too much faith in man and all too little faith in God" (*Papers* 2:519).

King later credited Tillich's work as a major influence on his religious thinking, having convinced him that "existentialism, in spite of the fact that it has become all too fashionable, had grasped certain basic truths about man and his condition that could not be permanently overlooked" (*Papers* 5:421). He frequently used Tillich's cautioning view that "sin is separation" to illustrate the inherently evil nature of segregation in speeches in his later years (King, "The Negro Is Your Brother"). Commenting on Tillich's view of God in this context of modern alienation, King observed: "His Christian existentialism gave us a system of meaning and purpose for our lives in an age when war and doubt seriously threatened all that we had come to hold dear" (King, October 1965).

SOURCES

King, "A Comparison of the Conceptions of God in the Thinking of Paul Tillich and Henry Nelson Wieman," 15 April 1955, in *Papers* 2:339–544.

King, "The Negro Is Your Brother," *Atlantic Monthly* 212 (August 1963): 78–81; 86–88.

King, "Pilgrimage to Nonviolence," 13 April 1960, in *Papers* 5:419–425.

King, Statement on death of Tillich, October 1965, MLKJP-GAMK.

Macleod, *Paul Tillich*, 1973.

Pauck and Pauck, *Paul Tillich*, 1976.

Tillich, *My Search for Absolutes*, 1967.

TIME MAGAZINE'S "MAN OF THE YEAR" (1963)

In its January 1964 issue, *Time* named Martin Luther King, Jr., "Man of the Year" for 1963, making the civil rights leader the first African American recipient of this honor. This was not King's first appearance on the cover of *Time*. In 1957 he was featured on the cover for his role in the **Montgomery bus boycott**.

One of the first news magazines in the United States, *Time* was founded in 1923 as a weekly publication. Over the years, the "Man of the Year" issue (later "Person of the Year"), in which the magazine recognizes the individual, group, or object that had the greatest influence on the year's news, has grown to be one of its most popular features.

Time's tribute to King included a photograph of the civil rights leader on the magazine's cover, along with a seven-page feature that included pictures of King during some of the most memorable moments of his civil rights career, including a meeting with President Lyndon B. **Johnson** and King's arrest in **Birmingham**, Alabama, in 1963. King received many congratulatory telegrams, notably from Roy **Wilkins**, secretary of the **National Association for the Advancement of Colored People**; A. Philip **Randolph**, president of the Brotherhood of Sleeping Car Porters; and Nelson A. **Rockefeller**, governor of New York.

Although many of King's supporters celebrated the tribute, King was privately incensed by some of the comments in the story. His clothing style was described as "funereal conservatism," and he was said to have "very little sense of humor." King, who had garnered considerable fame from his speeches and oratorical skills, was criticized for his use of metaphors, which the author called "downright embarrassing" ("Man of the Year," 13).

To those outside his inner circle, King said he was pleased to receive the honor. In a 27 February 1964 letter to Homer **Jack**, executive director of the **National Committee for a Sane Nuclear Policy**, he maintained that it was not just a personal honor but a tribute bestowed upon the entire civil rights movement. "The fact that *Time* took such cognizance of the social revolution in which we are engaged is an indication that the conscience of America has been reached and that the old order which has embraced bigotry and discrimination must now yield to what we know to be right and just," King wrote. In a letter to *Time* founder Henry R. Luce, King thanked him for the honor and commended the magazine for its inclusion of other professional African Americans. "This image of the Negro is certainly one that many of us like to see carried in the pages of our national periodicals," King wrote. "For it does much to help grind away the granite-like notions that have obtained for so long that the Negro is not able to take his place in all fields of endeavor and that he is lazy, shiftless and without ambition" (King, 16 January 1964).

SOURCES
King to Jack, 27 February 1964, HAJP-PSC-P.
King to Luce, 16 January 1964, MLKJP-GAMK.
"Man of the Year; Never Again Where He Was," *Time*, January 1964, 13–27.
"The South: Attack on the Conscience," *Time*, 18 February 1957, 17–20.

TRENHOLM, HARPER COUNCILL, JR. (1900–1963)

H. Councill Trenholm, president of Alabama State College during the height of the student **sit-in** movement, was criticized by Martin Luther King, Jr., after the embattled president expelled students and fired faculty for their protest participation.

Born on 14 November 1942, in Montgomery, Alabama, Trenholm received his BA from **Morehouse College** (1920) and his baccalaureate in philosophy from the University of Chicago (1921). In 1926 he succeeded his father as president of Alabama State College, a position he held until 1960.

A deacon at **Dexter Avenue Baptist Church**, Trenholm invited King to give the baccalaureate sermon at Alabama State's commencement in 1955. King agreed to speak and accepted an offer to be a dinner guest at Trenholm's home prior to the ceremony. The congenial relationship between the men continued when, in 1957, King applied for membership in the Sigma Phi Phi fraternity. As a member of the fraternity, Trenholm was "very pleased to have this application" (Trenholm, 9 May 1957).

After sit-ins began in Montgomery during 1960, Alabama Governor John **Patterson** threatened to fire Trenholm if he could not maintain order on the campus. Responding to Patterson's pressures, Trenholm threatened to expel any students or faculty who demonstrated. This threat had particular importance to King because of his close friendship with several targeted faculty members, including Lawrence **Reddick** and Dexter congregation members Jo Ann **Robinson** and Mary Fair Burks. Calling Trenholm's actions "cowardly," King expressed disappointment in the college president's response to Patterson: "I had hoped that Dr. Trenholm would emerge from this total situation as a national hero. If he would only stand up to the Governor and the Board of Education and say that he cannot in all good conscience fire the eleven faculty members who have committed no crime or act of sedition, he would gain support over the nation that he never dreamed of" (King, 9 August 1960; *Papers* 5:407). Reddick was fired and Robinson and Burks resigned. Trenholm left his position at Alabama State College in 1960 as well, and died three years later.

Sources

Introduction, in *Papers* 5:25.
King, "Other Mountains," Baccalaureate speech at Alabama State College, 15 May 1955, in *Papers* 6:214.
King to Burks, 5 April 1960, in *Papers* 5:406–408.
King to Patterson, 9 August 1960, in *Papers* 5:495–496.
King to Roy Wilkins, 9 August 1960, NAACPP-DLC.
Trenholm to King, 2 May 1955, in *Papers* 2:550–551.
Trenholm to King, 9 May 1957, MLKP-MBU.

TRUMAN, HARRY S. (1884–1972)

Following the death of Franklin D. Roosevelt in April 1945, Harry S. Truman became the 33rd president of the United States, after serving only 83 days as vice president. Martin Luther King had admired Truman's record on civil rights until 1960, when Truman made defamatory statements linking the **sit-in** demonstrations with **communism**.

Truman was born 8 May 1884, in Lamar, Missouri. After graduating from high school in 1901, when his family could not afford to send him to college, Truman worked a variety of jobs before enlisting in the Missouri National Guard in 1907. He was discharged as a corporal in 1911, and shortly after the United States entered World War I Truman enlisted in the Missouri Field Artillery, serving in France and later achieving the rank of colonel in the reserves. Returning to Missouri after the war, in 1922 Truman was elected judge of the Jackson County Court, a position he held for two years. He later served as presiding judge of the same court from 1926 to 1934.

Following his judgeship, Truman was elected to the U.S. Senate to represent Missouri. During his 10 years in the Senate, Truman supported Roosevelt's New Deal programs, as well as legislation that aided farmers and labor unions. Although he was openly racist when among his Senate peers, he lobbied for an end to legalized racial discrimination because it violated basic American ideals. Truman served as Roosevelt's running mate in the 1944 election, and the two men won 53 percent of the popular vote. After Roosevelt's death Truman assumed the presidency, and served until 1953.

During his presidency, Truman issued Executive Order 9808 (1946), which established the President's Committee on Civil Rights; Executive Order 9980 (1948), which established a fair employment board to eliminate discriminatory hiring within the federal government; and Executive Order 9981, which desegregated the U.S. armed forces. Truman's civil rights record was well received by African Americans, including King, who sent Truman an autographed copy of his first book, **Stride Toward Freedom**, in 1958.

A few years later Truman made public accusations that southern lunch counter demonstrations were orchestrated by Communists, and argued that: "If anyone came into my store and tried to stop business I'd throw him out. The Negro should behave himself and show he's a good citizen" (*Papers* 5:437). In response to Truman's comments, King wrote him, acknowledging his previous admiration for Truman's civil rights record and expressing his confusion and disappointment over the former president's statement. King stated: "It is a sad day for our country when men come to feel that oppressed people cannot desire freedom and human dignity unless they are motivated by Communism.... When the accusations come from a man who was once chosen by the American people to serve as the chief custodian of the nation's destiny then they rise to shocking and dangerous proportions" (*Papers* 5:438). King then asked Truman for a public apology, but no reply from Truman has been located. Following his tenure as president, Truman retired to Independence, Missouri. He died on 26 December 1972.

SOURCES
King to Truman, 19 April 1960, in *Papers* 5:437–439.
Miller, *Truman*, 1986.

TRUMPET OF CONSCIENCE, THE (1968)

The Trumpet of Conscience features five lectures that Martin Luther King, Jr., delivered in November and December 1967 for the Canadian Broadcasting Corporation (CBC) Massey Lectures. Founded in 1961 to honor Vincent Massey, former Governor General of Canada, the annual Massey Lectures served as a venue for earlier speakers such as John Kenneth Galbraith and Paul Goodman. The event, sponsored by the University of Toronto's Massey College, is broadcast each year on the CBC Radio One show "Ideas." Prior to King's **assassination**, the book was released under the title *Conscience for Change*, through the CBC. After King's death in 1968, the book was republished as *The Trumpet of Conscience*, and included a foreword written by Coretta Scott **King**. The book reveals some of King's most introspective reflections and his last impressions of the movement.

Each of the five orations encompasses a distinct theme pertinent to the African American civil rights struggle. In his first talk, "Impasse in Race Relations," King notes that although "the white backlash declared true equality could never be a reality in the United States," he felt that "mass civil disobedience as a new stage of struggle can transmute the deep rage of the ghetto into a constructive and creative force" (King, *Trumpet*, 10; 15). The second lecture, "Conscience and the Vietnam War," is a close parallel to the "**Beyond Vietnam**" speech that King gave at New York City's Riverside Church in April 1967, in opposition to the war. "Youth and Social Action,"

King's third lecture, envisions the mobilized power of a united youth front in which "hippies," "radicals," and other youth activists work in tandem to combine their strengths (King, *Trumpet*, 49). In "Nonviolence and Social Change," King defends nonviolent resistance as a political tool to convince "the wielders of power" to respond to national poverty (King, *Trumpet*, 62).

King's concluding speech was a live broadcast of his 1967 Christmas Eve sermon at **Ebenezer Baptist Church**, "A Christmas Sermon on Peace." The sermon illuminates King's long-term vision of **nonviolence** as a path to world peace and contains many of King's classical oratorical set pieces, including his description of **agape**. In his concluding comments, King refers to his remarks at the **March on Washington for Jobs and Freedom** and admits, "Not long after talking about that dream I started seeing it turn into a nightmare" (King, *Trumpet*, 76). He reviews the recent setbacks the movement faced, including violence during the **Birmingham Campaign**, persistent poverty, urban race riots, and an escalation of the war in **Vietnam**, and notes, "I am personally the victim of deferred dreams, of blasted hopes" (King, *Trumpet*, 76). In spite of these hurdles, King reassures his congregation: "I still have a dream. I have a dream that one day men will rise up and come to see that they are made to live together as brothers" (King, *Trumpet*, 76–77).

SOURCES

King, *A Call to Conscience*, ed. Carson and Shepard, 2001.
King, *Conscience for Change*, 1967.
King, *Trumpet of Conscience*, 1968.

UNITED PACKINGHOUSE WORKERS OF AMERICA (UPWA)

An early supporter of the **Montgomery bus boycott**, the United Packinghouse Workers of America (UPWA) raised funds for civil rights groups and participated in civil rights campaigns throughout the country during the 1950s and 1960s. At the 1962 UPWA Annual Convention, King told union members, "If labor as a whole, if the administration in Washington matched your concern and your deeds, the civil rights problem would not be a burning national issue, but a problem long solved, and in its solution a luminous accomplishment in the best tradition of American principles" (King, 21 May 1962).

The UPWA was created in 1943 from the Congress of Industrial Organizations' Packinghouse Workers Organizing Committee. In contrast to its rival union, the more conservative Amalgamated Meat Cutters, the UPWA was aligned with the radical Left and committed to interracial cooperation. In 1949 the union began pursuing anti-discrimination activities. The following year it created an Anti-Discrimination Department, dedicated to ending racial discrimination in meat packing plants and working against segregation in local communities.

In February 1956, two months after the start of the **Montgomery bus boycott**, the UPWA arranged a meeting in Chicago for King to address supporters of the boycott. UPWA local and district conventions passed resolutions in support of the boycott, arguing that "the enemies of Negroes are also the enemies of organized labor" (Russell Bull, 13 March 1956). The head of the Anti-Discrimination Department, UPWA Vice President Russell Lasley, attended the founding meeting of the **Southern Christian Leadership Conference** (SCLC) in January 1957, calling it "an extreme honor and privilege to represent UPWA in a conference of leaders who have dedicated their lives to the cause of freedom and the establishment of a society free of racial injustice and second class citizenship" (Lasley, 11 January 1957).

SCLC members promised to help the UPWA organize in southern plants, and the union launched a Fund for Democracy in the South, which raised $11,000 in local union contributions to SCLC. Presenting King with the check at the Anti-Discrimination Department's annual convention in October 1957, UPWA president Ralph **Helstein** told King that the union had joined the "battle for civil rights" because its members "have felt that freedom, like peace, is indivisible" (Helstein, 2 October 1957).

In the late 1950s and early 1960s, the U.S. Congress accused the UPWA of being a Communist-dominated organization. The union set up a Public Advisory Review Commission to oversee the UPWA's compliance with the **American Federation of Labor and Congress of Industrial Organizations'** (AFL-CIO) Ethical Practices Code, which banned Communists from holding union offices and prohibited the union from adopting communist doctrine. King sat on the commission.

The union's contribution to the movement went beyond financial donations to SCLC. The UPWA donated scholarship funds to support students involved in civil rights, and became a key benefactor of the **Student Nonviolent Coordinating Committee**. The union also wrote telegrams and letters of support during SCLC's various campaigns, and UPWA members participated directly in civil rights actions, including the 1963 **March on Washington for Jobs and Freedom** and the 1966 **Chicago Campaign**. Even after his controversial statements about the **Vietnam War** in 1967, the UPWA continued to support King.

In 1968, suffering from massive job cuts in the packinghouse industry due to technological changes, the UPWA was forced to merge with its old rival, Amalgamated Meat Cutters, forcing the organization to tone down its radical activism. During King's life, however, the union served as a role model for organized labor and a pioneer in the civil rights movement.

SOURCES

Russell Bull to Richard Durham, 13 March 1956, UPWP-WHi.

Halpern, *Down on the Killing Floor*, 1997.

Halpern and Horowitz, *Meatpackers*, 1996.

Helstein, Remarks at the UPWA conference, 2 October 1957, UPWP-WHi.

Horowitz, *"Negro and White, Unite and Fight!"*, 1997.

King, Address at the Thirteenth Constitutional Convention of the UPWA, 21 May 1962, UPWP-WHi.

Lasley, "Report on the Southern Leaders Conference on Transportation and Non-violent Integration," 11 January 1957, UPWP-WHi.

UPWA. *See* United Packinghouse Workers of America.

VANDIVER, SAMUEL ERNEST, JR. (1918–2005)

Upon learning of Martin Luther King's proposed move to Atlanta in December 1959, Georgia's Governor, Ernest Vandiver, declared that King was disruptive to the state's "good relations between the races" and vowed that the civil rights leader would be kept under surveillance. Vandiver claimed that "wherever M. L. King, Jr., has been there has followed in his wake a wave of crimes including stabbings, bombings, and inciting riots, barratry, destruction of property, and many others" ("Vandiver Says").

Vandiver was born in Canon, Georgia, on 3 July 1918. After graduating from Darlington Preparatory School in Rome, Georgia, he earned both his AB and LLB degrees at the University of Georgia. Vandiver served during World War II and, after returning to Georgia, he was elected mayor of Lavonia, Georgia, in 1946. Utilizing his father's connections to the Talmadge family's Democratic Party political machine, he then moved on to other positions within state government. In 1948 he managed Herman Talmadge's successful gubernatorial campaign, and went on to become both adjutant general and state director of selective service of Georgia. Vandiver was elected lieutenant governor under Marvin Griffin in 1954, and subsequently ran for and won Griffin's office in 1958.

Once elected, Vandiver proposed successful legislation requiring the withdrawal of state funds from public schools ordered to desegregate by federal courts, and preventing local property tax revenue from funding integrated schools. In January 1961, upon word that Vandiver planned to enforce Georgia law and close the University of Georgia, an additional federal injunction prevented him from doing so. At a special joint session of the Georgia Assembly, Vandiver urged the legislature to alter state law to authorize local communities to integrate or close their own public schools, warning that the issue would otherwise "blight our state.... Like a cancerous growth, it will devour progress ... denying the youth of Georgia their proper educational opportunity" (Sitton, "Vandiver Offers").

Tensions between King and Vandiver peaked upon news of King's relocation to Atlanta in early 1960. Vandiver expressed his discontent publicly, maintaining that King was not welcome in Georgia. In response to the governor's statement that King's arrival would bring violence to Atlanta, King wrote to a supporter: "Why Governor Vandiver made such an extreme accusation I do not know, other than the fact that he probably felt the need to appeal to some of the reactionaries who vote to keep him in office" (King, 23 December 1959).

Following King's arrest in October 1960 for his participation in a **sit-in** at a department store restaurant in Atlanta, Democratic Party presidential candidate John F. **Kennedy** made a phone call to Coretta Scott **King** expressing his concern for her jailed husband. Publicly, Vandiver told reporters: "It is a sad commentary on the year 1960 and its political campaign when the Democratic nominee for the presidency makes a phone call to the home of the foremost racial agitator in the country" ("King Hurt Demos"). Privately, Vandiver had suggested to Robert F. **Kennedy** that he make the personal phone call to DeKalb County Judge J. Oscar Mitchell, which led Mitchell to free King on bail. Vandiver's tactical recommendation was kept quiet.

Georgia's restrictions on serving consecutive terms forced Vandiver to leave office in 1963, and a heart attack during his 1966 reelection campaign forced him to withdraw from the race. Vandiver resumed his legal practice, and in 1971 served as Governor Jimmy Carter's adjutant general. He later held leadership positions with several institutions, including Atlanta's Rapid Transit Committee and the Lavonia Development Corporation. Vandiver died in 2005 at the age of 86.

SOURCES

Branch, *Parting the Waters*, 1988.
Bradford Daniel, "Martin Luther King says: 'I'd Do It All Again,'" *Sepia*, December 1961.
Henderson, *Ernest Vandiver*, 2000.
Introduction, in *Papers* 5:20–21; 36–40.
King, Address at NAACP Mass Rally for Civil Rights, 10 July 1960, in *Papers* 5:485–487.
"King Hurt Demos, Vandiver Asserts," *Atlanta Journal*, 31 October 1960.
King to Lee Perry, 23 December 1959, MLKP-MBU.
Claude Sitton, "Vandiver Offers Integration Plan," *New York Times*, 19 January 1961.
"Vandiver Says Rev. King Not 'Welcome' Here," *Atlanta Daily World*, 2 December 1959.

VEP. *See* Voter Education Project.

VIETNAM WAR (1961–1975)

Four years after President John F. **Kennedy** sent the first American troops into Vietnam, Martin Luther King issued his first public statement on the war. Answering press questions after addressing a Howard University audience on 2 March 1965, King asserted that the war in Vietnam was "accomplishing nothing" and called for a negotiated settlement (Schuette, "King Preaches on Non-Violence").

While King was personally opposed to the war, he was concerned that publicly criticizing U.S. foreign policy would damage his relationship with President Lyndon B. **Johnson**, who had been instrumental in passing civil rights legislation and who had declared in April 1965 that he was willing to negotiate a diplomatic end to the war in Vietnam. Though he avoided condemning the war outright, at the August 1965 annual **Southern Christian Leadership Conference** (SCLC) convention King called for a halt to bombing in North Vietnam, urged that the United Nations be empowered to mediate the conflict, and told the crowd that "what is required is a small first step that may establish a new spirit of mutual confidence … a step capable of breaking the cycle of mistrust, violence and war" (King, 12 August 1965). He supported

Johnson's calls for diplomatic negotiations and economic development as the beginnings of such a step. Later that year King framed the issue of war in Vietnam as a moral issue: "As a minister of the gospel," he said, "I consider war an evil. I must cry out when I see war escalated at any point" ("Opposes Vietnam War").

King's opposition to the war provoked criticism from members of Congress, the press, and from his civil rights colleagues who argued that expanding his civil rights message to include foreign affairs would harm the black freedom struggle in America. Fearful of being labeled a Communist, which would diminish the impact of his civil rights work, King tempered his criticism of U.S. policy in Vietnam through late 1965 and 1966. His wife, Coretta Scott **King**, took a more active role in opposing the war, speaking at a rally at the Washington Monument on 27 November 1965 with Benjamin **Spock**, the renowned pediatrician and anti-war activist, and joined in other demonstrations.

In December 1966, testifying before a congressional subcommittee on budget priorities, King argued for a "rebalancing" of fiscal priorities away from America's "obsession" with Vietnam and toward greater support for anti-poverty programs at home (Semple, "Dr. King Scores Poverty"). King led his first anti-war march in Chicago on 25 March 1967, and reinforced the connection between war abroad and injustice at home: "The bombs in Vietnam explode at home—they destroy the dream and possibility for a decent America" ("Dr. King Leads Chicago"). A few days later, King made it clear that his peace work was not undertaken as the leader of the SCLC, but "as an individual, as a clergyman, as one who is greatly concerned about peace" ("Dr. King to Weigh Civil Disobedience").

Less than two weeks after leading his first Vietnam demonstration, on 4 April 1967, King made his best known and most comprehensive statement against the war. Seeking to reduce the potential backlash by framing his speech within the context of religious objection to war, King addressed a crowd of 3,000 people at Riverside Church in New York City. King delivered a speech entitled "**Beyond Vietnam**," pointing out that the war effort was "taking the black young men who had been crippled by our society and sending them eight thousand miles away to guarantee liberties in Southeast Asia which they had not found in southwest Georgia and East Harlem" (King, "Beyond Vietnam," 143).

Although the peace community lauded King's willingness to take a public stand against the war in Vietnam, many within the civil rights movement further distanced themselves from his stance. The **National Association for the Advancement of Colored People**, for example, issued a statement against merging the civil rights and peace movements. Undeterred, King, Spock, and Harry **Belafonte** led 10,000 demonstrators on an anti-war march to the United Nations on 15 April 1967.

During the last year of his life, King worked with Spock to develop "Vietnam Summer," a volunteer project to increase grassroots peace activism in time for the 1968 elections. King linked his anti-war and civil rights work in speeches throughout the country, where he described the three problems he saw plaguing the nation: racism, poverty, and the war in Vietnam. In his last Sunday sermon, delivered at the National Cathedral in Washington, D.C., on 31 March 1968, King said that he was "convinced that [Vietnam] is one of the most unjust wars that has ever been fought in the history of the world" (King, "Remaining Awake," 219). Nearly five years after

King's **assassination**, American troops withdrew from Vietnam and a peace treaty declared South and North Vietnam independent of each other.

SOURCES

Branch, *At Canaan's Edge*, 2006.

"Dr. King Leads Chicago Peace Rally," *New York Times*, 26 March 1967.

"Dr. King to Weigh Civil Disobedience If War Intensifies," *New York Times*, 2 April 1967.

"Dr. Martin Luther King: Beyond Vietnam and Remaining Awake through a Great Revolution," 90th Cong., 2d sess., *Congressional Record* 114 (9 April 1968): 9391–9397.

Garrow, *Bearing the Cross*, 1986.

King, "Beyond Vietnam," in *A Call to Conscience*, ed. Carson and Shepard, 2001.

King, Excerpts, Address at mass rally during the 1965 SCLC convention, 12 August 1965, MLKJP-GAMK.

King, "Remaining Awake Through a Great Revolution," in *A Knock at Midnight*, ed. Carson and Holloran, 1998.

(Scott) King, *My Life with Martin Luther King, Jr.*, 1969.

"Opposes Vietnam War," *New York Times*, 11 November 1965.

Paul A. Schuette, "King Preaches on Non-Violence at Police-Guarded Howard Hall," *Washington Post*, 3 March 1965.

Robert B. Semple, Jr., "Dr. King Scores Poverty Budget," *New York Times*, 16 December 1966.

VIVIAN, CORDY TINDELL (1924–)

As a minister, educator, and community organizer, C. T. Vivian has been a tenacious advocate for civil rights since the 1940s. After joining the **Southern Christian Leadership Conference** (SCLC) in the early 1960s, he became the Director of Affiliates and participated in numerous protests. Known for his sharp tongue and unflinching courage, Vivian recalled what movement veterans felt after serving time in jail: "They had triumphed, that they had achieved, that they were now ready, they could go back home, they could be a witness to a new understanding. Nonviolence was proven in that respect" (Hampton and Fayer, 96).

Vivian, who was born on 28 July 1924, in Boonville, Missouri, relocated with his family to Macomb, Illinois, when he was six years old. After graduating from Macomb High School in 1942, he enrolled at Western Illinois University. Upon moving to Peoria, Illinois, Vivian worked as assistant boys' director at Carver Community Center and later participated in a successful lunch counter **sit-in** in 1947. He served as pastor of the First Community Church in Nashville from 1956 to 1961, while completing his BD at American Baptist Theological Seminary and editing the *Baptist Layman*, a journal of the **National Baptist Convention**.

While organizing in Nashville, he became acquainted with James **Lawson**. Together with Kelly Miller **Smith**, they founded the Nashville Christian Leadership Conference. In early 1960 Vivian joined Diane **Nash**, James **Bevel**, John **Lewis**, and other students from local universities as they staged sit-ins and other nonviolent protests throughout the city. Nash recalled Vivian's presence: "He was an eloquent spokesperson. His fire was very much in evidence. He has a certain commitment in his personality that really pervades the things he does and says" (Hampton and Fayer, 66). In 1961 Vivian was among the Nashville activists who replaced injured freedom riders in Montgomery, Alabama. At the conclusion of the **Freedom Rides** in Jackson, Mississippi, police arrested Vivian and sent him to Parchman Prison, where he was brutally beaten by guards.

In 1963 King invited Vivian to join the executive staff of SCLC as the Director of Affiliates. In this capacity Vivian coordinated the activities of local civil rights groups nationwide. He also advised King and organized demonstrations during campaigns in **Birmingham** and Selma, Alabama, and **St. Augustine**, Florida. Vivian attracted national media attention in February 1965, when he was struck by Sheriff Jim **Clark** while leading a group attempting to register to vote at the Selma courthouse. The event was captured by television cameras and increased support for the protest.

In 1966 Vivian left SCLC and moved to Chicago to direct the Urban Training Center for Christian Mission. Two years later he organized the Coalition for United Community Action, a group of 61 black organizations aimed at ending racism in building trade unions. He later founded the Black Action Strategies and Information Center and the Center for Democratic Renewal, formerly known as the National Anti-Klan Network. His book, *Black Power and the American Myth*, was published in 1970.

SOURCES
Halberstam, *Children*, 1998.
Hampton and Fayer, with Flynn, *Voices of Freedom*, 1990.

VOTER EDUCATION PROJECT (VEP)

The Voter Education Project (VEP) coordinated the voter registration campaigns of five civil rights groups—the **Southern Christian Leadership Conference** (SCLC), the **Student Nonviolent Coordinating Committee**, the **National Association for the Advancement of Colored People**, the **Congress of Racial Equality**, and the **National Urban League**—under the auspices of the Southern Regional Council (SRC), a non-profit research organization. The creation of the VEP enabled foundations to make tax-free donations directly to voter registration efforts, which were then coordinated by SRC to prevent duplicate coverage areas. Martin Luther King believed the VEP to be a success, pledging to "continue to participate personally" in its registration efforts (King, 5 April 1962).

Established in April 1962, the VEP originated in discussions between U.S. Attorney General Robert F. **Kennedy**, Assistant Attorney General for Civil Rights Burke **Marshall**, the SRC's Harold C. Fleming, and philanthropist Stephen R. Currier. They believed that the creation of a nonpartisan, tax-exempt, and centrally organized agency would attract private contributions to the civil rights struggle and improve the efficiency of voter registration efforts already underway. In addition, they hoped the VEP would shift the efforts of civil rights groups away from confrontational direct action methods toward less controversial voter registration drives. Although civil rights groups were well aware of this motivation for advocating the VEP, they welcomed the additional funding and viewed participation in the project as a way to continue their work with increased federal protection.

VEP-funded projects had early successes in communities such as Albany, Georgia, where a VEP grant helped the **Albany Movement** register more than 500 new voters in two weeks during 1962. However, in early 1963 the VEP threatened to suspend SCLC from the program because of inadequate reporting on the use of grant funds. King hastily called a conference between VEP leadership and SCLC, during which he acknowledged that SCLC had to work harder to reach its reporting obligations and asked the VEP to renew its support. The VEP agreed, and SCLC continued its VEP-sponsored projects.

Although many registration campaigns achieved success, in some areas, notably Mississippi, the VEP concluded that discrimination was so entrenched that only federal intervention could significantly increase the number of black voters. By the end of 1964 VEP grants totaled almost $900,000, and nearly 800,000 new black southern voters had been added to the rolls since the VEP began. In October 1965, a few months after the passage of the **Voting Rights Act of 1965**, King told an SCLC administrative committee that more than 175,000 new black voters had been registered since the act passed, and that SCLC registration and canvassing was responsible for more than half of that increase.

In 1967 the VEP began a third operational phase that focused on channeling grants to local voter leagues. The VEP separated from the SRC in 1970, but continued voter education and registration work until it closed in 1992.

SOURCES
Fairclough, *Race and Democracy*, 1995.
King, Press conference after meeting with Lyndon B. Johnson, 5 August 1965, MLKJP-GAMK.
King, "Statement on intensified voter registration drive," 5 April 1962, MLKJP-GAMK.
Navasky, *Kennedy Justice*, 1971.
Parker, *Black Votes Count*, 1990.

VOTING RIGHTS ACT OF 1965

On 6 August 1965 President Lyndon B. **Johnson** signed the Voting Rights Act into law, calling the day "a triumph for freedom as huge as any victory that has ever been won on any battlefield" (Johnson, "Remarks in the Capitol Rotunda"). The law came seven months after Martin Luther King launched a **Southern Christian Leadership Conference** (SCLC) campaign based in Selma, Alabama, with the aim of pressuring Congress to pass such legislation.

"In Selma," King wrote, "we see a classic pattern of disenfranchisement typical of the Southern Black Belt areas where Negroes are in the majority" (King, "Selma— The Shame and the Promise"). In addition to facing arbitrary literacy tests and poll taxes, African Americans in Selma and other southern towns were intimidated, harassed, and assaulted when they sought to register to vote. Civil rights activists met with fierce resistance to their campaign, which attracted national attention on 7 March 1965, when civil rights workers were brutally attacked by white law enforcement officers on a march from **Selma to Montgomery**.

Johnson introduced the Voting Rights Act that same month, "with the outrage of Selma still fresh" (Johnson, "Remarks in the Capitol Rotunda"). In just over four months, Congress passed the bill. The Voting Rights Act of 1965 abolished literacy tests and poll taxes designed to disenfranchise African American voters and gave the federal government the authority to take over voter registration in counties with a pattern of persistent discrimination. "This law covers many pages," Johnson said before signing the bill, "but the heart of the act is plain. Wherever, by clear and objective standards, States and counties are using regulations, or laws, or tests to deny the right to vote, then they will be struck down" (Johnson, "Remarks in the Capitol Rotunda").

On the same day Johnson signed the bill, he announced that his attorney general, Nicholas **Katzenbach**, would initiate lawsuits against four states that still required a poll tax to register. Although King called the law "a great step forward in removing all of the remaining obstacles to the right to vote," he knew that the ballot would only be an effective tool for social change if potential voters rid themselves of the fear associated with voting (King, 5 August 1965). To meet this goal and "rid the American body politic of racism," SCLC developed its Political Education and Voter Registration Department (King, "Annual Report").

SOURCES

Carson, *In Struggle*, 1981.

John Herbers, "Alabama Vote Drive Opened by Dr. King," *New York Times*, 3 January 1965.

Johnson, "Remarks in the Capitol Rotunda at the Signing of the Voting Rights Act," 6 August 1965, in *Public Papers of the Presidents of the United States: Lyndon B. Johnson, 1965*, 1966.

E. W. Kenworthy, "Johnson Signs Voting Rights Bill, Orders Immediate Enforcement; 4 Suits Will Challenge Poll Tax," *New York Times*, 7 August 1965.

King, "Annual Report Delivered at SCLC's Ninth Annual National Convention, 11 August 1965," MLKPP.

King, Press conference after meeting with Lyndon B. Johnson, 5 August 1965, MLKJP-GAMK.

King, "Selma—The Shame and the Promise," *IUD Agenda* 1 (March 1965): 18–21.

"Provisions of Voting Bill," *New York Times*, 7 August 1965.

WACHTEL, HARRY H. (1917–1997)

Harry Wachtel, a prominent New York lawyer, began working for Martin Luther King in 1962. With King's endorsement, Wachtel co-founded the **Gandhi Society for Human Rights**, which, as a tax-exempt charitable organization, effectively raised substantial funds for the civil rights movement. In subsequent years King came to rely on Wachtel's legal advice and moral support, as Wachtel arranged meetings with prominent donors and government officials and met with King regularly.

Wachtel was born in New York City on 26 March 1917. A self-described student radical, Wachtel received his law degree from Columbia University in 1940. With the exception of his military service during World War II, Wachtel practiced continuously in New York firms throughout his career.

King was introduced to Wachtel through Clarence B. **Jones**, King's trusted legal advisor. Jones had contacted Wachtel because he represented the parent company of several segregated lunch counters and Jones was interested in pursuing back-channel negotiations on desegregation. Jones found a willing and able ally in Wachtel, who immediately offered his legal services directly to King. After a series of letter exchanges in late 1961, King and Wachtel met in early 1962 when King was in town for a fundraiser for the **Southern Christian Leadership Conference** (SCLC). Soon after, Wachtel wrote King: "I must confess that before our meeting I had a deep respect for your historic and selfless fight against encrusted injustice and inhumanity. The several hours spent with you stirred me and afforded me new perspectives" (Wachtel, 16 February 1962). The two immediately began collaborating on the formation of the Gandhi Society for Human Rights.

In 1963 Wachtel joined Jones in defending Ralph **Abernathy** and three other ministers in a libel suit stemming from an advertisement in the *New York Times*. Wachtel quickly became part of King's inner circle and was jokingly referred to as the twin of King's confidante Stanley **Levison**, also a Jewish lawyer from New York. In 1964 Wachtel formed a small advisory group for King that they called the Research Committee, which met regularly at Wachtel's office and included Jones, union leader Ralph **Helstein**, Bayard **Rustin**, and others. Later that year, Wachtel joined a group accompanying King to Norway to accept the **Nobel Peace Prize**.

Wachtel remained King's close advisor until his death in 1968, guiding him through matters ranging from interaction with **Federal Bureau of Investigation** director

J. Edgar Hoover, to gaining support from religious conservatives, to taking a public stance against the **Vietnam War**. Wachtel's Wall Street and legal connections gave King access to potential donors and high-level government and business contacts. Wachtel also played a key role in arranging meetings for King with Vice President Hubert Humphrey and President Lyndon B. **Johnson**.

After King's **assassination**, Wachtel became Coretta Scott **King's** personal lawyer. He also served as a trustee of SCLC and vice president and legal counsel for the **King Center** from 1969 to 1982. Wachtel died of Parkinson's disease in 1997.

SOURCES

Branch, *At Canaan's Edge*, 2006.
Branch, *Pillar of Fire*, 1998.
Jones, Interview by King Papers Project staff, 7 March 2007.
Wachtel to King, 16 February 1962, MLKJP-GAMK.

WALKER, WYATT TEE (1929–)

Described by Martin Luther King as "one of the keenest minds of the nonviolent revolution," Wyatt Tee Walker served as executive director of the **Southern Christian Leadership Conference** (SCLC) from 1960 to 1964 (Press release, 23 June 1964).

Walker was born 16 August 1929, in Brockton, Massachusetts, to John Wise and Maude Pinn Walker. Walker graduated Magna Cum Laude in 1950 from Virginia Union University in Richmond, Virginia, with a BS in both chemistry and physics. He then entered Virginia Union's Graduate School of Religion, serving as student body president before receiving his BD in 1953. At a meeting of the Inter-Seminary Movement, Walker met King, then a student at **Crozer Theological Seminary**.

In 1953 Walker accepted a position as minister at Gillfield Baptist Church in Petersburg, Virginia. Walker also held a number of leadership roles with local civil rights organizations. He served as president of the local chapter of the **National Association for the Advancement of Colored People** and as state director of the **Congress of Racial Equality**. He was also a founder of the Virginia Council on Human Relations, a biracial group working for desegregation, and led the Petersburg Improvement Association, which was modeled after the **Montgomery Improvement Association**.

In 1959 Walker organized and led the first local Prayer Pilgrimage for Public Schools, an event that protested Virginia state officials' attempts to block public school integration. The same year, Walker also joined the board of SCLC. In January 1960 King spoke at the second annual Prayer Pilgrimage and in March of that year Walker decided to remain in jail after being arrested protesting segregation in the Petersburg Library. Meanwhile, King had mailed him an offer to become SCLC's new executive director. King expressed confidence that Walker "would bring into full grown maturity an organization that is presently a sleeping giant" (*Papers* 5:385). Walker replaced Ella **Baker**, who had served as interim director since John Lee **Tilley's** resignation in 1959. Walker subsequently moved to Atlanta with his family. He brought Dorothy **Cotton** and James R. Wood, two of his closest assistants from the Petersburg Improvement Association, with him to SCLC.

A firm administrator, Walker worked to bring order to the organization's fundraising efforts and the wide-ranging activities of its staff. Walker was also a key tactician, authoring and evaluating protest strategies, including "Project C," the basis for

SCLC's **Birmingham Campaign** in 1963. SCLC benefited from Walker's advice on organizational structure and strategy. Walker described himself as someone "who didn't care about being loved to get it done—I didn't give a damn about whether people liked me, but I knew I could do the job," an attitude exemplary of a heavy-handed leadership style that occasionally fueled SCLC staff tensions (Eskew, 37). Walker's leadership style also alienated some young activists affiliated with the **Student Nonviolent Coordinating Committee**.

Such conflicts were the motivating forces behind Walker's eventual resignation from SCLC in 1964. When Walker was replaced by SCLC staff member Andrew **Young**, he went on to work as vice president of a new publishing venture, the Negro Heritage Library. In 1965 he became president of the organization, which sought to increase the attention paid to black history in school curricula. Walker and King maintained contact in the years following Walker's resignation, and King preached at his 1968 installation service at Canaan Baptist Church, praising Walker as "a tall man, tall in stature, tall in courage," who contributed significantly to SCLC (King, 24 March 1968).

Walker remained active in religion and social change activities after leaving SCLC. In 1975 he received his D.Min. from Colgate-Rochester Divinity School. Walker also served as New York Governor Nelson **Rockefeller**'s special assistant on urban affairs and held visiting professorships at Princeton Theological Seminary and New York University. An expert on gospel music, Walker published several books on the role music has played in the black religious tradition, including *Somebody's Calling My Name: Black Sacred Music and Social Change* (1979).

SOURCES
Eskew, *But for Birmingham*, 1997.
King, "A Knock at Midnight," 24 March 1968, MLKJP-GAMK.
King to Walker, 5 March 1960, in *Papers* 5:384–385.
Press release, Statement on Walker's appointment at Educational Heritage, 23 June 1964, SCLCR-GAMK.
Young, *An Easy Burden*, 1996.

WALLACE, GEORGE CORLEY, JR. (1919–1998)

After pledging "Segregation now! Segregation tomorrow! Segregation forever!" in his 1963 inaugural address, Alabama Governor George Wallace gained national notoriety by standing at the entrance to the University of Alabama to denounce the enrollment of two African American students. Martin Luther King described Wallace as "perhaps the most dangerous racist in America today" (King, "Interview"). In a 1965 interview King said: "I am not sure that he believes all the poison that he preaches, but he is artful enough to convince others that he does" (King, "Interview").

Wallace was born on 25 August 1919, in Clio, Alabama. The son of a farmer, he worked his way through the University of Alabama, earning his law degree in 1942. After a brief time in the Air Force, Wallace returned to Alabama to work as the state's assistant attorney general. He was elected to the state legislature in 1947, and served as a district judge from 1953 to 1959. In his early political career he maintained a moderate stance on integration; but after losing his first gubernatorial campaign to a candidate who was endorsed by the Ku Klux Klan, Wallace became an outspoken defender of segregation. In 1962 Wallace won the governorship on a segregationist platform, receiving the largest vote of any gubernatorial candidate in Alabama's history until that time.

In June 1963 Wallace fulfilled a campaign promise to stand in the schoolhouse door rather than accede to federal orders to integrate Alabama schools. Wallace blocked black students Vivian Malone and James Hood from entering the University of Alabama, but yielded when President John F. **Kennedy** federalized the Alabama National Guard to ensure their entrance. Three months later violence in the city erupted, concluding in the murder of four young black girls in a bombing at Sixteenth Street Baptist Church in Birmingham. King, who had been in Birmingham to desegregate public facilities, felt that Wallace's actions contributed to the violence in the city. Writing to President Kennedy in September 1963, King lamented: "A reign of terror continues in Birmingham. The atmosphere of violence and lawlessness has been fomented and created by the irresponsible actions of Governor George Wallace who persists in violating federal fiat in arrogant and blatant defiance." King warned Kennedy that if he did not "use the influence of [his] high office," Birmingham would "see the worst race riot in our [nation's] history" (King, 5 September 1963). Similar confrontations, repeated in other cities, bolstered Wallace's reputation. His first term was also marked by the violent responses of Alabama authorities to voting rights demonstrations in Selma, Alabama.

Wallace's position on civil rights and his anti-Washington rhetoric appealed not only to southern segregationists, but also to voters in other parts of the country. In 1964 he entered the Democratic Party's presidential primaries in Wisconsin, Indiana, and Maryland and made a strong showing in all three states, drawing up to 43 percent of the vote. In 1968 he launched a full-fledged national campaign for the presidency. Running as a third-party candidate, he won five southern states and 10 million votes, half of them from outside the South.

During Wallace's third bid for the presidency in 1972, an assassination attempt left him paralyzed below the waist and ended his campaign. He was eventually able to return to his duties as governor, and was reelected to a third term in 1974. As the black vote became more influential in Alabama, Wallace began to shift his stance on racial issues. After renouncing his former views on segregation and seeking reconciliation with civil rights leaders such as Ralph **Abernathy**, Jesse **Jackson**, and John **Lewis**, he won a fourth term as governor in 1982 with substantial support from African Americans. Wallace died in Montgomery on 13 September 1998 at the age of 79.

SOURCES

Carter, *Politics of Rage*, 2000.
King, "Interview with Martin Luther King, Jr.," *Playboy* (January 1965): 65–68; 70–74; 76–78.
King to Kennedy, 5 September 1963, DJG-GEU.
Lesher, *George Wallace*, 1994.

WATSON, MELVIN HAMPTON (1908–2006)

A long-standing friend of the King family, Melvin Watson was one of a group of ministers in Atlanta, Georgia, committed to preaching the **social gospel**.

The son of Peter O. Watson, clerk and Sunday school superintendent of **Ebenezer Baptist Church**, Watson graduated in 1930 from **Morehouse College** with Martin

Luther **King**, Sr. Encouraged to continue his religious education by theologian Howard **Thurman**, he studied at the Oberlin College Graduate School of Theology, where he received his BD (1932) and his MA in sacred theology (1934). Watson went on to obtain his doctorate in Theology (1948) at the Pacific School of Religion in Berkeley, California. He was dean of men and professor of Religion at Shaw and Dillard Universities before returning to Morehouse as dean and professor of Philosophy and Religion in the School of Religion, where he remained for many years. Praised by King, Sr., as someone who was "among the few teachers who are able to preach and carry a Church with ease," Watson became pastor of Liberty Baptist Church in Atlanta in 1958, where he served until his retirement in 1990 (King, Sr., 5 August 1955).

Watson's support of a socially and politically involved ministry was evident early in his career. Watson believed that the church could "provide the spiritual dynamics for social action" (Watson, "The Church and Political Action"). Reverend Calvin O. Butts, III, one of Watson's students, reminisced after Watson's death: "He was preparing us to go out and disturb the conscience and rebel against injustice" (Henry, "Melvin H. Watson").

As a young preacher King, Jr., looked to Watson's ministry for guidance. When King delivered the sermon "Communism's Challenge to Christianity" in August 1952, at Ebenezer, Watson was sitting in the congregation. Two days later Watson critiqued the sermon on **communism** in a letter to King. Disagreeing with King's interpretation of the concept of materialism, Watson cautioned him to differentiate between the Marxist and ancient Greek meanings of the term, but praised him generally for doing a "fine job" (*Papers* 2:157). After visiting the Kings in 1954 Watson praised King's pastorate: "You are definitely off to a promising start, and I believe the Lord is with you. You have my prayers and best wishes for continued growth in spiritual stature and in the capacity to serve the people" (*Papers* 2:321).

SOURCES

Derrick Henry, "Melvin H. Watson, 98, Trained Civil Rights Leader," *Atlanta Journal-Constitution*, 24 June 2006.

King, Sr., to Watson, 5 August 1955, EBCR.

Watson, "The Church and Political Action," *Journal of Religious Thought* 8, no. 2 (Spring/Summer 1951): 114–124.

Watson to King, 14 August 1952, in *Papers* 2:156–157.

Watson to King, 15 December 1954, in *Papers* 2:321.

WATTS REBELLION (LOS ANGELES, 1965)

On Wednesday, 11 August 1965, Marquette Frye, a 21-year-old black man, was arrested for drunk driving on the edge of Los Angeles' Watts neighborhood. The ensuing struggle during his arrest sparked off 6 days of rioting, resulting in 34 deaths, over 1,000 injuries, nearly 4,000 arrests, and the destruction of property valued at $40 million. On 17 August 1965, Martin Luther King arrived in Los Angeles in the aftermath of the riots. His experiences over the next several days reinforced his growing conviction that the **Southern Christian Leadership Conference** (SCLC) should move north and lead a movement to address the growing problems facing black people in the nation's urban areas.

Frye had been drinking and was driving with his brother, Ronald, in the car, when the two were pulled over two blocks from their home. While Marquette was being arrested, Ronald retrieved their mother from her house. When Mrs. Frye saw her son being forcibly arrested, she fought with the arresting officers, tearing one officer's shirt. An officer then struck Marquette's head with his nightstick, and all three of the Fryes were arrested.

By the time the Fryes were arrested, hundreds of onlookers had been drawn to the scene. Anger and rumors spread quickly through the black community, and residents stoned cars and beat white people who entered the area. A neighborhood meeting called by the Los Angeles County Human Relations Commission the following day failed to quell the mounting tension, and that evening rioting resumed. Firemen attempting to put out blazes were shot at by residents, and looting was rampant. All day Friday the riots intensified, prompting the California lieutenant governor to call in the National Guard. By Saturday night a curfew had been set, and nearly 14,000 National Guard troops were patrolling a 46-mile area. By the time King arrived on Tuesday, having cut short his stay in Puerto Rico, the riots were largely over and the curfew was lifted. Fueling residual anger, however, police stormed a Nation of Islam mosque the next night, firing hundreds of rounds of ammunition into the building and wounding 19 men.

While deploring the riots and their use of violence, King was quick to point out that the problems that led to the violence were "environmental and not racial. The economic deprivation, social isolation, inadequate housing, and general despair of thousands of Negroes teeming in Northern and Western ghettos are the ready seeds which give birth to tragic expressions of violence" (King, 17 August 1965). Although California Governor Edmund Brown hoped King would not go to Watts, King went to support those living in the ghetto who, he claimed, would be pushed further into "despair and hopelessness" by the riot (King, 17 August 1965). He also hoped to bolster the frayed alliance between blacks and whites favoring civil rights reform. He offered to mediate between local people and government officials, and pushed for systematic solutions to the economic and social problems plaguing Watts and other black ghettos.

King told reporters that the Watts riots were "the beginning of a stirring of those people in our society who have been by passed by the progress of the past decade" (King, 20 August 1965). Struggles in the North, King believed, were really about "dignity and work," rather than rights, which had been the main goal of black activism in the South (King, 20 August 1965). During his discussions with local people, King met black residents who argued for armed insurrection, and others who claimed that "the only way we can ever get anybody to listen to us is to start a riot" (King, 19 August 1965). These expressions concerned King, and before he left Los Angeles he spoke on the phone with President Lyndon B. **Johnson** about what could be done to ease the situation. King recommended that Johnson roll out a federal anti-poverty program in Los Angeles immediately. Johnson agreed with the suggestion, telling King: "You did a good job going out there" (Branch, 308).

Later that fall, King wrote an article for the *Saturday Review* in which he argued that Los Angeles could have anticipated rioting "when its officials tied up federal aid in political manipulation; when the rate of Negro unemployment soared above the depression levels of the 1930s; when the population density of Watts became the worst in the nation," and when the state of California repealed a law that prevented discrimination in housing (King, "Beyond the Los Angeles Riots").

After SCLC initiated its **Chicago Campaign** that fall, King asked an audience there: "What did Watts accomplish but the death of thirty-four Negroes and injury to thousands more? What did it profit the Negro to burn down the stores and factories in which he sought employment? The way of riots is not a way of progress, but a blind ally of death and destruction which wrecks its havoc hardest against the rioters themselves" (King, 12 March 1966).

SOURCES

Branch, *At Canaan's Edge*, 2006.

King, Address at the Chicago Freedom Festival, 12 March 1966, CULC-ICIU.

King, "Beyond the Los Angeles Riots: Next Step, The North," *Saturday Review* (13 November 1965): 33–35; 105.

King, Statement on Los Angeles, 20 August 1965, MMFR.

King, Statement on riots in Watts, Calif., 17 August 1965, SCLCR-GAMK.

King, Statement to the people of Watts, 19 August 1965, MLKJP-GAMK.

WCC. *See* White Citizens' Councils.

WEST, IRENE (1890–1975)

Irene West was an active participant in the African American freedom struggle who, according to Jo Ann **Robinson**, dedicated her life to "fighting for the cause of first-class citizenship" for blacks (Robinson, 70). A prominent woman in Montgomery, Alabama, who was married to Dr. A. W. West, Sr., a wealthy dentist, Martin Luther King referred to West as "the real mother of the Movement" (Seay, i).

West was born in 1890 and raised in Perry County, Alabama. She graduated from Alabama State College, which is now called Alabama State University. She also attended Tuskegee and Hampton Institutes. West was a member of numerous civic organizations, including the **National Association for the Advancement of Colored People** and the Women's League for Peace and Freedom. She joined the **Women's Political Council** (WPC) shortly after it was founded in 1946, and became its treasurer. As a WPC organizer, West was involved in voter registration projects, educational issues, efforts to improve the treatment of African Americans on city buses, and efforts to improve the poor quality of segregated parks and recreational facilities.

Although West was in her sixties at the start of the **Montgomery bus boycott**, she was one of the most involved activists—distributing information about the boycott, calling civic leaders to meetings, and driving in the carpool. In *Stride Toward Freedom*, King's memoir of the boycott, he recalled West's enthusiasm for the campaign and how she spent the days driving people to work and home again. Interviewed early in the boycott, West was already impressed with the youthful King and **Montgomery Improvement Association** (MIA) lawyer Fred **Gray**, stating: "Their minds are much older than they are biologically" (West, 23 January 1956).

West and several others, including E. D. **Nixon**, were appointed to the executive board of the MIA because, according to Robinson, "MIA members felt [they] would speak out without fear and speak with authority as representatives of the black protesters" (Robinson, 65). She, King, Robinson, and several other MIA members made up a special delegation of representatives who met with city commissioners and bus company officials during the boycott to resolve concerns about the treatment of African Americans on transportation. West was secretary of the MIA Transportation Committee and was also one of the MIA members arrested for operating the carpool on 22 February 1956, along with her friend, Robinson. Robinson later recalled that during the finger-printing at the jail, Mrs. West joked with the officers and "the interchange was good for all of us, and we felt wonderful, relaxed, at peace with ourselves" (Robinson, 151).

SOURCES
King, *Stride Toward Freedom*, 1958.
Robinson, *Montgomery Bus Boycott*, 1987.
Seay, *I Was There by the Grace of God*, 1990.
West, Interview by Willie Mae Lee, 23 January 1956, PV-ARC-LNT.

WHERE DO WE GO FROM HERE (1967)

While vacationing in the Caribbean in January and February 1967, King wrote the first draft of his final book *Where Do We Go from Here: Chaos or Community?* Accompanied by Coretta Scott **King**, Bernard **Lee**, and Dora **McDonald**, King rented a secluded house in Ocho Rios, Jamaica, with no telephone. This was one of the very few times in King's adult life that he was completely isolated from the demands of the movement and could focus entirely on his writing. He labored on the initial manuscript for a month, sending chapters to Stanley **Levison** in New York for his revisions.

Where Do We Go from Here was King's analysis of the state of American race relations and the movement after a decade of U.S. civil rights struggles. "With Selma and the Voting Rights Act one phase of development in the civil rights revolution came to an end," he observed (King, 3). King believed that the next phase in the movement would bring its own challenges, as African Americans continued to make demands for better jobs, higher wages, decent housing, an education equal to that of whites, and a guarantee that the rights won in the **Civil Rights Act of 1964** and the **Voting Rights Act of 1965** would be enforced by the federal government. He warned that "the persistence of racism in depth and the dawning awareness that Negro demands will necessitate structural changes in society have generated a new phase of white resistance in North and South" (King, 12).

King assessed the rise of **black nationalism** and the increasing use of the slogan "**Black Power**" in the movement. While he praised the slogan as "a call to black people to amass the political and economic strength to achieve their legitimate goals," he also recognized that its implied rejection of interracial coalitions and call for retaliatory violence "prevent it from having the substance and program to become the basic strategy for the civil rights movement in the days ahead" (King, 36; 44). Condemning the advocacy of black separatism, King maintained that there would be no genuine progress for African Americans "unless the whole of American society takes a new turn toward greater economic justice" (King, 50). Despite King's impatience with Black Power proponents, he ended the book on an optimistic note, calling for continued faith in "mass nonviolent action and the ballot" and including his own "Program and Prospects" for black advancement (King, 129; 193–202).

After the book's publication in June 1967, King used its promotional tour to reinforce points raised in its pages, speaking out on the living conditions of many black Americans and against U.S. involvement in the **Vietnam War**. At a luncheon in his honor, King chided the nation for doing nothing to eradicate slum conditions: "Everyone is worrying about the long hot summer with its threat of riots. We had a long cold winter when little was done about the conditions that create riots" ("Dr. King Deplores"). During a July television appearance, King repeated his assertion, made in the book and in his April 1967 speech "**Beyond Vietnam**," that "the war in Vietnam is clearly an unjust war" (King, 6 July 1967).

Where Do We Go from Here received mixed reviews. One critic called the book "incisive," while another hailed it for its ability to speak "to the inner man" in a "moderate, judicious, constructive, pragmatic tone" (*Where Do We Go from Here?*, ad). One of the most scathing reviews appeared in the 24 August 1967 *New York Review of Books*: "Martin Luther King once had the ability to talk to people, the power to change them by evoking images of revolution," the author said. "But the duty of a revolutionary is to make revolutions (say those who have done it), and King made none." The review asserted that the **Chicago Campaign** was King's last as a national leader. King has been "outstripped by his times, overtaken by the events which he may have obliquely helped to produce but could not predict. He is not likely to regain command" (Kopkind, "Soul Power").

SOURCES
Garrow, *Bearing the Cross*, 1986.
Display ad, *Where Do We Go from Here?*, *New York Times*, 11 July 1967.
"Dr. King Deplores 'Long Cold Winter' on the Rights Front," *New York Times*, 20 June 1967.
King, Interview on the Merv Griffin Show, 6 July 1967, MLKJP-GAMK.
King, *Where Do We Go from Here*, 1967.
Milton R. Konvitz, Review of *Where Do We Go from Here*, *Saturday Review* (July 1967), 28–29.
Andrew Kopkind, "Soul Power," *The New York Review of Books* (24 August 1967): 3–6.

WHITE CITIZENS' COUNCILS (WCC)

In response to the 1954 **Brown v. Board of Education** decision ending school segregation, white segregationists throughout the South created the White Citizens' Councils (WCC). These local groups typically drew a more middle and upper class membership than the Ku Klux Klan and, in addition to using violence and intimidation to counter civil rights goals, they sought to economically and socially oppress blacks. Martin Luther King faced WCC attacks as soon as the **Montgomery bus boycott** began and was a target of these groups throughout his career.

In January 1956, a month after the start of the boycott, W. A. Gayle, the mayor of Montgomery, joined the WCC, publicly declaring, "I think every right-thinking white person in Montgomery, Alabama and the South should do the same. We must make certain that Negroes are not allowed to force their demands on us" (Azbell, "Council Official Says"). By the next month WCC membership had doubled. The WCC attempted multiple strategies to stop the boycott, from prosecuting the boycott organizers to pressuring insurance agencies throughout the South to cancel policies for church-owned vehicles. King appealed to President Dwight D. **Eisenhower** to investigate violence perpetrated by WCC members after **Montgomery Improvement Association** members' homes were bombed, and effigies of a black man and a white man "who 'talked integration'" were hung in downtown Montgomery (*Papers* 3:357). The attorney general responded to King's appeal, writing that "the activities of the White

Citizens Council … [do] not appear to indicate violations of federal criminal statutes" (*Papers* 3:365).

In a 1956 New York speech, King described the WCC as a modern Ku Klux Klan, targeting black and white people supportive of civil rights. "They must be held responsible for all of the terror, the mob rule, and brutal murders that have encompassed the South over the last several years," King said. "It is an indictment on America and democracy that these ungodly and unethical and un-Christian and un-American councils have been able to exist all of these months without a modicum of criticism from the federal government" (*Papers* 3:475).

King encountered WCC groups all over the South, from Selma, Alabama—the first Alabama town to create a White Citizens' Council—to Jackson, Mississippi, where Medgar **Evers**, the local **National Association for the Advancement of Colored People** chairman, was killed by a WCC member. King feared that WCC activities would prevent white moderates from becoming involved in desegregation issues. WCC groups, King argued, "demand absolute conformity from whites and abject submission from Negroes.… What channels of communication had once existed between whites and Negroes have thus now been largely closed" (King, 16 October 1959).

As late as 1966, the White Citizens' Council teamed up with the virulently anti-Communist John Birch Society to petition the federal government to investigate whether King and over 100,000 other rights activists had Communist connections. Yet King believed that their power was fading: "Two years ago Americans, in a presidential election, overwhelmingly rejected representatives of Birchism and the White Citizens Council," he said, referring to Barry **Goldwater**'s defeat by Lyndon B. **Johnson**. "It is my honest opinion that this same majority still finds repulsive persons who strive to impose 19th Century standards upon our society" (King, 26 May 1966).

SOURCES

Joe Azbell, "Council Official Says Negro 'Bloc' No Longer Threat in Elections Here," *Montgomery Advertiser*, 26 January 1956.

King, "Desegregation and the Future," 15 December 1956, in *Papers* 3:471–479.

King, "The Future of Integration," 16 October 1959, MLKP-MBU.

King, Statement on petition sponsored by the John Birch Society and the White Citizens' Council, 26 May 1966, MLKJP-GAMK.

King to Dwight D. Eisenhower, 27 August 1956, in *Papers* 3:357–358.

Warren Olney, III, to King, 7 September 1956, in *Papers* 3:364–365.

WHY WE CAN'T WAIT (1964)

After the conclusion of the **Birmingham Campaign** and the **March on Washington for Jobs and Freedom** in 1963, Martin Luther King commenced work on his third book, *Why We Can't Wait*, which told the story of African American activism in the spring and summer of 1963.

In July 1963 King published an excerpt from his "**Letter from Birmingham Jail**" in the *Financial Post*, entitling it, "Why the Negro Won't Wait." King explained why he opposed the gradualist approach to civil rights. Referring to the arrival of African Americans in the American colonies, King asserted that African Americans had waited over three centuries to receive the rights granted them by God and the U.S.

Constitution. King developed these ideas further in *Why We Can't Wait*, his memoir of what he termed "The Negro Revolution" of 1963 (King, 2).

With the aid of his advisors Clarence **Jones** and Stanley **Levison**, King began work on the book in the fall of 1963. To explain what King called the "Negro Revolution," he drew on the history of black oppression and current political circumstances to articulate the growing frustration of many African Americans with the slow implementation of the **Brown v. Board of Education** decision, the neglect of civil rights issues by both political parties, and the sense that the liberation of African peoples was outpacing that of African Americans in the United States (King, 2). King pointed in particular to President Abraham Lincoln's **Emancipation Proclamation**, observing that the "milestone of the centennial of emancipation gave the Negro a reason to act—a reason so simple and obvious that he almost had to step back to see it" (King, 13).

Several chapters detailed the costs and gains of the "nonviolent crusade of 1963" (King, 30). In a chapter titled "The Sword That Heals," King wrote that nonviolent direct action was behind the victory in Birmingham. Later in the book, King reflected on the sight of hundreds of thousands participating in the March on Washington for Jobs and Freedom, commenting: "The old order ends, no matter what Bastilles remain, when the enslaved, within themselves, bury the psychology of servitude" (King, 121). King concluded the book by calling for a "Bill of Rights for the Disadvantaged" that would affect both blacks and poor whites (King, 151).

Harper & Row published the book in June 1964. New York Governor Nelson **Rockefeller** told King the volume was "an incisive, eloquent book," and King's mentor Benjamin **Mays** called it "magnificently done. In fact the last chapter alone is worth the book" (Rockefeller, 23 May 1964; Mays, 20 July 1964). Other reviewers applauded the book as "a straightforward book that should be read by both races," and "one of the most eloquent achievements of the year—indeed of any year" (Hudkins, "Foremost Spokesman for Non-violence"; Poling, Book review).

SOURCES

Lonnie Hudkins, "Foremost Spokesman for Non-violence," *Houston Post*, June 1964.

King, "Why the Negro Won't Wait," *Financial Post*, 27 July 1963.

King, *Why We Can't Wait*, 1964.

Mays to King, 20 July 1964, MLKJP-GAMK.

Daniel A. Poling, Book review of *Why We Can't Wait*, for *Christian Herald*, 12 May 1964, MLKJP-GAMK.

Rockefeller to King, 23 May 1964, MLKJP-GAMK.

WILKINS, ROY OTTAWAY (1901–1981)

As executive secretary of the **National Association for the Advancement of Colored People** (NAACP) from 1955 to 1977, Roy Wilkins collaborated with Martin Luther King on many of the major campaigns of the civil rights movement. Although Wilkins favored a legal approach to achieving racial equality over King's nonviolent direct action campaigns, the two leaders recognized that both methods were critical to advancing the civil rights cause. On the occasion of Wilkins' 30th anniversary with the NAACP, King wrote to him: "You have proved to be one of the great leaders of our time. Through your efficiency as an administrator, your genuine humanitarian concern, and your unswerving devotion to the principles of freedom and human dignity, you have carved for yourself an imperishable niche in the annals of contemporary history" (King, 3 January 1962).

Wilkins was born on 30 August 1901, in St. Louis, Missouri. Raised in St. Paul, Minnesota, Wilkins attended an integrated high school and graduated from the University of Minnesota in 1923. While in college he was shocked to learn of the lynching of three black men in nearby Duluth, and became dedicated to the cause of civil rights. Wilkins joined the NAACP, and after graduating, took a job at the *Kansas City Call*, an influential black newspaper. His editorial work captured the attention of then NAACP executive secretary Walter White, who brought him to New York as his chief assistant in 1931. In this capacity Wilkins investigated working conditions for southern blacks in Mississippi River levee labor camps and advocated anti-lynching laws. In 1934 Wilkins succeeded W.E.B. Du Bois as editor of *The Crisis*, the NAACP's magazine. Later Wilkins served as the NAACP's administrator of internal affairs. When White died in 1955, Wilkins was selected to replace him.

In the second month of the **Montgomery bus boycott**, Wilkins sent King a donation to aid the **Montgomery Improvement Association** (MIA) in its efforts. By February 1956, three months into the boycott, the NAACP had offered the MIA legal counsel and urged chapters to raise funds for the boycott. King was "quite conscious of [the MIA's] dependence on the NAACP," whose legal support was instrumental in allowing the boycott to continue (*Papers* 3:244). King wrote to Wilkins, "I have said to our people all along that the great victories of the Negro have been gained through the assiduous labor of the NAACP" (*Papers* 3:244).

Wilkins took pride in his organization's diligent legal work and institutional presence. Although he recognized that "the Montgomery protest … caught the eyes and hearts of the world and probably stirred more unity and pride among Negroes than anything that has happened in a quarter-century," he believed that "the thing which won the Montgomery case was not the walking of the brave people, but a decision in the Supreme Court … secured through the skill of [an] NAACP lawyer" (Wilkins, 14 February 1957). In 1963, following the assassination of NAACP field secretary Medgar **Evers**, Wilkins was angered by King's decision to launch a fundraiser for his own organization as a memorial to the slain civil rights leader. King's plans for the fundraiser were dropped, and the two men were able to make common cause to help organize the **March on Washington for Jobs and Freedom** several weeks later.

Despite their private struggles, the two leaders were always careful to publicly stress their cooperation and mutual admiration. King told one reporter: "I think we can work together in a very cooperative and creative manner. There need be no conflict" (King, "TV Interview"). Wilkins similarly praised King's work, acknowledging that King's **Birmingham Campaign** had "made the nation realize that at last the crisis had arrived" (Wilkins, 23 July 1963).

Like many moderate civil rights leaders, Wilkins disagreed with King's decision to speak out against the **Vietnam War**, and went as far as to send a memorandum to NAACP chapters instructing them not to use the NAACP's name during demonstrations against the war. Despite tensions over the war, the two leaders remained closely aligned in their commitment to integration and fought to counter rising calls for "**Black Power**."

In 1967 Wilkins was appointed by President Lyndon B. **Johnson** to serve on his National Advisory Commission on Civil Disorders, which was charged with investigating the causes of urban riots. The commission's report, released 29 February 1968, warned: "Our nation is moving toward two societies, one black, one white—separate and unequal" (Herbers, "Panel on Civil Disorders"). Although King called the commission's findings "timely," he argued that the recommendations "have been made before almost to the last detail and have been ignored almost to the last detail" (Zion, "Rights Leaders").

In the last two months of King's life, King and Wilkins both lent their support to the **Memphis Sanitation Workers' Strike**. Wilkins' speech to the workers drew a crowd of several thousand people. After King's **assassination**, Wilkins continued to lead the NAACP for nearly a decade. Throughout the 1970s he was critical of Presidents Richard **Nixon** and Gerald Ford, writing in his autobiography: "I thought Mr. Nixon would try to be President of all the people; instead, he allied himself with the worst enemies of black children" (Wilkins, *Standing*, 339). The 1970s were also turbulent times for the NAACP, as several key national staff passed away or retired. Wilkins retired from the NAACP in 1977, and died in September 1981.

SOURCES

John Herbers, "Panel on Civil Disorders Calls for Drastic Action to Avoid 2-Society Nation," *New York Times*, 1 March 1968.

King, Address at the Fiftieth Annual NAACP Convention, 17 July 1959, in *Papers* 5:245–250.

King, "Remarks in Acceptance of the Forty-Second Spingarn Medal at the Forty-Eighth Annual NAACP Convention, in *Papers* 4:228–233.

King, "TV interview with the Reverend Martin Luther King, Jr.," *Afro American*, 4 March 1961.

King to Wilkins, 28 January 1956, in *Papers* 3:108–109.

King to Wilkins, 1 May 1956, in *Papers* 3:243–244.

King to Wilkins, 3 January 1962, MLKJP-GAMK.

Roger Wilkins, *A Man's Life*, 1982.

Wilkins, Interview on "For Freedom Now," 23 July 1963, MLKJP-GAMK.

Wilkins and Mathews, *Standing Fast*, 1982.

Wilkins to Barbee William Dunham, 14 February 1957, NAACPP-DLC.

Wilkins to King, 22 February 1956, in *Papers* 3:134–135.

Sidney E. Zion, "Rights Leaders Support Criticism of Whites," *New York Times*, 2 March 1968.

WILLIAMS, ADAM DANIEL (A. D.) (c. 1861–1931)

Although likely born in 1861, A. D. Williams, the grandfather of Martin Luther King, Jr., celebrated 2 January 1863, the day after the effective date of the **Emancipation Proclamation**, as his birthday. Williams was one of the pioneers of a distinctive African American version of the **social gospel**, endorsing a strategy that combined elements of Booker T. Washington's emphasis on black business development and W.E.B. Du Bois' call for civil rights activism. As pastor of **Ebenezer Baptist Church** for over 25 years, Williams infused his ministry with social activism by helping found the Atlanta chapter of the **National Association for the Advancement of Colored People** (NAACP).

Born in Greene County, Georgia, to slaves Willis and Lucretia Williams, A. D. spent his childhood on the William N. Williams plantation. After the death of his father in 1874, he and his family moved to nearby Scull Shoals, a rural community on the Oconee River. Williams' desire to follow his father, "an old slavery time preacher," into the ministry was evident even as a child, when "it was his greatest pleasure to preach the funeral of snakes, cats, dogs, horses, or any thing that died.

The children of the community would call him to preach the funeral and they would have a big shout" (*Papers* 1:1; 4). Although he was unable to attend school because of the demands of sharecropping, the seven-year-old Williams reportedly "attracted the people for miles around with his ability to count" (*Papers* 1:4). Taught by several ministers in the community, Williams earned his license to preach in April 1888.

During the late 1880s and early 1890s A. D. Williams tried to make a living as an itinerant preacher while supplementing his income with other work. An injury in a sawmill accident left him with only the nub of a thumb on his right hand. Seeking better opportunities elsewhere Williams joined the black exodus from Greene County. In January 1893 he left for Atlanta, where he was called to the pastorate of Atlanta's Ebenezer Baptist Church.

Although Ebenezer had only 13 members when he arrived, the congregation grew to 400 members by 1903. Recognizing that his long-term success as an urban minister required that he overcome his academic limitations, Williams enrolled at Atlanta Baptist College (later named **Morehouse College**) and, in May 1898, received his certificate from the ministerial program. While in Atlanta Williams met Jennie Celeste Parks. The two were married on 29 October 1899. On 13 September 1903 she gave birth at home to their only surviving child, Alberta Christine Williams, the mother of Martin Luther King, Jr.

In September 1895 Williams joined 2,000 other delegates and visitors at Friendship Baptist Church to organize the **National Baptist Convention**, the largest black organization in the United States. By 1904 Williams was president of the Atlanta Baptist Ministers' Union and chairman of both the executive board and finance committee of the General State Baptist Convention.

In 1906 Williams helped organize the Georgia Equal Rights League to protest the white primary system. Early in 1917 he became involved in an effort to organize a local branch of the NAACP. Williams—described in one account as "a forceful and impressive speaker, a good organizer and leader, a man of vision and brilliant imagination, which he sometimes finds it necessary to curb" (*Papers* 1:15)—experienced early success as an NAACP leader, becoming branch president in 1918. During his tenure the branch grew to 1,400 members within five months, and the newly invigorated NAACP spearheaded a major effort to register black voters. In a speech to the NAACP national convention the following year, he convinced the delegates to meet in Atlanta in 1920, the first national NAACP convention to meet in the South.

In 1926 Williams' daughter Alberta Christine married Martin Luther **King**, Sr., who eventually succeeded him as pastor of Ebenezer. When Williams died in 1931, his obituary was effusive: "'A. D.' was a sign post among his neighbors, and a mighty oak in the Baptist forest of the nation.... He was a preacher of unusual power, an appealing experimentalist, a persuasive evangelist, and a convincing doctrinarian" (*Papers* 1:28).

SOURCE
Introduction, in *Papers* 1:1–4; 6–7; 9–11; 15; 25–26; 28.

WILLIAMS, HOSEA (1926–2000)

Hosea Williams described himself as the "thug" of the **Southern Christian Leadership Conference** (SCLC). Martin Luther King affectionately called him "my wild man, my Castro," in recognition of Williams' skills as a protest organizer (Branch, 124).

Williams was born 5 January 1926, in Attapulgus, Georgia. His mother, a blind, unmarried teenager, died soon after, leaving Williams to be raised by his grandparents. At age 14, Williams moved on his own to Tallahassee, Florida, where he worked odd jobs for three years before returning to Georgia. When the United States entered World War II, Williams enlisted in the Army, working his way up to staff sergeant in an all-black unit. He was wounded by shrapnel and spent over a year recovering in a British hospital. Once back in the United States, Williams completed high school, earned a bachelor's degree at Morris Brown College in Atlanta, and a master's from Atlanta University. He worked for the U.S. Department of Agriculture in Savannah, Georgia, from 1952 to 1963.

Upon moving to Savannah Williams joined the **National Association for the Advancement of Colored People** (NAACP) and began grassroots organizing. He became widely known for giving speeches against segregation in a public park during his daily lunch break. By 1960 he had become the president of the Southeastern Georgia Crusade for Voters, an affiliate of SCLC. The following year he spoke on the power of the ballot at SCLC's annual meeting. At SCLC's board meeting in 1962 King personally recommended that Williams join the SCLC executive board, an honor Williams accepted.

In 1962 Williams began positioning for a seat on the Georgia NAACP national board. When NAACP director Roy **Wilkins** told Williams that he could advance no further in the NAACP because of his family background, Williams complained to King. King supported Williams and when he was arrested in Savannah the following summer, offered SCLC's backing "100 percent" (King, 11 June 1963). In 1964, SCLC voted Williams "Man of the Year," and King hired him on a trial basis to work in **St. Augustine, Florida**, where on the eve of the city's 400th anniversary, SCLC was collaborating with local activists to protest segregation. There, Williams taught **nonviolence** to volunteers, led marches, and was arrested along with his wife and two of their five children.

Later that year Williams formally joined SCLC staff as the director of voter registration. King personally raised funds for his salary, writing a potential donor that Williams' "talents need a broader horizon [than Savannah, Georgia], and his energies need to be made available to other communities across this nation" (SCLC, 9 November 1964). One such community was Selma, Alabama, where SCLC began work in January 1965, supporting local voting rights activists. After three months of groundwork, Williams and **Student Nonviolent Coordinating Committee** leader John **Lewis** jointly led the first attempt at a **Selma to Montgomery March**. This effort became known as "Bloody Sunday" after state troopers and local law enforcement officers brutally beat the demonstrators as they attempted to cross the Edmund Pettus Bridge. King came to Selma to lead a successful march three days later.

In March 1965 King named Williams the head of SCLC's **Summer Community Organization and Political Education** (SCOPE) **Project**, where he oversaw a half-million-dollar budget and several thousand volunteers. Promoted to the role of southern project director by 1966, Williams toured projects, often rallying supporters with King, and walked in the March against Fear to protest the shooting of James **Meredith**.

In November 1966 King asked Williams to come to Chicago, where SCLC was working with the Coordinating Council of Community Organizations on the **Chicago**

Campaign. Although Williams did not want to leave the South, he grudgingly complied and moved north to run the campaign's voter registration project.

Williams returned to the South to work as field director for SCLC's **Poor People's Campaign** in early 1968. He attended multiple rallies a day, flying with King from town to town to build support for the Washington campaign. At King's urging, Williams and other SCLC staff joined King in Memphis to support the **Memphis Sanitation Workers' Strike** that April. He was with King at the Lorraine Motel when King's **assassination** took place on 4 April 1968.

After King's death Williams became executive director of SCLC, a position he held until 1979, when he was forced to leave because of differences within SCLC. Williams entered mainstream politics, winning election to the Georgia General Assembly in 1974. After a decade of service, he resigned and his wife Juanita won his seat. Williams was later elected to the Atlanta City Council and then became the De Kalb County commissioner. In 1987 Williams led the largest civil rights march in Georgia history into all-white Forsyth County, approximately 30 miles north of Atlanta. Hundreds of Ku Klux Klan members and white supremacists greeted an estimated 20,000 marchers, including King's widow, Coretta Scott **King**, and veteran civil rights colleagues Jesse **Jackson**, Andrew **Young**, Ralph **Abernathy**, Dick **Gregory**, and Benjamin **Hooks**. Williams died of cancer in 2000.

SOURCES

Branch, *Pillar of Fire*, 1998.

Carson, *In Struggle*, 1981.

Dudley Clendinen, "Thousands in Civil Rights March Jeered by Crowd in Georgia Town," *New York Times*, 25 January 1987.

"Hosea Williams, a Civil-rights Campaigner, Died on November 16th, Aged 74," *The Economist*, 25 November 2000.

King to Williams, 11 June 1963, MLKJP-GAMK.

Daniel Lewis, "Hosea Williams, 74, Rights Crusader, Dies," *New York Times*, 17 November 2000.

SCLC, "Proposal to the United Presbyterian Church," 9 November 1964, NCCP-PPPrHi.

WILLIAMS, ROBERT FRANKLIN (1925–1996)

Robert F. Williams, president of the local branch of the **National Association for the Advancement of Colored People** (NAACP) in Monroe, North Carolina, became embroiled in a 1959 controversy surrounding remarks he made following the acquittal of a white man accused of attempting to rape a black woman. An article appearing in the 7 May 1959 *New York Times* claimed that Williams had asserted that the failure of the courts demanded that African Americans "meet violence with violence.... We are going to have to try and convict these people on the spot" ("N.A.A.C.P. Leader Urges 'Violence'"). Martin Luther King condemned Williams' comments, sparking a debate between the two leaders on the efficacy of **nonviolence**.

Born in Monroe, North Carolina, in February 1925, Williams was the grandson of a former slave. Through his grandmother's tales and political observations, he was made aware of racial injustice at an early age. As a young man Williams went north to find work. During World War II he was drafted into the Army and served 14 months. He returned to Monroe and married Mabel Robinson in 1947. During the next several years Williams enrolled in various college programs. Unable to secure a job, Williams enlisted in the Marine Corps in 1954, where he was an outspoken opponent of racial segregation in the armed forces. His candor concerned the Marines, who placed Williams under investigation and gave him an "undesirable" discharge.

In 1955 Williams returned to Monroe with a renewed vigor for race relations. He was hopeful about the May 1954 Supreme Court decision in **Brown v. Board of Education**. "I was sure that this was the beginning of a new era in American democracy," Williams said (Tyson, 73). With membership dwindling in the Monroe NAACP branch, Williams got involved with the organization and was elected president. In 1956 news of the **Montgomery bus boycott** bolstered Williams' spirits. He called those involved with the bus protest the "patriots of passive revolution" (Tyson, 78). Addressing those who attempted to stifle the revolution in Montgomery, Williams quipped: "Has an American no right to walk when to ride would degrade his dignity? Has our beloved Republic reached the stage that the jails have no room for criminals, because they are filled with liberty-loving citizens whose only crime is that there voices cry out for freedom?" (Tyson, 78).

From 6 members at the beginning of Williams' term, the Monroe NAACP branch grew to 121 members in late 1959. After his controversial statement calling for armed retaliation against racial injustice in May 1959, NAACP Executive Secretary Williams found himself suspended from his post by Roy **Wilkins**. Williams unsuccessfully appealed his suspension to delegates attending the group's national convention in July.

In King's address at the July convention he reaffirmed his commitment to nonviolence: "We all realize that there will probably be some sporadic violence during this period of transition, and people will naturally seek to protect their property and person, but for the Negro to privately or publicly call for retaliatory violence as a strategy during this period would be the gravest tragedy that could befall us" (*Papers* 5:248). The press quickly seized on "The Great Debate," and Anne and Carl **Braden**'s *Southern Patriot* published King's and Williams' views on the role of violence in the struggle for integration in early 1960.

In 1961 a representative of the **Southern Christian Leadership Conference** (SCLC) was sent to Monroe to investigate the racial situation there and to support the early **Freedom Rides**. When King declined an offer from the **Student Nonviolent Coordinating Committee** to participate in the rides, Williams sent King a scathing telegram: "No sincere leader asks his followers to make sacrifices that he himself will not endure. You are a phony…. If you lack the courage, remove yourself from the vanguard…. Now is the time for true leaders to take to the field of battle" (31 May 1961).

As racial tensions increased in Monroe, the town erupted into violence fueled by white racists. Williams and his wife fled to Cuba in late 1961 to escape the **Federal Bureau of Investigation** (FBI), which sought to arrest them on kidnapping charges related to the violence in Monroe. Once in Cuba Williams wrote his memoir, *Negroes with Guns* (1962). In the book's prologue Williams attempted to clarify what he believed was a distortion of his position on violence: "I do not advocate violence for its own sake, or for the sake of reprisals against whites…. My only difference with Dr. King is that I believe in flexibility in the freedom struggle" (Williams, 40).

From Cuba, the couple continued to publish their newspaper, *The Crusader*, and aired a radio program called *Radio Free Dixie*. In 1965 they moved to China, returning to the United States in 1969. While in exile Williams was elected president of the

Republic of New Africa, a revolutionary organization aimed at establishing a separate black nation in the southern United States. He resigned from the organization after his return to the United States.

In 1976 North Carolina dropped remaining criminal charges against Williams. In 1996, he died of Hodgkin's disease at age 71.

SOURCES

Introduction, in *Papers* 5:2; 17.
"The Great Debate: Is Violence Necessary to Combat Injustice?" January 1960, in *Papers* 5:300.
King, Address at the Fiftieth Annual NAACP Convention, 17 July 1959, in *Papers* 5:245–250.
King, "The Social Organization of Nonviolence," October 1959, in *Papers* 5:299–304.
"N.A.A.C.P. Leader Urges 'Violence,'" *New York Times*, 7 May 1959.
Tyson, *Radio Free Dixie*, 1999.
Williams, *Negroes with Guns*, 1962.
Williams to King, 31 May 1961, MLKP-MBU.

WOFFORD, HARRIS LLEWELLYN (1926–)

Harris Wofford was the **Kennedy** administration's civil rights expert and an ally of Martin Luther King. Wofford believed in employing a mix of direct action and legal techniques to combat segregation. He applauded King's leadership in Montgomery: "You have already proven yourselves master artists of non-violent direct action" (*Papers* 3:226).

Born in New York City to a line of southern aristocrats, Wofford graduated from the University of Chicago in 1948. A lifelong advocate of Gandhian **nonviolence**, Wofford studied in India before returning to the United States and enrolling at Howard Law School, making him the first white student to do so since the suffragist movement of the early 1900s. While at Howard Wofford toured Alabama doing research on the status of civil rights in the South.

Like many of King's other advisors, Wofford first heard of King during the **Montgomery bus boycott**. Wofford wrote to King, sent him a copy of his book, *India Afire*, and offered his perspectives on the application of the techniques of Mohandas Karamchand **Gandhi** to Montgomery. King recalled reading a copy of a talk on the application of nonviolent tactics against segregation that Wofford gave at Hampton Institute in October 1955. King later stated, "This talk and other talks … were widely distributed in the South, helping to create better understanding of what we were doing in Montgomery" (King, March 1961). Although initially not part of King's inner circle of advisors, Wofford urged King to go on his **India trip** and was instrumental in arranging funding for the trip from the Christopher Reynolds Foundation.

Wofford participated, along with King, in a convocation at Howard University in November 1957. Speaking on "Non-Violence and the Law," Wofford told the gathering that "what Martin Luther King has given us is the unadulterated message of non-violence which Gandhi wanted the Negroes finally to deliver to the world." King used some of the ideas expressed in this speech in his chapter, "Where Do We Go from Here?" in **Stride Toward Freedom**. King wrote in the preface to this book that he was grateful to Wofford "for significant suggestions and real encouragement" (King, 11).

After several years on the Civil Rights Commission established by President Dwight D. **Eisenhower**, Wofford joined the staff of presidential candidate John Fitzgerald

Kennedy in 1960. Eager to win the black vote, Wofford managed a meeting between King and Kennedy on 23 June 1960. Several months later, when King was arrested for his participation in an Atlanta **sit-in**, Wofford suggested that Kennedy phone Coretta Scott **King**, an action that made a crucial difference in the election.

Kennedy appointed Wofford as a special assistant on civil rights in his new administration, despite Wofford's interest in joining the Peace Corps. In his White House role, Wofford recognized the political realities of the day. In a memo sent to Kennedy soon after his 1960 victory, he noted that "although it is heresy in the civil rights camp to say this ... you can do without any substantial civil rights legislation this session of Congress *if* you go ahead with a substantial executive action program" (Wofford, 30 December 1960). Political realities would also force Wofford into uncomfortable situations with old allies, particularly when the Kennedys asked him to inform King of **Federal Bureau of Investigation** suspicions that longtime King advisor Stanley **Levison** had Communist affiliations. Wofford later wrote that "what Kennedy liked best in my role, and I liked least, was my function as a buffer between him and the civil rights forces pressing for presidential action" (Wofford, 164).

After two years Wofford left the White House staff to go to Africa with the Peace Corps and then became the group's associate director, serving until 1966. He participated in the **Selma to Montgomery March**, and after several university positions and jobs in law, became a senator from Pennsylvania in 1991. He served until 1995.

SOURCES

King, Letter to the editor, March 1961, CSKC.
King, *Stride Toward Freedom*, 1958.
Wofford, *India Afire*, 1951.
Wofford, "Non-Violence and the Law," 7 November 1957, CSKC.
Wofford, *Of Kennedys and Kings*, 1980.
Wofford to Kennedy, 30 December 1960, JFKPP-MWalK.
Wofford to King, 25 April 1956, in *Papers* 3:225–226.

WOMEN'S POLITICAL COUNCIL (WPC) OF MONTGOMERY

The Women's Political Council (WPC) of Montgomery, Alabama, was established in 1946 by Mary Fair Burks to inspire African Americans to "live above mediocrity, to elevate their thinking ... and in general to improve their status as a group" (Robinson, 23). The WPC sought to increase the political leverage of the black community by promoting civic involvement, increasing voter registration, and lobbying city officials to address racist policies. The group's work expanded to include public protest in 1955, when it helped initiate the **Montgomery bus boycott**, the event that brought Martin Luther King and the civil rights struggle into the national spotlight.

The original WPC chapter was made up of middle class professionals, most of whom were educators and taught at the all-black Alabama State College or in the city's public schools. Burks, who was head of Alabama State's English Department, served as WPC president until 1950, when she was succeeded by Jo Ann **Robinson**. By 1955 the WPC counted over 200 members in three neighborhood chapters.

The WPC had been planning for a citywide boycott of buses long before the historic boycott of 1955. In 1953 the WPC approached Montgomery city commissioners about unfair practices, such as having African Americans enter through the back of the bus after paying their fare up front. On 21 May 1954 Robinson sent a letter suggesting a city law, much like the one already implemented in other cities, in which black passengers would be seated from back to front and white passengers seated from front to back, until all seats were filled. The WPC's concerns were consistently dismissed by city commissioners, even following Robinson's statement that "even now plans are being made to ride less, or not at all, on our buses" (Robinson, 21 May 1954). After the March 1955 arrest of Claudette Colvin for refusing to give up her seat, King, Rufus **Lewis**, E. D. **Nixon**, Robinson, Irene **West**, and Burks met with the city commissioners but made little headway.

On 1 December 1955, the arrest of Rosa **Parks** gave the WPC the opportunity it had been waiting for. After Nixon, with the help of Virginia and Clifford **Durr**, gained Parks' release from jail and secured her approval to use her arrest as a test case to challenge bus seating policies, Nixon called King and other black leaders to inform them of the effort, already under way, to boycott Montgomery's buses. By this time Robinson and the WPC had already drafted, mimeographed, and begun circulating leaflets across the city, announcing the boycott. Throughout the boycott the WPC engaged in the daily activities of driving in the carpools, organizing mass meetings, and communicating with protesters.

Burks later stated that "members of the Women's Political Council were trailblazers" and credited the WPC for its ability "to arouse black middle-class women to do something about the things they could change in segregated Montgomery" (Burks, "Trailblazers," 76). Their role in the boycott, however, was not without consequences. Many WPC members were also teachers at Alabama State College, where officials closely investigated everyone involved in the boycott and in other student demonstrations. Tensions on the campus, especially after the **sit-ins** of 1960, caused many of the women, including Robinson and Burks, to resign from the college and find employment elsewhere, an event that dispersed key members throughout the nation.

SOURCES

Burks, "Trailblazers: Women in the Montgomery Bus Boycott," in *Women in the Civil Rights Movement*, 1990.
Garrow, *Walking City*, 1989.
Introduction, in *Papers* 3:3.
Robinson, *Montgomery Bus Boycott*, 1987.
Robinson to W. A. Gayle, 21 May 1954, MCDA-AMC.

WPC. *See* Women's Political Council of Montgomery.

WURF, JEROME (1919–1981)

As president of the nation's largest union of public employees—the American Federation of State, County, and Municipal Employees (AFSCME)—Jerome Wurf provided the support of his union to various civil rights causes, including the October 1958 **Youth March for Integrated Schools**, an event co-chaired by Martin Luther King. In a 4 December 1958 letter to Wurf, King expressed his gratitude: "The support given to the Youth March by Local 420 and the other local unions of District Council 37, and their success in achieving such wide participation by their members and the children of their members, offers eloquent testimony to the fact of their devotion to the cause of human freedom and the brotherhood of man" (*Papers* 4:544).

The son of immigrants, Wurf was born in New York City in May 1919. Following his graduation from New York University in 1940, he took a job working in a cafeteria. After working in the cafeteria for three years, Wurf organized his fellow workers into Local 448 Hotel and Restaurant Employees. His experience organizing labor convinced AFSCME President Arnold Zander to hire Wurf in 1947 to build District Council 37, the public employee's union in New York City. In 1964 Wurf defeated Zander for the AFSCME presidency, a position he held for 17 years, until his death in 1981.

Throughout his career, Wurf worked to provide union representation throughout the United States. In 1964 he helped form Local 1733, which included black sanitation workers in Memphis, Tennessee, who were protesting racial discrimination and poor job conditions. When Local 1733 went on strike in 1968, Wurf and others attempted to negotiate with city officials refusing to recognize the legitimacy of the union. At the urging of James **Lawson** and another AFSCME official, King reluctantly agreed to come to Memphis to show his support of the striking workers.

The day before King's **assassination** on 4 April 1968, Wurf addressed several thousand people at Mason Temple in Memphis. Nearly two weeks after King's death, the city council finally recognized that Local 1733 was the rightful bargaining agent of the sanitation workers. At the ratification meeting, Wurf paid homage to King: "Let us never forget that Martin Luther King, on a mission for us, was killed in this city. He helped bring us this victory" (Goulden, 181).

In 1969 Wurf was named **American Federation of Labor and Congress of Industrial Organizations** (AFL-CIO) vice president despite his sharp criticism of the **Vietnam War**, which put him at odds with much of domestic labor leadership, including AFL-CIO President George Meany. In 1978 AFSCME became the largest unit of the AFL-CIO when it merged with the Civil Service Employees Association of New York.

SOURCES

Goulden, *Jerry Wurf*, 1982.

Honey, *Going Down Jericho Road*, 2007.

King, "Give Us the Ballot," Address delivered at the Prayer Pilgrimage for Freedom, 17 May 1957, in *Papers* 4:208–215.

King to Wurf, 4 December 1958, in *Papers* 4:544.

Y

YOUNG, ANDREW (1932–)

Andrew Young's work as a pastor, administrator, and voting rights advocate led him to join Martin Luther King, Jr., and the **Southern Christian Leadership Conference** (SCLC) in the civil rights struggle. Young, who entered electoral politics shortly after King's **assassination**, credited King with giving "purpose and sustenance" to his life (Young, 474). "He left his mark on me, both in indelible memories and in the spiritual and practical lessons of our trials and triumphs," Young recalled. "It is by the quality of those days that I have come to measure my own continuing journey" (Young, 474).

Born in New Orleans, Louisiana, on 12 March 1932, into a middle-class family, Young earned a BS (1951) in biology from Howard University before studying to become a minister. In 1955 he earned a divinity degree at Hartford Theological Seminary and was ordained as a minister in the United Church of Christ. In 1957, after serving as a pastor at Bethany Congregational Church in Thomasville, Georgia, Young joined the **National Council of the Churches of Christ in America** in New York as an associate director of the Youth Division of Christian Education.

In his memoir *An Easy Burden* (1996), Young recalls meeting King in 1957, when the two shared the podium at the Alpha Phi Alpha fraternity's annual program at Talladega College in Alabama. After the event, King invited Young to visit him in Montgomery. Young was excited about the possibility of speaking with King about his philosophy of **nonviolence** and "about how he had applied his academic training to the practical situation in the South," but to Young's dismay, King was not interested in talking about his academic studies: "He was mostly interested in talking about Yoki, his and Coretta's new baby … and he didn't feel like acting out the role of the Reverend Dr. Martin Luther King, Jr." (Young, 97).

Moved by the student movement in Nashville in 1960, Young considered relocating to the South to run the **Highlander Folk School** Citizenship Training Program and solicited King's advice. Although King had high praise for Highlander's program, he cautioned Young that Tennessee officials were attempting to close the school. "Certainly I would not advise you to leave the position that you are now holding unless you can be sure that Highlander will remain open" (King, 25 April 1961). Young accepted Highlander's offer, but, as King warned, Highlander closed in 1961 before Young and his wife, Jean, arrived. The program moved its administrative offices to

SCLC headquarters in Atlanta, while the United Church of Christ renovated facilities in Dorchester, Georgia, to host the citizenship schools. Young took over the program, which gradually became an integral part of SCLC. In 1963 Young was a key figure on the biracial negotiating committee that forged the hard-won agreement that ended the **Birmingham Campaign**.

In 1964 King promoted Young to executive director of SCLC after the departure of the embattled Wyatt Tee **Walker**. For the next several years Young became one of King's most trusted advisors and confidantes and worked with him during campaigns in **St. Augustine**, **Selma**, and **Chicago**. He recalled that, in executive meetings, King wanted to hear conservative as well as radical viewpoints, "and it almost always fell to my lot to express the conservative view" (Young, 16 July 1968).

In April 1968 Young was with King at the Lorraine Motel in Memphis when the civil rights leader was slain. Young recalled that King was in a jovial mood on the evening before his **assassination**, even engaging Ralph **Abernathy** and Young in a pillow fight. Late in the afternoon of 4 April, shortly after a limousine arrived to pick up King and his entourage for dinner, Young heard a sound like a car backfiring and saw that King was no longer standing on the hotel balcony. Young's first thought was that King was "still clowning" (Young, 464). Young was devastated by King's assassination: "It seemed unfair that he was 'free' from innumerable problems, while we, the living, were left to try to cope without him. We had been just getting by with him, how could we get along without him?" (Young, 466).

Young left SCLC in 1970 to run for Congress. Although defeated in his first bid, he ran successfully in 1972, and represented his Georgia district for three terms before being appointed ambassador to the United Nations by President Jimmy Carter. Noted for his sympathetic approach in dealing with developing nations, Young was pressured to resign in 1979, after an unauthorized meeting with a representative of the Palestinian Liberation Organization. In 1981 President Carter awarded Young the Congressional Medal of Freedom. Young served as mayor of Atlanta from 1982 to 1990 before launching an unsuccessful bid for governor of Georgia in 1990.

SOURCES
King to Young, 25 April 1961, MLKP-MBU.
Young, *An Easy Burden*, 1996.
Young, Interview by Katherine Shannon, 16 July 1968, RBOH-DHU.

YOUNG, WHITNEY MOORE (1921–1971)

Whitney Young served as the executive director of the **National Urban League** from 1961 to 1971, the critical years in the civil rights movement. Although the National Urban League was not involved in direct action protests, Young often collaborated with Martin Luther King, who appreciated that each leader played a different role in the movement and praised Young's "creative vitality" (King, 31 July 1963).

Young was born on 31 July 1921, in Lincoln Ridge, Kentucky. He grew up on the campus of the Lincoln Institute, a black high school where his father served as president. After graduating from the Lincoln Institute he enrolled at the all-black Kentucky State College, becoming president of his senior class and vice president of the **Alpha Phi Alpha fraternity**, which King would later join. After graduation he enlisted in the Army. Young had his first experience as a racial mediator in France during World War II, a role that inspired him to pursue a career in social work when he was discharged.

Young began to volunteer with the National Urban League while at the University of Minnesota, where he obtained his master's degree in social work in 1947. In 1954 Young moved to Atlanta to become the dean of the School of Social Work at Atlanta University, and also co-chaired the Atlanta Council on Human Relations.

On 21 June 1958 King solicited Young's suggestions for topics to discuss at a meeting he had requested between President Dwight D. **Eisenhower** and prominent African American leaders. Young wired King the same day, expressing his "complete confidence in you representing us" (Young, 21 June 1958).

Young was handpicked by a representative of the Rockefeller Foundation, a major donor to the National Urban League, to succeed Lester **Granger** as the organization's head. After spending a year at Harvard University on a fellowship from the Rockefeller Foundation, Young was elected executive director of the National Urban League in February 1961. King congratulated Young, writing: "I am convinced that they could not have found a better person for the job," and offering his full assistance (King, 13 February 1961).

The following year King invited Young to speak at the annual convention of the **Southern Christian Leadership Conferences** (SCLC). Young's speech was such a success that SCLC reproduced it for all of the conference participants. In 1963, at the instigation of philanthropist Stephen Currier, King, Young, and representatives from five other civil rights groups began to meet regularly to discuss the possibility of collaborating in the movement. The group later became known as the Council for United Civil Rights Leadership, or the Unity Council. Although the Urban League was more committed to social service than direct action, Young made the controversial decision to co-sponsor the 1963 **March on Washington for Jobs and Freedom** with other Unity Council members.

Like other moderate civil rights leaders, Young did not agree with King's opposition to the **Vietnam War**, saying that the first priority of black people was "survival in this country," and that the issues of civil rights and the war "should remain separate" (King, "Man's Relation to Man," 1964). King's opposition to the war led to his alienation from President Lyndon B. **Johnson**, but Young's stance brought him closer to the administration. At Johnson's request, Young traveled to Vietnam twice, returning with positive accounts of race relations in the military. Only after Johnson left office in 1969 did Young begin to call for a speedy withdrawal from Vietnam.

In his mediating role between whites and blacks, Young was often labeled a moderate, despite his own belief that "nobody who's working for black people is a moderate. We're *all* militants in different ways" (Buckley, "Whitney Young"). Young's sudden death in 1971 in Lagos, Nigeria, shocked the nation. President Richard **Nixon** sent a special Air Force jet to retrieve his body, and his funeral was attended by over 6,000 people, including Coretta Scott **King**.

SOURCES

Tom Buckley, "Whitney Young: Black Leader or 'Oreo Cookie'?" *New York Times*, 20 September 1970.

Dickerson, *Militant Mediator*, 1998.

King, "Man's Relation to Man: Beyond Race and Nation," *Current* 86 (May 1967): 32–40.

King to Officers and delegates of the National Urban League, 31 July 1963, MLKJP-GAMK.

King to Young, 21 June 1958, in *Papers* 4:425.

King to Young, 13 February 1961, WMYC-NN-Sc.

Weiss, *Whitney M. Young, Jr.*, 1989.

Young, Draft, Telegram to King, 21 June 1958, WMYC-NN-Sc.

YOUTH MARCH FOR INTEGRATED SCHOOLS (25 OCTOBER 1958 AND 18 APRIL 1959)

In 1958 and 1959, Martin Luther King, Jr., served as an honorary chairman of two youth marches for integrated schools, large demonstrations that took place in Washington, D.C., aimed at expressing support for the elimination of school segregation from American public schools.

In August 1958 a small committee headed by labor leader A. Philip **Randolph** began organizing the first Youth March for Integrated Schools, to take place on 25 October 1958. Born out of the "need for a project that would combine a moral appeal, reveal the support of liberal white people and Negroes together, and generally to give people in the North an opportunity to show their solidarity with Negro children in the South who have become the first line of defense in the struggle for integrated schools," the march represented a convergence of organizations and individuals interested in a common cause (*Papers* 4:484). A diverse group of leaders planned the march; the six honorary chairmen involved in the marches both years were King, Randolph, Roy **Wilkins**, Ruth Bunche, Jackie **Robinson**, and Daisy **Bates**.

On the day of the 1958 march, an integrated crowd of 10,000 marched down Constitution Avenue in Washington, D.C., to the Lincoln Memorial. There, Coretta Scott **King** delivered a speech on behalf of her husband, who was recovering from being stabbed by Izola **Curry** while in New York. Although King could not attend the march, he was enthusiastic about its possibilities, saying that "such a project will do much to give courage, support, and encouragement to our [beleaguered] children and adults in the south. Simultaneously it will have a profound moral effect upon the nation and world opinion" (*Papers* 4:484–485). During the march, Harry **Belafonte** led a small, integrated group of students to the White House to meet President Dwight D. **Eisenhower**, but was unable to meet with the president or any of his assistants. After staging a half-hour picket, the students left a list of demands to be forwarded to the president.

The second youth march was intended to build upon the efforts of 1958 by holding a large event and circulating a petition to urge "the President and Congress of the United States to put into effect an executive and legislative program which will insure the orderly and speedy integration of schools throughout the United States" (Youth March for Integrated Schools, January 1959). On 18 April 1959, an estimated 26,000 participants marched down the National Mall to a program at the Sylvan Theatre, where speeches were given by King, Randolph, Wilkins, and Charles Zimmerman, chairman of the **American Federation of Labor and Congress of Industrial Organizations** Civil Rights Committee. A delegation of students again went to the White House to present their demands to Eisenhower, but this time they met with his deputy assistant, Gerald D. Morgan, who reportedly said that "the president is just as anxious as they are to see an America where discrimination does not exist, where equality of opportunity is available to all" (Report on the Youth March on Washington, 18 April 1959).

The 1959 march was marred by accusations of Communist infiltration. The day before the march was to take place, Randolph, Wilkins, and King released a statement denying such involvement: "The sponsors of the March have not invited Communists or communist organizations. Nor have they invited members of the Ku Klux Klan or the White Citizens' Council. We do not want the participation of these groups, nor of individuals or other organizations holding similar views" (Youth March for Integrated Schools, 17 April 1959).

While Eisenhower and Congress failed to pass additional legislation that would have enhanced the 1957 Civil Rights Act and speeded up school integration, the two marches had symbolic power. King told the 1959 marchers that the events' successful outcomes were a sign of how, "in your great movement to organize a march for integrated schools, … you have awakened on hundreds of campuses throughout the land a new spirit of social inquiry to the benefit of all Americans" (*Papers* 5:188).

SOURCES

Introduction in *Papers* 5:14–15.

King, Address at the Youth March for Integrated Schools, 18 April 1959, in *Papers* 5:186–188.

King to Gardner C. Taylor, 2 September 1958, in *Papers* 4:483–485.

(Scott) King, Address at Youth March for Integrated Schools in Washington, D.C., 25 October 1958, in *Papers* 4:514–515.

Report on the Youth March on Washington, 20 April 1959, WONS-KAbE.

Youth March for Integrated Schools, "Anti-American Groups Not Invited to Youth March for Integrated Schools," 17 April 1959, NAACPP-DLC.

Youth March for Integrated Schools, "A Petition for Integrated Schools," January 1959, GMF-DAFL.

Bibliography

Below is a listing of published sources, including biographies and autobiographies, that were used in compiling the entries in this volume.

Abelove, Henry, and E. P. Thompson, eds. *Visions of History*. New York: Pantheon Books, 1983.

Abernathy, Ralph. *And the Walls Came Tumbling Down: An Autobiography*. New York: Harper & Row, 1989.

Adams, Frank, with Myles Horton. *Unearthing Seeds of Fire: The Idea of Highlander*. Winston-Salem, NC: J. F. Blair, 1975.

Albert, Peter J., and Ronald Hoffman. *We Shall Overcome: Martin Luther King, Jr., and the Black Freedom Struggle*. New York: Pantheon, 1990.

Ambrose, Stephen E. *Nixon*. New York: Simon & Schuster, 1987.

Anderson, Jervis. *Bayard Rustin: Troubles I've Seen: A Biography*. Berkeley: University of California Press, 1998.

Angelou, Maya. *The Heart of a Woman*. New York: Random House, 1981.

———. *I Know Why the Caged Bird Sings*. New York: Random House, 1970.

Ansbro, John J. *Martin Luther King, Jr.: Nonviolent Strategies and Tactics for Social Change*. Lanham, MD: Madison Books, 2000.

Arsenault, Raymond. *Freedom Riders: 1961 and the Struggle for Racial Justice*. New York: Oxford University Press, 2006.

Ashby, Warren. *Frank Porter Graham: A Southern Liberal*. Winston-Salem, NC: John F. Blair, 1980.

Baldwin, James. *The Fire Next Time*. New York: Dial Press, 1963.

———. *Go Tell It on the Mountain*. New York: Dial Press, 1953.

———. *Nobody Knows My Name: More Notes from a Native Son*. New York: Dial Press, 1961.

Baldwin, Lewis V. *The Legacy of Martin Luther King, Jr.: The Boundaries of Law, Politics, and Religion*. Notre Dame, IN: University of Notre Dame Press, 2002.

———. *There Is a Balm in Gilead: The Cultural Roots of Martin Luther King, Jr.* Minneapolis: Fortress Press, 1991.

———. *To Make the Wounded Whole: The Cultural Legacy of Martin Luther King, Jr.* Minneapolis: Fortress Press, 1992.

———. *Toward the Beloved Community: Martin Luther King, Jr., and South Africa*. Cleveland: Pilgrim Press, 1995.

Barth, Karl. *The Epistle to the Romans*. Edwyn Clement Hoskyns, trans. London: Oxford University Press, 1933.

Bates, Daisy. *The Long Shadow of Little Rock: A Memoir*. New York: David McKay, 1962.

Beifuss, Joan Turner. *At the River I Stand: Memphis, the 1968 Strike, and Martin Luther King*. Brooklyn, NY: Carlson Publishing, 1989.

Bennett, Lerone. *What Manner of Man: A Biography of Martin Luther King, Jr.* 3rd rev. ed. Chicago: Johnson Publishing, 1968.

Birnbaum, Johnathan, and Clarence Taylor, eds. *Civil Rights since 1787: A Reader on the Black Struggle.* New York: New York University Press, 2000.

Blumberg, Janice Rothschild. *One Voice: Rabbi Jacob M. Rothschild and the Troubled South.* Macon, GA: Mercer University Press, 1985.

Borders, William Holmes. *Seven Minutes at the "Mike" in the Deep South.* Atlanta: Logan Press, 1943.

Bowles, Chester. *Mission to India: A Search for Alternatives in Asia.* New Delhi: B. I. Publications, 1974.

Braden, Anne. *The Wall Between.* New York: Monthly Review Press, 1958.

Branch, Taylor. *At Canaan's Edge: America in the King Years, 1965–1968.* New York: Simon & Schuster, 2006.

———. *Parting the Waters: America in the King Years, 1954–1963.* New York: Simon & Schuster, 1988.

———. *Pillar of Fire: America in the King Years, 1963–1965.* New York: Simon & Schuster, 1998.

Brightman, Edgar Sheffield. *A Philosophy of Religion.* New York: Prentice-Hall, 1940.

Buhle, Paul. *C. L. R. James: The Artist as Revolutionary.* London: Verso, 1988.

Burner, Eric R. *And Gently He Shall Lead Them.* New York: New York University Press, 1994.

Burns, Stewart. *To the Mountaintop: Martin Luther King, Jr.'s Sacred Mission to Save America, 1955–1968.* San Francisco: Harper San Francisco, 2004.

Burns, Stewart, ed. *Daybreak of Freedom: The Montgomery Bus Boycott.* Chapel Hill: University of North Carolina Press, 1997.

Carawan, Guy, with Candie Carawan. *We Shall Overcome! Songs of the Southern Freedom Movement.* New York: Oak Publications, 1963.

Carmichael, Stokely, and Charles V. Hamilton. *Black Power: The Politics of Liberation in America.* New York: Vintage Books, 1967.

Carmichael, Stokely, with Michael Thelwell. *Ready for Revolution: The Life and Struggles of Stokely Carmichael (Kwame Ture).* New York: Scribner, 2003.

Carr, Johnnie Rebecca, Randall Williams, and Jeffrey Hurst. *Johnnie: The Life of Johnnie Rebecca Carr, with Her Friends Rosa Parks, E. D. Nixon, Martin Luther King, Jr., and Others in the Montgomery Civil Rights Struggle.* Montgomery, AL: Black Belt Press, 1996.

Carson, Clayborne. *In Struggle: SNCC and the Black Awakening of the 1960s.* Cambridge, MA: Harvard University Press, 1981.

Carson, Clayborne, David J. Garrow, Gerald Gill, Vincent Harding, and Darlene Clark Hine, eds. *The Eyes on the Prize Civil Rights Reader: Documents, Speeches, and Firsthand Accounts from the Black Freedom Struggle, 1954–1990.* New York: Penguin, 1991.

Carter, Dan T. *The Politics of Rage: George Wallace, the Origins of the New Conservatism, and the Transformation of American Politics.* Baton Rouge: Louisiana State University Press, 2000.

Carter, Weptanomah W. *Born to Be President: The Story of the Life of Dr. T. J. Jemison, President, National Baptist Convention, USA, Inc.* Pikesville, MD: Gateway Press, 1984.

Chireau, Yvonne Patricia, and Nathaniel Deutsch. *Black Zion: African American Religious Encounters with Judaism.* New York: Oxford University Press, 2000.

Christopher, Maurine. *America's Black Congressmen.* New York: Crowell, 1971.

Clark, Septima. *Ready from Within: Septima Clark and the Civil Rights Movement.* Cynthia Stokes Brown, ed. Navarro, CA: Wild Trees Press, 1986.

Clark, Septima, with LeGette Blythe. *Echo in My Soul.* New York: Dutton, 1962.

Colburn, David R. *Racial Change and Community Crisis: St. Augustine, Florida, 1877–1980.* New York: Columbia University Press, 1985.

Collier-Thomas, Bettye, and V. P. Franklin, eds. *Sisters in the Struggle: African American Women in the Civil Rights–Black Power Movement.* New York: New York University Press, 2001.

Cone, James H. *Martin and Malcolm and America: A Dream or a Nightmare.* Maryknoll, NY: Orbis Books, 1991.

Crawford, Vicki L., Jacqueline Anne Rouse, and Barbara Woods, eds. *Women in the Civil Rights Movement: Trailblazers and Torchbearers, 1941–1965*. New York: Carlson Publishing, 1990.

Davis, Ossie, and Ruby Dee. *With Ossie and Ruby: In This Life Together*. New York: Morrow, 1998.

Davis, Sammy, Jr. *The Sammy Davis, Jr., Reader*. Charles W. Eagles, ed. New York: Farrar, Straus & Giroux, 2001.

Davis, Sammy, Jr., Jane Boyar, and Burt Boyar. *Yes I Can: The Story of Sammy Davis, Jr.* New York: Farrar, Straus & Giroux, 1965.

Deats, Paul, and Carol Robb, eds. *The Boston Personalist Tradition in Philosophy, Social Ethics, and Theology*. Macon, GA: Mercer University Press, 1986.

D'Emilio, John. *Lost Prophet, the Life and Times of Bayard Rustin*. New York: Free Press, 2003.

DeWolf, L. Harold. *The Case for Theology in Liberal Perspective*. Philadelphia: Westminster Press, 1959.

———. *Crime and Justice in America: A Paradox of Conscience*. New York: Harper & Row, 1975.

———. *Responsible Freedom: Guidelines to Christian Action*. New York: Harper & Row, 1971.

———. *A Theology of the Living Church*. New York: Harper, 1953.

Dickerson, Dennis C. *Militant Mediator: Whitney M. Young, Jr.* Lexington: University Press of Kentucky, 1998.

Draper, Alan. *Conflict of Interests: Organized Labor and the Civil Rights Movement in the South, 1954–1968*. Ithaca, NY: ILR Press, 1994.

Durr, Virginia Foster, and Hollinger F. Barnard. *Outside the Magic Circle: The Autobiography of Virginia Foster Durr*. Tuscaloosa: University of Alabama Press, 1985.

Dyson, Michael Eric. *I May Not Get There with You: The True Martin Luther King, Jr.* New York: Free Press, 2000.

Eagles, Charles W. *Outside Agitator: Jon Daniels and the Civil Rights Movement in Alabama*. Chapel Hill: University of North Carolina Press, 1993.

English, James W. *The Prophet of Wheat Street: The Story of William Holmes Borders, a Man Who Refused to Fail*. Elgin, IL: D. C. Cook Publishing, 1973.

Eskew, Glenn T. *But for Birmingham: The Local and National Movements in the Civil Rights Struggle*. Chapel Hill: University of North Carolina Press, 1997.

Evans, Zelia Stephens, and James T. Alexander, eds. *The Dexter Avenue Baptist Church, 1877–1977*. Montgomery, AL: Dexter Avenue Baptist Church, 1978.

Evers, Charles, and Andrew Szanton. *Have No Fear: The Charles Evers Story*. New York: Wiley & Sons, 1997.

Evers, Medgar Wiley. *The Autobiography of Medgar Evers: A Hero's Life and Legacy Revealed through His Writings, Letters, and Speeches*. Myrlie Evers-Williams and Manning Marable, eds. New York: Basic Civitas, 2005.

Fager, Charles E. *Selma, 1965*. New York: Scribner, 1974.

Fairclough, Adam. *Martin Luther King, Jr.* Athens: University of Georgia Press, 1995.

———. *Race and Democracy: The Civil Rights Struggle in Louisiana, 1915–1972*. Athens: University of Georgia Press, 1995.

———. *To Redeem the Soul of America: The Southern Christian Leadership Conference and Martin Luther King, Jr.* Athens: University of Georgia Press, 1987.

Farmer, James. *Lay Bare the Heart: An Autobiography of the Civil Rights Movement*. New York: Arbor House, 1985.

Farris, Christine K. *My Brother Martin: A Sister Remembers Growing Up with the Rev. Dr. Martin Luther King, Jr.* New York: Simon & Schuster Books for Young Readers, 2003.

Fendrich, James Max. *Ideal Citizens: The Legacy of the Civil Rights Movement*. Albany: State University of New York Press, 1993.

Ferm, Vergilius Ture Anselm, ed. *Contemporary American Theology: Theological Autobiographies*. Second series. New York: Round Table Press, 1933.

Fierman, Morton C. *Leap of Action: Ideas in the Theology of Abraham Joshua Heschel*. Lanham, MD: University Press of America, 1990.

Foner, Eric, and John Arthur Garraty, eds. *The Reader's Companion to American History*. Boston: Houghton Mifflin, 1991.

Forman, James. *The Making of Black Revolutionaries: A Personal Account*. New York: Macmillan, 1972.

————. *Sammy Younge, Jr.: The First Black College Student to Die in the Black Liberation Movement*. New York: Grove Press, 1968.

Fosdick, Harry Emerson. *The Hope of the World: Twenty-Five Sermons on Christianity Today*. New York: Harper & Brothers, 1933.

————. *The Living of These Days: An Autobiography*. New York: Harper, 1956.

————. *On Being Fit to Live With: Sermons on Post-War Christianity*. New York: Harper & Brothers, 1946.

Fosl, Catherine. *Subversive Southerner: Anne Braden and the Struggle for Racial Justice in the Cold War South*. New York: Palgrave Macmillan, 2002.

Fox, Richard Wightman. *Reinhold Niebuhr: A Biography*. New York: Pantheon Books, 1985.

Frady, Marshall. *Jesse: The Life and Pilgrimage of Jesse Jackson*. New York: Random House, 1996.

————. *Martin Luther King, Jr.* New York: Penguin Group, 2002.

Friedly, Michael, and David Gallen, eds. *Martin Luther King, Jr.: The FBI File*. New York: Carroll & Graf, 1993.

Friedman, Murray, with Peter Binzen. *What Went Wrong? The Creation and Collapse of the Black-Jewish Alliance*. New York: Free Press, 1995.

Gandhi, Mohandas. *The Gandhi Reader: A Source Book of His Life and Writings*. Homer A. Jack, ed. Bloomington: Indiana University Press, 1956.

————. *The Wit and Wisdom of Gandhi*. Homer A. Jack, ed. Boston: Beacon Press, 1951.

Garrow, David J. *Bearing the Cross: Martin Luther King, Jr., and the Southern Christian Leadership Conference*. New York: Morrow, 1986.

————, ed. *Chicago 1966: Open Housing Marches, Summit Negotiations, and Operation Breadbasket*. Brooklyn, NY: Carlson Publishing, 1989.

————. *The FBI and Martin Luther King, Jr.: From "Solo" to Memphis*. New York: W. W. Norton, 1981.

————, ed. *Martin Luther King, Jr.: Civil Rights Leader, Theologian, Orator*. Brooklyn, NY: Carlson Publishing, 1989.

————. *Protest at Selma: Martin Luther King, Jr., and the Voting Rights Act of 1965*. New Haven, CT: Yale University Press, 1978.

————, ed. *St. Augustine, Florida, 1963–1964: Mass Protest and Racial Violence*. Brooklyn, NY: Carlson Publishing, 1989.

————, ed. *The Walking City: The Montgomery Bus Boycott, 1955–1956*. Brooklyn, NY: Carlson Publishing, 1989.

Glen, John M. *Highlander, No Ordinary School: 1932–1962*. Lexington: University Press of Kentucky, 1988.

Goldman, Peter Louis. *The Death and Life of Malcolm X*. New York: Harper & Row, 1973.

Goldwater, Barry, and Jack Casserly. *Goldwater*. New York: Doubleday, 1988.

Goulden, Joseph C. *Jerry Wurf: Labor's Last Angry Man*. New York: Atheneum, 1982.

Graetz, Robert. *Montgomery: A White Preacher's Memoir*. Minneapolis: Fortress Press, 1991.

Graham, Billy. *Just As I Am: The Autobiography of Billy Graham*. San Francisco: Harper San Francisco, 1997.

Grant, Joanne. *Ella Baker: Freedom Bound*. New York: Wiley & Sons, 1998.

Gray, Fred D. *Bus Ride to Justice: Changing the System by the System: The Life and Works of Fred D. Gray, Preacher, Attorney, and Politician*. Montgomery, AL: Black Belt Press, 1995.

Gray, Fred D., and Willy S. Leventhal, eds. *The Children Coming On: A Retrospective of the Montgomery Bus Boycott*. Montgomery, AL: Black Belt Press, 1998.

Greenberg, Jack. *Crusaders in the Courts: How a Dedicated Band of Lawyers Fought for the Civil Rights Revolution*. New York: Basic Books, 1994.

Greene, Melissa Fay. *The Temple Bombing*. Reading, MA: Addison-Wesley, 1996.

Gregg, Richard Bartlett. *The Power of Nonviolence*. Nyack, NY: Fellowship Publications, 1959.

Gregory, Dick. *Nigger: An Autobiography*. New York: Dutton, 1964.

Haberman, Frederick W., ed. *Nobel Lectures Including Presentation Speeches and Laureates' Biographies*. Vol. 3, *Peace: 1951–1970*. New York: Elsevier, 1972.

Halberstam, David. *The Children*. New York: Random House, 1998.

Hall, Mitchell K. *Because of Their Faith: CALCAV and Religious Opposition to the Vietnam War*. New York: Columbia University Press, 1990.

Halpern, Rick. *Down on the Killing Floor: Black and White Workers in Chicago's Packinghouses, 1904–1954*. Urbana: University of Illinois Press, 1997.

Halpern, Rick, and Roger Horowitz. *Meatpackers: An Oral History of Black Packinghouse Workers and Their Struggle for Racial and Economic Equality*. New York: Twayne Publishers, 1996.

Hamilton, James Wallace. *Ride the Wild Horses! The Christian Use of Our Untamed Impulses*. Westwood, NJ: Revell, 1952.

Hampton, Henry, and Steve Fayer, with Sarah Flynn. *Voices of Freedom: An Oral History of the Civil Rights Movement from the 1950s through the 1980s*. New York: Bantam, 1990.

Hansen, Drew D. *The Dream: Martin Luther King, Jr., and the Speech That Inspired a Nation*. New York: Ecco, 2003.

Harding, Vincent. *Martin Luther King: The Inconvenient Hero*. Maryknoll, NY: Orbis Books, 1996.

Hassler, Alfred. *Diary of a Self-Made Convict*. Chicago: H. Regnery, 1970.

———. *Saigon, U.S.A.* New York: R. W. Baron, 1970.

Height, Dorothy I. *Open Wide the Freedom Gates: A Memoir*. New York: Public Affairs, 2003.

Henderson, Harold P. *Ernest Vandiver, Governor of Georgia*. Athens: University of Georgia Press, 2000.

Henry, Aaron, and Constance Curry. *Aaron Henry: The Fire Ever Burning*. Jackson: University Press of Mississippi, 2000.

Heschel, Abraham Joshua. *God in Search of Man: A Philosophy of Judaism*. New York: Farrar, Straus & Cudahy, 1955.

———. *Man Is Not Alone: A Philosophy of Religion*. New York: Farrar, Straus & Young, 1951.

———. *No Religion Is an Island: Abraham Joshua Heschel and Interreligious Dialogue*. Harold Kasimow and Byron L. Sherwin, eds. Maryknoll, NY: Orbis Books, 1991.

Honey, Michael. *Black Workers Remember: An Oral History of Segregation, Unionism, and the Freedom Struggle*. Berkeley: University of California Press, 1999.

———. *Going Down Jericho Road: The Memphis Strike, Martin Luther King's Last Campaign*. New York: W. W. Norton, 2007.

Hooks, Benjamin L., with Jerry Guess. *The March for Civil Rights: The Benjamin Hooks Story*. Chicago: ABA, 2003.

Hopkins, Charles Howard. *The Rise of the Social Gospel in American Protestantism, 1865–1915*. New Haven, CT: Yale University Press, 1940.

Horowitz, Roger. *Negro and White Unite and Fight! A Social History of Industrial Unionism in Meatpacking, 1930–1990*. Urbana: University of Illinois Press, 1997.

Horton, Myles, with Judith Kohl and Herbert R. Kohl. *The Long Haul: An Autobiography*. New York: Doubleday, 1990.

Houser, George M. *No One Can Stop the Rain: Glimpses of Africa's Liberation Struggle*. New York: Pilgrim Press, 1989.

Howlett, Duncan. *No Greater Love: The James Reeb Story*. New York: Harper & Row, 1966.

Ivory, Luther D. *Toward a Theology of Radical Involvement: The Theological Legacy of Martin Luther King, Jr*. Nashville, TN: Abingdon Press, 1997.

Jackson, Jesse. *Make a Joyful Noise unto the Lord! The Life of Mahalia Jackson, Queen of Gospel Singers*. New York: Thomas Y. Crowell, 1974.

James, C. L. R. *The Black Jacobins: Toussaint Louverture and the San Domingo Revolution*. New York, Dial Press, 1938.

Jenkins, Mary Royal. *Open Dem Cells: A Pictorial History of the Albany Movement*. Columbus, GA: Brentwood Academic Press, 2000.

Johnson, Lyndon B. *Public Papers of the Presidents of the United States: Lyndon B. Johnson, 1965,* vol. 1, *January 1 to May 31, 1965.* Washington, DC: U.S. Government Printing Office, 1966.

———. *Public Papers of the Presidents of the United States: Lyndon B. Johnson, 1965,* vol. 2, *June 1 to December 31, 1965.* Washington, DC: U.S. Government Printing Office, 1966.

———. *The Vantage Point: Perspectives of the Presidency, 1963–1969.* New York: Holt, Rinehart & Winston, 1971.

Kaplan, Edward K. *Spiritual Radical: Abraham Joshua Heschel in America, 1940–1972.* New Haven, CT: Yale University Press, 2007.

Kapur, Sudarshan. *Raising Up a Prophet: The African-American Encounter with Gandhi.* Boston: Beacon Press, 1992.

Katz, Milton S. *Ban the Bomb: A History of SANE, the Committee for a Sane Nuclear Policy, 1957–1985.* Westport, CT: Greenwood Press, 1986.

King, Coretta Scott. *My Life with Martin Luther King, Jr.* New York: Holt, Rinehart & Winston, 1969.

King, Dexter Scott. *Growing Up King: An Intimate Memoir.* New York: IPM, 2003.

King, Martin Luther, Jr. *Autobiography of Martin Luther King, Jr.* Clayborne Carson, ed. New York: IPM, 1998.

———. *A Call to Conscience: The Landmark Speeches of Dr. Martin Luther King, Jr.* Clayborne Carson and Kris Shepard, eds. New York: IPM, 2001.

———. *Conscience for Change.* Toronto: Canadian Broadcasting Co., 1967.

———. *A Knock at Midnight: Inspiration from the Great Sermons of Reverend Martin Luther King, Jr.* Clayborne Carson and Peter Holloran, eds. New York: IPM, 1998.

———. *The Measure of a Man.* Philadelphia: Christian Education Press, 1959.

———. *The Papers of Martin Luther King, Jr.,* Volume 1: *Called to Serve, January 1929–June 1951.* Clayborne Carson, Ralph Luker, and Penny A. Russell, eds. Berkeley: University of California Press, 1992.

———. *The Papers of Martin Luther King, Jr.,* Volume 2: *Rediscovering Precious Values, July 1951–November 1955.* Clayborne Carson, Ralph Luker, Penny Russell, and Peter Holloran, eds. Berkeley: University of California Press, 1994.

———. *The Papers of Martin Luther King, Jr.,* Volume 3: *Birth of a New Age, December 1955–December 1956.* Clayborne Carson, Stewart Burns, Susan Carson, Peter Holloran, and Dana L. H. Powell, eds. Berkeley: University of California Press, 1997.

———. *The Papers of Martin Luther King, Jr.,* Volume 4: *Symbol of the Movement, January 1957–December 1958.* Clayborne Carson, Susan Carson, Adrienne Clay, Virgina Shadron, and Kieran Taylor, eds. Berkeley: University of California Press, 2000.

———. *The Papers of Martin Luther King, Jr.,* Volume 5: *Threshold of a New Decade, January 1959–December 1960.* Clayborne Carson, Tenisha Armstrong, Susan Carson, Adrienne Clay, and Kieran Taylor, eds. Berkeley: University of California Press, 2005.

———. *The Papers of Martin Luther King, Jr.,* Volume 6: *Advocate of the Social Gospel, September 1948–March 1963.* Clayborne Carson, Susan Carson, Susan Englander, Troy Jackson, and Gerald L. Smith, eds. Berkeley: University of California Press, 2007.

———. *Strength to Love.* New York: Harper & Row, 1963.

———. *Stride Toward Freedom: The Montgomery Story.* New York: Harper, 1958.

———. *A Testament of Hope: The Essential Writings of Martin Luther King, Jr.* James Melvin Washington, ed. San Francisco: Harper & Row, 1986.

———. *The Trumpet of Conscience.* New York: Harper & Row, 1968.

———. *Where Do We Go from Here: Chaos or Community?* New York: Harper & Row, 1967.

———. *Why We Can't Wait.* New York: Harper & Row, 1964.

King, Martin Luther, Sr., with Clayton Riley. *Daddy King: An Autobiography.* New York: Morrow, 1980.

King, Mary. *Mahatma Gandhi and Martin Luther King, Jr.: The Power of Nonviolent Action.* Paris: UNESCO Publishing, 1999.

Kluger, Richard. *Simple Justice: The History of Brown v. Board of Education and Black America's Struggle for Equality.* New York: Knopf, 1975.

Kotz, Nick. *Judgment Days: Lyndon Baines Johnson, Martin Luther King, Jr., and the Laws That Changed America*. Boston: Houghton Mifflin, 2005.

Kunstler, William Moses. *Deep in My Heart*. New York: Morrow, 1966.

Kunstler, William Moses, with Sheila Isenberg. *My Life as a Radical Lawyer*. Secaucus, NJ: Carol Publishing, 1994.

Landess, Thomas H., and Richard Quinn. *Jesse Jackson and the Politics of Race*. Ottawa, IL: Jameson Books, 1985.

Langum, David J. *William M. Kunstler: The Most Hated Lawyer in America*. New York: New York University Press, 1999.

Lee, Chana Kai. *For Freedom's Sake: The Life of Fannie Lou Hamer*. Urbana: University of Illinois Press, 1999.

Lesher, Stephan. *George Wallace: American Populist*. Reading, MA: Addison-Wesley, 1994.

Levine, Daniel. *Bayard Rustin and the Civil Rights Movement*. New Brunswick, NJ: Rutgers University Press, 2000.

Lewis, Anthony. *Make No Law: The Sullivan Case and the First Amendment*. New York: Random House, 1991.

Lewis, David L. *King: A Critical Biography*. New York: Praeger, 1970.

Lewis, John, with Michael D'Orso. *Walking with the Wind: A Memoir of the Movement*. New York: Simon & Schuster, 1998.

Lichtenstein, Nelson. *Walter Reuther: The Most Dangerous Man in Detroit*. Urbana: University of Illinois Press, 1995.

Ling, Peter J. *Martin Luther King, Jr.* New York: Routledge, 2002.

Lischer, Richard. *The Preacher King: Martin Luther King, Jr., and the Word That Moved America*. New York: Oxford University Press, 1995.

Logan, Rayford Whittingham. *Howard University: The First Hundred Years, 1867–1967*. New York: New York University Press, 1969.

Lomax, Louis E. *When the Word Is Given: A Report on Elijah Muhammad, Malcolm X, and the Black Muslim World*. Cleveland: World, 1963.

Loveland, Anne C. *Lillian Smith, a Southerner Confronting the South: A Biography*. Baton Rouge: Louisiana State University Press, 1986.

Macleod, Alistair M. *Paul Tillich: An Essay on the Role of Ontology in His Philosophical Theology*. London: Allen & Unwin, 1973.

Malcolm X. *Malcolm X Speaks: Selected Speeches and Statements*. George Breitman, ed. New York: Merit, 1965.

———. *Two Speeches by Malcolm X*. New York: Pioneer Publishers, 1965.

Malcolm X, with Alex Haley. *The Autobiography of Malcolm X*. New York: Grove Press, 1965.

Manis, Andrew Michael. *A Fire You Can't Put Out: The Civil Rights Life of Birmingham's Reverend Fred Shuttlesworth*. Tuscaloosa: University of Alabama Press, 1999.

Marshall, Thurgood. *Thurgood Marshall: His Speeches, Writings, Arguments, Opinions, and Reminiscences*. Mark V. Tushnet, ed. Chicago: Lawrence Hill Books, 2001.

Martinez, Elizabeth Sutherland. *Letters from Mississippi*. New York: McGraw-Hill, 1965.

Maynard, Aubré de L. *Surgeons to the Poor: The Harlem Hospital Story*. New York: Appleton-Century-Crofts, 1978.

Mays, Benjamin E. *Born to Rebel: An Autobiography*. New York: Scribner, 1971.

———. *Dr. Benjamin E. Mays Speaks: Representative Speeches of a Great American Orator*. Freddie C. Colston, ed. Lanham, MD: University Press of America, 2002.

Mboya, Tom. *Freedom and After*. Boston: Little, Brown, 1963.

McAdam, Doug. *Freedom Summer*. New York: Oxford University Press, 1988.

McKnight, Gerald. *The Last Crusade: Martin Luther King, Jr., the FBI, and the Poor People's Campaign*. Boulder, CO: Westview Press, 1998.

McWhorter, Diane. *Carry Me Home: Birmingham, Alabama, the Climactic Battle of the Civil Rights Revolution*. New York: Simon & Schuster, 2001.

Meier, August, and Elliot M. Rudwick. *Black Detroit and the Rise of the UAW*. New York: Oxford University Press, 1979.

————. *CORE: A Study in the Civil Rights Movement*. New York: Oxford University Press, 1973.

Miller, Keith D. *Voice of Deliverance: The Language of Martin Luther King, Jr., and Its Sources*. New York: Free Press, 1992.

Miller, Richard Lawrence. *Truman, the Rise to Power*. New York: McGraw-Hill, 1986.

Moreno, Paul D. *Black Americans and Organized Labor: A New History*. Baton Rouge: Louisiana State University Press, 2006.

Morgan, Charles. *A Time to Speak*. New York: Harper & Row, 1964.

Morris, Aldon D. *Origins of the Civil Rights Movement: Black Communities Organizing for Change*. London: Collier Macmillan, 1984.

Moses, Robert P., and Charles E. Cobb. *Radical Equations: Civil Rights from Mississippi to the Algebra Project*. Boston: Beacon Press, 2001.

Muste, Abraham Johannes. *The Essays of A. J. Muste*. Nat Hentoff, ed. Indianapolis: Bobbs-Merrill, 1967.

————. *What the Bible Teaches about Freedom: A Message to the Negro Churches*. New York: Fellowship of Reconciliation, 1943.

Natwar-Singh, K. *The Legacy of Nehru: A Memorial Tribute*. New York: John Day, 1965.

Navasky, Victor S. *Kennedy Justice*. New York: Atheneum, 1971.

Neary, John. *Julian Bond: Black Rebel*. New York: Morrow, 1971.

Nehru, Jawaharlal. *Toward Freedom: The Autobiography of Jawaharlal Nehru*. New York: John Day, 1941.

Niebuhr, Reinhold. *Moral Man and Immoral Society: A Study in Ethics and Politics*. London: Scribner, 1932.

Nkrumah, Kwame. *Ghana: The Autobiography of Kwame Nkrumah*. New York: Nelson, 1957.

————. *Kwame Nkrumah: The Conakry Years:; His Life and Letters*. June Milne, comp. London: Atlantic Highlands, 1990.

Nunnelley, William A. *Bull Connor*. Tuscaloosa: University of Alabama Press, 1991.

Nygren, Anders. *Agape and Eros: A Study of the Christian Idea of Love*. London: Society for Promoting Christian Knowledge, 1932.

O'Reilly, Kenneth. *Racial Matters: The FBI's Secret File on Black America, 1960–1972*. New York: Free Press, 1989.

Parascandola, Louis J., ed. *Look for Me All Around You, Anglophone Caribbean Immigrants in the Harlem Renaissance*. Detroit: Wayne State University Press, 2005.

Paris, Peter J. *Black Religious Leaders: Conflict in Unity*. Louisville, KY: Westminster/John Knox Press, 1991.

Parker, Frank R. *Black Votes Count, Political Empowerment in Mississippi after 1965*. Chapel Hill: University of North Carolina Press, 1990.

Parks, Rosa, and Jim Haskins. *Rosa Parks: My Story*. New York: Dial Books, 1992.

Pauck, Wilhelm, and Marion Pauck. *Paul Tillich: His Life and Thought*. New York: Harper & Row, 1976.

Payne, Charles M. *I've Got the Light of Freedom: The Organizing Tradition and the Mississippi Freedom Struggle*. Berkeley: University of California Press, 1995.

Pearson, Hugh. *When Harlem Nearly Killed King: The 1958 Stabbing of Dr. Martin Luther King, Jr.* New York: Seven Stories Press, 2002.

Peck, James. *Freedom Ride*. New York: Simon & Schuster, 1962.

Pepper, William F. *An Act of State: The Execution of Martin Luther King*. London: Verso, 2003.

————. *Orders to Kill: The Truth Behind the Murder of Martin Luther King*. New York: Carroll & Graf, 1995.

Pfeffer, Paula F. *A. Philip Randolph, Pioneer of the Civil Rights Movement*. Baton Rouge: Louisiana State University Press, 1990.

Pomerantz, Gary. *Where Peachtree Meets Sweet Auburn: The Saga of Two Families and the Making of Atlanta*. New York: Scribner, 1996.

Posner, Gerald L. *Killing the Dream: James Earl Ray and the Assassination of Martin Luther King, Jr.* New York: Random House, 1998.

Quill, Shirley. *Mike Quill, Himself: A Memoir*. Greenwich, CT: Devin-Adair, 1985.

Rabby, Glenda Alice. *The Pain and the Promise: The Struggle for Civil Rights in Tallahassee, Florida*. Athens: University of Georgia Press, 1999.

Raines, Howell. *My Soul Is Rested: Movement Days in the Deep South Remembered*. New York: Penguin, 1983.

Ralph, James R. *Northern Protest: Martin Luther King, Jr., Chicago, and the Civil Rights Movement*. Cambridge, MA: Harvard University Press, 1993.

Ramachandran, G., and T. K. Mahadevan, eds. *Gandhi, His Relevance for Our Times*. New Delhi: Gandhi Peace Foundation, 1967.

Ransby, Barbara. *Ella Baker and the Black Freedom Movement: A Radical Democratic Vision*. Chapel Hill: University of North Carolina, 2003.

Rauschenbusch, Walter. *Christianity and the Social Crisis*. New York: Macmillan, 1907.

Reddick, Lawrence Dunbar. *Crusader without Violence: A Biography of Martin Luther King, Jr.* New York: Harper, 1959.

Robinson, Jackie, and Alfred Duckett. *I Never Had It Made*. New York: Putnam, 1972.

Robinson, Jo Ann Gibson. *The Montgomery Bus Boycott and the Women Who Started It: The Memoir of Jo Ann Gibson Robinson*. Knoxville: University of Tennessee Press, 1987.

Robinson, Jo Ann Ooiman. *Abraham Went Out: A Biography of A. J. Muste*. Philadelphia: Temple University Press, 1981.

Robinson, Rachel. *Jackie Robinson: An Intimate Portrait*. New York: Abrams, 1996.

Rosenberg, Rosalind, and Eric Foner, eds. *Divided Lives: American Women in the Twentieth Century*. New York: Hill & Wang, 1992.

Ross, Rosetta E. *Witnessing and Testifying: Black Women, Religion, and Civil Rights*. Minneapolis: Fortress Press, 2003.

Rothschild, Janice O. *As But a Day: The First Hundred Years, 1867–1967*. Atlanta: Hebrew Benevolent Congregation, 1967.

Schuyler, George Samuel. *Black and Conservative; The Autobiography of George S. Schuyler*. New Rochelle, NY: Arlington House, 1966.

Seale, Bobby. *Seize the Time: The Story of the Black Panther Party and Huey P. Newton*. New York: Random House, 1970.

Seay, Solomon Snowden. *I Was There by the Grace of God*. Montgomery, AL: S. S. Seay, Sr. Educational Foundation, 1990.

Smith, Kenneth L., and Ira G. Zepp. *Search for the Beloved Community: The Thinking of Martin Luther King, Jr.* Valley Forge, PA: Judson Press, 1974.

Smith, Lillian Eugenia. *The Journey*. Cleveland: World, 1954.

———. *Killers of the Dream*. New York: W. W. Norton, 1949.

———. *Now Is the Time*. New York: Viking Press, 1955.

———. *Strange Fruit*. New York: Reynal & Hitchcock, 1944.

Sunnemark, Fredrik. *Ring Out Freedom! The Voice of Martin Luther King, Jr., and the Making of the Civil Rights Movement*. Bloomington: Indiana University Press, 2004.

Taylor, Clarence. *The Black Churches of Brooklyn*. New York: Columbia University Press, 1994.

Taylor, Cynthia. *A. Philip Randolph: The Religious Journey of an African American Labor Leader*. New York: New York University Press, 2006.

Taylor, Gardner. *Chariots Aflame*. Nashville, TN: Broadman Press, 1988.

———. *How Shall They Preach?* Elgin, IL: Progressive Baptist Pub. House, 1977.

———. *The Scarlet Thread: Nineteen Sermons*. Elgin, IL: Progressive Baptist Pub. House, 1981.

Tedford, Thomas L. *Freedom of Speech in the United States*. New York: Random House, 1985.

Theoharis, Athan G., ed. *From the Secret Files of J. Edgar Hoover*. Chicago: Ivan R. Dee, 1991.

Thomas, Gerald Lamont. *African American Preaching: The Contribution of Dr. Gardner C. Taylor*. New York: Peter Lang, 2004.

Thornton, J. Mills. *Dividing Lines: Municipal Politics and the Struggle for Civil Rights in Montgomery, Birmingham, and Selma*. Tuscaloosa: University of Alabama Press, 2002.

Thurman, Howard. *Jesus and the Disinherited*. New York: Abingdon-Cokesbury Press, 1949.

————. *With Head and Heart: The Autobiography of Howard Thurman*. New York: Harcourt Brace Jovanovich, 1979.

Tillich, Paul. *My Search for Absolutes*. New York: Simon & Schuster, 1967.

————. *Shaking the Foundations [Sermons]*. New York: Scribner, 1948.

Travers, Len, ed. *Encyclopedia of American Holidays and National Days*. Westport, CT: Greenwood Press, 2006.

Tyson, Timothy B. *Radio Free Dixie: Robert F. Williams and the Roots of Black Power*. Chapel Hill: University of North Carolina Press, 1999.

Urquhart, Brian. *Ralph Bunche: An American Life*. New York: W. W. Norton, 1993.

Viorst, Milton. *Fire in the Streets: America in the 1960s*. New York: Simon & Schuster, 1979.

Vivian, C. T. *Black Power and the American Myth*. Philadelphia: Fortress Press, 1970.

Walker, Wyatt Tee. *Somebody's Calling My Name: Black Sacred Music and Social Change*. Valley Forge, PA: Judson Press, 1979.

Ward, Brian, and Anthony J. Badger. *The Making of Martin Luther King and the Civil Rights Movement*. Basingstoke, NH: Macmillan, 1995.

Washington, James Melvin, ed. *A Testament of Hope: The Essential Writings of Martin Luther King, Jr.* San Francisco: Harper & Row, 1986.

Watson, Goodwin Barbour. *Action for Unity*. New York: Office of Jewish Information, 1946.

Watters, Pat, and Reese Cleghorn. *Climbing Jacob's Ladder*. New York: Harcourt, Brace, & World, 1964.

Weatherby, William J. *James Baldwin: Artist on Fire: A Portrait*. New York: D. I. Fine, 1989.

Webster, John, ed. *The Cambridge Companion to Karl Barth*. Cambridge: Cambridge University Press, 2000.

Weiss, Nancy J. *Whitney M. Young, Jr., and the Struggle for Civil Rights*. Princeton, NJ: Princeton University Press, 1989.

Werner, Craig Hansen. *A Change Is Gonna Come: Music, Race, and the Soul of America*. New York: Plume, 1998.

Wexler, Sanford. *The Civil Rights Movement: An Eyewitness History*. New York: Facts on File, 1993.

Wilkins, Roger W. *A Man's Life: An Autobiography*. New York: Simon & Schuster, 1982.

Wilkins, Roy, and Tom Mathews. *Standing Fast: The Autobiography of Roy Wilkins*. New York: Penguin, 1982.

Williams, Juan. *Eyes on the Prize: America's Civil Rights Years, 1954–1965*. New York: Viking, 1987.

————. *Thurgood Marshall: American Revolutionary*. New York: Times Books, 1998.

Williams, Robert F. *Negroes with Guns*. New York: Marzani & Munsell, 1962.

Wilson, Joseph F., ed. *Tearing Down the Color Bar: A Documentary History and Analysis of the Brotherhood of Sleeping Car Porters*. New York: Columbia University Press, 1989.

Wofford, Clare, and Harris Wofford. *India Afire*. New York: John Day, 1951.

Wofford, Harris. *Of Kennedys and Kings: Making Sense of the Sixties*. New York, Farrar, Straus & Giroux, 1980.

Worcester, Kent. *C. L. R. James: A Political Biography*. Albany: State University of New York Press, 1996.

Yolles, Melanie A., and Norman Thomas. *The Norman Thomas Papers Guide, 1904–1967*. Cambridge: Chadwick-Healey, 1985.

Young, Andrew. *An Easy Burden: The Civil Rights Movement and the Transformation of America*. New York: HarperCollins, 1996.

Index

Page numbers in **bold** indicate main entries.

About the Authors

TENISHA ARMSTRONG, associate director of the King Institute's Martin Luther King, Jr., Papers Project, holds an MA from Stanford University. A former King Summer Research Fellow, she joined the Institute staff in 1998 and was the lead editor of *The Papers of Martin Luther King, Jr.*, vol. 5: *Threshold of a New Decade, January 1959–December 1960* (2005).

CLAYBORNE CARSON, a Stanford University history professor, is founding director of the Martin Luther King, Jr., Research and Education Institute. In 1985 Coretta Scott King named him to direct the King Papers Project, and he has co-edited six of the projected 14-volume edition of *The Papers of Martin Luther King, Jr.* In addition, he has also edited *The Autobiography of Martin Luther King, Jr.* (1998); *A Call to Conscience: The Landmark Speeches of Dr. Martin Luther King, Jr.* (2001); and *A Knock at Midnight: Inspiration from the Great Sermons of Rev. Martin Luther King, Jr.* (1998).

SUSAN CARSON, former managing editor of the King Institute, holds an MA in library science from San Jose State University. She co-edited *The Papers of Martin Luther King, Jr.*, vol. 3: *Birth of a New Age, December 1955–December 1956* (1997); vol. 4: *Symbol of the Movement, January 1957–December 1958* (2000); vol. 5: *Threshold of a New Decade, January 1959–December 1960* (2005); and vol. 6: *Advocate of the Social Gospel, September 1948–March 1963* (2007).

ERIN COOK is the former associate director of the King Institute's Liberation Curriculum initiative. She served as a teaching assistant for Professor Carson's undergraduate course on the African American freedom struggle and currently teaches history at an independent high school in California.

SUSAN ENGLANDER earned a PhD in U.S. history from the University of California–Los Angeles in 1999 and has been an editor at the Martin Luther King, Jr., Papers Project since 2001. She was the lead editor for *The Papers of Martin Luther King, Jr.*, vol. 6: *Advocate of the Social Gospel, September 1948–March 1963* (2007).